NATIONAL GEOGRAPHIC LEARNING

Life Intermediate Student's Book, **2nd Edition**

Helen Stephenson, Paul Dummett, John Hughes

Vice President, Editorial Director: John McHugh

Executive Editor: Sian Mavor

Publishing Consultant: Karen Spiller

Project Manager: Sarah Ratcliff

Development Editor: Liz Driscoll

Editorial Manager: Claire Merchant

Head of Strategic Marketing ELT: Charlotte Ellis

Senior Content Project Manager: Nick Ventullo

Manufacturing Manager: Eyvett Davis

Senior IP Analyst: Ashley Maynard

Senior IP Project Manager: Michelle McKenna

Cover: Lisa Trager

Text design: emc design ltd.

Compositor: emc design ltd.

Audio: Tom Dick and Debbie Productions Ltd

Contributing Writer: Graham Burton (Grammar summary)

© 2019 National Geographic Learning, a Cengage Learning Company

ALL RIGHTS RESERVED. No part of this work covered by the copyright herein may be reproduced or distributed in any form or by any means, except as permitted by U.S. copyright law, without the prior written permission of the copyright owner.

"National Geographic", "National Geographic Society" and the Yellow Border Design are registered trademarks of the National Geographic Society ® Marcas Registradas

---

For product information and technology assistance, contact us at
Cengage Learning Customer & Sales Support, cengage.com/contact

For permission to use material from this text or product, submit all requests online at **cengage.com/permissions**
Further permissions questions can be emailed to
permissionrequest@cengage.com

ISBN: 978-1-337-28591-9

National Geographic Learning
Cheriton House, North Way,
Andover, Hampshire, SP10 5BE
United Kingdom

National Geographic Learning, a Cengage Learning Company, has a mission to bring the world to the classroom and the classroom to life. With our English language programs, students learn about their world by experiencing it. Through our partnerships with National Geographic and TED Talks, they develop the language and skills they need to be successful global citizens and leaders.

Locate your local office at **international.cengage.com/region**

Visit National Geographic Learning online at **NGL.Cengage.com/ELT**
Visit our corporate website at **www.cengage.com**

CREDITS

Although every effort has been made to contact copyright holders before publication, this has not always been possible. If notified, the publisher will undertake to rectify any errors or omissions at the earliest opportunity.

Text: p15: source: 'A world together', by Erla Zwingle, National Geographic, August 01, 1999. www.nationalgeographic.com; p36: source: 'Return to Titanic', Titanic: The Final Secret, National Geographic, National Geographic Channel; p39: source: 'Love and death in the sea', by Enric Sala, National Geographic, June 08, 2011. http://newswatch.nationalgeographic.com; p51: source: 'A better life', by Peter Hessler, National Geographic, May 2008. http://ngm.nationalgeographic.com/2008/05/china/whats-next/hessler-text; p58: source: 'Pizza with a pedigree', National Geographic Magazine, August 2008; p60: source: 'Imaginary eating', by Christine Dell'Amore, National Geographic, December 2010. http://news.nationalgeographic.com/news/2010/12/101209-chocolate-obesity-science-mind-diet-weight-loss-eat-food/; p63: source: 'A caffeine-fuelled world', by T.R. Reid, National Geographic. http://science.nationalgeographic.com/science/health-and-human-body/human-body/caffeine-buzz/; p75: source: 'Amelia Earhart Spit Samples to Help Lick Mystery?', by Ker Than, National Geographic, February 18, 2011. http://news.nationalgeographic.com/news/2011/02/110218-amelia-earhart-spit-dna-mystery-disappearance-saliva-science/, and source: 'Where is Amelia Earhart? - Three theories Lost and found', by John Roach, National Geographic, December 15, 2003. http://news.nationalgeographic.com/news/2003/12/1215_031215_ameliaearhart.html; p77: source: 'Georgian woman cuts off web access to whole of Armenia', Guardian News and Media Limited. http://www.guardian.co.uk/world/2011/apr/06/georgian-woman-cuts-web-access/; p82: source: 'Before New York', by Peter Miller, National Geographic. http://ngm.nationalgeographic.com/2009/09/manhattan/miller-text; p87: source: 'Sweet songs and strong coffee', by Àitor Garrido Jiménez, allgristthemill.blogspot.co.uk; p94: source: 'Holidays and memories', NG Traveler, National Geographic, April 2013; p96: sources: 'Walking for wildlife', by Mike Fay, National Geographic. http://www.nationalgeographic.com/explorers/bios/michael-fay/, http://kids.nationalgeographic.com/explore/explorers/interview-with-mike-fay/ and http://radio.nationalgeographic.com/radio/ng-weekend-archives/1205/; p111: source: 'The art of the deal', by Andrew McCarthy, National Geographic, January/February 2011, http://travel.nationalgeographic.com/travel/countries/morocco-traveler/; p123: source: 'Diane Van Deren', by Andrea Minarcek, National Geographic, 2009. http://adventure.nationalgeographic.com/, and source: 'John Bul Dau, Humanitarian', National Geographic. www.nationalgeographic.com/; p142: source: 'Want to search for the Northwest Passage like

Printed in Greece by Bakis SA
Print Number: 01 Print Year: 2017

a 19th-century British explorer? Bring your sterling silverware and hubris', by Mary Anne Potts, National Geographic, April 07, 2010. ngadventure. typepad.com/blog/2010/04/want-to-seach-for-the-northwest-passage-like-a-19thcentury-british-explorer-bring-your-sterling-silv.html; p144: source: 'Experts in the wild', by Emma Stokes, National Geographic. http://www.nationalgeographic.com/field/explorers/emma-stokes/, and source 'Experts in the wild', by Beth Shapiro, National Geographic. http://www.nationalgeographic.com/field/explorers/beth-shapiro/; p147: source: 'The Samurai Way', by Tom O'Neill, National Geographic, December 2003, p. 98.

Cover: © Atlantide Phototravel/Getty Images.

Photos: 6 (t) Andrew Wilson/Alamy Stock Photo; 6 (m) © TebNad/Shutterstock.com; 6 (bl) © NurPhoto/Getty Images; 6 (br) © Cory Richards/National Geographic Creative; 7 (tl) © NASA; 7 (tr) © Krystle Wright/National Geographic Creative; 7 (bl) © Aaron Huey/National Geographic Creative; 7 (br) © Chris Caldicott/Design Pics/Getty Images; 8 (tl) © Erika Larsen/National Geographic Creative; 8 (tm) © Austin Beahm; 8 (tr) © Kos Picture Source/Getty Images; 8 (mtl) © Charles Stinson Photography; 8 (mtm) © Brian Finke c/o Everybody Somebody Inc/National Geographic Creative; 8 (mtr) © Andrew Lever/4Corners Image Library; 8 (mbl) © Brian Skerry/National Geographic Creative; 8 (mbm) © Jonathan & Angela Scott/AWL Images/Getty Images; 8 (mbr) © Arcansel/Shutterstock.com; 8 (bl) © Pierre Verdy /AFP/Getty Images; 8 (bm) © Chris Rainier; 8 (br) © Jim Richardson/National Geographic Creative; 9 © Erika Larsen/National Geographic Creative; 10 (t) © Passakorn sakulphan/Shutterstock.com; 10 (mt) © Miau/Shutterstock.com; 10 (m) © Joachim Wendler/Shutterstock.com; 10 (mb) © dan_chippendale/Getty Images; 10 (b) chris brignell/Alamy Stock Photo; 12 Keren Su/China Span/Alamy Stock Photo; 13 (t) © Tim Laman/National Geographic Creative; 13 (b) LOOK Die Bildagentur der Fotografen GmbH/Alamy Stock Photo; 15 © Adriana Zehbrauskas/Bloomberg/Getty Images; 16 © Rawpixel.com/Shutterstock.com; 17 © Design Pics Inc/National Geographic Creative; 18 © Chris Caldicott/Design Pics/Getty Images; 20 © sharptoyou/Shutterstock.com; 21 © Austin Beahm; 22 © Laura Boushnak/AFP/Getty Images; 23 © Fisher Photostudio/Shutterstock.com; 24 © Tanya Kirnishi; 27 © R.M. Nunes/Shutterstock.com; 29 Photos 12/Alamy Stock Photo; 30 robertharding/Alamy Stock Photo; 32 © Paul Whitton; 33 © Kos Picture Source/Getty Images; 34 (l) © Stuart Westmorland/Getty Images; 34 (r) © Sportstock/Shutterstock.com; 35 © John Stanmeyer/National Geographic Creative; 36 © Emory Kristof/National Geographic Creative; 37 © Mansell/The LIFE Picture Collection/Getty Images; 38 © hadynyah/iStockphoto; 39 (t) © Rebecca Hale/National Geographic Creative; 39 (b) © xavierarnau/Getty Images; 40 © Cesar Badilla/REX Shutterstock; 41 © Jorge Fajl/National Geographic Creative; 42 © Krystle Wright/National Geographic Creative; 44 (l) © Max Earey/Shutterstock.com; 44 (tm) © Catalin Petolea/Shutterstock.com; 44 (tr) © Elena Elisseeva/Shutterstock.com; 44 (bm) © Filipe Frazao/Shutterstock.com; 44 (br) © Andrew Mayovskyy/Shutterstock.com; 45 © Charles Stinson Photography; 46 © Monty Rakusen/Getty Images; 47 © Yoshikazu Tsuno/AFP/Getty Images; 48 (t) ZUMA Press, Inc./Alamy Stock Photo; 48 (m) © Abraham Nowitz/National Geographic Creative; 48 (b) Reuters/Alamy Stock Photo; 49 © arek_malang/Shutterstock.com; 51 (t, b) © Fritz Hoffmann/National Geographic Creative; 54 © Aaron Huey/National Geographic Creative; 56 (l) © Fritz Hoffmann/National Geographic Creative; 56 (tm) © Andrey_Popov/Shutterstock.com; 56 (tr) © freedomnaruk/Shutterstock.com; 56 (bm) © gpointstudio/Shutterstock.com; 56 (br) © 135pixels/Shutterstock.com; 57 © Brian Finke c/o Everybody Somebody Inc/National Geographic Creative; 58 © Rebecca Hale/National Geographic Creative; 59 (l) jeremy sutton-hibbert/Alamy Stock Photo; 59 (ml) © mypokcik/Shutterstock.com; 59 (mr) Arctic Images/Alamy Stock Photo; 59 (r) © Bork/Shutterstock.com; 60 © Photography by Fernando de Otto/Getty Images; 63 © TommL/Getty Images; 64 (tl) © Rob White/Getty Images; 64 (tr) © Foodpictures/Shutterstock.com; 64 (bl) Alexander Mychko/Alamy Stock Photo; 64 (br) © Rohit Seth/Shutterstock.com; 66 Malcolm Wray/Alamy Stock Photo; 68 © Abraham Nowitz/National Geographic Creative; 69 © Andrew Lever/4Corners Image Library; 70 © ThomasVogel/Getty Images; 72–73 © Robert Clark/National Geographic Creative; 75 © Keystone-France/Getty Images; 76 (l) © 2licht/Getty Images; 76 (m) © Ken Welsh/age fotostock/Photo Library; 76 (r) © Paul Chesley/National Geographic Creative; 77 © Sebastian Tomus/Shutterstock.com; 78 Andrew Wilson/Alamy Stock Photo; 80 andrew parker/Alamy Stock Photo; 81 © Brian Skerry/National Geographic Creative; 82–83 (t) © Markley Boyer/National Geographic Creative; 82–83 (b) © Robert Clark/National Geographic Creative; 84 (tl) © Apurva Madia/Shutterstock.com; 84 (tr) © David Edwards/National Geographic Creative; 84 (bl) © Claudiovidri/Shutterstock.com; 84 (br) © Frans Lanting/National Geographic Creative; 87 (all) © Amy Toensing/National Geographic Creative; 88 Image Source/Alamy Stock Photo; 90 © TebNad/Shutterstock.com; 92 © Donald Miralle/Getty Images; 93 © Jonathan & Angela Scott/AWL Images/Getty Images; 94 © Sean Gallagher/National Geographic Creative; 96 © Michael Nichols/National Geographic Creative; 99 © Fabi Fliervoet; 100 © koh sze kiat/Shutterstock.com; 101 © William Perugini/Shutterstock.com; 102 © Cory Richards/National Geographic Creative; 104 (l) © Pius Lee/Shutterstock.com; 105 © Arcansel/Shutterstock.com; 106 (t) keith morris/Alamy Stock Photo; 106 (b) © Chris Ratcliffe/Bloomberg/Getty Images; 107 © Mariana Greif Etchebehere/Bloomberg/Getty Images; 108 © Matt McClain/The Washington Post/Getty Images; 109 Roger Davies/Alamy Stock Photo; 110 © Chirs Rainer/National Geographic Creative; 111 © Angiolo Manetti: 112 © pcruciatti/Shutterstock.com; 113 (t) LAMB/Alamy Stock Photo; 113 (b) © topnatthapon/Shutterstock.com; 114 © Jonathan Knowles/Getty Images; 116 (tl) © withGod/Shutterstock.com; 116 (tr) © Sylvie Bouchard/Shutterstock.com; 116 (bl) © Salvador Aznar/Shutterstock.com; 116 (br) © Peter Wollinga/Shutterstock.com; 117 © Pierre Verdy /AFP/Getty Images; 118 titoOnz/Alamy Stock Photo; 120 © Michael Buholzer/AFP/Getty Images; 121 © Bryan Christie Design; 123 (t) © Masterfile Royalty Free; 123 (b) © Mark Thiessen/National Geographic Creative; 124 mark phillips/Alamy Stock Photo; 125 © Martin Valigursky/Shutterstock.com; 126 (inset) ITAR-TASS Photo Agency/Alamy Stock Photo; 126 © NASA; 128 © Jimmy Chin and Lynsey Dyer/National Geographic Creative; 129 © Chris Rainier; 130 © Ricardo Stuckert; 131 © Michael Nichols/National Geographic Creative; 132 © STRDEL/Stringer/Getty Images; 135 © Matthieu Paley/National Geographic Creative; 136 © Dragon Images/Shutterstock.com; 138 © NurPhoto/Getty Images; 139 Illustration by www.british-sign.co.uk; 140 Arina Habich/Alamy Stock Photo; 141 © Jim Richardson/National Geographic Creative; 142 © 2011 by Anchor Books, a division of Penguin Random House Group Inc., from "The Man Who Ate His Boots: The Tragic History of the Search for the Northeast Passage" by Anthony Brandt. Used by permission of Alfred A. Knopf, a division of Random House Inc.; 142–143 © Paul Nicklen/National Geographic Creative; 144 (t) © John Goodrich/National Geographic Creative; 144 (b) © Beth Shapiro/National Geographic Creative; 145 © Lynn Johnson/National Geographic Creative; 147 © Ira Block/National Geographic Creative; 148 © Birgid Allig/Getty Images; 149 © Image Source/Getty Images; 150 Danita Delimont/Alamy Stock Photo; 152 © Steve Winter/National Geographic Creative.

Illustrations: 28 (l, r) Matthew Hams; 28 (m) emc design; 70 Laszlo Veres/Beehive Illustration.

ACKNOWLEDGEMENTS

The *Life* publishing team would like to thank the following teachers and students who provided invaluable and detailed feedback on the first edition:

Armik Adamians, Colombo Americano, Cali, Colombia; Carlos Alberto Aguirre, Universidad Madero, Puebla, Mexico; Anabel Aikin, La Escuela Oficial de Idiomas de Coslada, Madrid, Spain; Pamela Alvarez, Colegio Eccleston, Lanús, Argentina; Manuel Antonio, CEL – Unicamp, São Paolo, Brazil; Bob Ashcroft, Shonan Koka University, Japan; Linda Azzopardi, Clubclass, Malta; Éricka Bauchwitz, Universidad Madero, Puebla, Mexico; Paola Biancolini, Università Cattolica del Sacro Cuore, Milan, Italy; Laura Bottiglieri, Universidad Nacional de Salta, Argentina; Richard Brookes, Brookes Talen, Aalsmeer, Netherlands; Maria Cante, Universidad Madero, Puebla, Mexico; Carmín Castillo, Universidad Madero, Puebla, Mexico; Ana Laura Chacón, Universidad Madero, Puebla, Mexico; Somchao Chatnaridom, Suratthani Rajabhat University, Surat Thani, Thailand; Adrian Cini, British Study Centres, London, UK; Andrew Clarke, Centre of English Studies, Dublin, Ireland; Mariano Cordoni, Centro Universitario de

Idiomas, Buenos Aries, Argentina; Monica Cuellar, Universidad La Gran Colombia, Colombia; Jacqui Davis-Bowen, St Giles International, UK; Nuria Mendoza Dominguez, Universidad Nebrija, Madrid, Spain; Robin Duncan, ITC London, UK; Christine Eade, Libera Università Internazionale degli Studi Sociali Guido Carli, Rome, Italy; Leopoldo Pinzon Escobar, Universidad Catolica, Colombia; Joanne Evans, Linguarama, Berlin, Germany; Juan David Figueroa, Colombo Americano, Cali, Colombia; Emmanuel Flores, Universidad del Valle de Puebla, Mexico; Sally Fryer, University of Sheffield, Sheffield, UK; Antonio David Berbel García, Escuela Oficial de Idiomas de Almería, Spain; Lia Gargioni, Feltrinelli Secondary School, Milan, Italy; Roberta Giugni, Galileo Galilei Secondary School, Legnano, Italy; Monica Gomez, Universidad Pontificia Bolivariana, Colombia; Doctor Erwin Gonzales, Centro de Idiomas Universidad Nacional San Agustin, Peru; Ivonne Gonzalez, Universidad de La Sabana, Colombia; J Gouman, Pieter Zandt Scholengemeenschap, Kampen, Netherlands; Cherryll Harrison, UNINT, Rome, Italy; Lottie Harrison, International House Recoleta, Argentina; Marjo Heij, CSG Prins Maurits, Middelharnis, Netherlands; María del Pilar Hernández, Universidad Madero, Puebla, Mexico; Luz Stella Hernandez, Universidad de La Sabana, Colombia; Rogelio Herrera, Colombo Americano, Cali, Colombia; Amy Huang, Language Canada, Taipei, Taiwan; Huang Huei-Jiun, Pu Tai Senior High School, Taiwan; Nelson Jaramillo, Colombo Americano, Cali, Colombia; Jacek Kaczmarek, Xiehe YouDe High School, Taipei, Taiwan; Thurgadevi Kalay, Kaplan, Singapore; Noreen Kane, Centre of English Studies, Dublin, Ireland; Billy Kao, Jinwen University of Science and Technology, Taiwan; Shih-Fan Kao, Jinwen University of Science and Technology, Taipei, Taiwan; Youmay Kao, Mackay Junior College of Medicine, Nursing, and Management, Taipei, Taiwan; Fleur Kelder, Vechtstede College, Weesp, Netherlands; Dr Sarinya Khattiya, Chiang Mai University, Thailand; Lucy Khoo, Kaplan, Singapore; Karen Koh, Kaplan, Singapore; Susan Langerfeld, Liceo Scientifico Statale Augusto Righi, Rome, Italy; Hilary Lawler, Centre of English Studies, Dublin, Ireland; Eva Lendi, Kantonsschule Zürich Nord, Zürich, Switzerland; Evon Lo, Jinwen University of Science and Technology, Taiwan; Peter Loftus, Centre of English Studies, Dublin, Ireland; José Luiz, Inglês com Tecnologia, Cruzeiro, Brazil; Christopher MacGuire, UC Language Center, Chile; Eric Maher, Centre of English Studies, Dublin, Ireland; Nick Malewski, ITC London, UK; Claudia Maribell Loo, Universidad Madero, Puebla, Mexico; Malcolm Marr, ITC London, UK; Graciela Martin, ICANA (Belgrano), Argentina; Erik Meek, CS Vincent van Gogh, Assen, Netherlands; Marlene Merkt, Kantonsschule Zürich Nord, Zürich, Switzerland; David Moran, Qatar University, Doha, Qatar; Rosella Morini, Feltrinelli Secondary School, Milan, Italy; Judith Mundell, Quarenghi Adult Learning Centre, Milan, Italy; Cinthya Nestor, Universidad Madero, Puebla, Mexico; Peter O'Connor, Musashino University, Tokyo, Japan; Cliona O'Neill, Trinity School, Rome, Italy; María José Colón Orellana, Escola Oficial d'Idiomes de Terrassa, Barcelona, Spain; Viviana Ortega, Universidad Mayor, Santiago, Chile; Luc Peeters, Kyoto Sangyo University, Kyoto, Japan; Sanja Brekalo Pelin, La Escuela Oficial de Idiomas de Coslada, Madrid, Spain; Itzel Carolina Pérez, Universidad Madero, Puebla, Mexico; Sutthima Peung, Rajamangala University of Technology Rattanakosin, Thailand; Marina Pezzuoli, Liceo Scientifico Amedeo Avogadro, Rome, Italy; Andrew Pharis, Aichi Gakuin University, Nagoya, Japan; Hugh Podmore, St Giles International, UK; Carolina Porras, Universidad de La Sabana, Colombia; Brigit Portilla, Colombo Americano, Cali, Colombia; Soudaben Pradeep, Kaplan, Singapore; Judith Puertas, Colombo Americano, Cali, Colombia; Takako Ramsden, Kyoto Sangyo University, Kyoto, Japan; Sophie Rebel-Dijkstra, Aeres Hogeschool, Netherlands; Zita Reszler, Nottingham Language Academy, Nottingham, UK; Sophia Rizzo, St Giles International, UK; Gloria Stella Quintero Riveros, Universidad Catolica, Colombia; Cecilia Rosas, Euroidiomas, Peru; Eleonora Salas, IICANA Centro, Córdoba, Argentina; Victoria Samaniego, La Escuela Oficial de Idiomas de Pozuelo de Alarcón, Madrid, Spain; Jeanette Sandre, Universidad Madero, Puebla, Mexico; Bruno Scafati, ARICANA, Argentina; Anya Shaw, International House Belgrano, Argentina; Anne Smith, UNINT, Rome & University of Rome Tor Vergata, Italy; Suzannah Spencer-George, British Study Centres, Bournemouth, UK; Students of Cultura Inglesa, São Paolo, Brazil; Makiko Takeda, Aichi Gakuin University, Nagoya, Japan; Jilly Taylor, British Study Centres, London, UK; Juliana Trisno, Kaplan, Singapore; Ruey Miin Tsao, National Cheng Kung University, Tainan City, Taiwan; Michelle Uitterhoeve, Vechtstede College, Weesp, Netherlands; Anna Maria Usai, Liceo Spallanzani, Rome, Italy; Carolina Valdiri, Colombo Americano, Cali, Colombia; Gina Vasquez, Colombo Americano, Cali, Colombia; Andreas Vikran, NET School of English, Milan, Italy; Helen Ward, Oxford, UK; Mimi Watts, Università Cattolica del Sacro Cuore, Milan, Italy; Yvonne Wee, Kaplan Higher Education Academy, Singapore; Christopher Wood, Meijo University, Japan; Yanina Zagarrio, ARICANA, Argentina.

9th Fast Bomber Aviation Regiment (9 SBAP) 107
10th Fast Bomber Aviation Regiment (10 SBAP) 108
11th Light Bomber Aviation Regiment (11 LBAP) 109
13th Fast Bomber Aviation Regiment (13 SBAP) 109
14th Recconnaissance Aviation Regiment (14 RAP) 112
14th Transport Aviation Regiment (14 TAP) 112
15th Fighter Aviation Regiment (15 IAP) 112
16th Fighter Aviation Regiment (16 IAP) 114
16th Fast Bomber Aviation Regiment (16 SBAP) 114
18th Fast Bomber Aviation Regiment (18 SBAP) 116
19th Fighter Aviation Regiment (19 IAP) 118
20th Fighter Aviation Regiment (20 IAP) 120
21st Long-Range Bomber Aviation Regiment (21 DBAP) 120
23rd Fighter Aviation Regiment (23 IAP) 124
24th Fast Bomber Aviation Regiment (24 SBAP) 125
25th Fighter Aviation Regiment (25 IAP) 128
26th Fighter Aviation Regiment (26 IAP) 135
27th Fighter Aviation Regiment (27 IAP) 138
31st Fast Bomber Aviation Regiment (31 SBAP) 138
33rd Fast Bomber Aviation Regiment (33 SBAP) 140
34th Fighter Aviation Regiment (34 IAP) 141
35th Fast Bomber Aviation Regiment (35 SBAP) 141
38th Fighter Aviation Regiment (38 IAP) 144
39th Fast Bomber Aviation Regiment (39 SBAP) 148
41st Fast Bomber Aviation Regiment (41 SBAP) 149
42nd Long-Range Bomber Aviation Regiment (42 DBAP) 155
43rd Light Bomber Aviation Regiment (43 LBAP) 159
44th Fighter Aviation Regiment (44 IAP) 161
44th Fast Bomber Aviation Regiment (44 SBAP) 163
45th Fast Bomber Aviation Regiment (45 SBAP) 167
48th Fighter Aviation Regiment (48 IAP) 167
48th Fast Bomber Aviation Regiment (48 SBAP) 168
49th Fighter Aviation Regiment (49 IAP) 170
49th Fast Bomber Aviation Regiment (49 SBAP) 176
50th Fast Bomber Aviation Regiment (50 SBAP) 176
52th Fast Bomber Aviation Regiment (52 SBAP) 178
53rd Long-Range Bomber Aviation Regiment (53 DBAP) 178
54th Fast Bomber Aviation Regiment (54 SBAP) 186
58th Fast Bomber Aviation Regiment (58 SBAP) 188
60th Fast Bomber Aviation Regiment (60 SBAP) 189
63rd Fast Bomber Aviation Regiment (63 SBAP) 190
68th Fighter Aviation Regiment (68 IAP) 190
69th Fighter Aviation Regiment (69 IAP) 195
72nd Mixed Aviation Regiment (72 SAP) 196
80th Mixed Aviation Regiment (80 SAP) 201
85th Special Purpose Aviation Regiment (85 AP ON) 203
145th Fighter Aviation Regiment (145 IAP) 206
146th Fighter Aviation Regiment (146 IAP) 207
147th Detached Fighter Aviation Regiment (147 OIAP) 207
148th Fighter Aviation Regiment (148 IAP) 208
149th Fighter Aviation Regiment (149 IAP) 209
152nd Fighter Aviation Regiment (152 IAP) 214
153rd Fighter Aviation Regiment (153 IAP) 216

Detached Aviation Squadrons (OAE) 217
1st Air Defense Fighter Aviation Squadron (1 IAE PVO) 217
1st Long-Range Reconnaissance Squadron (1 DRAE) 217
4th Long-Range Reconnaissance Squadron (4 DRAE) 219
8th Detached Night Aviation Squadron (8 ONAE) 220
12th Detached Fighter Aviation Squadron (12 OIAE) 220
12th Detached Special Purpose Aviation Squadron (12 OAE ON) 221
19th Detached Aviation Squadron (19 OAE) 221

29th Detached Liaison Aviation Squadron (29 OAES) 221
31st Military Reconnaissance Aviation Squadron (31 VRAE) 222
32nd Reconnaissance Aviation Squadron (32 RAE) 222
33rd Reconnaissance Aviation Squadron (33 RAE)... 223
34th Long-Range Reconnaissance Squadron (34 DRAE).. 223
38th Heavy Transport Aviation Squadron (38 TTAE) 225
41st Reconnaissance Aviation Squadron (41 RAE) 225
50th Detached Aviation Squadron (50 OAE) 226
56th Detached Army Corps Aviation Squadron (56 OKAE) 226
Detached Aviation Units (OAO) 226
1st Army Corps Aviation Unit (1 KAO) 226
2nd Army Corps Aviation Unit (2 KAO) 227
5th Detached Army Corps Aviation Unit (5 OKAO or 5 KAO) 228
9th Army Corps Aviation Unit (9 KAO)... 228
11th Army Corps Aviation Unit (11 KAO) 229
15th Army Corps Aviation Unit (15 KAO) 229
16th Army Corps Aviation Unit (16 KAO) 232
18th Army Corps Aviation Unit (18 KAO) 232
23rd Army Corps Aviation Unit (23 KAO) 234
33rd Liaison Aviation Unit at 9th Army HQ (33 AO svyazi Shtaba 9.A)... 234
Liaison Flights *(Aviazveno Svyazi)* 235
29th Liaison Flight (29 AZv sv) 235
36th Liaison Flight (36 AZv sv) 235
61st Liaison Flight (61 AZv sv) 235
69th Liaison Flight (69 AZv sv) 235
85th Liaison Flight (85 AZv sv) 235
Aviation Groups 236
Aviation Group Tkachenko *(Aviagruppa Tkachenko)* 236
Aviation Group Filin *(Aviagruppa Filina)* 237
Aviation Group Spirin *(Aviagruppa Spirina)* 238
Civil Air Fleet Special Aviation Group (OAG GVF)... 239
1st Combined Aviation Unit of the Civil Air Fleet 246
2nd Special Unit of the Civil Air Fleet (2 OO GVF) 246
3rd Special Unit of the Civil Air Fleet, also 3rd Combined Special Air Unit of the Civil Air Fleet (3 OO
   GVF) 247
Baltic Fleet Air Force (VVS KBF) 248
VVS KBF Organisation 248
8 Bomber Aviation Brigade (8 BAB) 250
1 Aviation Regiment (1 AP) 250
57 Aviation Regiment (57 AP) 256
11 Detached Fighter Aviation Squadron (11 OIAE) 259
12 Detached Fighter Aviation Squadron (12 OIAE) 260
13 Detached Fighter Aviation Squadron (13 OIAE) 261
61 Fighter Aviation Brigade (61 IAB).. 263
5 Fighter Aviation Regiment (5 IAP) 266
Night Fighter Group... 267
13 Fighter Aviation Regiment (13 IAP) 267
10 Aviation Brigade (10 AB) 268
1 and 2 Detached Fast Bomber Aviation Squadron (1 and 2 OSBAE) 269
3 Detached Bomber Aviation Squadron (3 OBAE, also called 3 Detached Long-Range Bomber
   Aviation Squadron 3 OBDAB).. 272
30 Detached Fighter Aviation Squadron (30 OIAE) 275
12 Detached Maritime Close Reconnassaince Aviation Squadron (12 OMBRAE)................... 276
43 Detached Maritime Reconnaissance Aviation Squadron (43 OMRAE) 276
44 Detached Maritime Reconnaissance Aviation Squadron (44 OMRAE) 276
Detached Units 277
15 Detached Maritime Reconnaissance Aviation Regiment (15 OMRAP)................................ 277
18 Maritime Close Reconnaissance Aviation Squadron (18 OMBRAE) 279
19 Maritime Close Reconnaissance Aviation Squadron (19 OMBRAE) 279
58 Detached Aviation Squadron (58 OAE) 279
12 Detached Maritime Reconnaissance Aviation Unit (12 OMRAO) 279

71 Detached Fire-Control Aviation Unit (71 OKAO)	279
Ladoga Military Flotilla (VVS LVF)	280
41 Detached Maritime Reconnaissance Aviation Squadron (41 OMRAE)	281
Northern Fleet Air Force (VVS SF)	282
118 Maritime Reconnaissance Aviation Regiment (118 MRAP)	283
72 Aviation Regiment (72 AP)	283
White Sea Flotilla	284
49 Detached Naval Close-Reconnaissance Aviation Squadron (49 OMBRAE)	284
Claims and Losses	284
Aviator POWs	287
Finnish POWs in Soviet Union	289
Finnish War Booty Aircraft	289
Winter War Impact on the Soviet Air Forces	293
Finnish Air Force during the Winter War 1939–1940	295
Introduction	295
Aircraft procurement in October 1939	300
30 November 1939 – the Winter War breaks out	302
Finnish Air Force operations summary:	302
International assistance during the Winter War	307
Assistance offered by allied countries (England, France, Poland)	312
Colour Profiles	329

English abbreviations

A-A	AntiAircraft (Artillery)
C.O.	Commanding officer
c/n	Construction number
CoS	Chief of Staff
DOW	Died of wounds
GPW	Great Patriotic War (Soviet term for the conflict with Germany and its allies 22.6.1941–9.5.1945)
HQ	Headquarter(s)
HSU	Hero of the Soviet Union
KIA	Killed in action
MD	Military district
MG	Machine gun
MIA	Missing in action
POW	Prisoner of war
WIA	Wounded in action

Finnish abbreviations

KoeL	Koelentue (Test flight)
LeR	Lentorykmentti (Aviation regiment)
LLv, LLv	Lentolaivue (Aviation squadron)
MHR	Mannerheim-ristin ritari (Mannerheim Cross Knight)
VL	Valtion lentokonetehdas (State Aircraft Factory, Tampere)

Soviet Army and Air Force ranks, Officers

Soviet		English	Finnish
Before 7 May 1940	From 7 May 1940		
Marshal	*Marshal*	Marshal	*Marsalkka*
Komandarm	*General armii*	Army General	*(Armeijakenraali, not applicable)*
Komkor	*General-polkovnik*	Colonel General	*(Kenraaliversti, not applicable)*
Komdiv	*General-lejtenant (g-l)*	Lieutenant General	*Kenraaliluutnantti (kenrl)*
Kombrig	*General-major (g-m)*	Major General	*Kenraalimajuri (kenrm)*
Polkovnik (polk)	*Polkovnik (polk)*	Colonel	*Eversti (ev)*
Podpolkovnik (podp)	*Podpolkovnik (podp)*	Lieutenant Colonel	*Everstiluutnantti (evl)*
Major	*Major (maj)*	Major	*Majuri (maj)*
Kapitan	*Kapitan (kapt)*	Captain	*Kapteeni (kapt)*
Starshiy leitenant (st.lt)	*Starshiy leitenant (st.lt)*	Senior Lieutenant	*Yliluutnantti (ylil)*
Leitenant (lt)	*Leitenant (lt)*	Lieutenant	*Luutnantti (luutn)*
Mladshiy leitenant (ml.lt)	*Mladshiy leitenant (ml.lt)*	Second Lieutenant (Ensign)	*Vänrikki (vänr)*

Soviet Army and Air Force ranks, NCOs

Soviet		English	Finnish
Before 7 May 1940	After 7 May 1940		
(not applicable)	*(not applicable)*	Flight Master	*Lentomestari (lentom)*
Starshina (star)	*Starshina (star)*	Master Sergeant	*Vääpeli (vääp)*
Mladshiy komzvod (ml.kzv)	*Starshiy serzhant (st.ser)*	Senior Sergeant	*Ylikersantti (ylik)*
(not applicable)	*Serzhant (ser)*	Sergeant	*Kersantti (kers)*
(not applicable)	*Mladshiy serzhant (st.ser)*	Junior Sergeant	*Alikersantti (alik)*
Otdelennyy komandir	*Yefrejtor (yefr)*	Corporal	*Korpraali (korp)*
Krasnoarmeyets (kr-ts)	*Krasnoarmeyets (kr-ts)*	Private	*Sotamies, (puna-armeijalainen)*

Soviet Navy ranks

Soviet		English	Finnish
Before 7 May 1940	From 7 May 1940		
Flagman flota	*Admiral*	Admiral	*Amiraali*
Flagman 1.ranga	*Vitse-admiral*	Vice Admiral	*Vara-amiraali*
Flagman 2.ranga	*Kontra-admiral*	Rear Admiral	*Kontra-amiraali*
Kapitan 1.ranga (kapt 1.r)	*Kapitan 1.ranga (kapt 1.r)*	Commodore	*Kommodori*
Kapitan 2.ranga (kapt 2.r)	*Kapitan 2.ranga (kapt 2.r)*	Commander	*Komentaja*
Kapitan 3.ranga (kapt 3.r)	*Kapitan 3.ranga (kapt 3.r)*	Lieutenant Commander	*Komentajakapteeni*
Kapitan-leitenant (kapt-lt)	*Kapitan-leitenant (kapt-lt)*	Senior Lieutenant	*Kapteeniluutnantti*
Starshiy leitenant (st.lt)	*Starshiy leitenant (st.lt)*	First Lieutenant	*Yliluutnantti*
Leitenant (lt)	*Leitenant (lt)*	Lieutenant	*Luutnantti*
Mladshiy leitenant (ml.lt)	*Mladshiy leitenant (ml.lt)*	Ensign	*Aliluutnantti*
Michman	*Michman*	Chief Petty Officer	*Ylipursimies*
Starshina (star)	*Starshina (star)*	Petty Officer	*Pursimies*
Krasnoflotets (kr-ts)	*Krasnoflotets (kr-ts)*	Seaman	*Matruusi*

Soviet Political officer ranks

Soviet	English	Finnish
Armeyskiy komissar (arm.komiss)	(Army Commissar)	(Armeijakomissaari)
Korpusnoy komissar (korp.komiss)	(Army Corps Commissar)	(Armeijakuntakomissaari)
Divizionnyy komissar (div.komiss)	(Division Commissar)	(Divisioonakomissaari)
Brigadnyy komissar (brig.komiss)	(Brigade Commissar)	(Prikaatikomissaari)
Polkovoy komissar (polk.komiss)	(Regiment Commissar)	(Rykmenttikomissaari)
Bataljonnyy komissar (bat.komiss)	(Battalion Commissar)	(Pataljoonakomissaari)
Starshiy politruk (st.politr)	(Senior Politruk)	(Vanhempi politrukki)
Politruk (politr)	(Politruk)	(Politrukki)
Mladshiy politruk (ml.politr)	(Junior Politruk)	(Nuorempi politrukki)

Foreword

The Winter War, which started on 30 November 1939 with the brutal attack by the Soviet Union, Finland's eastern neighbour and superpower, is for ever written into the collective memory of the Finnish people. To the surprise of the outside world and of all Finns, the lightning war planned by Stalin did not take place.

After three months of hopeless resistance a peace treaty was signed on 13 March 1940. Although the peace terms were extremely harsh and vast territories were handed over to the former enemy, the most important thing was nevertheless achieved: Finland did not capitulate nor was it occupied.

In the Kremlin's war planning important tasks were allocated to the Red Air Forces: to crush Finnish fighting ability and will by bombing rear areas, and to give the Red Army ground forces support on the battlefield.

The unexpectedly difficult Winter War was to have a deep impact on the Soviet Air Force and the future careers of Soviet aviation officers. Initially only the Leningrad Military District and the Baltic Fleet were allocated for the anticipated short campaign. Soon reinforcements, in particular fresh aviation units, had to be sent to the front. Later, aviation units were dispatched from practically all over the Soviet Union, even from the Far East and Pacific Fleet. Many large Air Force formations were split up into smaller units to be able to operate from temporary bases north of Lake Ladoga, in Northern Karelia and in the Arctic Murman region.

Several aviation officers who later served in prominent positions in the Great Patriotic War got their baptism of fire in the Winter War. The impact of the war's experience was still significant during the Cold war.

For the first time ever all Soviet aviation units on both land and sea fronts are presented in this book with as much detail of organisation, combat history and losses as possible. Some elements of the book were published by the Finnish Apali Publishing Co. in 2004 (Soviet Naval Air Forces in the Winter War, co-authored by Samuil Tirkeltaub and Gennadiy Petrov), and 2011 (Red Army Air Forces in the Winter War, translated into Russian in 2014), but are here significantly updated and expanded with previously unpublished material. The book draws heavily on documents from the Russian State War Archive (RGVA, Moscow) and Russian State Naval Archive (RGAVMF, St.Petersburg), published aviation regiment histories, aviator's memoirs, and also Finnish intelligence information, captured Soviet documents, POW interrogation reports etc.

Although the Winter War was very seldom explicitly referred to in the Soviet Union, interesting facts and references and even detailed descriptions of air combats can be found in the rich literature of memoirs.

Among my Russian friends I want to thank the renowned aviation historians Sergej Abrosov and Oleg Kiselev, whose research and publications provided valuable additions to my own work. Ilya Prokofyev generously provided his loss lists.

My friend of many years Gennadiy Petrov has again provided a mass of unique, previously unpublished photographs. The late Samuil Tirkeltaub worked for many years in the RGAVMF, collecting material about the history the Baltic Fleet Air Force (VVS KBF), to which Dr. Pavel Petrov has added exact loss information. Photos and information are also provided by the historians Kirill Aleksandrov, Viktor Kulikov, Aleksandr Makhalin (+), Andrei Nikitin, Denis Sivach, Konstantin Strelbitskiy, Dmitriy Khazanov, Yevgeniy Balashov, Leonid Karankevich, Vyacheslav Nikitin, Nina Stolepova and Bair Irincheev. Colonel Yulij Stojlik (+) provided unique photos from the collection of his aviator father Boris Stojlik (who was killed in aerial combat over Finland on 25 June 1941).

I have also got significant assistance from the following institutions: Finnish National Archive, Photo Archive of Finnish Defence Forces (SA-kuva), Finnish Aviation Museum and Finnish Air Force Museum; friends and colleagues Lennart Andersson, Göran Bruun, Mikael Forslund, Matti Haapavaara (+), Pentti Mannincn, Kyösti Partonen, Pekka Simula, Kari Stenman, Antero Uitto and Jukka Vesen.

Finnish Cultural Fond, Finnish Air Force Support Fond, Finnish Non-Fiction Writers and Swedish Cultural Fond have supported my research in the Russian archives. The color profiles are made by Vasiliy Zolotov and Valeriy Bulba. I am personally responsible for all conclusions, possible misunderstandings and errors.

Helsinki 30 November 2019
(80 years from the outbreak of the Winter War)
Carl-Fredrik Geust

The Winter War – General Outline

For over 500 years Finland was a part of the Kingdom of Sweden, but after the Swedish-Russian war 1808–1809 Finland was separated from Sweden and became an autonomous Grand Duchy of the Russian Empire. After the Russian Revolution in 1917 Finland declared its independence on 6 December 1917.

ReconnaissanceWorld War Finland attempted to solve its security issues by turning to the leading Western European nations (England, France and Germany), and also the neighbouring countries around the Baltic Sea (in particular Sweden) for support.

However, Finland's strategic position changed dramatically on 23 August 1939, when the infamous Molotov-Ribbentrop pact was signed in Moscow, and opened the way for the German attack against Poland on 1 September 1939. The Red Army advanced in its turn into eastern Poland on 17 September 1939, after which vast Polish territories were attached to the Byelorussian and Ukrainian Socialist Soviet Republics. In Soviet terminology this process was cynically named "liberalization of western parts of Byelorussia and Ukraine".

On 28 September 1939 a second Soviet-German Treaty, now concerning "Friendship and Borders", was signed in Moscow. Simultaneously the Kremlin turned to the other countries within its "sphere of interest" in accordance with the top-secret German-Soviet additional protocol, first to the Baltic republics and then to Finland.

The world was shocked when German Foreign Minister Joachim von Ribbentrop unexpectedly flew to Moscow 23 August 1939 and signed the infamous Nonagression Pact with his Soviet colleague Vyacheslav Molotov. Komandarm Boris Shaposhnikov (Head of Red Army General Staff), Ribbentrop, Stalin and Soviet interpreter Vladimir Pavlov were witnesses when Molotov signed the Pact. (Archiwum Docendo)

Baltic bases

The Soviet-Estonian Mutual Assistance Treaty was signed in Moscow on 28 September 1939, permitting Soviet naval and Air Force bases in Estonia. Details of the Soviet garrisons were elaborated in a protocol signed in Tallinn on 10 October 1939.

Soviet Air Force units were thus to be located in Estonia as follows:
- Paldiski area: one fighter and one bomber aviation regiment
- Haapsalu area: an aviation brigade HQ and one bomber aviation regiment
- Saaremaa island: one fighter aviation regiment

Rear airfields were additionally to be constructed in Kuusiku and Kehtna (near Rapla). Entrance of Soviet troops into Estonia was to begin on 18 October 1939, with 255 aircraft to be based in Estonia. Detailed protocols desciribing naval bases were signed on 11 October 1939, and included naval aviation bases at Kihelkonna and Koiguste (at the western and eastern shores of Saaremaa respectively).

Similar Mutual Assistance Treaties were signed with Latvia and Lithuania in Moscow 5 and 10 October 1939 respectively, with detailed protocols signed in Riga on 23 October and in Kaunas on 28 October. In Latvia fighter aviation regiments were to be located in Ventspils-Piltene and in Liepaja-Grobina and a bomber regiment in Vainode-Ezere. Entrance of Soviet troops into Latvia was to commence 29–31 October 1939.

In Lithuania a bomber unit (personnel up to 900 soldiers) and a fighter unit (max. 600 soldiers) were to be located in Gaiziunai (25 km north-east of Kaunas) and Alytus (50 km south of Kaunas), and additional reserve bases in the Skuodas-Jurbarkas-Alytus and Siauliai-Jonava-Vilnius directions. Entrance of Soviet troops into Lithuania was to commence on 3 November 1939.

Negotiations with Finland

Meanwhile the Finnish government was invited on 5 October 1939 to negotiations concerning so-called "territorial problems". Stalin wanted to eliminate potential interference by third parties in Finland, which might threaten Soviet security interests. A confidential request to move the Soviet-Finnish border on the Karelian Isthmus about 150 km to the north-west had already been presented to Finland in March 1939. Furthermore the Hanko peninsula with its ice-free port at the mouth of the Gulf of Finland and Kalastajasaarento ("Fisherman's peninsula"; Rybachyi and Srednyi Peninsulas in Russian) in the Barents Sea should – partly or entirely – be transferred to the Soviet Union.

The Hanko region was of special historical significance for the Soviet Navy. The naval victory of Czar Peter the Great over the Swedish Navy on 26–27 July 1714 at Hanko became the starting point for the development of Russian sea power. Since that time one of the big ships of the Russian/Soviet Navy has always proudly carried the name *Gangut* (Russian variant of Swedish *Hangö udd*), and the last Sunday in July is celebrated as Navy Day in Russia.

A Soviet Naval base in Hanko would thus ensure total control of the entrance to the Gulf of Finland. In case Finland might refuse to permanently transfer Hanko to the USSR, a 30-year lease of the territory would also be acceptable. In exchange Finland was offered double the amount of territory in Soviet Karelia.

From 12 October 1939 Soviet-Finnish negotiations were held in Moscow. The Soviet Government presented a proposal concerning the territorial exchange, and also proposed a mutual assistance treaty enabling Soviet military units to enter Finnish territory under certain conditions. Both proposals were rejected by the Finns. The negotiations were finally interrupted on 13 November 1939, after which the situation escalated rapidly.

"The deal is closed" – Stalin congratulated Ribbentrop after signing the pact 23 August 1939. (Archiwum Docendo)

War Preparations

War preparations had already been initiated in October 1939, simultaneously with the negotiations in Moscow. On 10 October 1939 the Finnish Army was discretely mobilized under cover of *extraordinary manoeuvres*. Moscow had naturally started preparations even before Finland was invited to negotiations.

On 26 October 1939, the Baltic Fleet Air Force (VVS KBF) was ordered to perform regular reconnaissance patrols over the Gulf of Finland. Also on the same day two SB bombers led by Captain V.I. Rakov (squadron commander of 57 AP) performed a daring mission searching for the Finnish coastal armoured ships *Väinämöinen* and *Ilmarinen*, seriously violating Finnish air space. The ships were located at anchor near Nagu (in the archipelago between Turku and the Åland island). Because of the complete surprise of Rakov's low-level dash no opposing fire took place.

After this overflight the armoured ships moved to the well-camouflagued Högsåra anchorage. On the western shore of Lake Ladoga Soviet overflights of the Finnish coastal artillery forts at Konevitsa-Ylläpäänniemi-Taipale (Järisevä) were observed on 7 and 22 November. Gradually Soviet aircraft were met by Finnish ground fire.

On 11 November 1939 a Soviet MBR-2 flying boat (of 15 OMBRAE) took photos of Hogland (Suursaari), the central island in the Gulf of Finland.

The Finnish Air Force had also performed similar reconnaissance flights in the eastern part of Gulf of Finland (even up to the approaches to Kronstadt). In summer and autumn 1939 Captain Armas Eskola of LeR 4 performed several clandestine high-altitude photo reconnaissance missions deep into Soviet Karelia and the Kronstadt and Leningrad areas with specially equipped Blenheim bombers (BL-114, BL-118 and BL-110). The intention of Eskola's top secret flights was to check the possible build-up of Soviet armed forces along roads and railways leading towards Finland.

Operational plans were subseqently tentatively updated and forwarded to Army, Naval and Air Force units. On 3 November 1939 the Soviet Baltic and Northern Fleets were instructed to be ready for war against Finland. The Baltic Fleet was further ordered to prepare "forward bases" at Ust'-Luga (in the Luga Bay) and Peipiya (in the Koporskaya Bay) by 12 November 1939. Large-scale movements of troops

Soon after Germany attacked Poland on 1 September 1939, and 17 September 1939 the Red Army advanced into Eastern Poland. The new allies met in Lublin and organized a joint parade in Brest. The parade was reviewed by Maj.Gen. Heinz Guderian and kombrig Semyeon Krivoshein. (Archiwum Docendo)

and air force units to North-West Russia were already initiated, on 5 November 1939 lists of bombing targets were compiled, and on 17 November attack orders were distributed to Long-Range Bomber Regiments.

The Soviet Government (or Council of People's Commissars) Defence Committee had already decided in 1938 to subordinate the Naval Air Forces to the terrestrial Military Districts in case of war. The Baltic Fleet AF (VVS KBF) was consequently to be subordinated to the Leningrad Military District (LVO), all orders were however to be given by the Baltic Fleet HQ. In order to simplify the distribution of responsibility, a "demarcation line" between Baltic Fleet and "Military District" Air Forces was defined. Leningrad Military District AF was thus responsible for all air operations east of Viipuri (except the Finnish Koivisto Coastal Artillery Fort, which was repeatedly attacked and strafed by Soviet Naval aircraft).

On 23 November 1939 detailed orders were issued to the Baltic Fleet Air Force (VVS KBF), listing tasks in the coming war:
- defence of Leningrad city and industries, Kronstadt Naval base, and "forward bases" against enemy air and seaborne attacks;
- destruction of enemy naval vessels (in particular the Finnish armoured ships *Ilmarinen* and *Väinämöinen* and submarines),
- destruction of enemy aircraft, airfields and AF bases west of Kotka-Suursaari longitude (27° east);
- destruction of coastal batteries and fortified positions at Hanko;
- support to a special reconnaissance operation against Suursaari (*Hogland*, in Russian spelled *Gogland*), and invasion operations of Lavansaari (now *Moshchnyy*) and Seiskari (*Seskar*) islands in the Gulf of Finland;
- anti-submarine patrolling up to 27° eastern longitude;
- readiness to destroy enemy defensive fortifications of Helsinki and Kotka, Koivisto and Ino coastal batteries, and ships transporting troops bound for the Åland Islands.

VVS KBF was also ordered to avoid bombing of enemy cities and villages without troop concentrations.

On 26 November 1939 the Soviet Government accused Finland of artillery shelling of Soviet troops at Mainila, just east of the Soviet-Finnish border on the Karelian Isthmus. The Soviet Government demanded Finland withdraw all troops to 20–25 km from the border. Finland responded immediately that no artillery batteries were able to shell Mainila, and proposed that both parties should mutually withdraw their troops from the vicinity of the border. The events had now escalated out of control, and two days later the Soviet Government renounced the Soviet-Finnish non-aggression treaty of 1932. Moscow even refused to receive the Finnish proposal to set up a joint commission to investigate the Mainila incident, as diplomatic relations were already broken off by the Kremlin.

On the night of 30 November 1939 all Soviet military radio stations transmitted the coded signal *FAKEL* – the attack order – to all units and ships. In the morning the Red Army crossed the Soviet-Finnish border between the Gulf of Finland and the Arctic Ocean, and bomber aviation regiments attacked virtually all large cities in southern Finland, including Helsinki – Finland's capital.

This development in fact followed a staff war game performed some eight months earlier in Leningrad, starting with border incidents at Mainila (sic!), after which the Red Army was to cross the border to Finland and advance towards Viipuri, Lappeenranta and Mikkeli. The Baltic Fleet would occupy Suursaari, Lavansaari and Seiskari islands in order to "ensure the security of Leningrad". Full-scale ma-

On 28 September 1939 Ribbentrop made another trip to Moscow and signed a Friendship and Border Treaty with Molotov, German interpreter Gustav Hilger watching the handshake. Stalin and Ribbentrop signed the map with the new Soviet-German border. (Archiwum Docendo)

noeuvres were to follow in September 1939. Because of the changed political situation (as the former "probable enemy" Germany had became a friend and ally) and the outbreak of the Second World War, all manoeuvres were cancelled and a real war was initiated.

The next day after the attack, on 1 December 1939 the People's Government of the Democratic Republic of Finland was set up in the small city of Terijoki (now *Zelenogorsk*), very close to the border on the shore of Gulf of Finland. This new Finnish "Government" was headed by O.W. Kuusinen, a Finnish communist and Komintern secretary living in exile in the Soviet Union since 1918. Kuusinen signed a Friendship and Mutual Assistance Treaty with the Soviet Government on 2 December, happily accepting the proposed territorial exchange. Thus Stalin's territorial problem was solved – but only on paper.

To the apparent surprise of Moscow the Finns continued fighting. The bizarre Kuusinen episode in fact only strengthened Finnish resistance, and contributed considerably to reunifying the Finnish people – only two decades earlier divided in a blood-spilling civil war between White and Red Finns.

As Finland received in the main only sympathy and practically no military assistance from other countries, it was only too obvious that the war would result in a military catastrophy for Finland.

Discreet contacts with the Soviet Government were established via Sweden, and in late January 1940 Stalin was ready to quietly forget "Kuusinen's Government". Recent research indicates that Anglo-French plans to bomb the Soviet oil fields at Baku may have contributed to Stalin's decision to accept the Finnish government at the negotiation table, before he would face a multi-front war against England and France.

After the Soviet break-through of the Mannerheim Line on the Karelian Isthmus on 10 February 1940, Moscow's very harsh peace conditions were received on 23 February via Sweden. A final futile attempt was made to get military assistance from England and France, but because of the hopeless military situation Finland was ready to send a delegation to Moscow for peace negotiations. Prime Minister Risto Ryti's delegation departed for Moscow via Stockholm on 6 March 1940 on board Swedish ABA airliner Ju 52/3m SE-AFB.

The Red Army entered Estonian territory on 18 October 1939.

In late September-early October 1939 Mutual Assistance Pacts were signed with the three Baltic states. On 5 October 1939 the Latvian Pact was signed by Molotov, witnessed by Stalin and Latvian Foreign Minister Vilhelms Munters. (Archiwum Docendo)

Soviet territorial demands in the Gulf of Finland October 1939.

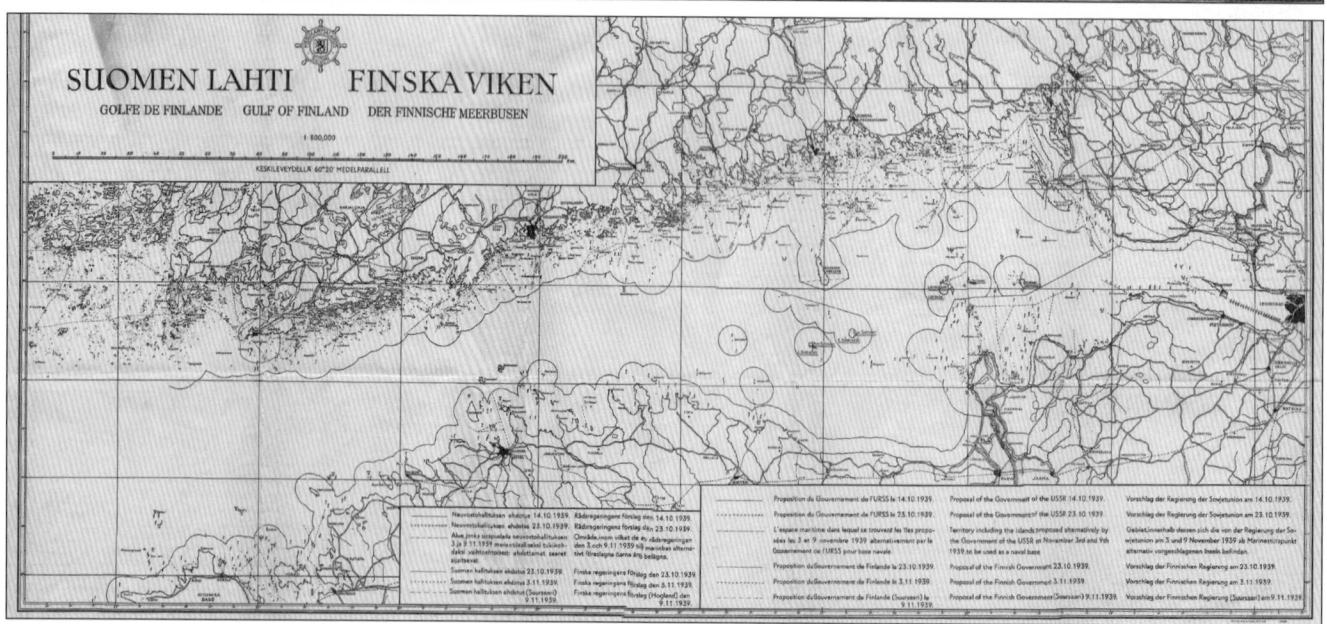

The aircraft was piloted by Sixten Barenthein, performing an "unscheduled flight" from Stockholm to Moscow via Riga. For security reasons the Finns were entered on the passenger list with false Swedish names. The passengers Arngren, Bronander, Eskilsson, Bergkvist, Sundström, Blomgren and Karlkvist were in fact Prime Minister Risto Ryti, Minister J.K. Paasikivi, *Maj.Gen.* Rudolf Walden, Parliament Member Professor Väinö Voionmaa, Counsellor Rafael Hakkarainen, Miss Polvinen and Mr. Johan Nykopp (the last three of the Foreign Ministry).

The peace treaty was signed in Moscow on the night of 12/13 March 1940. In line with the preliminary conditions Finland was forced to cede the Karelian Isthmus (including the city of Viipuri), the north-western shore of Lake Ladoga (the so-called Ladoga Karelia with the cities of Käkisalmi and Sortavala), Salla (Kuolajärvi) and arctic Kalastajasaarento (Rybachiy and Sredniy Peninsulas) on the Barents Sea. Hanko was leased for 30 years to the USSR as a Naval base.

Some 24,000 Finnish soldiers were killed in action and 44,000 more wounded, and about 1,000 Finnish civilians died

Finnish Minister Väinö Tanner and J.K. Paasikivi returning from one of the resultless negotiating rounds in Kremlin in October 1939. (SA-kuva)

Captain A. Eskola performed several photo-reconnaissance flights deep into Soviet territory with specially equipped Blenheims of LLv 46 in summer 1939. The super-secret photos were taken early morning on 19.8.1939 from 8,000 m altitude on the return leg from Leningrad towards Finland. Eskola was piloting Blenheim I BL-110, equipped with a Zeiss Rb 3030/50 camera. The photos depict Levashovo (left photo, with tens of aircraft, ready for the Air Force Day Annual parade next day, visible in the original print) and on the right photo Kasimovo AF bases. (Finnish National Archive)

13

from Soviet bombs. According to the Soviet Government Red Army losses were 220,000 soldiers, of which 49,000 were killed in action. Exact figures are not available; actual losses may have been greater.

Soviet Military Supreme Command

The Soviet supreme leader – in all categories – was Iosif Stalin (1879–1953), formally Secretary General of the Central Committee of the Bolshevik Party. His closest compatriot and aide was Vyacheslav Molotov (1890–1986), formally Chairman of the Council of People's Commissars and simultaneously People's Commissar of Foreign Affairs, or both Prime and Foreign minister.

Another old bolshevik, Mikhail Kalinin (1875–1946) served as titular Soviet Head of State (Chairman of the Presidium of the Supreme Soviet) from 1919 to 1946, mainly performing ceremonial tasks only, such as handing out high decorations like the Golden Star of the Hero of Soviet Union awards etc.

The Commander of the Red Army, or People's Commissar of Defence from 1925 was Marshal of the Soviet Union Klim Voroshilov (1881–1969). On 7 May 1940 he was replaced by Marshal Semyon Timoshenko (1895–1970). The General Staff was headed by *komandarm 1.r* Boris Shaposhnikov (1882–1945) from 10 May 1937 to August 1940.

On 9 December 1939 a special command for all military actions against Finland, Stavka of the Supreme Command of the Red Army was set up, consisting of Stalin, Voroshilov, Shaposhnikov and *flagman 2.r* Nikolai Kuznetsov (1904–1974), People's Commissar of the Naval Forces. On 5 January 1940 the name of this Command organ was changed to Stavka of Supreme Military Council of the Red Army. It is noteworthy that the Soviet Air Force was not represented in the Stavka.

Notes:
In summer 1940 international style General and Admiral ranks were introduced, *komandarm* (Army Commissar), *komkor* (Army Corps Commander) becoming Lt General, *komdiv* (Division Commander) and *kombrig* (Brigade Commander) becoming Major General and Brigade General respectively, while *flagman* ranks were converted to corresponding Admiral ranks. The old ranks were however not always exactly converted, so some discrepances can be observed.

On 15 March 1946 the denomination People's Commissar (and Commissariate) was replaced by the modern terms Minister and Ministry.

11.11.1939 kapitan F.A. Usachev (15 OMRAP) made a low level reconnaissance flight over Hogland and photographed Suurkylä (upper) and Kiiskinkylä (lower) fishing villages. (RGAVMF)

Red Army in the Winter War

On 30 November 1939 the USSR mobilized four ground armies (consisting of up to 9 infantry divisions, artillery and tank units, in addition to various special units such as signals, pioneers etc), along the 1,000 km Finnish border. During the Winter War two more Armies, 13th and 15th, were formed.

The strongest 7th Army was grouped at the Karelian isthmus, which was anticipated to be the main direction of attack, leading directly to Viipuri (the main city in Karelia) and further to Helsinki, the Finnish capital.

- 7th Army was formed in the Kalinin Military District 14 September 1939, and subordinated to Leningrad Military District. On 26 September 1939 7th Army was transferred to Idritsa at the Latvian border in order to secure the establishment of Soviet garrisons in the Baltic republics, and moved on to the Karelian isthmus 15 November 1939.
  Commander: *komandarm 2. r.* Vsevolod Yakovlev (1895–1974), to 9.12.1939.
  komandarm 2. r. Kirill Meretskov (1897–1968), from 9.12.1939.
  7th Army was dissolved after the Winter War, but was soon reorganized in Soviet Karelia.
- 13th Army was established on 25 December 1939 on the eastern part of the Karelian isthmus with *komkor* Grendal's Operative group as nucleus (originally part of 7th Army):
  Commander: *komkor* (16.1.1940 *komandarm 2. r*) Vladimir Grendal' (1884–1940), to 2.3.1940.
  komkor Filipp Parusinov, from 2.3.1940.
  13th Army was dissolved on 5 April 1940. In late December 1939 a new command structure, the North-Western Front (incorporating 7th and 13th Armies) was formed on the Karelian isthmus.
- 8th Army was also formed on 14 September 1939, and transferred to Pskov on 23 September to secure the establishment of Soviet garrisons in the Baltic republics. The 8th Army moved on to Petrozavodsk, arriving from 29 October 1939.
  Commander: *komdiv* Ivan Khabarov, to 4.12.1939.
  komkor Vladimir Kurdyumov, to 10.1.1940.
  komandarm 2.r. Grigoriy Shtern, from 10.1.1940.
  After the Winter War 8th Army moved to Novgorod in late April 1940.
- 15th Army was formed on 11 February 1940 from the southern part of the 8th Army. Both 15th and 8th Armies operated north of Lake Ladoga.
  Commander: *komandarm 2.r.* Mikhail Kovalev (1897–1967), to 11.2.1940
  komandarm 2.r. Vladimir Kurdyumov (1895–1970), from 25.2.1940.
  15th Army was dissolved on 28 March 1940.
- 9th Army was formed on 17 November 1939 in Kem' on the White Sea, and operated at Finland's narrowest part, aiming to advance to Oulu and cut Finland into two parts.
  Commander: *komkor* Mikhail Dukhanov (1896–1969), to 17.12.1939.
  komkor Vasiliy Chuikov (1900–1982), from 22.12.1939.
  9th Army was dissolved 5 April 1940.
- 14th Army was formed on 16 September 1939 as Murmansk Group, it expanded to 14th Army on 19 November 1939.
  Commander: *komdiv* Valerian Frolov (1895–1961)
  14th Army remained in the Murmansk region after the Winter War.

North-West Front (SZFr)

On 7 January 1940 a new command level, North-West Front was established in the main combat theatre, the Karelian Isthmus, with the task to command the operations of 7th and 13th Armies. The North-West Front was subordinated to Marshal Voroshilov.

North-West Front Top Command
Commander: *komandarm 1.r.* Semyon Timoshenko (1895–1970)
War Council Member: Andrej Zhdanov (1896–1948)
korp. komiss A.P. Mel'nikov
Chief of Staff: *komandarm 2.r.* Ivan Smorodinov

Red Army Air Force (VVS RKKA)

High Command

From 19 November 1939 the Red Army Air Force (VVS RKKA, or terrestrial Air Force) was commanded by *komkor* Yakov Smushkevich (1902–1941). His predecessor was *komandarm 2.r.* Aleksandr Loktionov (1893–1941), VVS Commander and Deputy People's Commissar of Defence from November 1937.

After participation in the Russian civil war 1918–1920, Smushkevich served as political officer in various AF units. During the Spanish Civil War he served as chief aviation adviser to the Republican government under the cover name "General Douglas". On 21 June 1937 he received the HSU Golden Star, and from May to August 1939 commanded the AF component in the border conflict with Japan at the Khalkin-Gol river in Mongolia. On 17 November 1939 he was awarded a second HSU award, and appointed Commander of the Soviet Air Force two days later. His term as AF Commander ended on 27 August 1940 when *Lt Gen.* Pavel Rychagov was appointed Commander. Thereafter Smushkevich served as General Inspector of the Air Force until arrested by the NKVD as "enemy of the people and foreign agent" on 8 June 1941. He was executed on 28 October 1941 near Kuibyshev (now Samara) without legal proceedings together with Loktionov and several other senior AF officers, all of whom were posthumously rehabilitated in 1954–1955.

Military Commissar — *div.komiss* F.A. Agal'tsov (1900–1980). Spanish Civil War veteran. Commanded 1 SAK 1945, commanded DA 1962–1969. HSU 21.2.1978.

Chief of Staff — *komdiv* F. K. Arzhenukhin (1920–1941). Arrested 28.6.1941 and executed 28.10.1941.

Below and below middle: People's Defence Commissar K.Ye. Voroshilov approved new fighter combat regulations BUIA-40 and bomber combat regulations BUBA-40 on 26.1.1940.(Finnish National Defence University)

Below, right: One month before the Soviet attack (29.10.1939) the SB instruction manual KLB-SB-40 was approved. The manual was classified For Official Use Only, and all examples were numbered. (Finnish National Defence University)

Aircraft industry

On 11 January 1939 the People's Commissariate for Defence Industry was split into separate Peoples' Commissariates for the Aviation Industry, Shipbuilding, Military Equipment and Armament. The new People's Commissariate of Aircraft Industry (NKAP) was headed by the old bolshevik Mikhail Kaganovich (1888–1941). Exactly one year later a younger generation took over: Aleksandr Shakhurin (1904–1975) was appointed People's Commissar, and the brilliant aircraft designer Aleksandr Yakovlev (1906–1989) Deputy Commissar for experimental aircraft design.

The Red Army Air Force (VVS RKKA) on 1 October 1939 disposed of 12,677 aircraft in 136 aviation regiments. Over 2,350 combat aircraft (primarily I-15bis, I-16 and I-153 fighters; SB, DB-3 and TB-3 bombers, and R-5 and SSS reconnaissance aircraft) were concentrated against Finland in November 1939. The aircraft were organized into the Air Forces of 7th, 8th, 9th and 14th Armies (or VVS 7.A, VVS 8.A, VVS 9.A and VVS 14.A; primarily formed from Leningrad Military District Air Force VVS LVO), and Baltic and Northern Fleet Air Forces (VVS KBF and VVS SF). Furthermore obsolete aircraft (R-6, I-15, UT-2 and U-2 etc.) were available for secondary tasks. In March 1940 the number of combat aircraft concentrated against Finland rose to 3,253.

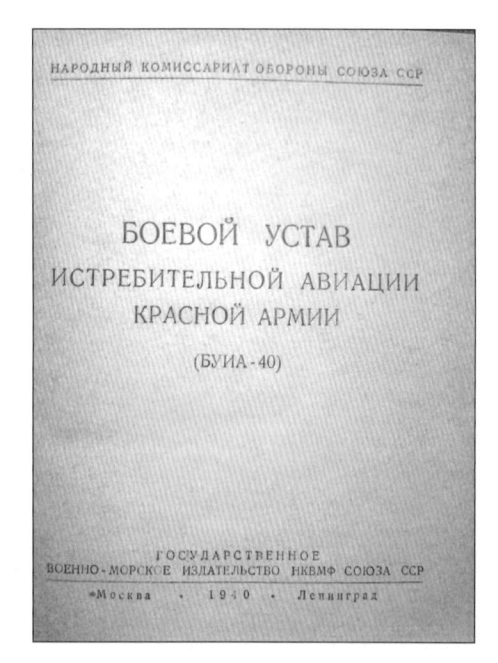

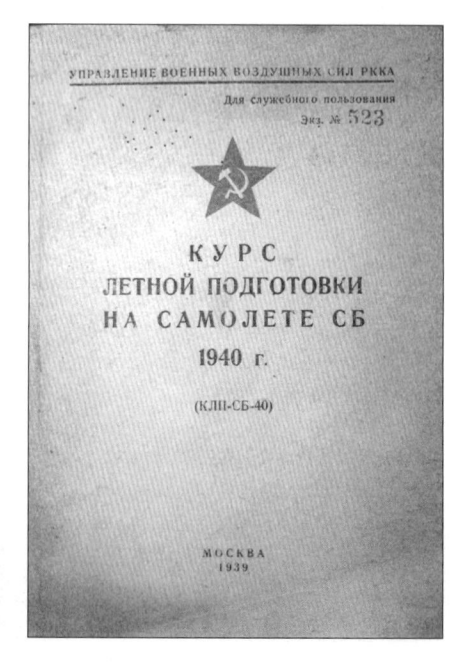

Downtown Helsinki was seriously damaged by Soviet bombs 30 November 1939. (SA-kuva)
Above left: *Seriously damaged Helsinki Technical University and burning apartment houses. (SA-kuva)*

Aviation Regiment Structure

Regiment type	Abbreviation	*Escadrilles*/Squadrons	Aircraft
Fighter	IAP	4–5	63–77
Fast bomber	SBAP	5	62
Light bomber	LBAP	5	62
Long-range bomber	DBAP	3–4	38–42
Heavy bomber	TBAP	3–4	38–42
Ground attack	ShAP	5	67

In late 1937 the Soviet Air Force had 18 aviation and 6 technical schools, educating 22,707 cadets (of which 9,201 were pilot students and 2,850 gunner and observer trainees), 7,880 aviation mechanics and 2,776 armament trainees. The aviation schools were equipped with 3,007 aircraft. By 1939 the number of air force schools had risen to 32.

Senior Air Force officers were primarily educated in Zhukovskiy Air Force Academy (named in honor of aviation theoretician and pioneer Nikolai Zhukovskiy) and also in the Frunze Military Academy, while political officers were educated in the Lenin Military-Political Academy. Furthermore 5,670 high-ranking officers were transferred to the Air Force in 1928–1938 from other arms. On 1 January 1939 Air Force personnel numbered 203,600, or 10.4 % of all military personnel.

However, competence and quality of the aviators was not on appropriate levels, which was clearly shown by numerous accidents, losses of orientation and technical malfunctions and inappropriate tactical preparation.

The Red Air Force furthermore suffered severely from the party purges and repressions in 1937–1939, when 5,616 high-ranking air force officers (including consecutive AF Commanders *komandarm 2.r.* Jan Alksnis and *general-polkovnik* Aleksandr Loktionov, six consecutive AF Chiefs of Staff, eleven Military District Air Force commanders, two Aviation Army commanders, almost all Aviation Army Corps commanders, twelve Aviation Division commanders and every other Aviation Regiment commander) were expelled from the Air Force, imprisoned and in many cases executed.

While Soviet society was suffering from the inhuman party purges, more than 300 Soviet aviators took part in the Spanish Civil War 1936–1939, at first as "advisors" to the Republican side, but gradually also actively participating in air combat. The new I-16, I-153 and SB aircraft got their combat baptism in the Spanish sky, where they fought against German Bf 109 and He 111 combat aircraft. 35 Soviet aviators were appointed Heroes of the Soviet Union due to combat in Spain, while 93 aviators were killed in action there.

In 1938–1939 several armed conflicts were fought against Japan: in China and Mongolia from February 1938, at Lake Khasan 29 July – 11 August 1938 and at Khalkhin-Gol 11 May – 16 September 1939. Several aviators were decorated with the Golden Star (14, 1 and 25 aviator Heros respectively). In

Four high-ranking AF officers with combat experience from China 1937–1938 held responsible commands in the Winter War: from left A.S. Blagoveshchenskiy (54 IAB Commander), A.G. Rytov (VVS 8.A political Deputy Commander), P.V. Rychagov (VVS 9.A Commander, also a Spanish Civil War veteran) and F.V. Polynin (VVS 13.A Commander). (G.F. Petrov)

autumn 1939 several aviation units which had participated in these border conflicts were transferred to Northwest Russia, where preparations for a possible campaign against Finland were undertaken. Thus considerable numbers of Soviet aviators had experience from combat with skilled pilots in modern German and Japanese aircraft. At the same time it was clear that Soviet-made fighters and bombers were inferior to the opposing aircraft, so active development of new aircraft types was initiated in the USSR.

In 1939 several new military airfields were constructed in the vast and relatively thinly populated Leningrad Military District, which stretched from the Arctic sea in the north to Pskov and Novgorod in the south. In late 1939, 71 airfields were ready to receive aviation units (compared to only 12 airfields in 1938), of which 10 were constructed in the Murmansk and Petrozavodsk regions (where no airfields existed in 1938). New aviation units were correspondingly set up (in early 1938 Leningrad Military District counted only 99 SB-bombers and 130 fighters).

Nevertheless the base situation remained unsatisfactory in the northern Karelian ASSR and southern Kola peninsula (which was to become the operational area of 9th Army, an area of almost 200,000 km²), where only two airfields were capable of handling modern combat aircraft: Chiksha (150 x 800 m; some 10 km east of Karelian Uhtua, Russian Uhta; from 1963 *Kalevala*) and Afrikanda (200 x 1,000 m). Poduzhemye (in Finnish *Usmana*, 18 km west of Kem') was clearly unfit for operations, and located over 200 km from the Finnish border. As the Soviet Air Force had no experience of ice bases, numerous accidents occurred before the frozen ice of the improvised bases became thick enough to carry heavy aircraft.

As already mentioned, Finland's strategic position changed dramatically after the Molotov-Ribbentrop pact was signed 23 August 1939. The Soviet Union was granted air force and naval bases in the

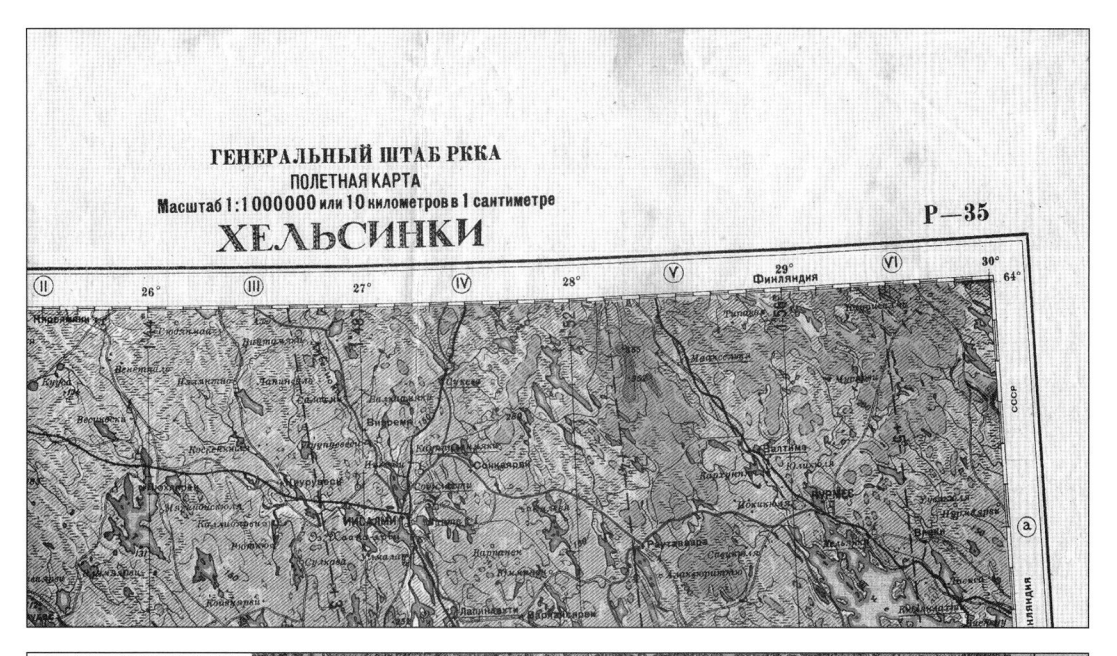

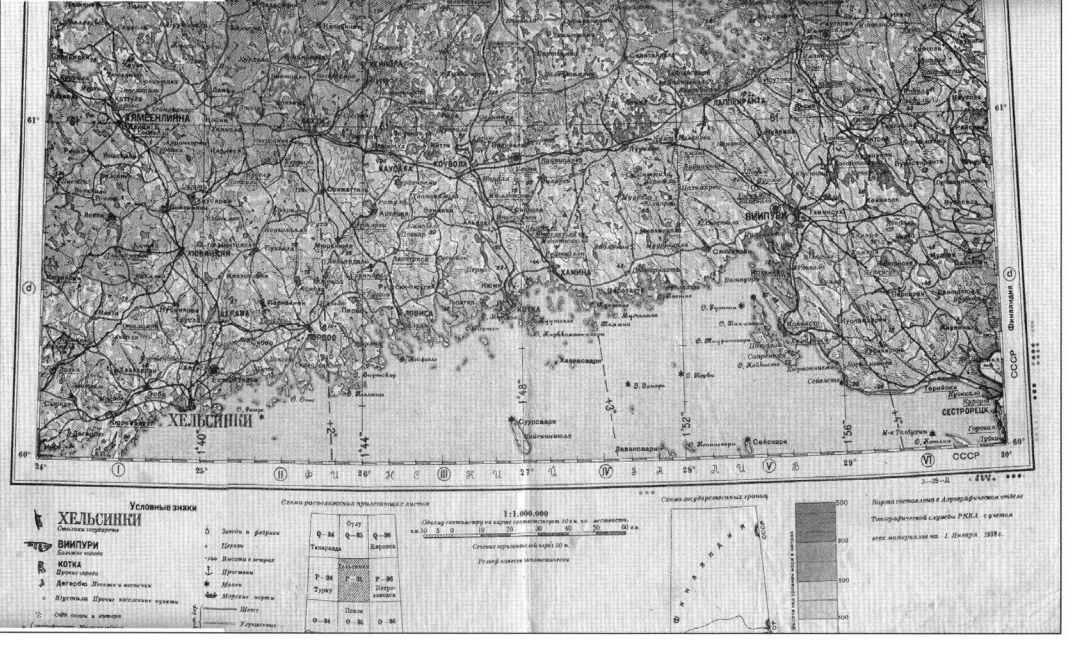

The navigation map P-35 Helsinki (scale 1:1,000,000) showed most of the Soviet AF operational area in SE and southern Finland. The Turku-map was coded P-34. Connecting maps of northern Finland were Oulu (Q-35) and Gaparanda (Q-34). Map P-35 was created by the Aerografic Dept. of the Red Army Topographic Service, and finished on 1.1.1938. (C-F. Geust)

This and next page: Helsinki was bombed three times 30.11.1939. From 9 o'clock three SBs of 35 SBAP searched for Helsinki-Malmi airport without result. Somewhat later naval 57 SBAP bombed Santahamina (killing four persons), aiming at the destruction of the naval air station. The station was empty, as all Ripon and Kotka a/c of LLv 36 were secretly moved to Kallvik some weeks before. In the afternoon naval 3./1 AP bombed the Hietalahti ship yard and Helsinki western port. In downtown Helsinki major damage was caused, and 91 persons were killed. (SA-kuva)

Baltic countries. Finland's "political negotiations" were interrupted without results on 13 November 1939, and large-scale troop movements to North-West Russia were initiated.

E.g. 6 DBAP received the first attack order as early as 17 November 1939, and aviation units were transferred to North-West Russia at an accelerating pace, as is seen from the chronology.

In the early morning of 30 November 1939 the Red Army crossed the Soviet-Finnish border from the Gulf of Finland up to the Arctic Ocean. Red AF bomber regiments attacked virtually all large cities in southern Finland, including the capital Helsinki.

Bombing attacks went on the next day, but after this non-flyable weather commenced, which continued until 19 December 1939. Meanwhile land attacks were bogged down at Finland's main defense line, the so-called Mannerheim Line. Now Stalin tried to destroy Finland's defensive will and capacity with heavy bombing of rear targets, however with only modest success.

In early January 1940 the number of Soviet troops on the Karelian Isthmus considerably increased. Fresh, well-equipped and trained units were prepared to break through the Mannerheim Line. On the eve of 10 February 1940 some 760 bombers, 157 light bombers and 393 fighters were concentrated for immediate support of the 7th and 13th Armies (subordinated to NW Front) on the Karelian Isthmus. During preparations for the attack on the Mannerheim Line 7,532 combat missions (4,087 bomber and 3,445 fighter missions) were performed.

Main Soviet Combat Aircraft in the Winter War

In the Spanish Civil War Soviet aviators met modern German aircraft (Bf 109, He 111 etc) in combat, and had to admit that their own aircraft were inferior. Development of new combat aircraft was subsequently initiated, but was still not yet finished when the Winter War broke out.

The biplane I-15bis fighter, equipped with fixed undercarriage, had been in production since 1937. Up until early 1939 2,408 I-15bis fighters were produced, after which production of more modern I-153s was initiated. The I-15bis was powered by the M-25 engine (licence-produced Wright Cyclone R-1829-F3; 750 hp), armament two or four PV-1 7.62 mm machine guns. In the Winter War the I-15bis was the main Soviet fighter north of Lake Ladoga.

Production of I-153 fighters was begun in 1939, 1,013 aircraft were produced but only 192 I-153 were operational on 1 October 1939.

The most important Soviet fighter in the main theatre, the Karelian Isthmus, was the monoplane I-16, with 6,384 produced from 1934 (*tip* 5, 6, 10, 12 and 17; and two-seater trainers UTI-1 and UTI-4). The I-16 was powered by 750 hp M-25A or M-25V engines, top speed 425–448 km/h at 3,000 m altitude, climbing to 5,000 m in 6 min 45 sec to 8 min 50 sec. All three fighter types (I-15bis, I-153 and I-16) were designed by Nikolai Polikarpov and initially produced by *Zavod* No.1 in Moscow.

On 1 November 1939 the Soviet Air Force had 13 Long-Range Bomber Aircraft Regiments (DBAP), equipped with DB-3s designed by Sergei Ilyushin (bomb load 1,050 kg, flight distance 1,500–2,000 km, max. speed 400 km/h, powerplant M-85 760 hp radial engine). DB-3 production was begun in 1937. When production ceased in 1940 *Zavod* No. 39 in Moscow and *Zavod* No. 18 in Voronezh had produced 1,528 aircraft.

Forty Fast Bomber Aircraft Regiments (SBAP) were operational on 10 February 1939, equipped with 1,614 SB-bombers. The SB bomber (designed by Andrei Tupolev) carried a 1,000–1,500 kg bomb-load at 1,000–1,500 km range, was powered by two Klimov M-100 or M-103 (860–960 hp liquid-cooled engines, based on a Hispano-Suiza 12Y license), and reached a top speed of 420–450 km/h. SB was produced by *Zavod* No. 22 in Moscow (from 1936) and from 1937 also by *Zavod* No.122 in Irkutsk.

Heavy and slow TB-3 bombers (top speed only 177–300 km/h) were still operational in Heavy Bomber Regiments (TBAP), carrying bomb-loads up to 5,000kg (including FAB-2000 bombs). The Tupolev-designed TB-3 were soon transferred to supply dropping tasks, supporting Soviet divisions surrounded by small Finnish units in *mottis*[1]. Supply dropping was mostly performed at night. 321 TB-3 missions (total flight time 1,194 hours) were performed in the Winter War.

Reconnaissance and liaison aircraft, including slow R-5 and U-2 biplanes (both designed by Nikolai Polikarpov) were also given supply dropping tasks.

---

1   *Motti* is Finnish military slang for a totally encircled enemy unit. The tactic of encircling it is called motitus, literally meaning the formation of an isolated block or "motti", but in effect meaning an entrapment or envelopment.

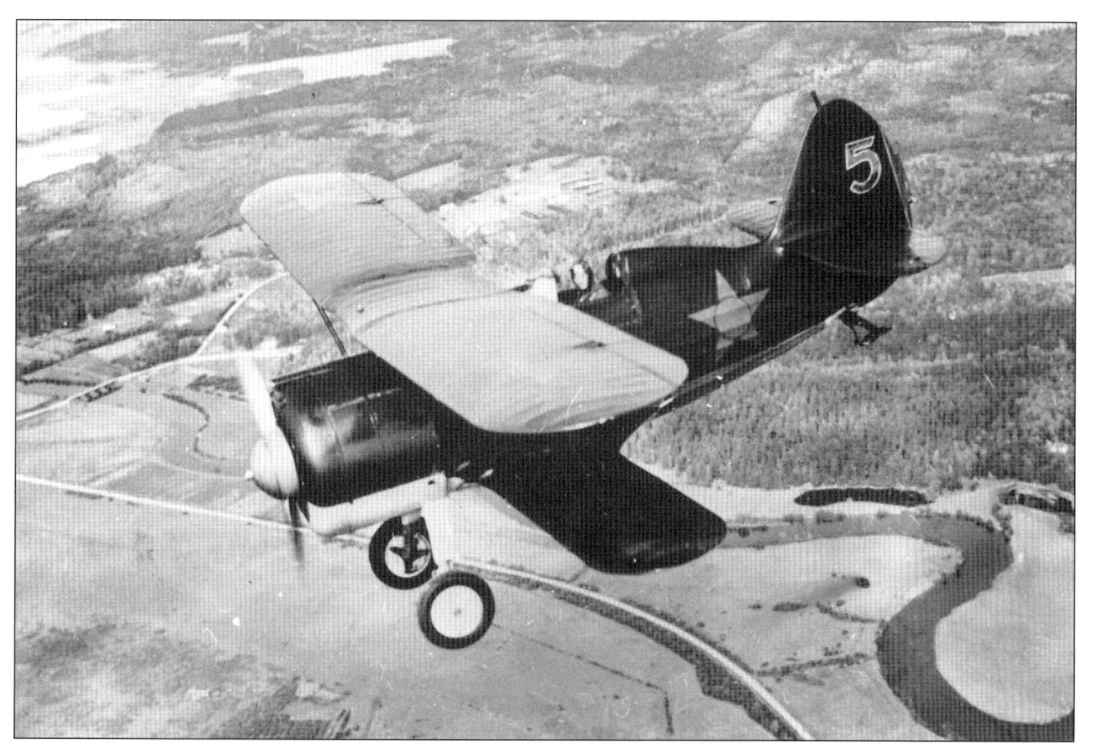

This and next page: The fixed undercarriage I-15bis was the main Soviet fighter in late 1930s. After heavy losses in the opening phase of the war many I-15bis units were transferred north of Lake Ladoga, where no Finnish fighters operated. Note bomb racks and starter cart. (G.F. Petrov)

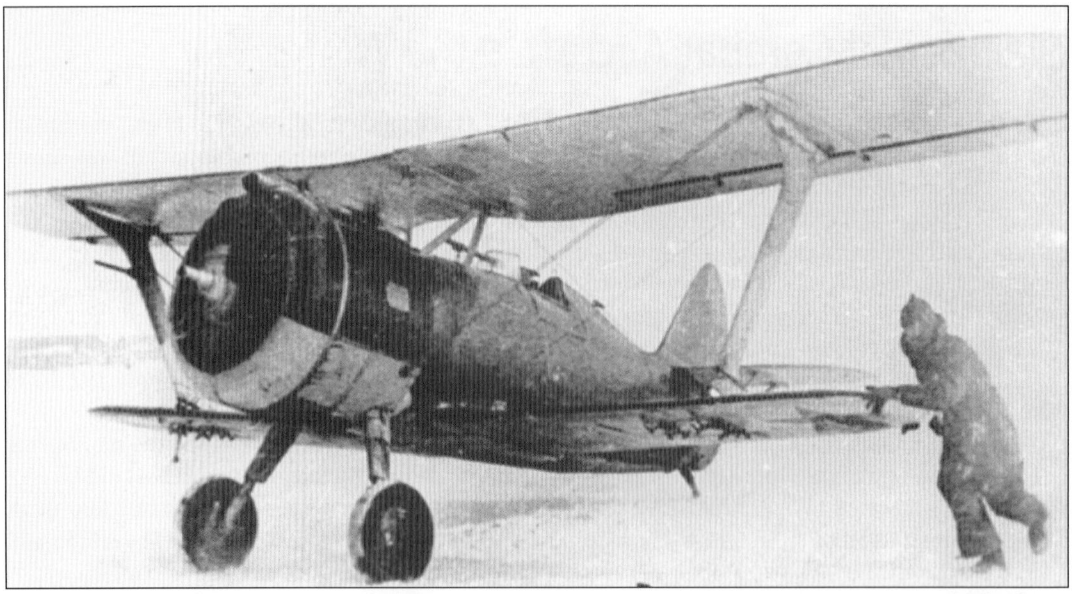

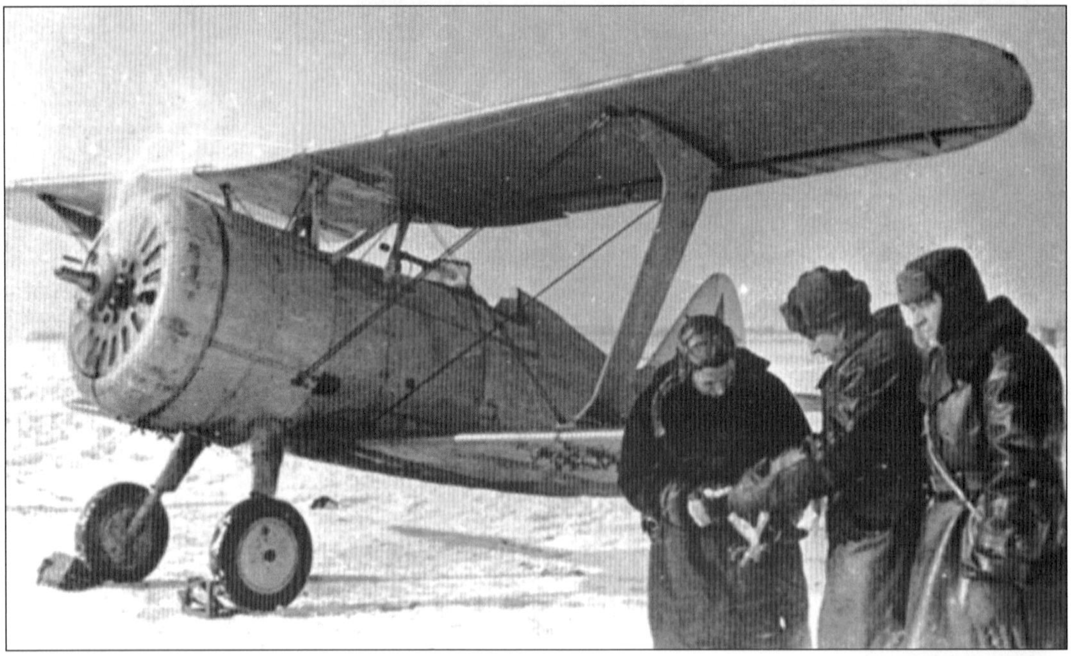

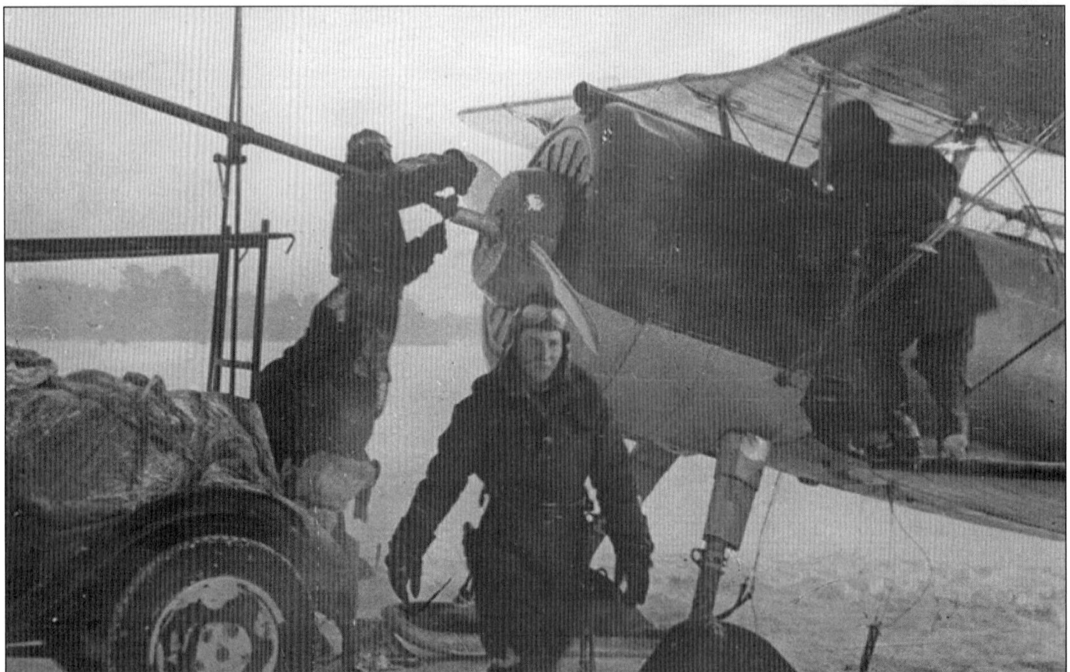

I-16 was one of the best Soviet fighters in the Winter War, tip 5 (above) and tip 10 (below). (G.F. Petrov)

I-16 tip 29 with gun-camera (usually installed in the leading aircraft of a fighter formation). (G.F. Petrov)

The I-153 biplane carried considerable armament and could be equipped with retractable skis. With auxiliary fuel tanks the fighter was able to escort bombers deep into the Finnish rear. Warbooty I-153 fighters were still successfully used by Ilmavoimat in 1942–1943. (G.F. Petrov)

Below: TsAGI published the I-153 manual in late 1940. Editing of the secret manual was finished 11.4.1940, and it was accepted for printing 3.7.1940. All I-(istrebitel) fighters (I-15bis, I-16 and I-153) were designed by Nikolai Polikarpov. (C-F. Geust)

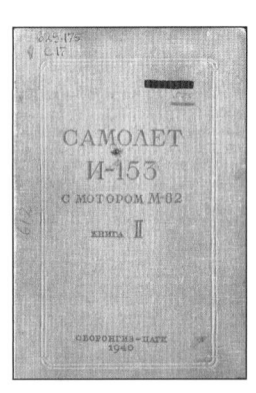

This and next page: Lack of ready constructed airfields and covered hangars, and exceptionally severe winter conditions considerably hampered all Soviet AF operations. Mission preparation and maintenance was often performed in the open air. The units of the SB bombers depicted are still to be identified. (G.F. Petrov)

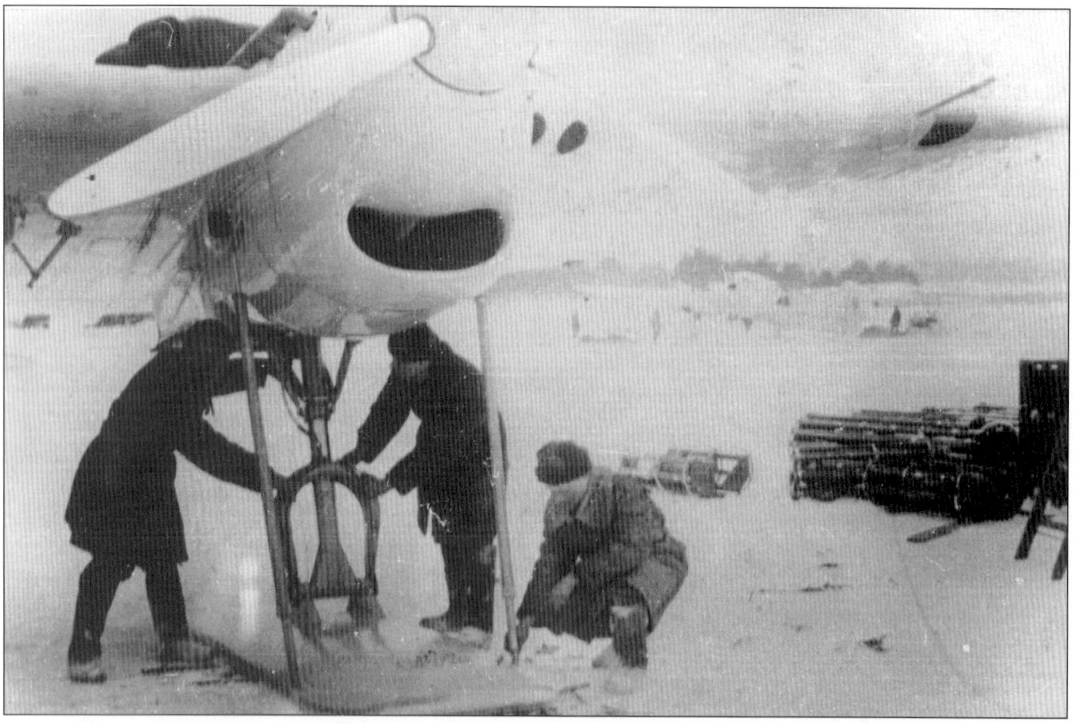

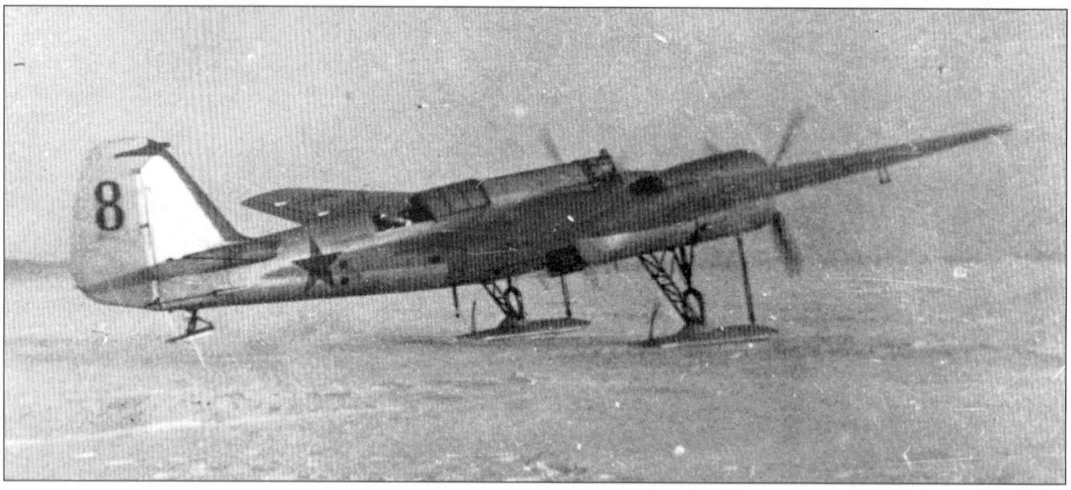
8

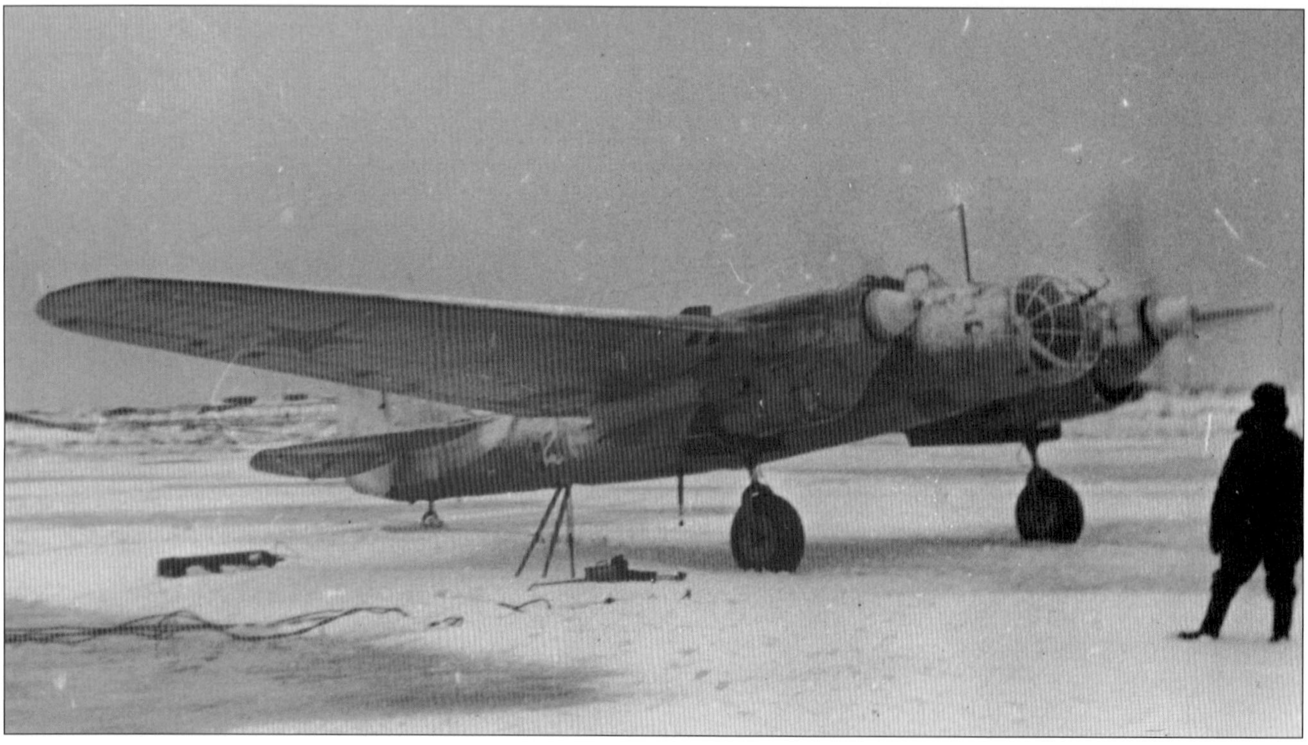

Left: SB ski detail. (G.F. Petrov)

Above: VAP chemical bomb is seen under an SB wing. (G.F. Petrov)

Andrei Tupolev also designed the dual control bomber trainer USB. Note the fixing of the bomber to the frozen airfield surface. Photo dated January 1940. (G.F. Petrov)

27

Long-range DB-3 bombers (designed by Sergei Ilyushin) were used both by Red Army AF (VVS RKKA) and Baltic Fleet AF (VVS KBF). The repeated DB-3 attacks were intended to break the Finnish defensive will and capability, and to prevent supply deliveries from Sweden, however with only moderate results. Engine maintenance of the DB-3 shown seem to be interrupted. (G.F. Petrov)

The slow and vulnerable heavy four-engine TB-3 bombers were soon reallocated to transport tasks. Although many TB-3s were ski-equipped, several accidents occurred on slippery and narrow runways. (G.F. Petrov)

Four VAP-500 liquid bombs are seen under the fuselage of this ski-equipped TB-3. Note different propellers on outer and inner engines. (G.F. Petrov)

R-5, R-Z and R-5SSS biplanes were used for reconnaissance, light bomber and ground attack tasks. (G.F. Petrov)
Battle damages of R-5 "66" are inspected, right upper wing is already dismounted. (G.F. Petrov)

Virtually all aircraft types were used for supply of Soviet units surrounded in "mottis". Soft G-6 under-wing containers (design by P.I. Grokhovskiy) were carried by various aircraft, an R-5 is depicted. The 80 kg payload G-6 container was parachute-dropped. (G.F. Petrov)

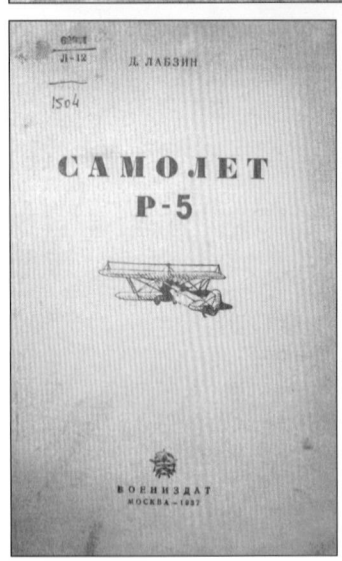

Left: *The R-5 manual written by D. Labzin was published in 1937. (Finnish National Defence University)*

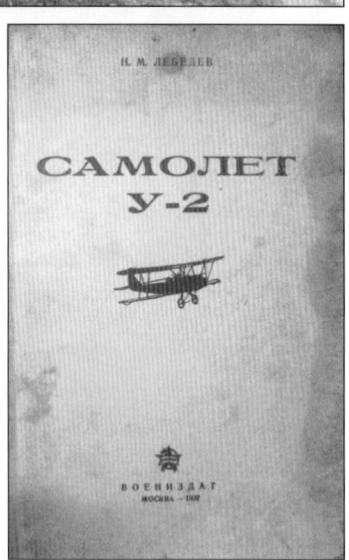

Right: *The U-2 manual written by N.M. Lebedev was published in 1937, print run 60,000 copies. (Finnish National Defence University)*

Below: *VVS RKKA published in 1939 a classified identification manual, with silhouettes and national insignia of possible future enemy aircraft. Regardless of the big print run (note manual no. 9767!) identification mistakes were numerous. (C-F. Geust)*

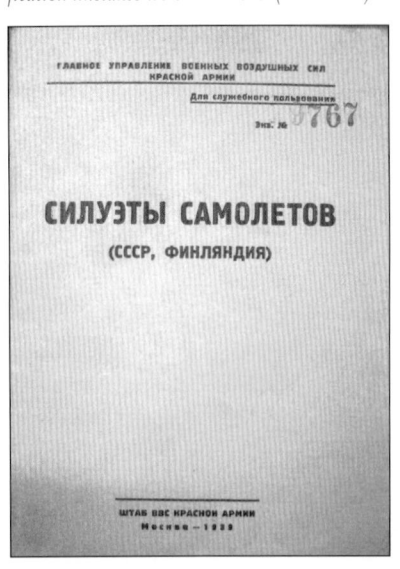

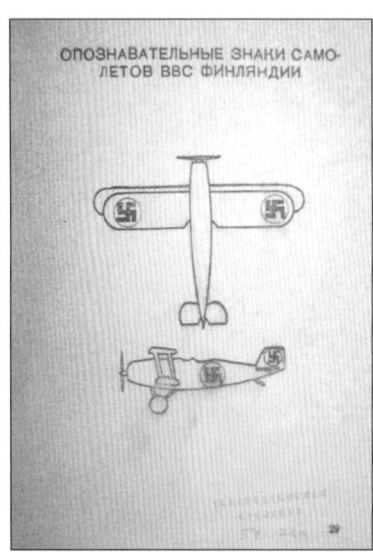

Below: *A classified and numbered manual (For Official Use Only) describing the Finnish AF was published in 1940. (C-F. Geust)*

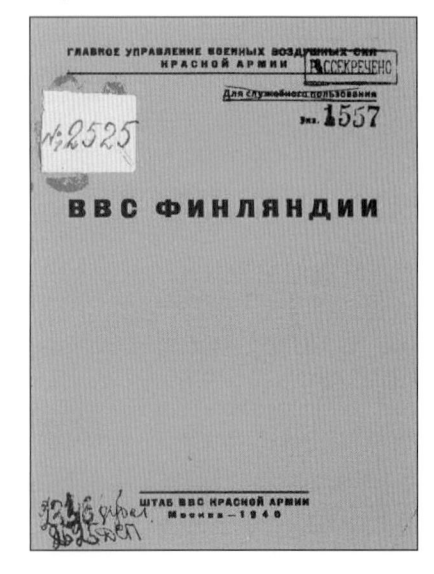

Different versions of the U-2 aircraft designed by Polikarpov were used for liaison and fire control tasks. Several S-1 ambulance aircraft of the Civil Air Fleet (GVF) were also mobilized. (G.F. Petrov)

Several U-2 and SB aircraft were equipped with ABK-1 containers (named Onisko's bucket) filled with small explosive bombs. Container use was however hazardeous, as tightly packed bombs often exploded at release with fateful consequences for the carrying aircraft. (G.F. Petrov)

Army for Special Purpose (AON)

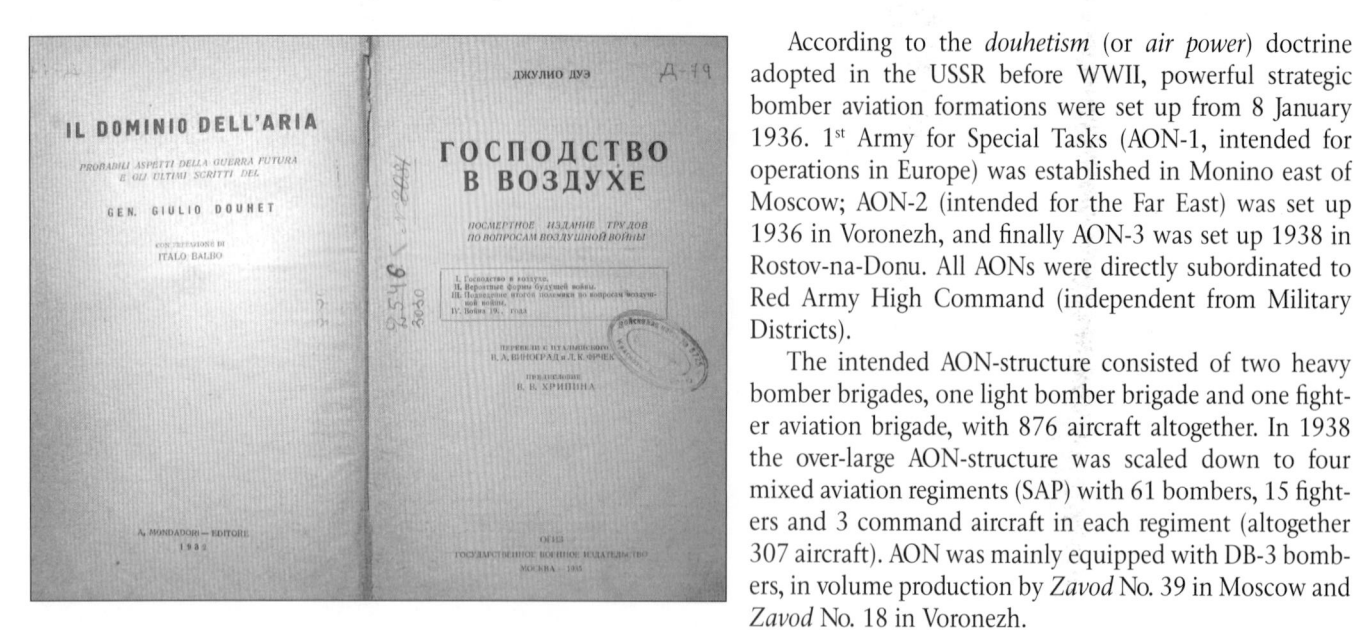

According to the *douhetism* (or *air power*) doctrine adopted in the USSR before WWII, powerful strategic bomber aviation formations were set up from 8 January 1936. 1st Army for Special Tasks (AON-1, intended for operations in Europe) was established in Monino east of Moscow; AON-2 (intended for the Far East) was set up 1936 in Voronezh, and finally AON-3 was set up 1938 in Rostov-na-Donu. All AONs were directly subordinated to Red Army High Command (independent from Military Districts).

The intended AON-structure consisted of two heavy bomber brigades, one light bomber brigade and one fighter aviation brigade, with 876 aircraft altogether. In 1938 the over-large AON-structure was scaled down to four mixed aviation regiments (SAP) with 61 bombers, 15 fighters and 3 command aircraft in each regiment (altogether 307 aircraft). AON was mainly equipped with DB-3 bombers, in volume production by *Zavod* No. 39 in Moscow and *Zavod* No. 18 in Voronezh.

Italian General Giulio Douhet's book Il domino dell'aria *(Command of the Air) was published in Russian in 1935, with foreword written by V.V. Khripin (future AON-1 Commander). (Finnish National Defence University)*

The entire AON-1 and almost all units of AON-2 participated in the Winter War.

21 and 53 DBAP of 27 AB and 6 DBAP of 13 AB relocated on 14–16 November 1939 to Yedrovo (AON-1/HQ and 21 DBAP), Krestsy (53 DBAP) and Krechevitsy (6 DBAP). From these bases 559 missions were performed in December 1939.

SB-equipped 41 SBAP of 27 AB relocated to Gorelovo, operationally attached to 15 SBAB.

The AON-structure was far too big and clumsy for operations in the Arctic region, with only small and poorly equipped AF bases. Thus AON-1 was dissolved on 24 January 1940, and all subordinated DB (long range) regiments were directly attached to the Northwest Front Air Force (VVS SZFr). AON-2 was dissolved on 12 January 1940. Some elements of AON-3 were also dispatched to the Finnish front from February 1940.

AON-1 Organisation 20.10.1939

HQ Monino

13 AB (Kalinin)
    6 DBAP (Ivanovo). To 27 AB in Krechevitsy 14.11.1939.
    41 SBAP (Kalinin). To 27 AB in Gorelovo late November 1939.
Note: 13 AB/HQ was transferred on 1.1.1940 to VVS 8.A in Lodejnoye Pole (Lotinapelto), where new units were attached (13 AB section, page 49).

M.N. Izotov, AON-1 war council member. (G.F. Petrov)

27 AB (Monino). To Yedrovo 14.11.1939.
    21 DBAP (Monino). To Yedrovo 16.11.1939.
    53 DBAP (Monino). To Krestsy 14.11.1939; and 7.1.1940 to OAG in Kuusiku, Estonia.

AON-1 High Command

Commander	*kombrig* A.V. Nikitin. Commanded AON-1 until December 1939.
	polkovnik Ye. M. Beletskiy (1905–1984). AON-1 acting commander until 24.1.1940, then Deputy Commander of VVS LVO. In GPW commanded VVS 51.A, 1 IAK etc.
Military Commissar	*brig.komiss* I.T. Chernyshev
War Council Member	*kombrig* M.I. Izotov. Commanded 1 DBAK in 1941.
Chief of Staff	*kombrig* P.P. Belichenko

AON-2 Organisation 20.10.1939

Deputy Commander of AON-2 S.V. Slyusarev (HSU 22.2.1939) was appointed Deputy Commander of VVS 8.A in January 1940. (G.F. Petrov)

HQ Voronezh

30 AB (Kursk)
    45 SBAP (Orel). To 13 AB (VVS 15.A) in Lodejnoye Pole 15.2.1940.
    51 SBAP (Kursk)

64 AB (Voronezh)
>7 DBAP (Voronezh). To OAG in Kuusiku, Estonia 21.1.1940.
>42 DBAP (Voronezh). To VVS SZFr in Kretchevitsy 21.1.1940.

AON-2 Top Command

Commander	*komdiv* S.P. Denisov (1909–1971; to January 1940). Participated in Spanish Civil War. From January 1940 commanded VVS 7.A. In GPW commanded 283 IAD etc. HSU 4.7.1937 and 21.3.1940.
	komkor P.S. Shelukhin (from January 1940)
Deputy Commander	S.V. Slyusarev (1906–1981). In China 1938–1939. Deputy Commander of VVS 8.A January-March 1940. In GPW commanded 5 SAK, 3 SAK and 2 GShAK. Commanded 12th Air Army 1947–1950. Military advisor in China 1950, commanded 64 IAK 1953–1955. HSU 22.2.1939.
Military Commissar	*kombrig* I.P. Abramov
War Council Member	*brig.komiss* Shimko
Chief of Staff	*polkovnik* I. Belov
	kombrig P.L. Kotel'nikov

AON-3 Organisation 20.10.1939

HQ Rostov-na-Donu

3 AB (Rostov-na-Donu)
>1 TBAP (Rostov-na-Donu). 1st Squadron to AG Spirin (VVS 9.A) in Fedosejevka 1.3.1940.
>12 DBAP (Novocherkassk)

7 AB (Zaporozhe)
>8 DBAP (Khabarovsk). One squadron to 53 DBAP (OAG) in Kuusiku, Estonia 13.2.1940.
>11 DBAP (Zaporozhe). One squadron to 53 DBAP (OAG) in Kuusiku, Estonia 13.2.1940.

AON-3 Top Command

Commander	*komdiv* T.I. Butorin
Deputy Commander	S.G. Korol' (1894–1975). In GPW commanded 9 IAK etc.
War Council Member	*div.komiss* Ovchinkin
Chief of Staff	*polkovnik* Malyshev

Above: Douhetism was widely discussed in the 1930s in the USSR. *Aviatsija v sovremennoj vojne (Air force in the modern war)* was written by A. Algazin in 1936. *(Finnish National Defence University)*

Right: Winter War veteran, DB-3 pilot I.G. Serebryakov 1.6.1940. Fur clothing was required even in summertime for high altitude flights. *(G.F. Petrov)*

Soviet Naval Air Forces (VVS VMF) in the Winter War

The Red Army Air Force (VVS RKKA) also included naval air units until 30 December 1937, when a separate People's Commissariat for Navy (NKVMF, or *Narodnyy komissariat Voyenno-Morskogo Flota* (headed by *flagman 2.kl.* Nikolaj Kuznetsov) was established, and Naval Air Forces (*VVS VMF*, with aviation units attached to each fleet) were correspondingly formed. Both Baltic and Northern Fleet Air Forces (*VVS KBF* and *VVS SF*) participated in the Winter War, with considerable reinforcements during the short period. The Baltic and Northern Fleet Air Forces (VVS KBF and VVS SF) are described in detail after the description of the Red Army Air Force (VVS RKKA), starting on page 248.

Note:
1. In Russian literature the acronym "KBF" (*Krasnoznamennyy Baltiyskiy Flot*, or Red Banner Baltic Fleet) is generally used for the Baltic Fleet, which was awarded the Red Banner Order on 23.2.1928. In connection with the 20-year anniversary of victory in the Great Patriotic War the Baltic Fleet was awarded another Red Banner Order 7.5.1965, after which the official acronym became DKBF (*Dvazhdy Krasnoznamennyj Baltijskij Flot*, or Double Red-Banner Baltic Fleet).
2. On 15.3.1946 the denomination *People's Commissariat* was replaced by the modern word *Ministry*.

VVS VMF Commander S.F. Zhavoronkov. (G.F. Petrov)

VVS VMF Top Command
Commander   *kombrig* S.F. Zhavoronkov (1899–1967). Commanded VVS VMF from August 1939.
Military Commissar   *brig.komiss* V.P. Alekseyev
Chief of Staff   V.V. Suvorov

Leningrad Military District Air Force (VVS LVO)

Leningrad Military District Air Force (VVS LVO) consisted on 20 October 1939 of seven Aviation Brigades: 14 AB (Pskov), 15 AB (Novgorod), 29 AB (Yedrovo), 54 IAB (Gorelovo) 55 AB (Staraya Russa), 59 IAB (Pushkin), 68 LBAB (Krasnogvardejsk) and 71 AB (Siverskaya). 54 and 59 AB were fighter brigades, all others were primarily bomber brigades.

In October and November 1939 VVS LVO received considerable reinforcements from other military districts (in particular from Byelorussian and Kiev MD, corresponding acronyms BOVO and KOVO). Also AON-1 (27 and 13 AB) moved to Northwest Russia in mid-November 1939 as mentioned above. Many aviators already had combat experience from the Spanish Civil War 1936–1938, and from the recent conflicts in China and Khalkhin-Gol.

The main part of VVS LVO was on 30 November 1939 converted into 7th Army Air Force (VVS 7.A), except for long-range bombing aviation regiments (DBAP), which remained subordinated to VVS LVO until January 1940 when the Northwest Front (SZFr) was established.

VVS LVO was commanded by Ye.S. Ptukhin, who was appointed Commander of the new VVS SZFr in early 1940 (HSU 21.3.1940). (G.F. Petrov)

VVS LVO Top Command
Commander   *komkor, komandarm 2.r.* Ye.S. Ptukhin (1902–1942). Participated in Spanish Civil War. HSU 21.3.1940. In GPW commanded VVS SZFr until 27.6.1941 when arrested. Executed 23.2.1942.
Deputy Commander   *kombrig* I.I. Kopets (1908–1941). Participated in Spanish Civil War, 2 victory claims. HSU 21.6.1937. In GPW commanded VVS ZapFr, committed suicide 23.6.1941.
Assistant Commander   *kombrig* Ye.M. Beletskiy (from February 1940, see AON-1, page 32).
Military Commissar   *korp.komiss* N.S. Shimanov (1901–?)
Chief of Staff   *kombrig* A.A. Novikov (1900–1976). In GPW commanded VVS RKKA 1942–1945. HSU 17.4.1945 and 8.9.1945. Commanded DA 1953–1955 etc.

VVS LVO Commander Ptukhin with his Deputy I.I. Kopets (HSU 21.6.1937, VVS 8.A Commander in the Winter War). In 1941 Ptukhin and Kopets commanded the AF of the Kiev and Western (Belorussian) Military Districts respectively. After the enormous losses suffered on 22.6.1941 Kopets committed suicide the following day, while Ptukhin was arrested one week later and executed 23.2.1942. (G.F. Petrov)

Northwest Front Air Force (VVS SZFr)

Because of the only moderate combat success during December 1939, the Soviet high command *Stavka* (consisting of People's Commissar for Defense Marshal Klim Voroshilov, the Secretary General of the CC of VKP(b) Iosif Stalin and the Chief of General Staff of the Red Army *komandarm 1.r.* Boris Shaposhnikov) on 7 January 1940 established a new command level, Northwest Front, on the Karelian isthmus. The Northwest Front was commanded by *komandarm 1.r.* Semyon Timoshenko, directly reporting to Marshal Voroshilov. Both the 7th Army on the left flank and 13th Army on the right flank (western and eastern Karelian Isthmus respectively), were put under Timoshenko's direct command.

Simultaneously AON-1 (commanded by *komandarm 2.r.* Yevgeniy Ptukhin and attached to the Leningrad Military District Air Force VVS LVO), was converted into the Northwest Front Air Force (VVS SZFr), to which VVS 7.A and VVS 13.A were subordinated.

This new Air Force Command was directly responsible for bombing strategic targets in the Finnish rear with DB-3 long-range bombers, which on 25 January 1940 were concentrated in 27 DBAB. The special night and all-weather squadron 12 OAE, which had arrived 25 December 1939 in Pushkin, and 29 DBAB were also transferred to VVS SZFr. The DB-3s of the Baltic Fleet continued to operate separately and were used for attacks on the Finnish armoured ships *Väinämöinen* and *Ilmarinen*, and for dropping mines in the waters of Finland's south-western coast.

Strategic bombing in western and central Finland was performed by Estonia-based OAB, while the tasks of VVS 7.A and VVS 13.A included ground forces support and destruction of Finnish fortifications close to the front line (by SB-bombers and ground-attack fighters).

VVS SZFr bomber targets included the administrative and industrial centers Viipuri, Kotka, Hamina, Mikkeli, Imatra, Lappeenranta etc., plus railway and communication junctions at Kouvola, Antrea, Simola, Elisenvaara, Pieksämäki, Vuoksenniska etc.

After heavy losses of 16 SBAB (31 and 54 SBAP) on 17 January 1940 Yevgeniy Ptukhin prohibited bombing attacks on Kouvola, Suur-Merijoki, Lappeenranta, Viipuri, Hiitola and Elisenvaara without fighter escort. "*If the planned rendezvous with escort fighters does not take place, bombers are to turn back and land at their bases with bombs. I am immediately to be informed of such incidents.*" Ptukhin also repeated the Stavka Order of 27 December 1939, which explicitly prohibited use of the same outward and inward flight routes and crossing points.

On the eve of the main attack on the Mannerheim Line on 10 February 1940 VVS SZFr had 351 bombers (DB-3, SB and a few TB-3), and some 45 fighters for immediate ground force support (see below for details). In mid-February 1940 bombing of Finnish rear areas was resumed, and 911 bombing missions against Finnish industrial objects and 168 missions against bridges were performed by VVS SZFr in February 1940.

The long-range DB-3 bombers of VVS SZFr performed altogether 2,129 missions (of which 1,733 were during the breakthrough of the Mannerheim Line), or 47% of all bombing missions of the frontal Air Forces. Target type distribution of long-range bomber missions:
- railway targets   1,374
- military industries   259
- ports   496

A.A. Novikov, VVS LVO Chief of Staff. Novikov commanded Soviet Air Force in GPW (HSU 17.4 and 8.9.1945). (G.F. Petrov)

VVS SZFr Organisation
- **16 SBAB** (Chernevo). Late January 1940 to VVS SZFr from VVS 7.A.
    - **31 SBAP** (Chernevo). Arrived 29.12.1939 from Smolensk (18 AB, VVS BOVO).
    - **54 SBAP** (Smuryayevo). Late January 1940 to VVS SZFr from VVS 7.A.
- **27 DBAB** (Krestsy). 25.1.1940 from VVS LVO to VVS SZFr.
    - **6 DBAP** (Kretchevitsy). 25.1.1940 from VVS LVO to VVS SZFr.
    - **21 DBAP** (Pushkin). 25.1.1940 from VVS LVO.
    - **42 DBAP** (Kretchevitsy). Arrived 20.1.1940 from Voronezh (64 AB, AON-2).
- **29 DBAB** (Yedrovo). Late January 1940 to VVS SZFr from AON-1.
    - **7 TBAP** (Yedrovo). Late January 1940 to VVS SZFr.
- **2 SBAP** (Ropsha-Vitino). To VVS SZFr from 15 SBAB 10.1–18.1.1940, then back to 15 SBAB.
- **9 ShAP** (Pushkin). Split up in January 1940; 3rd Squadron to VVS SZFr from VVS 7.A.
- **38 IAP**. To VVS SZFr 12.1.1940, later converted into 149 IAP.
- **149 IAP**. Set up 1.2.1940 in Pushkin, with 38 IAP as nucleus.
- **12 OAE ON** (Pushkin). Arrived 25.12.1939 from Monino (VVS MVO). 1.2.1940 expanded to **85 OAP ON**.

VVS SZFr Top Command
Commander *komandarm 2.r.* Ye.S. Ptukhin (see VVS LVO, page 34).
Military commissar *korp.komiss* N.S. Shimanov, Soviet AF Deputy Commander 1943–1945.
  polk.komiss Silantyev
Chief of Staff *kombrig* A.A. Novikov (see VVS LVO).

Air Force of the 7th Army (VVS 7.A)

The main attack against Finland was to be made on the Karelian Isthmus by 7th Army, which primarily consisted of units of the Leningrad Military District (commanded by *komandarm 2.r.* Konstantin Meretskov), and incorporated its corresponding aviation forces (VVS 7.A). According to Meretskov's attack plan of October 1939, VVS 7.A was to include 292 combat aircraft from 68 LBAB, 29 TBAB, 7 and 25 IAP, 32 RAE (reconnaissance squadron) and 9 KAO (army corps aviation detachment).

Primary tasks included attacks against strategic targets in the rear (up to 320 km from the Finnish-Soviet border), including Mannerheim Line fortifications, the Finnish Ladoga flotilla, railway stations and junctions, Lahti broadcasting station, Tampere aircraft factory, transport infrastructure, Ristniemi coastal forts etc.), artillery fire control, own ground forces protection and support, and prevention of Finnish attacks against Soviet defense lines. Up until 27 December 1939 the operational area was limited to Tampere in the west, Kuopio in the north and Lahdenpohja in the east.

It soon became evident that the aviation units allocated were unable to perform the tasks given, considerable reinforcements were required.

VVS 7.A (Commander *kombrig* S.K. Goryunov) and aviation units directly subordinated to VVS LVO counted on 30 November 1939 805 bombers (SB, DB-3 and TB-3), 630 fighters (of which 265 were attached to 54 IAB, primarily responsible for Leningrad air defense), 67 ground attack aircraft and light bombers and some 50 reconnaissance aircraft. Thus almost 1,300 aircraft were available for operations on the Karelian Isthmus. (Some aviation units were still being re-equipped or in transfer to new bases.)

As available reconnaissance aircraft (R-5, R-Z and SSS) were clearly insufficient, a number of reconnaissance units were urgently sent to the Finnish front (e.g. 18 KAO was dispatched from Ural MD and 15 KAO from Volga MD). R-5 equipped 3 LBAP was soon split up: on 10 December 1939 4th Squadron (five R-5) was sent to VVS 8.A, on 12 December 1939 2nd Squadron (nine SSS) remained in VVS 7.A, and 5th Squadron with 10 R-5 was allocated to the new VVS 13.A. The remaining two Squadrons were re-equipping with SBs.

Frequent accidents and losses of orientation due to weather conditions drew attention to insufficient all-weather training. An order to set up a special aviation squadron able to operate at night and in adverse weather conditions was issued 11 December 1939. After two weeks 12 OAE, which consisted of experienced test and long-range pilots from the Air Force Research Institute (NII VVS), the blind-flying center in Ryazan, pilot inspectors of various units etc. arrived in Pushkin with eight DB-3s and three SBs. All aircraft were equipped with special navigation instruments, blind-flying systems, radio compasses and night bombsights. 12 OAE performed its first bombing operation on the next day. In January 1940 12 OAE was attached to VVS SZFr, and expanded to regiment strength.

On the eve of the main attack on the Mannerheim Line on 10 February 1940 VVS 7.A numbered 210 SB, 95 light bombers (R-Z and SSS) and some 120 fighters for immediate support of 7th Army on the western Karelian Isthmus.

VVS 7.A Commander S.P. Denisov (HSU 4.7.1937 and 21.3.1940). (G.F. Petrov)

VVS 7.A Organisation

- **1 LBAB** (Suulajärvi). Arrived 11.2.1940 from Kirovograd (VVS KOVO).
    5 SBAP (Suulajärvi). Arrived 26.2.1940 from Kirovograd (VVS KOVO).
    7 ShAP (Halolanjärvi, Uusikirkko). Arrived 13.2.1940 from Kiev (VVS KOVO).
    43 LBAP (Suulajärvi). Arrived in February 1940 from Vitebsk (70 AB, VVS BOVO).

- **15 SBAB** (Novgorod). 30.11.1939 transferred from VVS LVO to VVS 7.A.
    2 SBAP (Ropsha and Vitino). Arrived 9.12.1939 from Solt'sy (VVS 7.A).
    24 SBAP (Gorelovo). Arrived late November from Kretshevitsy (VVS 7.A).
    41 SBAP (Gorelovo). Arrived late November from Kalinin (13 AB, AON-1), attached to 27 AB. Transferred late December 1939 to Tshiksha (VVS 9.A).

- **16 SBAB** (Chernovo). Arrived late November 1939 from Seshchinskaya (VVS BOVO).
    13 SBAP (Chernovo). Arrived 30.11.1939 from Seshchinskaya (VVS BOVO).
    31 SBAP (Chernovo). Arrived 31.12.1939 from Smolensk (18 AB, VVS BOVO).

54 SBAP (Smuravyevo). Arrived 30.11.1939 from Shejkovka (VVS BOVO).
18 SBAB (Siverskaya). Transferred 16.1.1940 from VVS SZFr.
48 SBAP (Siverskaya). Arrived 1.1.1940 from Uman' (VVS KOVO), attached to 18 SBAB.
50 SBAP (Siverskaya). Transferred 1.1.1940 from 71 AB.

- 29 TBAB (Yedrovo). Also attached to AON-1.
   7 TBAP (Pushkin). Arrived in December 1939 from Jelgava, Latvia.
   9 SBAP (Yedrovo). In December 1939 split up into detached squadrons.

- 54 IAB (Gorelovo)
   19 IAP (Gorelovo and Vitino). 4th Squadron to Chiksha (VVS 9.A) in December 1939.
   26 IAP (Uglovo and Manushkino)
   44 IAP (Ropsha and Vitino)

- 55 SBAB (Staraya Russa). In January 1940 to Sestroretskiy zaliv.
- 44 SBAP (Staraya Russa, Zajtsevo, Krasnogvardejsk). In January 1940 to Sestroretskiy zaliv.
- 58 SBAP (Sivoritsy, Staraya Russa). In January 1940 to Sestroretskiy zaliv.

- 59 IAB (Pushkin)
   7 IAP (Levashovo, Kasimovo). Early November 1939 1st (I-16P) and 3rd (I-15bis) Squadrons moved from Pushkin to Levashovo, and 2nd (I-15bis) and 4th (I-16) Squadrons to Kasimovo. 25.12.1939 2nd Squadron was transferred to 68 IAP (a new I-16 equipped 2nd Squadron was formed by reinforments from various regiments). Two Squadrons moved 30.12.1939 to Rieskjärvi, and the other two squadrons moved 15.1.1940 to Vammeljärvi (also other ice bases used). 3rd Squadron exchanged its I-15bis fighters for I-153s by 20.1.1940.
   23 IAP (Kaukjärvi). Arrived 4.3.1940 from Zhitomir (69 AB, VVS KOVO).
   25 IAP (Komendantskoye, Gorskaya, Levashovo). Late December 1939 3rd and 4th Squadrons (I-153) were transferred to 38 IAP (and further to OAG), and 1st and 2nd Squadrons (I-16) moved to Kanneljärvi. 5th (?) Squadron (I-15bis) moved 18.12.1939 from Pushkin to Murmashi (VVS 14.). One I-153 Squadron moved 27.12.1939 from Pushkin to Suulajärvi. A new 3rd Squadron (I-16) arrived 1.1.1940, and a new 4th Squadron (I-16) arrived 28.1.1940, both from 68 IAP to Suulajärvi. Late February two I-16 Squadrons arrived from 22 IAP and 70 IAP in Mongolia and formed 5th and 6th Squadrons at Suulajärvi.
   38 IAP (Pushkin, Vyskatka). Late November 1939 38 IAP was divided into two parts, with 1st and 4th Squadrons (I-16 and I-15bis) in Pushkin and Vyskatka, and 2nd and 3rd Squadrons in Pushkin (I-16 and I-153). The I-15bis fighters of 1st and 4th Squadrons were transferred to Uhtua (VVS 9.A) 20.12.1939, and the I-16s were divided between 7 IAP (Kasimovo) and 68 IAP (Levashovo). The I-16s of 2nd and 3rd Squadrons were transferred to Klooga and Sinalepa, Estonia (OAG) 1.1.1940. In January 1940 I-153s were received from 4./43 IAP and 4./2 IAP (VVS KOVO), and also from 2. and 4./25 IAP. 20.2.1940 a squadron arrived from 56 IAP in Mongolia, and formed 5th Squadron.
   68 IAP (Pushkin). To Kasimovo 19.12.1939. Transferred 27.12.1939 to VVS 13.A.
   148 IAP (Rieskjärvi). Arrived 27.2.1940 from Lyubertsy (VVS MVO).

- 68 LBAB (Krasnogvardejsk). In early January 1940 transferred from VVS 7.A to VVS 13.A.
   3 LBAP (Krasnogvardejsk). In December 1939 split up. 2nd Squadron remained in VVS 7.A (frequent base changes: Levashevo, Kanneljärvi, Suuri Särkijärvi, Suulajärvi and Kanneljärvi). 4.3.1940 named 19 OAE, which next day moved to Kaukjärvi. 4th Squadron moved 10.12.1939 to Nurmolitsa (VVS 8.A), and 5th Squadron moved to Lempaala (VVS 13.A).
   10 SBAP (Krasnogvardejsk). 19.1.1940 to VVS 13.A.
- 9 ShAP (Krestsy, Kretshevitsy, Yedrovo, Grivochki). 2nd Squadron was transferred to VVS 14.A 14.12.1939. 9 ShAP was split up in January 1940; 1st Squadron to Vammeljärvi (VVS 7.A), 3rd Squadron to Pushkin (VVS SZFr) and 4th Squadron to VVS 13.A.
   1 DRAE (Kretshevitsy). In January 1940 to Kaukjärvi.
- 10 OAE. Supported ground forces, in January 1940 based at Kirkkojärvi.
- 31 VRE (Novoseltsy). In winter 1940 to Kirkkojärvi.
- 32 RAE (Krasnogvardejsk). To Southern Lempaala Ozero 29.1.1940, and attached to VVS 13.A.
- 50 OAE. Supported ground forces, in January 1940 based at Kirkkojärvi.
- 56 KAE (Novotsherkassk, VVS SKVO). In winter 1940 to VVS 7.A?
- 1 KAO (Yegorevsk, VVS MVO). In January 1940 to VVS 7.A, bases Vammeljärvi, Kaukjärvi and Suulajärvi.

S.K. Goryunov commanded VVS 7.A at the beginning of the Winter War. (G.F. Petrov)

- 9 KAO (Komendantskoye). To Kanneljärvi 24.12.1939, then split up: partly to VVS 9.A, and partly 1.1.1940 to Metsäpirtti (VVS 13.A).
- 16 KAO (Korostovichi). In winter 1940 to Kanneljärvi.
- 36 Aviazveno svyazi

VVS 7.A High Command

Commander	*kombrig* S.K. Goryunov (1899–1967). In GPW commanded 5th Air Army etc. Commanded 69th Air Army 1951–1956. HSU 28.4.1945.
	komdiv S.P. Denisov from January 1940 (former Commander of AON-2).
Deputy Commander	*major* N.S. Gerasimov (1911–1960). Participated in Spanish Civil War. HSU 22.2.1939. In GPW commanded 256 IAD etc.
Military Commissar	*polk.komiss* Korolev
Chief of Staff	*polkovnik* Lvov
	polkovnik S.A. Lavrik. Chief of Staff of 13th Air Army 1944–1945.

Air Force of the 13th Army (VVS 13.A)

After all attempts to break through the Mannerheim Line were interrupted in mid-December 1939, a new attack plan was developed by the Stavka from 28 December 1939. *Komkor* V.D. Grendal's army group on the right flank of 7th Army (eastern Karelian Isthmus) was transformed into the separate 13th Army. HSU, *polkovnik* F.P. Polynin was on 31 December 1939 appointed Commander of VVS 13.A.

Tasks of VVS 13.A included: destruction of fortifications in the Taipale-sector of the Mannerheim Line (at Muolaa-Ilves, Heikurila, Riiska), transport infrastructure and Käkisalmi, Immola and Vuoksenniska AF bases; reconnaissance flights to a depth of 150 km, fighter escort of own reconnaissance, bomber and artillery control aircraft.

In January 1940 68 SBAB (5th Squadron/3 LBAP and 10 SBAP) and 4th Squadron/9 ShAP were attached to VVS 13.A. In February 1940 60 SBAP, 4 LBAP and 41 RAE arrived.

On the eve of the main attack on the Mannerheim Line on 10 February 1940 VVS 13.A numbered 199 SB, 62 R-Z light bombers and some 60 fighters for immediate support of the 13th Army on the eastern Karelian Isthmus.

VVS 13.A organisation

Units	Bases	Aircraft 31.12.1939	Comments
15 SBAB – 2 SBAP – 24 SBAP	Gorelovo, Ropsha, Vitino	107 SB	From VVS 7.A (15 SBAB formally transferred 7.1.1940).
68 LBAB – 5./3 LBAP – 10 SBAP – 4 LBAP – 60 SBAP	Lempaala Levashovo Kaukolovo Kasimovo		In January 1940 from VVS 7.A. 5.1.1940 from VVS 7.A. 19.1.1940 from Krasnogvardejsk (VVS 7.A). 13.2.1940 from Kharkov 1(19 AB, VVS KhVO). 21.1.1940 from Lebedin (VVS KhVO). 68 LBAB renamed 68 SBAB.
2./7 IAP	Metsäpirtti	13 I-15bis	25.12.1939 from Kasimovo (VVS 7.A); attached to 68 IAP.
4./9 ShAP			In January 1940 from VVS 7.A to VVS 13.A.
68 IAP	Kasimovo	51 I-16	27.12.1940 from VVS 7.A; 12.1.1940 to Lempaalanjärvi.
31 RAE	Metsäpirtti		29.1.1940 from VVS 7.A.
41 RAE			17.2.1940 to VVS 13.A.
2 KAO	Nurmijärvi, Valkjärvi		9.1.1940 from Mogilev (VVS BOVO) to Nurmijärvi, later to Valkjärvi.
9 KAO	Metsäpirtti	2 R-5	1.1.1940 from Kanneljärvi (VVS 7.A) to Metsäpirtti (VVS 13.A); 10.1.1940 to Kanneljärvi.
11 KAO			Winter 1940 to VVS 13.A from Mogilev (VVS BOVO).
23 KAO	Metsäpirtti	10 R-5, 3 SSS	25.12.1940 from Podolsk (VVS MVO). 1.1.1940 to VVS 13.A.
29 Aviazveno svyazi		6 U-2	
85 Aviazveno svyazi			Supported 49. Division at Taipale.

VVS 13.A Top Command

Commander	*kombrig* F.P. Polynin (1906–1981). In China 1937–1938. HSU 14.11.1938. In GPW commanded 6th Air Army 1943–1944. Commanded 13th Air Army 1947–1950 etc.
Deputy commander	*polkovnik* V.I. Klevtsov (1909–1998). HSU 7.4.1940. In GPW commanded 60 SAD 1941–1942.
Military commissar	F.I. Bragin
Chief of Staff	*polkovnik* G.F. Mikhel'son

VVS 13.A Commander F.P. Polynin (HSU 14.11.1938). (G.F. Petrov)

Special Aviation Brigade (OAB), later Special Aviation Group (OAG)

As the Baltic Fleet Air Force (VVS KBF) also turned out to be unable to fulfill all tasks ordered, a powerful task force, the Special Aviation Brigade (OAB) was dispatched to Estonia, where bases were established according to the Soviet-Estonian agreement of 11 October 1939.

OAB HQ was formed from HQ of 71 AB, and was located at Haapsalu. AF bases included Sinalepa (south of Haapsalu), Kuusiku (Rapla), Klooga (7 km east of Paldiski) and Kuressaare in Saaremaa. Double HSU, *polkovnik* G.K. Kravchenko (with combat experience from China and Khakhin-Gol) was appointed commander of OAB, directly subordinated to the Soviet AF Commander *komkor* Ya.V. Smushkevich, while the Baltic Fleet command was only "informed" of OAB's operations (although naval AF units were also located in Estonia).

Tasks of OAB included bombing of administrative and industrial centres and railway junctions in southwest Finland (up to the 25° meridian in the east), and up to 800 km long reconnaissance flights. Baltic Fleet Air Force (VVS KBF) continued its operations against ports and shipping in the northern Baltic Sea and the southern Gulf of Bothnia.

On 18 December 1939 three squadrons of 35 SBAP (commanded by *major* G.A. Sukhorebnikov, former Commander of 71 AB) and two squadrons of 38 IAP (commanded by *major* T.V. Ledenev) took off from Siverskaya and Pushkin to Sinalepa and Klooga respectively. From 6 January 1940 also DB-3 equipped 53 DBAP was transferred to Estonia, and six days later OAB numbered some 60 bombers and 65 I-153 fighters.

In early January 1940 OAB was ordered to intensify its attack against "strategic" targets in western and central Finland, including Turku, Tampere, Riihimäki, Lahti, Vaasa, Seinäjoki etc.

In late February 1940 15 IAP, 7 DBAP and 52 SBAP were also attached to OAB, which was renamed OAG (Special Aviation Group), now numbering over 200 bombers and over 100 fighters. The main task

Soviet photo of Turku bombing 13.1.1940. Target no. 4 is the port storage area, size 275 x 175 m. (RGAVMF)

of the fighters was bomber escort, but independent ground-attack missions were also performed. In order to increase effective range many fighters were equipped with under-wing fuel tanks.

OAG operation regions and tasks:
Operation regions:
Southern and south-western Finland
Tasks:
Destruction of industrial facilities
Destruction of transport infrastructure
Reconnaissance missions up to 800 km from coastline

OAG Commander G.P. Kravchenko (HSU 22.2 and 29.8.1939). (G.F. Petrov)

OAG organisation

Unit	Arrival date	Aircraft	Location	Comments
38 IAP (LVO)	18.12.1939	32 I-153	Sinalepa	
1, 2 and 3/35 LBAP (LVO)	18.12.1939	38 SB	Sinalepa	
4 and 5/35 LBAP	29.12.1939	24 SB		
4/2 IAP (KOVO)	4.1.1940	15 I-153		Became 2/38 IAP
53 DBAP (AON-1)	9.1.1940	43 DB-3		
4/43 IAP (KOVO)	12.1.1940	15 I-153	Klooga	Became 1/38 IAP
15 IAP	11.2.1940	59 I-153		12 I-153 to 38 IAP
OAE/11 DBAP (AON-3)	13.2.1940	(only crews)		To 53 DBAP
7 DBAP	17.2.1940	39 DB-3	Kuusiku	
52 SBAP	26.2.1940	51 SB, 1 USB	Kuresaare	
OAE/8 DBAP	1.3.1940	6 DB-3		To 53 DBAP
4/7 DBAP (LVO)	3.3.1940	12 DB-3	Kuusiku	
Zv/7 IAP	10.3.1940	3 I-16P		

7 DBAP (Kuusiku). Arrived 17.2.1940 from Voronezh (64 AB, AON-2).
14 TAP. Arrived winter 1940 from Borispol (VVS KOVO), and from Pushkin (7 TBAP, 29 AB, AON-1).
15 IAP (Klooga, Sinalepa, Kuusiku). Arrived 17.2.1940 from Parubanok, Lithuania (VVS BOVO).
35 SBAP (Haapsalu). Arrived 18.12.1939 from Siverskaya (VVS 7.A).
38 IAP (Klooga). Arrived 18.12.1939 from Pushkin (59 IAB, VVS 7.A).
52 SBAP (Kuressaar). Arrived 26.2.1940 from Ovruch (VVS KOVO).
53 DBAP (Kuusiku). Arrived 6.1.1940 from Kretshevitsy (27 AB, AON-1).

OAG loss summary

Type	Combat losses	Missing in action	Accidents	Total
I-153	4 (Finnish fighters 2, Finnish A-A 2)	-	3	7
SB	13 (Finnish fighters 8, Finnish A-A 5)	-	1	14
DB-3	10 (Finnish fighters 7, Finnish A-A 3)	1	8	19
Total	27 (Finnish fighters 17, Finnish A-A 10)	1	12	40

Some damaged aircraft apparently later returned to service, as the number of destroyed DB-3 is also indicated as 13, while 29 damaged DB-3 were repaired.

63 OAG aviators were killed, and 17 shot down and imprisoned in Finland. Only one OAG aviator became the Golden Star. The HSU criteria were apparently rather strict in OAG!

OAG High Command

Commander	*polkovnik* G.K. Kravchenko (1912–1943). In China and Khalkin-Gol 1937–1939. HSU 22.2. and 29.8.1939.
Assistant Commander (fighter aviation)	*major* Ye.I. Antonov
Assistant Commander (bomber aviation)	*polkovnik* A.M. Kravtsov. HSU-proposal, not accepted.
Assistant Commander	*polkovnik* N.P. Kretov (1901–1952). HSU-proposal, not accepted. In GPW commanded 214 ShAD etc.
Navigation officer *(flagshturman)*	N.V. Sokolov. HSU-proposal, not accepted.

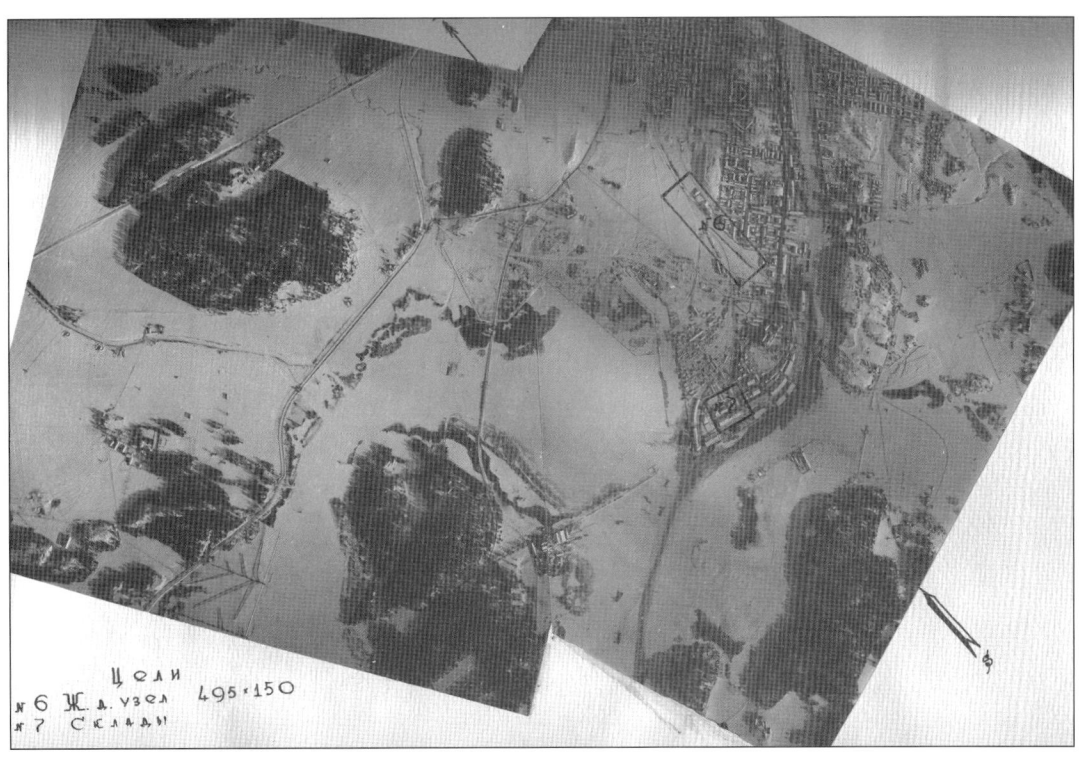

Turku bombing 14.2.1940. Railway yard is target no. 6 (size 495 x 150 m), port storage area is target no. 7. (RGAVMF)

Turku bombing 17.2.1940, photo altitude 3,750 m. Target no. 8 is an armament store (size 200 x 125 m), targets 9 and 10 are harbour stores (size 212 x 220 m and 225 x 185 m).

The main Soviet photo journal Ogonek presented the double-HSU aviators in the Aviation Day issue 20 August 1940 with the title Stalinskiye sokoly (Stalin's Falcons). From left to right: G.P. Kravchenko, Yu.V. Smushkevich and S.P. Denisov. (Finnish National Library)

Right: Locations and numbers of anti-aircraft guns in Turku are indicated on this Soviet photo. (RGAVMF)

Bottom, right: Turku air defence artillery map (compiled from air photos). (RGAVMF)

Below, two photos: Soviet bombings caused large-scale devastation in Turku. (Åbo Akademi)

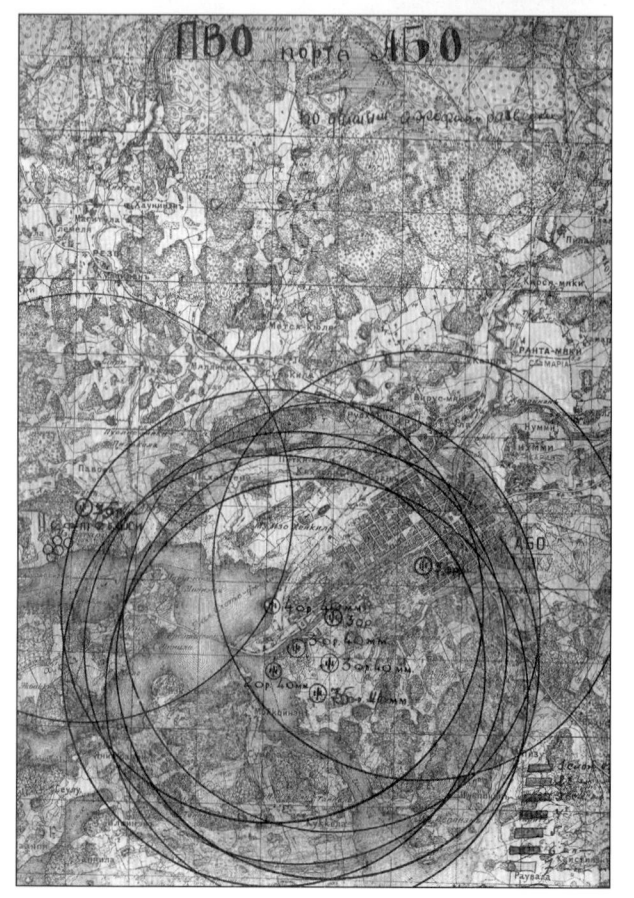

42

Air Force of the 8th Army (VVS 8.A)

VVS 8.A was initially located on the southeastern shore of Lake Ladoga, and consisted of 49 IAP, 72 SAP and 18 SBAP (total 164 combat aircraft). Only 20 SB (3rd and 4th Squadrons/72 SAP) in Besovets, and 33 I-16 (2nd and 4th Squadrons/49 IAP) in Nurmolitsa were combat ready (see 49 IAP and 72 SAP, pages 170 and 196).

Tasks of VVS 8.A included destruction of transport infrastructure and Värtsilä AF base, reconnaissance flights up to 100 km from the front line, fighter escort of own reconnaissance, bomber and artillery spotting aircraft, ground force protection and support, and supply of surrounded units.

In December 1939 and early January 1940 VVS 8.A received considerable reinforcements: 13 SBAP (45 SB) and 4th Squadron/3 LBAP (5 R-5) were transferred from VVS 7.A; 3 TBAP (26 TB-3) arrived from Borovskoye (VVS BOVO), 5 KAO (10 SSS) from Korostovichi (VVS LVO) and 15 KAO (7 R-5) from Saratov (VVS PrivVO or Volga MD).

HQ/13 SBAB with subordinated 13 SBAP, 18 SBAP and 3 TBAP arrived 1 January 1940. The subordination of 13 SBAP ended 7 January 1940, but was replaced by 39 SBAP with 62 SB from VVS BOVO in Staraya Bykhov.

Brigade HQ soon faced serious logistic problems. As no machine gun spare parts were available for the heavy TB-3 bombers, and the bomb racks were worn out, TB-3s were mainly used for transport and supply dropping. Coordination of bomber and fighter operations left much to be desired, and communication between ground and air forces was unsatisfactory.

Ilmavoimat's fast Blenheims performed strategic reconnaissance tasks for several weeks without interference from the fighters of 49 IAP and 72 SAP. Finally on 6 January 1940 three I-16 of 49 IAP shot down BL-112 (LLv 46), which force-landed at Polvijärvi. The Blenheim crew was able to reach their own lines.

In late January 1940 the main task of VVS 8.A became supply of surrounded ground forces (18th and 168th Divisions and 34th Tank Brigade; in Russian terminology "garrisons fighting in the enemy's rear"). All aviation units (except 18 SBAP) were given supply tasks, using aircraft of all types from heavy lift capacity TB-3 bombers to I-15bis fighters with under-wing containers.

1st Fighter Aviation Squadron (1 IAE; equipped by 11 I-153 fighters) was responsible for air defense of Lodejnoye pole AF base from 2 February 1940. The squadron was initially subordinated to VVS 8.A, but later transferred to VVS 15.A.

On 12 February 1940 the left flank of 8th Army was converted into 15th Army, and correspondingly VVS 15.A was formed. In February 1940 *kombrig* I.I. Kopets proposed dropping OV liquid bombs before ground attacks. Preparations to use VAP-500 bombs were initiated by 13 SBAP and 72 SAP, but combat ended before such bombs were used.

VVS 8.A Commander I.I. Kopets (HSU 21.6.1937).

VVS 8.A Political Commissar A.G. Rytov.

VVS 8.A Commander A.I. Gusev (HSU 14.11.1938). (all photos G.F. Petrov)

VVS 8.A Organisation

- **13 SBAB (Lodejnoye pole).** Staff arrived 1.1.1940 from Kalinin (AON-1).
    - **1. and 3./3 TBAP (Lodejnoye pole).** Arrived late December 1939 from Borovskoye (VVS BOVO). 5.1.1940 to 13 SBAB; 18.2.1940 13 SBAB to VVS 15.A.
    - **13 SBAP (Besovets)** In 13 SBAP 1–7.1.1940, then to 14 AB.
    - **18 SBAP (Lodejnoye pole).** Arrived 18.12.1939 from Olsufyevo (VVS BOBO); to Nurmolitsa 14.1.1940. Attached 21.2.1940 to 19 LBAB, VVS 15.A.
    - **39 SBAP (Lodejnoye pole).** Arrived 2.2.1940 from Staraya Bykhov (65 AB, VVS BOVO). With 13 SBAB 13.2.1940 to VVS 15.A. 39 SBAP returned 1.3.1940 to VVS 8.A.
    - **45 SBAP (Lodejnoye pole).** Arrived 15.2.1940 from Orel (30 AB, AON-2).
- **14 AB**
    - **13 SBAP (Besovets).** Arrived 21.12.1939 from Chernevo (16 SBAB, VVS 7.A). To 13 SBAB 1–7.1.1940, then to 14 AB.
    - **49 IAP (Nurmolitsa, Lodejnoye pole, Novaya Ladoga).** Arrived 22.11.1939 from Krestsy (14 AB, VVS LVO). To Karkunlampi 17.12.1939; 3./49 IAP to Käsnäselkä and Uomaa 18.12.1939, to Karkunlampi 27.12.1939. 49 IAP transferred to VVS 15.A 15.2.1940. 5./49 IAP formed AG Tkachenko, to Suojärvi 16.12.1939.
- **AG Tkatshenko (Suojärvi).** 16.12.1939 transformed from 5./49 IAP.
- **4./3 LBAP (Nurmolitsa).** Arrived 10.12.1939 from Krasnogvardejsk (VVS 7.A).
    - **72 SAP (Besovets).** 1./72 SAP to Uhtua (VVS 9.A) 26.11.1939. 4 DRAE attached to 72 SAP in March 1940.
- **1 IAE (Lodejnoye pole).** Arrived 2.2.1940 to VVS 8.A, later to 153 IAP, VVS 15.A.
- **4 DRAE (Besovets).** Arrived 28.2.1940 from Smolensk (VVS BOVO).
- **12 OIAE (Besovets).** Attached 2.2.1940 to VVS 8.A (possibly subordinated to 72 SAP).

- **5 KAO** (Lodejnoye pole). Arrived 6.12.1939 from Lisino (VVS 7.A); to Prääsä 1.1.1940; later to Suvilahti, Suojärvi.
- **15 KAO** (Besovets). Arrived 5.12.1939 from Saratov (VVS PrivVO); late December 1939 to Uomaa and Kolatselkä. 18.2.1940 to VVS 15.A.
- **54 Aviazveno Svyazi**. Supported 18. Division at Lemetti.
- **69 Aviazveno Svyazi**. Supported 56. Division in the Loimola direction.

VVS 8.A Command

Commander	*kombrig* I.I. Kopets (1908–1941). HSU 21.6.1937. In GPW commanded VVS ZFr. Committed suicide 23.6.1941 after heavy losses the day before.
Deputy commander	*polkovnik* S.V. Slyusarev (1906–1981). Deputy Commander of AON-2 to January 1940.
Military commissar	*polk.komiss* A.G. Rytov (1907–1966). In China 1938. In GPW political deputy commander of 8th Air Army. Soviet AF Chief Political Officer 1955–1967.
Chief of Staff	*polkovnik* I.V. Zirkov

Air Force of the 15th Army (VVS 15.A)

On 11 February 1940 the left flank of 8th Army was converted into 15th Army, commanded by *komandarm 2.r.* Mikhail Kovalev, who on 25 February 1940 was replaced by *komandarm 2.r.* Vladimir Kurdyumov. The main part of VVS 8.A was correspondingly converted into VVS 15.A.

Tasks of VVS 15.A included destruction of Finnish fortifications, transport infrastructure, reconnaissance flights up to 150 km from the front line, fighter escort of own reconnaissance, bomber and artillery spotting aircraft, ground force protection and support, and supply of surrounded Red Army units.

VVS 15.A operational area was limited to the north by Loimola, Matkaselkä, Jänisjärvi, and in the south by north and northwest shore of Lake Ladoga. The main task of VVS 15.A gradually became supply of Red Army units encircled north of Ladoga.; e.g. 13 SBAB dropped 296,904 kg foodstuff to 168th Division in the Kitelä *motti*.

VVS 15.A organisation 19.2.1940
- **13 SBAB** 175 SB-bombers in three regiments:
    - **18 SBAP** (Nurmolitsa)
    - **39 SBAP** (Lodejnoye pole)
    - **45 SBAP** Arrived 15.2.1940 from Orel (AON-3) to Lodejnoye pole.
- **1 IAE** (Lodejnoye pole; 15 I-153)
- **3 TBAP** (Lodejnoye pole; TB-3)
- **Detached units**
- **2 LBAP** (Nurmolitsa). 56 R-Z arrived 21.2.1940 from 62 AB VVS KhVO.
- **49 IAP** (Nurmolitsa and Karkunlampi; 29 I-153, 21 I-16 and 12 I-15bis)
- **153 IAP** (Karkunlampi). 60 I-153 arrived 22–26.2.1940 from 2 IAB, VVS MVO.
- **15 KAO** (Kolatselkä; 7 R-5)

19 LBAB Staff arrived late February 1940 from VVS 9.A to Nurmolitsa, where 2 LBAP and 18 SBAP were attached to 19 LBAP.

VVS 15.A Top Command

Commander	*polkovnik* A.I. Gusev (1910–1978). Spanish Civil War veteran. HSU 14.11.1938.
	polkovnik A.P. Khrustalov
	polkovnik N.N. Semenov
	kombrig Ya.S. Shkurin (1898–1971). In GPW 8th Air Army Chief of Staff etc.

Air Force of the 9th Army (VVS 9.A)

Tasks of VVS 9.A included destruction of transport infrastructure (including railway junctions and bridges at Kemi, Oulu and Kontiomäki), destruction of Oulu and Kemi AF bases, reconnaissance flights up to 300 km from the front line, fighter escort of reconnaissance, bomber and artillery correction aircraft, ground forces protection and support, supply of surrounded units and personnel evacuation.

VVS 9.A operational area was limited in the north at Kemijärvi, in the west at Puolanka, and in the south at Kajaani. Distribution of aviation units to the North was very difficult because of very scarce airfields. As Poduzhemye and Chiksha were the only permanent airfields in the operation area, temporary ice bases had to be set up, which required enormous efforts in sub-zero conditions.

The aviation elements of 9th Army consisted on 30 November 1939 of only 14 I-15bis of 1st Squadron/72 SAP, which had arrived to Chiksha only four days earlier. Two TB-3s with I-15bis spare parts, tools and fuel crashed on route to Chiksha 26–27 November 1939, one of which was c/n 22482 (7 TBAP), which crashed 26 November 1939 at Volozero, 60 km east of Medvezhegorsk.

9th Army also had an R-5 courier aircraft, which together with the fighter squadron formed "Aviation Group of 9th Army" (commanded by *polkovnik* Mel'nikov), capable of operating in the area of 163rd Division only. With only six flyable fighters left on 12 December 1939 (two were lost 2 December, and two more 6 December 1939), the Aviation Group was absolutely unable to perform active operations. 54th Mountain Division, attacking towards Kuhmo, was "supported" by 61 *Aviazveno svyazi* (61st liaison flight; only equipped with one U-2 biplane and three Sha-2 amphibians, lacking combat aircraft).

A few days later considerable reinforcements were dispatched to 9th Army, which enabled formal establishment of VVS 9.A 13 December 1939. *Komdiv*, HSU Pavel Rychagov was appointed VVS 9.A Commander, and *polkovnik* Mel'nikov Deputy Commander.

12 December 1939 33 AOS arrived with nine U-2 biplanes in Kem', and three days later more I-15bis fighters arrived. 17 December 1939 six SBs arrived from 9 SBAP and formed a special reconnaissance squadron directly attached to 9th Army HQ. Two days later 41 SBAP (which had suffered heavy losses on the Karelian Isthmus) landed in Chiksha, and 4th Squadron/19 IAP (I-15bis) arrived by train to Kem'. After assembly in Poduzhemye, the fighters flew to Chiksha.

After the attacks of 163rd and 44th Divisions on Suomussalmi were interrupted in mid-December 1939, VVS 9.A was urgently ordered to assist the encircled units with all means.

Late December 1939 VVS 9.A received also seven R-5 (9 KAO), two I-16 squadrons (of 20 IAP, VVS BOVO), 30 I-15bis of 38 IAP (which later formed 145 and 152 IAP), and also 14 I-153, 18 I-15bis, 3 DB-3 and 18 SB of 80 SAP in Arkhangelsk. Most new aircraft were based on the ice of Lake Sredneye Kuito (Keski-Kuittijärvi) south of Uhtua. Before the ice was thick enough two SB bombers sank through the ice after landing.

In January 1940 152 IAP (formed from ex-38 IAP I-15bis fighters and R-5 reconnaissance aircraft of 9 KAO) supported 163rd and 44th Divisions at Suomussalmi. In the northernmost sector 122th Division at Salla-Kemijärvi was supported by AG Filin (formed by 23 I-15bis of 145 IAP) and three DB-3 of 80 SAP. Directly subordinated to VVS 9.A were 17 I-15bis (80 SAP) and 46 SB (of 41 SBAP and 80 SAP).

9 January 1940 five TB-3 (3 TBAP) and 33 VRE from Krasnogvardejsk arrived in Chiksha. 30 I-16 from 20 IAP (VVS BOVO) were divided between 80 SAP and 145 IAP.

27 January 1940 VVS 9.A and 2 OO GVF (two detached aviation units of the Civil Aviation Fleet) were ordered to drop supplies to the encircled 54th Mountain Division. In late January 1940 more reinforcements arrived: 16 SBAP arrived 22–25 January 1940 from Rzhev (Kalinin MD) to Uhtua and on 27 January 1940 19 AB HQ arrived from Kharkov, and next day 10 SBAB HQ arrived from Kiev. 4th Squadron/27 IAP which arrived from Moscow Military District, and was attached to 19 AB, while 16 SBAP, 41 SBAP and 2nd Squadron/3 TBAP were attached to 10 SBAB. After these reinforcements the strength of VVS 9.A was 1 February 1940 110 SB, 10 DB-3, 4 TB-3, 13 R-5 and 143 fighters (55 I-153, 25 I-16 and 63 I-15bis).

In February 1940 almost all aircraft of 10 SBAB, heavy TB-3 bombers and I-15bis fighters included, were engaged in supporting the surrounded 54th Mountain Division at Kuhmo, by supply-dropping and harassing the Finnish 9th Division. VVS 9.A performed 1,434 supply-dropping missions in February 1940 (or 29% of all missions).

54th Mountain Division was also supported by 80 SAP, which furthermore attacked targets in the Finnish rear (including Kajaani and Kontiomäki with 17 SB, 15 I-15bis and 13 I-16). Up to 13 March 1940 VVS 9.A performed 2,443 supply missions and delived some 5,000 supply containers to the surrounded troops. Almost 2,500 officers, soldiers and medical personnel were flown by VVS 9.A into the *mottis*, while over 4,000 wounded were evacuated. Three aircraft were lost in supply operations.

In the opinion of modern Russian historians 54th and 168th Divisions (which were surrounded in the *mottis* at Kuhmo and Lemetti-Kitelä respectively) were saved from complete annihilation by air support. However, improvised air supply operations were not able to save 44th or 18th Division nor 34th Tank Brigade. The post-mortem Kremlin hearings in April 1940 paid considerable attention to the lack of specialized transport aviation units and aircraft.

In early February 1940 a special blind-flying group was formed (commanded by *kombrig* Spirin), consisting of 12 DB-3 (from 80 SAP), 8 I-16 (145 IAP), and 5 SB from the Air Force Academy in Moscow. AG Spirin received reinforcements from 29 February 1940, when 34 DRAE arrived from Gostomil (VVS KOVO). Next day six TB-3 arrived from 1 TBAP in Rostov-na-Donu at the Black Sea. AG Spirin was located at Fedoseyevka ice base near Kandalaksha.

As the two Aviation Brigades (10 and 19 AB) attached to VVS 9.A in February 1940, were lacking adequate communication means, their role was only passive, and were often only informed afterwards

VVS 9.A Commander P.V. Rychagov (HSU 31.12.1936). Rychagov commanded VVS RKKA 1940–1941, was arrested 24.6.1941 and executed 28.10.1941. (G.F. Petrov)

of orders given directly by VVS 9.A to the aviation regiments. Late February 1940 19 AB HQ moved to VVS 8.A in Nurmolitsa.

VVS 9.A Organisation
- **Staff/10 SBAB**. Arrived 27.1.1940 from Kiev (VVS KOVO).
- **Staff/19 LBAB**. Arrived 26.1.1940 from VVS KhVO.
- **1./1 TBAP**. Arrived 1.3.1940 from Rostov-na-Donu (VVS KOVO), attached to AG Spirin.
- **2./3 TBAP**. Arrived 9.1.1940 from Lodejnoye pole (VVS 8.A).
- **16 SBAP**. Arrived 25.1.1940 from VVS KalVO to Uhtua; attached to 10 SBAB.
- **4./19 IAP**. Arrived in December 1939 to Chiksha.
- **20 IAP**. Two squadrons arrived in December 1939 from VVS BOVO.
- **4./27 IAP**. Arrived from VVS MVO, attached to 19 LBAB.
- **38 IAP**. Two squadrons arrived in December 1939; in January 1940 formed 145 and 152 IAP.
- **41 SBAP**. Arrived 19.12.1939 from Gorelovo (15 SBAP, VVS 7.A) to Chiksha. Attached to 10 **1./72 AP** (Chiksha)
- **80 SAP**. Arrived 9.1.1940 from Borovskoye (VVS BOVO) to Chiksha. Attached to 10 SBAB in February 1940.
- **145 IAP**. (Kairala etc.) Set up 17.1.1940 with elements from 38 IAP, 20 IAP etc. Attached to AG Filin 7.3.1940.
- **152 IAP** (Vuonninen). Set up 2.1.1940 with elements from 19 IAP, 27 IAP, 38 IAP, 72 SAP and 80 SAP. 18 KAO was attached in January 1940.
- **ORAE VVS 9.A**. Arrived 17.12.1939 from Yedrovo (9 SBAP, 29 AB, VVS 7.A). SBAB in February 1940.
- **33 VRE**. Arrived 9.1.1940 from Krasnogvardejsk (VVS 7.A) to Chiksha.
- **34 DRAE**. Arrived 29.2.1940 from Gostomil (VVS KOVO), attached to AG Spirin.
- **9 KAO**. Split up in December 1939, seven R-5s arrived in December 1939 from Kanneljärvi (VVS 7.A).
- **18 KAO** (Vuonninen). Arrived 28.12.1939 from Sverdlovsk (VVS UrVO). In January 1940 attached to 152 IAP.
- **33 AOS** (Uhtua). Arrived 5.1.1940 to Uhtua from Krasnogvardejsk (VVS 7.A).
- **61 Aviazveno svyazi**. Supported 54. Mountain Division in the Kuhmo direction.
- **AG Spirin**. Formed early February 1940 from parts of 80 SAP, 145 IAP and VVA (Air Force Academy) in Moscow, based at Fedoseyevka.

VVS 9.A Top Command

Commander	*komdiv* P.V. Rychagov (1911–1941). Participated in Spanish Civil War, 6 victory claims. HSU 31.12.1936. In China 1938. Commanded VVS 1940–1941, executed 28.10.1941.
Military Commissar	*bat.komiss* G.P. Politykin
Chief of Staff	*polkovnik* P.P. Yusupov

Air Force of 14th Army (VVS 14.A)

Tasks of VVS 14.A included protection of Murmansk and the Barents Sea coastline against possible invasion by western powers (in particular surveillance of Barents Sea shipping), destruction of Finnish transport infrastructure, reconnaissance flights up to 150 km from the front line, fighter escort of own reconnaissance, bomber and artillery correction aircraft and own ground forces protection.

VVS 14.A operational area was limited in the west by the Norwegian and Swedish borders and in the south by the Polar circle.

Formation of the future 14th Army, including aviation units, already was initiated in September 1939 in the Murmansk area. VVS 14.A consisted initially only of Murmansk Aviation Brigade, incorporating only the mixed aviation regiment 5 SAP (equipped with SB and DB-3 bombers, and also with some fighters). After arrival of more fighters in December 1939 147 IAP was formed 9 January 1940.

On 30 November Murmansk Aviation Brigade was based at Shongui, Murmashi and Vayenga. Later bases in occupied Finnish territory were used, eg. Luostari and Salmijärvi.

VVS 14.A (Murmansk aviation brigade) 12.1.1940

	Aircraft	Base
VVS 14.A HQ	1 SB, 1 DB-3	Luostari
Murmansk aviation brigade HQ	2 I-153, 1 unidentified	Murmansk
5 SAD HQ	1 I-15bis	Luostari
1st SB Squadron	12 SB	Luostari
2nd SB Squadron	12 SB	Luostari
3rd SB Squadron	11 SB	Murmashi
DB-group (2 escadrilles/squadrons)	15 DB-3	Murmashi
5 SAP total	1 I-15bis, 35 SB, 15 DB-3	
147 IAP HQ		
1st Squadron	17 I-153	Vayenga
2nd Squadron	18 I-16	
3rd Squadron	14 I-15bis	Luostari
4th Squadron	14 I-15bis	Murmashi
5th Squadron	14 I-15bis	Murmashi
147 IAP total	42 I-15bis, 18 I-16, 17 I-153	
Total	133 (43 I-15bis, 18 I-16, 19 I-153, 36 SB, 16 DB-3 and 1 unidentified)	

VVS 14.A Commander S.A. Krasovskiy (HSU 29.5.1945).

T.T. Khryukin commanded VVS 14.A from January 1940 (HSU 22.2.1939 and 19.4.1945). (both G.F. Petrov)

33 SBAP arrived from Kiev military district to Luostari with 59 SB in February 1940, after which VVS 14.A numbered 96 bombers (in 5 OSBAP and 33 SBAP), and 86 fighters in 147 IAP.

The reason why such powerful air force units were transferred to Pechenga (Petsamo) has been subject to discussion both in Russia and in Finland, as neither the Finnish Air Force nor the Swedish volunteer Wing F 19 were able to attack this region. Neither were Soviet fighters based in Pechenga and on the coast of the Arctic Ocean able to escort their own bombers on attacks to targets in Finnish Lapland. The motive was apparently fear of Allied invasion on the Arctic coast, which was in fact considered in London and in Paris during the final phase of the Winter War.

VVS 14.A Top Command
Commander S.A. Krasovskiy (1897–1983), commanded VVS 14.A to January 1940. In GPW commanded 2nd and 17th Air Armies. HSU 29.5.1945. Commanded 26th Air Army 1955–1956.
polkovnik T.T. Khryukin (1910–1953). Commanded VVS 14.A from January 1940. Spanish Civil War and China veteran. In GPW commanded Karelian Front AF, VVS 8th and 1st Air Armies. HSU 22.2.1939 and 19.4.1945. Deputy Commander of VVS 1950–1953, died after traffic accident 19.7.1953.
A.S. Osipenko (1910–1991). Spanish Civil War veteran, HSU 22.2.1939. Acting VVS 14.A commander from February 1940. In GPW commanded 8 IAK etc.
Military Commissar *bat.komiss* Berkutov
Chief of Staff *kombrig* P.P. Ionov. Head of VVS Academy 1944–1946.

Aviation Brigades

Brigade type (I, LB, SB, TB etc) is explicitly indicated below; this attribute is often left out in contemporary documents.

1st Light Bomber Aviation Brigade (1 LBAB)
Autumn 1939 1 LBAB was based in Kirovograd (VVS KOVO). 1 LBAB arrived 11 February 1940 in Suulajärvi (in occupied Karelian Isthmus).

During the attacks against the Mannerheim Line from 11 to 27 February 1940 1 LBAB performed 795 combat missions (mainly at night), and dropped 319.4 t (8 to 100 kg) bombs.

1 LBAB Subordination
VVS KOVO (to 11.2.1940)
VVS 7.A (from 11.2.1940)

R-5 was also tested for troop or passenger transport duty, carrying up to seven persons in each under-wing Grokhovskiy G-61 container. After flight tests 8.12.1936 the G-61 container was produced in limited numbers. No details about Winter War use are available, but propaganda photos were distributed. (G.F. Petrov)

1 LBAB Regiments
5 SBAP. Already by autumn 1939 in 1 LBAP, arrived 26.2.1940 from Kirovograd to Suulajärvi.
7 LShAP. Arrived 13.2.1940 from Kiev (51 AB, VVS KOVO) to Halolanjärvi, Uusikirkko.
43 LBAP. Arrived in February 1940 from Vitebsk (70-AB, VVS BOVO) to Suulajärvi.

1 LBAB Command
Commander   P.G. Zhuravlev
Military Commissar   F.I. Zhmulev
Chief of Staff   P.N. Solovyev

10th Fast Bomber Aviation Brigade (10 SBAB)

In autumn 1939 10 SBAB was based in Belaya Tserkov' (VVS KOVO). 10 SBAB HQ arrived 28 January 1940 to VVS 9.A, where various aviation units were attached (see below).

On 1 February 1940 10 SBAB was ordered by VVS 9.A Commander *komdiv* Rychagov to *destroy the railway station and city of Kajaani* on 2–6 February 1940 (exact day to be determined by weather conditions) with six nine-bomber squadrons. Calculated bomb amount: 245 FAB-50 500kg explosive bombs and 1,874 ZAB-2 500kg incendiary bombs, total weight 35.3 tons.

Note: this order is apparently a very rare order, explicitly prescribing destruction of an entire city, without any references to military targets whatsoever!

The Commander of 10 SBAB *polkovnik* Vadimir Shevchenko ordered 16 and 41 SBAP to perform the attack with three squadrons each. Because of weather conditions the Kajaani bombing was performed 7 February 1940 by 56 SB-bombers. 41 SBAP attacked at 1515–1525 hours with 25 SBs, and 16 SBAP attacked at 1510–1517 hours with 19 SBs, altogether 28.3 ton bombs were dropped. In Kajaani 64 houses, shops and production facilities were destroyed. Fortunately only four persons were killed.

10 SBAB Commander V.I. Shevchenko (HSU 14.3.1938). (G.F. Petrov)

10 SBAB Subordination
VVS KOVO (until 28.1.1940)
VVS 9.A (from 28.1.1940)

10 SBAB Regiments
16 SBAP. Arrived 23–25.1.1940 from Rzhev (VVS KalVO) to Chiksha.
41 SBAP. Arrived late December 1939 from Borovskoye from 15 SBAB, VVS 7.A to Kem' and Sholopovo.
80 SAP. Arrived late December 1939 from Arkhangelsk (VVS LVO) to Uhtua.
2. Squadron/3 TBAP. Arrived 9.1.1940 from Borovskoye (VVS BOVO) to Uhtua.

Elements/9 SBAP. Arrived late December 1939 from Yedrovo (29 AB, VVS 7.A) to Uhtua. Later reinforcements from various units.

10 SBAB Command
Commander	*polkovnik* V.I. Shevchenko (1908–1972). HSU 14.3.1938. In GPW commanded VVS 37.A, 1 SAK etc.
Military commissar	*polk.komiss* Vyvolokin
Chief of Staff	*polkovnik* Kuznetsov

13th Fast Bomber Aviation Brigade (13 SBAB)

In autumn 1939 13 SBAB was based in Kalinin (AON-1). 13 SBAB HQ arrived 1 January 1940 to Lodejnoye pole on the southern bank of the River Svir, and was attached to VVS 8.A. On 19 February 1940 13 SBAB was transferred to the new VVS 15.A with 175 SB bombers.

Because of extreme cold with temperatures down to –45° or – 50° in January 1940, combat missions were performed only on 5, 6, 21, 23, 28 and 29 January 1940. In March 1940 13 SBAB supported Soviet troops fighting in the northern part of Ladoga at Vuoratsu, Maksimansaari and Kuivaniemi.

13 SBAB Commander B.K. Tokarev. (G.F. Petrov)

13 SBAB Subordination
AON-1 (as 13 AB. The Aviation Brigade was later renamed 13 SBAB.)
VVS 8.A (from 1.1.1940 to 19.2.1940)
VVS 15.A (from 19.2.1940)

13 SBAB Regiments
3 TBAP. Arrived 5.1.1940 from Borovskoye (VVS BOVO) to Lodejnoye pole.
13 SBAP. Arrived 21.12.1939 from Chernevo (16 SBAB, VVS 7.A) to Besovets (VVS 8. A). Subordinated to 13 SBAB 1.-7.1.1940, later to 14 AB.
18 SBAP. Arrived 18.12.1939 from Bobrujsk (65 AB, VVS BOVO) to Lodejnoye pole (VVS 8.A). 18 SBAP was 1.1.1940 attached to 13 SBAB, and 21.2.1940 to 19 LBAB (VVS 15.A).
39 SBAP. Arrived 2.2.1940 from Staraya Bykhov (65 AB, VVS BOVO) to Lodejnoye pole (13 SBAB). 39 SBAP was 13.2.1940 attached to VVS 15.A as part of 13 SBAB. 39 SBAP was 1.3.1940 transferred back to VVS 8.A.
45 SBAP. Arrived 15.2.1940 from Orel (30 AB, AON-2) to Lodejnoye pole, and was attached to 13 SBAB.

Former regiments of 13 AB were transferred as follows:
6 DBAP arrived 14.11.1939 from Ivanovo to Krechevitsy, and was attached to VVS LVO. 6 DBAP was 25.1.1940 attached to 27 DBAB (VVS SZFr).
41 SBAP arrived late November 1939 from Kalinin to Gorelovo, and was attached to 15 SBAB (VVS 7.A).

13 SBAB Command
Commander	*polkovnik* B.K. Tokarev (1907–1977). In GPW commanded 1 ShAK, 6 ShAK etc.
Military commissar	*polk.komiss* Korolev
Chief of Staf	*polkovnik* P.S. Popov

14th Aviation Brigade (14 AB)

In autumn 1939 14 AB was based in Krestsy near Novgorod (VVS LVO). 14 AB arrived in November 1939 to Lodejnoye pole at the River Svir, and in January 1940 moved to Karkunlampi ice base (north of Lake Ladoga, some 10 km west of the Finnish-Soviet border).

Finnish Blenheim BL-119 (*luutn* Andreas Platan, *kers* Unto Oksala (MHR) and *ylik* Antti Unto Lattunen) of LLv 44 photographed the Lodejnoye pole, Nurmolitsa and Karkunlampi AF bases on 4 February 1940 at 1207–1235 hours. Of the 29 photos taken only one photo of Lodejnoye pole AF base has been found (see page 73).

14 AB Subordination
VVS LVO (until 30.11.1939)
VVS 8.A (from 30.11.1939)

14 AB Regiments

13 SBAP. Arrived late December 1939 from 16 SBAB (VVS 7.A) in Chernevo to Besovets, 1.1.1940 attached to 13 SBAB (VVS 8.A). Later transferred to 14 AB.

49 IAP. Arrived 22.11.1939 from Krestsy to Nurmolitsa, Lodejnoye pole and Novaya Ladoga, and attached to VVS 8.A. 49 IAP was 15.2.1940 transferred to VVS 15.A.

14 AB Command

Commander	*polkovnik* Ye.Ya. Kholzakov. In 1941 commanded 39 IAD.
Assistant commander	*major* I.V. Yakubovich. 12.12.1939–12.1.1940 commanded 49 IAP.
Military commissar	F.F. Morozov. In 1941 55 SAD commissar.

15th Fast Bomber Aviation Brigade (15 SBAB)

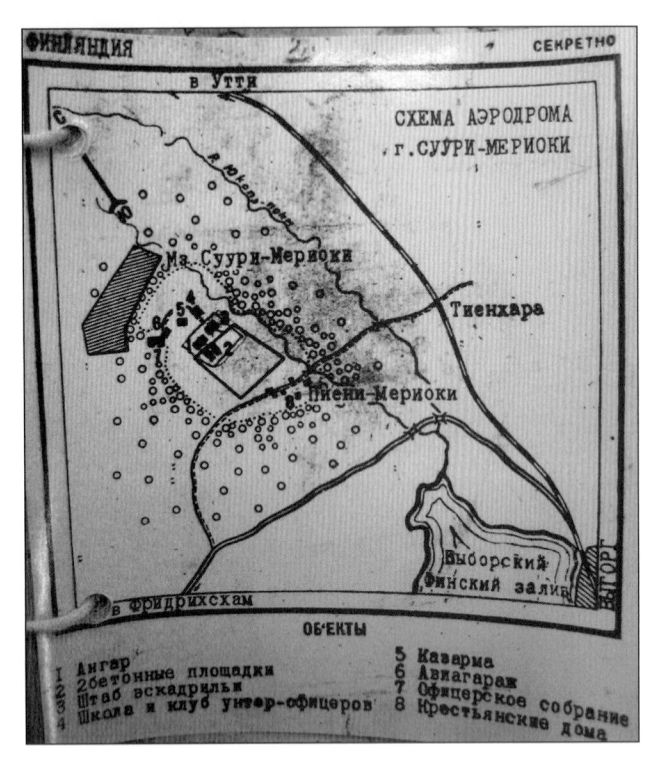

In autumn 1939 15 SBAB was based in Novgorod (VVS LVO).

30 November 1939 eight SBs from 2 SBAP bombed Imatra hydro-electric power station, and six SBs of 24 SBAP bombed Viipuri railway junction.

1 December 1939 147 SB-bombers attacked Immola and Suur-Merijoki AF bases, Viipuri, Hiitola, Kiviniemi, Raivola and Mustamäki railway stations. Only Moth MO-111 was damaged in Suur-Merijoki, but eleven bombers were shot down by Finnish Fokker fighters (SB c/n 13/223 of the Deputy Commander of 15 SBAP *polkovnik* I.I. Kuznetsov, six SBs of 41 SBAP and four SBs of 24 SBAP). Furthermore SB c/n 3/220 of 24 SBAP belly-landed in Vitino with 159 bullet holes; this aircraft was still under repair in Ropsha on 25 February 1940.

According to *Osobyi otdel* (Special Department) of Leningrad Military District, bombing from only 400 m altitude (not 2,000 m as ordered) led to loss of five SB-bombers.

The Special Department's report referred apparently to 24 SBAP. The correlation between flight altitude and losses indicates that the bombers were believed to have been shot down by Finnish A-A artillery. Most SBs lost by 24 SBAP were however shot down in air combat, at both 2,000 m and 400 m altitude!

After this snow and fog prevented air operations until 18 December 1939, when 15 SBAB performed 79 missions against fortifications at the eastern end of the Mannerheim Line (Taipale,

A map of Suur-Merijoki (Finnish AF base west of Viipuri) found in an SB shot down 1.12.1939 at Säiniö. (Finnish National Archive)

Kaarnajoki and Kelja). Next day 15 SBAB performed two attacks with full strength. The first attack was made against fortifications at Summa, and the second against targets at the NW shore of Ladoga (from Käkisalmi to Sortavala). In December 1939 819 combat missions were performed by 15 SBAB.

Early January 1940 15 SBAB was attached to the new VVS 13.A. Despite non-flying weather *polkovnik* Pyatykhin ordered a combat mission to be made on 7 January 1940, resulting in the loss of three SBs.

Because of the extreme cold (temperatures down to – 45° or – 50°) in January 1940, combat missions were made only on 12, 18, 20, 22, 29 and 30 January 1940, when only 18 missions were

RRAB Rotativno-rasseivajushshaja aviabomba, (Rotating-spreading aviation bomb) was a cylindrical container filled with small bombs. The rear wings caused the container to rotate. When critical rotating speed was reached, the bombs were released over a wide area. In Finland RRAB-3 (length 2.3 m, diameter 0.52 m, weight empty 65 kg, weight loaded 250–450 kg) were soon given the nickname Molotov's bread basket. In the photo a young soldier is standing beside an undetonated RRAB-3. (SA-kuva)

50

flown. However, combat intensity grew fast: on 1 February 1940 88 missions were flown, and two days later 180 missions! It is remarkable that an order to *destroy Sortavala* was given on 1 February 1940 to 15 SBAB. Because of poor weather the reserve target was bombed, but next day 84 bombers dropped over 48 tons of explosive and incendiary bombs and 33,200 leaflets on the small garden town, entirely lacking military objectives. 15 SBAB reported *Sortavala destroyed...*

From 13 February 1940, 15 SBAB bombed Finnish troops and fortifications between Muolaa and Äyräpää, supporting Soviet 15th and 23rd Army Corps. From 13 to 16 February 1940 467 t of bombs were dropped. 19 February 1940 a massive attack against Käkisalmi was performed, with 85.2 t bombs dropped.

15 SBAB performed altogether 4,704 combat missions.

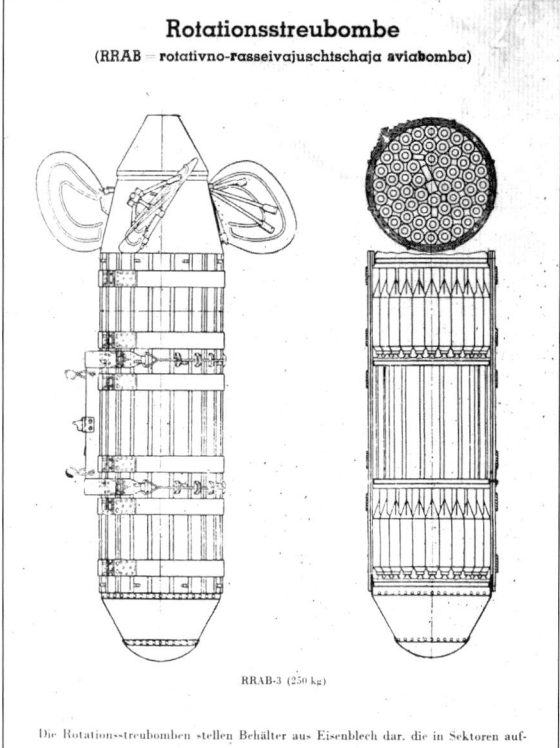

15 SBAB Subordination
VVS LVO, Novgorod
VVS 7.A (until 6.1.1940)
VVS 13.A (from 6.1.1940)

15 SBAB Regiments
2 SBAP. Arrived 29.11–9.12.1939 from Solt'sy to Ropsha and Vitino. To VVS SZFr 10.1–18.1.1940, then back to 15 SBAB.
24 SBAP. Arrived late November 1939 from Krechevitsy to Gorelovo.
41 SBAP. Arrived late November 1939 from Kalinin (13 AB, AON-1) to Gorelovo, attached to 27 DBAB (operatively subordinated to 15 SBAB). Late December 1939 transferred to 10 SBAB (VVS 9.A).
68 IAP. To 15 SBAB from VVS 13.A 11.-19.1.1940, then back to VVS 13.A.

15 SBAB Command
Commander — *polkovnik* I.G. Pyatykhin (1904–1971). Performed 25 combat missions in the Winter War. HSU 7.4.1940. In GPW commanded 15th Air Army 1942–1943.
Military commissar — F.F. Verov. In GPW deputy Commander of 4th Air Army 1943–1945.

German description of the RRAB-3 bomb container. (Finnish National Archive)

Loading of a RRAB-3 bomb container. (G.F. Petrov)

RRAB-3 function was rather unreliable, so undetonated containers could often be found. The tightly packed bombs might also explode at release, causing serious damage to their own bombers. In the photo Finnish soldiers are seen collecting undetonated AO-2.5 bombs.

Undetonated FAB-100 bombs in Sortavala. (SA-kuva)

Typical posed HSU propaganda photo: from left 15 SBAB Commander I.G. Pyatykhin (HSU 7.4.1940) with A.Ya. Letuchiy (3 LBAP squadron CO, HSU 19.5.1940) and A.N. Kostylev (50 SBAP Commissar, HSU 21.3.1940). (G.F. Petrov)

16th Fast Bomber Aviation Brigade (16 SBAB)

In autumn 1939 16 SBAB was based in Seshchinskaya (VVS BOVO), and arrived in late November 1939 to Chernevo, 26 km SE Gdov (VVS 7.A). The first operations by 16 SBAB were performed 19 December 1939. Before 1939 ended 16 SBAB performed 229 combat missions, and dropped 56.2 t of explosive, 8,022 splinter and 424 incendiary bombs.

In January 1940 16 SBAB was attached to VVS SZFr.

17 January 1940 the task was to bomb Lappeenranta together with practically all bombers of VVS SZFr. According to the order received the previous night *"the military target of the railway station at Lappeenranta was to be set afire and destroyed by a massive attack"*. However, in the morning many AF bases were covered by thick fog, with temperatures down to even -41°, so only 31 and 54 SBAP of 16 SBAB were able to participate, but not with full strength. At 1328 to 1339 hours 20 SB-bombers took off: 11 a/c from 31 SBAP, 8 a/c from 54 SBAP, and the SB piloted by 16 SBAB Commander, *major* Borisenko (who dropped his 1,000kg bomb load on the bridges at Viipuri). The intention was that 25 IAP should escort the bombers, but five minutes before take-off a message was received that Kanneljärvi AF base was covered by fog, so fighter escort was out of question. Three SBs were forced to turn back for various reasons, and only 16 bombers reached Lappeenranta. After the bombs were dropped ten Fokkers of 1st and 4th Flight/LLv 24 from Joutseno and Ruokolahti appeared and downed five bombers without own losses. In addition several bombers were seriously damaged. Only nine SBs (of which two were damaged) returned to their bases.

16 SBAB Commander M.Kh. Borisenko. (G.F. Petrov)

After the heavy losses the Commander of VVS SZFr *komandarm* Yevgeniy Ptukhin prohibited bombing attacks to Kouvola, Suur-Merijoki, Lappeenranta, Viipuri, Hiitola and Elisenvaara without escort fighters. Ptukhin also repeated the Stavka order of 27 December 1939, which categorically prohibited the reuse of routes and entry point on approach and return flights. (See also VVS SZFr, 31 and 54 SBAP; pages 35, 138 and 186). The 1 February 1940 bombing target of 16 SBAB was Imatra. Immediately before take-off new orders were received from VVS SZFr with Neuvalo as the new target. However, these orders were also changed, now back to Imatra! The final target was Neuvalo (to be attacked by three nine-bomber squadrons, or by one entire aviation regiment), while the other squadrons were to bomb Imatra.

From 15 February 1940 the task of 16 SBAB was to prevent the transport of Finnish reinforcements to the Karelian Isthmus by bombing railway stations and junctions between Kouvola and Vuoksenniska.

16 SBAB mission statistics

	Missions Total	Missions Task performed	Bombs dropped (t)	Flight time (h)
Staff	34	28	22	71
13 SBAP	45	36	14	64
31 SBAP	940	799	472	2,699
54 SBAP	1,046	988	578	3,351
Total	2,065	1,851	1,086	6,185

16 SBAB losses

	Aircraft losses Enemy fighters	Personnel losses Enemy A/A	MIA	Not combat lossses	Pilots	Navigators	MG-gunners
13 SBAP	2		4	6	4	5	4
31 SBAP	5			6	8	9	6
54 SBAP	7	4	1	1	10	12	11
Total	14	4	5	7	22	26	21

16 SBAB machine-gunners claimed 43 enemy fighters (however only one Finnish aircraft can be considered shot down by 16 SBAB gunners).

After the Winter War 16 SBAB formed 47 SAD, which on 22 June 1941 was attached to the Air Force of the Western Front (VVS ZFr); see 13, 31 and 54 SBAP; pages 109, 138 and 186.

16 SBAB Subordination
VVS BOVO (until 30.11.1939)

VVS 7.A (from 30.11.1939)
VVS SZFr (from late January 1940)

16 SBAB Regiments

13 SBAP. Arrived 30.11.1939 from Seshchinskaya (16 AB, VVS BOVO) to Chernovo. To VVS 8.A 20.12.1939.
31 SBAP. Arrived 31.12.1939 from Smolensk (18 AB, VVS BOVO) to Chernovo.
54 SBAP. Arrived 30.11.1939 from Shejkovka (VVS BOVO) to Smuravyevo.

16 SBAB command

Commander	*polkovnik* N.G. Belov
	M.Kh. Borisenko (1904–1958). In GPW commanded 6 SAK and 5 BAK.
Chief of Staff	*polkovnik* S.I. Fedulyev
Military Commissar	*polk.komiss* M.M. Moskalev

18th Fast Bomber Aviation Brigade (18 SBAB)

In autumn 1939 18 SBAB was based in Smolensk (VVS BOVO), and in November 1939 relocated to Latvia, from where 18 SBAB/HQ arrived in Siverskaya late December 1939.

16 January 1940 18 SBAB started systematic bombing of the central sector of the Mannerheim Line between Summa and Muolaanjärvi, where 123rd Division was to perform its breakthrough with 126 SB bombers. Before 10 February 1940 681,5 tons of explosive, incendiary and 50 500 kg splinter bombs were dropped by 18 SBAB. Before the main attack of 123rd Division in the Lähde-sector, 18 SBAB bombed the Finnish fortifications for 20 minutes. Some days later 18 SBAB concentrated its efforts somewhat more to the east in the Perkjärvi-Kämärä direction, supporting the Soviet 19th Army Corps.

From 28 February 1940 18 SBAB supported 10th and 28th Army Corps advancing on the frozen Bay of Viipuri.

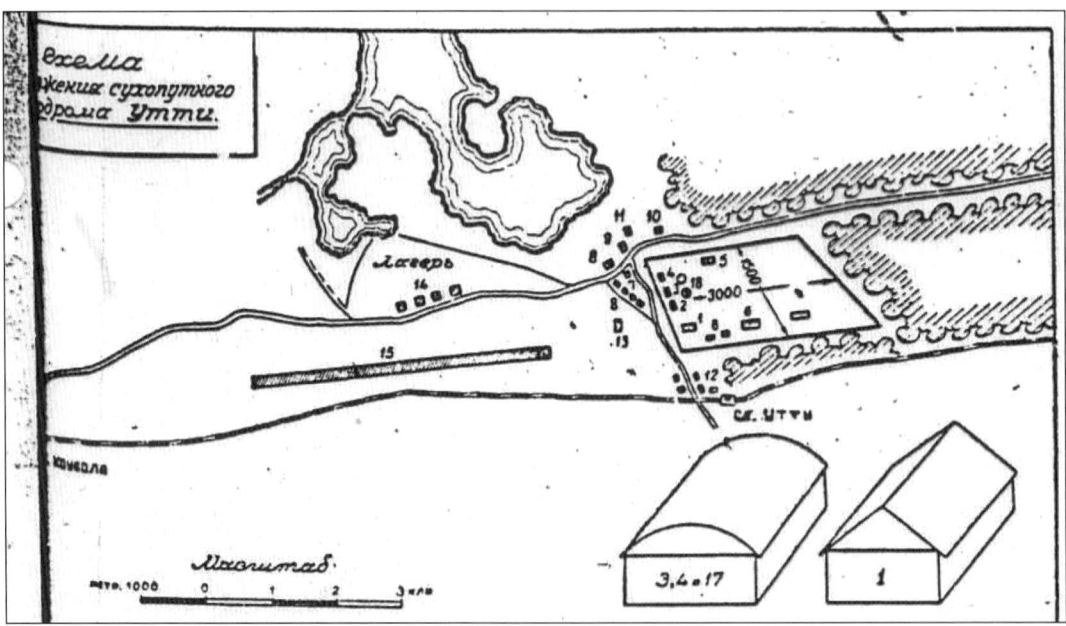

18 SBAB Commander V.V. Naneishvili (HSU 21.3.1940). (G.F. Petrov)

Soviet map of Utti AF base. (Finnish National Archive)

18 SBAB missions

Month	Missions
December 1939 (50 SBAP)	151
January 1940	383
February 1940	2,810
March 1940	885
Total	4,229

18 SBAB Commissar F.I. Bogatyrev congratulating an SB-crew after a successful bombing mission. (G.F. Petrov)

18 SBAB performed 68 "brigade missions" (or 4,229 individual combat missions, total flight time 4,857.35 hours), and dropped 2,494.5 t bombs. Targets included Utti AF base, Kouvola and Helsinki.

18 SBAB Bombing Targets

Target type	Bomber regiment		Total
	48 SBAP	50 SBAP	
Fortifications	762	847	1,629
Railway targets	418	320	738
Enemy troops and population centres	740	1,130	1,870
Total	1,940	2,297	4,239

Kouvola bombing. The photo was taken between 20 and 25 February 1940. (RGVA)

18 SBAB Subordination
VVS SZFr (1.-16.1.1940)
VVS 7.A (from 16.1.1940)

18 SBAB Base-area
Siverskaya (1.-25.1. 1940), Sestroretskiy razliv from 25.1.1940.

18 SBAB Regiments
48 SBAP. Arrived from Uman' (VVS KOVO) to Siverskaya. 1.1.1940 attached to 18 SBAB.
50 SBAP. 20.10.1939 in Siverskaya subordinated to 71 AB. 1.1.1940 attached to 18 SBAB.

18 SBAB Command
Commander	*polkovnik* V.V. Nanejshvili (1903–1978; Georgian). HSU 21.3.1940. In GPW commanded VVS 46. and 47. A, and 8 ShAK 1944–1945. Commanded 34th Air Army 1950–1951. Nanejshvili is said to have participated in bombing Marshal Mannerheim's residence, after which the Finnish Supreme Commander was forced to retreat to the rear…
Military commissar	*polk.komiss* F.I. Bogatyrev (?–1940, previously in 71 LBAB)
	polk.komiss Malyshkin
Chief of Staff	*major* A.Ye. Rasskazov (1898–?, previously in 71 LBAB)

19th Light Bomber Aviation Brigade (19 LBAB)

In Autumn 1939 19 LBAB was based in Kharkov (VVS KhVO). 19 LBAB/HQ arrived on 28 January 1940 at VVS 9.A in northern Karelian ASSR. The subordinated units arrived later, and on 21 February 1940 19 LBAB was attached to VVS 15.A in Nurmolitsa (Nurmoila).

19 AB Commander N.P. Kamanin (HSU 20.4.1934). (G.F. Petrov)

19 LBAB Subordination
VVS KhVO (until 28.1.1940)
VVS 9.A, (28.1.–21.2.1940)
VVS 15.A (from 21.2.1940)

19 LBAB Regiments
2 LBAP. Arrived 21.2.1940 from Konotop (62 AB, VVS KOVO) to Nurmolitsa, attached to 19 LBAB.
18 SBAP. Transferred 21.2.1940 from 13 SBAP (VVS 8.A) to 19 LBAB (VVS 15.A).

Note: 4 LBAP (formerly subordinated to 19 AB) arrived 13.2.1940 from Kharkov to Kaukolovo and was attached to 68 LBAB.

4. Squadron/27 IAP arrived from VVS MVO to VVS 9.A, and was attached to 19 LBAB. It is not known whether this subordination continued after 21.2.1940.

19 LBAB Command
Commander	*polkovnik* N.P. Kamanin (1908–1982). HSU 20.4.1934. In GPW commanded 8 SAK 1943 and 5 ShAK 1943–1945. Commanded 73th Air Army 1957–1958. Head of Cosmonaut training centre *Zvezdnyi gorodok* (Star city) 1966–1971.
Military commissar	*polk.komiss* Kozlov
Chief of Staff	*major* Yarov (Yarovskiy?)

27th Long-Range Bomber Aviation Brigade (27 DBAB)

In autumn 1939 27 DBAB was based in Monino (AON-1), and arrived on 14 November 1939 at Yedrovo and Krestsy.

The DB-3 regiments of 27 DBAB performed 2,085 combat missions with 8,511 h flight time. 49 DB-3 were lost (17 shot down by enemy fighters, 5 by A-A artillery, 11 went missing and 16 were destroyed in non-combat accidents). Furthermore 12 seriously damaged DB-3s were written off, but 52 damaged DB-3 returned to service after repairs.

27 DBAB Subordination
AON-1 (until 14.11.1939)
VVS LVO (from 14.11.1939)
VVS SZFr (from 25.1.1940)

27 DBAB Regiments
6 DBAP. Arrived 14.11.1939 from 13 AB (AON-1) in Ivanovo to Krechevitsy. Attached to 27 DBAB 25.1.1940.
21 DBAP. Arrived 16.11.1939 from AON-1 in Monino to Yedrovo, and 29.12.1939 to Pushkin.
41 SBAP. Arrived late November 1939 from 13 AB (AON-1) in Kalinin to Gorelovo. 41 SBAP was formally attached to 27 DBAB, but operatively subordinated to 15 SBAB. Late December 1939 41 SBAP was transferred to VVS 9.A.
42 DBAP. Arrived 15–21.1.1940 from 64 AB (AON-2) in Voronezh to Krechevitsy.
53 DBAP. Arrived 14.11.1939 from AON-1 in Monino to Krestsy. Transferred 7.1.1940 to OAG in Kuusiku, Estonia.

27 DBAB Strength
11.1.1940 (6, 21 and 53 DBAP): 111 DB-3
11.2.1940: 142 DB-3
3.3.1940: 167 DB-3

27 DBAB Command
Commander	*kombrig* M.P. Kaz'min
	polkovnik V.A. Sudets (1904–1981.) Acting 27 DBAB commander from 21.12.1939, performed 14 combat missions. HSU 28.4.1945. In GPW commanded 17th Air Army etc. Commanded DA 1955–1962.
Military commissar	*polk.komiss* N.I. Petrov
	polk.komiss Terentyev
Chief of Staff	*polkovnik* V.A. Sudets
	I.M. Sokolov (1900–1982). 27 DBAB CoS from January 1940. In GPW commanded 7th Air Army etc.

27 AB Deputy Commander V.A. Sudets (HSU 28.4.1945). He commanded Dalnyaya Aviatsiya (Soviet Long-Range Aviation) 1955–1962, and the Air Defence Forces 1962–1966 as Soviet Deputy Minister of Defence. (G.F. Petrov)

27 AB Commander I.M. Sokolov. He served as Deputy Chief of Air Force General Staff 1955–1959. (G.F. Petrov)

Vladimir Sudets (at left) with serious-looking officers. Note stylized number 21. (G.F. Petrov)

29th Heavy Bomber Aviation Brigade (29 TBAB), also 29th Long-Range Bomber Aviation Brigade (29 DBAB)

In autumn 1939 29 TBAB was based in Yedrovo (VVS LVO). 29 TBAB (also called 29 DBAB) was in December 1939 apparently subordinated to both AON-1 and VVS 7.A. In January 1940 29 TBAB was attached to VVS SZFr.

29 TBAB Subordination
VVS LVO
AON-1 (operationally subordinated to VVS 7.A)
VVS SZFr (from January 1940)

29 TBAB Regiments
7 TBAP. Arrived in October 1939 from Yedrovo to Jelgava (Latvia). In December 1939 to Pushkino.
9 SBAP, Yedrovo. Conversion from TB-3 to SB initiated 12.12.1939. 9 SBAP was later split up into squadrons.

29 TBAB Command
Commander	*polkovnik* Zhukov
	polkovnik Abanin, from 24.1.1940.
Military commissar	*polk.komiss* Antonov
Chief of Staff	I.M. Sokolov, to January 1940. (See 27 DBAP, page 57.)

Some TB-3 aircraft were equipped with ski undercarriages. Ground operating instructions were given by signal flags which were acknowledged by the navigator standing in the aircraft nose. (G.F. Petrov)

54th Fighter Aviation Brigade (54 IAB)

In autumn 1939 54 IAB was based in Gorelovo (Leningrad MD), and subordinated to both VVS 7.A and 2nd Air Defense Army Corps (2 AK PVO).

Tasks

54 IAB was responsible for the air defense of Leningrad (PVO) and also of 7th Army HQ in Ropsha. 30 November 1939 54 IAB disposed of 183 I-16, of which there were 15 new *tip 18* and *30* 20-mm cannon-equipped *tip 17*, 45 I-153 and 37 I-15bis; totaling 265 fighters. Unusually some fighters were equipped with radios, enabling direct contact with air observation and command centers.

As no enemy intrusions into the air space of Leningrad were recorded, several squadrons were soon sent elsewhere. 54 IAB was later escorting the bombers of 15 SBAB and reconnaissance aircraft of 1 DRAE, and also performing train hunting. 10 February 1940 54 IAB numbered 168 fighters. Twelve Finnish fighters were claimed destroyed in air combat and ground attacks against enemy AF bases, and 82 locomotives, 32 trains and 51 wagons were destroyed.

54 IAB Commander A.S. Blagoveshchenskiy (HSU 14.11.1938) with one of "his" I-153 fighter pilots. (G.F. Petrov)

54 IAB Aircraft

Type	30.11.1939 Total	13.3.1940 Serviceable	Total	Serviceable
I-16 tip 5	137	158	173	160
I-16 tip 10	1			
I-16 tip 17	30			
I-16 tip 18	15			
I-16 tip 24	-	-	28	28 (no combat missions)
I-153	45	39	42	30
I-15bis	37	36	14	13
Total	265	233	257	231

54 IAB Combat Missions

Combat flights				
I-16	I-153	I-15	Total
8434	1438	261	10133

Attack missions	Ground forces protection	Bomber Escort	Enemy bases attack	Air combat	Leningrad air defence
786	291	462	18	18	85848,584

Flying days: 68, total flight time 10,918 h 20 min.
Missions per day: on average 149, maximum 393 missions (2.2.1940).
Active pilots per day: 190–195.
Operable aircraft per day: 175–180

54 IAB Subordination
VVS LVO
VVS 7.A

54 IAB Regiments and main bases
19 IAP, Gorelovo and Vitino
26 IAP, Uglovo and Manushkino
44 IAP, Ropsha and Vitino

54 IAB Command
Commander — *polkovnik* A.S. Blagoveshchenskiy (1909–1994). In China 1938. HSU 14.11.1938. NII VVS test pilot from October 1938. In GPW commanded 2 IAK 1942–1945. Head of NII VVS 1952–1959.
Military commissar — *polk.komiss* Zvanskiy

55th Fast Bomber Aviation Brigade (55 SBAB)

In autumn 1939 55 SBAB was based in Staraya Russa (VVS LVO), and was partly relocated to Estonia from 18 October 1939.

55 SBAB performed combat missions as early as 30 November 1939, when one squadron of 44 SBAP bombed Utti AF base. Next day 18 bombers of 58 SBAP attacked Simola railway station, Lahti broadcasting station and Kotka fuel storage tanks, but did not find the main target, Suur-Merijoki AF base.

Because of snow and foggy weather no more operations were performed by 55 SBAB before 19 December 1939, when the western part of the Mannerheim Line was attacked by 116 aircraft. Most attacking aircraft (96 SB) approached in nine-aircraft squadron formations with 5–10 minute intervals on identical routes and altitude, which according to Russian post-attack analysis led to the loss of seven SBs to Finnish A-A artillery.

23 December 1939 55 SBAB lost five SBs of 44 SBAP in air combat.

In late January 1940 55 SBAB relocated to an ice base (south of Kuokkala on the frozen Gulf of Finland), from where maximum support to ground forces was given during new attacks on the Mannerheim Line.

From 2 to 18 February 1940 55 SBAB dropped 152 FAB-500, 1,263 FAB-250, 4,791 FAB-100, 2,988 FAB-50 and thousands of smaller bombs on the westernmost part of the Mannerheim Line and in its immediate rear. Handling and maintenance of large aircraft formations in sub-zero conditions was a permanent problem. E.g. 4 February 1940 55 SBAB was unable to dispatch full nine-aircraft squadrons. Only incomplete squadrons with four, five and seven aircraft took off, with individual missions stretching to excessive lengths.

In February 1941 55 SBAB was converted into 2 SAD.

55 SBAB Subordination
VVS LVO, Staraya Russa
VVS 7.A

55 SBAB Regiments and Main Bases
44 SBAP, Staraya Russa, Zajtsevo, Krasnogvardejsk
58 SBAP, Sivoritsy, Staraya Russa

55 SBAB Commander N.F. Naumenko (G.F. Petrov)

55 SBAB Military Commissar A.A. Ivanov. (G.F. Petrov)

55 SBAB Command

Commander	*polkovnik* I.G. Pyatykhin, later commanded 15 SBAB.
	polkovnik N.F. Naumenko (1901–1967). Perfomed 25 combat missions in Winter War. In GPW commanded 4th and 15th Air Armies. Commanded 15th Air Army 1945–1950.
Military commissar	*bat.komiss* Vikhoryev
	polk.komiss Tolmachev
	A.A. Ivanov. In GPW Deputy Commander of 13th Air Army etc.
Chief of Staff	*polkovnik* S.I. Tishchenko

59th Fighter Aviation Brigade (59 IAB)

In autumn 1939 59 IAB was based in Pushkin (VVS LVO). At the outbreak of the Winter War the 59 IAB inventory counted 296 fighter pilots and 317 fighter aircraft. Some 60 combat missions were performed on 1 December 1939.

Before the year's end 2,110 combat missions were performed, of which 405 were bomber escort missions and 965 ground force protecting missions. In January 1940 59 IAB performed 474 ground-attack missions, and 228 bomber escort missions.

1 January 1940 59 IAB HQ moved from Levashovo to Kanneljärvi on occupied Finnish territory.

On 3 and 4 February 1940 59 IAB-fighters dropped 124,000 leaflets, towing special bags holding 15,000 leaflets. 2 March 1940 *kapitan* Belousov's Squadron was moved from Kerstovo and attached to 68 IAP at Lake Lempaala.

In order to increase ground-attack mission efficiency DER-7 bomb racks for FAB-100 bombs were installed on 28 I-16 fighters in Pushkin 28 January to 8 March 1940. The first fighter-bomber mission was performed 7 February 1940, when an I-16 group led by 7 IAP military commissar N.D. Antonov bombed Näykki.

59 IAB fighter pilots claimed 101 aircraft, with an additional 30 aircraft destroyed on the ground.

59 IAB Commander Ye.Ye. Yerlykin (HSU 21.3.1940). (G.F. Petrov)

I-16 fighters of 59 IAB 12.1.1940

Unit	Base	Serviceable I-16s	Non-serviceable I-16s
7 IAP			
Staff, 1st and 2nd Squadrons	Vammeljärvi	13 (cannon-equipped) 12 (M-62 engine)	2 (cannon-equipped)
4th Squadron	Rieskjärvi	14 (M-25 engine)	2 (cannon-equipped)
	Levashovo		1 (M-62 engine) 2 (cannon-equipped)
25 IAP			
Staff, 1st and 2nd Squadrons	Kanneljärvi	29 (M-25 engine)	2
3rd Squadron	Suulajärvi	14 (M-25 engine)	1
68 IAP (in VVS 13.A from 27.12.1939!)			
	Lempaala	39 (M-25 engine)	1
	Nurmijärvi	3 (M-25 engine)	
	Kasimovo	2 (M-25 engine)	3
	Pushkin		2 (M-25 engine)
Total		126	16

59 IAB Combat missions in January 1940

Regiment	Ground attack	Ground force protection	Bomber Escort	Enemy AF base attacks	Air combat	Reconnaissance	Total missions	Aborted missions
7 IAP	281	66	211	12	9	20	599	-
25 IAP	193	162	194	-	-	20	575	6
Total	474	228	405	12	9	40	1,174	6

59 IAB and 68 IAP fighters 30 January 1940

Type	Regiments			
	7 IAP	25 IAP	68 IAP	Total
I-16 tip 5	9	28	44	81
I-16 tip 10	4	17	1	22
I-16 tip 17	19	-	-	19
I-16 tip 18	13	-	1	14
I-16 tip 27	-	7	-	7
I-153	21	9	-	30
I-15bis	4	4	15	23
Total	70	65	61	196

59 IAB Subordination
VVS LVO, Pushkin
VVS 7.A

59 IAB Regiments and Main Bases
7 IAP, Levashovo, Kasimovo, Kanneljärvi and Vammeljärvi.
25 IAP, Pushkin, Kanneljärvi and Suulajärvi.
38 IAP, Pushkin. Late December 1939 38 IAP was split up; two squadrons to VVS 9.A. In January 1940 rest of 38 IAP to OAB in Estonia.
68 IAP, Pushkin and Kasimovo. To VVS 13.A 27.12.1939.
148 IAP. Arrived 27.2.1940 from Lyubertsy (VVS MVO) to Rieskjärvi.
23 IAP. Arrived 4.3.1940 from Zhitomir (69 AB, VVS KOVO) to Boboshino (Kaukjärvi).

59 IAB Command
Commander	*polkovnik* Ye.Ye. Yerlykin (1909–69). Participated in Spanish Civil War. HSU 21.3.1940. In GPW commanded 7 IAK 1941–1943 and 6 IAK 1943–1944.
Military commissar	*polk.komiss* Gubanov
Chief of Staff	A.S. Pronin In GPW 1st Air Army CoS 1942–1944, 2nd Air Army CoS 1944–1945.
	polkovnik Parvov

The Soviet fighters, like this I-16 tip 17 were urgently equipped with ski-under-carriges for operations from temporary ice bases. (G.F. Petrov)

Kaukjärvi and Suulajärvi ice bases of 59 IAB were photographed 1.3.1940 by LLv 44. Tens of different fighters are seen on the frozen lakes. (Finnish National Archive)

I-16 and I-153 fighters could carry two FAB-100 bombs. (G.F. Petrov)

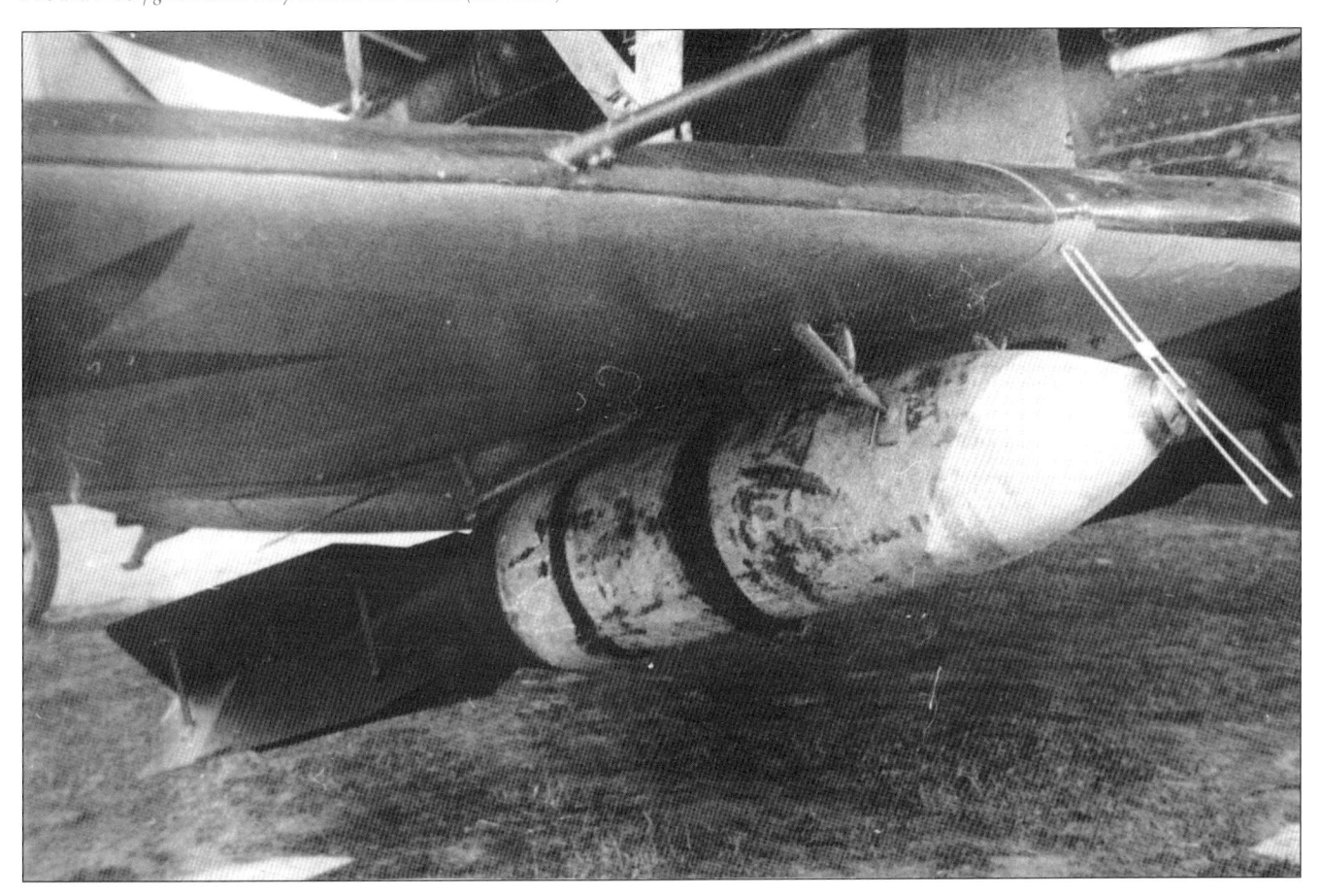

68th Light Bomber Aviation Brigade (68 LBAB), later 68th Fast Bomber Aviation Brigade (68 SBAB)

In autumn 1939 68 LBAB was based in Krasnogvardejsk (VVS LVO). When VVS 13.A was formed early in January 1940 68 LBAB (including part of 3 LBAP and 10 SBAP) was transferred from VVS 7.A to the new AF command. Subsequent to the arrival of 60 SBAP the aviation brigade was renamed 68 SBAB. From 18 February 1940 68 SBAB supported the attacks by 49th and 150th Divisions at Taipale.

68 LBAB Assistant Commander V.N. Zhdanov. (G.F. Petrov)

68 LBAB/SBAB Subordination
VVS LVO
VVS 7.A
VVS 13.A (from January 1940)

68 LBAB/SBAB Regiments and Main Bases
3 LBAP, Krasnogvardejsk. In December 1939 split up into detached squadrons.
4 LBAP. Arrived 13.2.1940 from Kharkov (19 LBAB, VVS KhVO) to Kaukolovo.
10 SBAP, Krasnogvardejsk and Siestarjoki (Sestroretsk). To VVS 13.A 19.1.1940.
60 SBAP. Arrived 21.1.1940 from Lebedin (VVS KhVO) to Kasimovo.

68 LBAB/SBAB Command
Commander	*polkovnik* Novikov
Assistant commander	V.N. Zhdanov (1896–1946). Performed 30 combat missions in Winter War. Commanded 8th Air Army 1944–1945.
Military commissar	*polk.komiss* Antontsev
Chief of Staff	*polkovnik* Shumilov

71st Light Bomber Aviation Brigade (71 LBAB)

In autumn 1939 71 LBAB was based in Siverskaya (VVS LVO). In October-November 1939 71 LBAB/HQ moved to Estonia and Latvia, and subsequently formed the Detached Aviation Brigade (OAB) HQ.

71 LBAB Subordination
VVS LVO

71 LBAB Regiments
35 SBAP. Late December 1939 transferred to OAB in Estonia.
50 SBAP. Remained in VVS 7.A, attached to 18 SBAB.

71 LBAB Command
Commander	
Military commissar	*polk.komiss* F.I. Bogatyrev (?–1940, later in 18 SBAB)
Chief of Staff	*major* A.Ye. Rasskazov (1898–?, later in 18 SBAB)

REGIMENTS

1st Heavy Bomber Aviation Regiment (1 TBAP)

Autumn 1939 1 TBAP was based in Rostov-na-Donu on the Azov Sea.

Subordination
3 AB, AON-3 (until 28 January 1940)
1. Squadron/1 TBAP: AG Spirin, VVS 9.A (from 1 March 1940)

Combat Chronicle
Six TB-3s of 1st Squadron departed on 28 January 1940 from Rostov-na-Donu. Before departure the selected crews got special training, and were inspected by VVS *flagshturman*, HSU A.V. Belyakov (participant in the transpolar ANT-25 flight to USA in June 1937). The detachment (commanded by *st.lt* Paramonov) was organized into three flights, commanded by Paramonov, Maslov and N.F. Gastello. After a long and troublesome ferry flight the TB-3 bombers landed on 1–4 March 1940 at Fedoseyevka ice base (west of Kandalaksha), and was attached to AG Spirin.

On 10 March 1940 TB-3 c/n 22198 (pilot *st.lt* S.T. Karepov) was intercepted and shot down by Swedish volunteer, *fänrik* Gideon Karlsson (F 19) in a Gladiator. The TB-3 had participated in the first bombing mission to Rovaniemi, and crashed on the ice at Murtoselkä near Posio. Five crew members were killed and three MG-gunners were taken prisoner.

Note: Flight C.O. N.F. Gastello became legendary after his fatal "burning taran" against advancing German tanks near Minsk 26 June 1941, then *kapitan* and Squadron C.O. in 207 DBAP. He was posthumously appointed HSU on 26 July 1941.

1 TBAP command (remained in Rostov)
Commander	Filippov
Military commissar	Bragin
1st Squadron C.O.	*major* Shchelkin

In GPW 1 TBAP was on 5 March 1942 attached to ADD (Soviet Long-Range Air Forces), and on 18 August 1942 elevated to Guards status as 1 GvAP DD. After conversion of ADD to 18th Air Army 6 December 1944 the regiment's designation was changed to 194 GvBAP.

TB-3 bomber of 1 TBAP (downed by G. Karlsson of F 19) at Kemijärvi 10.3.1940. (DigitaltMuseum)

TB-3 bomber of 1 TBAP (downed by G. Karlsson of F 19) at Kemijärvi 10.3.1940. (DigitaltMuseum)

This and opposite page: A group of officers from F 19 arrived 24.3.1940 in a Junkers F13 liaison aircraft (OH-SUO) to inspect the TB-3. From left G. Karlsson, Å. Nettelbladh-Hollsten, F 19 CoS kapten B. Bjuggren, M. Wennerström and R. Martin. (all photos DigitaltMuseum)

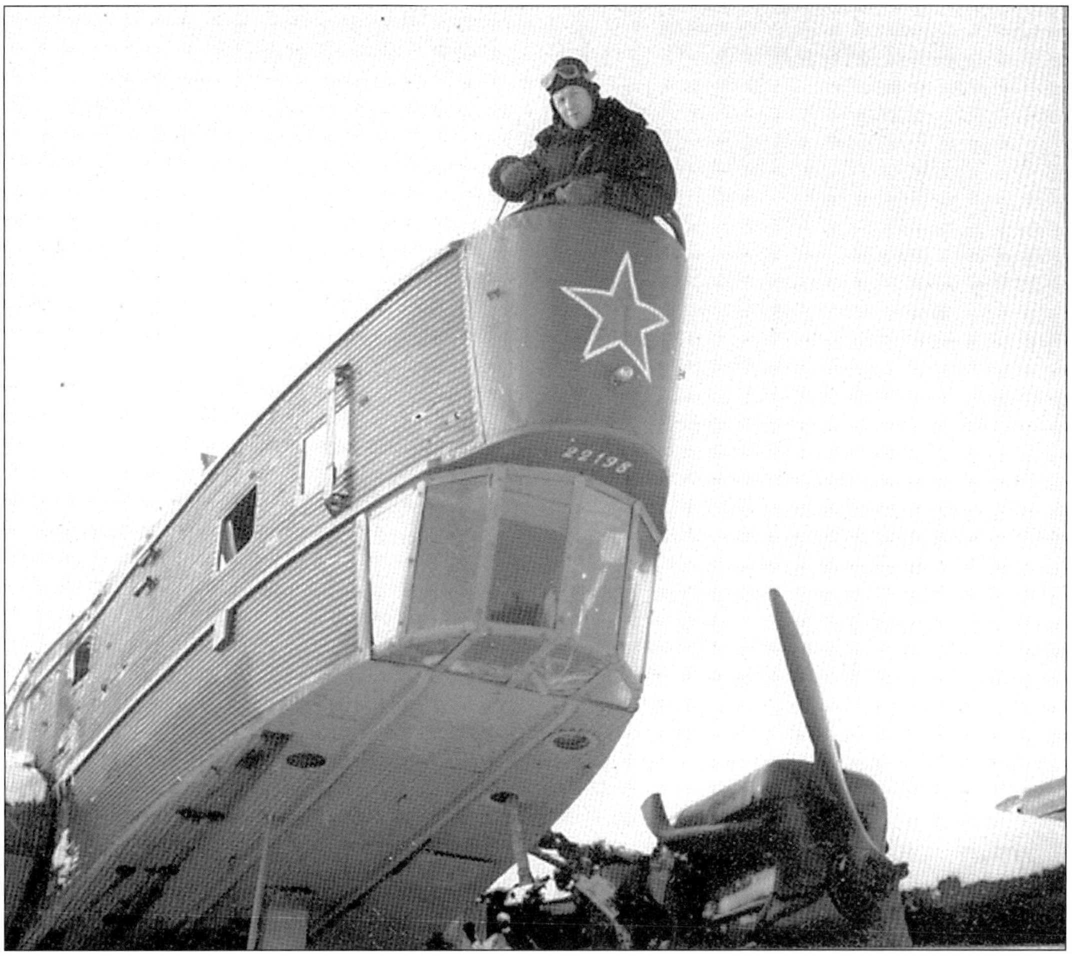

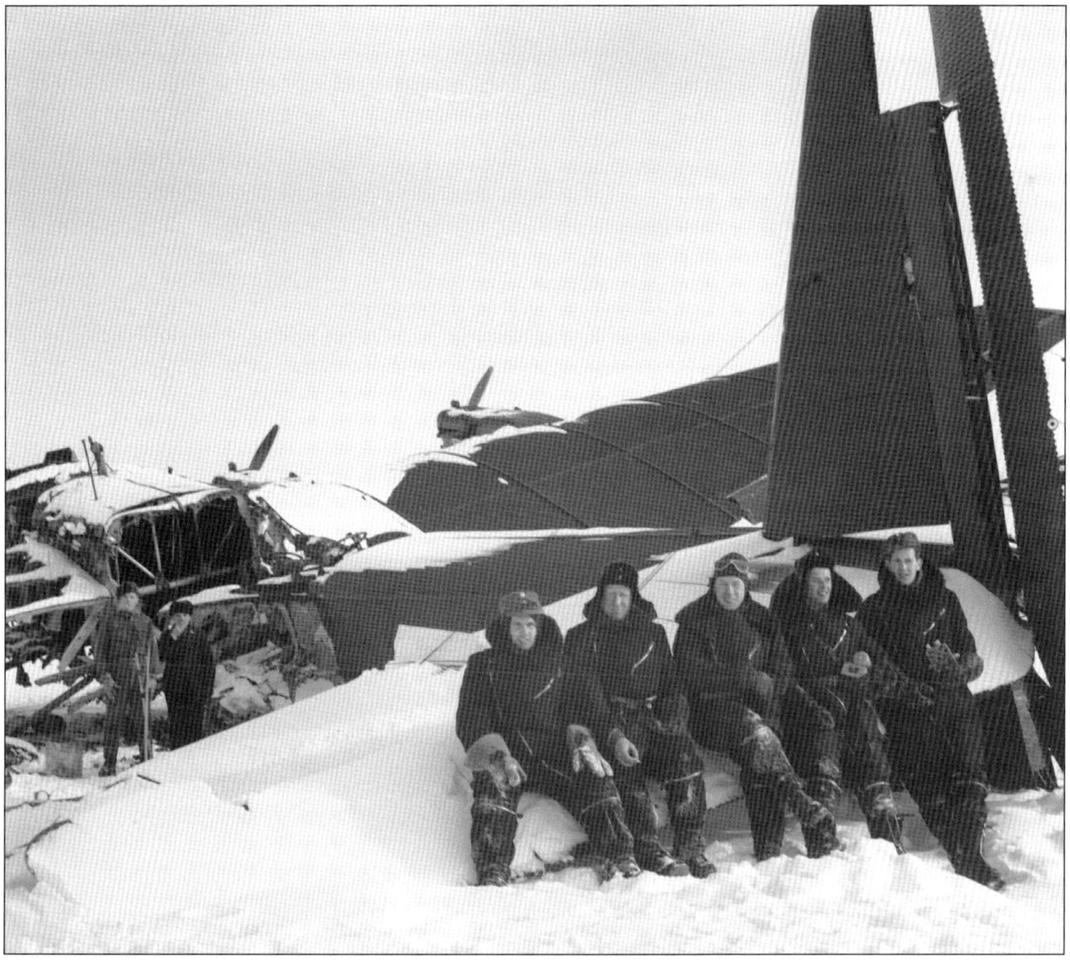

2nd Fast Bomber Aviation Regiment (2 SBAP)

In Autumn 1939 2 TBAP was based in Sol'tsy; five Squadrons with 45 SB. 2 TBAP converted from heavy TB-3s to fast SBs in September 1939. The regiment name was correspondingly changed on 23 December 1939 from 2 TBAP to 2 SBAP.

Subordination
15 AB, VVS LVO
15 SBAB, VVS 7.A (until 6 January 1940)
VVS 13.A (from 6 January 1940)

Combat Chronicle

2 TBAP was put on war alert 14 November 1939. 3rd Squadron moved from Sol'tsy to Ropsha on 29 November 1939. The other Squadrons followed on 5–9 December 1939 to Ropsha and Vitino.

On 30 November 1939 nine SBs attacked Imatra hydro-electric power station. Upon return interception by seven biplanes (apparently own I-15bis fighters!) was reported. Hits on at least one bomber were recorded. SB c/n 16/222 (tactical no. "5", 4th Squadron) was 70% destroyed on take-off from Ropsha.

On 1 December 1939 38 missions were performed. 2nd Squadron bombed Suvantojärvi (south of Sakkola, between Kiviniemi and Taipale). Seven SBs took off from Sol'tsy and landed at Vitino. Three SBs got hits on Muolaa-Räisälä.

Because of poor weather no combat missions were made until 18 December 1939, when 40 missions were flown from Ropsha. Now mission preparations were made very hastily. E.g. P.A. Vovna (C.O. 2nd Squadron) was informed of the bombing target only one minute before his four-aircraft formation was to take-off, resulting in bombing the wrong target (instead of the intended *target nr. 8*, i.e. Koukunniemi). *Lt* Malyshev (1st Squadron) got lost and force-landed on the frozen Nikolskoye Ozero. His SB c/n 17/222 partly sank, but was later lifted and repaired.

SB tactical 5 (c/n 16/222) piloted by V.G. Glazunov (4./2 SBAP) was destroyed on take-off from Ropsha 30.11.1939 (RGVA).

SB tactical 1 (c/n 11/222) piloted by P.G. Ovcharenko (3./2 SBAP Commander) was damaged on take-off from Ropsha 26.12.1939. (RGVA)

19 December 1939 58 missions performed. SB c/n 12/224 (2nd Squadron) was shot down by two fighters at Muolaanjärvi-Uusikirkko. The pilot *st.lt* A.D. Malinin escaped by parachute and reached his own lines, *shturman* T.K. Ilyin was killed. MG-gunner *ml. komzvod* V.P. Bakhvalov scored hits on two Fokker fighters (one of which was claimed shot down) before he jumped. Bakhvalov reached his own lines next day, and was appointed HSU 15 January 1940. The same day 2nd and 4th Squadrons relocated to Vitino. Vänr E. *Enroth (LLv 26, FR-103)*, kers *L. Aaltonen (LLv 26, FR-114)*, lentom *V. Pyötsiä (LLv 24, FR-110)*, vänr *P. Kokko (LLv 24, FR-90) and* kers *P. Mannila (LLv 26, FR-96) claimed SB bombers at Lake Muolaanjärvi.*

25 December 1939 three squadrons were based at Ropsha and two Squadrons at Vitino, with 48 serviceable bombers altogether.

27 December 1939 2nd Squadron was ordered to destroy the Hiitola railway bridge. Three SBs (c/n 2/224, 14/224 and 16/224) were shot down by "*12 attacking Finnish fighters*", and crashed at Hiitola-Jääski. Soviet gunners claimed three Finnish fighters. Two aviators were taken prisoner (*lt* I.D. Krakhmal, pilot of c/n 2/224; and *st.lt* A.D. Pyankov, navigator of c/n 16/224), the other four crew members were killed. Pyankov's SB (tactical 5) was exhibited in the war booty exhibition in Helsinki from mid-February 1940. This severely irritated the Soviet leadership, so Pyankov who "permitted the Finns to capture his aircraft virtually intact" was after repatriation condemned to 10 years in a GULAG camp, where he died. *The bombers were shot down by* kers *L. Nissinen in FR-98,* kers *M. Sillanpää in FR-81 and* vänr *H. Ilveskorpi in FR-78 (all from LLv 24). No Finnish aircraft were lost.*

On 6 January 1940 2 SBAP was transferred to VVS 13.A with 32 SB in Ropsha and 13 SB in Vitino.

Ten days later (6.1.1940) two SB-bombers collided on the ground in Ropsha. SB tactical 6 (c/n 6/222) piloted by lt N.V. Vasilyev got 80% damage, the other SB (c/n 7/60) was only slightly damaged. (RGVA)

SB blue 3 (c/n 1/224) piloted by Lt A.A Kostin (2./2 SBAP) was destroyed on take-off from Vitino 2.2.1940. (RGVA)

4 February 1940 SB c/n 2/236 (*lt* A.M. Vorobyev, 2nd Squadron) crashed in foggy weather at Valamo monastery on Lake Ladoga, all the crew was killed.

15 February 1940 four SBs returned with up to 165 bullet holes after air combat with Fokkers. These SBs were back in service between 16 February and 2 March 1940.

18 February 1940 SB c/n 14/222 (pilot *lt* Saburov) belly-landed at Sestroretsk (Siestarjoki, just east of the 1920 year Finnish-Soviet border) after air combat. *Saburov's SB was shot down by* lentom *Y. Turkka in FR-83, LLv 24.*

On 21 February 1940 SB c/n 3/72 (*lt* F.M. Volgayevskiy, 6th Squadron) was downed by A-A artillery at Hotokka (5 km north of the Mannerheim-line at the northern shore of Lake Muolaanjärvi). The bomber crashed in flames 500 m NE Hotokka, the crew was killed.

27 February 1940 SB c/n 15/224 (*lt* S.A. Goryunov, 4th Squadron) was shot down by A-A artillery at Marjaniemi, and crashed in flames in the Koprala-Mälkölä region (north of Äyräpäänjärvi, some 10 km north of the Mannerheim-line). The crew was killed.

2 March 1940 SB c/n 15/221 (2nd Squadron) was shot down by A-A artillery at Jääski railway station (on the River Vuoksi, some 30 km SE Imatra), the crew was killed. The pilot, Squadron C.O. *kapitan* P.A. Vovna was posthumously appointed HSU 7 April 1940.

5 March 1940 SB c/n 5/224 (*lt* V.G. Glazunov, 4th Squadron) was shot down by A-A artillery at Mäkelä and crashed at Vuosalmi, Äyräpää, the crew was killed.

2 SBAP command

Commander	*polkovnik* B.P. Pisarskiy. Commanded 46 BAD in 1941.
Military commissar	*bat.komiss* Politykin
	bat.komiss Plakhottya
Chief of Staff (CoS)	*polkovnik* I.S. Morunov. 14 VA CoS in 1943.
	major Bruslavskiy

Squadron C.O. and commissars
- 1st — *major* Spiridonov
  - *st.politr* Khryastalov
- 2nd — *kapitan* P.A. Vovna (1906–2.2.1940). HSU posthumously 7.4.1940.
  - *st.politr* Suvit
- 3rd — *major* N.S. Starkov
  - *kapitan* P.G. Ovcharenko
  - *st.politr* Badulin
- 4th — *kapitan* A.V. Svirin
  - *st.politr* Belous
- 5th — *kapitan* Pervukhin
  - *major* N.S. Starkov
  - *st.politr* Dubinin
- 6th — *kapitan* Pervukhin

2 SBAP performed 2,237 missions in the Winter War, flight time 3,356 h 11 min. The regiment lost eight SBs; three were shot down in air combat and the others by A-A artillery. Nine Finnish fighters were claimed by the MG-gunners of 2 SBAP.

Two aviators of 2nd Squadron were appointed HSUs: *ml.komzvod* V.P. Bakhvalov (15 January 1940) and *kapitan* P.A. Vovna (7 April 1940, posthumously).

After the Winter War 2 SBAP relocated to Kresty, and was attached to 2 SAD of Leningrad MD.

In GPW 2 SBAP was on 3 September 1943 elevated to Guards status, and became 119 GvBAP.

2nd Light Bomber Aviation Regiment (2 LBAP)

Autumn 1939 2 LBAP was based in Konotop (Kiev MD).

Subordination
- 62 AB, VVS KOVO (in Konotop until 18 February 1940)
- 19 LBAB, VVS 15.A (from 21 February 1940)

Combat Chronicle

18 February 1940 departed from Konotop, and arrived 21 February 1940 in Nurmolitsa with 59 R-Z.

On the night of 5/6 March 1940 Jänisjärvi railway junction (40 km north of Lake Ladoga) was attacked. Six R-Z were destroyed and several aviators were injured when they got lost in a snow storm. Three R-Z (c/n 1592, 1801 and 2039) crashed at Karkunlampi ice base, c/n 2023 crashed at Nurmolitsa, c/n 2017 at Andryusovo and c/n 2043 at Kaukojärvi (just east of the Finnish-Russian border, 20 km E Karkunlampi).

10 and 11 March 1940 56 FAB-100 bombs were dropped at Jänisjärvi railway bridge, which was destroyed by three hits. Seven more hits were observed on the bridge foundations.

25 May 1940 2 LBAP was renamed 138 SBAP.

2 LBAP command

Commander	*major* Mozgovoi
Military commissar	*bat.komiss* Paltsev
Chief of Staff	*major* Reshetov

Squadron C.O. and commissars
- 1st — *kapitan* Yevdokimov
  - *st.politr* Privezentsev
- 2nd — *kapitan* Metelkin
  - *st.politr* Mamayev
- 5th — *kapitan* Nesmeyankov
  - *kapitan* Lugovskoi

3rd Light Bomber Aviation Regiment (3 LBAP)

Autumn 1939 3 LBAP was based in Krasnogvardejsk, and equipped with various R-5 subtypes. Late November 1939 1st and 2nd Squadrons (both equipped with SSS) were based in Grivochki, 3rd Squadron (R-Z) in Lisino, 4th and 5th Squadrons (both with R-5) in Krasnogvardejsk.

Subordination
68 LBAB, VVS 7.A (until 5 January 1940)
3 LBAP was split up 5 January 1940: 2. Squadron (nine SSS) remained in VVS 7.A, and was on 5 March 1940 renamed 19 OAE.

Bases: Levashevo 12–18 December 1939, Kanneljärvi 18 December 1939 – 4 January 1940, Suuri Särkijärvi 4–10 January 1940, Suulajärvi 10 January-8 February 1940 and Kaukjärvi from 8 February 1940.
4. Squadron (four R-5) was on 10 December 1939 dispatched to VVS 8.A in Nurmolitsa (later transferred to VVS 15.A).
5. night Squadron (ten R-5) was transferred to VVS 13.A in Lempaala.
1. and 3. Squadrons received SB bombers from 5 January 1940. After type training 63 SBAP (46 SB bombers) was formed with these Squadrons as nucleus, and on 10 March 1940 was subordinated to VVS SZFr.

Combat Chronicle
In December 1939 seven R-5 were handed over to 23 KAO, which arrived without aircraft from Podolsk (VVS MVO).
18 or 19 December 1939 an SSS of 2nd Squadron was damaged in air combat at Ristseppälä, Heinjoki (over 60 bullet hits) and became a write-off. Pilot *lt* Ye.V. Zdesenko and observer *starshina* A.G. Ivanov were seriously wounded. A "two-engine Finnish fighter" was claimed by 3 LBAP.
1 February 1940 when dropping supplies to the encircled Soviet 168th and 18th Divisions and 34th Tank Brigade in the Lemetti *motti*, an R-5Sh of 4th Squadron C.O. *kapitan* A.S. Topaller was hit by A-A artillery, and force-landed at Ylä-Lavajärvi (25 km E Lemetti). Topaller's deputy *st.lt* A.Ya. Letuchiy and observer *st.lt* K.P. Prisyazhnyuk performed a daring landing next to the damaged R-5Sh, and picked up Topaller and his observer *st.lt* M.G. Bliznyuk. Two other R-5s protected the rescue operation.
On the night of 2/3 February 1940 *st.lt* Ignatov was blinded by a searchlight and collided with a high-voltage line, the crew was unhurt.
7 February 1940 an R-5 of 4th Squadron forced-landed in the Lemetti *motti* after A-A hits. The crew (*st.lt* A.I. Britov and *lt* P.I. Karateyev) stayed in the *motti* until the end of the war.
9 February 1940 Letuchiy's R-5 (4th Squadron) was also hit while supply dropping, and force-landed in no man's land 15 km SW Uomaa. Letuchiy and the wounded observer *st.lt* M.G. Bliznyuk (see 1 Feb-

R-5SSS tactical 11 (c/n 1347) piloted by st.lt A.A. Podvornov (3 LBAP) was destroyed on landing in Lisino 16.12.1939. (RGVA)

ruary 1940 above) were rescued by *st.lt* N.G. Braginets in another R-5. In order to enable a fast take-off from the forced-landing site (subject to Finnish infantry fire), Braginets' observer *starshina* M.M. Chikunov gave his rear seat to Letuchiy and Bliznyuk, while himself lying tied to the wing! The daring rescue operations of 1 and 9 February 1940 immediately became Soviet heroic legends, and were among the very few published air combat episodes of the Winter War in Soviet times.

The rescue operation heroes Topaller, Letuchiy and Braginets were appointed HSUs 19 May 1940.

3 LBAP command

Commander	*major* Novikov
Military commissar	*bat.komiss* Kosarev
Chief of Staff	*polkovnik* Belen'kov
Squadron C.O. and commissars:	
1st	*st.lt* Shcherbatykh
2nd (= 19 OAE, VVS 7.A)	*kapitan* V.V. Totskiy
4th (VVS 8.A)	*kapitan* A.S. Topaller (1911–1996). HSU 19 May 1940.
5th (VVS 13.A)	*kapitan* G.S. Ravenskiy
military commissar	*st.politr* Verstov

3 LBAP mission summary

Squadron	Combat missions	Flight time	Losses
2nd Squadron	200 (194 night missions)	288 h	2
4th Squadron	138 (11 night missions)	278 h	4
5th Squadron	265 (240 night missions)	304 h	2
Total	603 (445 night missions)	870 h	8

3rd Heavy Bomber Aviation Regiment (3 TBAP)

In Autumn 1939 3 TBAP was based in Borovskoye (75 km NW Voroshilovgrad, Byelorussian MD), equipped with TB-3 heavy bombers.

Subordination
VVS BOVO
VVS 8.A (1. and 3. Squadrons from late December 1939)
VVS 9.A (2. Squadron, from 9 January 1940)
3 SBAB, VVS 8.A (1. and 3. Squadrons, from early January 1940)
VVS 15.A (1. and 3. Squadrons from 18 February 1940)

Combat Chronicle
Late December 1939 3 TBAP departed from Borovskoye, and arrived 18 December 1939 in Lodejnoye pole (Lotinanpelto) with 26 TB-3 (of which only ten remained in VVS 8.A).

By 20 December 1939 *kapitan* Kalinin's detachment had departed to Murmashi, and was attached to 5 OSAP (VVS 14.A). During the ferry flight two TB-3s (piloted by Squadron C.O. *kapitan* I.P. Kalininchenko and deputy regiment C.O. *major* A.G. Mel'nikov) crashed at Kildin Island in the Barents Sea. 13 March 1940 5 OSAP had four TB-3s in its inventory. The heavy and clumsy four-engine TB-3 was clearly difficult to handle on snowy and slippery runways:

25 December 1939 TB-3 *red 7* (*kapitan* Prygunov, 3rd Squadron) collided with a civil PS-9 transport aircraft on take-off from Besovets. Two other pilots of 3rd Squadron collided with SB bombers at Lodejnoye pole (5 January and 14 February 1940), and on 18 January 1940 two TB-3s collided on the ground at Lodejnoye Pole.

5 January 1940 1st and 3rd Squadrons were attached to 13 SBAB (VVS 8.A). The Squadrons operated independently, serving the Soviet armies north of Lake Ladoga, which were stuck in roadless forests and swamps. As Soviet units were surrounded by agile Finnish ski patrols in *mottis*, the main task of the heavy TB-3 bombers became delivery of foodstuffs,

Lodejnoye pole AF base at River Svir was photographed 4.2.1940 by kapt A. Platan in BL-119 (LLv 44). TB-3s, SBs and fighters are seen in large numbers. (A. Juhola)

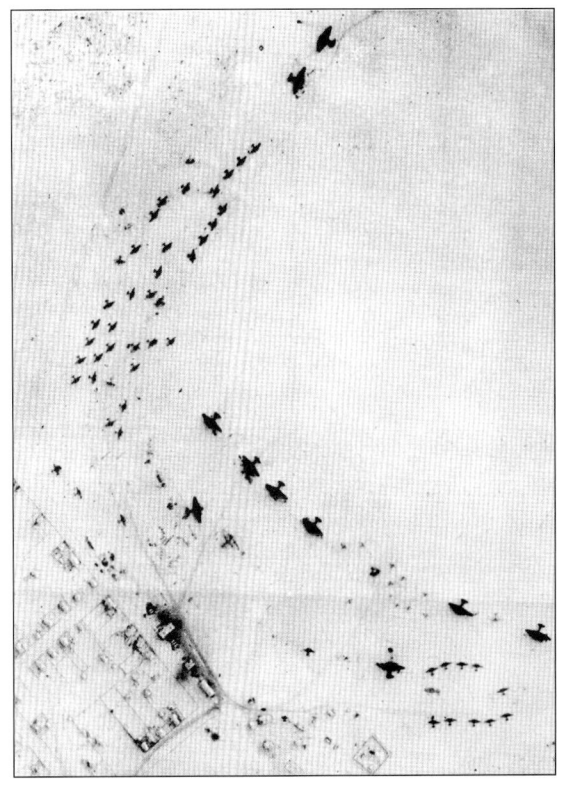

Two TB-3s of 3 TBAP white 7 (c/n 22545) and yellow 7 (c/n 22604) collided in Lodejnoye pole 18.1.1940, two aviators were seriously injured. (RGVA)

ammunition and other supplies, while bombing Finnish targets was only of secondary priority. The difficult and unknown operation area, and the complicated handling of big and slow aircraft in the primitive Karelian bases led to heavy losses (as mentioned above at least five TB-3 were destroyed in ground collisions and accidents at Lodejnoye pole and Besovets). Although Finnish fighters were rarely encountered, slow TB-3s on supply dropping missions were rather easy targets for Finnish A-A machine guns. In order to drop supplies accurately, bombers had to descend to only 50–100 m altitude, resulting in frequent combat losses. A considerable amount of the supplies dropped also went missing, and were picked up by Finnish ski troops.

5 January 1940 TB-3 c/n 307 (pilot *st.lt* V.A. Kashentsev) collided with SB c/n 4/94 of 18 SBAP at Lodejnoye Pole. Both aircraft were destroyed, the TB-3 was disassembled for spares.

From 9 January 1940 2nd Squadron arrived with eight TB-3s in Uhtua, and was attached to VVS 9.A. The transfer was detected by Finnish radio intelligence on 4 January 1940 when the message *"10 TB-3 bombers will be transferred to 9th Army"* was intercepted. Three days later another message *"5 TB-3 and 3 SB have today departed to bases at Uhtua and Afrikanda"* was intercepted. In late January 1940 this Squadron was attached to 10 SBAB.

The other Squadrons remained in Lodejnoye pole and Besovets (at first attached to VVS 8.A, and from 18 February 1940 to VVS 15.A).

12 January 1940 TB-3 c/n 22223 *red 3* (*st.lt* T.I. Pozhilayev, 3rd Squadron) on a supply dropping mission was hit by anti-aircraft fire and Finnish railway artillery at Impilahti. The heavy TB-3 (loaded with 940 kg of foodstuffs etc.) force-landed on frozen Lake Ladoga SW Vuoratsu, and gradually sank through the ice. In addition to supply of the encircled Soviet 168th Division, according to Finnish intelligence the task was to evacuate *komdiv* A.I. Cherepanov, C.O. 56th Army Corps. The crew reached their own lines at

TB-3 tactical 1 (probably c/n 22527 of 2./3 TBAP) was left behind on Lake Saunajärvi, and inspected by Finnish troops 14.3.1940. (SA-kuva)

75

Pitkäranta (several aviators were seen moving on the ice). Documents, armament, parachutes and radio equipment were removed from the abandoned TB-3 by Finnish patrols.

18 January 1940 TB-3s *yellow 9* (*st.lt* I.P. Krasiyev, 4th Squadron) and *white 7* (*st.lt* V.N. Bunin-Sokolov, 3rd Squadron) collided on the ground at Lodejnoye pole after the failure of two engines of the latter aircraft on take-off. Both aircraft were destroyed.

19 January 1940 at least two TB-3s were lost on supply flights: c/n 22323 (*kapitan* A.F. Tsesarenko, 3rd Squadron) was hit at Lavajärvi and crashed on the return leg at Olonets, and *blue 8* (c/n 22125, *lt* Shashurkin) was hit by A-A artillery and force-landed on the ice at the north-eastern shore of Lake Ladoga. The big TB-3 was observed by Fokker C.X-dive bombers of LLv 10 which then and next day attacked the paper pulp factory in occupied Pitkäranta. The TB-3 partly sunk through the ice which prevented evacuation, but the crew reached their own lines. The gunner *starshina* S.I. Titov of a third TB-3 was killed by ground fire. This TB-3 returned to a Soviet base.

25 January 1940 3 TBAP had only five airworthy TB-3 bombers at Lodejnoye Pole, with ten bombers being repaired. 1st and 3rd Squadrons were completely devoid of serviceable aircraft.

29 January 1940 all crews of 3 TBAP had performed 3–5 supply dropping missions each, some crews had performed up to 7 or 8 missions.

In January 1940 3 TBAP performed 31 supply-dropping flights (approx. 30% of all flights). Losses were very great: two TB-3s were shot down by A-A artillery, and nine bombers were lost in accidents.

1 February 1940 TB-3 *red 12* (Squadron C.O., *kapitan* N.M. Monakov) was shot down by AA-artillery and crashed 2 km W Nietjärvi, all nine crew members were killed. Two other TB-3s were damaged by ground fire.

6 February 1940 Finnish A-A artillery shot down a TB-3 (2nd Squadron, attached to 10 SBAB of VVS 9.A) dropping supplies to the encircled 54th Mountain Division SE Kuhmo. The TB-3 crashed on the eastern shore of Lake Leksozero (Lieksanjärvi) 4 km west of Chalki (Tsholkka). Pilot *st.lt* N.I. Susarev was killed, several other crew members were injured.

14 February 1940 SB c/n 17/65 (pilot Orabinskiy, 39 SBAP) collided at take-off with TB-3 *red 2* (*lt* V.N. Ishkov, 3rd Squadron) at Lodejnoye Pole. Factory repair of both aircraft was required.

17 February 1940 Finnish AF issued an order to bomb Lodejnoye pole AF base. Due to unfavorable weather conditions the attack was only performed on 26 February 1940, when eight Blenheims (led by kapt *K. Kepsu, LLv 46) attacked at 0300 hours. Because of bad visibility only three Blenheims (BL-130, BL-128 and BL-126) found the target, the others bombed reserve targets: Lodejnoye pole warehouse (BL-133), Videlitsa (Vitele; BL-129 and BL-131), Kovkanitsa (BL-132) and Krasnaya Gorka (BL-124). Three Blenheims (BL-130, BL-133 and BL-128) repeated the attack in the afternoon. Eight Soviet aircraft were reported destroyed, one building was left burning, and the railway broken.* According to Russian sources nine bombs were dropped on Volhovstroi power plant, and four enemy aircraft dropped six bombs on Lodejnoye pole AF base, where three aircraft were damaged and two pilots injured.

18 February 1940 3 TBAP was transferred to VVS 15.A (still based in Lodejnoye pole). At the end of the Winter War an almost intact TB-3 (tactical no. "4", probably c/n 527 of 2nd Squadron) was found left on the ice of Saunajärvi, SE Kuhmo.

3 TBAP performed 262 missions serving 8th and 15th armies, including 81 supply missions to encircled Soviet troops (73.3 t of foodstuff, 1.3 t of medicines and 68 ammunition boxes were dropped). 139 bombing missions were performed (247.3 t bombs dropped). 12 TB-3 battle-worn bombers were written off after the war.

3 TBAP Strength and locations

Date	Base	Subordination	Equipment
1.1.1940	Lodejnoye Pole, Uhtua, Besovets (LVO); Borovskoje (BOVO)	VVS 8.A, VVS 9.A	50 TB-3: 22/Lodejnoye Pole, 6/Uhtua, 14/Besovets, 8/Borovskoye
1.2.1940	Lodejnoye Pole, Uhtua, Besovets (LVO)	VVS 8.A, VVS 9.A	48 TB-3: 24/Lodejnoye Pole, 12/Uhtua, 12/Besovets
1.3.1940	Lodejnoye Pole, Uhtua, Besovets (LVO)	VVS 8.A, VVS 9.A, VVS 15.A	46 TB-3: 16/Lodejnoye Pole, 14/Uhtua, 16/Besovets
1.4.1940	Borovskoye (BOVO)	39 AB	50 TB-3

3 TBAP command

Commander	*polkovnik* M.R. Belousov
Military commissar	*bat.komiss* F.I. Khutoryanskiy
Chief of Staff	*kapitan* I.I. Tanygin
Squadron C.O	
1st	*kapitan* N.M. Strebulayev

2nd	*kapitan* V.G. Kitayev
	kapitan G.B. Prygunov
3rd	*kapitan* N.M. Monakov (KIA 1.3.1940)
Unknown	*kapitan* I.P. Kalinintshenko

In GPW 3 TBAP was on 5 March 1942 attached to ADD (Soviet Long-Range Air Forces), and 18 September 1943 elevated to Guards status as 23 GvAP DD. After conversion of ADD to 18th Air Army the regiment's designation was changed to 239 GvBAP.

4th Light Bomber Aviation Regiment (4 LBAP)

Autumn 1939 4 LBAP was based in Kharkov.

Subordination
19 LBAB, VVS KhVO (until 13 February 1940)
68 SBAB, VVS 13.A (from 13 February 1940)

Combat Chronicle

27 January 1940 departed from Kharkov with six Squadrons, and arrived 13 February 1940 at Kaukolovo ice base with 62 R-Z. 4 LBAP was attached to 68 SBAB (VVS 13.A).

13 February 1940 R-Z (c/n 2001, *kapitan* P.V. Spitsyn) crashed at Ristseppälä, Heinjoki. Spitsyn reached his own lines, while *shturman* D.G. Kalinichenko was killed.

17 February 1940 4 LBAP bombed Finnish troops north of the River Vuoksi. Two R-Z were shot down by Finnish A-A artillery. R-Z c/n 2290 was hit at Äyräpää; *lt* L.V. Kashelenko and *ml.lt* D.M. Petrishev escaped by parachute and were taken prisoner. R-Z c/n 2035 was hit at Ojajärvi railway station in Kirvu, the crew went missing. *Kashelenko's name was originally Bellmans. His father was a Belgian industrialist in Imperial Russia. Both his parents were murdered by the Bolsheviks during the Russian Civil War. The orphaned boy was able to hide his real identity, using the name Kashelenko, became a civil mail pilot (despite his "capitalist background"), and was later admitted into the Red Air Force. According to Kashelenko/Bellmans 4 LBAP bombed its own troops by mistake north of the River Taipale 15 February 1940. When Kashelenko departed for his last mission 4 LBAP was being investigated by the NKVD. Kashelenko was questioned by Finnish Intelligence representatives at least five times 18–23 February 1940. He told his interrogators exceptionally detailed information about the organization, tactics, aircraft, maintenance, bases etc. of VVS. One interesting detail concerned the fuel types used: either a mixture of 85% "Baku" and 15% "Groznyi" gasoline, or 65% "Baku" gasoline and 35% benzole, to which 2.5 cm^3 tetraethylene per litre is added.*

18 February 1940 three Squadrons (27 aircraft) bombed their own lines by mistake, and destroyed six Soviet artillery positions. Three R-Z participated in the rescue operation of the crew of an SB of 31 SBAP which on 17 February 1940 had force-landed between the lines at Muolaa after air combat. One R-Z was damaged and was unable to take off from the forced-landing site. I-16 pilot *kapitan* P. Geras (68 IAP) who protected the rescue operation landed and tied wounded R-Z pilot N.L. Kosichkin to the I-16 ski body and flew to Lempaala (see 31 SBAP, page 138).

25 February 1940 nine R-Z escorted by six I-153 fighters were intercepted by three Gladiators of LLv 26. Three R-Z were shot down in air combat at Muolaa. c/n 2083 (*ml.lt* A.R. Krykhtin) force-landed at Muolaanjärvi, c/n 2253 (*ml.lt* F.Z. Boldyrikhin, observer *st.lt* V.G. Belyayev perished of his wounds two days later) force-landed in Suulajärvi, and c/n 2058 (*lt* G.T. Meshcherakov, 3rd Squadron) force-landed at Kanneljärvi. *The opposing Gladiators of LLv 26 claimed four "R-5". The Finnish participants were* alik M. Sukanen, GL-258; luutn P. Tevä, GL-254 (two claims) *and* alik I. Joensuu, GL-256. *On the Finnish side* luutn P. Tevä *and* alik M. Sukanen *were shot down by escorting I-153 fighters and killed.*

On the night 27/28 February 1940 R-Z c/n 2053 (*lt* G.T. Meshcherakov, 3rd Squadron) got lost on a mission to Heinjoki, Sintola, and crashed in Pushkinskoye, Karelian ASSR.

29 February 1940 R-Z c/n 2033 of 4th Squadron was shot down by A-A artillery, and crashed 2 km SE Heinjoki. The crew was killed.

3 March 1940 2nd Squadron C.O. *major* N.G. Lin'kov and *st.lt* I.F. Kozin were killed when R-Z c/n 2294 stalled during take-off for a night mission from Kaukolovo.

4 LBAP command
Commander *polkovnik* M.I. Gorlachenko (1905–1976). Spanish Civil War veteran; in GPW commanded 3 ShAK etc.

4 LBAP Commander M.I. Gorlachenko. (G.F. Petrov)

Military commissar	*bat.komiss* Ryabov
Chief of Staff	*major* P.N. Poluektov
Squadron C.O. and commissars	
1st	*major* M.A. Kolokolov
	st.politr S.Ya. Dryukov
2nd	*major* N.G. Lin'kov (KIA 3.3.1940)
	st.politr Largin
3rd	*kapitan* V.V. Kiselev
4th	*st.lt, kapitan* I.M. Dvoinyh
5th	*kapitan* M.T. Nikolayev
	st.politr F.Ye. Vasilenko (1911–1983). HSU 13.3.1944 in 10 GAP DD.

4th Fighter Aviation Regiment (4 IAP)

4 IAP was formed in April 1938 in Bobrujsk (Byelorussian MD).

Subordination
56 IAB, VVS BOVO (until 27 December 1939)
VVS 8.A (from late December 1939)

Combat Chronicle
17 September – 7 October 1939 4 IAP participated in the "Western Byelorussia campaign", or the German-Soviet division of Poland.

27 December 1939 4 IAP was ordered to move to Petrozavodsk, and was partly reorganized with Squadrons of other BOVO aviation regiments:
- 1st Squadron – former 3rd Squadron (I-153)
- 2nd Squadron – former 4th Squadron (I-15bis, later I-153)
- 3th Squadron – 4th Squadron/35 IAP (of 56 AB in Pruzhan, I-15bis, later I-153)
- 4th Squadron – 1st Squadron/20 IAP (of 18 AB in Smolensk, I-15bis, later I-153).

Thus two squadrons (35 aircraft) came from the "old" 4 IAP in Bobrujsk, one squadron (14 aircraft) from 35 IAP, and one squadron (17 aircraft) from 20 IAP. Total strength 64 aircraft (18 I-153 and 46 I-15bis fighters). 1st and 2nd Squadrons of 4 IAP exchanged their I-16 for I-15bis and I-153 biplanes only 7 days before the transfer.

The pilots' experience of the new aircraft types was rather modest; average 30 min – 1 hour in 1st Squadron, and max. 30 min in 2nd Squadron. Six pilots had no previous experience with the new fighters!

The Squadrons from Bobrujsk (4 IAP) and Pruzhan (35 IAP) were dispatched 8 January 1940 by train and only arrived on 4 February 1940 in Petrozavodsk. Upon arrival the squadrons were attached to VVS 8.A, and after assembly took off to Suojärvi (in occupied Finnish territory) 16 February 1940.

The Smolensk Squadron (20 IAP) arrived in Petrozavodsk 18 January 1940 and was combat-ready 27 January 1940.

Although 4 IAP was ordered to support 75th Division (Loimola direction), no direct communications were organized between 4 IAP and the ground forces!

17 February 1940 *lt* A.A. Morozov force-landed with I-15bis (c/n 5366) at Riuttasenjärvi (on the Finnish side of the front-line) after an engine malfunction. He was picked up by *kapitan* A.G. Karmanov in another I-15bis. Karmanov was subsequently awarded the Red Star Order.

20 February 1940 *lt* A.V. Murashov in I-15bis (c/n 4344) was shot down by Finnish A-A fire on a supply dropping flight to Lemetti.

1 March 1940 *kapitan* I.I. Kozlov (I-153) force-landed on Finnish-held territory at Vieksijärvi after A-A hits. Kozlov was picked up by *st.lt* Bochkov (I-153, also of 4 IAP), Kozlov's I-153 was left behind. Two days later *kapitan* Kozlov force-landed with another I-153 just east of the front line after Finnish A-A hits.

18 February-13 March 1940 4 IAP performed 2,590 missions (of which 2,050 were I-15bis missions and 540 I-153 missions), total flight time 2,438 h. One pilot, one technician and five aircraft were lost.

4 IAP combat missions

Ground forces protection	274
Railway targets	136
Population centres	21
Enemy forces	451
Own ground forces protection	183
Ground attack	732
Reconnaissance missions	216
Bomber escort	334
Supply dropping	235

4 IAP command

Commander *major* N.F. Demidov
Military commissar *bat.komiss* Mironov
Chief of Staff *major* Lokhov

Squadron C.O.
4th (ex 1./20 IAP) *kapitan* P.P. Ledyayev
 kapitan Ivchenko
Unknown *kapitan* A.G. Karmanov
Unknown *kapitan* D.A. Gusarov
Unknown *kapitan* A.A. Tereshkin
Squadron commissars
Unknown *st.politr* S.K. Toporkov
Unknown *st.politr* A.M. Gorin

5th Detached Mixed Aviation Regiment (5 OSAP), from January 1940 5th Detached Fast Bomber Aviation Regiment (5 OSBAP)

5 OSAP formed the nucleus of Murmansk Aviation Brigade, and included separately operating DB-3, SB and fighter squadrons. Two long-range bomber Squadrons (22 DB-3, led by *major* Gajkovich) were in late November 1939 transferred from 53 DBAP in Monino and AON-2 in Voronezh to Murmansk Aviation Brigade, and based in Murmashi and Shongui. The two SB squadrons counted 28 SB.

Subordination
VVS LVO
VVS 14. A

Combat Chronicle
At the beginning of the Winter War the fighter squadrons of 5 OSAP (initially 18 I-16, 15 I-15bis and I-153) were based at Vayenga, and relocated to Luostari and Salmijärvi in occupied Finnish territory, while the SB and DB-3 bomber Squadrons relocated to Notozero (90 km SW Murmansk).

In November 1939 I-15bis fighters arrived from 26 IAP in Uglovo, north of Leningrad. Next month also *kapitan* Savchenko's I-15bis Squadron arrived from 38 IAP in Pushkin.

30 November 1939 1st DB-Squadron was ordered to bomb Kemijärvi. Because of insufficient preparation and bad weather the Squadron lost five (!) DB-3 bombers and 11 aviators: one aircraft crashed on take-off without crew losses (c/n 391802), while four bombers disappeared in a snow storm in Pirenga-Monchegorsk-Kirovsk region: c/n 392114 (*st.lt* A.S. Kulikov), c/n 392111 (*st.lt* A.P. Yakushev), c/n 391820 (*st.lt* P.A. Semenov) and c/n 392106 (*st.politr* V.A. Orlov). MG-gunner T.Ya. Lukanchik of Orlov's bomber was found on 6 December 1939 alive but badly frozen at Chuna Tundra, 25 km W Monchegorsk.

5 December 1939 a group of I-15bis fighters led by *lt* I.M. Belov strafed the Petsamo-Salmijärvi road; I-15bis c/n 3843 (5th Squadron) was shot down by A-A – fire, *lt* M.I. Sidorov was killed. During the next four weeks the regiment lost at least five aircraft (U-2, USB and UTI-4) in accidents.

5 OSBAP Commander N.G. Serebryakov (HSU 7.5.1940). (G.F. Petrov)

DB-3 tactical 9 (c/n 391802) piloted by st.lt M.P. Burykh (5 OAP) crashed on take-off from Murmashi 30.11.1939. (RGVA)

USB c/n 22287 piloted by st.lt G.D. Vladimirov (5 OAP) force-landed in Vayenga 31.12.1939. (RGVA)

20 December 1939 six TB-3 headed for Murmashi from 3 TBAP (VVS KOVO) in Borovskoye, and were loosely attached to 5 OSAP. During the ferry flight two bombers crashed on Kildin Island in the Barents Sea (see also 3 TBAP, page 73).

2 January 1940 I-15bis c/n 5670 (5th Squadron) collided on take-off with a PS-9 courier aircraft in Luostari. *Lt* A.V. Chizenkov was killed.

9 January 1940 the fighter elements of 5 OSAP formed the new 147 IAP at Vayenga and Murmashi, after which 5 OSAP became a pure bomber formation with the regiment's name correspondingly changed to 5 OSBAP.

12 January 1940 Norwegian löytnant Karl Jacobsen was patrolling on the Norwegian side of the Norwegian-Soviet border in a Tiger Moth, when an SB bomber and an escort fighter opened fire 1–2 km west of the border at Svanvik, Pasvik. Later the same day 11 Soviet aircraft were observed over Pasvik. The Norwegian Foreign Ministry filed a protest. Next day oberst W.N. Faye (responsible for the defense of the Eastern Finnmark district) asked for permission to open fire against future intruders.

13 January 1940 1st Fighter Squadron (I-16) moved to Luostari (15 km south of Pechenga), and 2nd Fighter Squadron (also equipped with I-16) moved to Salmijärvi19 January 1940. SB and DB-3 bomber Squadrons moved to Notozero (90 km southwest of Murmansk).

14 January 1940 the target of 2nd DB Squadron was Kemi. *Lt* L.F. Zubov got lost and force-landed with c/n 391505 "8" at Sodankylä, Vaalajärvi, he was taken prisoner. The almost intact bomber was disassembled and transported to the State Aircraft Factory (VL) in Tampere for overhaul, and was later used by Finnish Air Force. The target of 1st Squadron was Rovaniemi. The leading DB-3 lost its orientation on the return leg, and force-landed at Sköytfoss in Norway! After a fast check of the landing site, the aircraft took off before the Norwegian border guards were able to prevent the take-off, and landed in the dark on the ice of Lake Bezymannoye, 45 km NE Murmansk. On the same day flights over Norwegian territory continued: 32 Soviet planes were observed over Svanvik.

DB-3 tactical 8 (5 OAP, c/n 391505) crashed at Sodankylä 14.1.1940 and is seen in Rovaniemi four days later on its way to VL in Tampere. (Flygvapenmuseum)

Lt L.F. Zubov was taken prisoner at the crash-landing site 14.1.1940. (Flygvapenmuseum)

14 January 1940 three I-15bis fighters got also lost on route to strafing Sangelsk (Suonikylä), and force-landed at Labdshjaur, Hihnakylä (east of Nautsi). The pilots were captured five days later. (See 147 OIAP, page 207.)

18 January 1940 two SB bombers (c/n 19/96 piloted by *kapitan* C.O. Alekseyev and c/n 20/66 piloted by *st.lt* Yermakov) were lost in a snow storm on the return leg from Nautsi to Luostari. The first bomber crashed at Kalastajasaarento (Rybachiy Peninsula), however apparently without casualties, while the second force-landed on the frozen Lake Malaya Lopatka, and partly sank through the ice. *Shturman kapitan* I.P. Kiselev was killed. *The same day the Norwegians again observed four Soviet fighters over their territory. The Soviet authorities also answered the Norwegian note of 12 January 1940, regretting the border crossing, which was "due to navigation problems".* After this crossings of the Norwegian border practically ceased until 31 January 1940, when three Soviet bombers dropped six bombs north of Grensefoss on the Norwegian side of the Pasvik-border river. Five bombs fell in the river and the sixth exploded on the Norwegian shore, however not causing any damage.

81

1 February 1940 Swedish volunteer *fänrik* P-J. Salwén (in a Gladiator of F 19) shot down SB c/n 15/59 of 3rd Squadron, the target of which was Rovaniemi. The bomber crashed at Käyrämöjärvi, all crew (*st.lt* B.M. Babkin, *st.lt* A.U. Mel'nik and *ml.komzv.* B.I. Batorin) were killed.

4 February 1940 SB c/n 16/210 (5th Squadron) did not return. The bomber was allegedly shot down by Finnish A-A artillery at Ivalo, but Finnish investigations indicated that the bomber was hit by splinters from its own bombs. The SB force-landed in Koivuvaara, 45 km E Ivalo. The stranded crew (*st.lt* Alagurov, *lt* Losev and *starshina* Glushenkov) were picked up by *st.lt* A.Ye. Fatyanov who landed nearby in another SB. The empty SB was found practically undamaged by Finnish troops, and was apparently later used by Finnish AF. Fatyanov was decorated with the Golden Star 7 May 1940.

17 February 1940 TB-3 c/n 22330 (pilot *lt* B.V. Frajdenberg) got lost on a bombing mission to Ivalo-Nautsi, and crashed 40 km S Notozero. The 8-man crew was later rescued.

21 February 1940 a mixed SB and DB formation took off to bomb Rovaniemi. Swedish volunteer *fänrik* C-O. Steninger (piloting a Gladiator of F 19) bravely intercepted the bombers, of which he claimed two shot down. A DB-3 force-landed almost without substantial damage 18 km NW Vuotso. This aircraft (c/n 391695, *red 11*) was also later used by Finnish AF (Finnish code apparently VP-14). *St.lt* A.N. Isachev (pilot) and *lt* F.P. Zapryagayev (navigator) were taken prisoner, gunner *starshina* V.F. Volkov was killed on capture. Steninger's second victory claim was an SB, which disappeared emitting smoke and

Swedish volunteers A. Frykholm and C-O. Steninger (F 19) downed 21.2.1940 DB-3 red 11 (5 OAP, c/n 391695) north of Vuotso. The aircraft was later repaired and apparently became VP-14 in Ilmavoimat. (Flygvapenmuseum)

Interesting details of DB-3 red 11. (Flygvapenmuseum)

Left and below left: Details of DB-3 red 11. (Flygvapenmuseum)

Left: Inspection of the interior of DB-3 red 11. (Flygvapenmuseum)

VP-14 after repair at VL in Tampere March 1941. (K. Stenman)

Pajala bombat av sju ryska flygplan.

Fruktansvärd förödelse i kyrkbyn. Dödsoffer?

The captured aviators of DB-3 red 11 (A.N. Isachev and F.P. Zapryagayev) did not believe that they had bombed Swedish territory. A great catastrophy was imminent in Swedish Pajala, but fortunately no persons were killed. (Flygvapenmuseum)

was believed to have crashed on its return leg. This was apparently SB c/n 5/95 (3rd Squadron) which did not return from Rovaniemi (crew *lt* I.D. Danilenko, *lt* A.A. Losev and *starshina* A.P. Petrov).

This day Pajala in northern Sweden (!) was bombed by seven bombers, dropping 48 explosive and over 100 incendiary bombs, which was categorically denied by POWs. In Pajala six buildings burned including a cottage, a sawmill and a cattle-shed. Luckily only two persons were slightly injured. The Swedish minister to Moscow Vilhelm Assarsson filed a protest, which at first was bluntly refuted by foreign minister Vyacheslav Molotov, but after substantial evidence (e.g. bomb fragments with inscriptions in Russian) was presented by the Swedes, the Kremlin admitted a "navigation mistake" on 6 March 1940, and compensation of 40,000 Swedish kronor was paid for the damage in Pajala. A peculiar fact is that F 19 was visited 3 March 1940 by *kapten* Stig Wennerström (future GRU-super spy, who was arrested summer 1963!) from the Swedish Defense HQ, with the task to investigate the Pajala incident.

9 March 1940 two SB bombers (3rd Squadron) were lost: *st.lt* Troshin force-landed with c/n 14/114 10 km west of the Finnish-Soviet border at the right bank of River Lutto. Squadron C.O. *kapitan* D.D.

SB "yellow 6" (c/n 15/59) was shot down by fänrik P-J. Salwen 1 February 1940 at Kayramojarvi. All crew was killed. The only slightly damaged aircraft is on the way to VL in Tampere. (Flygvapenmuseum)

Troshin's SB red 2 (c/n 14/114) was located by Finnish troops in summer 1940. (SA-kuva)

85

Valentik landed nearby with c/n 11/114 in order to pick up Troshin's crew. Valentik unfortunately crashed into a tree, and his unserviceable bomber was set on fire. Both crews were later picked up by a PR-5 liaison aircraft.

5 OSAP Strength and locations

Date	Base	Subordination	Equipment
1.12.1939	Vayenga, LVO	Murmansk AB, VVS SZFr	24 SB, 18 I-16, 44 I-15bis
1.1.1940	Vayenga, LVO	VVS SZFr	9 SB, 7 DB-3, 18 I-16, 16 I-153, 30 I-15bis
1.2.1940	Vayenga and Notozero, LVO	VVS SZFr	30 SB, 19 DB-3
1.3.1940	Vayenga and Notozero, LVO	VVS SZFr	31 SB, 18 DB-3
1.4.1940	Vayenga, LVO	VVS LVO	33 SB, 18 DB-3

5 OSBAP performed 567 bombing missions, usually deep into the enemy rear. The main target was Rovaniemi, where five enemy fighters were claimed. The Rovaniemi bombings of 23 January, 31 January, and 1 February 1940 were particularly heavy. 31 January 1940 direct hits were scored on an exploding train and a railway bridge. Also Sodankylä (23 January 1940), Kemijärvi, Kemi and Ivalo (4 February 1940) were bombed. As all targets were rather distant the bombers operated without escorting fighters, which was not considered necessary as no Finnish fighter units existed in the north. After arrival of the Swedish volunteer unit F19 12 January 1940 the situation changed, and 5 OSBAP War Diary mentions explicitly encounters with enemy Fokker fighters(!).

As is well known F19 was equipped with 12 Gladiators only.

The fighter Squadrons of 5 OSBAP repeatedly performed ground attacks on closer targets (Petsamo, Salmijärvi, Nautsi).

5 OSBAP command

Commander	*major* N.G. Serebryakov (1913–1988). Participated in Spanish Civil War. HSU 7 May 1940.
Military commissar	*bat.komiss* Kazarinov
Chief of Staff	*kapitan* Polikarpov
Squadron C.O. and commissars	
DB group	*major* Gajkovich
1st DB Squadron	*kapitan* V.G. Tikhonov
	major Gaikovich
2nd DB Squadron	Dashkevich
	politr Kirillov
3rd SB Squadron	*kapitan* D.D. Valentik (1907–1969). HSU 7 May 1940. In GPW commanded 284 BBAP.
	st.lt V.I. Ivashkin (1908 – 8.5.1942, KIA). In GPW in 608 BAP, VVS KarFr. HSU 22.2.1943.
SB Squadron	*kapitan* Alekseyev
SB Squadron	*kapitan* A.V. Ivanov
I-153 Squadron	*major* Galitsyn
2nd IAE (I-16)	*kapitan* S.A Tryapichkin
TB-3 detachment (from 3 TBAP)	*kapitan* Kalinin

5 OSBAP was awarded Red Banner Order 7 May 1940. Despite a very small number of combat missions five aviators became HSUs: 5 February 1940 *lt* I.M. Belov (10 combat missions) and *st.politr* S.Ye. Ponomarchuk (10 combat missions), and on 7 May 1940 *major* N.G. Serebryakov (7 combat missions), *st.lt* A.Ya. Fatyanov (6 missions; rescue operation of force-landed crew 4 February 1940) and *kapitan* D.D. Valentik (26 combat missions; unsuccessful rescue operation 9 March 1940).

20 May 1940 the two SB squadrons were expanded into 137 KSBAP: 3rd Squadron became 1st Squadron/137 KSBAP, and 4th Squadron became 2nd Squadron. 137 KSBAP was thus already from the beginning a *Krasnoznamennyi polk* (or *Red Banner regiment*, indicated by "K" in the Russian acronym **KSBAP**, as it inherited the Red Banner Order of 5 OSBAP.

In GPW 137 KSBIAP was elevated to Guards status 24 August 1943 and named 114 GvBAP.

5th Fast Bomber Aviation Regiment (5 SBAP)

5 SBAP was established in July 1938 in Odessa Military District with 58 OAE as nucleus. Autumn 1939 5 SBAP was based in Kirovograd (Kiev MD).

Subordination
1 LBAB, VVS KOVO
1 LBAB, VVS 7.A (from 26 February 1940)

Combat Chronicle
5 SBAP moved together with 1 LBAB on 14 February 1940 from Kirovograd to Suulajärvi (in occupied Finnish territory), combat ready 26 February 1940 (38 SB).

27 February 1940 SB c/n 10/209 crashed at Ristseppälä (east of Heinjoki on the Karelian isthmus) after A-A hits. The crew *kapitan* V.I. Chufrin, *st.lt* V.D. Yegorov and radioman/gunner Ye.A. Tselodub were killed.

In 1948 three villages near the crash site were given names honoring the dead crew (the territory was ceded to the USSR in the peace treaties of 13 March 1940 and 19 September 1944):
- Voipiala = Chufrino
- Harju = Yegorovo
- Kaukolempiälä = Tsvelodubovo

5 March 1940 SB c/n 19/201 of 2nd Squadron was shot down by enemy A-A. *Kapitan* M.I. Kozyrev, *st.lt* F.N. Malov and *starshina* S.N. Kuznetsov were killed.

8 March 1940 SB c/n 18/201 of 2nd Squadron was shot down by enemy A-A. *St.politr* A.K. Suvorov, *kapitan* N.A. Shalin and *starshina* K.P. Lakoshin were killed. The Soviet legation in Helsinki inquired on 25 November 1940 whether Shalin had been taken prisoner.

5 SBAP performed 36 bombing missions. According to a brief unit history published in 2000 in Odessa, 5 SBAP lost seven aircraft in combat and another two in accidents.

Squadron C.O.
Unknown	*major* M.I. Belov
Unknown	*kapitan* V.I. Chufrin (KIA 27 February 1940)
5th	*major* Prokoin

In summer 1940 5 SBAP participated in the "liberation" of Bessarabia, based at Belgorod-Dnestrovskiy (former Akkerman).

In GPW 5 SBAP was elevated to Guards status 7 March 1942 and renamed 8 GvBAP.

Orders are given in 5 SBAP in Suulajärvi ice base, early March 1940. Note: 5 SBAP operated only on the Karelian isthmus at the end of the Winter War, and was NOT related to 5 OSBAP which operated during the entire war in the far North. (G.F. Petrov)

Above: The grave of Chufrin's crew (5 SBAP) at Kaukolempiälä (now Tsvetodubovo) at the eastern shore of Lake Suulajärvi. (SA-kuva)

Above right: Bomb bay of an SB-bomber. (G.F. Petrov)

6th Long-Range Bomber Aviation Regiment (6 DBAP)

Autumn 1939 6 DBAP was based in Ivanovo (Moscow MD).

Subordination
    13 AB, AON-1 (until 25 January 1940)
    VVS SZFr, 27 AB (from 25 January 1940)

Combat Chronicle
6 DBAP arrived 14 November 1939 from Ivanovo to Krechevitsy with 55 DB-3 bombers and one TB-3.
    6 DBAP got its first combat order on 17 November 1939:
- 1st Squadron was to bomb Mikkeli airfield,
- 2nd Squadron Iisalmi airfield,

One of the DB-3s downed by Jorma Sarvanto. (SA-kuva)

- 3rd Squadron Kuopio airfield,
- 4th Squadron Joroinen airfield,
- 5th Squadron Puumala airfield.

Combat alert was to begin at 0700 hours 19 November 1939, with take-off according to separate orders.

27 November 1939 VVS *flagshturman*, *kombrig* A.V. Belyakov inspected 6 DBAP. However, because of poor weather the first combat mission was only performed on 19 December 1939.

6 DBAP bombed primarily strategic targets in the Finnish rear: armament factories (Jyväskylä, Kuopio) and railway junctions (Pieksämäki, Kouvola, Lappeenranta etc.), and also closer targets such as Viipuri railway bridge, Elisenvaara railway junction, Käkisalmi (Kexholm) etc. 6 DBAP was badly organized and suffered large losses, which led to the dismissal of regiment commander *polkovnik* V.S. Nikitin on 30 December 1939.

F.I. Lopatin (6 DBAP MG-gunner) claimed two enemy aircraft 25.12.1939 at Immola (HSU 15.1.1940) (G.F. Petrov)

6 DBAP combat missions

No.	Date	Target (bombers allocated)	Aircraft started/bombed	Flight hours	Enemy aircraft claimed	Own aircraft lost
1	19.12.39	Helsinki (4) Liimatta (16), Säiniö (8)	33/28	106		1
2	21.12.39	Elisenvaara (12), Käkisalmi (9), Lahti (6), Hiitola (9), Lahdenpohja (4)	44/40	137		3
3	25.12.39	Käkisalmi (3), Elisenvaara (7), Vuoksenniska (2), Järvelä (5), Lahti (4), Immola (5)	34/26	107	4	3
4	26.12.1939	Hiitola (9), Elisenvaara (11), Palojärvi (3)	28/23	85		
5	29.12.1939	Jyväskylä	16/7	61		
6	31.12.1939	Jyväskylä	16/15	73		
7	5.1.1940	Värtsilä	11/3	30		
8	6.1.1940	Kuopio	?/14	82	8	7
9	18.1.1940	Läskelä	18/6	50		
10	20.11940	Viipuri	25/23	129		
11	21.11940	Jyväskylä	27/-	86		
12	2.2.1940	Kuopio, Pieksämäki	25	140	2	2
13	3.2.1940	Kuopio	25	154		
14	4.2.1940		33	116		
15	13.2.1940	Hiitola	24/21	84		
16	14.2.1940		46	170		1
17	15.2.1940	Viipuri	43/41			--
18	17.2.1940	Käkisalmi	27/27			
19	18.2.1940		45/44			
20	20.2.1940	Hiitola, Elisenvaara	44/43		1	
21	21.2.1940	Elisenvaara (23), Hiitola (9)	32	147		
22	26.2.1940	Lappeenranta	45	180		
23	27.2.1940	Antrea	25			
24	29.2.1940	Pieksämäki	23	142		
25	1.3.1940	Pieksämäki, Tienhaara	41	205		1
26	5.3.1940	Mikkeli (7), Jyväskylä	43	245		
27	8.3.1940	Sorvali, Hiitola, Viipuri	36	123		
28	10.3.1940	Monrepos, Herttuala	36	108		
29	11.3.1940	Sorvali	36	54		
30	11.3.1940	Sorvali	36	54		

Ye. P. Fedorov (1./6 DBAP) was appointed HSU 7.4.1940. Fedorov got his second Golden Star 29.6.1945. (G.F. Petrov)

Combat missions total:	922, of which 809 aircraft bombed
Flight time, total:	3,653 hours
Bombs dropped:	14 FAB-500
	206 FAB-250
	4 512 FAB-100
	843 FAB-50
	1,210 ZAB-50
	164 RRAB-3
Leaflets dropped:	358,800
Combat losses ac/aviators:	11/37
Aircraft/aviators missing:	4/15
Enemy aircraft claimed shot down:	15

6 DBAP Strength and locations

Date	Base	Subordination	Base unit	Equipment
1.11.39	Ivanovo	13 AB, AON-1	14 RAB, 12 AB	73 DB-3, 1 TB-3
1.12.39	Krechevitsy	13 AB, AON-1	4 RAB, 139 AB	55 DB-3, 1 TB-3
1.1.40	Krechevitsy	13 AB, AON-1	4 RAB, 139 AB	47 DB-3, 1 TB-3
1.2.40	Krechevitsy	27 AB	4 RAB, 139 AB	45 DB-3, 1 TB-3
1.3.40	Krechevitsy	27 AB	4 RAB, 139 AB	56 DB-3, 1 TB-3
1.4.40	Kursk	27 AB	16 RAB, 12 AB	55 DB-3, 1 TB-3

Jorma Sarvanto downed six DB-3 of 6 DBAP during one mission 6.1.1940, and immediately became well-known in Finland and abroad. Sarvanto's heroic combat, together with the successful motti encirclements, symbolized Finland's fight against the numerically superior aggressor. Sarvanto's photo was published on the cover of Finnish weekly Hakkapeliitta no. 5/1940. (Finnish National Library)

Combat Chronicle

19 December 1939 6 DBAP performed its first attack. Of the 33 DB-3s taking off 28 bombed the targets given: 4 bombed Helsinki, 8 bombed Säiniö and 16 bombed Liimatta railway junction SE Viipuri. DB-3 c/n 819 (*kapitan* M.F. Zherdev, 1st Squadron) did not return. Luutn *J.* Karhunen (FR-112) and kers M. Alho (FR-117) shot down a DB-3 which crashed some kilometers south of Oravaniemi on the River Vuoksi.

21 December 1939 three aircraft were lost: The engines of DB-3 c/n 130 (*kapitan* Mustafa, 1st Squadron) malfunctioned on take-off from Selishche, the crew was unhurt; DB-3 c/n 529 (*kapitan* A.S. Svetelkin, 3rd Squadron) was shot down in air combat over the Karelian Isthmus, and DB-3 c/n 820 (*kapitan* M.A. Brusnitsin, 5th Squadron) went missing after air combat. The aircraft and wounded crew were later located near border pole nr. 237. Luutn *J.* Vuorela (FR-87), vänr A. Linnamaa (FR-114) and vänr *J.* Savonen (FR-93) *claimed jointly a DB-3 in air combat at Kämärä*.

25 December 1939 bombing targets were industries in South-East Finland, Lahti radio station and Immola AF base. At Immola five bombers led by polkovnik Niktin were intercepted by eleven (!) Finnish fighters. Radio-operator/gunners Lopatin and Tarasov claimed two fighters each. Three bombers were lost in air combat: c/n 623 red 7 (*lt* I.P. Lipin, 1st Squadron), c/n 226 green 6 (*st. lt* L.N. Starikov, 3rd Squadron and c/n 518 green 5 (*lt* G.I. Malygin). Furthermore c/n 624 and 218 returned with serious damages, which required factory repairs. The machineguns of the bombers malfunctioned because of congealed gun grease. *The DB-3 bombers were intercepted by LLv 24 pilots kers S. Ikonen (FR-102), kers L. Nissinen (FR-98), luutn P-E. Sovelius (FR-92), ylik O. Tuominen (FR-117) and ylik K. Virta (FR-101), who jointly claimed two DB-3s at Enso-Immola-Joutseno. No Finnish aircraft were lost.*

29 December 1939 *major* I.F. Balashov led two Squadrons (seven DB-3 each), the target of which was *Valtion Tykkitehdas* (State Cannon Factory) in Jyväskylä. Because of poor weather only one squadron located the target.

31 December 1939 *Valtion Tykkitehdas* (State Cannon Factory) in Jyväskylä was again a bombing target. Despite air combat with seven Finnish fighters at Pyhtää and fierce A-A fire at the target all bombers returned to their base, two with serious damage.

6 January 1940 6 DBAP bombed Kuopio railway junction with 17 bombers. *major* Balashov personally led 9 bombers (from 1st and 2nd Squadrons), which returned without losses. *major* Maistrenko led 8 bombers (from 1st and 3rd Squadrons), of which only *lt* Ageyev's DB-3 returned. On the approach to the target, an air combat

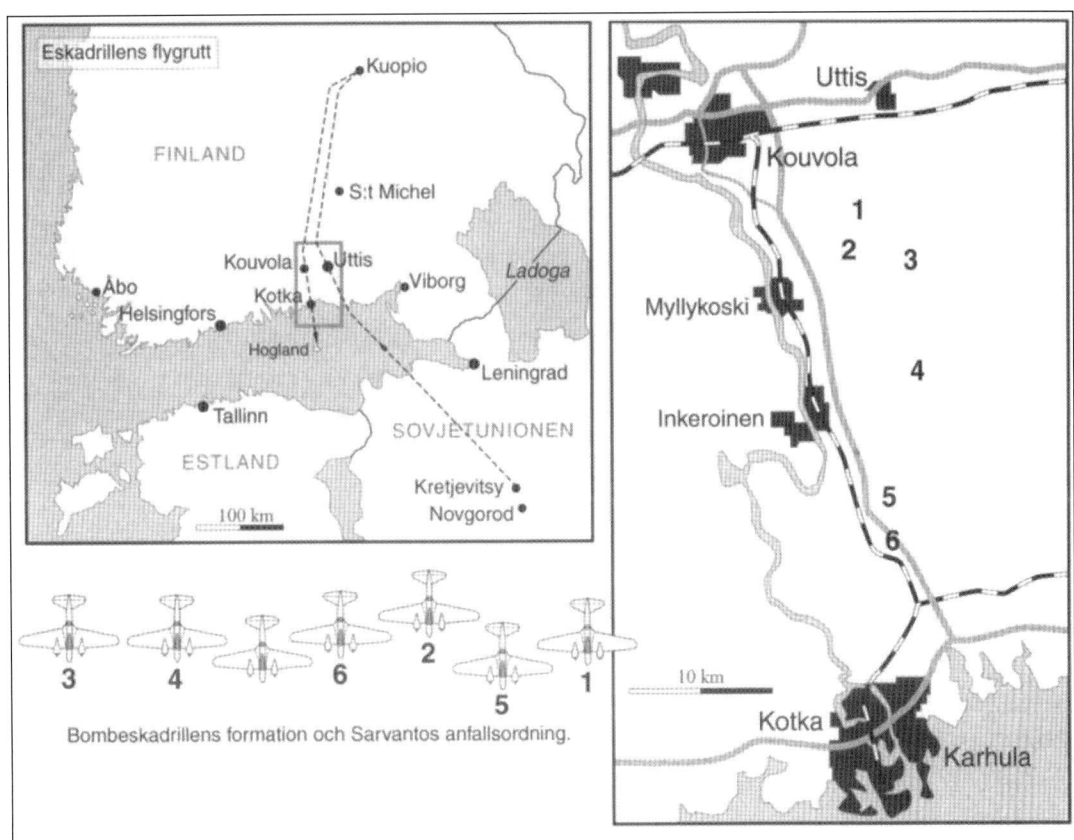

The route of 6 DBAP from Krechevitsy to Kuopio and back, Sarvanto's attack order on his 21st combat mission, and the location of the six DB-3 downed 6 January 1940. (From the Swedish version of Sarvanto's memoirs edited in 2005 by C-F. Geust.)

Sarvantos legendariska luftstrid den 6 januari 1940 kl. 11.55–12.25, då han kämpade ned sex DB-3-bombplan, var hans tjuguförsta stridsflygning. De sex DB-3-bombplanen störtade mellan Uttis och Kotka, eskadrillens sjunde plan sköts ned av Pelle Sovelius. Den högra kartan visar platserna där planen störtade.

was fought in which a bomber was shot down. On the return leg seven Finnish fighters shot down six bombers, including the leading aircraft of *major* Majstrenko. The MG-gunners of 6 DBAP claimed eight Fokker fighters shot down in air combat! Luutn *J. Sarvanto, FR-97 (LLv 24) shot down six bombers on their return leg, the seventh was shot down by luutn P-E. Sovelius (FR-92). Sarvanto was lucky to be able to return, as his Fokker got 35 bullet holes. St.lt* G.K. Nikulin (1st Squadron) and *kapitan* M.V. Malorodov (3rd Squadron) were taken prisoner in Heinoja and Inkeroinen respectively.

The exceptionally heavy losses of 6 DBAP led to detailed investigations. Partly based on *lt* Ageyev's reports the following conclusions were made:
1. Incoming and outgoing flight routes and crossing points had remained unchanged since the beginning of the war (almost six weeks), which gave the enemy the possibility to organise permanent surveillance at the crossing points.
2. Although the Squadron was already attacked during the approach route, on return *major* Majstrenko led his formation along the very same route and at the very same altitude.
3. The bombing task was performed without escort fighters.

The real reason of the losses was also detected: "*bad radio discipline and the joint radio tuning before take-off provided the enemy the possibility to intercept the tuning communication, and to deduce the number of aircraft, bombing target, and approach and return routes*". Furthermore technical deficiencies of the DB-3 bombers were observed: "*because of unprotected fuel tanks and lack of carbon dioxide emitting fire extinguishers the aircraft burst into flames, although enemy firing lasted only for 1.5–2 minutes*".

2 February 1940 25 bombers took off, with targets Kuopio and Pieksämäki. DB-3 c/n 119 (Tolmachev) crashed at take-off from Krechevitsy, and c/n 2702 (*ml.lt* M.M. Shukhtomov, 3th Squadron) crashed at Tuusniemi (between Kuopio and Joensuu). Four DB-3s were damaged. Luutn *P-E. Sovelius (FR-92) and kers M. Alho (FR-81) of LLv 24 claimed one DB-3 south of Virolahti (apparently one of the damaged DB-3s returning from Kuopio). Danish volunteer Løjtnant J. Ulrich, (GL-259) of LLv 26 claimed another bomber near Suursaari (Hogland), apparently SB c/n 8/238 of 57 AP KBF (crew lt G.S. Pinchuk, kapitan V.M. Kharlamov and st.ser A.I. Belogurov) which crashed on the ice near Koivisto-Someri. The crew was subsequently found and picked up (for details, see Appendix 15).*

3 February 1940 25 bombers attacked Kuopio, which suffered extensive damage. 37 civilians were killed.

American war reporter Martha Gellhorn visited Immola AF base 4.12.1939, and met some of Finland's best fighter pilots. From left Jorma Sarvanto, Sakari Ikonen, MG, Olli Mustonen, G-E. Magnusson, Pelle Sovelius and Lasse Heikinaro & Eero Kinnunen. Ms. Gellhorn's dramatic reports of the bombing of Helsinki 30.11.1939 and her Immola visit contributed considerably to American support for Finland. (C-F. Geust)

14 February 1940 DB-3 c/n 2710 (*st.lt* M. Pleshakov, 3rd Squadron) was destroyed at take-off from Krechevitsy, all three crew died.

18 February 1940 45 DB-3s were escorted by 18 fighters.

20 February 1940 targets Hiitola and Elisenvaara. MG-gunner Yevseyev (1st Squadron) claimed one Gladiator.

26 February 1940 two Fokkers were claimed in air combat at Lappeenranta.

29 February 1940 gunner *st.lt* I.A. Bitkovskiy escaped by parachute after air combat over Lake Ladoga and went missing. Pilot Tarasenko crash-landed at Charoj-Orefyeva Gora.

In February 1940 6th Squadron was formed from 12 DB-3 bombers from 7 AB (AON-3) in Zaporozhe.

1 March 1940 three Squadrons (27 bombers) took off from Krechevitsy via Shamozero, Koitere and Tuusniemi to bomb Pieksämäki railway junction (reserve target Kuopio railway station). A-A artillery got hits on a bomber of 2nd Squadron which crashed in Ilomantsi, Ala-Vieksi. Pilot *st.lt* A.Z. Melikhov, and MG-gunners M.Ye. Martsenyuk and N.A. Aseikin were captured five days later, *shturman* A. Gavrilov was killed on capture by Finnish soldiers.

6 DBAP command

Commander   *polkovnik* V.S. Nikitin, commanded 6 DBAP to 30 December 1939.
             polkovnik G.N. Tupikov (1907–1961). Commanded 6 DBAP from 30 December 1939. Former Flight Technics Inspector of AON-1. In GPW commanded 1 GvBAK DD etc. Commanded 43rd Air Army 1956–1960.

St.lt Ye.P. Fedorov gives instructions to his crew in Krechevitsy, January 1940. (G.F. Petrov)

Military commissar	*bat.komiss* N.I. Ivanov
Chief of Staff	*major* Lobakhin

major A.I. Kuznetsov must be replaced 23 January 1940, "was replaced" POW info 6 March 1940.

Squadron C.O. and commissars

1st	*kapitan* M.D. Zherdev (KIA 18 December 1939)
	kapitan G.F. Orlovskiy
	kapitan Ye.P. Fedorov (1911–1993). Performed 24 missions, duration 3–7 hours. HSU 7 April 1940 and 29 June 1945 as Deputy Commander of 2 GvAD DD.
2nd	*kapitan* Fedorov
	kapitan A.G. Kozhevnikov
	st.politr A.P. Chulkov
	st.politr Oshepkov
	st.politr Kozlov
3rd	*major* V.D. Maistrenko (KIA 6 January 1940)
	kapitan V.P. Shimarin
	st.politr P.I. Gramotkin (KIA 6 January 1940)
4th	*kapitan* Gorodilov
	kapitan N.I. Vinogradov
	st.politr I.N. Baranov
	st.politr Solomin
5th	*kapitan* F.P. Tunygin
	st.politr V.F. Salkonin
Commissar	*st.politr* V.V. Zotov
	st.politr Teperskiy

Three aviators became HSUs, 15 January 1940 MG-gunner *ml.kzv* F.I. Lopatin ("*shot down two enemy fighters at Immola 25 December 1939*"), 7 April 1940 Assistant Regiment C.O. *major* I.F. Balashov (performed 13 missions) and C.O. of 1st Squadron *kapitan* Ye.P. Fedorov (24 missions).

After the war 6 DBAP departed from Krechevitsy to Kursk with 62 DB-3 and one TB-3.

In 1969 the traditions of 6 DBAP were transferred to 117 OAPEP (Detached Aviation Regiment for Electroniv Jamming) which in 1974 became 117 VTAP (Military Transport Aviation Regiment).

7th Heavy Bomber Aviation Regiment (7 TBAP)

Autumn 1939 7 TBAP was based in Yedrovo (Leningrad MD).

Subordination
29 TBAB, AON-1
29 TBAB, VVS SZFr

Combat Chronicle
In October 1939 part of 7 TBAP moved to Jelgava, Latvia. In November 1939 main operational base was Pushkin (strength 43 TB-3).

26 November 1939 (or four days before the war) a "combat mission" is recorded in the War Diary: TB-3 c/n 22485 (*st.lt* I.Ye. Kosach, 3rd Squadron) crashed 60 km E Medvezhegorsk (Karhumäki) on a ferry flight (on behalf of 72 SAP) to Uhtua. Unfortunately no explanation for this "combat mission" has been found.

After 30 November 1939 two transport groups and one night bomber Squadron (4th Squadron with 15 TB-3s, led by *polkovnik* A.A. Kisel') were formed. 4th Squadron was subordinated to VVS 7.A and based at Pushkin. This Squadron was in action until 15 February 1940, performed 85 missions and dropped 123 t bombs, flight time 268 hours.

9 December 1939 was a bad day for 7 TBAP: four TB-3 bombers of 4th Squadron went missing on a night mission from Pushkin. The bombers tried to turn back after icing conditions over Lake Ladoga. *Polkovnik* A.A. Kisel's TB-3 c/n 22623 (carrying the entire regiment command, nine officers including regiment Chief of Staff, *flagshturman*, Head of Communications Services and Flight Inspector) went missing. Three other TB-3s bombers force-landed after loss of orientation and up to six hours in the

A spare M-34 engine is lifted into a TB-3 bomber. (G.F. Petrov)

A TB-3 transport aircraft on skis. (G.F. Petrov)

TB-3 bombers were equipped with twin 7.62 mm DA-2 machine-guns. (G.F. Petrov)

air: TB-3 c/n 22475 (N.A. Yevdak) landed 4 km from Mga with moderate damage, c/n 22591 (*st.lt* V.I. Kalygin) crashed at Mga-Sinyavino (50 km from Pushkin) and c/n 22598 (A.I. Vladimirov) crashed at Pudosh (27 km from Pushkin). Surprisingly no personnel losses were suffered in these crashes.

28 December 1939 TB-3 c/n 22455 (*kapitan* V.S.Yevtukh, 4th Squadron) crashed at take-off for a ferry flight to Yedrovo.

23 January 1940 three TB-3s were transferred to OAG in Estonia.

28 January 1940 TB-3 c/n 22469 ("6", M.A. Bazhenov, 2nd Squadron) was destroyed shortly after take-off from Pushkin for a nocturnal *spetszadanije* (special mission, possibly agent dropping in Finland).

29 January 1940 TB-3 c/n 22601 ("1", *st.lt* B.G. Yezerskiy, 4th Squadron) crashed in bad weather at night near Volkhovstroj, returning from a *spetszadanije* (probably repetition of the mission interrupted the night before). The crew was unhurt.

The transport groups (29 TB-3 bombers) transported 946 persons and 230 t cargo in January 1940, flight time 468 hours. Total flight time of 7 TBAP by end-February 1940 was 441 h 25 min (daytime) and 89 h 45 min (nighttime).

After *polkovnik* Kisel' went missing 9 December 1939, *major* Labudev was appointed regiment C.O.; *polkovnik* Zhukov (temporary C.O. 29 TBAB) was appointed C.O. of 4th (Night Bomber) Squadron.

27 February 1940 7 TBAP was inspected by the Political administration (*Politupravleniye*) of VVS SZFr. 48 aircraft incidents were recorded during the Winter War, 18 due to technical defects, and 30 due to incorrect handling by the technical staff.

17 March 1940 seven TB-3s returned to Yedrovo from Pushkin. In spring 1940 7 TBAP made a number of flights to the Hanko peninsula, which was leased to the USSR according to the peace treaty signed 13 March 1940. As there was no airfield in the Hanko area, an aviation bridge operated until the sea opened, the aircraft with troops and cargo landing on the ice.

7 TBAP command

Commander	*polkovnik* A.A. Kisel'. MIA 9 December 1939.
	major Labudev. From mid-December 1939.
Military commissar	*bat.komiss* Yastrebtsev
	bat.komiss Peshkov
Chief of Staff	*polkovnik* A.I. Pavlov. MIA 9 December 1939.
4th Squadron (night bomber)	*polkovnik* A.A. Kisel'. MIA 9 December 1939.
	polkovnik Zhukov (29 TBAB acting C.O.)
	polk.komiss Antonov (29 TBAB Military commissar)
Unknown Squadron	*kapitan* K.D. Belyakov. In GPW 122 IAD (PVO) deputy C.O.

In GPW 7 TBAP was merged with 750 DBAP in early December 1941, and on 5 March 1942 attached to ADD (Soviet Long-Range Air Forces). On 18 August 1942 7 AP DD was elevated to Guards status, becoming 3 GvAP ADD, and renamed 183 GvBAP in late 1944.

7th Long-Range Bomber Aviation Regiment (7 DBAP)

Autumn 1939 7 DBAP was based in Voronezh (Orel MD).

Subordination
64 AB, AON-2 (until 17 February 1940)
OAG (from 18 February 1940)

Combat Chronicle
7 DBAP (3 Squadrons, 39 DB-3 bombers) arrived 17–18 February 1940 1940 from Voronezh to Kuusiku (Rapla) in Estonia, where 53 DBAP was already based at the southern part of the airfield. The aviators of 7 DBAP were accommodated in Kehno, some 18 km from the base, while the technicians were accommodated near the airfield. After arrival of 4th Squadron on 1 March 1940 total strength was 51 DB-3s.

The vulnerability of DB-3 to enemy fighters attacking from behind and below was already well known, so regiment deputy C.O. A. Anisiforov was given the urgent task to install a rearward-firing machine-gun. This task was not easy, as available space was considerably limited by the tail wheel. After successful testing of an experimental DA-1 machine gun installation, rear MGs were retrofitted in all existing DB-3s, and all new DB-3 batches were equipped with factory-installed rear MGs, which significantly reduced combat losses.

2 March 1940 33 bombers attacked Tampere. 15 DB-3 bombed the "aircraft engine factory", dropping 36 bombs (16 FAB-500 and 20 FAB-250, total weight 13.0 t), while 17 DB-3 and one SB bombed Tampere railway junction, dropping 182 bombs (180 FAB-100 and 2 ZAB-50, total weight 18.2 t). 7 DBAP suffered no losses, but an attacking Fokker D.XXI was shot down by MG-gunner Yefimov. *St.lt* Sitnikov's aircraft was seriously damaged. Tampere was also bombed by 35 SBAP of OAG. A total of 104 bombers attacked Tampere in three waves, dropping some 600 bombs. 10 buildings were totally destroyed, and another 30 seriously damaged. Nine persons were killed and 27 injured. Considerable damage was caused to the railway yard and the city electricity network. *The test pilots of Koelentue (Test Flight) intercepted the attacking bombers, and shot down two SBs of 35 SBAP and seriously damaged a third SB (for details see 35 SBAP, page 141). Lentom U. Heiskala (FR-84) was shot down and killed by a Soviet MG-gunner (apparently Yefimov, 7 DBAP).*

11 March 1940 Kouvola railway junction was bombed by 45 DB-3s. 275 bombs (6 FAB-500, 59 FAB-250 and 210 FAB-100, total weight 38.8 t) were dropped. One DB-3 was shot down by A-A artillery at Kouvola, and another was shot down by a "Spitfire" during the return leg. One Fokker D.XXI and one "Spitfire" crashed in the Gulf of Finland were claimed by MG-gunners of 7 DBAP. 16 DB-3 were hit in air combat or by A-A artillery.

Vänr M. Inehmo (MS-304); vänr A. Linnamaa (MS-306) and luutn M. Linkola (MS-302) of LLv 28 and luutn O. Puhakka (FA-21) of LLv 26 claimed victories. Puhakka shot down DB-3 c/n 352 ("2", st.lt G.K. Bulava, 1ˢᵗ esc.) which crashed in Lappträsk, killing all crew.

DB-3 c/n 1749 (lt K.I. Pelikh, 2ⁿᵈ esc.) was shot down by A-A at Kouvola. Italian volunteer kers D. Manzocchi (FA-22) was hit and forced-landed on the ice of Lake Ikolajärvi. His FIAT G.50 turned over in the soft snow, and he perished before the aircraft was located. Vänr M. Inehmo force-landed at Ruuhijärvi after combat hits.

Both Moranes and FIATs were apparently wrongly identified as "Spitfires".

Another "Spitfire" was claimed 11 March 1940 by an escorting I-153 (15 IAP) at Lahti. Three Moranes of LLv 28 scrambled from Hollola to intercept the bombers. No losses were suffered. 7 DBAP also planned to bomb the Military Flying School (Ilmasotakoulu) in Kauhava, but the attack was cancelled after the peace treaty was signed in Moscow on the night of 12/13 March 1940.

(Note: in Finnish intelligence documents 7 DBAP is often mixed up with 7 TBAP).

7 DBAP performed four "regiment attacks", totaling 125 missions during 26 February-11 March 1940. 799 bombs (total weight 108.0 t) were dropped, total flight time 465 h.

7 DBAP combat missions

No.	Date	Target	Aircraft	Bombs	Comments
1	26.2.40	Riihimäki	14 DB-3, 1 SB	9 FAB-250, 38 FAB-100, total 6.0 t	
2	29.2.40	Haapamäki	26 DB-3, 1 SB	24 FAB-250, 230 FAB-100, 8 FAB-50, total 29.4 t	
3	2.3.40	Tampere	32 DB-3, 1 SB	(see above)	1 Fokker claimed
4	11.3.40	Kouvola	45 DB-3	(see above)	2 DB-3s lost, 2 fighters claimed

7 DBAP command

Commander	*polkovnik* N.N. Buyanskiy (1901–1953). In GPW commanded 8 AK DD etc.
Deputy Commander	*major* Ya.P. Prokofyev
	A.A. Anisiforov
Military commissar	*bat.komiss* N.V. Ochnev
Chief of Staff	K.N. Shevchuk
	kapitan Aristov

Squadron C.O. and commissars

1ˢᵗ Squadron	*kapitan* T.S. Sukach
	st.politr L.M. Rybakov
Unknown Squadron	*kapitan* I.F. Aleksandrov (His Squadron performed 44 missions without losses, one Fokker D.XXI was claimed.)
Unknown Squadron	*major* S.A. Dzamashvili, commanded 40 DBAD in 1942.
Unknown Squadron	*kapitan* A.I. Shcherbakov (1909–1986). Performed 3 combat missions in the Winter War. Commanded 65ᵗʰ Air Army 1951–1953.
Unknown Squadron	*kapitan* D.F. Klerfon
Unknown Squadron	*kapitan* Chernovolenko

In GPW 7 DBAP was attached to ADD on 5 March 1942. 7 AP DD was elevated to Guards status 25 March 1943 as 7 GvAP DD, and renamed 186 GvBAP after conversion of ADD to 18th Air Army in December 1944.

7th Fighter Aviation Regiment (7 IAP)

7 IAP was formed in Krasnogvardejsk (now Gatchina), Leningrad MD (LVO) in April 1938. In autumn 1939 7 IAP was based in Pushkin, and from 8 September 1939 was dispatched to Kiev MD (KOVO) and was assigned to Odessa air defense. In October 1939 7 IAP returned to Pushkin, where the fighter pilots landed 20 October 1939. In early November 1939 1st (15 I-16P) and 3rd (16 I-15bis) Squadrons moved to Levashevo, and 2nd (17 I-15bis) and 4th (15 I-16) Squadrons to Kasimovo. (I-16P was a ground attack fighter, equipped with 20 mm ShVAK-cannons.)

7 IAP was the main Soviet fighter regiment in the Winter War. In the first days of the war the main task was fighter interception and bomber escort. At the end of the war 7 IAP also performed ground attacks at the Bay of Viipuri.

Subordination
 59 IAB, VVS LVO
 59 IAB, VVS 7.A

Combat Chronicle

30 November 1939 early in the morning Finnish trains were attacked at Kiviniemi. I-15bis (c/n 4686, "483", 3rd Squadron) was shot down by Finnish infantry fire at 0930 hours at Sakkola, *ml.lt* S.I. Grigoryev was killed. This was the first Soviet aircraft shot down in the Winter War.

1 December 1939 4th Squadron (I-16; led by *st.lt* F.I. Shinkarenko) shot down a Bulldog at 1230 hours at Muolaa. *Lt* P.A. Pokryshev (4th Squadron, future double-HSU) force-landed at Kerrola, Muolaa after engine malfunction. Kers *T. Uuttu (BU-64, LLv 26) force-landed at Muolaanjärvi.*

18–25 December 1939 2nd Squadron (I-15bis, C.O. *kapitan* Postaush) moved from Kasimovo to Metsäpirtti (in occupied Finnish territory), and on 31 December 1939 was attached to 68 IAP (still based in Metsäpirtti).

18 December 1939 I-16 *tip* 10 c/n 1021727 (*ml.lt* V.A. Bogdanov, 4th Squadron) did not return from strafing Sakkola.

20 December 1939 at 1552 hours 9 I-15bis (2nd Squadron, led by *kapitan* Postaush) strafed Säiniö railway station. At Liimatta they were fired upon by A-A artillery, after which Suurpero and Pilppula were attacked. At Kämärä five Fokker D.XXI were seen, of which two attacked, one of which was shot down by *kzv* Mironov. The other Fokkers escaped.

On the same day at 1626 hours a group of I-16s led by *st.pol* G.V. Didenko (4th Squadron) escorted SB bombers. At Karpela three Fokker D.XXI were encountered at 2,500 m, of which two were claimed shot down. *St.lt* P.A. Pokryshev force-landed in Raivola, his I-16 burned. *No Finnish losses 20 December 1939.*

F.I. Shinkarenko (4./7 IAP Commander, HSU 21.3.1940). From 1951 Shinkarenko commanded the Baltic Air Defence region, and ordered the downing of a Swedish Tp 79 (C-47) radio intelligence aircraft in June 1952. (G.F. Petrov)

Fighter pilots of 4./7 IAP, in the middle F.I. Shinkarenko, and second from right future double-HSU (10.2.1943 and 24.8.1943) P.A. Pokryshev. (G.F. Petrov)

N.D. Antonov. 7 IAP Commissar (HSU 21.3.1940). (G.F. Petrov)

21 December 1939 I-16 *tip 17* c/n 172150 (7 IAP HQ) crashed on take-off from Levashovo. The regiment's *flagshturman st.lt* A.I. Davydov was killed.

23 December 1939 at 1140 hours 13 I-16s led by *st.lt* Shinkarenko (4th Squadron) fought against several Fokker D.XXI fighters, of which seven were claimed. At Honkaniemi-Pilppula two I-16 were shot down in combat: *lt* V.V. Zolotarev (I-16 *tip 10* c/n 1021779), and *lt* B.A. Grigoryev (unsuccessful parachute jump from I-16 *tip 5* c/n 5210836) were killed. Kers T. Kaarma, LLv 24 was wounded and force-landed with Fokker D.XXI (FR-111) in the forest at Lyykylä.

From 25 December 1939 to 20 January 1940 3rd Squadron (*kapitan* S.N. Polyakov) converted from I-15bis to I-153.

25 December 1939 future VVS Commander and double-HSU *lt* P.S. Kutakhov (3rd Squadron, I-15bis c/n 5101) was shot down by his own side's I-16 (piloted by *lt* A.N. Storozhakov, 26 IAP; HSU posthumously 10 February 1942).

Starting from 30 December 1939 1st and 4th Squadrons moved to Rieskjärvi ice base, and 15 January 1940 the other two Squadrons moved to Vammeljärvi (both locations in occupied Finnish territory).

6 January 1940 *ml.lt* B.S. Kul'batskiy (4th Squadron, I-16 *tip 5* c/n 5210823) did not return from ground attack at Kuolemajärvi. The I-16 was shot down by anti-aircraft machine-gun (*1. Ilmatorjuntakonekiväärikomppania*) at Närjänjärvi (NW Kuolemajärvi, southern Karelian isthmus).

6–20 January 1940 a new 2nd Squadron (with 14 I-16 M-62, commanded by *st.lt* V.D. Popov) arrived from 38 IAP. Reinforcement was also received from 68 IAP (I-16 Squadron), 25 IAP and VVS KOVO. Some I-16 *tip* 27 fighters equipped with 20 mm ShVAK-cannons were received.

12–15 January 1940 7 IAP staff, 1st, 2nd and 3rd Squadrons moved to Vammeljärvi.

Because of severe cold weather 7 IAP was forced to interrupt flight operations during several days in January 1940.

After the big SB-bomber losses on 17 January 1940 (see 31 and 54 SBAP, pages 138 and 186) the fighters of 59 IAB were ordered to protect bomber missions to the Finnish rear. On 20 January 1940 4th Squadron protected five SB groups, and 30 January 8–9 SB groups were escorted.

19 January 1940 LLv 12 attacked Kirkkojärvi ice base (where 12 I-16s were observed) after dark with nine FK biplanes (Fokker C.X), hits were scored on eight aircraft. (No fighters were based at Kirkkojärvi, only R-5 and SSS reconnaissance aircraft of 10 and 50 OAE.)

20 January 1940 three Fokker C.X bombed Suuri Särkijärvi ice base, and in the evening of 22 January 1940 Rieskjärvi ice base was bombed by three separate aircraft, damaging three or four Soviet aircraft.

The Finnish attack was in fact very efficient: 12 (!) fighters were damaged, of which three had to be sent for depot repairs, and three mechanics and one pilot were wounded. In the darkness the alerted I-15bis fighters did not find the Finnish aircraft, which were able to return to their base without losses.

One week after the surprise attack N.S. Shimanov, Military Commissar of the Northwest Front, arrived for an investigation of the matter. He found out that the fighters were parked less than 10 m from each other (to facilitate the work of the mechanics…) instead of 40–50 m as ordered, searchlight personnel were sleeping etc. The lorry drivers of the base did not bother about the blackout orders, but drove with full headlights after dark. One driver was even sentenced to 8 years in prison for breaking blackout regulations! Shimanov was also told about the obsolete and worked-out I-16 *tip* 5 versions, which were still widely used in 59 IAB.

7 IAP lost two aircraft and ten were damaged on the ground by Finnish bomber attacks in January.

1 February 1940 two Finnish fighters were claimed. *Lt* A.I. Kalinin (2nd Squadron, I-16) was shot down in air combat at Huumola. *Vänr* T. Harmaja (LLv 24, FR-115) was shot down near Viipuri. Kalinin's I-16 crashed at Kultakumpu; his personal documents were retrieved by Finnish troops.

4 February 1940 three Finnish fighters were claimed destroyed on the ground. No Finnish losses.

7 February 1940 *ml.lt* V.A. Kuzmichek (3rd Squadron) was killed when his I-153 (c/n 6718) carrying four AO-15 bombs stalled after take-off from Vammeljärvi.

8 February 40 5th Squadron (15 pilots led by *kapitan* A.Ye. Mol'bin) arrived from 18 IAP of Far East Army Corps (DVK) after departure 26 January 1940. Later also personnel of 70 IAP and 22 IAP (which had both fought at Khalhin-Gol in August 1939) arrived. *Kapitan* Mol'bin was shot down by A-A fire at Tikkola and killed on 14 February 1940, when he was escorting SB bombers. *St.lt* I.I. Geibo took over 5th Squadron, which received I-153s from 17 February 1940.

10 February 1940 SB *blue 1* (pilot *st.lt* M.F. Mazayev, 44 SBAP) force-landed at Kuolemajärvi after a direct hit by A-A fire. *Kapitan* Trusov of the same regiment landed nearby with SB *blue 10* and picked

I.I. Geibo, Commander of 5./7 IAP (HSU 28.4.1945). (G.F. Petrov)

Future double HSU (1.5.1943 and 15.8.1984), and long-time Soviet AF C-in-C (1969–1984), lt P.S. Kutakhov started his career in 3./7 IAP. His I-15bis c/n 5101 was shot down 25.12.1939 by one of his own side's I-16 in Riiska. (G.F. Petrov)

Soviet AF Commander, Chief Air Marshal Kutakhov made an official visit to Finland 30.8–3.9.1982. Finnish Defence Minister Juhani Saukkonen presented the first volume of the author's Red Stars-book series to Marshal Kutakhov 30.8.1982, General Lauri Sutela (Finnish Defence Forces C-in-C) watching at left. (SA-kuva)

7 IAP Commander Ye.G. Turenko (HSU 21.3.1940). (G.F. Petrov)

General-major P.A. Pokryshev retired in 1961, after which he was Head of Leningrad airport for some years. (G.F. Petrov)

A.F. Semenov (3./7 IAP Commander, HSU 21.3.1940) (G.F. Petrov)

up Mazayev's crew. The rescue operation was protected by 4th Squadron (commander F.I. Shinkarenko and commissar G.V. Didenko. The Golden Star was proposed to both fighter pilots, but only Shinkarenko became HSU on 21 March 1940).

13 February 1940 7 IAP was ordered by the Commander of VVS 7.A, *komkor* S.P. Denisov to escort artillery control aircraft of 1 KAO (co-located with 7 IAP at Vammeljärvi).

16 February 1940 a Finnish fighter was claimed. *No Finnish losses.*

19 February 1940 a Finnish fighter was shot down. An I-16 was hit by A-A fire at Karisalmi, and disappeared at Vammelsuu. *St.politr* I.V. Molochek went missing. *Danish volunteer Løjtnant E. Frijs (LLv 24, FR-80) was shot down at Viipuri. (Frijs was possibly downed by a DB-3 MG-gunner of 1 AP VVS KBF.)*

20 February 1940 six Finnish fighters were claimed, and two fighters on the ground. *Luutn P. Berg (LLv 26) escaped by parachute from GL-280 at Utti.*

27 February 1940 a Finnish fighter was shot down. *FA-12 was shot down near Utti,* vänr *E. Malmivuo (LLv 26) was killed.*

29 February 1940 a Finnish fighter was claimed, and eight fighters destroyed on the ground. *No Finnish losses in the operational area of 7 IAP, but considerable losses in an attack on 68 IAP at Ruokolahti ice base (see 68 IAP).*

5 March 1940 16 aircraft were claimed (10 fighters and three bombers). Only one claim can be identified: kapitan N.M. Kidalinskiy forced a Finnish Fokker down on the frozen Bay of Viipuri.

Kers M. Fräntilä reached his own lines, and Finnish ground forces claimed to have destroyed his FR-76! The rather slightly damaged Fokker was in fact evacuated by Soviet troops, and displayed in the war-booty exhibition in Leningrad until the beginning of the Great Patriotic War. The MG-gunner of BL-145, *ylik* T. Hämäläinen (LLv 42) claimed an I-16, which emitted smoke and dived between Teikarsaari and Säkkijärvi.

6 March 1940 three bombers were claimed. *No Finnish losses.*

7 March 1940 eight aircraft were claimed (one fighter and seven bombers).

BL-122 (LLv 46) was shot down by fighters and BL-144 (LLv 42) was shot down by A-A artillery at the Bay of Viipuri. The only survivors were luutn *N. Hakala, the wounded pilot of BL-122 and kokelas (aspirant) K. Nykänen (navigator of BL-144, who escaped by parachute, became a POW and was repatriated after the Winter War). As young Nykänen was the only Finnish aviator captured in the final phase of the war, he was extensively questioned by several command levels up to komdiv S.P. Denisov (Commander of VVS 7.A) and komandarm Ye.S. Ptukhin (Commander of VVS SZFr)! Information on the planned allied intervention had already reached the Soviet high command, but poor Nykänen was naturally unable to give any comments whatsoever!*

8 March 1940 three bombers were claimed. *No Finnish losses.* Alik Y. Hammarén (BL-139 MG-gunner, LLv 42) claimed two "possible" I-16 at Bay of Viipuri.

9 March 1940 nine aircraft were claimed (eight fighters and one bomber). *No Finnish losses.*

10 March 1940 three I-16P were transferred to OAG in Estonia. On this day *st.lt* I.I. Geibo (C.O. 5th Squadron, I-153) shot down one Blenheim, and also a fighter was claimed by 7 IAP. *Lt* Romanov (5th Squadron, I-153) was wounded in air combat, and force-landed at Bay of Viipuri. *BL-133 (*kapt *J. Piponius, LLv 46) was shot down at Ylämaa, all crew KIA.* The MG-gunner of BL-145 (*ylik* T. Hämäläinen) claimed one I-153 at Uuras, Bay of Viipuri. GL-279 (luutn T. Ollikainen, LLv 14) crashed into the ground in Kirvu, when evading attacks by three I-16 fighters.

16 March 1940 7 IAP returned to Pushkin with six Squadrons.

20–25 March 1940 three Squadrons (*st.lt* V.D. Popov, *st.lt* I.I. Geibo and *st.politr* Isayev) were transferred to Kiev MD (KOVO). From 28 June 1940 7 IAP was relocated to Suur-Merijoki (former Finnish AF base west of Viipuri), incorporating four I-153 Squadrons.

7 IAP locations 5 January 1940

Base	Pilots	I-16	I-16P	I-15
Rieskjärvi	33	12+2	16	1
Kanneljärvi	2	-	-	2
Levashovo	-	-	1+1	-
Pushkino	23	-	1	-
Total	58	12+2	18+1	3

7 IAP performed 4,885 missions (flight time 5 033 hours), and claimed 68 air victories (43 fighters, 21 bombers and 4 reconnaissance aircraft), additionally 14 aircraft were claimed destroyed on the ground.

7 IAP mission summary:

	Ground attack	Ground force protection	SB escort	Enemy AF bases	Air combat	Enemy A-A positions	Recon-naissance	Missions interrupted	Total
12.1939	199	177	314	10	35	122	110	39	967
1.1940	281	57	211	12	9		20		590
2.1940	453	358	759	77	17	16	232	13	1,912
3.1940	160	732	153	52	86	16	201		1,407
Total	1,093	1,324	1,437	151	147	154	563	52	4,885

The combat intensity in the last weeks of the Winter War can be clearly seen.

7 IAP was awarded Red Banner Order on 11 April 1940. Six pilots, regiment C.O. *major* Ye.G. Turenko, regiment commissar *voyenkom* N.D. Antonov, *st.lt* F.I. Shinkarenko (C.O. 4th Squadron), *kapitan* A.F. Semenov, *st.lt* V.M. Kurochkin and *st.lt* G.P. Larionov (4th Squadron), were appointed HSUs on 21 March 1940.

7 IAP Strength and locations:

Date	Base	Subordination	Base unit	Equipment
1.11.39	Pushkin	59 IAB	1 RAB, 150 AB	3 I-16, 18 I-16P, 40 I-15bis
1.12.39	Levashevo	59 IAB	1 RAB, 150 AB	3 I-16, 18 I-16P, 40 I-15bis
1.1.40	Rieskjärvi	59 IAB	150 AB	3 I-16, 17 I-16P, 38 I-15bis
1.2.40	Rieskjärvi	59 IAB	150 AB	2 I-16, 16 I-16P, 36 I-15bis, 17 I-153
1.3.40	Rieskjärvi	59 IAB	150 AB	2 I-16, 15 I-16P, 33 I-15bis, 16 I-153
1.4.40	Pushkin	59 IAB	1 RAB, 150 AB	2 I-16, 15 I-16P, 32 I-15bis, 15 I-153

7 IAP Fighter pilots:
– 23 February 1940: 84 pilots
– 3 March 1940: 69 pilots

Night fighter capable pilots in 59 IAB 26 January 1940

Unit	Squadron	Commander	Pilots
59 IAB	HQ	*Polkovnik* Yerlykin	3
7 IAP	HQ	*Major* Turenko	4
	1. Squadron	*Kapitan* Sotnikov	2
	3. Squadron	*Kapitan* Polyakov	4
	4. Squadron	*St.lt* Shinkarenko	4
	Total		14
25 IAP	Total		10
59 IAB	Total		26

7 IAP command

Commander	*major* Ye.G. Turenko (1905–1963). Performed 35 combat missions in Winter War. HSU 21.3.40. Later C.O. of Borisoglebsk Military Aviation School.
Assistant commander	*major* I.S. Khotelev, Red Banner order 7 April 1940.
Military commissar	*bat.komiss* N.D. Antonov (1909–1986). HSU 21.3.40. Personally led strafing of Vilajoki. In GPW C.O. of 7 IAK, later 2 GIAK.
Chief of Staff	*major* A.F. Kopytin

Squadron C.O. and commissars
1st   *kapitan* S.L. Sotnikov
2nd (I-15bis Squadron, 25 December 39 to 68 IAP)
        kapitan Postaush
2nd (new, 14 January 1940 from 38 IAP)
        st.lt V.D. Popov
        st.politr I.V. Molochek (from 38 IAP, KIA 19.2.40)
3rd (I-15bis Squadron, from 20 January 1940 I-153)
        kapitan S.N. Polyakov (1908–1941). Participated in Spanish Civil War. In GPW commanded 174 ShAP on Karelian isthmus. KIA 23.12.1941, HSU 10.2.1943.
        st.politr L.S. Chapchalov
4th (I-16)   *st.lt* F.I. Shinkarenko (1913–1994). Performed 46 combat missions, 3 victory claims in Winter War. HSU 21.3.1940. In GPW commanded 330 IAD. Com-

manded 15th Air Army 1968–1973.) After WW II commanded the Baltic Air Defence Area, and in June 1952 gave the order to shoot down a Swedish Tp 47 (C-47) ELINT-aircraft in the Baltic Sea.
st.politr G.V. Didenko

5th *kapitan* A.Ye. Mol'bin (from 18 IAP; KIA 14 February 40)
st.lt I.I. Gejbo (1910–1992). HSU 28 April 1945 as Commander of 6 GIAD.
st.politr K.S. Sorokin

In GPW 7 IAP was elevated to Guards status, becoming 14 GvIAP on 7 March 194

7 IAP victories (sources: Russian and Finnish Military archives; RGVA and Kansallisarkisto respectively)

Date, time, location	Fighter/ bomber/ reconnaissance ac/ unknown	Victors [Squadron]	Finnish information
1.12.39 1230–1315 Muolaanjärvi	-/-/1/-	Shinkarenko, Didenko, Grigoryev [4]	BU-64 force-landed, *ylik* T. Uuttu (LLv 26) OK.
20.12.39 1626 Karpela	3 FR/-/-/-	Didenko, Pokryshev, Mihajlyuk, Zobov, Zolotaryev [4]	No losses.
20.12.39 1552 Kämärä-Karpela	1 FR/-/-/-	Mironov [2]	No losses.
23.12.39 1140 Kaukjärvi-Uusikirkko; Lyykylä; Perkjärvi	7 FR/1 /-/-	Shinkarenko, Didenko, Bulayev, Mihajlyuk, Pokryshev, Larionov, Grigoryev [4]	FK-96 force-landed, *luutn* I. Salo OK, *kers* E. Saloranta KIA (LLv 12). FK-80 force-landed, *luutn* H. Kalaja WIA, *vänr* N. Lintunen KIA (LLv 10). FR-111 force-landed, *kers* T. Kaarma WIA (LLv 24).
24.12.39 Pienpero	-/-/1/-	Semenov	No losses.
1.2.40 Viipuri	2/-/-/-	Molotshek, Antonov [2]	FR-115 shot down, *vänr* T. Harmaja KIA (LLv 24).
4.2.40	3 (on ground)/-/-/-	Didenko, Mihajlyuk, Larionov, Pokryshev, Kulikov [4]	No losses.
16.2.40	1/-/-/-	Mihajlyuk, Zobov	No losses.
19.2.40 Viipuri	1/-/-/-	Shtanukhin, Kurotshkin	No losses.
20.2.40 Utti	4/-/-/-	Baranov (2), Ivanov (1), Masnikov, Dubovik (1)	GL-280 shot down, *luutn* P.Berg bailed out (LLv 26).
20.2.40	2 (on ground)/-/-/-	Ivanov (1), Baranov(1)	No losses.
20.2.40	2/-/-/-	Kalinichenko (1), Kachnovskiy (1)	No losses.
20.2.40	1 (on ground)/-/-/-	Kalinichenko's unit: Martynov, Kashrin, Isayev, Shurdukov, Ivanov, Kurochkin, Franchuk, Istaukhin	No losses.
27.2.40 Utti	1/-/-/-	Mihajlyuk	FA-12 shot down, *vänr* E. Malmivuo KIA (LLv 26).
29.2.40	1/-/-/-	Melnikov	No losses.
29.2.40	8 (on ground)/-/-/-	Bulayev (2), Larionov (2), Mihajlyuk (2), Borisov (1), Serezhenko (1)	No losses.
5.3.40 0717–0807 Nisalahti	-/-/1 TU/-	Seleznev, Karpov [1]	No losses.

Date/Time/Place	Claims	Pilots	Losses
5.3.40 0814–0926 Nuijamaa-Penttilä	1 GL/-/-/-	Bulayev, Melnik, Muravyev [4]	No losses.
5.3.40 1005–1105 Perimänki (?); Hypäälä (?)	2 GL/-/-/-	Malikov, Sayenko [2]	No losses.
5.3.40 1005–1105	-/-/1/-	Ketov, Semenishin, Vavilov [1]	No losses.
5.3.40 0858–1016 Teikarinsaari; Peltola	-/1 BL/-/1 DC	Kozlov, Sitnikov [2]	No losses.
5.3.40 1402–1507 Mitala; Lappeenranta	2/-/-/-	Bulayev, Zuyev, Muravyev [4]	No losses.
5.3.40 1401–1606	3 BU/-/-/-	Semenov, Myasnikov, Nikitin [3]	No losses.
5.3.40 1740–1900 Vilajoki; Karjannniemi	2 FR/-/-/-	Kidalinskiyj, Serezhenko [4]	FR-76 force-landed on the ice, *kers* M. Fräntilä reached own lines (LLv 24).
5.3.40 1630–1732 N Simola	-/1 BL/-/-	Isayev [1]	No losses.
5.3.40 1300–1415 Vanhakylä	-/1/-/-	Sayenko [2]	No losses.
6.3.40	-/2/-/-	Gejbo, Rybalov [5]	No losses.
6.3.40	-/1/-/-	Tikhomirov [5]	No losses.
7.3.40 Koivisto	-/1/-/-	Moshin (gunner), Sayenko, Malyshev [2]	BL-144 shot down, *kers* T. Hyytiäinen and *kers* E. Turunen KIA, *vänr* K. Nykänen bailed out, became POW (LLv 42).
7.3.40 Vilaniemi	-/1/-/-	Skryabin [2]	BL-122 shot down, *luutn* N. Hakala bailed out, *luutn* P. Salokoski and *kers* A. Pakkala KIA.
7.3.40	1/-/-/-	Kuzmenko [5]	No losses.
7.3.40	-/1/-/-	Golubev, Tikhomirov [5]	No losses.
7.3.40	-/1/-/-	Kainov, Balashov [5]	No losses.
7.3.40	-/1/-/-	Ketov, Semenikhin, Vavilov [1]	No losses.
7.3.40	-/1/-/-	Kainov, Rybalov [5]	No losses.
7.3.40	-/1/-/-	Shinkarenko [4]	No losses.
8.3.40	-/1/-/-	Antonov, Khotelev, Pavlov	No losses.
8.3.40	-/2/-/-	Glotov, Ivanov [3]	No losses.
8.3.40	-/1/-/-	Kainov, Romanov, Petrov [5]	No losses.
9.3.40	2/-/-/-	Kurochkin, Franchuk [1]	No losses.
9.3.40	-/1/-/-	Kidalinskiy [4]	No losses.
9.3.40	2/-/-/-	Zhujkov [3]	No losses.
9.3.40	1/-/-/-	Doletskiy [3]	No losses.
9.3.40	1/-/-/-	Karenukhin [3]	No losses.
9.3.40	1/-/-/-	Globov, Ivanov [3]	No losses.
9.3.40	1/-/-/-	Nikitin ("not confirmed")	No losses.
10.3.40 Ylämaa	-/1/-/-	Gejbo [5]	BL-133 shot down, *kapt* J. Piponius, *luutn* A. Sopenlehto and *kers* E. Tani KIA (LLv 46).
10.3.40	1/-/-/-	Marchenko [5]	No losses.
Total	42/20/4/1		

Gejbo and Kidalinskiy were credited with 2 personal victories each.

7th Light Ground Attack Aviation Regiment (7 LShAP)

Autumn 1939 7 LShAP was based in Kiev, and equipped with SSS light ground attack aircraft.

7 LShAP operated primarily as a night bomber unit with SSS aircraft (ground-attack version of R-5, with more powerful engine and armament), harassing Finnish ground forces, troop concentrations and preventing railway and truck transport at night.

Subordination
51 AB, VVS KOVO
1 LBAB, VVS 7.A (from 13 February 1940)

Combat Chronicle
31 December 1939 7 LShAP was ordered to relocate to the front. Its own flying personnel (35 aviators) were reinforced by 18 aviators from co-located 3 LShAP.

26 January 1940 7 LShAP started the slow ferry flight. At arrival at Halolanjärvi (in occupied Karelian Isthmus) on 13 February 1940 had 32 (50?) SSS. 7 LShAP was attached to 1 LBAB, VVS 7.A. Combat missions were initiated the same day.

20 February 1940 an SSS returned with 168 A-A hits. *st.lt* I.V. Malyi died of wounds 12 April 1940.

10 March 1940 SSS c/n 1260 ("46") was hit by A-A artillery at 2,000 hours. *St.lt* K.F. Kopyl and *st.lt* G.T. Turukin were killed.

3 March 1940 12 SSS-aircraft were transferred to VVS 8.A in Lodejnoye Pole.

7 LShAP performed 807 combat missions (786 night missions over 18 nights, flight time 1,090 h 22 min; and 21 daytime missions over 2 days, flight time 17 h 50 min). 17,609 bombs (of which almost 15,000 were small 8 and 10 kg splinter bombs) were dropped.

Up to 20 February 1940 main operation area was Koivisto-Kaislahti-Viipuri-Kaijala; after 20 February 1940 Viipuri-Lappeenranta-Hamina area.

7 LShAP command

Commander	*polkovnik* A.A. Kiselev
Military commissar	*bat.komiss* I.S. Kravtsov
Chief of Staff	*major* I.I. Sidorov

Officers and pilots of 7 LShAP. (G.F. Petrov)

Squadron C.O.
1st   *major* M.Ye. Ageyev
2nd   *major* A.A. Lozhechnikov
3rd   *kapitan* Ye.I. Sviridov
4th   *kapitan* N.S. Kukushka
5th   *major* A.M. Shust

Bombs are attached to a R-5SSS of 7 LShAP. (G.F. Petrov)

9th Light Bomber Aviation Regiment (9 LBAP)

According to the questioning of POW *lt* Kashelenko-Belmans (4 LBAP) 9 LBAP arrived from VVS KhVO to VVS 9.A in Poduzhemye.

9 LBAP command
  Commander   *major* Mironenko
  Military commissar *bat.komiss* Nemtinov
  Chief of Staff   *major* Voronov

9th Ground Attack Aviation Regiment (9 ShAP), also 9th Light Ground Attack Aviation Regiment (9 LShAP)

Autumn 1939 9 ShAP was based in Grivochki (Dno, Leningrad MD). From July to October 1939 9 ShAP converted from SSS reconnaissance aircraft to I-15bis fighters. Some SSS aircraft were transferred to 5 KAO, which was attached to VVS 8.A in December 1939. Late in November 1939 1st Squadron (14 I-15bis) was located in Krestsy, 2nd Squadron (15 I-15bis) in Krechevitsy (departed 14 December 1939 to VVS 14.A), 3rd Squadron (13 I-15bis) in Yedrovo (moved later to Pushkin) and 4th Squadron (21 I-15bis) in Grivochki.

  Subordination
    VVS LVO
    7 IAP, VVS 7.A (1st Squadron)

I-15bis (9 LShAP, c/n 4649) crashed on landing in Gribochki 9.1.1940. lt A.I. Torev was unhurt. (RGVA)

VVS 13.A (4ᵗʰ Squadron)
VVS SZFr (3ʳᵈ Squadron)

Combat Chronicle

In early January 1940 1ˢᵗ Squadron was attached to 7 IAP at Vammeljärvi (in occupied territory), tasked to protect 7ᵗʰ Army Command Post. 4ᵗʰ Squadron was attached to VVS 13.A in eastern Karelian Isthmus, while Pushkin-based 3ʳᵈ Squadron was attached to VVS SZFr.

16 February 1940 *ml.lt* N.I. Yerokhin (1ˢᵗ Squadron) did not return with I-15bis c/n 5562.

Also in February 1940 Murov (rank and initials unknown, also of 1ˢᵗ Squadron) disappeared with I-15bis c/n 4693.

9 ShAP command

Commander	*polkovnik* Filin
Military commissar	*bat.komiss* Nemtinov
Chief of Staff	*polkovnik* Vorobyev

Squadron C.O.
1ˢᵗ *kapitan* V.I. Belousov (1908–1981). Performed 30 combat missions, strafed Leipäsuo and Kämärä in the Winter War. In GPW commanded 235 ShAP and 65 ShAP/17 GShAP in East Karelia.
3ʳᵈ *major* Rutman
kapitan V.I. Belousov was awarded HSU 21 March 1940.

In August 1940 the regiment number was changed to 65 ShAP, which became 17 GvShAP on 7 March 1942.

The Commander of 17 GvShAP podpolkovnik V.I. Belousov is attaching a decoration to the uniform of an unidentified Senior Lieutenant in Eastern Karelia, spring 1942. In the rear Hurricanes can be seen. (G.F. Petrov)

9th Fast Bomber Aviation Regiment (9 SBAP)

Autumn 1939 9 SAP (subordinated to 29 AB) was based in Yedrovo (Leningrad MD), equipped with both I-15bis fighters and TB-3 heavy bombers. In September 1939 the fighter Squadron was transferred to 72 SAP in Karelian ASSR, after which the regiment (now named 9 SBAP) got the task to set up five own SB squadrons, and also one SB squadron each both for 5 SAP in Murmansk and for 72 SAP.

Subordination
29 AB, VVS LVO
VVS 9.A (from mid-December 1939)

Combat Chronicle

21 October 1939 almost 100 personnel moved to Besovets, Karelia, to set up 3rd Squadron of 72 SAP of VVS 8.A. 13 December 1939 8 SB bombers intended for this Squadron were flown to Besovets and Lodejnoye pole by pilots of 9 SBAP. Some ferry pilots moved on further north, and formed a Detached Reconnaissance Squadron (ORAE) directly attached to VVS 9.A. 9 SBAP apparently formed the reserve of the C.O. of VVS 9.A.

M.V. Kotel'nikov, Commander of 9. Army ORAE. (G.F. Petrov)

13 December 1939 3rd Squadron (9 SB, commanded by *kapitan* N.I. Ulasevich) moved to Uhtua, and was attached to 41 SBAP of VVS 9.A, which had suffered heavy losses during its first operations on the Karelian Isthmus, in VVS 7.A.

4 January 1940 SB (possibly c/n 13/217, piloted by *st.lt* I.S. Tsiganov) force-landed on own territory after A-A hits. The gunner was killed.

12 January 1940 SB c/n 13/139 was destroyed in an unsuccessful take-off from a force-landing site on the ice of Sredneye Kuito (Keski-Kuittijärvi). Injured MG-gunner *starshina* A.A. Vinogradov perished 15 January 1940.

In mid-January 9 SBAP moved from Uhtua to Sholopovo ice base, while 9 SBAP HQ was located in Kem'.

29 January 1940 the SB of C.O. of the detached reconnaissance squadron (ORAE; also referred to as 1./9 SBAP) *kapitan* S.I. Gorodetskiy (who was killed at his capture) was shot down at Kaitansalmi, Sotkamo by 20 mm A-A gun fire. *shturman kapitan* I.A. Kolomiyets and MG-gunner *starshina* A.S. Malyshev were taken prisoner.

In early February 1940 the personnel of 3rd Squadron were returned to 29 TBAB "because of cowardice", and the aircraft were handed over to VVS 9.A. (See also 10 SBAB and 41 SBAP, pages 48 and 149.)

3 February 1940 SB c/n 3/228 piloted by the new C.O. 1st Squadron *kapitan* K.S. Kozhinov was destroyed in a take-off collision with SB c/n 17/227 of the same Squadron (*lt* N.N. Buistov) at Budovo near Kalinin. All crew of c/n 3/228 were killed.

10 February 1940 SB c/n 20/240 disappeared 50 km SE Voknavolok (Vuokkiniemi). The pilot's body was found 23 February 1940. (This aircraft is also entered in the loss lists of 60 SBAP.) Bombing targets of 9 SBAP included Puolanka, Nurmes, Kuusamo, Hyrynsalmi, Taivalkoski, Pisto, and Kemijärvi.

In spring 1940 9 SBAP moved back to Yedrovo, and in late summer 1940 via Riga to Panavèzys in Lithuania.

9 SBAP Strength and locations

Date	Base	Subordination	Base unit	Equipment
1.11.39	Yedrovo	29 AB	2 RAB, 13 AB	36 SB, 18 TB-3
1.12.39	Yedrovo	29 AB	2 RAB, 13 AB	48 SB, 18 TB-3
1.1.140	Yedrovo, Nurmolitsa	29 AB, VVS LVO	6 RAB, 13 AB	50 SB, 14 TB-3
1.2.40	Yedrovo, Nurmolitsa	29 AB, VVS 8.A	6 RAB, 13 AB	59 SB, 10 TB-3
1.3.40	Yedrovo, Nurmolitsa	29 AB, VVS 8.A	6 RAB, 13 AB	57 SB, 5 TB-3
1.4.40	Yedrovo	29 AB	6 RAB, 13 AB	59 SB

9 SBAP command

Commander — *polkovnik* Val'kov
major Yegorov
Military commissar — *bat.komiss* Dorofeyev
Cheblikov
Chief of Staff — *polkovnik* Kovalevskiy
major Antonov

Squadron C.O.

1st (ORAE)	*kapitan* S.I. Gorodetskiy (KIA 29.1.40 in VVS 9.A, shot down by A-A at Kontiomäki.)
	M.V. Kotel'nikov (1904–1953). In GPW commanded 8 ShAK etc.
1st	*kapitan* K.S. Kozhinov (KIA 3.2.40, crash)
2nd	*major* Andreyev
	st.politr Zherebko
3rd	*kapitan* Ulasevich

10th Fast Bomber Aviation Regiment (10 SBAP)

Autumn 1939 10 LBAP was based in Krasnogvardejsk and Torosovo, and was converting from R-5 to new SB bombers; strength 30 November 1939 was 43 SB. Upon finishing conversion to SB (50 bombers) the name was changed to 10 SBAP. Early December 1939 10 SBAP moved to Levashovo, attached to VVS 7.A. 19 January 1940 10 SBAP was transferred to VVS 13.A.

Subordination
   68 LBAB, VVS LVO
   68 LBAB, VVS 7.A
   68 LBAB, VVS 13.A (from 19 January 1940)

10 SBAP Strength and location

Date	Base	Subordination	Base unit	Equipment
1.11.39	Krasnogvardeisk	68 AB, VVS LVO	1 RAB, 123 AB	38 SB
1.12.39	Krasnogvardeisk	68 AB, VVS 7.A	1 RAB, 123 AB	48 SB
1.1.40	Krasnogvardeisk	68 AB, VVS 7.A	1 RAB, 123 AB	52 SB
1.2.40	Levashevo	68 AB, VVS 13.A	1 RAB, 123 AB	57 SB
1.3.40	Levashevo	68 AB, VVS 13.A	1 RAB, 123 AB	54 SB
1.4.40	Krasnogvardeisk	68 AB, VVS LVO	1 RAB, 123 AB	54 SB

Combat Chronicle

Early December 1939 nine U-2 liaison aircraft with personnel were dispatched from 10 SBAP in Krasnogvardejsk to Poduzhemye (VVS 9.A), and formed 33 Otryad Svyazi.

18 December 1939 10 SBAP performed its first combat missions with nine SB, of which three bombers were damaged in force-landings on return to their home base. These aircraft were still being repaired on 13 March 1940.

21 December 1939 SB c/n 6/229 *red 5* of 1st Squadron exploded on take-off from Krasnogvardejsk.

25 December 1939 SB c/n 16/223 *red 4* was shot down by A-A artillery at Kipinola, Kuolemajärvi.

18–28 January 1940 10 SBAP performed 224 missions bombing the Mannerheim Line between Kämärä and Taipale, and 19 mission bombing railway targets.

19 January 1940 10 SBAP aircraft attacked enemy infantry soldiers with machine-gun fire.

11 February 1940 A-A artillery shot down SB c/n 14/228, which force-landed near the front line at Punnus, the crew reached their own lines. This was apparently c/n 4/228, which was later repaired.

15 February 1940 one a/c was hit in air combat at Variksenmäki, and force-landed at Vuotjärvi. *This SB was possibly shot down by* luutn *T. Huhanantti in FR-94.*

17 February 1940 A-A artillery downed one SB at Kuusa, Muolaa

Possibly 1 March 1940 A-A artillery downed one SB at Rautsuo

10 SBAP command

Commander	*polkovnik* G.I. Shumilov
	polkovnik Shornikov
	polkovnik Nichiporenko
Military commissar	*bat.komiss* Manukhin
Chief of Staff	*major* Panov

Squadron C.O.

1st	*kapitan* Shchukin
3rd	*kapitan* L.V. Mikhailov

10 SBAP was awarded Red Banner Order 11 April 1940.

In GPW 10 SBAP was elevated to Guards status 3 September 1943 and named 124 GvBAP.

11th Light Bomber Aviation Regiment (11 LBAP)

Autumn 1939 11 LBAP was based in Konotop (Kiev MD).

Subordination
  62 AB, VVS KOVO
  VVS 8.A (from 1 March 1940)

Combat Chronicle
11 LBAP arrived 1 March 1940 from Konotop to Iso-Pyhäjärvi ice base. The regiment's 63 R-Z aircraft performed 645 missions north of Ladoga "without observing enemy actions".

The only known female Soviet aviator in the Winter War, lt Yekaterina I. Zelenko fought in 11 LBAP. She was killed in a taran in the Great Patriotic War 12 September 1941 (then in 135 BBAP with Su-2), and posthumously became HSU 5 May 1990. Zelenko made an unsuccessful take-off with R-Z (c/n 1643) from Niemisenkylä 2 March 1940.

St.lt Yekaterina Zelenko (3rd Squadron/11 LBAP) destroyed a Finnish artillery position with her R-Z aircraft, and was decorated with the Red Banner-order in 1940. (G.F. Petrov)

Left: Unidentified pilot of a I-15bis of 11 LBAP. (G.F. Petrov)

11 LBAP command
  Commander   polkovnik Gubanov
  Military Commissar   bat.komiss Merkulov
  Chief of Staff   major Kovtunov

13th Fast Bomber Aviation Regiment (13 SBAP)

Autumn 1939 13 SBAP was based in Seshchinskaya (Byelorussian MD).

Subordination
  16 SBAB, VVS BOVO (until November 1939)
  16 SBAB, VVS 7.A (until 21 December 1939)
  VVS 8.A (from 21 December 1939)
  13 SBAB, VVS 8.A (1–7 January 1940)
  14 AB, VVS 8.A

Combat Chronicle
13 September 1939 13 SBAP was transferred to the Polish front. In November 1939 13 SBAP moved via Bobrujsk in Byelorussia to Chernevo (26 km SE Gdov), where 53 SB bombers arrived 30 November 1939 (subordinated to 16 SBAB, VVS 7.A).

The first war mission was only performed 19 December 1939 when 36 bombers attacked several targets on the Karelian Isthmus (i.e. Säiniö). Five bombers did not return after air combat, and a sixth returned badly damaged. Twelve aviators were killed. Note: one of the missing bombers is also listed as lost by 54 SBAP! *LeR 2 reported 19 December 1939 ten bombers "certainly" shot down on Karelian Isthmus, in addition to four possible claims. Note: in addition to the above mentioned losses of 13 SBAP, 44 SBAP lost nine and 50 SBAP two SB bombers on the Isthmus 19 December 1939.*

After two days 13 SBAP was unexpectedly ordered by 16 SBAB to immediately relocate from Chernevo to Besovets, subordinated to VVS 8.A. When the order was received 13 SBAP was preparing take-off for a bombing mission, so the new order could only be partly fulfilled. The bombers ordered to transfer had to be stripped of already loaded bombs etc. The ferry flight was made without thorough preparations, and ended tragically – two bombers (c/n 3/205 and 4/205) got lost in a snow storm, and eight aviators were killed. In addition several bombers were damaged in forced landings.

25 December 1939 SB c/n 5/115 of 3rd Squadron commander was shot down in air combat at Värtsilä; shturman st.lt A.M. Sukhin was taken prisoner. *Luutn J. Karhunen (FR-112) and kers T. Vuorimaa (FR-93) claimed two SB bombers each in the Korpijärvi-Korpiselkä-Ägläjärvi area.*

7 January 1940 the bomber regiment's subordination to 13 SBAB ended.

S.F. Ushakov, 13 SBAP Commander. (G.F. Petrov)

109

Orders are read to aviators of 13 SBAP. (G.F. Petrov)

An SB of 13 SBAP is warmed up by mechanic Morozov. (G.F. Petrov)

16 January 1940 eight SB bombers were attacked by one Fokker at Suistamo, but the MG-gunners fended off all attacks. Ylik *P. Tilli (FR-103)* claimed one SB over Ladoga.

17 January 1940 one SB did not return from a supply-dropping mission (apparently forced-landed successfully; the crew returned to Peski 22 January 1940). At least three other SBs were damaged by ground fire.

19 January 1940 one SB was shot down by ground fire, pilot *st.lt* Yakovlev returned to Peski after three days.

20 January 1940 SB c/n 11/115 crashed on a ferry flight due to pilot error by *lt* S.K. Snitko. *Shturman lt* I.G. Danilin was killed.

22 January 1940 one SB got 200 hits from ground fire, but was able to return to its base.

1 February 1940 part of the regiment moved to Shamozero, another part to Suojärvi ice base.

3 February 1940 one SB got 80 hits from own AO 2.5 bombs, pilot Bushnev force-landed at Säämäjärvi.

16 February 1940 one SB (c/n 3/218) went missing on the return leg, and was later found at Yalguba, 13 km NE Peski. Pilot and *shturman* were killed, the gunner was found alive. Another SB (piloted by *lt* I.I. Orlenko) forced-landed successfully 42 km SW Petrozavodsk, after a bombing mission to Jännejärvi.

18 February 1940 MG-gunner I.P. Borisov was killed by his own AO 2.5 bombs, which exploded under the aircraft immediately after dropping at Pojosvaara.

19 February 1940 navigator I.M. Moiseyev was killed by an A-A hit on a combat mission.

5 March 1940 over-sensitive AO-bombs again caused the death of an aviator of 13 SBAP: the MG-gunner of SB c/n 20/122 *starshina* I.I. Borisov was killed when bombing Samonjärvi (Säämäjärvi?).

7 March 1940 an SP liaison aircraft (modified U-2, civil registration L-2624) departed from Solomanni ice base to assist a forced-landed bomber. After loss of orientation the SP was shot down by ground fire at Pitkäranta, Aittojoki (near Vegarusjärvi). The civil pilot Moiseyenko was mortally wounded, military technicians A.N. Zakharov and I.A. Varivoda were taken prisoner.

The civil registered SP (SSSR-L2624) shot down at Pitkäranta, Aittojoki is apparently depicted in this photo. A red star is crudely painted over the civil registration. (SA-kuva)

13 SBAP Strength and locations

Date	Base	Subordination	Base unit	Equipment
1.11.39	Bobrujsk, BFr	16 AB, VVS BFr	9 RAB, 130 AB	66 SB
1.12.39	Bobrujsk, BOVO	16 AB, VVS BOVO	9 RAB, 130 AB	52 SB
1.1.40	Besovets, SZFr	13 AB, VVS 8.A	6 RAB, 130 AB	23 SB
1.2.40	Peski, SZFr	14 AB, VVS 8.A	6 RAB, 130 AB	34 SB
1.3.40	Peski, SZFr	14 AB, VVS 8.A	6 RAB, 130 AB	40 SB
1.4.40	Sescha, BOVO	16 AB, VVS BOVO	16 RAB, 106 AB	41 SB, 4 TB-3

13 SBAP performed a total of 1,433 combat missions, of which 33 missions were in VVS 7.A, and 1,400 missions in VVS 8.A. The regiment lost 11 aircraft (five in air combat, four in accidents, one bomber to explosion of own bombs and two bombers did not return). In addition two bombers had to be sent for factory repair. 30 aviators were killed.

After the Winter War 13 SBAP relocated to Ros' in Belorussian MD as part of 9 SAD. The regiment partly reequipped with Ar-2 and Pe-2 dive bombers supplementing the old SB bombers.

13 SBAP command

Commander   *polkovnik* S.F. Ushakov (1903–1986). In GPW commanded 2 BAK etc.
Military commissar   *bat.komiss* Morozov
Chief of Staff   *major* Taranenko

Squadron C.O. and commissars
1st   *kapitan* Kobets
2nd   *kapitan* Ilyuhin
         st.politr V.A. Zhulayev (KIA 21.12.1939)

3rd	*kapitan* B.M. Kalmychenko (KIA 25.12.1939) Chebyshev
4th	Gavril'chenko
5th	*kapitan* Chumakov (Chugunov?)

14th Recconnaissance Aviation Regiment (14 RAP)

Autumn 1939 14 RAP was based in Krasnogvardeisk. Its Squadrons 10, 30, 31, 32 and 33 VRAE operated independently on various front sectors, equipped with SSS, R-5 and I-15bis aircraft: 31 RAE in VVS 7.A, 32 VRAE in VVS 13.A and 33 VRAE in VVS 9.A. (See entries for Squadrons mentioned.)

Commander (acting 14 January 1940)   *major* Spiridovskiy

14th Transport Aviation Regiment (14 TAP)

Autumn 1939 14 TBAP was located at Borispol, Kiev (VVS KOVO), and equipped with TB-3 heavy bombers.

Subordination
 VVS KOVO
 OAG

23 January 1940 three TB-3 bombers were transferred to OAB in Estonia from 7 TBAP.
13 March 1940 14 TAP is included in OAG inventory. Following TB-3s were included in OAG inventory in spring 1940:
- c/n 22194   No.8 ("worn out")
- c/n 22352   No.9 ("worn out")
- c/n 22335   No.10 ("worn out")
- c/n 22272   No.12
- c/n 22234   "star"

15th Fighter Aviation Regiment (15 IAP)

15 IAP was formed in June 1938 in Byelorussian MD, and was based in Ulla in autumn 1939. 15 IAP was dedicated imeni Dzerzhinskiy (the infamous founder of the Soviet secret police, ChK or Cheka). This honorary title was inherited from the predecessor Squadron 7 OIAE, which received the "Dzerzhinsky"-title earlier in 1926.

15 IAP participated in the short Polish campaign from 17 September 1939 (officially called "liberation of Western Ukraine and Western Byelorussia"). 20 September 1939 15 IAP relocated to Parubanok in the Vilnius region (which was an object of conflict between Lithuania and Poland).

Subordination
 VVS BOVO
 OAB (from 17 February 1940)

In December 1939 2nd Squadron (15 I-15bis, commanded by *kapitan* A.V. Plotnikov) was dispatched to Vayenga and attached to the Northern Fleet, becaming the first fighter unit of VVS SF. (For details, see 72 AP in VVS SF section, page 283) A new 2nd Squadron of 15 IAP was formed in January 1940 from 33 IAP (66 AB in Mogilev, VVS BOVO).

In January 1940 OAB bombers in Estonia suffered heavy losses, and 15 IAP was ordered to relocate to Klooga, where escort fighters were urgently needed. 1st and 3th Squadrons received new I-153 fighters in Leningrad 20 January-15 February 1940. The first 35 I-153 fighters received were ordinary ones (without under-wing fuel tanks). Later 24 I-153s with under-wing tanks (PB) were received, of which twelve were subsequently transferred to co-located 38 IAP, in exchange for 12 war-weary ordinary I-153s. All former I-16s of 15 IAP were meanwhile transferred to 31 IAP in February 1940.

After re-equipment 2nd and 4th Squadrons were based in Klooga (with 33 I-153 fighters, of which 12 had additional fuel tanks). 1st Squadron (15 ordinary I-153s) was based in Sinalepa, and 3rd Squad-

I-153 fighter with under-wing fuel tanks. (G.F. Petrov)

ron (15 ordinary I-153s) in Kuusiku; total strength 63 I-153. 15 IAP performed combat missions from 28 February 1940; under-wing fuel tanks enabled bomber escort to Tampere, Kouvola and Lahti.

29 February 1940 an I-153 force-landed some 80 km south of Tallinn after running out of fuel. *Lt* Kuzenkov became unconscious at 6,200 m altitude when escorting SB bombers near Riihimäki, and lost his orientation. His virtually undamaged I-153 was moved to Klooga 5 March 1940.

2 March 1940 fighters of 15 IAP were escorting bombers to Tampere, when a number of Fokker D.XXI attacked. *Bat.komiss* Leshchenko was attacked by one Fokker. After dropping his fuel tanks he counter-attacked. The Fokker made a steep dive, after which Leshchenko rejoined the returning bomber formation, but was unable to see the ultimate fate of the Fokker. *Kers L. Aaltonen (LLv 26, FA-4) claimed one I-153 near Lahti.*

11 March 1940 *st.lt* S.F. Senkevich (C.O. 2nd Squadron) claimed a "Spitfire" 20 km south of Lahti, when escorting three bomber Squadrons (27 SB bombers; also DB-3s of 7 DBAP are mentioned), which attacked a railway bridge between Riihimäki and Lahti. After bombs were dropped from 2,000 m at 1255 (Moscow time) three "Spitfires" were observed. Senkevich attacked the left-most "Spitfire", opening fire from 200 m distance, and ceasing fire at 80 m. He followed his prey down to 300 m, after which "the aircraft crashed into the ground, but did not explode". His wingman *st.lt* S.V. Vasin attacked another "Spitfire", which evaded the attack. Flight leader Dmitriyev observed two "Spitfires", and ordered his flight to drop their under-wing fuel tanks, and attacked from 400 m distance. He also saw a "Spitfire" falling helplessly to the ground, after which he chased the third "Spitfire" away from Vasin's tail.

When another fighter group of 15 IAP escorted a DB-3 regiment to Kouvola later the same day, at 1445 hours two "Spitfires" attempted to attack the left-most and right-most flights of the last Squadron. The "Spitfires" were chased away by *bat.komiss* Leshchenko and Ovechkin. *A flight of three Morane 406 fighters of Osasto Siren (LLv 28) took off from Pyhänniemi, Hollola to intercept attacking bombers. Ilmavoimat did not lose any fighters on 11 March 1940.*

12 March 1940 *major* V.L. Bobrik (15 IAP commander) and *kapitan* I.N. Sharov were searching for two pilots of 38 IAP, missing since the day before. The search patrol landed on the frozen Gulf of Finland at 1705 hours, and picked up the missing pilots: *lt* Dobrov (who force-landed some 20 km south of Ingå with his

An unidentified fighter pilot at his I-153 aircraft. Note his thick fur boots. (G.F. Petrov)

I-153 after engine malfunction), and *lt* Romashkov (who landed next to Dobrov, in order to rescue him in his I-153, but was badly injured in a ground loop on the ice, and lost consciousness).

According to 15 IAP War Diary Dobrov towed the injured Romashkov lying on a parachute towards Estonia. After walking some 18–20 km (!) the open sea was reached, and the unfortunate aviators were forced to halt, and spend the night on the ice. Next day *major* Bobrik took the wounded *lt* Romashkov as a passenger in his I-153 (c/n 7172). Despite a collision with an ice block on take-off, he got airborne and landed safely. *Kapitan* Sharov took Dobrov on board, while *lt* M.V. Kuznetsov (4th Squadron; in GPW commanded 814 IAP, double-HSU 8 September 1943 and 27 June 1945) protected the rescue operation, and prevented a Finnish patrol from evacuating the crash-landed I-153.

15 IAP performed 514 combat missions (of which 346 were protecting take-off and landings of OAG bombers; 32 bomber escort missions by I-153PB fighters (with auxiliary fuel tanks), and 50 escort missions by ordinary I-153s, 34 independent strafing missions against railway targets (in particular the railway bridge at Koski, against which 30 FAB-50 and 30 AO-25 bombs were dropped – with poor results), 18 strafing missions against Turku airport, 26 railway and weather reconnaissance missions, and finally 12 missions searching for and rescuing missing aviators. 15 IAP participated in four air combats, and claimed one enemy fighter. Total flight time 433 h 30 min. 15 IAP suffered no personnel losses, but lost two I-153 fighters.

The HSU award was proposed to *major* V.L. Bobrik and *kapitan* I.N. Sharov, but the proposals were rejected.

15 IAP command

Commander	*major* V.L. Bobrik
Military commissar	*bat.komiss* P.S. Leshchenko
Chief of Staff	*kapitan* M.A. Lovkov

Squadron C.O. and commissars
1st	*kapitan* I.A. Dolzhenko
	bat.komiss Kiselev
2nd	*st.lt* S.F. Senkevich
Unknown	*kapitan* V.V. Andreyev
Unknown	*kapitan* A.T. Vasilyev
	kapitan S.T. Rozhkov

16th Fighter Aviation Regiment (16 IAP)

Autumn 1939 16 IAP was based in Lyubertsy (Moscow MD).

Subordination
VVS MVO

In January 1940 three Squadrons were dispatched to the Finnish front, for formation of new 146 and 148 IAP:
- 3rd Squadron (I-15), C.O. *major* S.S. Safiulin, and
- 4th Squadron (I-15), C.O. *kapitan* G.I. Brantsev, to 148 IAP.
- 15 pilots from various Squadrons were attached to 146 IAP.

16 IAP Command

Commander	*major* F.M. Prutskov

16th Fast Bomber Aviation Regiment (16 SBAP)

Autumn 1939 16 SBAP was based in Rzhev (Kalinin MD).

Subordination
VVS KalVO
10 SBAB, VVS 9.A (from 1 February 1940)

Combat Chronicle

16 SBAP arrived 23 January 1940 from Rzhev to Uhtua, and was at first subordinated directly to VVS 9.A, but after some days to 10 SBAB (arrived from VVS KOVO). According to orders given only experienced crews were to be chosen for transfer to the North, but of 52 chosen crews only 38 fulfilled the requirements. 12 crews had not attended bomber training courses: the pilots had not mastered the SB bomber, the navigators had never dropped bombs, and the MG-gunners had not mastered the aircraft guns.

28 January 1940 50 bombers had arrived in Uhtua, with another 2 aircraft arriving later. Strength 1 February 1940 was 52 SB, and 1 March 1940 55 SB bombers.

7 February 1940 1st and 3rd Squadrons of 16 SBAP attacked Kajaani at 15 October 1517 hours with 19 SB bombers. Altogether 16 FAB-250 and 82 FAB-100 explosive bombs, and 38 ZAB-50 and 28 ZAB-1e incendiary bombs from 2,000–3,200 m altitude. According to the daily report of VVS 9.A: "The city and railway station are burning". (See 10 SBAB and 41 SBAP, pages 48 and 149)

The destroyed centre of Kajaani 7.2.1940. (Kajaani museum)

14 February 1940 four SB of 5th Squadron bombed by mistake a tent with wounded soldiers of the surrounded 54th Mountain Division, killing 26 soldiers. Squadron C.O. *kapitan* Kotkin and *shturman kapitan* Melikhin were court-martialled.

17 February 1940 18 aviators arrived in Uhtua from 57 SBAP in Nezhin (Kiev Military District).

20 February 1940 3rd Squadron attacked Vaala railway bridge with six SB bombers. Swedish volunteer *fänrik* P-J. Salwén (F 19) intercepted the bombers and scored hits on two bombers. Lt A.Ya. Avrutskiy escaped by parachute and was captured next day at Luvanjärvi, Hyrynsalmi. The damaged SB forced-landed in Chiksha. The MG-gunner of the other SB hit by Salwén died of his wounds 27 February 1940.

22 February 1940 SB (c/n 12/236) of the same Squadron was hit by A-A artillery at Rovaniemi, and crashed 20 km SW of Uhtua, all crew were killed.

16 SBAP Combat missions:

January 1940	156
February 1940	733
March 1940	275
Total	1,164

16 SBAP Mission types:

Railway stations	382
Enemy transport and artillery positions	436
Enemy bases	141
Supply of 54th Division	91

The engines of an SB bomber are warmed up before take-off. (G.F. Petrov)

Weather reconnaissance	43
Photo reconnaissance	12
Fighter leading	9
Cancelled due to weather conditions	50
Bombs dropped	419.0 t

16 SBAP command

Commander	*podpolkovnik* S.P. Andreyev (1901 –). In 1940 C.O. 40 SBAB, 23 AD.
Military commissar	*bat.komiss* Dvinskiy
Chief of Staff	*major* Teplov

Squadron C.O.
1st A.S. Protasov
3rd *st.lt* V.V. Andrianov
4th *st.lt* I.S. Zaharchenko
5th *kapitan* Kotkin

18th Fast Bomber Aviation Regiment (18 SBAP)

Autumn 1939 18 SBAP was based in Olsufyevo (Byelorussian MD).

Subordination
VVS BOVO
VVS 8.A (from 18 December 1939)
13 SBAB, VVS 8.A (from 1 January 1940)
19 LBAB, VVS 15.A (from 21 February 1940)

Combat Chronicle

18 SBAP departed 29–30 November 1939 from Bobrujsk with 54 SB. Because of bad weather 18 SBAP only arrived in Lodejnoye Pole 18 December 1939, and was attached to VVS 8.A. Four Squadrons were located at Lodejnoye pole 18–26 December 1939.

18 SBAP initial strength was 53 SBs, one dual-control USB, and one U-2 liaison aircraft. The SB bombers were of different versions: one Squadron was equipped with new 201-series SB bombers (with M-103U engines), the other Squadrons had heavily used SBs (74 200 series, powered by M-100 engines with two-blade propellers, or by M-103 engines with three-blade propellers).

The Independent Night Bomber Squadron (in December 1939 commanded by I.P. Mazuruk) was apparently loosely attached to 18 SBAP. (See 72 SAP, page 196)

19 December 1939 three SB bombers (c/n 10/86, 3/100 and 6/118) were lost to ground fire at Tolvajärvi. Two aviators (*major* A.V. Yergunov, C.O. 3rd Squadron. and *starshina* M.S. Tabakov) were taken prisoner. *major* I.D. Antoshkin returned with a badly damaged bomber (103 hits).

21 December 1939 SB c/n 16/87 of 3rd Squadron made a belly-landing on the River Olonka after A-A hits. MG-gunner *starshina* I.A. Moiseyev was killed.

18 SBAP Commander I.D. Antoshkin (HSU 20.5.1940). (G.F. Petrov)

Flying and ground crew of 18 SBAP in January 1940. (G.F. Petrov)

1 January 1940 18 SBAP was attached to the newly arrived 13 SBAB. This day two SBs were lost in air combat. A Soviet fighter of 49 IAP (*lt* I.M. Glukhov) shot down SB c/n 20/99 of 5th Squadron, all crew were killed, and Finnish Fokkers downed SB c/n 16/93 of 2nd Squadron, which belly-landed. The crew was unhurt. *Luutn J. Karhunen (FR-110) shot down one SB at River Uuksu, in addition two possible victories were reported.*

In January-February 1940 at least four bombers on supply missions to surrounded troops at Lemetti were lost to Pitkäranta A-A artillery.

5 January 1940 SB c/n 4/94 (1st Squadron) collided on take-off with TB-3 c/n 307 (3 TBAP) in Lodejnoye Pole, both aircraft were destroyed.

6 January 1940 eight SB bombers were attacked by Fokker D.XXI fighters at Läskelä. One MG-gunner was wounded in his leg, one Fokker was claimed shot down. *Luutn E. Luukkanen (FR-108) reported one SB shot down at Uomaa, no own losses.*

14 January 1940 18 SBAP relocated from Lodejnoye pole to Nurmolitsa.

17 January 1940 SB c/n 10/101 landed 12 km from the shore of Lake Ladoga on return from a supply dropping mission, the crew was able to reach their own lines. The SB was later located on the ice of the Ladoga, and sunk through the ice on 4 February 1940. Another SB was hit by ground fire.

20 January 1940 SB c/n 13/210 (pilot *st.lt* Obojshchik) was shot down in air combat at Nietjärvi 5–6 km E Pitkäranta. The crew returned two days later. *Lentom V. Pyötsiä (FR-110) claimed two SB bombers (the other was apparently from 39 SBAP) at Korpiselkä.*

6 February 1940 two SB bombers were damaged by their own AO-2.5 bombs which exploded under the aircraft fuselages immediately after being dropped from so-called "Onisko's buckets". These were a container for transporting small bombs, but turned out to be very unreliable. Several aircraft were damaged by instantaneous bomb explosions.

After establishment of 15th Army 13 SBAB (including 18 SBAP) was transferred to VVS 15.A 19 February 1940. 18 SBAP was attached to 19 LBAB two days later, strength 43 SB.

1 March 1940 two SB bombers were received from 39 SBAP.

3 March 1940 three SB took off from Nurmolitsa (two SB of 18 SBAP and one SB ex-39 SBAP?) to bomb Syskyjärvi-Loimola road, railway crossing and bridges. SB c/n 18/215 (2nd Squadron) was shot down by A-A artillery at Loimola. The crew escaped by parachute, but only *shturman ml.lt* F.Ye. Nazarov survived, and was taken prisoner.

18 SBAP initially performed mainly bombing sorties, but was gradually also requested to support encircled Soviet troops by supply dropping.

18 SBAP performed 2,936 combat missions (of which 95 were at night) 19 December 1939–13 March 1940 ; flight time 4,002 hours (of which 151 hours were at night), and dropped 964 tons of bombs.

18 March 1940 18 SBAP moved back to Olsyfiyevo, and within one month to Kutiaisi in Georgia. The regiment was soon transferred to Armenian SSR, where an exceptionally detailed Winter War chronicle was printed in 1941.

18 SBAP Missions

Target type	Number	Comments
Enemy troops	2,113	
Railway targets	126	
Cities and population centres	81	Mostly nighttime missions
Bridges	18	
Reconnaissance missions	89	
Supply dropping	367	90.0 t (85.75 t on 350 missions on behalf of 15th Army)

18 SBAP command

Commander	*major* I.D. Antoshkin (1900–1944). HSU 20.5.1940. In 1944 commanded 6 SAK.
Military commissar	*bat.komiss* N.I. Kholodovskiy
Chief of Staff	*polkovnik* Mikhailov

Squadron C.O.
2nd *kapitan* Spitsyn
    kapitan N.M. Stetsenko
    st.politr A.F. Rybkin
3rd *major* A.V. Yergunov (POW 19.12.39)
    kapitan Chernisov
    st.lt Stebunov

	st.politr Shamshin
4th	*kapitan* I.V. Matrunchik (1903–1945). HSU 20.5.1940.
	st.politr Shakhmin
5th	*kapitan* A.S. Mozgovoj
	st.politr P.M. Kochetkov (KIA 1.1.1940)
	st.politr P.N. Aleksejchik
Independent Night Bomber Squadron	
	I.P. Mazuruk
	st.lt Karilov

18 SBAP was awarded Red Banner Order 20 May 1940. Regiment commander *major* I.D. Antoshkin and Squadron C.O. *kapitan* I.V. Matrunchik were appointed HSUs the same day.

19th Fighter Aviation Regiment (19 IAP)

19 IAP was formed in Gorelovo (Leningrad MD) in spring 1938. In autumn 1939 19 IAP was responsible for the air defense of Leningrad (PVO). Strength on 30 November 1939 was 56 I-16, 2 I-16P and 2 I-153.

Subordination
54 IAB, VVS LVO
54 IAB, VVS 7.A

Combat Chronicle
In 1939 19 IAP performed field tests of new I-16s with M-63 engines.

8 September 1939 19 IAP was transferred to Skomorokhi (Kiev MD) with three I-16 M-25 Squadrons and one I-15bis Squadron (total 60 fighters).

17 September-6 October 1939 participation in "liberation of Western Ukraine" (division of Poland jointly with Germany), with 1,420 war missions performed without losses, flight time 1,091 h.

19 IAP returned to Gorelovo from Ukraine. Main task of 19 IAP in the Winter War was air defense of Leningrad.

16 December 1939 4th (I-15bis) Squadron was dispatched to VVS 9.A in northern Karelia, and was attached to 152 IAP. In 19 IAP it was re-equiped with new I-16s which arrived late December 1939.

19 December 1939 I-16 (c/n 379) was destroyed in a take-off collision with I-16 "81" of *lt* Romanovich (1./38 IAP). *Lt* Yakobin (1st Squadron) was unhurt.

24 December 1939 I-15bis "173" of 4th Squadron force-landed on the ice at Oulunjärvi. *Lt* Ya.A. Andreyev was taken prisoner.

This and opposite page left: Ya.A. Andreyev (4./19 IAP) force-landed with I-15bis tactical 173 (c/n 4616) on frozen Oulunjärvi 24.12.1939. (both SA-kuva)

118

The intact I-15bis (tactical "173") was taken into use by the Finnish Air Force coded VH-11. Photos of this fighter are well-known, but are usually published without exact captions.

7 January 1940 one aircraft did not return from Suomussalmi.

In mid-January 1940 one Squadron moved to Vitino. In February 1940 Perkjärvi ice base (in occupied Finland) was used as intermediate base, in particular when trains were attacked by cannon-equipped I-16P.

Above: V.A. Matsiyevich, 1./19 IAP (HSU10.2.1943). (G.F. Petrov)

19 IAP Strength and locations

Date	Base	Subordination	Base unit	Equipment
1.11.39	Gorelovo, LVO	54 AB, LVO	1 RAB, 114 AB	30 I-16, 15 I-16P, 30 I-15bis
1.12.39	Gorelovo, LVO	54 AB, SZFr	1 RAB, 114 AB	40 I-16, 15 I-16P, 14 I-15bis, 14 I-153
1.1.40	Gorelovo and Vitino, LVO	54 AB, SZFr	1 RAB, 114 AB	57 I-16, 3 I-16P, 3 I-15bis
1.2.40	Gorelovo and Vitino, LVO	54 AB, SZFr	1 RAB, 114 AB	49 I-16, 15 I-16P, 5 I-15bis, 3 I-153
1.3.40	Gorelovo and Vitino, LVO	54 AB, SZFr	1 RAB, 114 AB	54 I-16, 15 I-16P, 7 I-15bis, 3 I-153
1.4.40	Gorelovo, LVO	54 AB, LVO	1 RAB, 114 AB	57 I-16, 15 I-16P, 5 I-15bis, 3 I-153

19 IAP command

Commander	*major* A.V. Tretyakov (1905 –). Participated in Spanish Civil War.
Military commissar	*bat.komiss* Gogolev
	bat.komiss V.A. Naumov
Chief of Staff	*major* Mizevich
Squadron C.O.	
1st	*kapitan* N.S. Vinogradov (1913 –). Participated in Spanish Civil War, 1 victory claim. In GPW commanded 199 and 231 AD etc.
	lt V.A. Matsiyevich (1913–1981). HSU 14 February 1943.
2nd	*kapitan* F.Ye. Maksimov (1911 –). Participated in Spanish Civil War.
3rd	*st.lt* P.G. Lebedinskiy
4th	*kapitan* M.G. Sorokin

19 IAP Mission statistics

Aircraft missions				Ground attack	Ground troops protection	Bomber escort	Air combats	Leningrad air defence	Total
I-16	I-153	I-15bis	Total						
3,346	20	93	3,459	387	6	98	5	2,968	3,459

19 IAP total flight time was 4,090 h. Leningrad air defense missions included 71 nighttime missions (I-15bis, flight time 70 h 25 min). Ground attack results of 19 IAP: 61 locomotives, 32 trains, 19 tank wagons, 14 passenger wagons, 3 railway station buildings, 51 vehicles and one store house destroyed. 19 IAP claimed three air victories at Viipuri and destroyed two enemy aircraft on the ground without own losses. 19 IAP was awarded Red Banner Order 11 April 1940.

19 August 1944 19 IAP was elevated to Guards status, becoming 176 GIAP (top ace triple-HSU I.N. Kozhedub), which also fought with distinction in the Korean war. When 176 GIAP was dissolved 15 March 1960 the traditions were transferred to 234 GIAP in Kubinka. This regiment is today the official Russian Air Force "Demonstration" unit 234 TsPAT (Tsentr Pokaza Aviatsionnoi Tekhniki). 234 TsPAT (with predecessors) was generally been the first VVS-unit to convert to new jet fighters, and also hosted several foreign AF visits. It was also the first Soviet AF unit to visit western countries with 12 MiG-21FL visiting Sweden in 1967. Finland and France were visited with MiG-23MLA (with pilots from 234 GIAP and 32 GIAP, both regiments based at Kubinka) in August and September 1978 and in 1982. A MiG-29 group from 234 GIAP visited Finland in 1986 and 1989. The well-known aerobatics groups *Russkiye Vityazi* (Su-27), *Strizhi* (MiG-29) and *Nebesnye Gusary* (Su-25) were also attached to 234 TsPAT. In summer 2009 234 TsPAT relocated from Kubinka to Lipetsk.

20th Fighter Aviation Regiment (20 IAP)

Autumn 1939 20 IAP was based in Smolensk (Byelorussian MD). In December 1939 the Squadrons were transferred to the front, and were attached to various regiments.

Subordination
 18 AB, VVS BOVO
 VVS 7.A (to 7 IAP)
 VVS 9.A (to 80 SAP and 145 IAP)

2nd and 3rd Squadrons were transferred from 18 AB in Smolensk to VVS 7.A (7 IAP).

1st and 4th Squadrons (I-16) were transferred to VVS 9.A at Kairala. On arrival on 24 December 1939 1st Squadron was attached to the new 145 IAP as 3rd Squadron, while 4th Squadron was attached to 80 SAP, keeping its number unchanged.

Squadron Commanders
1st   *kapitan* P.P. Ledyayev
4th   *major* F.A. Sukhorychenko

In GPW 20 IAP was elevated to Guards status 14 April 1944 and was named 139 GvIAP.

21st Long-Range Bomber Aviation Regiment (21 DBAP)

Autumn 1939 21 DBAP was based in Monino (Moscow MD).

Subordination
 27 AB, AON-1
 27 AB, VVS LVO (from 14 November 1939)
 27 AB, VVS SZFr (from 25 January 1940)

Combat Chronicle
During the Polish campaign in September 1939 21 DBAP moved to Seshchenskoye in Byelorussia, and returned to Monino the next month.

7 November 1939 21 DBAP was ordered to move from Monino to Yedrovo near Novgorod, where 56 DB-3s landed on 16 November 1939.

On the first combat missions of 21 DBAP 21 December 1939 the DB-3 machineguns malfunctioned because of insufficient frost-resistant gun grease. The initial intention was to use ski-undercarriages on the snow-covered airfield. As all DB-3s were not equipped with retractable skies and could not keep the same speed, the formations became scattered, and the ski-idea was abandoned.

21–29 December 1939 21 DBAP relocated from Yedrovo to Pushkin SW Leningrad.

25 December 1939 of 28 bombers departed only ten bombed the target. Because of defective bomb racks 18 bombers were forced to return to their base without having dropped a total of 108 bombs.

26 December 1939 because of an mistaken take-off command DB-3s c/n 915 and 1509 collided and caught fire in Yedrovo. Two aviators were killed. DB-3 c/n 2516 was lost in a take-off accident.

St.lt S.D. Spirin (4./21 DBAP) evaded a TB-3 and crashed at take-off 2.2.1940 with DB-3 (c/n 391618, tactical 3) from Pushkin. (RGVA)

Downtown Vaasa (the author's hometown) on fire 14.1.1940. (SA-kuva)

121

29 December 1939 Vaasa was attacked. Not all 13 DB-3 reached Vaasa, some aircraft bombed Turku and even Hiitola. One DB-3 did not return, and at least three were damaged in forced landings (of which one was hit by A-A artillery at Loviisa).

31 December 1939 Vaasa was attacked again by 25 DB-3s of 21 DBAP, and 8 DB-3s of 12 DBAE (co-located in Pushkin).[1] The return leg was difficult due to deteriorating weather: 19 DB-3s force-landed in various places, and three DB-3s were destroyed.

20 January 1940 the main target of 21 DBAP was Haapamäki railway junction, which was bombed by 1st and 4th Squadrons with 14 DB-3 bombers. Altogether 72 FAB-100 and 40 ZAB-50 bombs and 10 leaflet packages were dropped. One DB-3 of 1st Squadron dropped 10 ZAB-50 bombs at Suoniemi station and a bomber of 4th Squadron dropped 8 FAB-100 bombs in Porvoo. After the bombing 1st Squadron was attacked by nine Fokker fighters at Värtsilä. One DB-3 was lost (pilot *st.lt* I.M. Solovyev). The MG-gunners claimed 4 Fokkers. Three DB-3 bombers were hit (one aircraft had 22 bullet holes). 4th Squadron was attacked by 12 Fokkers. The navigator of the Squadron Commander's aircraft *lt* Kuz'min claimed one Fokker. *Lentom V. Pyötsiä (FR-110) shot down two "SB" aircraft 5 km south of Korpiselkä. No Ilmavoimat losses.*

2 February 1940 one DB-3 force-landed at Gumbaritsa at the eastern shore of Lake Ladoga, another was damaged in an unsuccessful take-off.

13 February 1940 one DB-3 crashed 15 km from the Finnish Fort Mustaniemi (near Verkkosaari at Lake Ladoga) and partly sunk through the ice. All four aviators were killed in the crash and were solemnly buried at Mustaniemi three days later. Documents, maps, navigation and flight instruments, radio equipment and machine guns etc. were retrieved by personnel from Mustaniemi.

14 February 1940 five DB-3s were hit in air combat at Lappeenranta. The MG-gunners claimed 5 Fokkers. The wounded *ml.kzv* B.R. Antilevskiy was appointed HSU 7 April 1940 as the sole "Hero" of 21 DBAP. (After getting fighter training in GPW, Antilevskiy served in 20 IAP on the Western front (Rzhev, Spas-Demensk etc.) as deputy Squadron C.O. He was shot down and captured by the Germans on 28 August 1943. In autumn 1943 Antilevskiy joined ROA, or "Vlasov's Army", where he commanded 2nd Bomber Squadron of VVS ROA. Like several other high-ranking officers of the ROA Antilevskiy was executed on 25 July 1946. Strangely his HSU-award was only cancelled officially on 12 July 1950.)

17 February 1940 "target no. 12" or Antrea railway station was attacked. As the escort fighters of 149 IAP did not show up, the bombers flew without cover. The prime target was also not found; when searching for the reserve target at 1545 hours the DB-3s were attacked by "six Finnish Fokkers". One DB-3 was shot down in air combat at Imatra. MG-gunner *ser* N.I. Slabkovich escaped by parachute and was taken prisoner, the other three aviators were killed. *Alik R. Heiramo (LLv 24, FR-104) shot down a DB-3 which exploded west of Enso.* Komandarm Ye.S. Ptukhin (VVS SZFr Commander) repeated his order prohibiting bomber attacks without fighter escort (see 54 SBAP, page 187), and severely criticized regiment commander *polkovnik* Novodranov and *kapitan* Men'shikov (C.O. 4th Squadron) for bad attack planning.

19 February 1940 One DB-3 (*lt* P.D. Bibichev, 3rd Squadron) was shot down by Fokker fighters at Simola, all four aviators were killed. Two Fokkers were claimed by the MG-gunners. *Majuri G-E. Magnusson shot down a DB-3 WSW of Joutseno.*

20 February 1940 two DB-3s were damaged by A-A artillery at Ristniemi, and another three were damaged in air combat at Lappeenranta. Three Fokkers were claimed, two by MG-gunners and one by escort fighters.

In February 1940 new DB-3s arrived to 21 DBAP from Monino and Krechevitsy. The combat performance of 21 DBAP (as with other regiments) suffered considerably by the fact that the crews were not permanently allocated specific aircraft. In February 1940 21 DBAP aviators were forced to use "unfamiliar" aircraft in 83 cases. In some cases the crews were allocated aircraft just immediately before take-off.

21 DBAP participated in combat from 21 December 1939, and performed 282 war missions (30 regiment missions). 21,324 bombs were dropped, total weight 561 t.

B.R. Antilevskiy was the only HSU in 21 DBAP, and his photo was published 28.4.1940 on the front page of Krasnaja zvezda. Antilevskiy was shot down 28.8.1943 As a POW in Germany he joined Vlasov's army (ROA), and subsequently served as a squadron Commander in VVS ROA. Antilevskiy is leftmost in the group of just decorated HSUs. (Finnish National Library)

---

1 The author's father Evald Geust (who served as an armament technician at a Military Depot in Vaasa) was seriously wounded by bomb splinters during this New Year's Eve attack.

21 December 1939–23 January 1940 5 attacks were performed by 116 a/c, which dropped 755 bombs. Targets included Viipuri, Kouvola, Elisenvaara and Haapamäki railway stations, military-industrial objects in Vaasa and Fort Koivisto.

21 DBAP Regiment Attacks:

Date	A/c ready	A/c started	A/c bombed target	A/c returned to own base	A/c losses	Bombs dropped	Comments, main targets
21.12.39	40	33	14	26 (13 with bombs)	3	16xFAB-250, 114xFAB-100, 20xFAB-50	
25.12.39	27	27	9	23	-	3xFAB-250, 64xFAB-100, 34xFAB-50	Several bombs not released
26.12.39					3		Ferry flight
29.12.39	15	13	10	5	2	129xFAB-100, 25 agitbombs	Vaasa
31.12.39	27	25	23	2	3	6xFAB-250, 178xFAB-100, 70xZAB-50	Vaasa
20.1.40		16			1		4 claims
2.2.40		33					
3.2.40		35					
4.2.40		27					
10.2.40		36					
13.2.40		36	35		1		Käkisalmi
14.2.40		36					Viipuri
14.2.40		18					Lappeenranta, 5 DB-3s damaged
15.2.40	36	36					
16.2.40	23	9					
17.2.40	35	34			1		Antrea
18.2.40	25	5					Simola
19.2.40	27	26			1		Simola
20.2.40	27	26		27			Simola
20.2.40	18	18		18			Lappeenranta
21.2.40	27	27					Savonlinna; reserve target Käkisalmi was bombed

21 DBAP lost three DB-3 in air combat, two bombers did not return and 11 aircraft were destroyed in accidents.

21 DBAP Strength and locations

Date	Base	Subordination	Base unit	Equipment
1.11.39	Monino, MVO	27 AB, AON-1	9 AB	69 DB-3
1.12.39	Pushkin, LVO	27 AB, AON-1	1 RAB, 9 AB	53 DB-3, 1 TB-3
1.1.40	Pushkin, LVO	27 AB, VVS SZFr	1 RAB, 9 AB	50 DB-3
1.2.40	Pushkin, LVO	27 AB, VVS SZFr	1 RAB, 9 AB	42 DB-3
1.3.40	Pushkin, LVO	27 AB, VVS SZFr	1 RAB, 9 AB	50 DB-3
1.4.40	Sescha, Kharkov VO	30 AB, VVS KhVO	17 RAB, 9 AB	51 DB-3, 1 TB-3

21 DBAP Strength 13 December 39

Staff	Yedrovo	3 DB-3
1st Squadron	Yedrovo	15 DB-3
2nd Squadron	Yedrovo	13 DB-3
3rd Squadron	Yedrovo	12 DB-3
4th Squadron	Yedrovo	13 DB-3

21 DBAP command

Commander	*polkovnik* N.I. Novodranov. Commanded 81 AD DD in 1942.
Assistant C.O.	*major* O.N. Borovkov (1908–1978). In China 1938. HSU 22.2.1939. In GPW deputy commander of ADD-division.
Military commissar	*bat.komiss* Mazepov ("must be replaced as guilty of ground collision of 2 a/c at Yedrovo 23 January 1940")
Chief of Staff	*major* Lobakin
	major Kalinin (from 24.1.1940)

Squadron C.O. and commissars

1st	*major* Mikryukov
	major Neklyudov
	st.politr Voronov
3rd	*kapitan* Belichenko
	kapitan Kozerov
	st.politr Koshmyakov
4th	*kapitan* Men'shikov
	st.politr Shoshin
5th	*kapitan* Gerasimov
	Grebennikov (?)
	st.politr Gerzon

After the Winter War 21 DBAP was attached to 22 SAD in Odessa MD.

In the GPW 21 DBAP was attached to ADD on 5 March 1942. 21 AP DD was elevated to Guards status 18 September 1943 as 24 GvAP DD, which was renamed 240 GvBAP after conversion of ADD to 18th Air Army in December 1944.

23rd Fighter Aviation Regiment (23 IAP)

Autumn 1939 23 IAP was based in Zhitomir (Kiev MD), and participated in the Polish campaign ("liberation of Western Ukraine") in September 1939, after which 23 IAP relocated to Sknilub (Lvov region).

Subordination
69 AB, VVS KOVO (until 16 February 1940)
59 IAB, VVS 7.A (from 4 March 1940)

Combat Chronicle

16 February 1940 23 IAP departed by train from Lvov to Boboshino (near Perkjärvi, on occupied Finnish territory), where it was attached to 59 IAB.

Before its departure to the front 23 IAP was reinforced with experienced Squadrons of two other regiments of VVS KOVO. The structure of 23 IAP was thus:
- 1st Squadron (14 I-153) from 28 IAP,
- 2nd Squadron (14 I-153) from 23 IAP,
- 3rd Squadron (16 I-15bis) from 23 IAP,
- 4th Squadron (19 I-15bis) from 12 IAP.

4 March 1940 23 IAP initiated its war missions from Boboshino, where full strength (34 I-15bis, 27 I-153 and 2 U-2) was reached four days later. The operational area included Perkjärvi, Leipäsuo, Kämärä, Revonsaari and Vilajoki.

6 March 1940 *ml.lt* V.I. Fadeyev (I-15bis c/n 4462, 4th Squadron) was hit by A-A at Vaalimaa on a ground attack, and crashed fatally.

10 March 1940 *kapitan* I.I. Kakutich (C.O. 1st Squadron) was killed when the propeller of I-153 c/n 6713 disintegrated at take-off from Kaukjärvi. The same day *lt* Shvetsov shot down a Finnish bomber which crashed at Raslahti (4 km W Viipuri, confirmed by Soviet ground forces). Also on the same day *kapitan* Popel'nushenko and *kapitan* Surnov attacked an enemy bomber at 2,000 m altitude. The bomber dived to ground level at Tervajärvi and disappeared behind the forest – "it was apparently hit and crashed in the forest". BL-133 was shot down and crashed at Ylämaa, *kapt* J. Piponius, *luutn* A. Sopenheimo and *kers* E. Tani were killed.

23 IAP performed 631 war missions, flight time 726 h 52 min, claimed 4 victories and dropped 49 FAB-50, 12 ZAB-50, 51 AO-10 and 69 AO-15 bombs during 10 days.

23 IAP command

Commander	*polkovnik* Sidorenko
Military commissar	*bat.komiss* Shumarin
Chief of Staff	*major* Ryabtsev
Squadron C.O.	
1st	*kapitan* I.I. Kakutich (1914–10.3.1940, KIA). Participated in Spanish Civil War.

24th Fast Bomber Aviation Regiment (24 SBAP)

Autumn 1939 24 SBAP was based in Krechevitsy (Leningrad MD).

Subordination
  15 SBAB, VVS LVO
  15 SBAB, VVS 7.A (until 6 January 1940)
  VVS 13.A (from 6 January 1940)

Combat Chronicle

Before the Winter War 24 SBAP was located in Krechevitsy, subordinated to 15 SBAB. In April 1938 24 SBAP converted from TB-3 bombers to new SB-aircraft.

In September 1939 1st Squadron moved to Vayenga to the Murmansk Aviation Brigade, and nine bombers participated in the Polish campaign (the so-called "liberation of Western Ukraine and Western Byelorussia") at the end of September 1939.

14 November 1939 24 SBAP was ordered to move to Gorelovo; ten bombers moved via Sol'tsy to Vitino.

29 November 1939 the first combat order was received: 3rd Squadron was ordered to destroy the enemy AF base at Suur-Merijoki (west of Viipuri) next day.

SB tactical 11 (3./24 SBAP, c/n 8/220) was shot down 1.12.1939 in Antrea, the crew was killed. (SA-kuva)

SB tactical 2 (ex 11) of 24 SBAP. The identity of this wreck is still unknown. (C-F. Geust)

30 November 1939 as no action was observed in Suur-Merijoki (due to snowy weather?), Viipuri railway junction was bombed.

1 December 1939 the task of 24 SBAP was to destroy Viipuri and "Kollakkala" (Kuokkala?) railway stations with 53 SB bombers. Four bombers of 24 SBAP were shot down by Finnish Fokkers. Ten aviators were killed and two were captured and taken prisoner (*st.lt* I.K. Storchilo and *st.lt* Ya.V. Yegorov). Storchilo's SB *yellow 4* was later exhibited in the war booty exhibition in Helsinki from February 1940, and was repaired by the Finnish State Aircraft Factory, becoming VP-10 in the Finnish Air Force. A fifth bomber was badly damaged, but was able to limp back to Vitino. This SB was still being repaired 25 February 1940. *LLv 24 shot down ten Soviet bombers, and claimed additionally two possible victories.*

20 December 1939 a number of aviators were dispatched by train to Petrozavodsk to join 72 SAP.

21 December 1939 the task of 24 SBAP was to destroy Immola AF base and railway station, and bomb the railway between Kämärä and Viipuri, and the road from Oivola to Kämärä. SBs (c/n 17/67, 13/96 and 15/96 were destroyed in air combat, six aviators were killed. Also SB c/n 2/97 was damaged but was able to return to its base on one engine. According the report by the special department of the Leningrad Military District (OO LVO) the main reason for the losses was the repeated approaches to the target performed by 5th Squadron, regardless of orders and warnings given to the Squadron commander, *kapitan* Kameshkov. *LLv 24 claimed one certain and three possible victories.*

23 December 1939 two aircraft were lost, five aviators were killed *On this day seven Soviet bombers were shot down by Finnish fighters.*

25 December 1939 Käkisalmi (Kexholm) railway station was bombed by 35 aircraft.

6 January 1940 24 SBAP was transferred to the newly formed VVS 13.A, with Gorelovo as its main base.

19 January 1940 six SBs bombed fortifications north of Suvantojärvi. A Fokker group chased the bombers to Rautu, or 15 km into the area occupied by the Red Army. Three SBs (c/n 3/96, 17/99 and

SB yellow 4 (3./24 SBAP, c/n 11/220) force-landed 1.12.1939 in Säiniö. St.lt I.K. Yegorov and st.lt Ya.V. Yegorov were captured, MG-gunner P.I. Petrov was killed. This aircraft apparently became VP-10 of Ilmavoimat. (SA-kuva)

10/135) were hit in air combat at Hiitola, and force-landed. The bombers had to be dispatched for lengthy repairs. MG-gunner D.M. Vorobyev (c/n 17/99) was killed.

2 February 1940 Sortavala was attacked by 44 SB. Before the main attack at 0900 hours *lentom* V. Pyötsiä (FR-110) shot down SB c/n 4/221 from a formation of three weather reconnaissance aircraft. The SB crashed at Hämekoski. The pilot *lt* N.A. Volkov escaped from the burning aircraft by parachute and was captured. He told his interrogators that the aircraft belonged to a Squadron based at Novaya Derevnya and subordinated directly to Leningrad Military District. Volkov died (like three other POW-aviators) of CO-suffocation in Otrakkala, Ruskeala POW-camp 8–9 February 1940. Squadron commander was *major* Yegorov, *kommissar* Cheblikov; unit number 6300.

21 February 1940 three aircraft were lost after A-A hits at Muolaanjärvi, including *kapitan* G.A. Timoshenko (C.O. 2nd Squadron) were killed.

26 February 1940 *kapitan* A.N. Kameshkov (C.O. 5th Squadron) took off from Gorelovo with locked trimmers. The outcome was tragic: SB c/n 2/234 crashed and all crew members were killed.

Wing structure of SB c/n 11/220 at VL. (SA-kuva)

127

VP-10, the first SB repaired by VL in April 1940. (K. Stenman)

24 SBAP Strength and locations

Date	Base	Subordination	Base unit	Equipment
1.11.39	Krechevitsy	14 AB, VVS KOVO	2 RAB, 139 AB	60 SB
1.12.39	Krechevitsy	14 AB, VVS KOVO	2 RAB, 139 AB	59 SB
1.1.40	Manushkino, LVO	15 AB, VVS SZFr	2 RAB, 139 AB	54 SB
1.2.40	Gorelovo, LVO	15 AB, VVS SZFr	2 RAB, 139 AB	62 SB
1.3.40	Gorelovo, LVO	15 AB, VVS SZFr	2 RAB, 139 AB	54 SB
1.4.40	Krechevitsy	15 AB, VVS KOVO	2 RAB, 139 AB	54 SB

24 SBAP command

Commander	*major* G.I. Belitskiy
Military commissar	*bat.komiss* Kalinin
	A.I. Vikhorev. In GPW political deputy commander of 8th Air Army.
Chief of Staff	*major* Suyakov

Squadron C.O. and commissars
1st   *kapitan* Lozenko
      st.politr Smirnov
2nd   *kapitan* I.A. Kolomijchenko
      kapitan G.A. Timoshenko (KIA 21.2.40)
3rd   *kapitan* N.A. Nikiforov
4th   *kapitan* Kotlyarov
      kapitan Suprun
5th   *kapitan* A.N. Kameshkov (KIA 26.2.40)
      kapitan Shasin
Unit 6300 (Novaya Derevnya)   *major* Yegorov
Military commissar   Cheblikov

25th Fighter Aviation Regiment (25 IAP)

25 IAP was formed in summer 1938 in Pushkin (Leningrad MD).

Subordination
59 IAB, VVS LVO
59 IAB, VVS 7.A

Combat Chronicle

25 IAP participated in the Polish campaign ("liberation of Western Ukraine") 17–28 September 1939, and returned to Pushkin 29 September-2 October 1939.

29 November 1939 25 IAP Command, 3rd (15 I-153, 34 I-15bis and 1 U-2) and 4th Squadrons (15 I-153 and 1 U-2) were located at Komendantskiy aerodrome, Leningrad, 1st Squadron (14 I-16) was

Fighter pilots of 25 IAP in December 1939. (G.F. Petrov)

located in Gorskaya, and 2nd Squadron (14 I-16) in Levashovo. Only I-153 and 11 I-15bis fighters were equipped with protected fuel tanks, while all I-16s had unprotected tanks.

30 November 1939 *lt* N.S. Bannikov in I-153 c/n 6437 was killed in an accident at Leningrad in bad weather conditions.

From 18 December 1939 3rd and 4th Squadrons (with 30 I-153) were transferred to 38 IAP (OAB) in Estonia, while Regiment Command, 1st and 2nd Squadrons (30 I-16) moved to Kanneljärvi (on occupied Finnish territory).

19 December 1939 "an enemy flight was downed", two light bombers and four fighters were claimed. *FK-95 of LLv 12 was shot down at Johannes, vänr K.I. Rintala and kers S.O. Mäkelä were killed.*

23 December 1939 78 missions were performed by 28 I-16s. Between 0900 and 1000 hours a flight led by *kapitan* A.S. Kostenko shot down one fighter and two reconnaissance aircraft. It was observed that I-16s with fixed ski undercarriage are slower than Fokker D.XXI. *Fokker C.X. FK-96 of LLv 12 was shot down at Kaukjärvi-Uusikirkko, luutn I. Salo and kers E. Saloranta were killed. At Perkjärvi FK-80 of LLv 10 was attacked by up to 30 enemy fighters, the observer vänr N. Lintunen was killed, but the badly wounded luutn H. Kalaja was able to return to Lappeenranta with his damaged aircraft.*

Orders read by kapitan *N.I. Zhuravlev, 2./25 IAP Commander. (G.F. Petrov)*

Kapitan Zhuravlev and st.lt Yakov A. Antonov. At rear I-16 tactical 11 can be seen. (G.F. Petrov)

Yakov Antonov (HSU 21.3.1940) with his father and daughter in spring 1940. (G.F. Petrov)

27 December 1939 14 I-153 (led by *major* Fatnev) relocated from Pushkin to Suulajärvi (also on occupied Finnish territory).

1 January 1940 10 I-16 arrived from 68 IAP to Suulajärvi, and formed a new 3rd Squadron (commanded by *kapitan* T.I. Kochetkov).

Early January 1940 1st Squadron led by *kapitan* A.T. Kostenko received new I-16 *tip* 27 (equipped with 20 mm ShVAK-cannons), and was soon transferred to 38 IAP.

Because of severe cold 25 IAP was forced to cease flight operations 2, 7–10, 15, 17, 21, and 23–27 January 1940. During the rest of January only limited operations could be performed (8–12 missions per day), but at the end of the month 36–61 missions per day.

11 January 1940 two I-16 fighters were lost to A-A artillery at Äyräpää. *lt* P.N. Bogomolov (I-16 *tip* 5 c/n 5210866) was injured, and taken prisoner after force-landing in the forest. Bogomolov had apparently been transferred from 26 IAP to 25 IAP in autumn 1939.

A.A. Ivashkin (2./25 IAP politruk) giving orders to a pilot taking off for a leaflet-dropping mission. (G.F. Petrov)

Commissar F.S. Zakharov, 1./25 IAP. (G.F. Petrov)

Major N.S. Toropchin, 25 IAP Commander (HSU 21.3.1940). (G.F. Petrov)

28 January 1940 9 I-153 arrived from Pushkin to Suulajärvi (led by *st.lt* P.K. Kozachenko); c/n 6732 w/o at landing. One Squadron (7 a/c, Bushev) arrived from Komendantskiy to Kanneljärvi.

In January 1940 reinforcements arrived also from 38 IAP and from Kiev Military District (KOVO).

2 February 1940: "12 Soviet and 18 Finnish aircraft" participated in air combat at Imatra. 12 (twelve!) Finnish aircraft were claimed shot down. *Danish volunteer Løjtnant F. Rasmussen of LLv 24 was killed, his Fokker D.XXI FR-81 crashed at Ruokolahti.*

13 February 1940 25 IAP was ordered by *komkor* S.P. Denisov (VVS 7.A Commander) to escort and protect artillery control aircraft of 9 and 16 KAO, co-located at Suulajärvi and Kanneljärvi respectively.

17 February 1940 *st.lt* G.M. Sokolov claimed two victories. *Vänr I. Törrönen (LLv 24, FR-80) was injured and force-landed in Korvenkylä.*

19 February 1940 Sokolov and Kozachenko claimed four Finnish fighters in combat against twelve Fokkers *This day only Danish volunteer Løjtnant E. Frijs of LLv 24 was killed. His FR-80 was apparently hit by MG-guns of DB-3s of 3rd Squadron of 1 AP (VVS KBF), and crashed at Viipuri.*

Late February 1940 two Squadrons with combat experience from arrived Khalkin-Gol: one Squadron of 22 IAP (which become 5th Squadron), and one Squadron of 70 IAP (which became 6th Squadron, which performed combat missions from 29 February 1940). Both 22 IAP and 70 IAP belonged to 1 IAG.

27 February 1940 strafing mission against Hamina railway station. One Fokker was claimed shot down in air combat. *kapitan* Toropchin's fighter was hit by ground fire, but he was able to return to his base with the damaged aircraft. *No Finnish aircraft losses.*

28 or 29 February 1940 *st.lt* I.I. Rybkin (I-16 *tip* 17 c/n 1721192, 5th Squadron) did not return from Vakkala after A-A hits.

5 March 1940 *lt* F.I. Duvanov (6th Squadron, who arrived on 26 February 1940 from 70 IAP in Mongolia) was killed when I-16 *tip* 18 c/n 1821K31 crashed SW Ventelä, Äyräpää (north of Vuosalmi).

6 March 1940 a Blenheim was attacked by two I-16 (*major* Bushev and *kapitan* Nikolayev), but the Finnish bomber was able to escape.

7 March 1940 a Blenheim was shot down jointly by I-153s of 7 IAP and *st.lt* Dyachenko. The Blenheim crashed in square 093 in the sector of 28th (Infantry) Army Corps. *BL-122 (LLv 46) was shot down by Soviet fighters over the Bay of Viipuri. Pilot luutn N. Hakala) escaped by parachute and reached his own lines, the other two aviators were killed. On the same day BL-144 (LLv 42) was shot down by A-A artillery.* (See 7 IAP, page 100)

9 March 1940 when protecting 28th Army Corps *st.politr* Shabanov attacked a two-engine aircraft which emitted smoke, but escaped in the direction of Viipuri. *ml.lt* Kazak attacked a fighter, but after all his ammunition was used, the enemy escaped. *lt* Pustynnykh attacked a Blenheim four times, but nevertheless the bomber escaped. *BL-139, BL-140 and BL-137 (all of LLv 42) performed repeated attacks against Soviet troops at Vilaniemi (on western shore of Bay of Viipuri).*

10 March 1940 at noon flight leader Zavarukhin attacked a Fokker D.XXI twice without success. When returning to the base he detected a two-engine aircraft, but was unable to intercept. *major* Bushev intercepted the Blenheim. Also *lt* Smolkin opened fire at the bomber, the left engine of which emitted smoke, but the bomber escaped at low altitude (20–30 m) in the direction of Säkkijärvi. *The Blenheim*

attacked by lt Smolkin was apparently BL-139 of LLv 42 (piloted by vänr P. Lumme), which escaped by diving to tree-top level. Also BL-145, BL-140 and BL-142 (all of LLv 42) were attacked by fighters over the Bay of Viipuri, but were able to return, after which the mechanics had much work to repair the combat damage as soon as possible.

11 March 1940 BL-139 and BL-140 (both LLv 42) were also on the same morning attacked by fighters at Bay of Viipuri, but were able to escape. Alik Y. Hammarén (BL-139 MG-gunner) claimed two I-153 fighters, one of which was reported crashing in Kiiskilä. (See 148 IAP, page 209) Kokelas E. Vuorenko (BL-140 navigator) was seriously wounded and perished in the evening.

At the end of the Winter War 25 IAP was also given ground attack tasks, e.g.:
18–19 February 1940 strafing of Leipäsuo and Kämärä.
27 February 1940 strafing of Tali.
29 February 1940 Sokolov destroyed 8 wagons.

According to a Soviet source a fighter formation led by 1st Squadron C.O. A.S. Kostenko intercepted a Finnish bomber attack against Leningrad in February 1940 (!). This (unfortunately undated) interception happened after an enemy aircraft was detected on the night of 5 February 1940 entering Leningrad airspace, was caught by searchlight beams and shot down by 115th Anti-aircraft artillery regiment.

The following Finnish intrusions in Leningrad airspace are known:

17 February 1940 two bombers of LLv 46 flew into the air space of Leningrad in the early morning: BL-130 flew between Kronstadt and Leningrad, and BL-124 bombed Krasnaya Gorka.

On the night of 25–26 February 1940 Finnish bombers attacked Lodejnoye pole AF base, approaching over Leningrad. BL-124 bombed reserve target Krasnaya Gorka.

1 March 1940 BL-106 and BL-120 of LLv 44 bombed Terijoki railway station in the evening, causing air alarms in Kronstadt and Leningrad. BL-132 (LLv 46) bombed Beloostrov (Valkeasaari) railway station, some 13 fighters attacked. The Blenheims were able to escape the Soviet fighters due to high-grade 100 octane fuel in special tanks, giving extra power!

Main operational base of 25 IAP was located in Kanneljärvi in occupied Finnish territory.

This propaganda poster depicts the air combat against 12 Fokkers 19.2.1940, in which G.M. Sokolov and P.K. Kozatshenko (both 25 IAP) claimed four Finnish aircraft. Sokolov was appointed HSU 21.3.1940, and Kozatshenko got the Golden Star 1.5.1943 (KIA in a taran attack 18.3.1945). (A. Uitto)

Major Yakov Antonov (then 84th IAP Commander) was shot down at Mozdok 25.8.1942 and captured. In the photo German aces Gordon Gollob (II./JG 3) and Adolf Dickfeld are questioning Antonov, who exceptionally wore all his decorations during his last mission. (C-F. Geust)

132

25 IAP Strength

Date	Base	Subordination	Base unit	Equipment
1.11.39	Pushkin, LVO	59 AB, VVS LVO	1 RAB, 150 AB	33 I-16, 30 I-15bis
1.12.39	Kanneljärvi, Suulajärvi, LVO	59 AB, VVS LVO	1 RAB, 150 AB	36 I-16, 10 I-153, 17 I-15bis
1.1.40	Kanneljärvi, Suulajärvi, LVO	59 AB, VVS LVO	1 RAB, 150 AB	35 I-16, 10 I-153, 4 I-15bis
1.2.40	Kanneljärvi, Suulajärvi, LVO	59 AB, VVS LVO	1 RAB, 150 AB	35 I-16, 19 I-16P, 10 I-153, 4 I-15bis
1.3.40	Kanneljärvi, Suulajärvi, LVO	59 AB, VVS LVO	1 RAB, 150 AB	33 I-16, 19 I-16P, 10 I-153, 6 I-15bis
1.4.40	Kanneljärvi, Suulajärvi, LVO	59 AB, VVS LVO	1 RAB, 150 AB	33 I-16, 19 I-15bis, 10 I-153, 6 I-15bis
1.5.40	Nasosnaja (45 km NW Baku), ZakVO	60 AB, VVS ZakVO	150 AB	43 I-16, 19 I-16P

25 IAP victory claims

Date, time, location	Fighter/bomber/reconnaissance/unknown	Victories	Finnish info
19.12.39 0950 Kaijala	-/1/-/-	*St.lt* Antonov's I-16 flight shot down one light bomber.	FK-95 was shot down at Johannes. *Vänr* K. Rintala and *alik* S. Mäkelä KIA (LLv 12).
19.12.39	2/-/-/-	I-16 flight of *kapitan* Zhuravlev's I-16 flight shot down two Fokker D.XXI.	No losses.
19.12.39 1130 Kämärä; 5 km E Viipuri	2/-/-/-	*Lt* V.F. Vilchik and *lt* Filippov shot down two fighters.	No losses.
19.12.39 1600	-/1/-/-	*St.lt* Antonov shot down a light bomber.	No losses.
23.12.39 0900–1000 Kämärä; Leipäsuo; Tyeppälä (?)	-/3/-/-	*Kapitan* A.T. Kostenko and *st.politr* F.S. Zakharov shot down three light bombers.	FK-96 was shot down at Kaukjärvi-Uusikirkko. *Luutn* I. Salo and *kers* E. Saloranta KIA (LLv 12). FK-80 was hit in air combat, *luutn* H. Kalaja WIA, *vänr* N. Lintunen KIA (LLv 10).
2.2.40 1615–1715 Imatra	12/-/-/-	10 I-16 and 3 I-153 led by assistant C.O. Bushev shot down 12 Fokkers without own losses.	No losses.
4.2.40 Rauhava	-/-/-/1	AF base Rauhava (100 km from the frontline) was strafed by 9 I-16 and 3 I-153 led by C.O. Toropchin. 1 enemy aircraft destroyed.	No losses.
17.2.40 1520–1625	3/-/-/-	*Kapitan* Nikolayev and *st.lt* Sokolov shot down 3 Fokker D.XXI. One FR crashed in Sulvalahti.	No losses.
18.2.40 1215–1325	1/2/-/-	I-16 flight led by *st.politr* Kopylov shot down one two-engined bomber and 2 fighters.	No losses.
19.2.40 Hamina	4/-/-/-	*Lt* Kozachenko and *lt* Sokolov (I-153) shot down four Fokkers.	No losses.
19.2.40 1640–1730 Viipuri	2/-/-/-	3 I-16 (*St.lt* Antonov, *kapitan* Nikolayev and *lt* Svitchenok (I-16) shot down two Fokkers.	FR-80 shot down, *luutn* E. Frijs KIA (LLv 24). Frijs was possibly shot down by DB-3 MG-gunner of 1 AP VVS KBF).

25.2.40	3/-/-/-	Three fighters shot down (FR and BU).	GL-256 shot down at Kämärä, *alik* T. Bergman OK (LLv 26). GL-254 shot down at Muolaanjärvi, *luutn* P. Tevä KIA (LLv 26).
26.2.40	2/-/-/-	Two Fokkers shot down.	FR-85 shot down at Immola, *kers* T. Kaarma OK (LLv 24).
27.2.40 Hamina	1/-/-/-	One Fokker shot down. *Kapitan* Toropchin's fighter was hit by A-A Artillery, but he was able to return and land at the base.	FA-12 shot down at Utti, *vänr* E. Malmivuo KIA (LLv 26).
7.3.1940	-/1/-/-	*St.lt* Dyachenko and I-153s of 7 IAP shot down one Blenheim.	See 7 IAP, page 100: either BL-122 (LLv 46) or BL-144 (LLv 42).

Fighter pilots of 26 IAP. (G.F. Petrov)

25 IAP command

Commander	*major* N.S. Toropchin (1904–1987). HSU 21.3.40. In GPW commanded 125 IAD.
Deputy Commander	*major* V.V. Bushev (replaced kapitan Oleinik, who was dispatched to 68 IAP)
Military commissar	*bat.komiss* A.N. Koblikov (1909–1945). HSU 21.3.40.
Chief of Staff	*major* B.P. Kaloshin
Squadron C.O. and commissars	
1st	*kapitan* A.T. Kostenko (I-16 Squadron; in January 1940 to 38 IAP)
	kapitan V.S. Mukhin
	st.politr F.S. Zakharov
2nd	*kapitan* N.I. Zhuravlev
	st.politr A.A. Ivashkin
3rd (from 1 January 1940, ex-68 IAP)	*kapitan* T.I. Kochetkov
4th	*st.lt* P.K. Kozachenko (21.1.40 from 38 IAP)
	st.lt Grishin (subordinated to Kravchenko's OAG, based at Paldiski, Estonia)
Unknown	V.M. Najdenko (1915–1969). HSU 21.4.43 as C.O. 126 IAP.
	kapitan Savchenko (I-15bis Squadron, 18.12.39 to Murmashi, and attached to 5 OSAP, later formed nucleus of 147 IAP)
Unknown	V.M. Najdenko (1915–1969). HSU 21.4.43 as C.O. 126 IAP.
	major Fatnev (I-153 Squadron, 27.12.39 from Pushkin to Suulajärvi)

25 IAP and 7 IAP were the most important Soviet fighter units on the Karelian Isthmus, together claiming "more than" 52 victories.

25 IAP performed 3,860 missions (3,786 flight hours) during the Winter War:

- 855 missions escorting SB bombers, fire control and ground attack aircraft, strafing of enemy ground forces and AF bases
- 1,094 missions covering own ground forces
- 441 reconnaissance missions;
- and fought 25 air combats, in which 45 enemy aircraft were claimed shot down (2 bombers, 4 reconnaissance aircraft and 39 fighters). Own losses were one aviator and one fighter.

17 March 1940 25 IAP moved back to Pushkin with 47 I-16, 9 I-153 and 4 I-15 aircraft. 11 April 1940 25 IAP was transferred from Leningrad Military District to Transkaukasian Military District, and arrived 19 April 1940.

25 IAP was awarded Red Banner Order 21 March 1940. Four pilots (*major* N.S. Toropchin, *bat. komiss* A.N. Koblikov, *st.lt* Ya.I. Antonov and *ml.lt* G.M. Sokolov, who had arrived from 34 IAP) were appointed HSU on the same day. Lt A.F. Moshin had already been awarded the Golden Star on 29 August 1939 (in 56 IAP at Khalkhin-Gol).

In the GPW HSU, *major* Yakov Antonov (Commander of 84 IAP) was shot down at Mozdok on 25 August 1942 and taken prisoner by the Germans.

26th Fighter Aviation Regiment (26 IAP)

26 IAP was formed in Gorelovo (Leningrad MD) in spring 1938. In autumn 1939 26 IAP was based in Gorelovo (Leningrad MD).

Subordination
54 IAB, VVS LVO
54 IAB, VVS 7.A

In November 1939 one I-15bis Squadron was transferred to 5 OSAP in Murmansk, and became 5th Squadron.

30 November 1939 1st and 2nd Squadrons equipped with 45 I-16 were based at Manushkino, while 3rd and 4th Squadrons (5 I-16, 18 I-153 and 12 I-15bis aircraft) were located in Uglovo.

Combat Chronicle
26 IAP performed ground attacks 18, 19, 20 and 27 December 1939.
19 December 1939 2nd Squadron claimed one Fokker at Käkisalmi.
21 December 1939 one fighter of 26 IAP was fired upon by own-side SB bomber at Koivisto.
24 December 1939 one "Gladiator" was claimed 3 km SW Käkisalmi, and another "Gladiator" 5 km SE Käkisalmi. *The "Gladiators" were Bulldog fighters of Osasto Heinilä/LLv 26, which relocated from Mensuvaara to Käkisalmi 19 December 1939. No Bulldog losses were suffered.*
25 December 1939 Käkisalmi AF base was attacked. This day I-16 *tip 5* c/n 521A399 was shot down by A-A artillery and crashed 5–8 km south of Rahkajärvi, *ml.lt* I.F. Masurenko (4th Squadron) was killed in air combat. *Note: kers V. Porvari (LLv 26, BU-68) reported a possible I-16 claim.*
26 December 1939 *lt* V.S. Tsyganenko crashed into a aircraft line when landing at Manushkino in I-16 *tip 5* c/n 531A378. In the crash four I-16s, one UTI-4 and one U-2 were destroyed.
16 February 1940 I-16 *tip 5* c/n 521A449 crashed on an aerobatics training flight, *ml.lt* N.A. Ogorodnikov (3rd Squadron) was killed.
26 IAP lost seven aircraft (of which one in air combat and six in accidents). Two pilots were killed.
26 IAP Strength and locations

26 IAP Strength and locations

Date	Base	Subordination	Base unit	Equipment
1.11.39	Gorelovo, LVO	54 AB, VVS LVO	1 RAB, 114 AB	35 I-16, 36 I-15bis
1.12.39	Gorelovo, LVO	54 AB, VVS SZFr	1 RAB, 114 AB	54 I-16, 15 I-153, 19 I-15bis
1.1.40	Uglovo, LVO	54 AB, VVS SZFr	1 RAB, 114 AB	59 I-16, 22 I-153, 14 I-15bis
1.2.40	Uglovo and Manushkino, LVO	54 AB, VVS SZFr	1 RAB, 114 AB	66 I-16, 21 I-153, 5 I-15bis, 6 I-15
1.3.40	Uglovo and Manushkino, LVO	54 AB, VVS SZFr	1 RAB, 114 AB	57 I-16, 21 I-153, 5 I-15bis, 4 I-15 (with RS-82 rockets)
1.4.40	Levashovo, LVO	54 AB, VVS LVO	1 RAB, 114 AB	55 I-16, 21 I-153, 5 I-15bis

When landing I-16 c/n 521A378 in Manushkino 26.12.1939 lt V.S. Tsyganenko (1./26 IAP) crashed into a row of parked aircraft. Four I-16s (including numbers 221 and 230), one UTI-4 and the U-2 in the foreground were written off. (RGVA)

26 IAP Strength 13 March 1940

Squadron	I-16	I-153	I-15bis	I-15	Combat missions
Staff	5				162
1st	14+4				467
2nd	15+3				844
3rd	14+3				737
4th		15+6	3+1	3+1	892
Total	38+10	15+6	3+1	3+1	3,102

26 IAP Mission statistics

Aircraft missions				Ground attack	Ground troops coverage	Bomber escort	AF base attacks	Air combats	Leningrad air defence
I-16	I-153	I-15	Total						
2,453	756	160	3,369	52	29	129	17	6	3,142

Bomber pilots HSU lt N.M. Stol'nikov and V.P. Pshenichnyi, 31 SBAP. (G.F. Petrov)

Three enemy aircraft were claimed in air combat, and six vehicles were destroyed on the ground. Own losses were one aviator and one aircraft.

26 IAP command

Commander   *major* A.I. Kirillov (1908 –). Participated in Spanish Civil War.
Military commissar   *bat.komiss* A.P. Sukhanov
Chief of Staff   *kapitan* Zanozdra

Squadron C.O.
1st   *st.lt* V.G. Turenko
2nd   *st.lt* A.M. Gorokhov (1912 –). Participated in Spanish Civil War.
3rd   *kapitan* K.P. Dobronitskiy (1910 –). Participated in Spanish Civil War.
4th   *kapitan* A.L. Matyukov

In GPW 26 IAP was elevated to Guards status 21 November 1942, becoming 26 GvIAP (the regiment number remained unchanged).

27th Fighter Aviation Regiment (27 IAP)

Autumn 1939 27 IAP was based in Pereslavl-Zalesskiy (Moscow MD).

Subordination
  57 IAB, VVS MVO
  19 AB, VVS 9.A

Combat Chronicle

1 October 1939 3rd Squadron and 16 December 1939 4th Squadron were transferred to Northwest and Finnish fronts respectively.

3rd Squadron started its combat missions on 30 November 1939 on the Karelian Isthmus. 25 December 1939–15 January 1940 the squadron was relocated by trucks to the Uhtua direction in sub-zero temperatures (down to – 46°). After assembly and testing of its five I-153 the squadron was attached to VVS 9.A in Poduzhemye (Usmana) 19 January 1940. Two days later the squadron was attached to 152 IAP at Vojnitsa (Vuonninen), and become 3rd Squadron of 152 IAP, with the task of supporting the surrounded 44th and 163rd Divisions from the ice base at Verkhneye Kujto (Ylä-Kuittijärvi).

In particular 3rd Squadron of 27 IAP escorted Soviet bombers dropping supplies to an infantry regiment (337th Mountain Infantry Regiment), which was surrounded some 40 km west of the Soviet-Finnish border at Saunajärvi.

4th Squadron of 27 IAP (eight I-153) arrived 19 January 1940 to VVS 9.A in Poduzhemye. Late January 1940 this Squadron was attached to 19 AB, which had arrived from Kharkov. The task of 4th Squadron was to protect Kirov (Murmansk) railway, including protection of Kem', Kochkoma and Louhi stations.

3rd Squadron of 27 IAP performed 434 missions and dropped 464 bombs, total flight time 512 h.

27 IAP Command

Commander	*major* I.D. Klimov
Military commissar	D.G. Avelev
Squadron C.O.	
3rd	*major* M.I. Korolev
4th	*kapitan* V.I. Nenashev

In GPW 27 IAP was elevated to Guards status 9 October 1943 as 129 GvIAP.

31st Fast Bomber Aviation Regiment (31 SBAP)

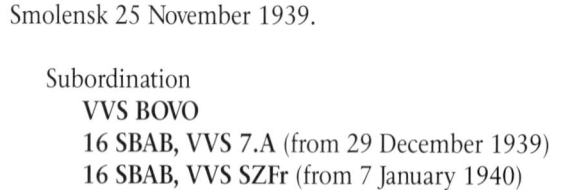

In autumn 1939 31 SBAP was based in Smolensk (Byelorussian MD), and participated in the "Polish campaign" from 17 to 28 September 1939, after which the regiment returned via Balbasovo arriving in Smolensk 25 November 1939.

Subordination
  VVS BOVO
  16 SBAB, VVS 7.A (from 29 December 1939)
  16 SBAB, VVS SZFr (from 7 January 1940)

Relocation to Chernevo was initiated on 18 Deecember 1939, and four Squadrons arrived from Smolensk 26–31 December 1939, and 5./39 SBAP arrived from Staraya Bykhov. By 16 December 1939 the best, night-trained 5th Squadron moved to 5 OSAP in Murmansk.

31 SBAP was combat-ready in Chernevo 5 January 1940 with 36 SB bombers, and was attached to 16 SBAB. Chernevo AF base turned out to be very small for the rather large number of arriving SB bombers with several mishaps on the ground.

Because of bad weather 12 SB bombers (arrived from 39 SBAP and formed 5th Squadron) and 5 bombers of 3rd Squadron only arrived on 20 January 1940, increasing strength to 53 SB aircraft. 6th Squadron was subsequently formed from aircraft and crews from 55 SBAP. 31 SBAP received on 1 February 1940 8 SB from Moscow, and on 16 February 1940 12 SB from Far East. Almost half of the regiment's SBs were new versions, equipped with M-103 engines.

31 SBAP Commander Fedor I. Dobysh. (G.F. Petrov)

SB yellow 8 (c/n 20/203) piloted by politr *I.B. Blagochnikov (3./35 SBAP) was shot down 1.12.1939 by A-A artillery, and crashed in Munkkiniemi, Helsinki. (SA-kuva)*

Combat Chronicle

5 January 1940 two SB collided in the air at Chernevo. The same day 31 SBAP bombed Mikkeli, Kouvola, Imatra and Viipuri railway stations.

17 January 1940 the bombing target of 16 SBAB was military objectives and the railway station at Lappeenranta. Only 11 SB bombers of 31 SBAP (from 3rd, 4th and 5th Squadrons) led by regiment Commander *major* Dobysh were able to take off in the foggy and very cold weather. 31 SBAP dropped from 2,200 m altitude four FAB-250, 32 FAB-100, four FAB-50 and 336 ZAB-1e bombs, and 65,000 leaflets which prevented ground visibility. On the return leg the bombers were attacked by 10 Fokkers, which shot down two SBs of 31 SBAP (c/n 18/114, *luutn* V. Karu, FR-107; and c/n 7/3, *luutn* J. Sarvanto, FR-99) in Heikurila and Harvala. All six aviators (including Squadron commissar N.P. Petrov) were killed. After the heavy losses *komandarm* Ye.S. Ptukhin (Commander VVS SZFr) issued an order prohibiting bombing attacks to Kouvola, Suur-Merijoki, Lappeenranta, Viipuri, Hiitola and Elisenvaara without escort fighters. Ptukhin also repeated the Stavka order of 27 December 1939, which categorically prohibited use of same routes and waypoints on approach and return flights. (See VVS SZFr, 16 SBAP, 31 and 54 SBAP; pages 35, 53, 138 and 186.)

5th Squadron (formed by bombers of 39 SBAP, which had arrived 20 January 1940 to 31 SBAP) lost three aircraft in air combat on 13 February 40 at Suistamo. The pilot of c/n 11/219 *lt* I.S. Khramtsov escaped by parachute and was taken prisoner the next day *(six SB bombers were shot down at the Jänisjärvi-Loimola region)*.

17 February 1940 Kouvola was bombed. SB c/n 13/104 was downed by Finnish fighters, and force-landed in no man's land in Muolaanjärvi. The crew was picked up next day by three R-5 biplanes protected by an I-16. The SB-crew *lt* N.M. Stol'nikov, wounded *lt* I.S. Khudyakov and *st.ser* G.D. Guslev, and the protecting I-16 pilot *kapitan* P. Petrov (68 IAP) were subsequently awarded the Golden star 7 April 1940. *Luutn* P-E. Sovelius (LLv 24, FR-94) *shot down a "DB" bomber, which crashed in Muolaanjärvi.*

3 March 1940 one SB was lost in air combat at Utti, all three aviators were killed.

5 March 1940 two SB bombers of 6th Squadron crashed on the ice south of Kotka after a mid-air collision, all six aviators were killed.

11 March 1940 an SB of C.O. of 4th Squadron was shot down at Säkkijärvi. According to Soviet historiography *kapitan* K.N. Orlov directed his burning aircraft against an enemy strongpoint at Säkkijärvi, thus performing a "blazing taran", for which he was posthumously made HSU 7 April 1940.

The wreck was located in 2002 near the Finnish-Russian border at Kotilamminkangas, Ylämaa.

31 SBAP Command

Commander — *major* F.I. Dobysh (1906–1980). In GPW commanded 1 GBAD. Commanded 50th Air Army 1955–1960 (military advisor in China 1957) and 50th Rocket Army 1960–1972.

Military commissar	*bat.komiss* V.I. Zubarev
Chief of Staff	*major* V.Ye. Kochekov

Eskadrille C.O. and Military Commissars
1st	*kapitan* Starodumov
2nd	*kapitan* Moryashov
3rd	*major* Prosvirin
	st.politr N.P. Petrov (KIA 17.1.1940)
4th	*kapitan* K.N. Orlov (1908–11.3.1940). HSU 7.4.1940.
5th	*kapitan* Zhuravskiy

31 SBAP performed 901 combat missions in the Winter War, dropped 11,807 bombs and claimed 13 air victories (17 victories according to some sources). 23 aviators and 16 SBs were lost.

Four aviators of 31 SBAP (*lt* N.M. Stol'nikov, *lt* I.S. Khudyakov, *starshina* V.D. Guslev and *kapitan* K.N. Orlov posthumously) on 7 April 1940 were decorated with the Golden Star. In 1967 a second Golden Star was proposed to Nikolai Stol'nikov, who performed 192 bomber missions with SB and Pe-2 in GPW, but this proposal was not accepted.

After the Winter War 31 SBAP returned to Smolensk, and in early June 1940 was attached to 18 SBAB, and transferred to Mitava (Mitau, later Jelgava) in Latvia.

In GPW 31 SBAP was among the first aviation regiments to be elevated to Guards status 6 December 1941 and named 4 GvPBAP (Dive Bomber Aviation Regiment).

33rd Fast Bomber Aviation Regiment (33 SBAP)

In GPW Vasily Yefremov was the first Soviet bomber pilot to be decorated with two Golden Stars. He performed over 380 combat missions with SB, Ar-2 and A-20 Boston aircraft. (G.F. Petrov)

In autumn 1939 33 SBAP was based in Belaya Tserkov (Kiev MD), and participated in the "liberation of Western Ukraine" in September 1939.

Subordination
10 AB, VVS KOVO
VVS 14.A (from late February 1940)

Combat Chronicle
33 SBAP arrived in late February 1940 from Belaya Tserkov to Luostari (in occupied Finnish Petsamo) with 59 SB, and was attached to VVS 14.A.

24 February 1940 nine SBs flew from Murmansk to Luostari (where already four or five TB-3s, three R-5s and two ANT-9s were located at 6th Reserve Aviation Base).

26 February 1940 eight aircraft took off for an attack against Nautsi (five bombers returned with bombs).

9 March 1940 SB c/n 6/126 of C.O. of 2nd Squadron was shot down by A-A at Virtaniemi, Nautsi. The navigator *kapitan* V.D. Sheremetyev and MG-gunner *starshina* V.F. Dorozhko were taken prisoner (they arrived in Petsamo on 24 February 1940 from Belaya Tserkov).

"Bombing of [the nickel mine and power station at] Jäniskoski was prohibited, because the mine operated with a British concession" (war diary of 33 SBAP).

33 SBAP Command
Commander	*polkovnik* I.Z. Mel'nikov
	major F.S. Pushkarev
Military commissar	*bat.komiss* Fadeyev
Chief of Staff	*major* Bochkarov
Squadron C.O.	
2nd	*kapitan* V.A. Muravyev (KIA 9.3.40)

33 SBAP performed 318 missions in the Winter War and dropped 125 t bombs.

In GPW 33 SBAP was elevated to Guards status 7 March 1942 and named 10 GvBAP.

Ex-33 SBAP *Lt* V.S. Yefremov (1915–1980) was appointed HSU on 1 May 1943 and for the second time on 24 August 1943.

34th Fighter Aviation Regiment (34 IAP)

34 IAP was formed based in Lyubertsy (Moscow MD) in spring 1938.

Subordination
57 AB, VVS MVO

2nd Squadron (*kapitan* N.P. Anistratenko) was dispatched to Arkhangelsk in October 1939.
In February 1940 34 IAP staff and two I-153 Squadrons were attached to the new 148 IAP.
In combat with seven Finnish fighters at Perkansaari *st.lt* I.P. Rybkin claimed one enemy aircraft, and major Gavrilov two.

34 IAP Command
Commander   *major* N.A. Sbytov (1905–1997). In GPW commanded VVS MVO etc.
Squadron C.O.
2nd   *kapitan* N.P. Anistratenko
Unknown   *major* N.V. Gavrilov (Red Banner Order 7 April 1940)

One former pilot of 34 IAP, *st.lt* G.M. Sokolov was awarded the Golden Star on 21 March 1940. In 25 IAP he claimed 4 victories in 3 combats on 75 missions. Sokolov was killed in action 27 December 1941.
Major N.V. Gavrilov and *st.lt* I.P. Rybkin were awarded the Red Banner Order 7 April 1940.

35th Fast Bomber Aviation Regiment (35 SBAP)

Autumn 1939 35 SBAP was based in Siverskaya (Leningrad MD); five squadrons (of which one was an all-weather/night squadron) with 62 SB bombers.

Subordination
71 AB, VVS LVO
71 AB, VVS 7.A (until 18 December 1939)
OAB, later OAG (from 18 December 1939)

Combat Chronicle
30 November 1939 three SBs attacked Helsinki. Because of the low clouds, the target Malmi airport was not found, so the reserve target Pasila railway station was bombed. During the first two days of the war Helsinki railway station and Malmi airport were the main targets.
1 December 1939 SB c/n 20/203 ("yellow 8", pilot *st.politr* I.B. Blagochnikov, 3rd Squadron) was shot down by A-A and crashed in Munkkiniemi, Helsinki. All crew were killed. According to persistent Finnish rumors one crew member was a woman – however this is not verified by crew lists in Russian archives. In addition also SB c/n 14/203 got A-A hits, MG-gunner P.F. Shornikov died of wounds.
16 December 1939 35 SBAP was attached to OAB (commanded by *polkovnik* G.K. Kravchenko), and ordered to relocate to Estonia. Three squadrons (1st, 2nd and 3rd Squadrons) landed two days later in Sinalepa, Haapsalu, and performed their first combat missions 21 December 1939.
One Squadron of 44 SBAP arrived from Staraya Russa, and was apparently merged with 35 SBAP. At least 2nd Squadron was temporarily located at Kuusiku, but returned to Sinalepa.
4th and 5th Squadrons arrived late to Estonia. The 5th Squadron bomber which had taken off from Gatchina and crashed at Pälkäne 20 January 1940 had just before received orders to relocate to Haapsalu. The pilot of 4th Squadron who was taken prisoner at Läyliäinen had taken off from Rakvere.
The prime task of OAB was to bomb strategic targets in southern Finland. First attacks were made without fighter protection (no enemy interceptors were anticipated in the Finnish rear, and the range of own fighters did not enable escort to given targets), which soon proved to be a mistake. After heavy losses on 20 January 1940 the need for fighter escort became acute. For instance I-153 fighters (of 15 and 38 IAP, also located in Estonia) were equipped with additional fuel tanks, enabling bomber escort during the last phase of the Winter War.
According to a "romantized" Soviet-era Kravchenko-biography the OAB was ordered to destroy the railway bridge of Turku on 21 December 1939, which was Stalin's 60th birthday! Despite attacks by over 20 aircraft no hits were scored, but surrounding buildings were severely damaged. Eight bombers bombed Tampere, dropping 23 bombs. Four civilians were killed in Tampere.

I.L. Turkel, 4./35 SBAP Commander. (G.F. Petrov)

In GPW Squadron Leader Pavel Taran (5 GvAP of ADD) was decorated with his second Golden Star on 13.3.1944 after the bombings of Helsinki in February 1944. (G.F. Petrov)

Christmas Day 25 December 1939 Tampere and Lahti railway stations were bombed. In Tampere five SB dropped 20 bombs, causing damage to the railway yard and several buildings, three persons were wounded. Three aircraft bombed suburbs west of Helsinki-Malmi airfield (which apparently was the intended target).

4th and 5th Squadrons arrived in Sinalepa from 29 December 1939.

1 January 1940 SB c/n 1/202 of 5th Squadron crashed on the return leg at Risti, Estonia (40 km south of Paldiski). The crew was killed.

12 January 1940 Turku railway station was bombed, SB c/n 13/204 *yellow 6* (3rd Squadron) was shot down by A-A, and crashed in Lill-Tervo, Parainen. MG-gunner *starshina* I.S. Grishin was taken prisoner, the pilot committed suicide and the navigator was killed on capture. Two Finnish home guard soldiers were injured. Grishin had arrived in Haapsalu 23 December 1939 from 44 SBAP. This day 35 SBAP performed 102 combat missions, or all bombers performed two missions. *36 bombers in two waves were observed over Turku, 250 bombs were dropped, main targets port, Crichton-Vulcan shipyard and city center. The inhabitants were forced to stay in bomb shelters for over six hours. Several buildings were destroyed, one civilian killed and four wounded.*

13 January 1940 Tampere was bombed by one Squadron, 80 bombs were dropped, the railway junction was severely damaged. Kapt O. Ehrnrooth (C.O. of Koelentue, in FA-1) attacked the last bomber of a nine aircraft formation at Pälkäne-Hauho. Luutn J. Visapää (also of KoeL, FR-91) scored hits on another SB which emitted smoke.

14 January 1940 35 SBAP bombed Riihimäki and Tampere with 84 bombers. At least one SB crashed on the return leg. Both SB c/n 11/81 and 8/109 exploded after direct A-A hits, and crashed at Koski and Janakkala respectively.

15 January 1940 Tampere and Riihimäki were bombed. *SB c/n 2/203 was downed at Tampere by* ylik A. Siltavuori (of KoeL, in FR-91), *who hit the rudder of the SB with his propeller (his guns were malfunctioning in the severe cold). The SB crashed in Vesilahti, all crew were killed. Although Siltavuori was badly injured, he force-landed successfully on the ice of Lake Pyhäjärvi.*

20 January 1940 35 SBAP attacked Tampere with some 32 bombers led by major Sukhorebnikov, some 380 bombs were dropped. Twelve buildings were set on fire, and several factories were damaged. Some 40 bombs fell on the territory of Tampere air field, however without any damage. Tampere city hospital was seriously damaged.

4th Squadron bombed Riihimäki railway junction. Four SB bombers (c/n 16/76, 20/110, 3/111 and 7/203) were shot down in air combat in southern Finland. One SB had taken off from Krasnogvardejsk, two from Haapsalu and one from Kuusiku. Four aviators were killed and eight taken prisoner. In Turku eleven bombers were observed, which dropped 215 bombs (mainly on houses). Two persons were killed and 21 injured. An SB bomber was hit by two Bulldogs from Littoinen (near Turku) and emitted smoke. SB c/n 20/110 (piloted by *lt* Ivan Maksimenko) was later exhibited in the War booty exhibition in Helsinki. Luutn E. Itävuori (FR-91, *which was due for testing after the repair of the damage received during* ylik Siltavuori's *taran-attack five days earlier – see 15 January 1940 above) and* lentom U. Heiskala (FR-101, *both of KoeL) claimed four bombers plus one probable. They in fact downed c/n 3/111 and 16/76 (of 2nd Squadron in Haapsalu) which crash-landed in Pälkäne and Hämeenlinna respectively. All crew of the two bombers were taken prisoner.*

The bomber of 5th Squadron which crashed in Pälkäne 20 January 1940 had taken off from Gatchina, and had only received the order to transfer to Haapsalu, while likewise the captured pilot of 4th Squadron took off from Rakvere.

Air surveillance personnel in Helsinki Stadium tower. In cold and clear "bombing weather" furs and sunglasses were necessary. (SA-kuva)

Soviet map of Helsinki-Malmi airport. (Finnish National Archive)

142

Ylik O. Marttila (of Fokker C.X. equipped LLv 12) happened to be in Tampere to fetch a repaired aircraft from VL. As he had received fighter training, he took off in the airworthy FR-76 and intercepted c/n 7/203 of 5th Squadron. This SB (which had taken off from Krasnogvardejsk) crashed in Janakkala, the navigator was captured, while the pilot and MG-gunner were killed. *Luutn* T. Huhanantti of LLv 24 had also arrived to pick up a Fokker D.XXI, and jumped into FR-91 (which had already been successfully "test-flown" by *luutn* Itävuori) and claimed two bombers, of which c/n 20/110 crashed in Läyliäinen. The pilot was captured, and said that he had arrived only three days before from Novgorod (Krechevitsy?) to Kuusiku.

5th Squadron was still based at Krasnogvardejsk, but was due to transfer to Haapsalu after the Tampere raid and join the rest of the regiment.

17 February 1940 35 SBAP bombed Tampere with 42 SB, dropping some 330 bombs. Some 20 buildings were damaged. Three persons were injured. *Kapt* O. *Ehrnrooth (KoeL, in FA-1) hunted a returning SB from Tampere to Loviisa (on the coast of the Gulf of Finland), setting the bomber on fire.*

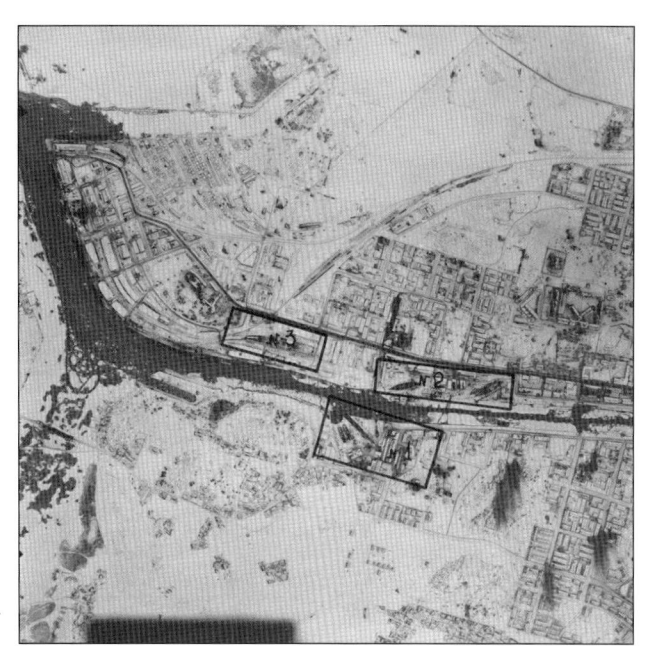

35 SBAP bombed Turku 12.1.1940 (target areas indicated in photo). (RGAVMF)

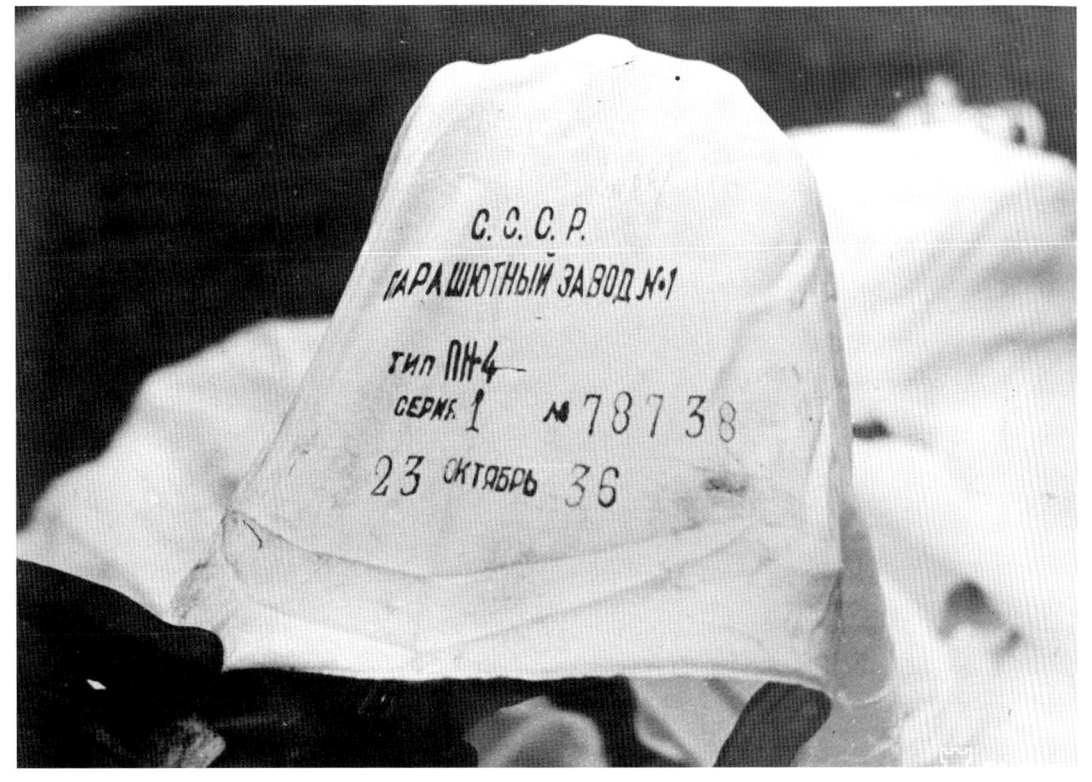

Most of the shot down bombers of 35 SBAP were very badly destroyed, and rather few usable parts could be evacuated. However, an unused parachute was found in one of the wreck. The parachute was produced 23 October 1936 by Parachute Factory No. 1. (SA-kuva)

19 February 1940 twelve SB bombers with crews arrived from 56 SBAP (based in Obo-Somon, Mongolia; with combat experience from the Khalkhin-Gol border clashes in summer 1939) to Sinalepa and joined 35 SBAP.

2 March 1940 35 SBAP and 7 DBAP bombed Tampere. Two SBs did not return from Tampere, and a third SB belly-landed at Paldiski after serious combat damage. 104 bombers attacked Tampere in three waves, and dropped some 600 bombs. 30 buildings were damaged and 10 more totally destroyed. Nine persons were killed and 27 injured. Considerable damage were caused to the railway yard and the electricity network.

35 SBAP lost two SB to pilots of Koelentue (Test Flight). *Kapt* O. Ehrnrooth (FR-101) shot down c/n 1/249 which crashed at Nokia, and *luutn* J. Visäpää (FR-106) damaged c/n 13/108 at Vesilahti. This SB tried to limp home but crashed at Kiikala, 18 km NE Salo. (This bomber was apparently also attacked by *alik* U. Lehtovaara in MS-326.) All six aviators were killed. c/n 5/99 was hit at Tampere, returned on one engine, and crash-landed in Paldiski. The gunner was killed. Koelentue however also suffered a loss as *lentom* U. Heiskala (FR-84) was shot down and killed by an air gunner (of 7 DBAP?) at Tampere. (Ehrnrooth and Visapää in fact claimed DB-3s.)

143

Bombing targets of 35 SBAP included Turku, Tampere, Lahti and Riihimäki, which were all bombed repeatedly. 35 SBAP 1,709 sorties (1,358 bombing missions, of which 48 at night), total flight time over 3,500 hours (82 hours at night), and lost twelve SB in combat (six at Tampere, two at Riihimäki, and one each at Helsinki, Turku, Koski and Lahti), and four SB in accidents. The air gunners of 35 SBAP claimed 18 Finnish fighters, *ml.lt* Ya.Ya. Yelizarov claimed two enemy fighters! *Major* G.A. Sukhorebnikov claimed one ship sunk. Only one Finnish fighter (FR-84, *lentom* U. Heiskala, KIA 2 March 1940) was shot down by OAG bombers (apparently by 7 DBAP).

Somewhat surprisingly 35 SBAP is the only OAG-unit with a HSU award. Several pilots (including *major* G.A. Sukhorebnikov) were proposed HSU-awards, but only *kapitan* N.S. Saranchev was decorated with the Golden Star 19 January 1940.

35 SBAP Command

Commander	*major* G.A. Sukhorebnikov (HSU-proposal, not accepted)
Military commissar	Zajchenko
	bat.komiss Kirenyshev
Chief of Staff	*major* Bogatyryev

Squadron C.O. and Commissars

1st	*kapitan* N.G. Saranchev (1906–1944). HSU 19.1.1940.
2nd	*kapitan* F.F. Zvontsov
3rd	*major* M.I. Skitev
	st.politr I.B. Blagochnikov (KIA 1.12.39)
4th	*major* I.L. Turkel' (1903–1983). Performed 34 combat missions in Winter War. In GPW commanded VVS 14.A etc. Commanded Polish AF 1950–1956.
Unknown	V.M. Najdenko (1915–1969). HSU 21 April 1943 as C.O. 126 IAP.
Unknown	*kapitan* P.F. Borisov
Unknown	*kapitan* K.I. Larionov
Unknown	*kapitan* M.K. Kolesnikov

In GPW ex-35 SBAP *Lt* P.A. Taran served in the Long-Range Aviation ADD. He was appointed HSU on 20 June 1942, and for the second time on 13 March 1944.

38th Fighter Aviation Regiment (38 IAP)

Autumn 1939 38 IAP was based in Pushkin (Leningrad MD), and in September 1939 was dispatched to Zhitomir in Kiev MD. 38 IAP participated in the Polish campaign from 17 to 28 September 1939, after which the regiment returned to Pushkin.

Subordination
59 IAB, VVS LVO
59 IAB, VVS 7.A (to 18 December 1939)
OAB, later OAG (from 18 December 1939)

Double-HSU recipient A.V. Vorozheikin was one of the most successful Soviet fighter aces. He had participated in the Khalkhin-Gol battle 1939, where he claimed six aircraft. During GPW he claimed 52 personal and 14 shared victories in 728 IAP. In his memoirs he mentions the Winter War only spuriously. The photo is taken post war when he served in the Naval AF. (G.F. Petrov)

In late November 1939 38 IAP was split up into two parts, commanded by *major* N.T. Syusyukalov (1st and 4th Squadrons in Pushkin/I-16 and I-15bis, and Vyskatka/I-15bis) and *major* T.V. Ledenev (2nd and 3rd Squadrons in Pushkin; I-16 and I-153) respectively.

In December 1939 38 IAP was completely reorganized: *major* Ledenev's part became a pure I-153 unit attached to *polkovnik* G.K. Kravchenko's OAB in Estonia, while *major* Syusyukalov's Squadrons were split up and dispatched in various directions.

16 December 1939 *major* Ledenev was ordered to relocate (with I-153 fighters only) to OAB in Sinalepa, Kuusiku (Rapla) and Klooga (near Paldiski), Estonia. Two days later the fighters took off for Estonia. Additional I-153s were received from 3rd and 4th Squadrons of 25 IAP, the latter Squadron arrived in Estonia from 21 January 1940.

The I-15bis fighters of 1st and 3rd Squadrons were transported by train 5–20 December 1939 from Pushkin to VVS 9.A at Uhtua, where two new fighter regiments were being set up:
- 145 IAP in Kairala (the 30 I-15bis aircraft of 38 IAP formed 1st and 2nd Squadrons),
- 152 IAP in Poduzhemye (only personnel for 4th Squadron).

St.lt N.P. Perevezentsev (2./38 IAP) crash-landed 20.2.1940 after ground fire with I-153 "16" (c/n 6804) in Kirkkkonummi. The pilot died of his wounds four days later. (SA-kuva)

Kapitan Savtshenko's 4th Squadron (I-15bis) starting on 13 December 1939 was dispatched by train from Pushkin to VVS 14.A at Murmashi, and was attached to 5 OSAP. The Squadron became the nucleus of 147 OIAP which was set up in January 1940. (This Squadron was apparently temporarily also attached to 25 IAP, as the pilots taken prisoner near Petchenga 19 January 1940 told that they came from 25 IAP. (See 147 OIAP, page 207)

From 19 December 1939 the I-16 fighters of 38 IAP were likewise divided between 7 IAP in Kasimovo and 68 IAP in Levashovo. *St.lt* P.K. Kozachenko got the task to set up a new I-153 Squadron for 25 IAP by 1 February 1940.

4 January 1940 4th Squadron of 43 IAP and 12 January 1940 4th Squadron of 2 IAP arrived with 15 I-153 each (both from VVS KOVO), which formed 1st and 2nd Squadrons of 38 IAP.

6–20 January 1940 *st.lt* V.D. Popov's Squadron (equipped with new I-16 *tip* 18 fighters) was transferred to 7 IAP, and became 2nd Squadron.

38 IAP was late December 1939 reinforced with 2nd and 4th Squadrons (I-153) of 25 IAP. The latter Squadron arrived in Estonia from 21 January 1940.

11 January 1940 *kapitan* A.T. Kostenko's I-16 Squadron arrived from 25 IAP.

The base location at Klooga enabled bomber escort to southern Finland. However, after heavy bomber losses at Tampere-Hämeenlinna, I-153s were also equipped with under-wing fuel tanks, which

N.I. Vydashenko (4./38 IAP) force-landed 11.3.1940 on frozen Gulf of Finland. He was rescued by his own side's aircraft, and the only slightly damaged I-153 (c/n 7275) was retrieved by Finnish troops. (Porvoo museum)

I-153 c/n 6776 of lt M.A. Bobrov (38 IAP) force-landed on the ice 20 km south of Inkoo. Lt G.I. Romashkov landed nearby with I-153 c/n 6795, but made a ground loop. Next day both pilots were picked up by their own aviators, and the aircraft wrecks were retrieved by Finnish troops. (C-F. Geust)

considerably increased safe escort range. One I-153 Squadron arrived also 20 February 1940 from 56 IAP (1 AG in Undur-Khan, Mongolia) to Kuusiku (possibly only pilots without aircraft).

M*ajor* Ledenev thus commanded the "renewed" 38 IAP in Estonia, while the nucleus of the original 38 IAP (commanded by *major* Syusyukalov) was on 12 January 1940 transferred to VVS SZFr. This element was subsequently expanded to the new 149 IAP set up in Pushkin 31 January 1940 (commanded by *major* Syusyukalov).

14 January 1940 I-153 c/n 6576 of 4th Squadron was hit and crashed in the Gulf of Finland, deputy Squadron leader *st.politr* M.Ya. Shishkin was killed.

20 January 1940 *major* Ledenev claimed a Fokker D.XXI at Riihimäki *Ilmavoimat did not suffer any losses.*

2 February 1940 *kapitan* V.P. Teplyakov shot down an enemy fighter when attacking Turku AF base. *kapitan* Sergeyev and *st.lt* Ivanov claimed three Bulldogs destroyed on the ground. *No Finnish losses suffered.* Luutn P. Berg of LLv 26 (in Gladiator GL-263 on transfer from Sweden) intercepted some ten I-153 south of Turku, and shot down I-153 c/n 6469 in Bromarf. St.lt N.I. Bedarev was taken prisoner; his original unit was 4th Squadron/25 IAP.

7 February 1940 *kapitan* Kashtanov and *st.lt* Shepetov claimed two Fokkers at Turku. Ilmavoimat *did not suffer any losses.*

20 February 1940 fourteen I-153 fighters led by 38 IAP deputy C.O. *bat.komiss* N. Kuligin took off with task to protect 53 DBAP bombers returning from Riihimäki, and to attack trains. A train was seen moving eastwards towards Kauniainen, and was attacked by *st.lt* N.P. Perevezentsev's flight. At Karvasmäki (1 km N of Espoo) fierce A-A machine-gun fire was encountered, and Perevezentsev's c/n 6804 was hit, and crashed on the ice south of Kirkkonummi. The seriously wounded pilot was captured, and said that his Squadron had relocated from the Leningrad area to Kuusiku in early February, while the other Squadrons had operated from Kuusiku already from early January. Perevezentsev perished four days later and was buried in Malmi cemetery in Helsinki. On 9 December 1940 his remains were handed over to the Russian legation in Helsinki, and subsequently buried in Hanko naval base.

2 March 1940 *st.lt* Lazarev and *st.lt* Shepetov claimed two Fokker D.XXI fighters shot down at Tampere. *No Fokker lost 2 March 1940 .*

5 March 1940 4th Squadron (led by *kapitan* V.G. Kashtanov) was searching for enemy aircraft at Parainen, when the leading I-153 (c/n 7271) was badly hit by A-A artillery. *kapitan* Kashtanov was however able to get the aircraft under control and fly back to Estonia. At the forced landing (on the ice?) the rear fuselage broke off. *Kashtanov's aircraft was shot down by 55.KevIt.Jaos, equipped with two 40 mm Bofors cannons, the prime task of which was defense of the factories of Pargas Kalkverk AB.*

11 March 1940 three I-153 fighters were lost: 4th Squadron *politr* N.I. Vydashenko force-landed with c/n 7275 on the ice near Långö (some 25 km south of Loviisa) after A-A hits. *Lt* G.L. Lobach landed

next to the force-landed I-153, and gave the stranded Vydachenko a ride home after his aircraft was set on fire. *According to Finnish documents an I-153 landed south of Norra Rönnskär, 1 km SO Bastö. Finnish patrols from Orrengrund and Bastö retrieved the I-153 which was captured almost intact.*

Lt G.I. Romashkov (flight leader, 5th Squadron) had less luck when he tried to pick up *lt* M.A. Dobrov (also of 5th esc.) After engine malfunction Dobrov force-landed with c/n 6776 also on the frozen Gulf of Finland, some 20 km south of Inkoo (12 km from Bågaskär lighthouse, direction 175°). Romashkov made a ground loop when landing with c/n 6795, and lost consciousness for a while. After a chilly night Romashkov tried to reach his own territory on foot, and was fortunately found after some ten kilometers by a patrol of the co-located 15 IAP (both 15 IAP and 38 IAP were based in Klooga). At 1705 hours *major* V.L. Bobrik (commander 15 IAP) landed on the ice and picked up *lt* Romashkov. *lt* Dobrov was waiting at the force-landing site, and was rescued by *kapitan* I.N. Sharov, who landed on the ice, while *st.lt* Kuznetsov was protecting the rescue operation. *According to Finnish archive documents the two crashed aircraft on the ice were detected from Bågaskär lighthouse 12 March 1940, and a patrol was sent out to investigate. Upon approach to the aircraft (which were 400 m apart) two other I-153 fighters arrived and strafed the Finnish patrol, killing one soldier. Next day the crashed aircraft were again investigated by a Finnish patrol, this time without interruption. The patrol noticed that two Soviet aviators (of which one was apparently seriously wounded) had walked on the ice some 12 km in a SE direction, and were then picked up by Soviet aircraft.*

38 IAP performed 2,288 combat missions (of which 742 were interception missions, 683 ground-attack and reconnaissance missions, 25 missions searching for "aircraft missing over enemy territory" and 6 night bombing missions), flight time 2,541 hours, and claimed 12 enemy aircraft shot down. During ground-attack missions 1,438 bombs (66.1 tons) were dropped. The railway station and railway yard in Karjaa was intensively attacked on 147 missions, with 16.2 tons of bombs dropped. Own losses were three aviators in combat and nine aircraft (of which seven were in combat).

Golden Stars were proposed to *major* T.V. Ledenev (who claimed two Fokker D.XXI on one mission), *lt* G.L. Lobach and *lt* M.A. Dobrov), but all proposals were rejected.

38 IAP Command

Commander	*major* N.T. Syusyukalov (1905–1942). Later commanded 149 IAP. Participated in Spanish Civil War, 2 victory claims. In GPW commanded 43 IAP.
	major T.V. Ledenev (HSU-proposal, not accepted)
	Loktionov
Military commissar	*bat.komiss* N.A. Kuligin
	st.politr A.V. Vorozhejkin (1912–2001; from February 1940). Khalkhin-Gol veteran 1939 (6 victories). One of the top fighter aces in GPW. Double HSU (4.3.1944 and 19.8.1944), with 52+14 victory claims in 728 IAP. After WW II Deputy Commander of PVO ChF etc. The Winter War is only spuriously mentioned in his memoirs.
Chief of Staff	*major* Sokolovskiy

Squadron C.O. and commissars

1st	*major* V.M. Fatnev
	st.politr Polkanov
2nd	*kapitan* N.G. Sobolev. Participated in Spanish Civil War, 2 victory claims. In Winter War 32 combat missions, and in GPW 193 combat missions, 9 + 8 victory claims.
	kapitan K.P. Sokol
	st. politr L.S. Chapchakhov
	kapitan Nikiforov
3rd	*st.lt* V.L. Grishin
	st.politr Mineyev
4th	*kapitan* V.G. Kashtanov (27 war missions)
	st.politr N.I. Vydashenko
5th	*kapitan* K.D. Kochetkov
	st.politr A.V. Vorozhejkin
Unknown	*st.lt* V.D. Popov (I-16; to 7 IAP 6–20.1.40)
Unknown	*kapitan* A.T. Kostenko

In GPW 38 IAP was elevated to Guards status 3 May 1942 and named 21 GvIAP.

39th Fast Bomber Aviation Regiment (39 SBAP)

Autumn 1939 39 SBAP was based in Staraya Bykhov (Byelorussian MD). 18 December 1939 39 SBAP arrived from Bobrujsk to VVS 8.A in Lodejnoye pole, and was attached to 13 SBAB 2 February 1940. After 15th Army was formed 13 SBAB (including 39 SBAP) on 18 February 1940 was transferred to VVS 15.A, strength 54 SB and returned to VVS 8.A 1 March 1940.

Subordination
VVS BOVO
VVS 8.A (from 18 December 1939)
13 SBAB, VVS 8.A (from 2 February 1940)
13 SBAB, VVS 15.A (from 18 February 1940)

Combat Chronicle
According to a decision late December 1939 5th Squadron of 39 SBAP was to be transferred to 72 AP of the Northern Fleet (VVS SF). In early January 1940 this Squadron was sent to Lodejnoye pole for installation of ski undercarriage, and was temporarily attached to 72 SAP of VVS 8.A (note that 72 SAP, which is described elsewhere in detail, is an entirely different unit than 72 AP of the Northern Fleet. The common number "72" is only coincidental.)

The local representative of 72 SAP Pankov was however unable (or unwilling) to arrange the ski installation. Only 18 January 1940 (during the absence of Pankov) skis were installed on explicit order by *polkovnik*, Commander of 13 SBAB, B.K. Tokarev, who also took the Squadron under his own command. Tokarev ordered two SB bombers to perform a local combat mission 20 January 1940.

20 January 1940 the SB piloted by 5th Squadron C.O., *kapitan* I.I. Legejda was shot down at Nietjärvi. Legejda was wounded, the MG-gunner was killed, the navigator escaped by parachute and returned after 8 days. *Lentom V. Pyötsiä (FR-110) claimed two SB bombers (the other SB apparently from 18 SBAP) at Korpiselkä.*

12 SB bombers of 39 SBAP formed 5th Squadron of 31 SBAP, and were dispatched to Chernevo 20 January 1940.

27 January 1940 *polkovnik* Tokarev ordered the rest of the Squadron to fulfill their original order to transfer to Vayenga near Murmansk. The ferry flight was undertaken next day, but at Medvezhegorsk (Karhumäki) a snowstorm was encountered. Five SB were able to turn back and landed in Petrozavodsk, while three SB bombers crashed, and one was damaged force-landing at Medvezhegorsk. Five aviators were killed, and several others severely injured.

2 February 1940 the main part of 39 SBAP was attached to 13 SBAP in Lodejnoye pole.

13 February 1940 5th Squadron of 39 SBAP lost three SBs (c/n 16/115, 14/217 and 11/219) in air combat at Suistamo, eight aviators were killed. Next day pilot *lt* I.S. Khramtsov, who had escaped by parachute from SB c/n 11/219, was taken prisoner, all the other eight crew members were killed. Khramtsov had taken off from Lodejnoye pole at 13.00 hours, with the task to bomb hill 108.8 east of Pyhäjärvi and to drop leaflets. *Gladiators of LLv 26 claimed five SBs at Jänisjärvi-Loimola: ylik O. Tuominen (3.5 SBs and an I-15bis with GL-255), lentom L. Lautamäki (0.5 SB with GL-253) and Danish volunteer Løjtnant J. Ulrich (2 SBs with GL-257). I-153s of 49 IAP in their turn shot down Løjtnant J. Ulrich (GL-257, WIA) and Løjtnant C. Kalmberg (GL-260, KIA); both were Danish volunteers.*

14 February 1940 SB c/n 17/65 piloted by Orabinskiy collided at take-off with parked TB-3 c/n 22312 red 2 (pilot *lt* V.N. Ishkov, of 3rd Squadron/3 TBAP) in Lodejnoye pole. Factory repair of both aircraft was required.

At night 25.-26 February 1940 two SB were damaged by enemy bombing of Lodejnoye pole AF base. *LLv 46 bombed Lodejnoye pole with three Blenheims on the night of 25–26 February 1940, and on 26 February 1940 afternoon with three Blenheims. According to Finnish observations next day eight aircraft were destroyed.*

29 February 1940 two SB bombers (c/n 18/65 of 39 SBAP and c/n 19/243 of 45 SBAP) were destroyed in a mid-air collision at Lodejnoye pole. All six aviators were killed.

1 March 1940 two aircraft of 39 SBAP were dispatched to 18 SBAP at Nurmolitsa.

3 March 1940 three aircraft (two from 18 SBAP and one ex-39 SBAP) took off from Nurmolitsa to bomb the main road, railway crossings and bridges between Syskyjärvi and Loimola. SB c/n 18/65 of 2nd Squadron was shot down by A-A artillery at Loimola, *shurman ml.lt* F.Ye. Nazarov escaped by parachute and was taken prisoner.

7 March 1940 the civil registered SP liaison aircraft L-2624 (mentioned in 13 SBAP section, see page 111), is also referred to in 39 SBAP documents.

39 SBAP performed 900 bombing missions during which 451.3 t of bombs were dropped. Furthermore 39 SBAP performed 59 supply dropping missions, during which over 65.3 tons food and other supplies were dropped to encircled Soviet troops of 56th Army Corps.

Strength and Locations

Date	Base	Subordination	Base unit	Aircraft
1.1.40	Staraya Bykhov	-	9 RAB, 116 AB	38 SB
1.2.40	Lotinapelto	13 AB, VVS 8.A	6 RAB, 116 AB	63 SB
1.3.40	Lotinapelto	13 AB, VVS 15.A	6 RAB, 116 AB	60 SB
1.4.40	Staraya Bykhov	41 AB	9 RAB, 116 AB	57 SB

39 SBAP command

Commander	*major* G.A Georgiyev
	major P.N. Zakharitsev
Military commissar	*bat.komiss* Seregin?
	Mokulin
Chief of Staff	*major* Altovich
Squadron C.O.	
1st	*kapitan* Mikryukov
	kapitan D.T. Zhuravskiy
2nd	*kapitan* Kosarev
	kapitan Sherbakov
3rd	*kapitan* A.A. Zayats
4th	*kapitan* Sergeyev?
	kapitan Kutryesov
5th	*kapitan* I.I. Legejda
	kapitan Debrov

41st Fast Bomber Aviation Regiment (41 SBAP)

Autumn 1939 41 SBAP was located in Kalinin (Kalinin MD).

Subordination
   13 AB, AON-1 (November 1939)
   VVS LVO (late November 1939)
   15 SBAB, VVS 7.A (December 1939)
   27 AB, AON-1 (December 1939)
   VVS 9.A (from 20 December 1939)
   10 SBAB, VVS 9.A (late January 1940)

Combat Chronicle
Considerable losses, frequent organization and subordination changes are typical for 41 SBAP.
   Late November 1939 41 SBAP (with three SB squadrons) arrived from 13 AB in Kalinin (according to POW questioning from Mozhajsk) via Krechevitsy to Gorelovo (20 km SW Leningrad), and was attached to VVS LVO. 3rd Squadron had relocated from Krechevitsy, Novgorod to Gorelovo on 29 November 1939, the other squadrons were still remaining in Krechevitsy. 1 December 1939 the regiment was subordinated to 27 AB (AON-1), but was operationally attached to 15 SBAB (VVS 7.A); strength 49 SB.
   1 December 1939 the first combat missions of 41 SBAP ended tragically: regiment commander I.Ye. Kolomiets led four bombers to destroy Suur-Merijoki AF base. 3rd Squadron attacked Rouhiala, Imatra and Lappeenranta; take-off from Gorelovo at 1300 hours. Particular task was to destroy the hydro-electrical power plant at Imatra, and the high-voltage power lines from Imatra to the west, reserve target Imatra railroad junction. SB c/n 16/101 (3rd Squadron) was shot down by A-A artillery and crashed in Montola, Lappee. The pilot *lt* N.G. Sapon and *shturman lt* P.G. Anichenko escaped by parachute and were taken prisoner, the MG-gunner was killed.
   SB c/n 2/72 of 5th Squadron did also not return. Although 1,216 bombs (2.5–100 kg) had been dropped (total weight 16.1 t), bombing results were only moderate. More significant were the heavy

This and opposite page: SB yellow 9 (2./41 SBAP, c/n 20/101) force-landed 1.12.1939 at Mansikkakoski, Imatra 1.12.1939. The only slightly damaged aircraft was repaired by VL, and later used by Ilmavoimat. (SA-kuva)

Above: Pilot Osetian lt *Zh. Tanklayev (photo) and navigator* st.lt *V.A. Demchinskiy of yellow 9 were captured. (G.F. Petrov)*

losses: of 29 bombers taking off 41 SBAP had lost six bombers and 18 aviators on its very first combat mission. Four aviators were Finnish POWs (which only became known in spring 1940).

2nd Squadron (led by *kapitan* Nazolin) took off from Krechevitsy at 1225 hours, task to destroy Immola AF base. Four SB were lost in air combat, of which three did not return, and the badly damaged fourth SB c/n 1/110 burned on forced-landing in Volosovo. Kapt G. Magnusson shot down c/n 2/48, which crashed in Rampalanjärvi. Kers L. Heikinaro and Løjtnant J. Karhunen shot jointly down SB c/n 13/110 (piloted by regiment commissar A.A. Anikeyev), which crashed in Mietinsaari, while luutn J. Räty shot down a third SB c/n 20/102 ("yellow 9") which landed at Mansikkakoski, pilot lt Zh.T. Tanklayev and shturman st.lt V.A. Demchinskiy were taken prisoner. In Immola DH Moth MO-111 liaison aircraft was burned.

After these huge losses the demoralized 41 SBAP virtually ceased to exist, and on 15 December 1939 some elements were attached to 44 SBAP in Staraya Russa.

As the regiment still formally existed, it was decided to reinstate 41 SBAP in VVS 9.A in northern Karelian ASSR, where no Finnish fighters threatened Soviet bombers.

The first reinforcements arrived from Kalinin Military District, and five SB were ferried to Chiksha, where operational readiness was reached 20 December 1939. Two days earlier Regiment Commander *polkovnik* I.Ye. Kolomiyets departed in SB c/n 12/110 from Leningrad region to Uhuta to receive his reinforcements. He did not however reach his destination, but disappeared during the ferry flight. The crashed SB was found after the war 3 km east of Tokari railway station (the accident report is dated 16 April 1940; the accident date is here 25 December 1939!).

20–31 December 1939 41 SBAP performed about 200 bombing missions in the Suomussalmi region, supporting the deteriorating situation of the Soviet 163rd Division.

28 December 1939 54 SB dropped a large number of small splinter bombs (total weight 6.1 ton) and 60 FAB-100, FAB-50 and ZAB-50 bombs on Finnish troops in Suomussalmi, and also strafed Finnish positions with machine-gun fire. This heavy bombing apparently enabled 163rd Division to withdraw from Suomussalmi to the north towards Juntusranta.

1 January 1940 41 SBAP numbered 28 SB. On this day SB c/n 4/103 of 4th Squadron (*ml.lt* V.M. Goryanin) was destroyed by own bomb splinters, all crew were killed. Another SB of 4th Squadron (*lt* Ye.N. Pavlov) crashed on the return leg on own territory; the injured crew were able to reach Uhtua.

Some bombers were attached to 9 SBAP, which late December 1939 was established in Kem', and in mid-January 1940 relocated to Sholopovo ice base.

7 January 1940 SB c/n 19/103 was destroyed in an unsuccessful night landing in Chiksha, pilot *st.lt* S.A. Bannikov (4th Squadron) was killed.

9 January 1940 SB c/n 20/225 force-landed after hits, MG-gunner *starshina* N.A. Konovalov was killed.

21 January 1940 44 SB of 41 SBAP (including some bombers of 80 SAP) took off from Uhtua in three waves during the afternoon and evening and bombed Oulu (according to Stalin's explicit order as revenge for the establishment of of the Swedish F19-aircraft base in the city). Four FAB-500, 33 FAB-250, 148 FAB-100 and over 1,400 smaller (1–50 kg) bombs were dropped at the city. Fortunately the damage was moderate: 17 houses destroyed and 10 houses damaged. Only one Danish volunteer soldier on guard was killed, and a few persons who went to the shelters too late were injured, but the invaluable

SB tactical no. 12 (3./41 SBAP, c/n 16/101) also crashed 1.12.1939 in Lappee. lt N.G. Sapon and lt P.G. Onishchenko bailed out and were captured. (SA-kuva)

collections of the Historical and Scientific Museums were destroyed. One SB-bomber of 2nd Squadron (*st.lt* N.I. Laukhin) did not return from the bombing mission to Oulu.

Late January 1940 41 SBAP was attached to 10 SBAB, which had arrived in Uhuta from Kiev.

7 February 1940 16 SBAP and 41 SBAP bombed Kajaani with 19 and 25 SBs respectively. Targets ordered: "the railway station and the city". 41 SBAP attacked at 1415–1425 hours. Altogether 41 SBAP dropped 2 FAB-500, 8 FAB-250, 60 FAB-100, 12 FAB-50, 2 AF-32 and 18 AO-25 explosive bombs, and 8 ZAB-50, 1344 ZAB 2.5 and 336 ZAB-1 incendiary bombs. The aviators observed five direct hits in the railway station. "*Several fires in the city. The target is destroyed.*" (See 10 and 15 SBAB, pages 48 and 50)

12 February 1940 SB (c/n 14/109?) of 3rd Squadron was hit by A-A fire at Ranta-Repola, MG-gunner G.M. Chudinov was killed.

20 February 1940 a bomber of 5th Squadron (*st.lt* A.N. Gordik) crashed at Repola because of pilot error at take-off. All crew were killed.

In addition several bombers were damaged in accidents.

41 SBAP Combat Missions

Base	Combat missions
Krechevitsy	40
Gorelovo	18 (9 returned without bombing)
Besovets	72
Chiksha	1,372 (200 returned)
Repola	1,053
Total	2,555 combat missions (209 failed), flight time 3,516 h 57 min.
Night missions	141 (36 failed)

41 SBAP Bombing targets

Targets	Missions
Railway stations	252
Rail transports	30
Railway bridges	47
Enemy troops	816
Population centres, industrial targets	152
Aerodromes	25
Food dropping to surrounded 54th Division	999
Reconnaissance	31

41 SBAP Aircraft/personnel losses

Date	Crashed in own territory	MIA	Catastrophies	Accidents	Missing during ferry flights	Force landings
1.12.39	1/-	6/18	-	-	-	3
2–31.12.39	-	-	-	4	¼	1
January 1940	2/-	1/3	1/1	1	-	11
February 1940	5/1	-	1/3	2		1
March 1940	-	-	-	-	-	-
Total	8/1	7/21	2/4	7	¼	16

One of the captured aviators is questioned in Enso 4.12.1939. (SA-kuva)

Comments:

Catastrophies: One at Chiksha (a night landing), and one at Reboly (spin).

Accidents: two accidents at Chiksha (short runway), two aircraft sank (ice at ice base too thin), one accident on a forced-landing, one accident in bad weather and one accident due to pilot error.

Forced-landings: loss of orientation 9, bad weather 9, darkness 3, enemy A-A 5.

41 SBAP Bomb attacks
- Immola, 11 missions 1.12.39
- Imatra, chemical plant and ammunition store, 9 missions 1.12.39
- Hovinmaa railway station, 8 missions 1.12.39
- Suurmerijoki AF base, 14 missions 1.12.39
- Suurpero railway station, 4 missions, 1.12.39
- Suomussalmi, enemy troops, 98 missions, 21.12.39–8.3.40
- Kontionmäki railway station, 37 missions 21.12.39–13.2.40
- Kemijärvi railway station and city, 18 missions 21.12.39–6.2.40
- 54.D; enemy troops, 463 missions 3.2–13.3.1940

- Kylänlahti railway station, 2 missions 4.2.40
- Vaala railway bridge, 3 missions 4.2.40
- Eno railway bridge, 27 missions 25.2.40
- Sortavala railway bridge, 25 missions 21–25.12.39
- Ilomantsi, 18 missions 24.12.39
- Läskelä railway station, 18 missions 27.12.39
- 163. D, Juntusranta, enemy troops, 9 missions 24–25.1.40
- Sija, Saukoski enemy troops, 30 missions 23–31.1.40
- Hiisjärvi, enemy troops, 8 missions 24.12.39
- Taivalkoski, 26 missions 1–23.1.40
- Oulu, 34 missions 3–22.1.40
- Vihanti, 1 mission 3.1.40, 6 FAB-100
- Sotkajärvi, 1 mission 3.1.40, 6 FAB-100
- Kajaani railway station, 21 missions 3.1–7.2.40, h 1,000–2,200 m, 2 FAB-500, 8 FAB-250, 36 FAB-100, 46 FAB-50, 13 ZAB-50, 336 ZAB-1, total 11,886 kg
- Kajaani city, 31 missions 4.1–23.2.40, height 1,000–2,200 m, 2 FAB-500, 48 FAB-100, 77 FAB-50, 26 ZAB-50, 1512 ZAB-2,5, 336 ZAB-1, total 15,078 kg
- Kuhmoniemi enemy troops, 35 missions 4.1–29.1.1940
- Hirvasvaara, enemy troops, 6 missions, 26.1.40
- Koski enemy troops, 9 missions, 27.1.40
- Vuokatti railway station, 10 missions, 23.1.-1.3.40
- Truck colonnes (Suomussalmi, Vaala station, Kajaani) 20 missions, 4.2–1.3.40, h 400–2,000 m, 22 FAB-100, 17 FAB-50, 106 FAB-32, 30 AO-25, 216 AO-15, 72 AO-10, 48 AO-8; total 8,530 kg
- Paliniemi railway station, 3 missions 18.2.40
- Murtomäki railway station, 3 missions 18.2.40
- Pielisjärvi railway station, 25 missions 19–22.2.40
- Jurikolahti railway station, 1 mission, 1.3.40
- Sotkamo, 13 missions 15–23.2.40
- Iisalmi railway station, 12 missions 17–19.2.40
- Kiehima railway station, 15 missions 16–18.1.40
- Tapaanivara, 1 mission 18.1.40
- Nurmes railway station, 38 missions 18.1.-22.2.40
- Lentiira, 5 missions, 21.1.40
- Kuusamo, 39 missions, 23–31.1.40
- Puolanka, 14 missions 3.1–26.2.40
- Salmijärvi, Kursu troops 73 missions 18–31.1.40
- Hyrynsalmi, 49 missions 18.1–27.2.40
- 54.D, food dropping, 999 missions, total 450,000 kg
  Information of 3rd and 5th Squadrons (Besovets) incomplete.

Kajaani city centre was almost entirely destroyed on 7.2.1940. (Kajaani museum)

41 SBAP command
Commander	*polkovnik* I.Ye. Kolomiyets (KIA 18.12.39)
	polkovnik G.A. Shanin
	polkovnik I.T. Batygin (1905-)
Military Commissar	*bat.komiss* M.M. Anikeyev (KIA 1.12.39)
	bat.komiss P.M. Teperskiy (1909-)
Chief of Staff	*major* Antonov (?)
	major F.A. Obojshchikov (1906-)

Squadron C.O. and Commissars
1st	*kapitan* Ye.M. Anikeyev
	st.politr Sokolov
2nd	*lt* Starikov
	kapitan Ye.P. Nazolin (1908-)
	politr Ivanov
	st.politr M.A. Didenko (1909-)
3rd	*kapitan* K.F. Katarkin (1912-)
	st.politr A.I. Nikitin (1908-)
	kapitan Solovyev (?)
	st.politr Bezits (?)
4th	*major* I.I. Avtonomov
5th	*major* I.N. Kozlov (1907-)
	bat.komiss P.V. Gal'chuk (1904-)
Unknown	*kapitan* Novikov

42nd Long-Range Bomber Aviation Regiment (42 DBAP)

Autumn 1939 42 DBAP was located in Voronezh (Orel MD).

Subordination
64 DBAB, AON-2 (until January 1940)
27 DBAB, VVS SZFr (from 25 January 1940)

Combat Chronicle
42 DBAP arrived 15–21 January 1940 with 58 DB-3 from 64 AB (AON-2) from Voronezh to Krechevitsy. Upon arrival 42 DBAP was attached to 27 DBAB, VVS SZFr. Operational readiness was reached 30 January 1940, strength 45 DB-3 bombers.

3 February 1940 targets of the first combat mission of 42 DBAP were Jyväskylä railway junction (4th Squadron, reserve target Joensuu railway junction) and Kuopio ammunition factory (5th Squadron).

The squadrons had been reinforced to formations of 18 aircraft each. 42 DBAP commander *major* Vyaznikov personally led the formation bound for Kuopio. The order to bomb Kuopio was given only 25 minutes before take-off at 1136 hours, so most navigators were still making their route calculations during take-off and flight towards the target. After Kuopio had been bombed *major* Vyaznikov's detachment returned via Sortavala, which had rather strong air defense, and was thus subject to A-A fire and attacks by Finnish fighters and A-A fire.

Six DB-3 were lost because for various reasons (two aircraft collided in mid-air, enemy fighters downed three bombers, and one went missing). Three aircraft were seriously damaged, and 17 (!) bombers force-landed in various places.

Kapitan F.S. Snobkov (5th Squadron C.O.) force-landed with DB-3 c/n 391450 ("9", ex "5") in Jääski at 14.00 hours because of engine malfunction. *kapitan* Snobkov and R/T operator/gunner *ml.lt* M.V. Mikhalin were killed by Finnish troops, *shturman kapitan* I.A. Solovyevich was taken prisoner.

After overhaul at VL the intact DB-3 was taken into use by Finnish Air Force, coded VP-12.

Late February 1940 a cold period with clear skies began, enabling the bombers to easily find their targets. 42 DBAP repeatedly bombed the important Elisenvaara railway junction, in order to prevent transport of troops and supplies to the Karelian isthmus. In this 26.2.1940 post-bombing photo the Elisenvaara junction area is covered by black smoke. (RGVA)

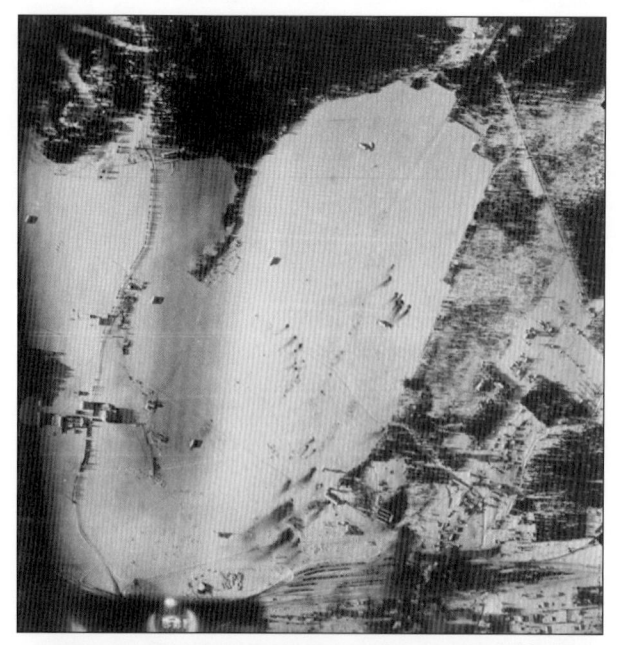

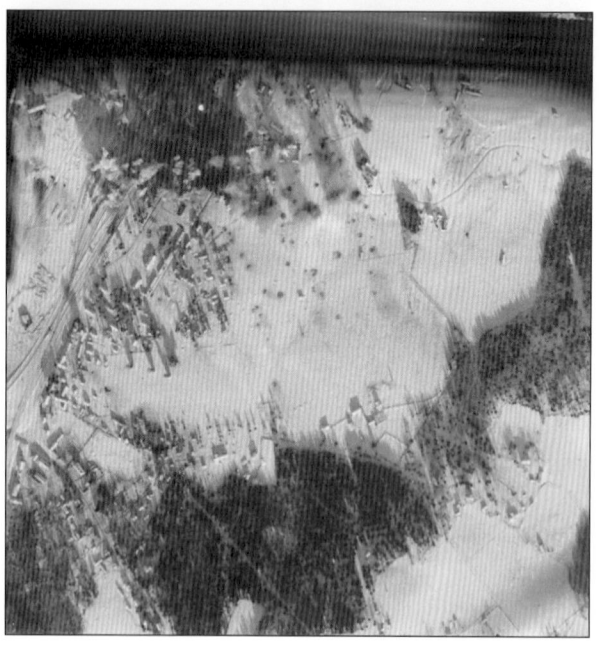

At Sortavala-Rapattila three bombers were shot down: DB-3 c/n 391151 *"14"* (also of 5th Squadron) force-landed at Salonlappaa, Läskelä at 1630 hours after hits in air combat. The wounded pilot *st.lt* N.H. Vorobyev (who made an unsuccessful suicide attempt) and RT-operator/gunner *ser.* V.Ya. Pal'chikov were taken prisoner, *shturman st.lt* K.N. Sokolov shot himself on capture. The prisoners told that the Squadron took off from *Voronezh* at 0900 hours (disinformation?) to bomb Jyväskylä railway station (reserve target Pieksämäki?).

Also DB-3 c/n 390538 (5th Squadron) did not return, and DB-3 c/n 390350 (1st Squadron) crashed at Rapattila. Vorobyev and Palchikov died (like two other POW-aviators) of CO-suffocation in the POW camp in Otrakkala, Ruskeala 8–9 February 1940. Majuri *G. Magnusson (FR-92) shot down one DB-3 south of Joutseno, and* luutn *J. Sarvanto (FR-80) shot down another DB-3 at Nuijamaa-Hanhijärvi.*

At least three aircraft headed east (after loss of orientation?), and force-landed at Lodejnoye pole. Two bombers collided, and *major* Vyaznikov's aircraft made a ground loop. S.F. Ushakov (later Colonel General in ADD) recollects in his memoirs: *"the regiment Commander was not familiar with DB-bombers, so numerous accidents happened in the regiment"*... Upon return four Finnish fighters were claimed shot down.

14 February 1940 DB-3 c/n 390838 (2nd Squadron) was destroyed after A-A hits, all four aviators were killed.

15 February 1940 DB-3 c/n 391451 (4th Squadron) was shot down in air combat at Ihantala. Luutn *J. Sarvanto (FR-80) shot down a DB-3 bomber at Kärstilänjärvi-Noskua, and* ylik *V. Porvari (LLv 26) in Gladiator GL-264 claimed another DB-3 bomber at Suulajärvi.*

15 February 1940 bombing target was Antrea. DB-3 c/n 391451 (4th Squadron) was shot down in air combat at Pilppula, the crew was killed. Luutn *J. Sarvanto (FR-80) shot down a DB-3 at Kärstilänjärvi-Noskua, and* ylik *V. Porvari (LLv 26; GL-264) claimed a DB-3 at Suulajärvi.*

19 February 1940 DB-3 c/n 391346 was hit by A-A artillery at Antrea, and crashed in Lake Kirkkojärvi.

25 February 1940 the DB-3 piloted by *ml.lt* A.M. Markov was hit. The seriously wounded Markov was able to make a successful forced-landing on Soviet-held territory, and thus saved his crew. Markov was appointed HSU 7 April 1940.

29 February 1940 nine bombers were heading for Elisenvaara railway junction, where DB-3 c/n 390448 (5th Squadron) was shot down by A-A artillery. Pilot *lt* A.I. Oblogin escaped by parachute and was taken prisoner, the other crew members were killed.

During the Elisenvaara bombings 29.2.1940 and 1.3.1940 Finnish A-A artillery was active, and on both days downed a DB-3 of 42 DBAP. (RGVA)

1 March 1940 DB-3 of 42 DBAP (pilot *lt* I.P. Popov) was shot down Elisenvaara, all crew were killed.

Possibly 5 March 1940 two Finnish fighters were claimed by MG-gunners N. Solonin and I. Plaksitskiy. *Finnish AF suffered no losses 5 March 1940.*

10 March 1940 one DB-3 was lost at Louko.

11 March 1940 a bomber of 2nd Squadron was hit by A-A artillery at Tali. The badly damaged DB-3 attempted to reach Pushkin AF base, but crashed in the forest 8 km east of Slutsk, both wings were broken off. Surprisingly the crew only got slight bruises.

42 DBAP performed 446 combat missions (including 17 "regiment attacks") from 2 February 1940.

42 DBAP Command

Commander	*major* F.M. Vyaznikov. In GPW commanded 90 AP, 820 NBAP and 257 SAD.
	major Avelyanov
Military commissar	*polk.komiss* Kolesnichenko
	bat.komiss Kozlov
Chief of Staff	*major* V.A. Stepanchenkov
Squadron C.O.	
1st	*kapitan* A.D. Babenko
	kapitan Ye. Lomakin

F.S. Snobko (5./42 DBAP Commander) force-landed 3.2.1940 in Jääski with DB-3 tactical 9 (c/n 391450). The pilot and the gunner were killed on capture, shturman kapitan I.A. Solonevich was captured. Lentom *Helge Laitinen* ferried the aircraft to VL in Tampere 11.3.1940. After overhaul the bomber became *VP-12 in* Ilmavoimat. (SA-kuva)

2nd	*kapitan* Khrustalev
3rd	*major* Pleskatov
5th	*kapitan* F.S. Snobkov (KIA 3 February 1940)
	kapitan Timofeyev

In GPW 42 DBAP was on 5 March 1942 attached to ADD (Soviet Long-Range Air Forces), and on 19 August 1944 elevated to Guards status and named 28 GvAP DD. After conversion of ADD to 18th Air Army 6 December 1944 the regiment designation was changed to 171 GvBAP.

VP-12 used by Ilmavoimat (LLv 46) summer 1941. (K. Stenman)

DB-3 c/n 391151 "14" of 5th Squadron/42 DBAP force-landed in Salonläppä, Läskelä after ground fire hit. Pilot st.lt N.H. Vorobyev and ml.kzv Palchikov were captured, while shturman st.lt K.N. Sokolov was killed. (SA-kuva)

Major F.M. Vyaznikov, Commander of 42 DBAP, was seriously criticised for the heavy losses of the regiment. (G.F. Petrov)

43rd Light Bomber Aviation Regiment (43 LBAP)

Autumn 1939 43 LBAP was located in Vitebsk (Byelorussian MD).

Subordination
70 AB, VVS BOVO
1 LBAB, VVS 7.A (from February 1940)

Combat Chronicle
43 LBAP arrived in February 1940 from Vitebsk to Suulajärvi ice base (on occupied Finnish territory) with 63 R-Z aircraft. 43 LBAP performed mainly night operations.

19 February 1940 R-Z c/n 2256 did not return.

6 March 1940 R-Z c/n 2238 was destroyed in an unsuccessful landing, the observer *st.lt* N.N. Pakhomov died of his injuries.

At night 11–12 March 1940 five R-Z got lost and force-landed in various places, the crews of R-Z c/n 2259 and 1891 were killed.

43 LBAP lost at least nine R-Z and seven aviators in night operations in the Karelian Isthmus, furthermore several R-Z were badly damaged.

43 LBAP Command
Commander	*major* G.I. Markov
Military commissar	*bat.komiss* A.F. Fedorov
Chief of Staff	*major* I.T. Leonenok
Squadron C.O.	
1st	*kapitan* I.V. Davydenko
2nd	*kapitan* V.S. Pakhnin
3rd	*kapitan* A.S. Fetisov
4th	*kapitan* I.I. Gvozdev
5th	*kapitan* V.N. Shvyndin

This and opposite page: Seven R-5SSS (43 LBSAP) were lost in a snowstorm on the night 10–11.3.1940. Tactical 10 and star (c/n 2251) crashed in Rahja, and tactical 6 (c/n 2260) crashed in Kontushi. (all photos RGVA)

44th Fighter Aviation Regiment (44 IAP)

Autumn 1939 44 IAP was located in Gorelovo (Leningrad MD).

Subordination
54 IAB, VVS LVO
54 IAB, VVS 7.A

30 November 1939 44 IAP was like 19 and 26 IAP of 54 IAB responsible for air defense of Leningrad. 1st and 3rd Squadrons (31 I-16) were located in Ropsha, 2nd Squadron (10 I-16 and 6 I-16P) in Vitino and 4th Squadron (14 I-153) in Gorskaya, where the entire regiment relocated in mid-January 1940.

Strength and Locations

Date	Base	Subordination	Base unit	Equipment
1.11.39	Gorelovo, LVO	54 AB, VVS LVO	1 RAB, 114 AB	38 I-16, 15 I-16P, 19 I-15bis
1.12.39	Gorelovo, LVO	54 AB, VVS SZFr	1 RAB, 114 AB	55 I-16, 15 I-16P, 15 I-153, 3 I-15bis
1.1.40	Ropsha, LVO	54 AB, VVS SZFr	1 RAB, 114 AB	36 I-16, 10 I-16P, 22 I-153, 18 I-15bis
1.2.40	Ropsha, LVO	54 AB, VVS SZFr	1 RAB, 114 AB	42 I-16, 10 I-16P, 17 I-153, 5 I-15bis
1.3.40	Ropsha, LVO	54 AB, VVS SZFr	1 RAB, 114 AB	42 I-16, 11 I-16P, 16 I-153, 3 I-15bis
1.4.40	Ropsha, LVO	54 AB, VVS LVO	1 RAB, 26 AB	40 I-16, 11 I-16P, 15 I-153, 2 I-15bis

44 IAP Mission statistics

Aircraft missions				Ground attack	Ground troops coverage	Bomber escort	Air combat	Leningrad air defence
I-16	I-153	I-15bis	Total					
2,565	625	8	3,198	333	256	227	12	2,381

Combat Chronicle

The war diary of 44 IAP, which mainly operated in the rear, contains such phrases as *"exceptionally many disorders in 3rd Squadron"*, entire 4th Squadron *"was drunk after New Year's celebrations"*.

19 January 1940 *ml.lt* M.B. Tuzhikov force-landed with an I-153 at Kanneljärvi ice base after engine malfunction. He was accidentally killed on the ground by a taxiing I-16 (*st.lt* Vostrov, Flight Inspector of 25 IAP!).

In February 1940 "train-hunting" on the Karelian Isthmus was started, using a temporary base at occupied Perkjärvi. 21 Finnish locomotives were claimed destroyed, and five Finnish aircraft were claimed shot down in air combat.

44 IAP lost five fighters and two pilots in accidents before the first losses in action. On 11 March 1940 *kapitan* F.S. Priyemov (C.O. of 2nd Squadron) forced-landed on Finnish held territory (or no-man's land?) at Pukalusjärvi with his I-16P fighter after A-A hits on a train strafing mission. (The I-16P version was equipped with two 20 mm ShVAK-cannons.) Squadron commissar A.S. Pasechnik and *lt* M.P. Tyurin attempted to pick up their stranded Squadron C.O. and landed nearby, but all three aviators were subsequently killed by Finnish fire. Tyurin and Pasechnik were posthumously appointed HSUs 7 April 1940. Tyurin was buried in Gorelovo, and a statue to his memory was erected in Serdobsk.

44 IAP performed 3,477 missions, claimed 3 enemy aircraft shot down in air combat, and 21 locomotives, 21 trains and 875 railway wagons destroyed on ground. Five aviators were lost (of which three were in combat and two in accidents).

44 IAP Command

Commander	*kapitan* A.M. Andreyev
Military Commissar	*bat.komiss* S.V. Shalyganov
Chief of Staff	*major* Fakov

Squadron C.O. and Commissars
1st *st.lt* L.S. Indyk
  st.politr Chishko
2nd *kapitan* F.S. Priyemov (KIA 11.3.1940)
  st.politr A.S. Pasechnik (1913 – 11.3.1940). HSU 7.4.1940.
3rd *st.lt* M.M. Kuz'min
4th *kapitan* G.N. Ivchenko
  st.politr Masliy

In GPW 44 IAP was elevated to Guards status 7 March 1942 and named 11 GvIAP.

Lt P.A. Mikhalskiy (2./44 IAP) crashed on landing in Ropsha 20.1.1940 I-16 (c/n 1721196, tactical 1). (RGVA)

44th Fast Bomber Aviation Regiment (44 SBAP)

Autumn 1939 44 SBAP was located in Staraya Russa (Leningrad MD).

Subordination
  55 AB, VVS LVO
  55 AB, VVS 7.A

Combat Chronicle
In October 1939 3rd Squadron of 58 SBAP (co-located in Staraya Russa) was transferred to 44 SBAP.

44 SBAP received its first War Order (No. 012) at Staraya Russa on 10 November 1939 at 1145 hours, according to which preparations for relocation to Zajtsevo (12 km north of Krasnogvardejsk, former Gatchina) were to be initiated immediately. Next evening at 1850 hours detailed operation order No.04 was received from HQ of 55 AB: *"44 SBAP shall destroy Kouvola railway station and the Lahti and Utti AF bases"*.

According to same order the co-located 58 SBAP was to destroy Lappeenranta and Kotka AF bases, Inkeroinen railway junction and fuel stores at Kotka. *"Attack time will be ordered separately"*.

The brigade order of 11 November 1939 was repeated two days later. 18 November 1939 tasks were slightly modified: task of 44 SBAP was still to destroy Utti AF base and Kouvola railway junction, while 58 SBAP was now to concentrate on destroying Lahti and Lappeenranta AF bases (targets at Kotka were now apparently allocated to the Baltic Fleet Air Force). The 18 November attack order was repeated on 30 November 1939 without changes.

This day 44 SBAP was still in Staraya Russa with 62 SB, with regiment HQ located in the Ivanovo manor house, 15 km west of Staraya Russa.

On approximately 15 December 1939 the remnants of 41 SBAP, which had suffered heavy losses, arrived in Staraya Russa and were attached to 44 SBAP.

18 December 1939 2nd Squadron moved from Staraya Russa to Krasnogvardejsk, while the other squadrons moved to Zajtsevo.

Next day, 19 December 1939, was to become a black day for 44 SBAP: nine aircraft and 22 aviators (of which three were taken prisoners by the Finns) were lost. (As the regiment numbered 55 SB, more than 16% of the strength did not return!)

Four of the missing aircraft belonged to 2nd Squadron, which had taken off from Krasnogvardejsk at 1050 hours, targets Äyräpää railway station (target no. 24) and Paakkola (target no. 25):
- a weather reconnaissance SB (c/n 7/134) aircraft was shot down in air combat (according to Soviet documents this aircraft also belonged to 2nd Squadron), *shturman lt* N.V. Poluyan was taken prisoner.

Luga Bay ice base of 44 SBAP was photographed by LLv 44 20.2.1940. (A. Juhola)

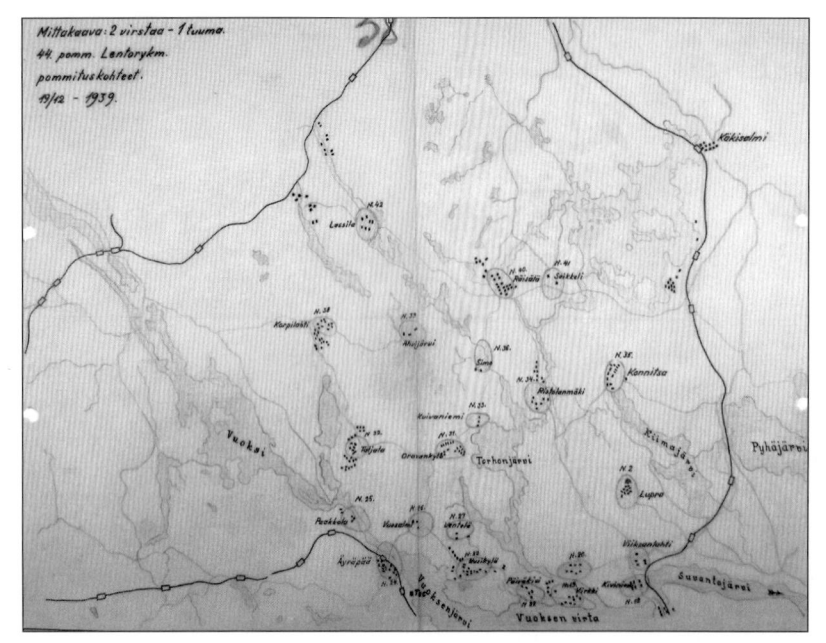

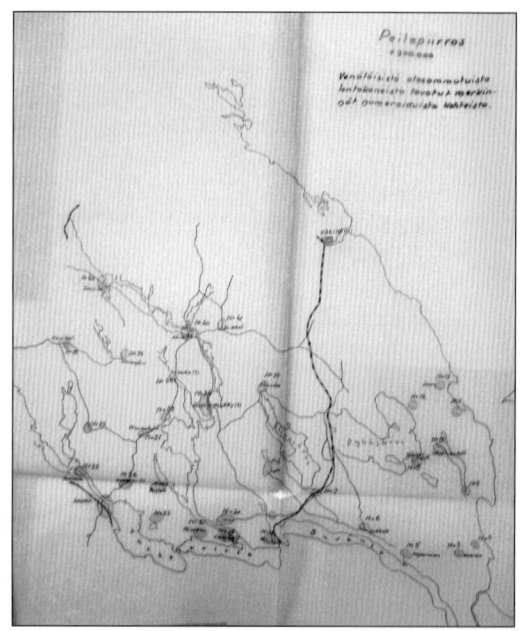

The 44 SBAP target maps were found in an SB which crashed 19.12.1939 in Kuparsaari, Antrea. The pilot lt N.D. Minyayev escaped by parachute and was captured. (Finnish National Archive)

(According to the questioning by Poluyan the crew originally belonged to 41 SBAP, and had been ordered to land in Staraya Russa or in Krasnogvardejsk after the bombing attack.)

- at Heinjoki another bomber was shot down by A-A artillery, pilot *lt* N.D. Minayev was taken prisoner.
- the SB of Squadron commissar *st.politr* G.S. Chernomaz did not return from Ristseppälä. The fourth lost SB of 2nd Squadron was c/n 7/137, which forced-landed badly damaged at Valkeasaari (at the Finnish-Soviet border), *shturman lt* A.G. Kulikov was killed.

3rd Squadron also lost four aircraft and 12 aviators (of which *st.lt* K.P. Strekalov became POW). Three bombers were shot down by A-A artillery and Finnish fighters (including the SB of the Squadron C.O.) at Muolaanjärvi and Heinjoki, the fourth aircraft limped back but was destroyed at landing in Krasnogvardejsk. As unknown aircraft piloted by the C.O. of 1st Squadron was destroyed in a forced landing on own territory. *kapitan* S.I. Kosyakin who returned with the damaged SB was appointed HSU 7 April 1940. *LeR 2 claimed ten certain bomber kills on 19 December 1940 over the Karelian Isthmus, and in addition four probable. Note: in addition to losses of 44 SBAP, this day 13 SBAP lost six and 50 SBAP two bombers over the Karelian Isthmus.*

21 December 1939 the other squadrons also moved to Krasnogvardejsk.

23 December 1939 was almost as black a day as 19 December, with at least five SB and 14 aviators lost (of which four were taken prisoner by the Finns, information on a fifth POW is unconfirmed):

- SB c/n 14/97 of regiment HQ was shot down by fighters at Äyräpää, and crashed at Heinjoki. Pilot *kapitan* I.Ye. Borodin escaped by parachute and became POW. The task was to attack an A-A battery presumed to be located at Suursaari (Hogland) in Muolaanjärvi.
- The target of 4th Squadron was Heinjoki railway station; SBs c/n 18/94 and 4/92 were lost. One pilot, *lt* I.K. Sorokin was taken prisoner. Next day, Christmas Eve, the MG-gunner of the other bomber *ml.kzv* N.I. Lyakhov was captured.

SB tactical 3 (c/n 19/136) piloted by lt N.I. Timoshenko (5./44 SBAP) was destroyed 26.12.1939 in Krasnogvardejsk. Note 44 SBAP emblem – the "finger" tail decoration. (RGVA)

164

5. Squadron lost two SBs in poor weather 30.1.1940. Blue 3 (c/n 2/92) crashed at Dudergof, navigator st.lt A.I. Apanosovich died of wounds. (RGVA, G.F. Petrov)

The task of 5th Squadron was to bomb a Finnish strongpoint at Oinala (SW Muolaanjärvi) with six bombers. Two SB – bombers (c/n 3/136 and 14/72) were shot down at Antrea, and c/n 3/136 crashed at Noisniemi. The pilot was able to reach his own lines; *shturman st.lt* A.G. Makarenko was killed, while MG-gunner K.I. Drozdetskiy was taken prisoner in the sector of Finnish Infantry Regiment 24 (8 Division). Finally a sixth SB was possibly shot down with pilot lt P. Smorodin becoming POW. *23 December 1939 LeR 2 claimed seven certain and one probable SB kills over the Karelian Isthmus.*

18 January 1940 at least two SBs of 4th Squadron got serious damage in air combat, one bomber was able to limp home on one engine. The pilot of the other SB *bat.komiss* I.I. Kozhemyakin was seriously wounded. He was subsequently appointed HSU 21 March 1940.

Late January 1940 44 SBAP relocated to an ice base south of Kuokkala on the frozen Gulf of Finland.

30 January 1940 5th Squadron lost SBs c/n 2/92 and 17/94 in bad weather, all six crew were killed.

In February 1940 the main task was to bomb Finnish fortifications ("Mannerheim Line") on the Karelian Isthmus.

2–26 February 1940 44 SBAP also used a base near Kurnosovo (near Luga Bay on the southern shore of Gulf of Finland).

10 February 1940 at 1605 hours 2nd Squadron (led by *kapitan* Lokotanov) attacked Finnish strongpoints at the Mannerheim Line with nine SBs escorted by 15 I-16 fighters (7 IAP). *St.lt* M.F. Mazayev's SB c/n 10/134 *blue 1* was hit by A-A at Yläkylä, and force-landed with a burning right engine and wing at Kuolemajärvi. *Lt* M.T. Trusov of the same Squadron landed nearby with SB *blue 10* and picked up the stranded crew while *lt* F.I. Shinkarenko and *st.politr* G.V. Didenko (4th Squadron/7 IAP) protected the rescue operation. Trusov and Shinkarenko subsequently became HSUs 21 March 1940. The Golden Star was also proposed for Didenko, but this proposal was not accepted.

Finnish soldiers inspecting SB tactical no. 10 of 44 SBAP. (C-F. Geust)

Lt M.T. Trusov (2./44 SBAP) landed 10.2.1940 with his SB at Kuolemajärvi next to a force-landed SB, and evacuated the stranded crew. Trusov was appointed HSU 21.3.1940. (G.F. Petrov)

Ivan P. Skok commanded 4./44 SBAP and 5./58 SBAP in the Winter War. (N. Stolepova)

11 February 1940 SB c/n 15/97 (3rd Squadron) crashed at Sestroretsk after A-A hits, two aviators were killed.

13 February 1940 44 SBAP bombed the Summa sector. At Leipäsuo SB c/n 1/135 (pilot *lt* F.M. Duyunov) of 1st Squadron got a direct A-A hit and crashed in flames.

19 February 1940 SB piloted by *lt* Drozdov (3rd Squadron) crashed after early explosion of his own AO-8 bombs.

26 February 1940 44 SBAP moved back to Zajtsevo.

5 March 1940 two SB (c/n 19/133 and 1/92) of 2nd Squadron collided over Gulf of Finland on the return leg. SB c/n 1/92 crashed onto the frozen sea. *St.lt* M.F. Mazayev and *lt* M.F. Bratyaga were killed, while gunner V. Shamshin escaped by parachute and was picked up by Lobayev (unit and a/c unknown).

44 SBAP performed 2,137 combat missions (flight time 2,658 h 25 min). 44 SBAP lost 23 aircraft and 52 aviators *(of which seven were POWs in Finland)*. According to its own estimates 44 SBAP lost 17 aircraft and 44 aviators in combat (other losses were considered accidental).

44 SBAP Command

Commander	*polkovnik* N.I. Dmitriyev (1901 –).
Military Commissar	*bat.komiss* A.I. Vikhoryev
	Vasilyev
Chief of Staff	*polkovnik* N.P. Dagayev
Squadron C.O. and Commissars	
1st	*kapitan* S.I. Kosyakin (1906–1941). HSU 21.3.1940.
	st.politr Gorshkov
2nd	*kapitan* S. Kuptsov
	kapitan V.S. Lokotanov
	st.politr G.S. Chernomaz (KIA 19.12.1939)
	st.politr Didenko
3rd	*st.lt* P.N. Shcherbakov (KIA 19.12.1939)
	kapitan I.P. Skok (1906–1977). Later deputy commander of 58 SBAP. In GPW commanded 72 SBAP (which suffered big losses at Joroinen 25.6.1941), Tu-2 equipped 334 BAD (which participated in the major attack on the Karelian isthmus in June 1944) and 6 BAK.
	st.politr Komissarov
4th	*major* M.N. Kolokol'tsev
	bat.komiss I.I. Kozhemyakin (1908 –). Seriously wounded in air combat 18.1.1940. HSU 21.3.1940.
5th	*kapitan* D.S. Cherchuk
	st.politr Burasnikov

Despite big losses 44 SBAP was awarded Red Banner Order 21 March 1940. Four aviators (*kapitan* S.I. Kosyakin, *bat.komiss* I.I. Kozhemyakin, *lt* M.T. Trusov and *shturman* of 1st Squadron *st.lt* V.Ye. Sharapa) were made HSUs on the same day.

In GPW 44 SBAP was elevated to Guards status 21 November 1942 and named 34 GvBAP.

45th Fast Bomber Aviation Regiment (45 SBAP)

Autumn 1939 45 SBAP was located in Orel MD.

Subordination
AON-2 (until 15 February 1940)
13 SBAB, VVS 15.A (from 15 February 1940)

Combat Chronicle
45 SBAP (equipped with 56 late-series SB) arrived 15 February 1940 from AON-2 in Orel to Lodejnoye pole, and was attached to 13 SBAB (which was transferred to the newly formed VVS 15.A). Some SB were furthermore transferred to 72 SAP (VVS 8.A) in Besovets.

23 February 1940 SB c/n 2/237 (5th Squadron, piloted by *lt* S.I. Golubev) was shot down by A-A artillery at Taipalsaari, all crew were killed.

29 February 1940 SB c/n 19/243 (4th Squadron) collided mid-air with SB c/n 18/65 of 39 SBAP some 6 km southwest of Lodejnoye pole; both bombers crashed. Only the pilot of the 39 SBAP bomber escaped by parachute, all the other five aviators were killed. The 45 SBAP crew was *st.lt* V.G. Dikolpolskiy, *lt* A.S. Druzhkin and *starshina* A.I. Kirilov.

4 March 1940 two bombers were destroyed after A-A hits:
- SB c/n 4/239 of 2nd Squadron (piloted by Squadron C.O. *kapitan* F.I. Yudin) was hit when dropping food supplies to 168th Division (encircled at Kitelä), and was destroyed in a crash-landing at Karkunlampi ice base.
- SB c/n 12/234 of 4th Squadron (piloted by Squadron C.O. *kapitan* M.I. Tolkachev) force-landed on the ice of Lake Ladoga 12 km west of Pitkäranta after A-A artillery hits.

Several Soviet aircraft and transport vehicles were observed on the ice evacuating the aviators, and apparently preparing retrieval of the aircraft. The Finnish coast battery at Ristisaari and railway battery at Impilahti shelled the crash-landed aircraft with some twelve shells, preventing the removal of the aircraft.

6 March 1940 SB c/n 12/239 of 3rd Squadron (pilot *ml.lt* S.I. Slobodin) crashed north of Vuoratsu after A-A hits, all crew were killed.

45 SBAP performed a total of 618 war missions and dropped 208.0 t bombs, also 140 supply dropping missions during which 26.0 t foodstuffs and medicines were dropped.

45 SBAP Command
Commander	*polkovnik* Kalametsin
	major Kuznetsov
Military commissar	*batl.komiss* Bogatatikov
Chief of Staff	*major* Zubarev
Squadron C.O.	
1st	*kapitan* Mikhajlov
2nd	*kapitan* F.I. Yudin
4th	*kapitan* M.I. Tolkachev

48th Fighter Aviation Regiment (48 IAP)

Autumn 1939 48 IAP was located in Ussuri, subordinated to 1st OKA (Detached Army), Far East Front.

Subordination
1 OKA
80 SAP and 145 IAP (VVS 9.A), from 15 February 1940.

Combat Chronicle
4th Squadron/48 IAP was (without aircraft) dispatched to the Finnish front.

16 February 1940 one half-Squadron (commanded by *kapitan* Bondarev) arrived from Spassk without aircraft, and was attached to 145 IAP (VVS 9.A). The other half-Squadron was attached to 80 SAP (VVS 9.A).

Personnel of another Squadron of 48 IAP had apparently arrived at VVS 8.A 15 February 1940, and received aircraft in Peski. Four fighters flew to Suojärvi 23 February 1940, and on 29 February 1940 11 aircraft arrived (this unit was possibly attached to 49 IAP).

Tasks:
- protection of Army HQ
- bomber escort
- reconnaissance and ground fighting.
  4./48 IAP performed 279 combat missions, flight time 328 h 16 min.

4./48 IAP command
Commander   *st.lt* Kulinich
Military Commissar   *lt* Pankratov

48th Fast Bomber Aviation Regiment (48 SBAP)

Autumn 1939 48 SBAP was located in Uman' (Kiev MD).

Subordination
VVS KOVO
18 SBAB, VVS SZFr (until 16 January 1940)
18 SBAB, VVS 7.A (from 16 January 1940)

Combat Chronicle
48 SBAP arrived in January 1940 from Uman' to Siverskaya, and moved on 18 January 1940 to Sestroretskiy razliv.

14 February 1940 SB c/n 9/G (2nd Squadron, pilot *lt* M.A. Astafyev) was shot down by own A-A artillery at Lähde, two aviators were killed, the gunner escaped by parachute. On the same day SB c/n 16/98 (also of 2nd Squadron) crash-landed after air combat hits, and became a write-off.

17 February 1940 27 SBs bombed Heinjoki. SB c/n 2/108 (pilot *st.politr* N.G. Sinitsyn) was lost to A-A artillery at Heinjoki-Säiniö, all crew were killed.

18 February 1940 SB c/n 13/98 (1st Squadron) was destroyed in a take-off accident at Sestroretsk, the crew was killed.

20 February 1940 15 SBs bombed Heinjoki. SB c/n 2/D (2nd Squadron, pilot *lt* N.A. Kalugin) was shot down by enemy A-A artillery, all crew were killed.

10 March 1940 SB c/n 20/98 (pilot *lt* V.P. Borisov) crashed at Naulasaari. All crew were killed. Finnish troops picked up the navigator *st.lt* N.G. Orlov's documents and personal flight diary, from which following information was read:
- 7.1.40 ferry flight Uman' – Bykov
- 30.1.40 ferry flight Bykov-Siverskaya (670 km)
- 4.2.40 combat mission Sestroretsk – target No.23 (132 km., 1 h)
- 9.2.40 combat mission (135 km, 1 h)
- 10.2.40 combat mission Sestroretsk-target No.11 (140 km, 1 h)
- 11.2.40 combat mission Sestroretsk-target No.23 (105 km, 50 min)
- 13.2.40 combat mission Sestroretsk-target No.23 (90 km, 48 min)
- 13.2.40 combat mission Sestroretsk-target No.23 (90 km, 50 min)
- 14.2.40 combat mission Sestroretsk-target No.X (85 km, 40 min)
- 14.2.40 combat mission Sestroretsk-target (85 km, 43 min)
- 14.2.40 combat mission Sestroretsk-target (85 km, 49 min)
- 15.2.40 combat mission Sestroretsk-target (90 km, 50 min)
- 15.2.40 combat mission Sestroretsk-target (90 km, 1 h 10 min)
- 20.2.40 combat mission Sestroretsk-target (110 km, 45 min)
- 21.2.40 combat mission Sestroretsk-Antrea station. (210 km, 1 h 27 min)
- 25.2.40 combat mission Sestroretsk-Peipiya (200 km, 1 h)
- 25.2.40 combat mission Sestroretsk-Karhusuo (200 km, 1 h)
- 27.2.40 combat mission Sestroretsk-Kämäränjärvi (120 km, 1 h)
- 27.2.40 combat mission Sestroretsk-Kämäränjärvi (120 km, 56 min)
- 27.2.40 combat mission Sestroretsk-Karisalmi station (230 km, 1 h 15 min)
- 29.2.40 combat mission Sestroretsk-Viipuri (215 km, 1 h)
- 1.3.40 combat mission Sestroretsk-Nurmi station. (250 km, 1 h 30 min)
- 3.3.40 combat mission Sestroretsk-Lappeenranta (300 km, 1 h 30 min)
- 3.3.40 combat mission Sestroretsk-Viipuri (250 km, 1 h 30 min)

Two SBs of 1./48 SBAP written off in Sestroretsk: tactical no. 7 (c/n 13/98) – crew was killed in a take-off accident 18.2.40, and on 25.2.1940 c/n 11/77 belly-landed. (RGVA)

48 SBAP Command
    Commander
    Military Commissar
    Chief of Staff

    Squadron C.O.
                    kapitan M.I. Martynov (1909–1986). HSU 21.3.1940.
                    kapitan V.V. Sharov (1909–1942). HSU 21.3.1940.

Squadron Commanders M.I. Martynov, and V.V. Sharov, and *st.lt* V.A. Khoroshilov were appointed HSUs 21.3.1940.

49th Fighter Aviation Regiment (49 IAP)

Autumn 1939 49 IAP was located in Krestsy (Leningrad MD).

Subordination
14 AB, VVS LVO
VVS 8.A (from 22 November 1939)
VVS 15.A (from 15 February 1940)

49 IAP arrived 22 November 1939 from Krestsy to southern Karelian ASSR, and was attached to VVS 8.A. 1st, 2nd and 4th squadrons were transferred to Nurmolitsa, 3rd Squadron to Lodejnoye pole and 5th Squadron to Novaya Ladoga. 1st Squadron was converting to I-153s, and became operational 9 December 1939. 3rd and 5th squadrons (I-15bis) were directly subordinated to VVS 8.A, with task to protect Svirstroi and Volkhov hydro-electric power plants (GES), and Lodejnoye pole AF base.

Future double-HSU (2.9.1943 and 1.7.1944) S.D. Luganskiy started his career in 49 IAP. (G.F. Petrov)

49 IAP Strength in November 1939

Squadron	Aircraft	Base
HQ	5 I-16	22.11.39 to Nurmolitsa (Nurmoila)
1st	15 I-153	9.12.39 to Nurmolitsa
2nd	15 I-16	22.11.39 to Nurmolitsa
3rd	15 I-15bis	22.11.39 to Lodejnoye pole
4th	13 I-16	22.11.39 to Nurmolitsa
5th	12 I-15bis	22.11.39 to Novaya Ladoga

49 IAP strength and locations

Date	Bases	Subordination	Base unit	Aircraft
1.11.39	Krestsy	14 AB, VVS LVO	3 RAB, 201 AB	38 I-15bis, 34 I-16
1.12.39	Nurmolitsa, Novaya Ladoga and ice base	VVS 8.A, VVS SZFr	6 RAB, 201 AB	38 I-15bis, 34 I-16
1.1.40	Nurmolitsa, Novaya Ladoga, ice base and Uomaa	VVS 8.A, VVS SZFr	6 RAB, 201 AB	36 I-15bis, 33 I-16
1.2.40	Nurmolitsa, Novaya Ladoga and ice base	VVS 8.A, VVS SZFr	6 RAB, 201 AB	35 I-15bis, 33 I-16, 22 I-153
1.3.40	Nurmolitsa, Novaya Ladoga and ice base	VVS 15.A, VVS SZFr	6 RAB, 201 AB	31 I-15bis, 30 I-16, 21 I-153
1.4.40	Nurmolitsa, Novaya Ladoga and ice base	VVS 15.A, VVS LVO	6 RAB, 201 AB	17 I-15bis, 27 I-16, 40 I-153
1.5.40	Krestsy	14 AB, VVS LVO	3 RAB, 201 AB	13 I-15bis, 25 I-16, 40 I-153

Combat Chronicle

49 IAP was given the task of supporting 56th AK (army corps)

3 December 1939 a Blenheim of LLv 44 flew over Nurmolitsa at 1300 hours. Fighters alerted from 49 IAP did not find the enemy.

6 December 1939 former 1 OIE (Detached Fighter Squadron, equipped with I-153s, and commanded by *kapitan* Popov) was sent to Nurmolitsa, and attached to 49 IAP.

The task of 2nd Squadron was strafing of Pitkäranta railway station. At Videlitsa (Vitele) on the eastern shore of Lake Ladoga four I-16 fighters located and shot down an MBR-2 flying boat of 41 AE of the Ladoga flotilla AF. Three of the four-person crew of the MBR-2 were killed (*lt* P.A. Tsiplakov, *kapitan* S.V. Belov and MG-gunner V.I. Grishkov), while wounded *shturman lt* Petrov was able to escape by parachute. The trigger-happy fighter group consisted of *kapitan* N.A. Sizov (C.O. 2nd Squadron), the regiment's *flagshturman* I.P. Murazanov, assistant Squadron C.O. G.A. Bobrov and Squadron adjutant I.S. Savushkin. The investigation of the tragic incident showed that VVS 8.A was not informed of the flight, and that VVS pilots in general did not know the configuration of naval aircraft! Otherwise the fighter pilots might well have all been executed. Murazanov was also wounded, but was able to land at Nurmolitsa (located only some 30 km east of Vitele).

8 December 1939 some 28 aircraft of VVS 8.A strafed Mantsinsaari (at NW shore of Lake Ladoga) in foggy weather. I-16 *tip* 10 c/n 1021592 and 1021601 of 4th Squadron collided mid-air when evading A-A

fire of Mantsi coast battery and crashed 1.5 km from Jänisniemi, *lt* P.M. Kozhakin and *st.lt* F.A. Samsonov were killed.

10 December 1939 the former Assistant Commander of 14 AB *major* I.V. Yakubovich was appointed Commander of 49 IAP. The former Commander *major* M.A. Budayev was placed at the disposal of the Commander of VVS 8.A.

10 December 1939 I-16 *tip 10* c/n 1021607 and 1021371 (*kapitan* I.A. Lavrenchuk and *ml.lt* P.A. Golovin, both of 2nd Squadron) disappeared in a snowstorm over Lake Ladoga. *ml.lt* V.A. Larionov (I-153 c/n 6491, 1st Squadron) crashed after damage from own bomb-splinters on a ground-attack mission.

16 December 1939 5th Squadron moved to Suojärvi (on occupied Finnish territory), and subsequently operated as detached Squadron *Aviagruppa Tkachenko*, directly subordinated to VVS 8.A. (See AG Tkachenko, page 236)

17 December 1939 49 IAP staff and 1st, 2nd and 4th squadrons moved from Nurmolitsa to Karkunlampi ice base (SE Salmi, on occupied Finnish territory), where these squadrons remained until the end of the war.

18 December 1939 3rd Squadron (operationally subordinated to 56th Army Corps) moved to Käsnäselkä and Uomaa (also on occupied Finnish territory). On the next day 20 I-16s were forced to return to Nurmolitsa as the ice in Karkku was not thick enough for a large number of aircraft, but 21 December 1939 a permanent base would be established at Karkunlampi. Also three I-16s flew to Suojärvi for protection of 8. Army HQ.

19 December 1939 *Ml.lt* S.P. Abramov (I-16 c/n 5219-B, 4th Squadron) was shot down in air combat at Uuksu, and M.A. Chemerichkin crashed with I-16 c/n 1021458 in Nurmolitsa.

20 December 1939 a lone Blenheim bombed Karkunlampi AF base, four mechanics from 201 AB were killed. This was BL-106 of LLv 46, which was attacked at Salmi by three I-16 fighters, which reported that the Blenheim crashed at Mantsinsaari. MG-gunner *kers* V. Mörsky claimed in his turn one I-16.

Because of increased enemy activity, on 27 December 1939 3rd Squadron was forced to move from Uomaa to Karkunlampi, where it remained for the rest of the war.

28 December 1939 a Blenheim of LeR 4 bombed the ice base of 49 IAP at Karkunlampi.

31 December 1939 *kers* Ilmari Juutilainen claimed an I-16 at Uomaa. 49 IAP did however not lose any aircraft this day, so the I-16 wreck located by Finnish ground forces was apparently one of the I-16s which disappeared 10 December 1939.

Ml.Lt V. Belyakov (49 IAP) at his I-153, to the left is Regiment Engineer P. Sukhov. (G.F. Petrov)

Fokker C.X. FK-81 was shot down in Uuksu 26.1.1940 by st.lt V.N. Peshkov (49 IAP, HSU 20.5.1940). Lentom, luutn T. Häilä and lt T. Vaittinen were killed. (G.F. Petrov)

Danish volunteer J. Ulrich force-landed after air combat 13.2.1940. (K. Stenman)

1 January 1940 flight leader, *lt* I.M. Glukhov by mistake shot down SB c/n 20/99 (18 SBAP) NW Pogrankondushi, the crew was killed.

5 January 1940 Blenheims BL-108 and BL-118 (LLv 46) were attacked by 49 IAP fighters at Suistamo and Salmi. Both Blenheims got hits, but thanks to their high-speed performance were able to escape from the Soviet fighters, and belly-landed at Joroinen. The MG-gunner *kers* P. Lumiala of BL-108 was lightly wounded.

6 January 1940 one Blenheim was sighted at Pitkäranta, but escaped by diving towards Valamo, another Blenheim was shot down by *st.lt* I.P. Murazanov and *ml.lt* S.T. Goryunov, and crashed 2–3 km NW Tolvajärvi/Polvijärvi. The apparently only slightly damaged wreck was located three days later at Riihilampi (7 km SW Uomaa), and "measures were taken for transport". *BL-112 of LLv 46 force-landed, right engine in flames, in Soviet-occupied territory at Riihilampi after air-combat with three I-16 fighters. The crew (Løjtnant O. Pesola, lentom M. Termonen and kers A. Pakkala) reached their own lines.*

12 January 1940 the frequent Regiment Commander changes continued, as *major* Yakubovich was placed at the disposal of the Commander of VVS 8.A (after commanding 49 IAP for only one month), and was replaced by *polkovnik* V.A. Kitayev.

15 January 1940 *st.lt* I.S. Savushkin and *ml.lt* S.T. Goryunov shot down a "Bulldog" at Pitkäranta. FK-87 of LLv 10 did not return from Pitkäranta (crew *luutn* L. Mustonen and *vänr* R. Turtiainen).

19 January 1940 Blenheim BL-121 (LLv 44) was shot down by three I-16 fighters led by *st.lt* I.P. Murazanov at Salmi (northeast shore of Lake Ladoga). This time the 49 IAP pilots were well prepared for the usual escape method of the Blenheim: when the fast bomber tried to escape by diving to tree-top level, *st.lt* I.S. Savushkin and *ml.lt* S.T. Goryunov were already alert at low altitude and shot down the Blenheim in flames. BL-121 crashed 5 km south of Alauuksu, all crew (*ylik* J. Toivonen, *vänr* T. Ranta and *kers* V. Toivio) were killed.

This day BL-106 (LLv 46) bombed and photographed Karkunlampi ice base. Some 60–70 aircraft were observed.

19 January 1940 3rd Squadron received 22 I-153 fighters, while all still serviceable I-15bis fighters were transferred to a new 5th Squadron (C.O. *kapitan* P.I. Kolomin), which thus numbered 12 I-15bis aircraft. The new Squadron was ordered to drop supplies to the encircled troops of 56th Army Corps at Uomaa, Lemetti and Lavajärvi. Two 100 kg PDMM-100 soft bags or two PDBB-100 hard-skin containers were attached to under-wing pylons of I-15bis fighters. This supply-dropping method was developed in the mid-1930s for Soviet parachute troops (*Voyenno-desantnyje vojska*, VDV). 49 IAP performed 264 supply-dropping missions, with 32.0 t supplies delivered.

20 January 1940 four Blenheims of LLv 44 (BL-106, BL-109, BL-115 and BL-119) bombed Karkunlampi ice base. According to Finnish information the bombs were well aimed and several aircraft were destroyed. *One I-15bis was damaged and one starter cart was destroyed.*

Two SB bombers (of 18 SBAP and 39 SBAP respectively) were seen shot down by two Finnish Fokker fighters. The bombers crashed between Nietjärvi and Mustalampi. Subsequently one of the Fokkers was shot down by *st.lt* I.S. Savushkin, *ml.lt* S.T. Goryunov and *st.lt* F.M. Fatkulin, and crashed 2–3 km SE Nietjärvi. *FR-107 of LLv 26 was shot down at Lohijärvi,* kers *P. Tilli was killed.*

22–23 January 1940 Karkunlampi was bombed at night by seven Fokker C.X of LLv 10. One I-15bis was damaged.

26 January 1940 *st.lt* V.N. Peshkov (I-153) shot down Fokker C.X FK-81 on a reconnaissance mission to Uuksu-Ylikylä-Salmi, *lentom* T.O. Heilä and *Løjtnant* R.K. Vaittinen (LLv 10) were killed.

29 January 1940 three I-153s led by *kapitan* I.I. Popov strafed and destroyed an armored train at Impilahti.

2 February 1940 I-15bis c/n 5196 of 5th Squadron was shot down by Finnish A-A artillery at Koivuselkä. *st.lt* V.D. Kuzmin escaped by parachute, but died of wounds. Another I-15bis force-landed because of engine malfunction at Pitkäranta, the pilot was lightly injured.

8 February 1940 at 11.40 hours two I-153 tried to intercept four Blenheims without success, and at 1230 hours two I-153 tried to intercept one Blenheim, also without success.

11 February 1940 I-153 c/n 6526 got hits at Pitkäranta, *ml.lt* S.V. Krivda was killed, and next day I-153 c/n 6790 was hit NW Pitkäranta, *ml.lt* D.Ya. Gerasimov was killed.

11–12 February 1940 two I-153 fighters crashed after A-A hits at Pitkäranta.

13 February 1940 the commissar of 5th Squadron *st.politr* M.A. Kochmala (I-15bis) was killed in air combat at Värtsilä. *Lt* Ya.F. Mikhin (AG Tkachenko/49 IAP) claimed a taran victory in his I-16 when he collided mid-air with a Finnish Fokker at Värtsilä. *Gladiators of LLv 26, led by Danish volunteer Løjtnant C.K. Kalmberg (GL-260) fought against 13 I-153 fighters which were escorting SB. Alik Joensuu shot down an I-15 and Havuvaara, Korpiselkä, but also Løjtnant Kalmberg was killed, and another Dane, Løjtnant J. Ulrich (GL-257) force-landed.* (See AG Tkachenko, page 236)

15 February 1940 49 IAP was attached to VVS 15.A in Karkunlampi, strength 29 I-153 (1st and 3rd Squadrons), 21 I-16 (2nd and 4th Squadrons) and 12 I-15bis (5th Squadron).

17 February 1940 an I-16 c/n 6534 of 1st Squadron was shot down by A-A artillery at Kuikka, *lt* G.T. Ivanov was killed.

18 February 1940 *st.lt* V.N. Peshkov shot down Blenheim BL-113 (LLv 44) on return from a photo-reconnaissance mission over Lake Ladoga. *Pilot* kers *K. Westermark escaped by parachute,* vänr *E. Laamanen and* ylik *T. Koivuneva were killed.*

21–22 February 1940 *ml.lt* V.D. Ratnikov (3rd Squadron, I-153 c/n 6488) was killed at Karkunlampi during a nighttime alarm mission.

24 February 1940 the commissar of 3rd Squadron *politr* V.S. Kobernik was killed in a forced-landing at Karkku after A-A artillery hits at Nietjärvi.

Possibly 27 February 1940 *Ml.lt* A.S. Petelov was killed in a landing accident at Pogrankondushi with I-16 *tip* 10 c/n 1021638.

28 February 1940 future double-HSU S.D. Luganskiy was shot down in air combat, but performed a successful forced-landing and was able to reach his own lines.

49 IAP performed 4,484 war missions, total flight time 4,097 h, of which 1,545 missions (of which 430 I-16 missions) were in VVS 15.A. Total flight time was 4,097 h. 49 IAP was one of the most efficient Soviet fighter regiments in the Winter War – the pilots were good shots, at least nine Finnish aircraft were brought down by 49 IAP (see table), but also two of their own aircraft were shot down with fatal results!

The rather few Finnish bombings of Karkunlampi, Lodejnoye pole and Repola (in the 9. Army sector) forced the Russians to organize almost continuous interceptor patrolling in the airspace of their AF bases, wearing aircraft, engines and pilots, and which led to excessive fuel consumption without corresponding results. In some cases the interceptors already patrolling did not detect the approaching lone Blenheim, which usually escaped because of its speed and diving characteristics. (See also 80 SAP, page 201)

As 49 IAP operated in extremely desolated regions, a separate unit with the somewhat clumsy name "1st Aviation Unit of the Northern Special Aviation Group at 49 IAP" (*1 Aviatsionnyi Otryad Severnoi Osobovoi AG pri 49 IAP*) for supply dropping and rescue missions, was also attached. The commander of this Aviation Group *lt* A.N. Yakovlev performed several supply dropping missions to encircled Soviet troops north of Lake Ladoga. Yakovlev became renowned for picking up the wounded four-person crew of a forced-landed SB-bomber with his U-2 on 14 March 1940 (one day after the signing of the Peace Treaty in Moscow), and transporting them to hospital in Petrozavodsk. This rescued crew is not yet identified, but presumably came from 18 or 72 SBAP.

Lt Yakovlev was awarded the Golden Star 20 May 1940.

Task Distribution

Ground forces protection	1,776
Ground-attack	1,201
Reconnaissance	632
Bomber escort	304
Supply dropping	264
Enemy aircraft interception	252
Other tasks	39
Total	4,468

49 IAP participated in 60 air combats, and claimed 28 enemy aircraft. In ground attack missions two trains, one armoured train wagon and one artillery battery were destroyed. Own losses were 13 aviators (of which six were in combat) and 11 aircraft.

49 IAP command

Commander	*major* M.A. Budayev, until 10.(12?).12.1939.
	major I.V. Yakubovich, from 10.(12?)12.1939 to 12.1.1940.
	polkovnik V.A. Kitayev, from 12.1.1940. Red Banner order. In GPW commanded 283 IAD.
Military Commissar	*bat.komiss* N.A. Kuligin, until 19.12.1939.
	bat.komiss F.I. Timoshenkov, from 19.12.1939.
Chief of Staff	*major* G.M. Vasil'kov (1905-). Red Banner order.

Squadron C.O. and Commissars

1st	*major* P.I. Nedelin (1910 –). Commanded 49 IAP from 16.3.40. 65 combat missions in Spanish Civil War. In Winter War 39 combat missions, Red Banner order.
	st.politr G. Kravtsov
2nd	*kapitan* N.A. Sizov (1901-). Red Star order.
3rd	*kapitan* I.I. Popov
	st.lt P.I. Kolomin, from 19.1.1940 C.O. 5th Squadron.
	st.politr V.S. Kobernik, KIA 24.2.1940.
4th	*kapitan* N.P. Baulin (1911–). Red Star order.
	st.politr A.S. Kajtshuk (1912–).
5th	*kapitan* A.G. Tkachenko (1917–1980). C.O. 5th Squadron until 16.12.1939 (when 5th Squadron was separated from 49 IAP and transformed into detached Gruppa Tkachenko). Performed 120 combat missions. Red Banner order; HSU 19.5.1940.
	st.lt P.I. Kolomin, from 19.1.1940.
	st.politr M.A. Kochmala; from 19.1.1940. KIA 13.2.1940.
1 AO GVF	*lt* A.N. Yakovlev (1908–1984). HSU 20.5.1940.

49 IAP strength 26 January 1940

Squadron	I-15bis	I-153	I-16	U-2
Staff	1	2	1	2
1st Squadron		8+5		
2nd Squadron			10+1	
3rd Squadron		8		
4th Squadron			7+3	
Kosyrev's group	12+2			
Tkachenko's group	10			
Total	23+2	18+5	18+4	2

49 IAP strength 13 March 1940

Squadron	I-15bis	I-153	I-16	Total
Staff		3+1	3	6+1
1st Squadron		11+3		11+3
2nd Squadron			11+2	11+2

3th Squadron		8		8
4th Squadron	--			-
5th Squadron	10+2	3		13+2
Total	10+2	25+4	14+2	49+8

49 IAP losses 30 November 1939 – 13 February 1940

Type	Combat losses			Non-combat losses
	A-A Artillery	MIA	Killed	Wounded
I-16	-	5	1	4
I-153	4	1	1	2
I-15bis	1	-	-	1
Total	5	6	2	7

49 IAP lost twenty aircraft (29.9% of its original strength), of which eleven were on combat missions (16.4%). Thirteen pilots (13.8%) were killed in action, of which five were shot down by A-A artillery, six missing in action and two killed in accidents.

16 March 1940 *major* P.I. Nedelin was appointed regiment Commander.

The regiment was awarded Red Banner Order 20 May 1940. Three pilots were appointed HSUs (*kapitan* A.G. Tkachenko 19 May 1940, and next day *st.lt* V.N. Peshkov and *lt* A.N. Yakovlev).

V.N. Peshkov was killed 8 September 1941 on a training flight in a Yak-1 fighter (271 IAP) at Batajsk, when he crashed into a storage building at take-off. He was buried in Rostov-na-Donu.

After the Winter War 49 IAP was relocated to Vil'no in the Lithuanian SSR as part of 57 IAD.

49 IAP victory claims until 1 March 1940

Date, time, location	Victors
6.12.1939 1132–1250 Vitele	Four I-16 (C.O. 2. esc *kapitan* N.A. Sizov, 49 IAP *flagshturman* I.P. Murazanov, G.A. Bobrov and I.S. Savushkin) shot down 41 AE:n MBR-2 (41 AE VVS LVF). *Lt* P.A.Tsiplakov, *kapitan* S.V. Belov and gunner V.I. Grishkov KIA, *st.lt* Petrov bailed out.
20.12.1939 1210 Salmi	*St.lt* I.P. Murazanov, *ml.lt* S.T. Goryunov, *ml.lt* B.I. Drozhbin (I-16) shot down 1 BL.
1.1.1940 2.5 km NW Rajakontu	I.M. Glukhov shot down SB (5./18 SBAP; *st.politr* P.Ya. Kochetov, *lt* K.A. Novikov and N.K. Skoselev KIA).
5.1.1940 1100 Läskelä, Juttulampi	*Lt* G.A. Bobrov and *ml.lt* S.T. Goryunov (I-16) shot down 1 BL.
5.1.1940 1200 Pitkäranta, Riihilampi	*Kapitan* A.S. Yegorov, *st.lt* G.P. Maslov, *st.politr* A.S. Kajchuk, *lt* A.J. Ananyin, *ml.lt* P.A. Dzhulaj and *ml.lt* N.K. Spiridenko (I-16) shot down 1 BL.
6.1.1940 1535 Salmi	*St.lt* I.S. Savushkin, *ml.lt* S.T. Goryunov and *st.lt* I.P. Murazanov (I-16) shot down 1 BL NW Tolvajärvi.
15.1.1940 1135 Pitkäranta	*St.lt* I.S. Savushkin and *ml.lt* S.T. Goryunov (I-16) shot down 1 FK
19.1.1940 1500 Salmi, Alauuksu	*St.lt* I.S. Savushkin and *ml.lt* S.T. Goryunov (I-16) shot down 1 BL.
20.1.1940 1600 Pitkäranta (FR); Nietjärvi (2 FK)	*St.politr* A.N. Permakov, *st.lt* I.S. Savushkin, *ml.lt* S.T. Goryunov and *ml.lt* L.M. Vinogradov (I-16) shot down 1 FR. *Kapitan* I.I. Popov, *kapitan* A.K. Karachentsev and *st.lt* F.M. Fatkulin (I-153) shot down 2 FK.
21.1.1940 Loimolanjärvi	*Kapitan* Lyutchenko and *ml.lt* Fedorov (I-16) shot down 1 BL.
22.1.1940 1645 Sortavala	*St.lt* I.P. Murazanov, *st.lt* I.S. Savushkin and *ml.lt* S.T. Goryunov (I-16); *polkovnik* V.N. Kitayev, *kapitan* I.I. Popov and *st.lt* V.N. Peshkov (I-153) shot down 1 FR and 1 biplane.

26.1.1940 1540 Uuksu	*St.lt* V.N. Peshkov (I-153) shot down 1 FK.
13.2.1940 Värtsilä	*St.politr* M.A. Kochmala (I-15) and *lt* J.F. Mikhin (I-16) shot down 2 GL and 1 FR.
18.2.1940 1150 Pitkäranta-Valamo	*St.lt* V.N. Peshkov (I-153) shot down 1 BL, one parachute was seen.
26.2.1940 0815 Syskyjärvi-Virakkalampi	*Kapitan* A.K. Karachentsev (I-153) shot down 1 BL.

Ml.lt S.T. Goryunov performed 101 missions and participated in 7 victories.

49th Fast Bomber Aviation Regiment (49 SBAP)

Autumn 1939 49 SBAP was located in Tain-Obo-Samon in Mongolia, attached to 1 AG.

A special Squadron was formed in 49 SBAP 30 January 1940, and departed 2 February 1940 to the Finnish front.

50th Fast Bomber Aviation Regiment (50 SBAP)

Autumn 1939 50 SBAP was located in Siverskaya, strength 30 November 1939 56 SB. In early December 1939 50 SBAP moved to Sestroretskiy razliv.

Subordination
71 AB, VVS LVO
18 SBAB, VVS SZFr (until 16 January 1940)
18 SBAB, VVS 7.A (from 16 January 1940)

Combat Chronicle
50 SBAP operated during the entire Winter War on the Karelian Isthmus. In January 1940 50 SBAP supported the Red Army's breakthrough of the Mannerheim Line at Summa, with 123rd Infantry Division as the spearhead unit, and in the final phase of the war 50 SBAP bombed Finnish fortifications in the Viipuri area. 50 SBAP performed 66 bombing attacks.

19 December 1939 Lähde was attacked by 30 bombers, of which SB c/n 3/42 and 1/43 were lost. SB c/n 1/43 of 2nd Squadron was set afire in air combat, but was able to reach Soviet-held territory, where the wounded pilot escaped by parachute, while the other crew members were killed. SB c/n 3/42 of 1st Squadron force-landed in Oranienbaum, the MG-gunner was killed. *This day LeR 2 claimed ten "certain" bomber kills in the Isthmus airspace, and furthermore four "probable". Note: in addition to the above-mentioned losses of 50 SBAP, 13 SBAP also lost six and 44 SBAP nine SB bombers in the indicated area 19 December 1939.*

Late December 1939 Makslahti and Antrea railway stations were bombed (Christmas Day 25 December and 29 December 1939 respectively). Continuous fog and falling snow interrupted all operations, many missions were canceled or targets could not be found.

25 December 1939 Lenkeri (?) was bombed by nine SBs, which were attacked by six Fokker fighters, of which one was claimed shot down by the gunners. No Finnish losses.

In December 1939 50 SBAP performed 151 combat missions.

11 January 1940 at least 3rd Squadron moved to Luga bay on the southern shore of Gulf of Finland.

18 January 1940 bombing of the Finnish fortifications of the Mannerheim Line in the Summa area was initiated (Summa, Hotokka and Leipäsuo strongpoints). Ilves was bombed by three SBs, which were attacked by a Fokker, which got hits on one SB.

19 January 1940 Säiniö railway station was bombed by two SBs, of which one was shot down and crashed on the return leg. Three SB were claimed by Finnish fighters on the Karelian Isthmus.

29 January 1940 Hotakka (north of Muolaanjoki) was bombed by nine SBs. According to Russian documents a Fokker flight made resultless counterattacks. Leipäsuo was bombed by another group of three SB, of which SB c/n 18/204 (4th Squadron) was shot down by Finnish A-A artillery, and crashed

Aleksandr N. Kostylev, 50 SBAP Military Commissar (HSU 21.3.1940). (G.F. Petrov)

south of Kangaspelto at 15.00 hours. *shturman lt* N.Ye. Gapeyev was taken prisoner, and said that four aircraft led by *st.lt* Ivanov had taken off from Siverskaya at 1320 hours, tasked to bomb the fortifications at Hotakka.

30 January 1940 Summa was bombed by 27 SBs. C/n 11/80 (*lt* M.M. Kulakov, 3rd Squadron) was shot down by A-A artillery at Hiitola.

17 February 1940 SB c/n 2/59 (3rd Squadron) was badly damaged by A-A artillery, but reached Soviet territory, and crashed at Sestroretsk. The wounded pilot *st.lt* N.Z. Zinchenko and killed MG-gunner *starshina* A.M. Salov were made HSUs 21 March 1940.

1 March 1940 nine SBs bombed Nurmi railway station. An SB was shot down by A-A artillery and force-landed at Kämärä on Finnish held territory. All crew were killed when attempting to reach own lines, and were buried on 10 March 1940 in Sestroretsk. All crew (*st.politr* V.V. Kojnash, *lt* B.A. Kornilov and *ml.kzv* F.Ya. Akkuratov) were posthumously appointed HSUs 21 March 1940.

50 SBAP Command

Commander	*major* V.V. Smirnov (1902–1943). HSU 21.3.40. In GPW commanded 233 ShAD.
Military Commissar	*bat.komiss* A.N. Kostylev (1908–1983). HSU 21.3.40. Later test pilot etc.
Chief of Staff	

Squadron C.O. and Commissars
1st	*st.politr* V.A. Orlov (KIA 30.11.39)
2nd	*st.politr* A.A. Budkin (KIA 19.12.39)
3rd	*st.politr* Polikarpov
4th	*kapitan* Sergeyev
5th	*kapitan* I.P. Vlasov (1912–1957). HSU 21.3.40, 52 combat missions in Winter War.
Unknown	*kapitan* M.M. Voronkov (1910–1999). HSU 21.3.40.
Unknown	*kapitan* Yu.N. Gorbko (1908–1942). HSU 21.3.40.

50 SBAP was awarded Red Banner Order, and ten aviators (Regiment commander Smirnov, Regiment commissar Kostylev, Squadron commanders Vlasov, Voronkov and Gorbko, pilot N.Z. Zinchenko and gunner/RT-operator A.M. Salov), and the three 1 March 1940 fallen aviators were appointed HSUs on 21 March 1940.

Pre-flight inspection at 50 SBAP. (G.F. Petrov)

52th Fast Bomber Aviation Regiment (52 SBAP)

Autumn 1939 52 SBAP was located in Ovruch (Kiev MD).

Subordination
VVS KOVO (until late February 1940)
OAG (from 26 February 1940)

Combat Chronicle

52 SBAP arrived from Ovruch to Kuressaare with 51 SB and one USB, and was attached to OAG. Operational readiness was reached 26 February 1940.

26 February 1940 2nd and 4th squadrons bombed Riihimäki. SB c/n 17/K (4th Squadron, pilot *st.lt* D.I. Matveyev) was shot down by A-A artillery, all crew were killed.

11 March 1940 52 SBAP bombed Riihimäki-Lahti railway. One SB (1st Squadron) was damaged at 1240 hours by attacking Finnish fighters at Hyvinkää, the MG-gunner was seriously wounded and died 14 March 1940.

52 SBAP dropped 82.3 t bombs on 132 combat missions, total flight time 431 h 42 min. Main bombing targets were Tampere, Riihimäki and Lahti railway junctions.

52 SBAP Command

Commander	*major* I.K. Kosenko
Military Commissar	*bat.komiss* F.S. Karpenkov
Chief of Staff	*polkovnik* Kuznetsov
Squadron C.O.	
1st	*kapitan* V.A. Morozov
3rd	*major* G.I. Yakimenko (Spanish Civil War veteran.)
4th	*kapitan* K.I. Larionov (Spanish Civil War veteran.)
5th	*kapitan* Borisov
Unknown	*kapitan* A.Z. Gajshunov

From the reminiscences of *politr* D.P. Dukhanin: "*Enemy air defense of Lahti railway station was badly organized. The A-A fire only reached approximately 2,000 m altitude, and our normal flight level was 4,000 m. At Tampere A-A defense was more effective. During one mission the bomber piloted by starshina (in fact lt D.I.) Matveyev of 2nd Squadron was shot down by A-A artillery; all crew was killed*".

53rd Long-Range Bomber Aviation Regiment (53 DBAP)

Autumn 1939 53 DBAP was located in Monino (Moscow MD). From May 1939 53 BAP re-equipped, and exchanged its SB for new DB-3 (of production batches 13 to 23). DB-3 conversion training was completed by 1 November 1939.

Subordination
27 AB, AON-1
OAB, later OAG (from 7 January 1940)

53 DBAP Commander S.S. Aleksandrov. (G.F. Petrov)

Combat Chronicle

Late autumn 1939 53 DBAP moved with 50 DB-3 to Krestsy, where operational readiness was reached 14 November 1939. Three bombing missions were made in full regiment strength from Krestsy. As Krestsy airfield (700 x 700 m) was too small for heavily loaded DB-3 bombers, 53 DBAP moved further to Krechevitsy 26 December 1939.

19 December 1939 27 DB-3 were ready for take off, but only six bombers of 1st Squadron were able to start. On the route to the target low visibility was encountered. Only three DB-3 dropped 20 bombs, and the other three landed with bombs (including regiment C.O. *polkovnik* S.S. Aleksandrov).

21 December 1939 36 bombers took off, only 26 bombed the target. Ten bombers were forced to interrupt the mission because of incorrect engine handling by inexperienced pilots, leading to engines overheating and malfunctioning. 30 minutes before take-off an order came to take two additional FAB-100 bombs in each aircraft, which considerable delayed the start. Ten bombers (including *polkovnik* S.S. Aleksandrov) returned with bombs, and 3 bombers force landed. Two DB-3 of 4th Squad-

ron (c/n 2306, piloted by Squadron C.O. *major* V.F. Dryanin, and c/n 1803, piloted by *lt* V.N. Kuzmin) collided in the air. Only *major* Dryanin was able to escape by parachute from c/n 2306 which crashed at Säiniö (the wreck was only located in summer 2006). DB-3 c/n 1803 was seriously damaged on crash-landing at Borki.

25 December 1939 33 DB-3 were to take off, but because of bad weather only six started. Two DB-3 (c/n 1711, *kapitan* A.A. Vdovin, 2nd Squadron and c/n 2312, *kapitan* N.S. Trutnev, 3rd Squadron) were lost in take-off accidents, no personnel losses.

26 December 1939 31 DB-3 took-off from Krestsy. After bombing 30 aircraft landed in Krechevitsy, where the regiment was located until 7 January 1940. 53 DBAP performed one unsuccessful attack 29 December 1939.

30 December 1939 reinforcement was received from 41 DBAP (7 bombers with crews and technical personnel, altogether 68 persons).

31 December 1939 an order was received from AON-1 to move on 7 January 1940 to Kuusiku, Estonia, and join OAG (commanded by *polkovnik* Kravchenko). A total of 45 bombers and 423 persons moved to Estonia (186 persons and seven bombers were left in Krechevitsy, subordinated to 27 AB of AON-1). Of nine DB-3 (5th Squadron) which took off from Krechevitsy 7 January 1940 only two arrived in Kuusiku. Two DB-3 crashed in bad weather (five aviators were killed), one DB-3 force-landed in Gdov, while the other four returned to Krechevitsy.

7 January 1940 5th Squadron took off to Kuusiku. Only two DB-3 arrived safely in Kuusiku in the bad weather, while two crashed (on DB-3 c/n 718 five aviators were killed, the crew of c/n 1809 were injured) during the ferry flight.

9 January 1940 three squadrons (1st, 2nd and 4th) took off from Kuusiku to bomb Vaasa. Because of bad weather the reserve target Tampere was bombed.

12 January 1940 Vaasa was bombed by three (3rd, 4th and 5th) DB-3 squadrons, which dropped 112 50 kg bombs, and Seinäjoki by two (1st and 2nd) squadrons. Two bombers crashed (at least one after A-A artillery/air combat hits) and force-landed in Estonia/NW Russia. *Ten bombers were observed in Vaasa, and 95 bombs counted (without serious damage)*.

DB-3 c/n 392313 crash-landed in Ulismainen, Korpijärvi in eastern Finland, 70 km north of Lake Ladoga, after which the crew tried to reach their own lines. After a night spent in the forest pilot *st.lt* N.F. Prikhodko requested that the bomber should be set on fire, and the crew must not surrender to the Finns, but be prepared to commit suicide. Then the navigator *st.lt* P.I. Pereskok shot the pilot

This and next page: Kapitan Pomazovskiy (4./53 DBAP Commander) got lost 29.1.1940 and landed with DB-3 red 15 (c/n 392320) on the frozen Lake Iso-Roine. Kapteeni Bo von Willebrand (T-LLv 29) ferried the aircraft to VL two days later. Note overpainted red stars and barely visible red 15. (all photos SA-kuva)

180

VP-101 in Helsinki-Malmi airport in spring 1940 after overhaul at VL. (SA-kuva)

dead, and continued the escape together with MG-gunner/RT-operator *ser.* I.F. Kostrov. Pereskok and the frost-bitten Kostrov were taken POW 14 January 1940 near the Soviet-Finnish border. According to their questioning the aircraft got lost on a ferry flight from Moscow via Tikhvin and Lodejnoye pole to Petrozavodsk.

13 or 14 January a DB-3 Squadron was to perform an attack against Ykspihlaja (port of Kokkola), simultaneously with an attack by the main part of 53 DBAP from Paldiski, Estonia to Vaasa. On the other hand, Soviet archive documents indicate that this bomber belonged to a formation which had taken off from Estonia heading for Vaasa! *Maybe the Finnish interrogators were not able to imagine such a loss of orientation? The forced landing was rather successful, with only the propellers slightly bent. From 18 January 1940 the aircraft was recovered by Finnish troops via Korpijärvi to Loimola, from where one week later the DB-3 was dispatched by train to the Aircraft Factory in Tampere. The recovery was detected on 22 January 1940 by Soviet aircraft which opened fire, however without serious damage. After this the difficult recovery was continued only during snowfall or at night.*

14 January 1940 Vaasa was attacked, with the task to destroy the port and the government administration in the city. 42 DB-3 took off from Kuusiku, of which 28 bombed the city center in two waves. 136 FAB-100 and 32 ZAB-50 bombs were dropped (*"the target was destroyed"*). Heavy A-A artillery fire was encountered, and M-G gunner Shevchenko claimed an *"unidentified fighter"*! *28 bombers were observed over Vaasa, and some 220 bombs counted (most of them FAB-100 splinter bombs and ZAB-50 incendiary bombs). Ten persons were killed. Some thirty houses were burning in the city, which completely lacked fighter defense!*

15 January 1940 22 bombers took off to bomb Tampere. Because of repeated engine failures the target was not reached, and the bombs were dropped at various places. DB-3 c/n 392601 (*st.lt* A.I. Fomin, 4th Squadron) returned from Tampere on one engine and crashed 25 km north of Rapla. *st.lt* Fomin and *kapitan* L.S. Demin were killed, and MG-gunner *starshina* V.I. Belousov was seriously wounded. Another DB-3 (Lomov) force-landed in Latvia after loss of orientation. Altogether 17 bombers suffered from engine problems on the return leg. After investigation it was established that the engine failures were due to careless fuel handling at Air Base Nr. 35 (Kuusiku), resulting in ice and dirt in the fuel systems.

Up to 21 January 1940 53 DBAP had performed 157 combat missions in OAG.

29 January 1940 was a dramatic day – the regiment lost seven bombers: *kapt* O. Ehrnrooth (of Koelentue – AF Test Flight, in FA-1) together with *vänr* O. Puhakka (FR-76) intercepted c/n 392316 of 3rd Squadron at Toijala, and forced the bomber to land at Lempäälä. On the ground the crew used their hand-guns against the alerted Finnish Home Guard patrol. Pilot and *shturman* were killed (one of them in the burning bomber, the other was killed at capture), but Home Guard officer *luutn* K. Tiili was also killed before *starshina* P.T. Danilenko was captured.

A combined formation (3rd and 4th Squadrons) led by *kapitan* Podmazovskiy got lost on the return leg. Four DB-3 landed on the frozen lake Iso-Roine at 1530 hours. When the Soviet aviators realized that they had landed on enemy territory, they took off immediately, except Podmazovskiy's *red 15* (c/n 392320), which was left behind because of lack of fuel. The stranded crew quickly boarded c/n 392303 (*lt* Timofeyev, 3rd Squadron) which had landed nearby. The stubborn *kapitan* Podmazovskiy

181

DB-3 red 3 (53 DBAP, c/n 392302) force-landed on the frozen Köyliöjärvi 29.1.40. After the aircraft was set on fire by the crew, only the navigator was captured. (C-F. Geust)

took now command of c/n 392303, resulting in his second aircraft loss the same day. After another loss of orientation he crash-landed in NE Pärnu, Estonia). Lentom P. Jääskeläinen (T-LeR 2) had been alerted from Parola in an obsolete Gloster Gamecock fighter trainer, and daringly tried to attack the Soviet bombers at Hauhonjärvi. According to Finnish information one of the Soviet aviators was hit by Jääskeläinen's gun fire, which however is not confirmed by Soviet documents. The intact "Red 15" was flown to Tampere via Lehijärvi 31 January – 1 February 1940 by kapt Bo von Willebrand (T-LLv 29) after the fuel tanks had been filled up. "Red 15" became VP-101 of Finnish AF (later renumbered VP-11), and on 1 March 1940 was allocated to naval squadron LLv 36. Because of lack of bombs no operational flights were made during the Winter War.

After loss of orientation DB-3 c/n 392302 *red 3* (2nd Squadron) force-landed on the frozen Lake Köyliöjärvi at 1536 hours. *Shturman lt* V.A. Ushakov was taken prisoner, while the other crew members committed suicide after setting the aircraft on fire. According to Finnish observations this bomber had circled for about one hour above Kokemäki, Peipohja and Säkylä. Half an hour later *luutn* J. Visapää (KoeL, FR-106) and *vänr* O. Puhakka (FR-76) forced down *red 12* (c/n 392525, *st.lt* G.A.Yandushev, 4th Squadron), which made a belly landing in Urjala, Kylmäkoski. After an exchange of fire the three-member crew was captured, and said that the bomber was on "a training flight". The repaired DB-3 was delivered to *Ilmavoimat* as VP-13 in February 1941.

DB-3 c/n 392520 (tactical 9, piloted by *st.lt* S.P. Sarayev) was shot down by A-A artillery on the return leg and crashed near the railway line in Helsinki-Pasila, all the crew were killed. The seventh DB-3 lost this day was c/n 392014 (*st.lt* Aruyunov, 3rd Squadron) which crash-landed 25 km north of Paide in Estonia, and was sent to Zavod 35 in Smolensk for repairs.

2 February 1940 DB-3 c/n 391712 of 2nd Squadron was shot down in air combat near Hanko. At 14.37 hours four Fokker D.XXI fighters made two attacks against nine DB-3 (2nd Squadron, commanded by *kapitan* Surov) near Bengtskär lighthouse. The attacks were made from the rear and below, concentrating on the outermost aircraft of the Squadron. The left-most bomber piloted by *st.lt* S.Ya. Rozhkov was set on fire (left engine), and the crew of three were seen to escape by parachute. The parachutes were closely followed by the Finnish fighters, which refrained from attacking the falling aviators, but they are not known to have been taken prisoner. One enemy fighter was claimed shot down by the MG-gun-

DB-3 tactical 9 was shot down by A-A artillery and crashed near the railway at Pasila, Helsinki. The wreck is seen loaded onto a railway car and on its way to VL. (SA-kuva)

ners. After the Squadron had landed a search party (one DB-3 and two I-153s) was dispatched at 1640 hours. Next day a similar search party was dispatched at 1530 hours, but neither search party found any traces of the DB-3 crew. After this loss the regiment command considered that bombers returning from Finland should be met by fighters patrolling in the Hanko, Turku and Åland regions. *LLv 24 claimed three DB-3 bombers on 3 February 1940 in the Nagu-Korpo region – is one of the documents wrongly dated? Vääp K. Virta (FR-84, LLv 24) shot down a DB-3 in this region (near Utö) 4 February 1940.*

In February-March 1940 53 DBAP received reinforcements:
- 11 February 1940 32 aviators arrived from Chkalov Aviation School in Orenburg,
- 13 February 1940 11 DB-3 arrived from 11 DBAP (7 AB, AON-3) in Zaporozhe (south Ukraine),
- 14 February – 1 March 1940 90 aviators and 8 DB-3 bombers arrived from 8 DBAP (formerly of 7 AB, AON-3) in Khabarovsk on the Pacific Ocean.

Note: Because of his combat experiences from China and Khalkhin-Gol, it can be assumed that *polkovnik* G. Kravchenko personally insisted on reinforcement of OAG with units well-known to him – despite the long and troublesome transport from Mongolia and the Far East to Estonia!

17 February 1940 53 DBAP bombed the *"exiled Finnish government"* in Ylistaro (39 km NW Seinäjoki). DB-3 c/n 391854 of 2nd Squadron was shot down in air combat at Keksfaarne (Kökar?) Island. The crew of this bomber had arrived from 11 DBAP. *There were absolutely no strategic targets in the parish of Ylistaro – the Finnish Government remained in Helsinki during the entire war. Soviet intelligence may have*

183

After air combat DB-3 c/n 392316 crash-landed and burned at Lempäälä on 29 January 1940. Pilot kapitan N.S. Trutnev (photo) and navigator kapitan I.P. Ivanov were killed, starshina P.T. Danilenko became POW. (C-F. Geust, G.F. Petrov)

got information about the evacuation of the Finnish Parliament to Kauhajoki, which however is located 50 km south-west of Seinäjoki! Three bombers attacked the port of Vaasa and Gåsgrund lighthouse, while five DB-3 attacked Ylistaro. No substantial damage was caused. A lone DB-3 of 2nd Squadron (ex-11 DBAP) returning from Ylistaro to Kuusiku was shot down over Korpo by luutn T. Hyrkki in MS-301. No losses were suffered by Finnish AF.

20 February 1940 4th Squadron bombed Haapamäki railway junction. Squadron Commander *kapitan* A.F. Seregin damaged four Finnish fighters, which were seen burning. DB-3 c/n 392417 (*st.lt* I.A. Bayev) (originally of 8 DBAP, AON-3 in the Far East) did not return. Luutn *V. Karu (LLv 28)* shot down two DB-3 bombers near the Estonian coast. Ylik *L. Nissinen (FR-98)* and vääp *L. Rautakorpi (FR-116, both of LLv 24)* shot down one bomber which crashed at Hyynilä, Mouhijärvi. An I-153 of 38 IAP force-landed on the ice at Porkkala. The seriously injured fighter pilot st.lt N. P. Perevezentsev was taken prisoner and died four days later. The task of the fighters was to secure the return of the bombers from Haapamäki.

By 1 March 1940 eight bombers had arrived from 8 DBAP (of AON-3 in Far East), making up the regiment's personnel strength to 575.

Eleven DB-3 (three shot down by fighters, three in accidents and five "did not return") and 33 aviators of 53 DBAP were killed in action. 53 DBAP performed 26 "regiment attacks", flight time 2,123 hours.

53 DBAP Regiment Attacks 19–29 December 1939

Date	Aircraft ready	Aircraft started	Aircraft bombed target	Aircraft returned to own base	Aircraft losses	Bombs dropped
19.12.39	27	6	-	6	-	20xFAB-100
21.12.39	36	36	26	32	2	40xFAB-100, 240xFAB-50
25.12.39	24	6	3	6	2	30xFAB-100
26.12.39	31	31	30	31	-	22xFAB-250, 120xFAB-100
29.12.39	29	12	-	12	-	30xFAB-100, 12xZAB-50
Total	147	91	59	87	4	22xFAB-250, 240xFAB-100, 240xFAB-50, 12xZAB-50

53 DBAP performed altogether 26 "regiment attacks".

53 DBAP Bombs Dropped

Target	FAB-50	FAB-100	FAB-250	FAB-500	ZAB-50
Vaasa	80	250	-	-	110
Seinäjoki	150	-	-	30	
Pori	10	468	-	-	51
Ylistaro	-	278	-	-	42
Haapamäki	518	-	-	88	
Riihimäki	288	24	-	118	
Tampere	80	316	-	14	50
Kouvola	-	-	66	22	-

DB-3 red 12 made a belly landing ar Urjala, Kylmäkoski on 29 January 1940. The only slightly damaged bomber was repaired at VL, and became VP-13 in Finnish AF (C-F. Geust, P. Manninen)

Lohja	-	20	-	-	34
Lahti	-	94	-	-	25
Viipuri	-	144	22	-	-
Ohters	368	812	33	-	144

53 DBAP Bombing targets
Railway junctions and yards:
Tampere   3 times (29.1.40 etc.)
Viipuri   1
Seinäjoki   1 (12.1.40)
Riihimäki   3
Haapamäki   4 (20.1.40 etc.)

Railway stations:
Pilppula   1
Pyhäjärvi   1
Salo   2
Vaasa   3 (12.1, 14.1 and 17.2.40)
Karjaa   1
Lahti   1
Ports:
Pori 2
Turku   2

Railway bridges:
Viipuri 2
Kouvola 1

Airforce bases:
Suur-Merijoki 1 (19.12.39)

Main storage depots:
Säiniö 1

Other targets:
Ylistaro (presumed location of the Finnish government!) 2 (17.2.40)
Maritime transport 1

53 DBAP Command

Commander	*polkovnik* S.S. Aleksandrov (1906–1971). In GPW commanded 335 ShAD etc. Commanded 34th Air Army 1951–1955.
Military Commissar	*bat.komiss* Samokhin
Chief of Staff	*major* Shejkhov
	major Poruchayev
Squadron C.O.	
2nd	*kapitan* S.S. Kurov
4th	*major* V.F. Dryanin
	kapitan Pomazovskiy
	major Alekseyev
	kapitan N.I. Repkin
	kapitan N.S. Gusarov
	kapitan A.F. Seregin
	kapitan V.Ya. Kryukov

54th Fast Bomber Aviation Regiment (54 SBAP)

54 SBAP was set up in May 1938, and all 56 SB were alerted in September of the same year because of the Czechoslovak crisis. In June 1939 12 aircraft were transferred to Mongolia. In autumn 1939 54 SBAP was located in Shejkovka, Byelorussian SSR.

Subordination
VVS BOVO
16 SBAB, VVS 7.A
16 SBAB, VVS SZFr (from 7 January 1940)

54 SBAP Strength and locations

Date	Base	Subordination	Base unit	Aircraft
1.11.39	Mogilev	58 AB	13 RAB, 121 AB	62 SB
1.12.39	Smuravyevo	16 AB	1 RAB, 121 AB	51 SB
1.1.40	Smuravyevo	16 AB	1 RAB, 121 AB	51 SB
1.2.40	Smuravyevo	16 AB	1 RAB, 121 AB	45 SB
1.3.40	Smuravyevo	16 AB	1 RAB, 121 AB	40 SB
1.4.40	Mogilev	41 AB	13 RAB, 121 AB	38 SB

Combat Chronicle

13 September 1939 54 SBAP had moved to Shejkovka (near Mogilev, Byelorussian SSR) with 63 SB, for participation in the final stage of the war against Poland (or "liberation of Western Ukraine and Byelorussia".) 54 SBAP performed 37 war missions (or one "regiment mission"), flight time 98 h 01 min.

In October 1939 the best 12 crews were relocated to Latvia. Late November 1939 the main part of 54 SBAP (53 SB) was relocated from Shejkovka via Vitebsk to Vyskatka, Smuravyevo (40 km NNE Gdov). At arrival 30 November 1939 54 SBAP was attached to 16 SBAB, VVS 7.A.

54 SBAP performed its first war missions 19 December 1939, when Finnish positions on the Karelian Isthmus were bombed without losses.

Early January 1940 3rd Squadron was relocated to Kingisepp (E Narva). 1st, 2nd and 4th Squadrons remained at Smuravyevo.

5 January 1940 54 SBAP bombed Kuparsaari and Mikkeli. Two SBs (c/n 1/218 and 11/93) of 1st Squadron were shot down in air combat at Jääski. c/n 1/218 crashed at Kuurnapohja, Imatra. *Shturman lt* F.Ye. Ivanov escaped by parachute and was taken prisoner, the other crew members were killed. LeR 2 claimed three "DB" over the Karelian Isthmus, and one uncertain kill. Entry – and return route was the Luga River at Luga Bay, then to the Finnish coast and north to Mikkeli.

17 January 1940 the bombing target of 16 SBAB was military objects and the railway station of Lappeenranta. Only eight SB of 54 SBAP (seven SB from 3rd Squadron and one from 4th Squadron) led by 3rd Squadron Commander *kapitan* Ivanov were able to take off in the foggy and very cold weather. The target of 54 SBAP was "military factories north of Lappeenranta". 54 SBAP dropped two FAB-250, 17 FAB-100 and 444 ZAB-1e bombs from 2,300 m altitude, and 22,400 leaflets, but was not able to destroy the target as most bombs fell in the city and the station area. The bombers continued their mission gaining altitude, and turned back to the northwest of the city. On the return leg the bombers were attacked by 10 Fokkers of 1st and 3rd flights of LLv 24, which shot down three SBs of 54 SBAP (c/n 4/71 crashed at Rättijärvi, 5 km NE Kilpeenjoki; c/n 12/93 red 10 crashed at Kavantsaari, the pilot *kapitan* A.N. Ivakin bailed out and was taken prisoner; c/n 10/93 crashed at Viipuri, *lt* D.N. Tarasov was taken prisoner). The other seven aviators were killed. SB c/n 12/68 was seriously damaged on crash-landing in Kamenka, gunner *starshina* K.A. Kas'ko died of wounds 22 January 1940 after his eighth combat mission. Kas'ko was posthumously awarded HSU 7 April 1940. Also *ml.kzv* V.G. Nechayev, who this day claimed four enemy aircraft in air combat, was awarded the Golden Star 7 April 1940. All other SBs of 54 SBAP received combat damage and force-landed in various locations, except SB c/n 10/124 which was the only a/c to return to its base, with 12 bullet holes in the fuselage. According to 54 SBAP War Diary *"24 enemy fighters attacked six Soviet bombers. 11 enemy fighters were shot down by the MG-gunners of the SB"*. LeR 2 claimed eight SB shot down, and six uncertain; no own losses.

Gunner V.G. Nechayev claimed four fighters 17.1.1940, and was awarded HSU 7.4.1940. He was killed in action 6.11.1941. (G.F. Petrov)

After the big losses *komandarm* Ye.S. Ptukhin (Commander VVS SZFr) issued an order prohibiting bombing attacks to Kouvola, Suur-Merijoki, Lappeenranta, Viipuri, Hiitola and Elisenvaara without escort fighters. Ptukhin also repeated the Stavka order of 27 December 1939, which categorically prohibited the use of same route and waypoints on the approach and return flights. (See VVS SZFr, 16 SBAB and 31 SBAP, pages 35, 53 and 138)

18 January 1940 SB c/n 10/217 was destroyed at take-off from Smuravyevo, navigator *kapitan* G.S. Stolyarov died of his injuries.

13 February 1940 at 1545 hours an aircraft dropped four bombs by mistake on the Estonian shore of Lake Peipus (Chudskoye ozero) without damage. The Estonian authorities filed a protest.

17 February 1940 reinforcements (72 aviators, some 25 pilots) from 57 LBAP (in Novo-Sosoyevko, Far East) arrived in Gdov.

20 February 1940 SB c/n 7/216 was shot down in air combat near Kouvola. *shturman lt* M.I. Maksimov was believed to have been taken prisoner after force-landing on the ice of the Gulf of Finland. *Luutn* P. Berg (GL-280, LLv 26) shot down an SB at Virolahti. *The Soviet legation in Helsinki inquired on 17 July 1940 whether Maksimov had been taken prisoner.*

21 February 1940 54 SBAP bombed Lappeenranta railway station. SB c/n 5/69 (6th Squadron) was shot down in air combat, and crashed in Rikkilä, Lappee (3 km W Simola), pilot *lt* V.A. Gavrilov was captured. *Luutn* T. Huhanantti (FR-94) and *vääp* W. Rimminen (FR-87) shot down an SB near Simola.

On both 10 and 11 March 1940 SBs of 7th and 1st Squadrons were shot down by A-A fire at Säkkijärvi; all crew were killed.

54 SBAP performed 1,131 war missions (33 "regiment missions"), flight time 3,249 h 22 min (of which combat missions 2,957 h 5 min). Targets primarily on Karelian Isthmus (in particular Säkkijärvi), but also cities and railway junctions in South-east Finland (Kouvola, Lappeenranta, Viipuri, Imatra, Hamina, Simola etc).

54 SBAP dropped 26,195 bombs (weight 558,284 kg). According to the combat report 54 SBAP bombers flew 743,953 km, of which 297,393 km over enemy territory (calculated from the theoretical medium speed 220 km/h) – there was apparently a mathematically skilled officer in the regiment HQ! Seven bombers were lost and 30 (38 according to some sources) enemy fighters were claimed shot down in air combat, and three bombers were shot down by Finnish A-A artillery. 54 SBAP lost 32 aviators in combat, or almost 20% of its personnel.

54 SBAP Command

Commander	*polkovnik* V.S. Leonov
	polkovnik Komarov
Military Commissar	*bat.komiss* F.N. Khorobryh
Chief of Staff	*major* S.T. Pisakov

Squadron C.O. and Commissars
1st	*st.lt* Yefimov
3rd	*kapitan* Ivanov
	politr Serbin
4th	*kapitan* Prochenko
	komiss st.lt D.I. Yas'ko (KIA 17.1.40)
	politr Punin
	st.politr N.S. Smolyak (KIA 21.2.40)
5th	*kapitan* M.I. Borisenko
6th	not known

54 SBAP was awarded Red Banner Order 21 March 1940. Two aviators (*ml.kzv* V.G. Nechayev and posthumously *starshina* K.A. Kas'kov) were appointed HSUs 7 April 1940.

After the Winter War 54 SBAP was relocated to Vil'no in the Lithuania, and together with 49 IAP formed 57 IAD.

58th Fast Bomber Aviation Regiment (58 SBAP)

Autumn 1939 58 SBAP was located in Staraya Russa (Leningrad MD).

Subordination
55 AB, VVS LVO
55 AB, VVS 7.A

58 SBAP Commander I.D. Udonin. (G.F. Petrov)

Combat Chronicle

17–28 September 1939 58 SBAP fought on the "Ukrainian front" against Poland, and performed 489 combat missions, flight time 1,079 h 38 min.

In October 1939 3rd Squadron was transferred to 44 SBAP, and a new 3rd Squadron was established in 58 SBAP.

29 November 1939 58 SBAP relocated to Sivoritsy, strength 53 SB (only seven bombers were of series 97 or newer; all other SBs came from earlier production batches). Targets of 58 SBAP included Kouvola and Simola railway junctions, Kotka (no airfield existed in Kotka!) and Utti airfields and Lahti radio station.

30 November 1939 because of bad weather only a reconnaissance flight to Muolaanjärvi was performed.

1 December 1939 58 SBAP attacked prime targets: 1st, 2nd and 3rd Squadrons bombed Simola (six trains destroyed), 4th Squadron silenced Lahti radio station and 5th Squadron set oil tanks in Kotka on fire. 17 of the 45 attacking SBs were hit by Finnish A-A fire.

Because of non-flying weather the next missions were only performed 19 December 1939, when the western part of the Mannerheim Line was attacked at Huumola, Karhula and Koivisto.

22 December 1939 an enemy fighter was claimed by *shturman st.lt* A.V. Kolchanov (2nd Squadron) at Supknila (?).

In January 1940 seven new SB were received.

7 January-28 February 1940 58 SBAP performed eleven attacks against the western part of the Mannerheim Line with full regiment strength; targets included fortifications at Huumola, Kaijala, Karhula, Lenkkeri, Liipola, Autio, Näykki and Järvelä; Kaislahti, Makslahti, Leipäsuo, Kämärä, Säiniö, Ala-Säiniö and Nuoraa railway stations, Rokkala railway bridge and Koivisto coast artillery positions. Later targets included Uuras (Trångsund), Lihaniemi, Ravansaari and Viipuri (Papula, Sorvali and Piikkiruukki).

29 January 1940 target was Viipuri AF base (= Suur-Merijoki). 58 SBAP attacked with its entire strength. The plan was to fly towards Helsinki, then turn back in two formations, one attacking from the north and the other from the south. Over the airfield 2nd Squadron approaching from the south was intercepted by six enemy fighters, of which one was claimed by *shturman lt* N.A. Bokman and *ml.kzv* L.M. Uglev in c/n 14/92, piloted by *lt* A.S. Gusev. However both c/n 14/92 and c/n 19/92 (pilot *ml.lt* B.I. Zirkin) went missing. Both crashed SB were found on the ice near Tolbukhin lighthouse 23 March

1940. *"The bomb attack left several Finnish fighters burning on the ground."* Twelve of the 36 attacking bombers were damaged by A-A fire.

At the end of January 1940 58 SBAP relocated to an ice base south of Uusikylä, Kuokkala (now Repino) on Gulf of Finland.

19 February 1940 Viipuri railway junction was attacked by 3rd Squadron; four trains with 120 wagons were bombed. One enemy fighter was claimed by the MG-gunners. The SB of *st.lt* A.Ye. Ostayev returned with 42 A-A hits.

20 February 1940 three squadrons repeated the attack on targets in Viipuri. SB (c/n 8/233, pilot *st.politr* I.F. Kvashnin, 3rd Squadron Commissar) exploded after a direct A-A hit. (In Soviet historiography Kvashnin is considered to have performed a "burning taran").

58 SBAP performed 2,350 combat missions (flight time 2,814 h 37 min), dropped 16,879 bombs (weight 1,048 t), and claimed destruction of 6 Finnish bunkers, 24 tanks, 17 artillery batteries, 16 A-A batteries and 250 railway wagons. Four enemy fighters were claimed shot down. Own losses were three SB and nine aviators. Four aviators were injured, and two persons were killed in accidents on the ground at the bases.

58 SBAP was awarded Red Banner Order 11 April 1940. Three aviators (*st.lt* A.Ye. Ostayev, *st.lt* B.P. Trifonov, and posthumously *st.politr* I.F. Kvashnin) became HSUs 21 March 1940.

58 SBAP Command

Commander	*polkovnik* I.D. Udonin. In 1943 commanded 261 SAD of 7th Air Army in Karelia.
Military Commissar	*bat.komiss* B.N. Smirnov
Chief of Staff	*polkovnik* A.Ye. Krasinskiy

Squadron C.O. and Commissars

1st	*kapitan* P.G. Danilov
	st.politr P.G. Nagavkin
2nd	*kapitan* A.N. Vitruk. In 1944 commanded 10 GvShAD.
	st.politr S.F. Litvyakov
3rd	*kapitan* K.A. Taranenko
	st.lt P.A. Zheleznyi
	st.politr D.D. Zherebko
	st.politr I.F. Kvashnin (1906–20.2.40). HSU 21.3.40.
4th	*kapitan* V.V. Markov
	st.politr A.I. Anikin
5th	*kapitan* I.P. Skok (1906–1977). In GPW commanded 72 SAP in 1941, 334 BAD in 1944 and 6 BAK in 1945.
	kapitan I.A. Platov
	st.politr R.M. Yemelyanov

60th Fast Bomber Aviation Regiment (60 SBAP)

Autumn 1939 60 SBAP was located in Lebedin (Kharkov MD).

Subordination
VVS KhVO
68 SBAB, VVS 13.A (from 11 February 1940)

Combat Chronicle

21 January 1940 60 SBAP moved from Lebedin to Kasimovo with 49 SB and one USB. 60 SBAP performed combat missions from 11 February 1940 (attached to 68 SBAB, VVS 13.A). Some elements of 60 SBAP were apparently also attached to VVS 9.A, and dropped supplies to encircled troops.

17 February 1940 two bombers were hit by A-A artillery on a supply-dropping mission (to the encircled 54th Mountain Division?); *shturman st.lt* G.V. Gmyzin was killed.

18 February 1940 SB c/n 11/224 (*kapitan* A.G. Bezdenezhnykh, C.O. 1st Squadron) was shot down at Teivonen. This day 12 SB of 5th Squadron bombed by mistake their own 469th and 674th Infantry Regiments (150th Division, 3rd Army Corps), which were to perform an attack at Taipale.

60 SBAP performed 1,245 combat missions, total flight time 1,348 h 27 min. 14,481 bombs (538.6 tonnes) were dropped.

60 SBAP Command

Commander	*major* Manturov (on sick leave from 4.2.40, replaced by assistant C.O. major Astafyev)
Military Commissar	*bat.komiss* Troshin
Chief of Staff	*kapitan* A.I. Orishshenko
Squadron C.O. 1st	*kapitan* A.G. Bezdenezhnykh (KIA 18.2.40)
2nd (?)	Ageyenko

63rd Fast Bomber Aviation Regiment (63 SBAP)

63 SBAP was the former 3 LBAP, 1st and 3rd Squadrons of which were converting to SB from 5 January 1940. When combat-ready 63 SBAP was on 10 March 1940 attached to VVS SZFr with 46 SB, based in Krasnogvardejsk. *St.lt* N.G. Braginets was appointed HSU 19 May 1940.

Subordination
VVS SZFr (from 10.3.40)

68th Fighter Aviation Regiment (68 IAP)

Autumn 1939 68 IAP was located in Pushkin (Leningrad MD).

Subordination
59 IAB, VVS LVO
59 IAB, VVS 7.A
15 SBAB, VVS 13.A (11–19 January 1940)
VVS 13.A (27 December 1939 – 11 January 1940, and from 19 January 1940)

Combat Chronicle
18–19 December 1939 68 IAP (47 I-16) moved from Pushkin to Kasimovo.

19 December 1939 nine I-16 of 68 IAP (led by *kapitan* Pershakov) escorted SB bombers to Viipuri and were intercepted by five Fokker D.XXI, which attacked from above. *Lt* Molchanov was injured in his leg, and I-16 of *lt* Chernetsov got 56 hits. The Fokkers escaped by steep dives.

20 December 1939 at 1500 hours fifteen I-16s led by *major* Gil' detected four Fokker D.XXI 500–600 m above. When two I-16 flights gained altitude the Fokkers escaped. At Viipuri an "apparently enemy aircraft" was seen falling in flames.

68 IAP fighter pilots in spring 1940, in the middle Regiment Commander V.V. Zelentsov (HSU 7.4.1940). (G.F. Petrov)

P.M. Petrov (3./68 IAP, HSU 7.4.1940) in 1941 as Commander of 254 IAP. (G.F. Petrov)

23 December 1939 at 1150 hours 13 I-16s led by *bat.komiss* Yakovenko fought against four Fokker D.XXI at Karhusuo. Two Finnish aircraft were claimed shot down, and one pilot escaped by parachute. Finnish troops observed a mid-air collision of two I-16, but only one parachute. Lt I.I. Koval'kov (3rd Squadron, I-16 number "228") was shot down at Ylä-Säiniö and captured by Finnish ground forces at Kangaspelto, Muolaa. Koval'kov had arrived to 68 IAP from 25 IAP. Kharchenko's I-16 received 30 hits. *The parachutist seen was apparently lt Koval'kov, as no Finn escaped by parachute this day. Koval'kov was downed by ylik L. Nissinen in FR-98.*

25–31 December 1939 the I-15bis Squadron commanded by *kapitan* Postaush arrived from 7 IAP, to which 4th Squadron (12 I-16) commanded by *kapitan* T.I. Kochetkov was transferred.

27 December 1939 68 IAP was transferred to the new VVS 13.A on the eastern Karelian Isthmus, and served as a detached regiment (OIAP), directly subordinated to VVS 13.A. This day 68 IAP supported the withdrawal of Red Army 220th Infantry Regiment (of 4th Division) from Kelja (on the northern shore of River Suvanto) with 27 I-16 and 12 I-15bis.

68 IAP was still based at Kasimovo until 12 January 1940, when the regiment moved to Lempaala. The three I-16 squadrons were located on the Southeast shore of Lake Lempaala. The regiment had also I-15bis fighters, which were received from 7 IAP in exchange for an I-16 Squadron.

Because of severe frost 68 IAP was forced to entirely cease flight operations 30 December 1939–11 January 1940, after which flight operations were possible only on 12–13, 16–22 and 29 January 1940.

Ml.Lt V.G. Masitsh (68 IAP) claimed four victories (HSU 7.4.1940). (G.F. Petrov)

M.I. Volosevich (2./68 IAP) bailed out and was captured 29.2.1940 at Ruokolahti. (G.F. Petrov)

191

13 January 1940 two I-15bis were fired upon by their own A-A artillery of 4th Division. I-15bis c/n 4347 caught fire, *lt* V.P. Timofeyev was killed after an unsuccessful parachute jump at Lapinlahti, Suvanto.

4th Squadron arrived 19 January 1940 from Pushkin to VVS 9.A in Vojnitsa, and formed 3rd Squadron of 152 IAP. 68 IAP got reinforcements by I-153 fighters, which arrived directly to Lempaala. The new 4th Squadron (the personnel of which arrived from 2nd Squadron/7 IAP) was located at Nurmijärvi, and was ordered to support 3rd and 15th Army Corps of 13th Army.

29 February 1940 six fighters departed for a reconnaissance mission to Antrea, and detected the Finnish ice base at Ruokolahti. After returning 24 fighters (6 I-153 and 18 I-16) took off to destroy the detected fighter unit. I-153 c/n 521 was shot down in air combat at Tainionkoski, *lt* M.I. Volosevich (2nd Squadron) escaped by parachute and was taken prisoner. *St.lt* D.P. Yefimov's I-16 did not level out from a steep dive to evade a chasing Finnish fighter, but crashed into the ground. *LeR 2 claimed four unverified victories.*

5 March 1940 *ml.lt* V.G. Semin (I-153) was killed in air combat at Äyräpää. Ylik *M. Perälä (LLv 14, GL-278)* shot down an I-153 fighter at Äyräpää.

13 March 1940 *st.lt* N.V. Potapov (I-16) did not return.

68 IAP Mission Summary

30 November-20 January 1940 (in 59 IAB)   557 missions
30 November 1939–13 March 1940   1,926 bomber escort missions

68 IAP claimed 68 victories, of which 20 (!) aircraft were claimed shot down at Ruokolahti 29 February 1940 (according to the attached combat report 18). Four pilots did not return.

L.I. Yakovenko, 68 IAP Commissar (HSU 7.4.1940). (G.F. Petrov)

Strength and locations

Date	Base	Subordination	Base unit	Equipment
1.11.39	Pushkin	59 AB, VVS LVO	1 RAB, 258 AB	33 I-16, 15 I-16P, 15 I-15bis
1.12.39	Pushkin	59 AB, VVS 7.A	1 RAB, 258 AB	33 I-16, 15 I-16P, 15 I-15bis
1.1.40	Manushkino	59 AB, VVS 7.A	1 RAB, 258 AB	36 I-16, 15 I-16P, 15 I-15bis
1.2.40	Lake Lempaala, Metsäpirtti	59 AB, VVS SZFr	1 RAB, 258 AB	34 I-16, 14 I-16P, 14 I-15bis
1.3.40	Lake Lempaala, Metsäpirtti	59 AB, VVS SZFr	1 RAB, 258 AB	31 I-16, 13 I-16P, 17 I-153, 4 I-15bis
1.4.40	Pushkin	59 AB, VVS LVO	1 RAB, 258 AB	31 I-16, 14 I-16P, 16 I-153

68 IAP command

Commander — *major* V.V. Zelentsov (1910–1978). HSU 7.4.1940. In GPW commanded 44 AD.

Military Commissar — *bat.komiss* L.I. Yakovenko (1909–1991). HSU 7.4.40. In GPW deputy commander of AF of Caukasian Front.

Chief of Staff — *major* A.Ye. Kleshchev

Squadron C.O.

1st — *st.lt* D.P. Yefimov (KIA 29.1.1940)

2nd — *kapitan* Pershakov

3rd — *kapitan* P.M. Petrov (1910–1941). HSU 7.4.1940. In GPW commanded 254 IAP.

4th — 1.1.1940 to 7 IAP, later to 25 IAP *kapitan* T.I. Kochetkov

Unknown — *st.lt* S.I. Mironov (1914–1964). Performed 40 combat missions, 2 victories claimed in Winter War. HSU 7.4.1940. In GPW commanded 193 IAP. Commanded 30th Air Army 1953–1957. Deputy commander of VVS 1962–1964.

Five aviators (regiment Commander V.V. Zelentsov, regiment Commissar L.I. Yakovenko, Squadron C.O. P.M. Petrov and S.I. Mironov and *ml.lt* V.G. Masich) were appointed HSUs 7 April 1940.

Ruoholahti Air Combat 29 February 1940

29 February 1940 Masich's flight (with wingmen Blinikhin and Kul'man) was observing road traffic at Antrea.

Five Finnish pilots were shot down and killed at Ruokolahti 29.2.1940. The wrecks of GL-263 (kers Jussi Tolkki, escaped by parachute) and GL-269 (alik Pentti Kosola, KIA) are depicted. (K. Stenman)

Near Antrea two Bulldog fighters were detected, which the flight leader decided to destroy. After chasing them to Imatra, Masich opened fire on the first fighter, which crashed in flames in the forest, after which the other enemy fighter was attacked. This had however landed on a lake 2 km north of Vuoksenniska. Several aircraft were seen taking off from the ice base. *lt* Blinikhin downed an aircraft taking off, which crashed on the northern shore of the lake. Immediately after 15 Bulldog and Fokker aircraft were observed, and Masich's flight escaped with great speed. After combat with the Bulldog there were more than 80 hits in Masich's aircraft, of which 3 hits were in the back shield. One incendiary bullet hit the parachute which started to burn. After the return of the reconnaissance group the Commander of 68 IAP decided to perform a general attack against the enemy base, which was accepted by the Commander of VVS 13.A.

23 aircraft took part in two formations:
1. *major* Gil's detachment, 12 fighters (9 I-16 and 3 I-153)
2. *st.lt* Yefimov's detachment, 11 fighters (8 I-16 and 3 I-153)

Take off at 1240 hours, route Lempaalanjärvi-Sairala-Target, altitude 2,000 m. 10–12 km from Target *major* Gil detected several aircraft taking off from the lake, and he decided to attack with his formation, which was protected by *st.lt* Yefimov's group. When diving *major* Gil observed 2,500–3,000 m above him up to 18 enemy aircraft. Gil's group interrupted their dive and started to gain altitude. Now Yefimov's formation attacked the enemies 5–6 km from Imatra, while the enemy top formation attacked *major* Gil's group. During the combat the formations of *major* Gil' and *st.lt* Yefimov shot down 18 enemy aircraft, of which 8 were Fokkers and 10 Bulldogs. After the first attack the combat turned into individual dogfights.

Combat details:

1. *Major* Gil shot down a Fokker in a head-on attack. The Fokker caught fire and went spinning down. A Bulldog was shot when it attempted to turn into *lt* Polukin's tail and crashed to the ground in flames. Gil's aircraft got four hits.
2. When attacking a Fokker *st.lt* Plotnikov noticed that a Bulldog was getting behind *major* Gil. He made a quick turn and shot down the Bulldog, which emitted smoke and crashed.
3. Despite that his fighter already had 28 hits *st.lt* Ivanov did not leave the formation. When he noticed a Bulldog at Plotnikov's tail, he shot it down. The Bulldog crashed, heavily emitting smoke.
4. At 3200 m altitude *lt* Sorokin and *lt* Nikitin shot down a Fokker in a left turn. The Fokker caught fire and crashed.
5. *St.lt* Yefimov, *lt* Shishov, *lt* Terpukhov, *lt* Orlov and *lt* Sapozhnikov shot down a Bulldog taking off at 70–100 m altitude. The Bulldog caught fire and crashed.
6. *Lt* Shishov noticed a Bulldog at 100 m altitude and performed his first high-speed attack. After a sharp turn he repeated the attack from above and behind. The Bulldog crashed emitting smoke.
7. *Lt* Polukhin and *ml.lt* Mazurenko observed a Fokker approaching from behind. After a quick turn they shot down the enemy attacking from opposite sides. The Fokker crashed in bright flames.
8. *Ml.lt* Mazurenko saw a Fokker approaching from behind. He quickly turned 45–50 degrees and was overtaken by the Fokker. After a right turn Mazurenko attacked and with a long burst shot down the enemy which crashed in flames. Mazurenko's fighters received 36 hits.
9. *Lt* Orlov dived steeply and attacked a Bulldog on the ground from behind. The Bulldog caught fire.
10. After ground strafing *lt* Platonov became engaged in a dogfight, in which he followed a Bulldog, which he forced downwards by long bursts. After a while the enemy crashed in a hopeless spin.
11. *Lt* Popov was gaining altitude after the ground attack against the enemy base, when he saw I-16 and I-153 chasing a Bulldog, which tried to escape by turning. He got into the enemy's tail and shot him down in a steep dive.
12. After his ground attack dive *lt* Mayev saw a Fokker turning into the tail of a I-16 and opening fire. Mayev attacked immediately and shot down the Fokker, which crashed in flames.
13. When strafing an enemy aircraft on the ground *ml.lt* Soldatov was attacked by two Fokkers. He made a quick turn and gained speed, and was able to climb above the enemy. When he saw a Fokker approaching an I-16 he attacked. The enemy tried to escape by turning, but the maneuverable I-153 got into the tail of the Fokker, and fired two long bursts, after which the enemy crashed in the forest.
14. *Lt* Konjukhov shot down a Fokker in a head-on attack. Strangely the enemy did not answer the fire, but emitted smoke and crashed.

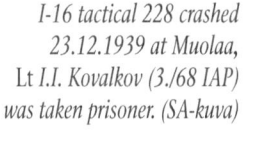

I-16 tactical 228 crashed 23.12.1939 at Muolaa, Lt I.I. Kovalkov (3./68 IAP) was taken prisoner. (SA-kuva)

15. *Lt* Nikitin (I-16) shot down a Bulldog after his strafing attack. He made two attacks from behind, and shot down the enemy, which crashed in the forest and caught fire. Nikitin's aircraft received four hits.
16. Over the target *st.lt* Fedorov saw a Bulldog at 2,200 m altitude. He got into the enemy's tail and fired two bursts, after which the enemy dived steeply and crashed north of Salvisaari. Thereafter he dropped his bombs on a taxiing Fokker, which crashed immediately after take-off.

Losses:
1. After a steep dive and because of a defective ski *st.lt* Yefimov (C.O. 1st Squadron) got into a negative-g dive and crashed into the forest.
2. *Lt* Volokhovich did not return.

The air combat was performed at levels between 500 and 2,500 m, and lasted 5–8 minutes. Our aircraft departed from the combat area only after the enemy. The formations assembled over the target were subject to A-A fire, after which return flight started.

Conclusions
1. The enemy did not fight actively despite his territorial and numerical superiority (27 enemy aircraft against our 23 aircraft)
2. The enemy used mixed formations (mono – and biplanes).
3. Fokker is a good fighter, but inferior to I-16 with M-62 engine.
4. Bulldog is good in horizontal manoeuvres.
5. The enemy tries to choose one-to-one combat.
6. Cooperation between I-16 and I-153 ensures excellent combat outcome.
7. In free dogfight I-16 tip 5 will enter a negative-g dive. Note loss of Yefimov 29 February 1940, and two other pilots, who escaped due to altitude reserve.

Note: The observed "Bulldogs" were in fact Gladiators. Although LLv 26 had used Gladiators for more than one month the enemy was not yet aware of the new biplane fighter! The Finns lost six Gladiators of LLv 26 and one Fokker of LLv 24, five fighter pilots were killed.

Finnish Losses at Ruokolahti 29 February 1940

Name	Aircraft	Fate	Notes
Alik P.V. Kosola	GL-269	KIA	
Ylik V.O. Lilja	GL-268	Parachute, KIA	
Luutn E.A.O. Halme	GL-262	KIA	
Løjtnant C.M.H. Kristensen	GL-259	KIA	Danish volunteer
Løjtnant P.B. Christensen	GL-261	Parachute	Danish volunteer
Kers J. Tolkki	GL-263	WIA	
Luutn T. Huhanantti	FR-94	KIA	

69th Fighter Aviation Regiment (69 IAP)

Autumn 1939 69 IAP was located in Odessa (Kiev MD).

Subordination
VVS KOVO

31 January 1940 1st and 2nd Squadrons (with 30 I-16 fighters and commanded by *kapitan* M.Ye. Astashkin and *kapitan* Matveyev respectively) were dispatched to the Northwest Front.

Astashkin's Squadron was apparently attached to 147 IAP at the Murmansk direction.

Astashkin became a posthumous HSU 10 February 1942 after a "blazing taran" near Odessa 14 September 1941.

72ⁿᵈ Mixed Aviation Regiment (72 SAP)

72 SAP was formed 10 April 1939, and based at Besovets (18 km W Petrozavodsk). However the first two squadrons with 15 I-15bis fighters only arrived from Gribochki and Krechevitsy 14 September 1939. One bomber squadron with 12 SB arrived later from 2 SBAP in Soltsy and another bomber squadron with 9 SB arrived from Siverskaya. The I-15bis fighter squadrons were soon dispatched to Kem'-Uhtua region for protection of the Detached Infantry Corps (commanded by *komdiv* Shmyryev) and attached to VVS 9.A. A new fighter Squadron (commanded by *st.lt* Zosima) with 15 I-153 arrived 11 January 1940 from Kiev Military District, and 16 February 1940 personnel for three SB-bomber squadrons arrived from 1ˢᵗ Separate Army in the Far East.

Subordination
VVS LVO
VVS 8.A
VVS 9.A (1ˢᵗ Squadron from 26 November 1939; became 1./152 IAP)

Orange-colored ANT-6 (coded SSSR-N170), piloted by polar aviator M.V. Vodopyanov (HSU 20.4.1934) was transferred to 72 SAP in December 1939 (photos taken in 1937). (G.F. Petrov)

72 SAP Strength and locations

Date	Base	Subordination	Base unit	Equipment
1.11.39	Besovets and Nurmolitsa, LVO	VVS 8.A, SZFr	6 RAB, 136 AB	29 I-15bis, 23 SB
1.12.39	Besovets and Nurmolitsa, LVO	VVS 8.A, SZFr	6 RAB, 136 AB	44 I-15bis, 23 SB
1.1.40	Besovets and Nurmolitsa, LVO	VVS 8.A, SZFr	6 RAB, 136 AB	42 I-15bis, 22 SB
1.2.40	Besovets and Nurmolitsa, LVO	VVS 8.A, SZFr	6 RAB, 136 AB	42 I-15bis, 15 I-153, 21 SB
1.3.40	Besovets and Nurmolitsa, LVO	VVS 8.A, SZFr	6 RAB, 136 AB	41 I-15bis, 40 I-153, 45 SB
1.4.40	Besovets and Nurmolitsa, LVO	VVS LVO	6 RAB, 136 AB	28 I-153, 45 SB

Combat Chronicle

The loss list of 72 SAP already began 19 October 1939(!), when a "special government task" was performed. Pilot S.F. Nikitin and navigator *lt* A.I. Yesakov were injured when landing in Petrozavodsk.

Was this a secret reconnaissance flight into Finnish territory during the negotiations in Moscow? Note the memoir phrase: "*Some days before the Mainila incident (26 November 1939) 72 SAP performed reconnaissance missions with single aircraft across the long border between Finland and the USSR.*" (M.F. Dryunin, head of operations department, 72 SAP)

30 November 1939 72 SAP consisted of 1st and 2nd fighter Squadrons; 3rd and 4th SB Squadrons (altogether 20 SB of 201-series, and older 200-series with 2-blade propellers and unprotected fuel tanks). On 26 November 1939 1st Fighter Squadron (14 I-15bis) flew from Besovets to Uhtua (and became later 1st Squadron/152 IAP of VVS 9.A).

2nd Fighter Squadron (with I-153) protected Besovets AF base, Petrozavodsk and the Murmansk ("Kirov") railway. This Squadron was possibly named 12 OAIE at the end of the war.

2 December 1939 SB (c/n 10/140, pilot *st.lt* A.P. Plakhov) took off with wrongly adjusted propellers and crashed (all crew were killed).

Polar aviator Mikhail Vodopyanov was one of the very first Heroes of the Soviet Union (20.4.1934). (G.F. Petrov)

ANT-6 (SSSR-N170) was equipped with state-of-the art navigation systems. (G.F. Petrov)

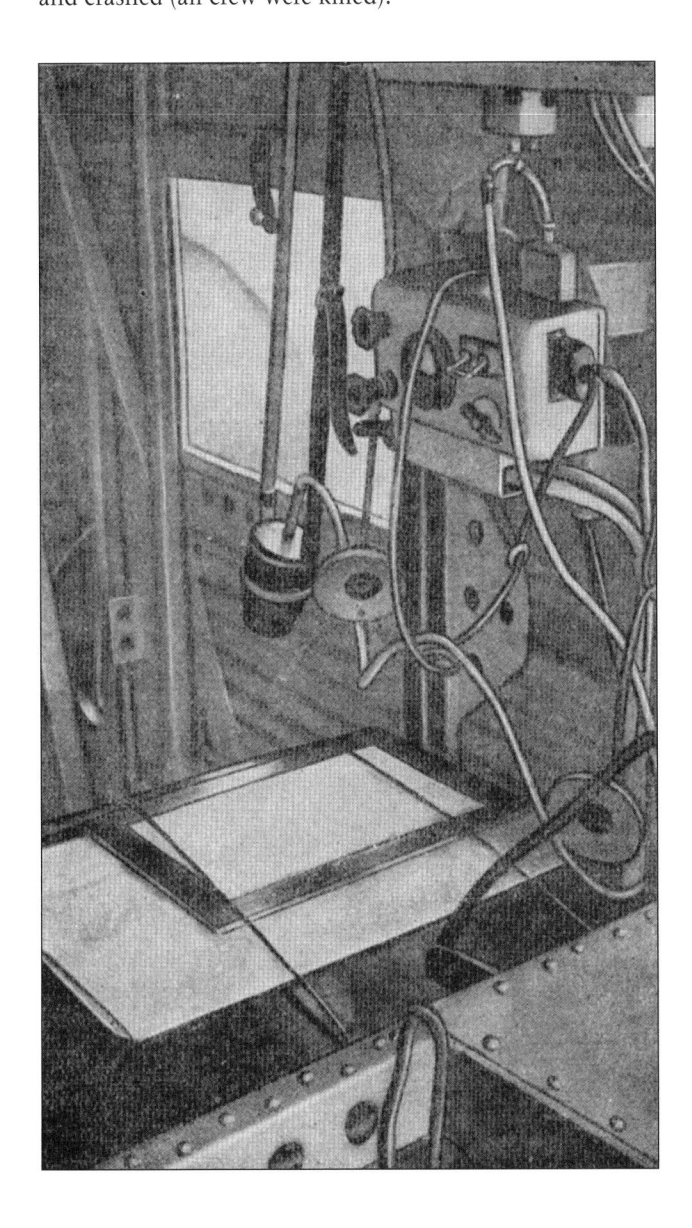

Polar aviator I.P. Mazuruk (HSU 27.6.1937, Commander of the night bombing squadron of 72 SAP) flew the specially equipped and brightly colored ANT-6 (SSSR-N169) and SB (inscribed AVIAARKTIKA) in the Winter War. (G.F. Petrov)

6 December 1939 Finnish forces at Kuusamo-Puolanka were strafed by an R-5 and four I-15bis fighters. Two I-15bis were hit by ground fire and disappeared. *St.lt* Sokolov (I-15bis c/n 5275) crashed at Kiantajärvi and was found badly frozen three days later. *lt* Krasnov force-landed on the ice of Lake Harmusjärvi (20 km from Uhtua) and was found four days later. Despite the arctic cold he was strangely enough OK. His aircraft was also serviceable after the fuel tank was filled up. Parts of *st.lt* Sokolov's I-15bis was lifted in 1972, and in 2018 the astonishingly well preserved M-25 engine was lifted. After conservation the M-25 engine and other I-15bis parts are displayed in the Karelian Aviation Museum in Lappeenranta.

In early December 1939 two four-engine ANT-6 (SSSR-N169 and SSSR-N170) of Avia-arktika (with special navigation equipment for all-weather operations, piloted by two of the first Heroes of Soviet Union, arctic veterans I.P. Mazuruk and M.V. Vodopyanov) arrived at 72 SAP in Besovets. The ANT-6 could take up over 4.0 t bombs (e.g. 8 FAB-250 and 26 FAB-100), and performed bombing attacks from 8 December 1939 (targets Miinisyrjä, Harmu, Kitsälä). The special unit was put under direct command of *kombrig* I.I. Kopets (Commander of VVS 8.A), much to the irritation of *polkovnik* G.A. Shanin (Commander of 72 SAP), who was clearly not pleased with his "uninvited" prominent guests. Shanin's negative attitude even attracted the attention of the feared NKVD *Osobyi Otdel*, which was meticulously watching all military units.

One of the brightly colored ANT-6 aircraft was sighted 20 December 1939 by BL-118. *Kapt* J. Piponius reported that "a big red-painted aircraft (TB-3?) was approaching from Suojärvi. Three I-16 fighters prevented further observations." Soon VVS 8.A command prohibited all combat missions of the prominent aviators with the slow and vulnerable ANT-6.

However, in late December 1939 Mazuruk was permitted to set up a separate Night Bombing Squadron with five specially equipped SB, which arrived 27 December 1939 from Moscow, and 14 January 1940 relocated to Nurmolitsa.

15 December 1939 I-15bis c/n 5219 (*lt* V.I. Vasilyev, 1st Squadron) did not return from Suomussalmi.

25 December 1939 SB c/n 4/135 and 4/134 of 3rd Squadron were shot down in air combat at Tolvajärvi-Ilomantsi. The MG-gunner of c/n 4/135 *starshina* N.V. Khlamin was taken prisoner. Furthermore SB c/n 4/81 of 4th Squadron lost control as its own bombs exploded under the belly, the crew escaped by parachute. *Starshina* O.G. Pugach was taken prisoner, the pilot and navigator reached their own lines. Luutn *J. Karhunen (FR-112)* and kers *T. Vuorimaa (FR-93)* claimed two bombers each at Korpijärvi-Äglajärvi-Suojärvi.

29 December 1939 I-15bis c/n 4452 (*st.lt* N.D. Surikov, 1st Squadron) did not return from a reconnaissance mission to Kiantajärvi, Suomussalmi.

1 January 1940 SB c/n 2/235 was shot down in air combat at Taivalkoski. According to documents found in the wreck the bomber arrived only the day before from 45 SBAP in Orel. Luutn *J. Karhunen (FR-112)* shot down an SB at Korpijärvi, Uuksunjoki. Furthermore Karhunen and Vuorimaa claimed two more bombers.

One of the ANT-6 pilots was polar-aviation veteran Valentin Akkuratov. (G.F. Petrov)

It is really cold up there! Lymarev's crew of 72 SAP. (N. Stolepova)

199

The extemely well preserved M-25V engine (No. 1911738) of Sokolov's I-15bis which force-landed on Lake Kientajärvi 6.12.1939, and subsequently sank to the bottom of the lake. The engine was lifted after almost 79 years in summer 2018. (P. Simula)

A.I. Tayurskiy commanded 72 SAP in the Winter War. (N. Stolepova)

14 January 1940 I-15bis c/n 3982 (?) force-landed at Suomussalmi. *st.politr* I.Ye. Yelyutin (1st Squadron) hid in a sauna, and was killed on capture. According to captured documents the aircraft was based in Vuonninen (Vodnitsa). The intact I-15bis was later used by Finnish AF.

19 January 1940 four SB of 3rd Squadron took off from Besovets for a reconnaissance mission to the encircled 18th and 56th Divisions. SB c/n 13/60 was shot down by *luutn* L. Ahola (FR-113) at Jänisjärvi (Uomaa), and crashed near Haahkajärvi (17 km E Syskyjärvi, 27 km S of Loimola). *lt* K.P. Gichak was taken prisoner, the other two crew members were killed.

20 January 1940 SB *red 2*, c/n 15/94 (piloted by Regiment Commissar, *bat.komiss* S.P. Kaminskiy) was hit by ground fire at Rauhala-Pojosvaara, and crashed 0.5 km from the home base after returning on one engine. The crew was unhurt.

22 January 1940 one SB of 4th Squadron (tactical *12*, c/n 9/231, pilot *lt* N.A. Brusentsev) was shot down by ground fire at Pojosvaara. The wreck was located by 80th Border Guard Unit (Suojärvi district) on 15 October 1940.

4 February 1940 SB c/n 2/240 was destroyed at take-off when *bat.komiss* S.P. Kaminskiy took off with fuel tanks closed. The crew suffered some injuries.

72 SAP also received reinforcements from 45 SBAP in Orel. In early January the fighter squadrons were separated and operated independently. In early February an I-153 Squadron was received (apparently the above mentioned 12 OIAE).

2 March 1940 SB of 5th Squadron was destroyed at landing in Besovets, two aviators were killed (date 3 March 1940?).

Early March 1940 long-distance reconnaissance Squadron 4 DRAE was attached to 72 SAP.

23 March 1940 72 SAP received 18 new I-153s, which formed 3rd Squadron.

In May 1940 72 SAP became 72 SBAP. The *Karelo-Finnish* 12 OIAE was possibly attached to 72 SAP 2 February 1940. (See 12 OIAE, page 220)

72 SAP Command

Commander	*polkovnik* G.A. Shanin. In GPW commanded 258 IAD, 7th Air Army.
	polkovnik A.I. Tayurskiy (1900–1942). In GPW Deputy Commander of VVS ZapFr. Arrested 8.7.41, executed 23.2.42.
Military Commissar	*polk.komiss* Kaminskiy
	bat.komiss Durov
Chief of Staff	*major* Nikolayev
	major P.I. Brajko

Squadron C.O. and Commissars

1st IAE (I-15bis)	*kapitan* A.I. Safronov
2nd IAE (I-153)	*st.lt* Zosima
3rd	*kapitan* F.I. Panyushin (KIA 25.6.41, 201 SBAP)
	st.politr M.I. Ivanov (KIA 25.12.39)
4th	*major* Khatminskiy

Unknown	*kapitan* G.D. Tyulenev (KIA 2.3.40)
ONBAE	I.P. Mazuruk, from 27.12.39. (1906–1989). HSU 27.6.1937. In GPW commanded the ALSIB – Lend-lease aircraft ferry route from Alaska to Siberia.

72 SAP Missions

Squadron	Combat missions	Flight time (hours)
1st	103	181 h
2nd	11	21 h 31
3rd	481	803 h 30
4th	487	793 h
5th	50	90 h 58
6th	176	176 h 22

72 SAP performed 1,308 combat missions (total flight time 2,066 h 21 min), dropped 650 t bombs, 965,000 leaflets and 120 food and medicine packages for the surrounded units of 56th Army Corps.

F.I. Panyushin commanded 3rd Squadron in the Winter War. He was shot down and killed on 25 June 1941, the first day of the Continuation War. In the photo he is instructing one of his pilot officers in the Winter War. (N. Stolepova)

80th Mixed Aviation Regiment (80 SAP)

80 SAP was formed in September 1939 in Orel as a two-Squadron SB-regiment, and in late autumn 1939 was transferred to Yagodnik near Arkhangelsk. 80 SAP was the only more or less permanent aviation regiment of VVS 9.A. By 16 October 1939 a DB-3 Squadron (from AON-2), an I-153 Squadron set up in Lyubertsy (commanded by kapitan Anistratenko), and an I-15bis Squadron from 7 TBAP (commanded by kapitan K.D. Belyakov) had arrived in Yagodnik.

Subordination
VVS LVO (until late December 1939)
VVS 9.A (from 28 December 1939)

Combat Chronicle
The task of 80 SAP was primarily to interrupt and destroy enemy railway traffic and stations in the Repola area, and later to support the surrounded 54th Mountain Division.

17 December 1939 SB c/n 8/221 (*st.lt* G.A. Karalkin, 2nd Squadron) went missing (on a ferry flight from Arkhangelsk to Uhtua). The wreck was only located in October 1998 near Severodvinsk.

24 December 1939 5th Squadron (18 I-15bis) arrived in Repola.

SB c/n 6/219 (80 SAP) was shot down by A-A artillery at Oulu 1.1.1940. (C-F. Geust)

28 December 1939 led by *major* Pleshivtsev 80 SAP (except the DB-3 Squadron) moved from Yagodnik to Uhtua. The regiment incorporated two SB squadrons, and was reinforced by two squadrons of 41 SBAP, and another two squadrons of 152 IAP.

30 December 1939 6th Squadron (14 I-153) arrived.

Late December 1939 14 I-153, 18 I-15bis, 3 DB-3 and 18 SB of 80 SAP were attached to VVS 9.A.

1 January 1940 Oulu was bombed by 17 SB from 4,500 m. SB c/n 6/219 (pilot *lt* A.A. Izyumchenko, 2nd Squadron) exploded after a direct A-A artillery hit.

Early January 1940 4th Squadron (15 I-16) was formed from 4th Squadron of 20 IAP, which had arrived 24 December 1939 by train from Smolensk to Kem'.

9 January 1940 1st Squadron (11 DB-3) arrived in Afrikanda, and was attached to AG Spirin in February 1940. 80 SAP was also reinforced by some SBs from 41 SBAP.

17 January 1940 three I-15bis fighters of 5th Squadron were destroyed with pilots: c/n 4474 crashed at Medvezhegorsk (Karhumäki) after air combat hits, c/n 4460 went missing after a reconnaissance mission to Koski-Kuhmoniemi road, and c/n 4357 made an unsuccessful forced landing in Segozero. Next day two I-16s were destroyed in force-landings at Sulostrov.

27 January 1940 I-15bis c/n 4460 (*starshina* K.I. Kochetkov, 5th Squadron) was shot down on a ground attack mission to Kuhmoniemi.

19 January 1940 a flight led by *major* Sukhoruchenko took off for a reconnaissance mission, but because of inaccurate information strafed his own troops, resulting in one soldier killed. On the return leg the Commander lost his orientation and the entire flight force-landed 40 km SE Repola. *Major* Sukhoruchenko also got lost on 22 January 1940, and next day his deputy got lost, which led to the firing of the Spanish Civil War veteran. *Major* Devochenko (from VVS 9.A HQ) was now appointed Commander of 4th Squadron.

21 January 1940 80 SAP participated in the major bombing of Oulu. (See 41 SBAP, page 149)

31 January 1940 an I-15bis (*kapt* K.D. Belyakov) went missing on a mission to Saunajärvi.

1 February 1940 80 SAP had 17 SB, 15 I-15 and 13 I-16 available for operations towards Kajaani. The 10 DB-3 bombers of 1st Squadron were subordinated to AG Spirin (VVS 9.A) at Fedoseyevka ice base.

2nd Squadron (ex 4th Squadron/19 IAP) and 3rd Squadron (ex 4th Squadron/68 IAP) of 152 IAP were attached to 80 SAP from 3 February 1940 and 13 February 1940 respectively.

From 1 to 22 February 1940 one Finnish Blenheim of LLv 44 was located at Kuluntalahti (8 km NE Kajaani), performing strategic photo reconnaissance and bombing Soviet ground forces and AF bases. The following Blenheims were located at Kuluntalahti: BL-117, 1–10 February 1940; BL-119, 9–17 February 1940 and BL-120, 20–22 February 1940.

3 February 1940 Blenheim BL-117 (lentom Salminen) bombed Repola AF ice base (where 12 SB-aircraft were observed) at 09.00 hours.

4 February 1940 Blenheim BL-117 (lentom Salminen) bombed Repola AF ice base (with 20 SB) and the command post of 80 SAP at 09.00 hours. Soviet fighters were warned too late and were not able to intercept the Blenheim.

4 February 1940 An SB (possibly c/n 1/205 of 2nd Squadron) was hit by ground fire, and crashed on the return leg 40 km NW Repola. Pilot *ml.lt* F.P. Volodin was injured, the other crew members were killed.

5 February 1940 BL-117 (lentom Salminen) bombed the Soviet 44th and 163rd Divisions on the Vasovaara road. All enemy bombing raids 3–5 February 1940 remained undetected by Soviet air surveillance.

12 February 1940 BL-119 (kers Westermark) performed the last bombing of Repola in the Winter War. One MG-gunner was injured. Two I-16s chased the bomber away.

12 February 1940 An SB of 3rd Squadron was hit by ground fire, MG-gunner N.S. Sobolev died of wounds.

Late February 1940 seven I-16 pilots and a mechanics group arrived from 48 IAP in the Far East. (See 145 IAP, page 206)

1 March 1940 80 SAP had 15 SB, 15 I-15 and 12 I-16 available for operations towards Kajaani, and 12 DB-3 bombers were subordinated to AG Spirin, VVS 9.A.

In March 1940 the fighters of 80 SAP repeatedly strafed Finnish troops surrounding 54th and 163rd Divisions.

11 March 1940 *lt* A.P. Moshin of 4th Squadron (I-16 c/n 562) went missing. Finnish troops handed over his body to Soviet authorities on 20 March 1940.

12 March 1940 SB c/n 13/217 of 3rd Squadron crashed on a supply mission after A-A hits, the crew was killed (Date possibly 11 March 1940?)

80 SAP bombed Oulu, Nurmes, Sotkamo, Kuhmo, Valtimo and Kajaani etc. and dropped supplies to the surrounded 54th Mountain Division. During the last weeks of the Winter War several aircraft were lost on supply-dropping missions to encircled units in *mottis*. 80 SAP performed 3,102 combat missions, and lost six pilots, six navigators, six gunners and three mechanics.

Major I.P. Firsov (C.O. 2nd Squadron) bombed Nurmes railway station at night and destroyed over 40 railway wagons, and attacked an enemy column on the Kuhmoniemi road, when *"over 30 trucks and considerable enemy troops were destroyed"*.

80 SAP Command

Commander	*major* B.I. Pleshivtsev
Military Commissar	*polk.komiss* G.D. Kolobkov
Chief of Staff	*major* Kubarev

Squadron C.O.
2nd SBAE *major* I.P. Firsov (1905–1943). HSU 21.5.40.
4th IAE (ex 4./20 IAP) *major* F.A. Sukhoruchenko (until 24.1.40). Spanish Civil War veteran, 3 victory claims. Red Banner order.
major Devotchenko (from 24.1.40)
5th IAE (ex-7 TBAP) *kapitan* K.D. Belyakov. MIA 31.1.40.
1st (?) Detached Reconnaissance Squadron *major* Chekalin (?)

80 SAP was awarded the Red Banner Order 21 May 1940, and on the same day *major* I.F. Firsov got the Golden Star – the very last HSU awarded for valor in the Winter War.

85th Special Purpose Aviation Regiment (85 AP ON)

After heavy losses and numerous losses of orientation during the first days of the Winter War, on the suggestion of the flight inspector of Red Air Force A.V. Belyakov Marshal K.Ye. Voroshilov gave the order to form a special night- and blind-flight capable unit for Supreme Command special tasks, including destruction of small-size, strategically important targets; railway bridges, the important Lahti radio sta-

12 OAE (predecessor of 85 OAP) lost SB c/n 7/236 on a nighttime take-off 19–20.1.1940, navigator kapitan A.I. Lyubavin was killed. (RGVA)

U-2 (c/n 15632) of 85 OAP was damaged on landing in Pushkin 9.2.1940, crew was injured. (RGVA)

85 OAP was established on a suggestion by VVS RKKA Flight Inspector, polar aviation veteran A.V. Belyakov (HSU 24.7.1936). (G.F. Petrov)

B.V. Sterligov (85 OAP Commander). (G.F. Petrov)

tion etc. The initiator, A.V. Belyakov had considerable personal experience of long-distance flights, and in 1937 had performed a non-stop flight with the ANT-25 from Moscow to the USA.

With test pilots and other personnel from AF Research Institute (NII VVS) at Chkalovskaya AF base (east of Moscow) as its nucleus a Special Aviation Group *(Osobaya Aviagruppa)* was formed from 12 December 1939. Additional personnel were recruited from the Blind Flying Center in Ryazan, pilot inspectors from AON-aviation armies, Military Districts and Aviation Brigades. Also famous polar aviators like A.V Yumashev (HSU 1 September 1937) were dispatched to the Special Aviation Group. 25 December 1939 eight DB-3 and three SB bombers of 12 AE ON (12. Special Aviation Squadron) landed in Pushkin. In early January 1940 more DB-3 arrived, and 19 January 1940 a decision was taken to expand the squadron to regiment strength 1 February 1940

Subordination
27 AB, VVS 7.A (12 OAE ON; from 25 December 1939)
VVS SZFr (from 7 January 1940)

85 AP ON (Aviation Regiment for Special Tasks) was directly subordinated to *komandarm* Jevgeniy Ptukhin, Commander of the Northwest Front. 85 AP incorporated three squadrons: 1st (DB-3), 2nd Night-Bombing (SB), and 3rd Dive-Bombing Squadron (three DB-3 and three SB, all specially modified). All dive-bombing pilots were former test-pilots. A special maintenance unit, 258 *Aviabaza* served the aircraft of 85 AP (co-located with 21 DBAP) in Pushkin.

All bombers of 85 AP were especially selected. Most DB-3 were of series 27 and 28 produced by *Zavod* No. 39 in Moscow, but some bombers came also from *Zavod* No.18 in Voronezh. The first ten aircraft allocated were thoroughly tested in NII VVS, and special navigation systems were installed before transfer to the front. The DB-3 bombers were equipped with *Chaika*-radiocompass, APG-1 autopilot, RO-1 or *Noch'*-1 blind landing system, NKPB night sight and propeller anti-freezing devices. *Chaika*-radiocompasses were also installed in the SB. The regiment Commander, *kombrig* B.V. Sterligov was the former head of the navigation systems department of NII VVS.

Additional structural modifications had to be made to DB-3 and SB dive bombers (as neither type was designed for dive bombing), and VISh-23 limited revs propellers, PAN-23 bomb sights, modified fuel pumps and bomb racks were installed.

As DB-3 was very vulnerable to enemy attacks from behind, a fuselage-mounted rearward firing machine-gun and a fourth crew member was added. The rear machine-gun was used for the first time on a night mission of three DB-3 to Mikkeli, with the gun technicians responsible on board.

From 26 December 1939 85 AP (and the predecessor 12 AE ON) performed combat missions over 48 days and 20 nights (only 26 days were non-flying days). Over 11 days the regiment flew "24 hours", while co-located 21 DBAP was only able to operate 25 days, and for 49 days was unable to take off because of non-flying weather.

85 AP performed 454 combat missions (1,134 h 43 min), of which 203 were night missions (flight time 556 h 52 min), 208 blind flights (438 h 11 min), and 19 dive-bombing missions (49 h 55 min). During the extremely cold January 1940, 107 missions were performed of which 55 were against railway targets, in particular Kouvola railway station was heavily bombed with 296 FAB-100 and 83 FAB-50 bombs dropped.

Repeated dive-bombing attempts were made to destroy the railway bridges at Koria and Savonlinna. FAB-250 and FAB-500 bombs were dropped in 70°-85° dives from 1,800–2,000 m altitude down to 1,000 m by 3rd Squadron. Koria bridge was bombed 14 times, a total of 30 FAB-500 and 25 FAB-250 bombs were dropped. Two FAB-500 bombs scored hits on the bridge supports, and 12 bombs (seven FAB-250) fell 20–50 m from the bridge.

Savonlinna bridge was bombed six times, five FAB-500 and four FAB-250 bombs were dropped, and another two FAB-500 at night. Two hits were observed in the water under the bridge, and one hit in the supports. The other bombs fell 10–40 m from the bridge. Although the bridges were not destroyed by dive bombing, the results were considerably better than by level bombing.

85 AP losses were considerable:

30 January 1940 two aircraft were lost: one DB-3 was shot down at Elisenvaara, and DB-3 c/n 392716 did not return from Kaitjärvi.

21 February 1940 DB-3 c/n 392705 did not return from Lappeenranta (the original units of the crews were 7 AP from Voronezh and 155 AP from Staraya Russa). Luutn *J. Sarvanto (FR-100)*, lentom *Y. Turkka (FR-83)* and alik *R. Heiramo (FR-104)* jointly shot down a DB-3 bomber at Simola.

4 March 1940 a SB attacking Juustila canal lock went missing.

8 March 1940 DB-3 was destroyed when force-landing after 37 mm A-A hits at Viipuri.

Several aircraft were furthermore destroyed in accidents, and at least 14 aviators were killed.

85 AP Command

Commander	*kombrig* B.V. Sterligov (1901–1971; former AF flight inspector, flew with ANT-3 to USA 1929. Director of ALSIB (Alaska-Siberia) lend-lease aircraft ferry route 1942–44.)
Military Commissar	*polk.komiss* Sushin
Chief of Staff	*major* V.L. Gerasimenko
Squadron C.O.	
1st	*major* Kurban
	major Gusev
2nd	*major* I.P. Zhuravlev (1905–1989). Performed 18 combat missions with SB in Winter War. HSU 7.4.40. Commander of 14th Air Army 1942–1944. Commanded 76th Air Army 1950–1956.
3th	*polkovnik* Shishkin
	kapitan Zhdanov

Combat experiences of 85 AP were not entirely satisfactory (considerable losses, unsuccessful dive bombing etc), which is reflected by the fact the regiment commander did not get the Golden Star after the Winter War (nor later). Three other aviators of 85 AP were decorated with this highest Soviet order on 7 April 1940 (*major* I.P. Zhuravlev, *kapitan* N.K. Leonchenko and *kapitan* L.V. Vinogradov).

Based on the experiences of 85 AP the Air Force Command and Navigation Academy (now Air Force Academy "*imeni Gagarina*") was established in Monino 29 March 1940, with A.V. Belyakov as Deputy Head.

Boris Sterligov served as navigator on board ANT-4 URSS-300, which perfomed an unique multi-leg flight from Moscow to New York in late autumn 1929. (G.F. Petrov)

145th Fighter Aviation Regiment (145 IAP)

145 IAP was established on 29 December 1939. 1st and 2nd Squadrons (formerly 1st and 3rd Squadrons of 38 IAP, equipped with 30 I-15bis) arrived 15–20 December 1939 by train from Pushkin. After assembly in Afrikanda the squadrons were ready for combat in Kairala 26 December 1939.

Two I-16 squadrons were also transferred to the north: 1st and 4th Squadrons/20 IAP (30 I-16) arrived 24 December 1939 from Smolensk by train to Kem', and more by truck to Poduzhemye, where the fighters were assembled. 1st Squadron was attached to 145 IAP (as 3rd Squadron), and 4th Squadron to 80 SAP in Repola. The squadrons were combat-ready 1 January 1940.

Organization of 145 IAP was completed by 17 January 1940. With 145 IAP as nucleus the Northern Aviation Group of VVS 9.A was set up. This unit is usually named Aviation Group (AG) Filin after its Commander *polkovnik* V.M. Filin.

16 February 1940 one half-squadron (commanded by *kapitan* Bondarev) arrived from 48 IAP of 1st Dedicated Red Banner Far East Army (1st *Otdel'naya Krasnoznamennaya Dal'nevostochnaya Armiya*).

The squadron commanded by *kapitan* Antonov (v/ch 6198) arrived 7 January 1940 from Kandalaksha to Kuolajärvi with five I-16 and ten I-15bis (according to interrogation report of POW Ishchenko 2 February 1940)

145 IAP was officially established 17 January 1940 in Kairala, and operated in the Kemijärvi area, strength 1 January 1940 23 I-15bis and 3 DB-3; 1 February 1940 23 I-15bis and 12 I-16 and 1 March 1940 24 I-15bis and 11 I-16.

Subordination
VVS 9.A
AG Filin, VVS 9.A (from February 1940)

145 IAP Strength and locations

Date	Base	Subordination	Base unit	Equipment
1.1.40	Uhtua, Mjatijarvi (LVO)	Shtab VVS 9.A	6 RAB, 262 AB	29 I-16, 26 I-15bis
1.2.40	Uhtua, Kantalahti, Mjatijarvi (LVO)	AG Filina, VVS 9.A	6 RAB, 262 AB	17 I-16, 25 I-15bis
1.3.40	Kantalahti (LVO)	10 AB, VVS 9.A	7 RAB, 262 AB	10 I-16, 24 I-15bis
1.4.40	Kantalahti (LVO)	27 AB, VVS 9.A	7 RAB, 262 AB	24 I-16, 23 I-15bis

St.lt A.M. Katyukhin (145 IAP) was shot down by A-A artillery at Kemijärvi 6.2.1940. His identification card was found in his pockets. (C-F. Geust)

Combat Chronicle

24 December 1939 *kapitan* K.P. Sokol (1st Squadron C.O.) shot down a "Junkers" at Märkäjärvi. *JU-126 of 3./LLv 16 was shot down at Kuolajärvi, pilot ylik K. Hyytiäinen escaped by parachute, luutn E. Hyytiäinen, kers P. Kaurto and mechanic M. Mauri were killed.*

25 December 1939 I-15bis c/n 4514 (*ml.lt* G.M. Terinenko, 1st, ex-38 IAP Squadron) did not return after a ground attack mission.

5 January 1940 1st Squadron commissar *st.politr* Yefimov went missing possibly in a I-15bis.

9 January 1940 I-15bis c/n 5105 (*ml.lt* I.A. Zudin, 2nd, ex-38 IAP Squadron) did not return from Märkäjärvi.

12 January 1940 Swedish volunteer F 19-Squadron performed its first combat mission, and attacked the base of 145 IAP at Märkäjärvi with four Hart light bombers and four Gladiator fighters. Two Harts collided mid-air and crashed. The I-15bis flight led by *lt* Kruchkov (with *lt* Gromov and *lt* Bondarenko as wingmen) shot down a third Hart 6 km south of Salla. The first attack by F19 was entirely unexpected by the Soviet infantry garrison at Märkäjärvi, and caused panic and uncontrolled opening of fire. Losses amounted to approx. 10 soldiers killed and wounded. Löjtnant Anders Zachau (leader of F19 bomb group) was killed, *fänrik* Arne Jung and *fänrik* Per Sterner were taken prisoner. The other three Swedes were able to reach their own lines. F19 claimed one I-15bis, which is not confirmed by 145 IAP documents.

17 January 1940 an I-15bis (2nd Squadron) force-landed after air combat 14 km west of Kuolajärvi, and two other I-15bis force-landed in Märkäjärvi, pilots were wounded. *The three I-15bis fighters were shot down by Swedish volunteers fänrik P-E. Salvén and fänrik R. Martin).*

23 January 1940 *lt* Konkin shot down an enemy aircraft, which caught fire and crashed 3–4 km north of Märkäjärvi. *A Gladiator of F19 was shot down, fänrik J. Sjökvist was killed.*

26 January 1940 I-16 tip 17 c/n 1721138 (*lt* N.G. Kozastryga, 3rd Squadron, ex 1./20 IAP) was shot down by A-A artillery in Savukoski.

28 January 1940 I-16 *tip* 5 c/n 5210517 (*lt* I.L. Ishshenko, 3rd Squadron) force-landed because of engine malfunction in Pelkosenniemi after a ground attack against Salmijärvi. Ishshenko was captured.

6 February 1940 I-16 *tip* 17 c/n 1721166 (*st.lt* A.M. Katyukhin, 3rd Squadron) was shot down by Swedish A-A artillery in Kemijärvi.

9 February 1940 three I-15bis were destroyed in Ahvenjärvi, pilots were unhurt.

18 February 1940 one Hawker Hart (Swedish F 19) bombed Kairala AF base (145 IAP) at night, one I-15bis was damaged.

145 IAP was attached to AG Spirin in February 1940.

145 IAP Command

Commander	*major* V.N. Shtoff. In GPW commanded 157 IAP, MIA 24.9.41.
Military Commissar	*st.politr* A.A. Ionin
Chief of Staff	*major* Kuskis
Squadron C.O.	
1st (ex 1./38 IAP; I-15bis)	*kapitan* K.P. Sokol
2nd (ex 3./38 IAP; I-15bis, later I-153)	
	kapitan V.A. Veklich (55 combat missions)
3rd (ex 1./20 IAP; I-16)	*kapitan* P.P. Ledyayev (1907–). Red Banner Order.
	kapitan Antonov
	st.politr Serdyutskiy

145 IAP performed 1,025 missions, dropped 1,468 AO-8 and AO-15, 36 FAB-50 and 308 FAB-100 bombs, fired 6,928 20 mm ShVAK-projectiles and 322,420 7.62 mm ShKAS-bullets.

145 IAP claimed five victories, own losses five aircraft. After the Winter War 2nd Squadron (I-153) of 145 IAP was swapped with 2nd Squadron (I-16) of 147 IAP.

In GPW 145 IAP was elevated to Guards status 4 April 1942 and named 19 GvIAP.

146th Fighter Aviation Regiment (146 IAP)

146 IAP was founded from elements of 57 IAB in Lyubertsy (VVS MVO), and equipped with I-16 fighters. In January 1940 15 pilots from 16 IAP in Lyubertsy were attached to 146 IAP, parts of which were dispatched to the Finnish fronts, and apparently attached to another IAP. The information about the involvement of 146 IAP in the Winter War is unfortunately still very sketchy. 146 IAP participated in the "liberation of Bessarabia" in early summer 1940, and was commanded by *major* P.A. Antonets.

147th Detached Fighter Aviation Regiment (147 OIAP)

147 OIAP was established 9 January 1940 in Vayenga and Murmashi from elements of former 5 OSAP (VVS 14.A).

147 OIAP consisted initially of five squadrons, of which 1st and 2nd Squadrons were transferred from 5 OSAP (15 I-16 and 15 I-153), and the other three squadrons arrived from 9 LShAP (11 I-15bis), 26 IAP (14 I-15bis) and 38 IAP (14 I-15bis); later a 6th Squadron was added. 147 OIAP initial organization was:
- 1st Squadron (15 I-153); Vayenga
- 2nd Squadron (15 I-16)
- 3rd, 4th and 5th squadrons (14 I-15bis each); Murmashi.

Total strength 85 fighters.

147 OIAP was set up by 17 January 1940 in Salmijärvi on occupied Finnish territory.

One of the I-15bis squadrons was later re-equipped with I-153 fighters, but did not participate in the war. The I-15bis squadrons commanded by Savchenko and Petrov were rather poorly prepared.

3rd Squadron was former 4th Squadron/38 IAP (C.O. *kapitan* Savchenko; 15 I-15bis fighters), which on 18 December 1939 was transferred by train from 25 IAP in Pushkin to Murmashi. The Squadron was attached to VVS 14.A, as a fighter element of 5 OSAP (together with some fighters of 26 IAP, which arrived in the north before the outbreak of the war). In early January 1940 this Squadron moved to Luostari (close to the frontline in occupied Finnish Petsamo; in Russian Pechenga).

14 January 1940 three ex-25/38 IAP I-15bis fighters strafed Suonikylä (Sangelsk), and force-landed at Labdshjaur, Hihnakylä (east of Nautsi, Pechenga area) after the fuel tank of the lead fighter was hit. All

three pilots (*kapitan* S.M. Borchevskiy, *lt* N.Ye. Kuznetsov and *ml.lt* A.N. Osipov) were taken prisoner five days later. The pilots were badly frozen after trying to reach their own lines in the arctic climate (with night temperatures falling down to –37° C!). The I-15bis aircraft were c/n 4647, 4672 and 4584; tactical "3", "13" and "492" (the correlation between the construction and tactical numbers is however unknown). The ultimate fate of the fighters is unclear. According to Soviet documents the pilots destroyed the aircraft after landing, but a Finnish ski patrol located the empty aircraft on the frozen Hihnajärvi two days later, and started to disassemble them, after which the aircraft were destroyed. Another patrol departed with horses and reindeers 25 January 1940 to Hihnajärvi to fetch more parts.

28 January 1940 I-15bis c/n 4528 of 6th Squadron was destroyed on a training flight at Murmashi, *st.lt* N.I. Voronskiy was killed.

In February 1940 a new 6th Squadron with 11 I-15bis was received (see above).

147 IAP Strength and locations

Date	Base	Subordination	Base unit	Aircraft
9.1.40	Vayenga and Murmashi	VVS 14.A	7 RAB, 102 AB	15 I-153, 15 I-16, 42 I-15bis
1.2.40	Salmijärvi and Luostari	VVS 14.A	7 RAB, 102 AB	14 I-153, 14 I-16, 39 I-15bis
1.3.40	Salmijärvi and Luostari	VVS 14.A	7 RAB, 102 AB	28 I-153, 14 I-16, 35 I-15bis
1.4.40	Salmijärvi and Luostari	14 AB	7 RAB, 102 AB	32 I-153, 18 I-16, 35 I-15bis
1.5.40	Salmijärvi and Luostari	27 AB	7 RAB, 102 AB	31 I-153, 16 I-16, 20 I-15bis

147 OIAP performed 830 combat missions (flight time 958 h), of which 136 were reconnaissance, 269 strafing, 40 ground troop protection, 68 bomber escort and 317 other missions. Five I-15bis were lost in combat losses, and five I-15bis and one I-153 were lost in accidents.

147 IAP Command

Commander   *major* N.S. Artemyev (1909 –). Spanish Civil War veteran.
Military Commissar *bat.komiss* A.A. Matveyev
Chief of Staff   *kapitan* K.I. Davydov

Squadron C.O. and Commissars
1st   *major* G.M. Galitsyn
2nd (ex 5 OSAP; I-16)   *kapitan* S.A. Tryapichkin
                            st.politr Kiselev
7th (I-15bis)   *kapitan* Savchenko (ex 4./25 IAP; also 7./5 OSAP?)
Unknown   *kapitan* Shevelev
Unknown (I-15bis)   Petrov
Unknown, commissar   *st.politr* Shimarev

After the Winter War 2nd Squadron (I-16) of 147 IAP was swapped with 2nd Squadron (I-153) of 145 IAP. In GPW 147 IAP was elevated to Guards status 4 April 1942 and named 20 GvIAP.

148th Fighter Aviation Regiment (148 IAP)

148 IAP was formed in February 1940, and like 146 IAP formed from squadrons of 16, 27 and 34 IAP (of 57 IAB) in Lyubertsy, Moscow MD. 57 IAB was named *"imeni V.G. Rakhova"* 28 December 1939 after *st.lt* V.G. Rakhov, who was awarded HSU 29 August 1939, and killed in action at Khakhin-Gol the very same day.

Subordination
57 IAB, VVS MVO
59 IAB, VVS 7.A (from 27 February 1940)

In January 1940 two squadrons of 16 IAP were dispatched to the Finnish front for formation of the new 148 IAP: 3rd Squadron (I-153), C.O. *major* S.S. Safiulin, and 4th Squadron (I-153), C.O. *kapitan* G.I. Brantsev.

148 IAP included also 3rd and 4th Squadrons of 27 IAP, 2nd Squadron of 34 IAP (C.O. *kapitan* A.P. Anistratenko) and the Staff of 34 IAP.

148 IAP departed from Lyubertsy 20 February 1940, and arrived 27 February 1940 to Rieskjärvi ice base (in occupied territory), and was attached to 59 IAB, strength 56 I-153.

3 March 1940 1st Squadron military commissar *st.politr* Kudryavtsev attacked a I-15bis flight by mistake, misidentifying them as Bulldogs.

7 March 1940 *major* N.V. Gavrilov and *st.lt* N.V. Rybin fought against seven Gladiators at Perkansaari. Gavrilov claimed two fighters and Rybin one. Both Soviet pilots were awarded Red Banner Order 7 April 1940. *Ml.lt* Y.I. Zaichikov did not return with I-153 c/n 7325, the wreck of which was located in Chulkovo (former Tervajoki) only in autumn 2009. *The task of LLv 14 was to protect Finnish ground forces at Tienhaara (west of Viipuri) with six Gladiator fighters. At Tervajoki three I-153 fighters attacked.* Luutn *T. Ollikainen (GL-267) and* vänr *K. Malinen (GL-276) claimed one Chaika-fighter each. Alik P. Roine (GL-278) made a successful force-landing at Löytöjärvi, Uuras, after a bullet hit in the fuel tank. The upper wingtip of GL-279 of* ylik *M. Perälä was broken after a mid-air collision with an I-153.*

11 March 1940 Finnish LLv 42 was bombing Turkinsaari in the Bay of Viipuri, when 12 I-153 fighters attacked (I-153 units: 7, 23 and 148 IAP). MG-gunner *alik* Y. Hammarén (BL-139) claimed one I-153 at Kiiskilä. This may be *ml.lt* Fomenko who escaped by parachute from I-153 c/n 6698 at Uuras (Trångsund).

18 March 1940 148 IAP moved to Levashevo and further to Liepaja in Latvia in April 1940.

148 IAP performed 1,120 missions, claimed three enemy aircraft, and lost one aviator and one aircraft.

Strength and Locations

Date	Base	Subordination	Base unit	Aircraft
1.2.40	Lyubertsy, MVO	57 AB, VVS MVO	259 AB	140 I-153, 12 I-15bis
1.3.40	Vammeljärvi	59 AB, VVS SZFr	1 RAB, 150 AB	57 I-153
1.4.40	Levashovo	59 AB, VVS LVO	1 RAB, 150 AB	56 I-153
1.5.40	Liepaja	18 AB, VVS LVO	15 RAB, 208 AB	55 I-153, 1 UT

148 IAP command
Commander   *polkovnik* N.K. Trifonov
Military Commissar   *bat.komiss* Golovachev
Chief of Staff

Squadron C.O. and Commissars
1st   *st.politr* Kudryavtsev
               kapitan A.P. Anistratenko (Red Banner order)
               kapitan G.I. Brantsev
               kapitan V.I. Nenashev (ex C.O. 4./27 IAP)
               kapitan S.S. Safiulin
3rd   *major* N.V. Gavrilov (ex 34 IAP; 7.4.1940 Red Banner order)

Future double-HSU (6 June 1942 and 24 August 1943; then in 198 ShAP) M.Z. Bondarenko (1913–1947) performed 17 combat missions in 148 IAP in I-153.

149th Fighter Aviation Regiment (149 IAP)

149 IAP was formed 31 January 1940 in Pushkin (based on elements from 38 IAP), and was attached to VVS SZFr. Reinforcements were received from 25 IAP (16 I-16 fighters for 1st Squadron), from three fighter regiments of Transbaikal MD: 32 IAP (I-153 fighters for 2nd Squadron), 8 IAP (I-15 for 3rd Squadron) and 51 IAP (I-16 for 4th Squadron).

1 February 1940 149 IAP moved to an ice base near Vejno west of Lake Peipus (Chudskoye ozero).

Tasks:
- 1st Squadron (I-16): escorting bombers of 16 SBAB and 85 OAP to Savonlinna, Kouvola, Lappeenranta, Luumäki, Koria, Koria-Simola, Imatra and Viipuri.
- 2nd Squadron (I-153): train strafing between Kouvola-Simola, attacks on Utti AF base.
- 3rd Squadron (I-15bis): reconnaissance to Viipuri, Antrea, Hiitola, Elisenvaara, Sortavala, Käkisalmi, Imatra.

VH-201 of Finnish AF was subtype (tip) 17 (c/n 27P21D54). Lt A.L. Kiselev (1./149 IAP) force-landed with this I-16 south of Kotka 2.2.1940. (SA-kuva)

Combat Chronicle

2 February 1940 two flights were escorting DB-3 bombers, the task of which was to destroy the railway bridge west of Kouvola. On the return leg Finnish Fokkers intercepted. I-16 tip 17 c/n 27P21D54 went missing; *lt* A.L. Kiselev of 1st Squadron (ex-25 IAP) was killed. *Kiselev was apparently shot down south of Kotka by* ylik *O. Tuominen (GL-258, LLv 26), who intercepted the attack of two SB and six fighters in the Inkeroinen-Elimäki region, and shot down one I-16 tip 17, south of Kotka at 1540 hours. The cannon-equipped I-16 was exhibited in the war trophy exhibition in Helsinki, and became VH-201 in* Ilmavoimat. *The 20 mm ShVAK cannons were later removed and replaced by 7.62 mm Browning machine guns. The code was later changed to VH-21, and the I-16 was sent to Germany for demonstration purposes in April 1941.*

10 February 1940 A.T. Kostenko's Squadron was intercepted by 4./LLv 24 at Lappeenranta, *vänr* H. Ikonen (FR-102) was wounded.

13 February 1940 I-16 c/n 27P21D58 was destroyed in a landing accident (*lt* A.A. Murashov was killed). A.I. Maslennikov (I-16 c/n 27P21D53) got lost on a bomber escort mission, and entered Estonian airspace. After running out of fuel he force-landed in Veipole in Estonia and set his aircraft on fire, as he believed that he had landed in enemy territory.

15 February 1940 seven I-16s and four I-153s were escorting 36 SB to target No. 20 (Imatra hydro-electric power station). At Lappeenranta six Fokkers tried to intercept. *Major* Syusyukalov's flight (*bat.komiss* Shalimov and *lt* Litvinenko as wingmen) claimed two Fokkers, of which one *"was set afire"*, and the other *"crashed uncontrolled to the ground"*. The other Fokkers escaped. Syusyukalov saw an *"SB-like aircraft"* in flames. Ilmavoimat *did not lose any fighters.*

VH-201 was exhibited in the war booty exhibition in Helsinki February 1940. (SA-kuva)

VL performed technical studies of all captured aircraft, including the I-16 retractable skis. (SA-kuva)

16 February 1940 14 I-153s led by *kapitan* Simonov moved from Komendantskiy to Vejno.

17 February 1940 11 I-16s were escorting 27 SB, and five I-16s protected two DB-3 which bombed the Kymi river bridge. On the return leg two "Bulldogs" intercepted without results.

18 February 1940 at 1100 hours 12 fighters were escorting 38 SBs to target No. 32 (Kouvola junction). Four Fokkers and two "Bulldogs" were encountered. *Major* Plygunov shot down one "Bulldog" and *major* Kuldin two Fokkers. *"The left wings of the "Bulldogs" were black"*. On one I-153 36 A-A and air combat hits were recorded. Ilmavoimat *did not lose any fighters. The "Bulldogs" were Gladiators of LLv 26, with characteristically black-white painted wings.*

19 February 1940 at 1145 hours 11 I-153s and I-16s were escorting 36 SB. At the target seven "Bulldogs" were encountered. During the air combat five enemy aircraft were claimed: *major* Syusyukalov and *bat.komiss* Shalimov shared one claim, *st.lt* Vilchik two claims, *st.lt* Pidyukov one and *lt* Pavlov one claim. Damaged 148 IAP aircraft: *major* Syusyukalov 38 bullet holes, *lt* Pavlov 33 holes, Litvinenko 15 holes and Pidyukov 6 holes. At 1540 hours seven I-153s and four I-16s were escorting 35 SB. After the bombs were dropped five "Bulldogs" attacked, with four I-153s responding. I-153s c/n 7142 and 7158 did not return from Sippola. *St.lt* N.Yu. Iyentish and *st.lt* V.S. Osipov (C.O. 2nd Squadron) became POW. *Lt* Makarov force-landed at Kotly after lack of fuel. *Lt* Semenov returned with 47 bullet holes. *The "Bulldogs" were Gladiators of LLv 26. In air combat at Sippola luutn P. Berg (GL-279) shot down one I-153, Danish volunteer Løjtnant P. Christensen (GL-261) and vänr L. Sihvo (GL-276) together shot down another I-153 without own losses.*

20 February 1940 six I-16s and 11 I-153s were escorting 36 SB to target No. 32 (Kouvola junction). Finnish fighters intercepted on the return leg south of Utti. Filatov claimed one Fokker, and got one hit on his own aircraft. *Luutn P. Berg shot down an SB-bomber of 54 SBAP. His own Gladiator (GL-280) was shot down in flames, and he was forced to bail out getting burns. No Fokkers were lost.*

21 February 1940 27 DB-3 were protected by 19 escort missions in bad weather. One I-16 was destroyed and another was damaged on landing, and two I-153s force-landed on the ice of Luga Bay. Four I-153s (Semenov, Grigoryev, Simonov and Raspevich) did not return. Next day information about the missing pilots was received: A.I. Raspevich had force-landed at Luga Bay, his I-153 c/n 7156 was destroyed. I-153 c/n 7183, 7179 and 7180 crashed in a snowstorm 25 km from the base. All three pilots *kapitan* S.A. Simonov, *lt* A.A. Grigoryev and *st.lt* V.I. Semenov were killed. *Fokkers of LLv 24 shot down an DB-3 of 85 AP at Simola, no own losses.*

25 February 1940 an SB-formation was escorted, target railway Kouvola-Utti-Kaipiainen. Large air combat at Utti: six I-16 and two I-153 of 149 IAP fought against eight enemy aircraft (*"two monoplanes and six biplanes"*). Pilot Kelin shot down one monoplane. Three biplanes (of which two caught fire) were shot down jointly by several fighters. One I-16 belly-landed 4 km north of Kurgolovo. *Vänr L. Sihvo (LLv 26, GL-279) claimed an uncertain victory south of Sippola, no own losses.*

26 February 1940 I-15bis c/n 4436 was hit by A-A artillery at Ristniemi, pilot P.G. Shirokov escaped by parachute at Narva. A.M. Ivakin (I-15bis c/n 5413) crash-landed on the ice between Hogland (Suursaari) and Lavansaari. Ivakin was picked up by *st.politr* Taranenko, who tied him to the wing of his I-15bis. After landing the injured Ivakin was sent to hospital. An I-16 belly-landed.

This and opposite page: I-16s of 149 IAP escorted bombers of VVS SZFr attacking cities in SW Finland in February-March 1940. 149 IAP moved 16.2.1940 to Vejno on the southern shore of Gulf of Finland (upper photo). (RGAVMF)

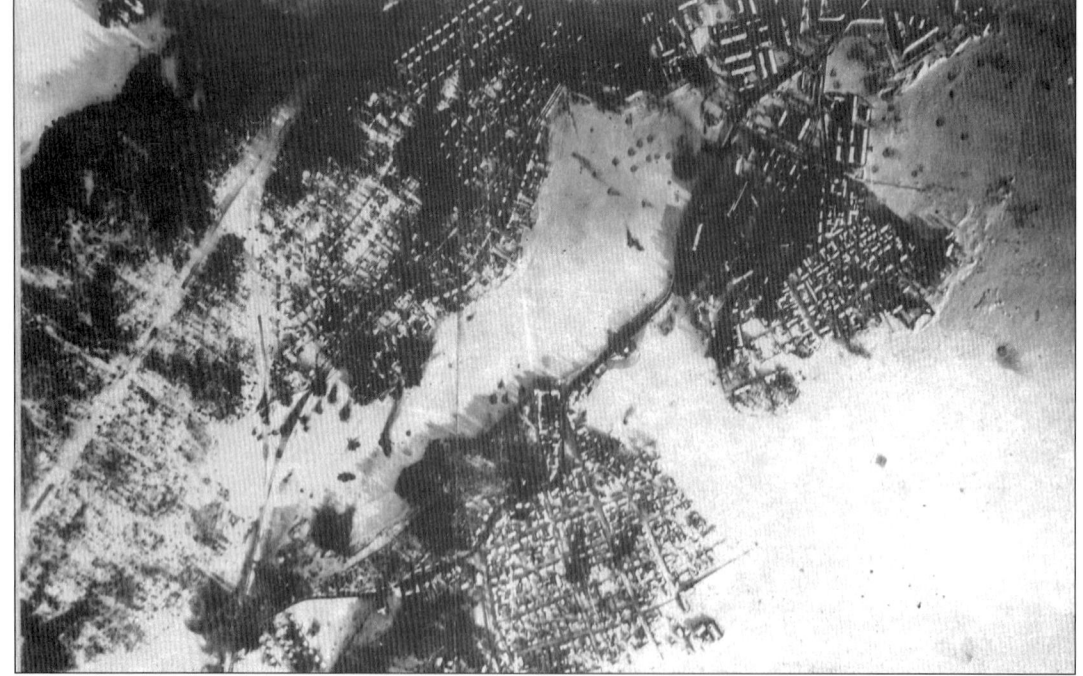

Post-bombing photo of Viipuri 20.2.1940. (RGVA)

Vilchik claimed a monoplane at Kouvola. *Lt* Kelin and *lt* Salov jointly claimed two Fokkers. *Lt* Begrov and *st.lt* Pindyukov jointly claimed a fighter *"equipped with open radial engine"* (this is clearly referring to a FIAT fighter). *In the air combat at Pyhtää* luutn O. Puhakka (FA-4) shot down an I-16 fighter and vänr K. Linnamaa (FA-9) downed an DB-3 bomber, no own losses.

2 March 1940 the Squadron of *kapitan* Belousov was transferred from Kerstovo to 68 IAP at Lake Lempaala.

3 March 1940 I-16 *tip 18* c/n 18P21M44 of S.M. Avdiyevich was destroyed when force-landing at Kaukjärvi.

5 March 1940 when escorting 30 SB (of 31 SBAP) to Kouvola *major* Plygunov (C.O. 2nd Squadron) claimed a "Bulldog", the pilot of which escaped by parachute at 5,500 m altitude. Plygunov fired at the escaped aviator down to 3,000 m altitude. *Lt* Surkov and *st.politr* Taranenko collided on landing. *No "compatible" Finnish accounts of this air combat have been found.*

18 March 1940 149 IAP (10 I-16, 14 I-153 and 8 I-15) returned from Vejno to Pushkin. In early GPW 149 IAP was attached to 64 IAD in Ukraine.

149 IAP performed 531 war missions (489 bomber escort missions, flight time 804 h 40 min), and claimed 19 enemy aircraft (six Fokkers, seven Gladiators, five monoplanes (type unidentified) and one Bulldog) in 11 air combats (26 claims according to M. Bykov).

V.F. Vilchik claimed 4 victories on 57 combat missions. 149 IAP lost one I-16 and two I-153 with pilots. Four pilots and six aircraft were lost in accidents.

Soviet post-bombing photos of Kouvola 29.2.1940 and Hamina 1.3.1940. (RGVA)

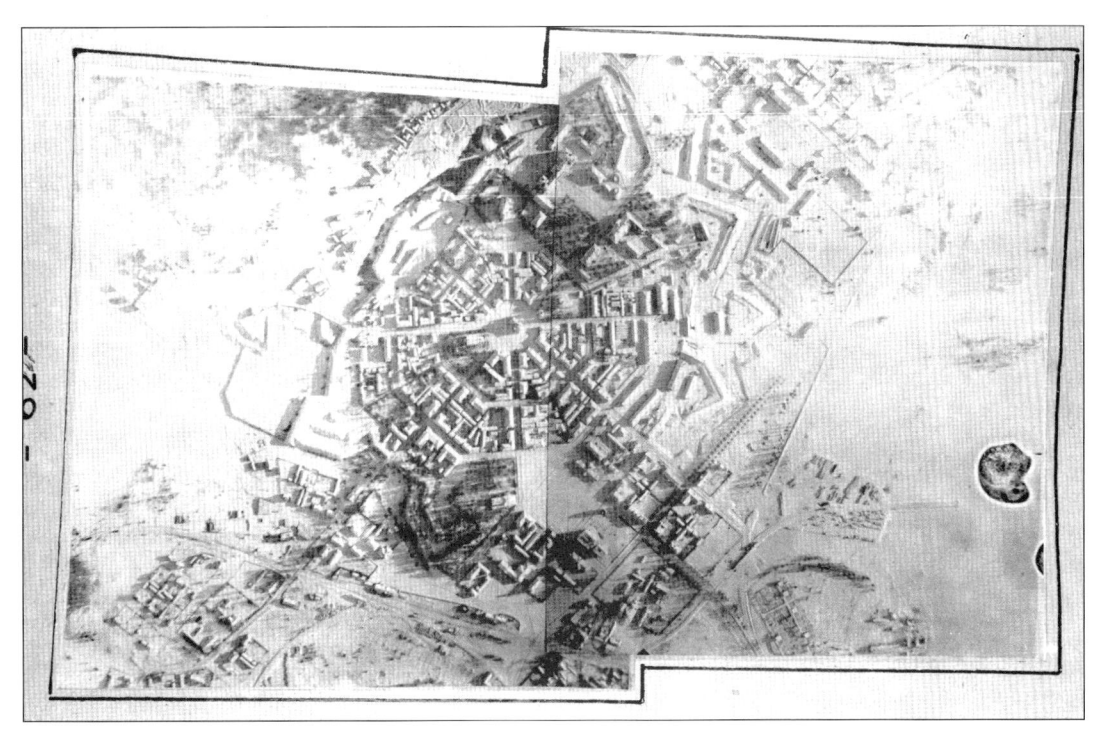

149 IAP Command

Commander	*major* N.T. Syusyukalov (ex-commander of 38 IAP)
Military Commissar	*bat.komiss* Shalimov
Chief of Staff	*major* Glyzin

Squadron C.O.
1st — *kapitan* A.T. Kostenko. In GPW commanded 37 IAK etc.
st.politr Zakharov
2nd — *kapitan* S.A. Simonov (I-153; ex 51 IAP, KIA 21.2.40)
major Plygunov
5th — *kapitan* K.A. Semenov (16 missions)
Unknown — *st.lt* V.S. Osipov (KIA 19.2.40)

213

152nd Fighter Aviation Regiment (152 IAP)

The HQ of 152 IAP was formally set up in Moscow 30 December 1939. 152 IAP was attached to VVS 9.A, and dispatched to Vojnitsa (Vuonninen) in the northern part of Karelian ASSR, arriving from 9 January 1940. 152 IAP incorporated five squadrons (of which two equipped with I-15bis and three with I-153).

152 IAP was formed from several squadrons which were transferred to the northern sector of the Soviet-Finnish front during the Winter War:

- 1st Squadron was ex-1st AE/72 SAP (14 I-15bis), which arrived 26 November 1939 from Besovets.
- 2nd Squadron was ex-4th AE/19 IAP (15 I-15bis), which arrived 16 December 1939 by train from Gorelovo. The aircraft were assembled in Poduzhemye, and were ready for combat 21 December 1939.
- 3rd Squadron was ex-4th AE/68 IAP, the mechanics of which arrived 22 December 1939. Three days before 18 new I-153s were delivered from Zavod No. 132, and the pilots arrived one month later (19 January 1940) from Pushkin to Poduzhemye. The nucleus of this Squadron was 3rd Squadron of 27 IAP (VVS MVO), commanded by *major* M.I. Korolev.
- 4th Squadron was ex-4th AE/38 IAP, which arrived simultaneously with 3rd Squadron.
- 5th Squadron was ex-4th AE/80 SAP.

Upon arrival in Karelia the liaison flight 18 KAO (equipped with R-5 aircraft) was also attached to 152 IAP. (See 18 KAO, page 232)

152 IAP operated *"at the disposal of the Central Direction Fighter Aviation Group commanded by major S.Ya. Simonenko"*. The tasks of this Aviation Group were protection of Uhtua, Chiksha and 9. Army HQ.

Combat Chronicle
24 December 1939 *lt* Ya.A. Andreyev (2nd Squadron, ex 4./19 IAP) force-landed at Manamansalo, Kaaresjärvi (at Lake Oulujärvi) with I-15bis c/n 4616 ("173") and was taken prisoner. This entirely intact aircraft was subsequently taken into use by Finnish AF as VH-11.

In January 1940 152 IAP (equipped with 29 I-15bis from 38 IAP and 7 R-5) operated mainly in the Kandalaksha-Salla area of 47th Army Corps.

3 January 1940 R-5 "31" of 18 KAO force-landed at Kiantajärvi, Suomusalmi (some 60 km north of Juntusranta). Lt A.A. Svedikov and *st.lt* V.I. Poryvkin were taken prisoners.

7 January 1940 I-15bis c/n 4453 (*st.lt* A.G. Shabalov, 2nd Squadron; ex 4./19 IAP) disappeared on a supply flight to the surrounded 44th Division along the Raate road.

23 January 1940 *st.lt* A.I. Puklin was captured at Suomussalmi after forced-landing with I-153 c/n 6862. He had lost his orientation on a ferry flight from Poduzhemye to Vojnitsa, and said that his unit was 4./68 IAP in Salessk, from where he was transferred 10 November 1939 together with five other aviators to Kem'; 3rd Squadron/27 IAP was also mentioned as his unit. The I-15bis possibly became VH-10 in Finnish Air Force.

31 January 1940 six aircraft took off to strafe enemy positions at Kiantajärvi, Suomussalmi. I-153 c/n 6819 of *ml.lt* V.S. Dunayevskiy (3rd Squadron) was shot down by enemy machine gun fire and crashed at Perankajärvi.

In January 1940 at least four aircraft were additionally lost in landing accidents.

3 February 1940 2nd and 3rd Squadrons were assigned to 80 SAP, which operated in the Repola direction, strafing Finnish positions at Suojärvi and Hautavaara and dropping supplies to surrounded Soviet units etc.

18 February 1940 I-153 c/n 6325 (*st.lt* V.A. Romanov, 4th Squadron) did not return to Uhtua. Another missing I-153 was located 20 km from Uhtua, which had force-landed because of early explosions of its own AO-8 bombs.

26 February 1940 two I-153s were lost on strafing missions: c/n 6820 of *ml.lt* V.I. Golubev, 4th Squadron went missing at Ristijärvi, 50 km north of Kajaani (probably due to splinters of its own FAB-50 bombs), while c/n 6326 of *st.politr* A.V. Soin (5th Squadron) was hit by ground fire at Parvavaara, south of Suomussalmi, and crashed 20 km from his base.

29 February 1940 *ml.lt* G.K. Bubnov was killed when I-153 c/n 6827 crashed because of splinters from its own FAB-50 bomb, which exploded on a training flight at Vojnitsa.

8 March 1940 I-15bis of *st.lt* G.G. Ayumov was shot down by A-A artillery at Saunajärvi. The fighter crashed some 400 m from the surrounded 54th Division. Next night the wounded pilot was rescued and brought into the motti, where the semiconscious Ayumov believed that he was taken prisoner by the Finns and refused to speak until the Military Commissar of 54th Division arrived.

12 March 1940 the sick tent was hit by a Finnish artillery shell, and several wounded Red Army soldiers including Ayumov were killed. In August 2004 parts of Ayumov's I-15bis were located, and are preserved in the Finnish Air Force Museum in Tikkakoski.

27 March 1940 1st and 5th Squadrons relocated to Besovets, while 2nd Squadron returned to Gorelovo, 3rd and 4th Squadrons to Pushkin and correspondingly to Klin.

152 IAP operated primarily in the Puolanka direction. Early January 1940 152 IAP was ordered to drop supplies to 44th Division, which was surrounded and cut into pieces ("*mottis*") by small Finnish ski units on the Raate road. 152 IAP performed only seven supply dropping missions, before 44th Division was virtually annihilated 10 January 1940.

According to Soviet documents the surrounded 44th Division lost 4,661 soldiers from 1–7 January 1940. The material losses amounted to 79 field guns (45 and 76 mm), 37 tanks (T-26 and T-38), 280 machine guns, 8 mortars (82 mm), about 150 trucks, all regiment, battalion and company radio transmitters etc. All this war booty was subsequently used by the Finnish Army.

High command of 44th Division, 662nd Infantry regiment and 3rd NKVD regiment (including Commanders, Political officers and Heads of Staff) were condemned to punishment by death at a court martial held 11–12 January 1940 in Vazhenvaara and Juntusranta. The court was chaired by the ill-reputed Lev Mekhlis (*armejskiy komissar 1.r.*, head of the Political Administration of the Red Army, and member of the War Council of 9th Army). The condemned were executed immediately in front of all troops.

Locations and Strength

Date	Subordination	Bases	Base units	Aircraft
1.1.40	VVS 9.A	Uhtua, Vuonninen and Poduzhemye	6 RAB, 261 AB	45 I-153, 24 I-15bis
1.2.40	VVS 9.A	Uhtua and Vuonninen	6 RAB, 261 AB	43 I-153, 23 I-15bis (10 I-15bis directly subordinated to VVS 9.A).
1.3.40	10 AB, VVS 9.A	Vuonninen	6 RAB, 261 AB	48 I-153, 24 I-15bis. Puolanka direction: 14 I-15bis and 29 I-153 Kajaani direction: 10 I-15bis and 9 I-153 10 I-153 direcly subordinated to VVS 9.A.
1.4.40	59 AB, VVS LVO	Besovets	6 RAB, 261 AB	33 I-153, 12 I-15bis

9 January-13 March 1940 152 IAP performed 1,435 missions (flight time 1,765 h 57 min), and lost eight aviators in combat.

3rd Squadron/27 IAP (C.O. *major* M.I. Korolev) performed 434 war missions, and dropped 464 bombs. One of the most talented pilots of this Squadron was Viktor Talalikhin, who performed 47 missions in the Winter War. During one mission Talalikhin protected his Squadron commander by attracting the attention of enemy A-A artillery onto himself. As 177 IAP deputy Squadron C.O. *ml.lt* Talalikhin performed the first nighttime taran in the Great Patriotic War by crashing into a German He 111-bomber. Talalikhin was exceptionally the next day appointed HSU. He was killed during his next taran-mission 27 October 1941.

A number of pilots and technicians of the "Karelo-Finnish" 12 OIAE were attached to 152 IAP after the war.

152 IAP Loss Summary

Squadron	In 152 IAP			Before 152 IAP		Note
	Accident	Catastrophy	Forced landing	Accident	Forced landing	
HQ	1					
1st			2	5	11	
2nd						(No data)
3rd			4			(Incomplete data)
4th		1	1	1		
5th			2	4	3	
18 KAO			3	1	4	
Total	1	1	12	11	18	

152 IAP command

Commander   *major* Ye.F. Kondrat (1911 –). Commanded 152 IAP from 2. to 9.1.40. Participated in Spanish Civil War, 3 + 3 claims. In GPW commanded 249 AD etc.
polkovnik S.Ya. Simonenko (from 9.1.40)

Military Commissar   *bat.komiss* Chirkov (??)
bat.komiss B.P. Lyubimov (from 9.1.40).

Chief of Staff *major* D.D. Ostromovskiy
(*major* Dobrovolskiy (?))

Squadron C.O.
1st (ex 1./72 SAP) *kapitan* A.I. Safronov
2nd (ex 4./19 IAP) *kapitan* P.I. Naumov
st.lt A.G. Shabalov
3rd (ex 4./68 IAP and 3./27 IAP)
kapitan M.I. Korolev
4th (ex 4./38 IAP) *st.lt* D.M. Novikov
5th (ex 4./80 SAP) *major* Shvetsov (?)
18 KAO *major* Borzov
bat.komiss Shokhrin

153rd Fighter Aviation Regiment (153 IAP)

153 IAP was established in Kubinka 23–26 January 1940 with four squadrons (based on 11 and 24 IAP of 2 IAB, VVS MVO), and received 65 new I-153 fighters. The pilots had in general 50–70 flight hours. 153 IAP took off 14 February 1940 from Kubinka to the Northwestern front. After intermediate landings in Yedrovo, Gorelovo and Nurmolitsa (20 February 1940) 16 I-153 arrived 22 February 1940 in Karkunlampi ice base, and were attached to VVS 15.A. 153 IAP fought its first combat subordinated to 49 IAP 23 February 1940. Two days later another 22 I-153 arrived in Karkunlampi, and on 26 February 1940 the last 22 I-153.

153 IAP performed 1,064 combat missions:
- 600 ground attack missions
- 200 reconnaissance missions
- 264 bomber escort and patrol missions.

Total flight time 1,115 h 48 min.

153 IAP Command

Commander *polkovnik* K.A. Katichev. In GPW commanded 57 SAD in 1941.
Deputy Commander *kapitan* M.F. Chernykh
Military Commissar *bat.komiss* I.A. Valujtsev
bat.komiss N. Kuligin
Chief of Staff *major* S.D. Kul'min

Squadron C.O. and Commissars
1st *kapitan* Shcholokhov
2nd *kapitan* Myakushev
3rd *kapitan* Afanasyev
4th *kapitan* V. Matveyev
st.politr A.F. Bystrov

After the war 153 IAP moved to Lodjenoye pole (attached to VVS 8.A), and later relocated to Kasimovo (attached to 59 IAB). Before GPW 59 IAB was converted to 5 SAD and attached to VVS 23.A. 22 June 1941 153 IAP was based in Helylä (Sortavala) and Käkisalmi.

153 IAP was elevated to Guards status 21 November 1942 and named 28 GvIAP.

In GPW ex-153 IAP fighter pilot *ml.lt* A.S. Smirnov (1917–1987) was appointed HSU on 28 September 1943 and for the second time on 23 February 1945.

Detached Aviation Squadrons (OAE)

1st Air Defense Fighter Aviation Squadron (1 IAE PVO)

1st Air Defense Fighter Aviation Squadron (1 IAE) was responsible for air defense of Lodejnoye pole AF base, equipped with 11 I-153 fighters from 2 February 1940. The Squadron was initially subordinated to VVS 8.A, then to VVS 15.A, and was finally attached to 153 IAP.

1st Long-Range Reconnaissance Squadron (1 DRAE)

Autumn 1939 1 DRAE was located in Krechevitsy. Strength on 30 November 1939 14 SB (of which ten were in Krechevitsy and four in Gorelovo, which were later transferred to 48 SBAP). In January 1940 1 DRAE moved to Kaukjärvi (in occupied Finnish territory), main equipment SB, but also a few I-15bis fighters were in use.

Subordination
VVS LVO
VVS 7.A

1 DRAE personnel (October 1935). (I. Stoilik)

19 December 1939 SB-pilot *st.lt* K.P. Strekalov was taken prisoner at Perkjärvi. On questioning he said that his unit was 1 DRAE. (According to archive documents his unit was however 3./44 SBAP) His observer and MG-gunner were killed.

30 January 1940 2 SBs (c/n 7/79 and 9/79) collided in the air at Kaukjärvi (one pilot was *st.lt* B.A. Stojlik); both bombers were flyable 2 February 1940.

6 February 1940 (or 16 February 1940?) one I-15bis was lost to enemy A-A artillery. This fighter was dispatched to 1st Squadron of 49 IAP at Karkunlampi.

15 February 1940 I-15bis c/n 5162 was hit by enemy fire, pilot *lt* I.F. Kremnev was injured. On the same day three new SB 2M-103 aircraft of batches 244 and 248 were received.

19 February 1940 *komkor* S.P. Denisov (Commander of VVS 7.A) ordered 2 I-16 flights (*zvenos*) of 59 IAB to protect the SBs of 1 DRAE. On the same day I-15bis c/n 4435 (tactical no. "161", piloted by Breyev) returned with bullet holes in the tail and fuselage. The fighter was disassembled, and some parts were used for repair of I-15bis c/n 5162 which was damaged four days earlier.

8 March 1940 seven SB were received.

13 March 1940 1 DRAE was based at Kaukjärvi with 12 SB and two I-15bis (equipped with AFA-cameras).

1 DRAE performed 385 combat flights, flight time 426 h 44 min. The Squadron took 34,200 air photos covering 8,100 km² territory, and dropped 150 FAB-100 bombs.

1 DRAE was awarded Red Banner Order 21 March 1940.

Above and right: 1 DRAE personnel (October 1935), squadron flag (January 1936) and a lesson (May 1936). Note that "enemies of the people" detected in the Party purges 1937–38 were to be painted out even in private photos! (I. Stoilik)

St.lt Boris A. Stojlik (ex-1 DRAE) was killed at Utti 25.6.1941 (then Commander of 3./201 SBAP). (I. Stoilik)

I-15bis tactical 161 (c/n 4435, piloted by Lt Breyev of 1 DRAE) was damaged by A-A fire 19.2.1940. (RGVA)

4th Long-Range Reconnaissance Squadron (4 DRAE)

Autumn 1939 4 DRAE was located in Smolensk (Byelorussian Military District).

Subordination
VVS BOVO
72 SAP, VVS 8.A (from 28 February 1940)

18 February 1940 4 DRAE received 12 new SBs in Moscow. Ten days later the Squadron arrived in Besovets, and was attached to the co-located 72 SAP.

11 March 1940 SB c/n 9/254 was shot down by A-A fire and crashed 3 km from Neidoja. *shturman kapitan* I.P. Kochkarev died of wounds 16 March 1940.

4 DRAE performed 120 combat missions, flight time 220 h 10 min. Combat missions/pilot max. 11–12 (average 10), flight time max. 21 h 40 min, average 17 h. Bombs dropped 4,559, total weight 94.5 t.

4 DRAE Commander
A.I. Pushkin (1915–2002). HSU 12.8.1942. In GPW commanded 135 BBAP, 188 BAD etc. In 1967 commanded 36th Air Army.

4 DRAE Commander A.I. Pushkin. (G.F. Petrov)

8th Detached Night Aviation Squadron (8 ONAE)

8 ONAE was formed 10 February 1940 on order of *komandarm* G.M. Shtern (Commander, 8th Army) and *kombrig* I.I. Kopets (Commander, 8th Army AF), and commanded by *major* Veber. Operations were initiated two days later from Peski ice base near Petrozavodsk in Karelian ASSR.

Personnel and SB bombers were received from 18 SBAP and 72 SAP.

8 ONAE Strength

Date	Aircraft	Notes
13.2.40	5 SB	
18.2.40	8 SB	
2.3.40	4 SB	Four ex-18 SBAP SB bombers were transferred to VVS 15.A
3.3.40	8 SB	Eight new SB bombers arrived from Zavod No. 22 in Moscow. Old SB bombers were returned to their former units.
8.3.40	10 SB	Reinforcement arrived from 72 SAP.

8 ONAE performed 255 combat missions, flight time 377 h 55 min. During the operation period (12 February–12 March 1940) there were 18 flyable nights. In one night (10 hours) up to 25–30 combat missions were performed; each crew performed up to four missions per night.

8 ONAE dropped 3,692 bombs (total weight 164.7 t) and 10,000 leaflets.

8 ONAE Bombing targets

Enemy troops and truck transports	220
Railway objects	162
War industries and population centres	82
Bridges	1
Reconnaissance missions	22

12th Detached Fighter Aviation Squadron (12 OIAE)

12 OIAE was set up in late November 1939 in Besovets (west of Petrozavodsk, Karelian ASSR), as a "national" AF unit. Ethnic "Finnish and Karelian" aviators were recruited from aviation clubs in Karelia and from various VVS units. When possible ground personnel was also recruited among local nationals.

Flight training was immediately initiated. Karelian Assistant Commissar *politr* Fedor Timoskainen, already had 30 flight hours experience. In January 1940 approximately 50% of the necessary technicians were available, but essential maintenance equipment was lacking. None of the technicians had previously seen the I-15bis fighters of the Squadron.

30 November 1939 Assistant Commander *kapitan* Pavel Ivanov (by nationality "Finnish") arrived. He was a former flight instructor in the local aviation club. Under his guidance the first I-15bis fighter course with six pupils started 15 December 1939. When the course ended 9 March 1940 the pupils were considered fit for war missions, and altogether had flight experience of 402 fighter hours. However, 12 OIAE (intended for the air defence of Petrozavodsk) apparently did not perform a single war mission.

12 OIAE Commander was *major* Semen Bamshin (former fighter Squadron commander in 72 SAP).[1]

During flight training the technicians got acquainted with I-15bis fighters, and managed to keep 6–8 aircraft serviceable (of a total inventory of some 20 fighters).

The organisation of 12 OIAE is clearly connected to the propagandistic *Democratic Republic of Finland* (DRF), led by exiled Finnish Communist O.W. Kuusinen. However 12 OIAE was never directly subordinated to the *Finnish Peoples' Army* (FPA), but on 2 February 1940 was attached to VVS 8.A (possibly via 72 SAP mentioned above). The first own liaison aircraft of FPA arrived only after the peace treaty of 13 March 1940, when a liaison flight was formed.

S.F. Bamshin (12 OIAE Commander) was taken prisoner by the Finns in June 1943 (then 957 ShAP Commander). (G.E. Strömberg)

---

[1] In June 1943 Bamshin commanded 957 ShAP, and was taken prisoner after force-landing 8 June 1943 near Mäkriä (near Olonets in Finnish occupied East Karelia). Bamshin admitted that he commanded a fighter squadron in the Winter War, but did not say that this was a "Karelo-Finnish" squadron (which the Finnish intelligence officers certainly did not ask either...). *Major* Bamshin was handed over to the German authorities 12 July 1943, and returned to the USSR from German captivity after WWII.

After the Winter War 12 OIAE was dissolved. Part of the personnel and equipment remained in Bessovets, and was attached to 152 IAP (which was set up during the war). The rest of the personnel returned to their original units, or were disbanded.

21 fighter pilots of 12 OIAE are known by name, of which 11 seem to be ethnic Karelian or Finnish, but of 48 technicians only 13 are known to be Karelo-Finnish.

12 OIAE Command

Commander	*kapitan* S.F. Bamshin. In 1943 commanded 957 ShAP; POW after forced landing at Olonets 8.6.1943. To Germany 12.7.1943.
Assistant Commander	*kapitan* P.N. Ivanov ("Finnish")
Assistant Commander	*vojentekhnik 1 r.* (Military Technician 1 cl.) M.Kh. Hovinen (Finnish)
Military Commissar	*st.lt* Vinogradov
Assistant Military Commissar	*politr* F.F. Timoskainen (Finnish)

12th Detached Special Purpose Aviation Squadron (12 OAE ON)

(Expanded to aviation regiment strength 1 February 1940. (See 85 AP ON, page 203)

19th Detached Aviation Squadron (19 OAE)

19 OAE was formerly 2nd Squadron/3 LBAP, which participated in the Winter War from 12 December 1939 with nine SSS. (See 3 LBAP, page 72)

From 5 March 1940 the Squadron was attached to VVS 7.A, and based at Kaukjärvi.

19 OAE performed mainly nighttime operations: of a total of 200 missions 194 were performed at night, flight time 288 h (280 h at night). Bombs dropped 4,830 (4,710 at night). (The statistics seem to include the missions performed by 2nd Squadron of 3 LBAP, predecessor of 19 OAE.)

The Golden Star was proposed to 19 OAE commander *kapitan* V.V. Totskiy, but the proposal was not supported.

19 OAE Command

Commander	*kapitan* V.V. Totskiy
Military Commissar	*st.politr* Savchenko

29th Detached Liaison Aviation Squadron (29 OAES)

9 December 1939 Leningrad Military District War Council established 29th Liaison Aviation Squadron (29 AES), attached to 8. Army HQ. 29 AES was organized with 29 OAKO and 5th Squadron/24 SBAP as nucleus. Main task of 29 OAES was supply dropping to surrounded troops at Lemetti.

Subordination
VVS 8.A

11 December 1939 the personnel were transported from Leningrad to Lodejnoye pole.

18 December 1939 12 new U-2 aircraft flew to Lodejnoye pole. Six U-2s were immediately transferred to Suojärvi, and the other six aircraft were distributed to various operational areas of 8. Army.

14 January 1940 29 OAES arrived from Leningrad to Kolatselga (Kolatselkä, just east of the Finnish-Soviet border) ice base with 12 U-2.

20 January 1940 three SSS arrived from Leningrad to be used for quick delivery of "operational documents", and later another four SSS-aircraft were received.

The first combat missions of 29 OAES were performed by *lt* P.L. Olejnikov to surrounded troops at Lemetti (dropping of 400 kg supply bags) on 20 January 1940. Despite A-A hits he was able to return to his base. On this day SSS c/n 1263 was shot down by enemy fire, crew OK.

10 February 1940 SSS c/n 1434 (pilot *lt* I.P. Kolesnikov) force-landed after enemy hits 6–8 km east of Uomaa. *Kapitan* Moskalev landed nearby with another SSS, and transported Kolesnikov and the

navigator, *lt* N.K. Zubik (both tied to the wings) back to base. Later the engine of the force-landed SSS was replaced, after which *kapitan* Moskalev was able to fly it away.

12 February 1940 an SSS on a supply mission from Kolatselga to Lemetti crashed at 1100 hours east of Nietjärvi after ground fire hits. *shturman st.lt* I.I. Gribov was killed on capture, pilot *lt* P.L. Olejnikov was captured next day.

In February 1940 145 combat missions were performed by SSS-aircraft (185 h 43 min), and 568 missions by U-2 aircraft (326 h). Altogether 208 supply dropping missions were performed, flight time 331 h 37 min.

The few pilots performed up to 55 missions (max. flight time 81 h 5 min), on average 35 missions/pilot (flight time 51 h 56 min/pilot).

Two SSS-aircraft were transferred to 5 OKAO in February 1940, and one U-2 to VVS 15. A.

29 OAES Command
Commander *kapitan* Moskalev
Military Commissar *st.politr* Bogdanovskiy

31ˢᵗ Military Reconnaissance Aviation Squadron (31 VRAE)

In autumn 1939 31 VRE was based in Novoseltsy (Leningrad Military District).

Subordination
VVS 7.A

6 February 1940 two I-15bis fighters of 31 VRAE collided in mid-air, and crashed in the frozen Bay of Viipuri between Tuppura and Ruonti. *lt* K.S. Chumachenko and *lt* V.V. Koksharov were killed.

13 March 1940 31 VRAE was located at Kirkkojärvi ice base, with four SSS, eight R-5 and six I-15bis.

31 VRAE Commande *major* Chinirdin

32ⁿᵈ Reconnaissance Aviation Squadron (32 RAE)

Autumn 1939 32 RAE was based in Krasnogvardejsk (Leningrad Military District).

Subordination
VVS 13.A (from 29 January 1940)

32 RAE performed front line photo reconnaissance missions from 29 January 1940 with nine 9 R-Z reconnaissance aircraft, based at Southern Lake Lempaala.

17 February 1940 32 RAE participated in the rescue operation of a force-landed crew of 31 SBAP, evacuating the injured *lt* I.S. Khudyakov (see 31 SBAP, page 139).

13 March 1940 32 RAE was based in Lempaala with 12 R-Z aircraft.

32 RAE performed 534 missions (of which 445 were bombing missions, 71 photo-reconnaissance missions and 18 visual reconnaissance missions), flight time 504 h.

11 April 1940 32 RAE was awarded Red Banner Order.

32 RAE Command
Commander *kapitan* Perepelitsa
Military Commissar *st.politr* Basargin

33rd Reconnaissance Aviation Squadron (33 RAE)

Autumn 1939 33 VRE was based in Krasnogvardejsk (Leningrad Military District).

Subordination
AG Filin, VVS 9.A (from 1 February 1940)

17 January 1940 33 VRE was dispatched from Krasnogvardejsk to VVS 9.A.
1 February 1940 33 VRE was divided into two separate flights operating in Kemijärvi (five R-5) and Kajaani directions (two R-5 aircraft). The latter flight was ordered to participate in the supply of the surrounded 54th Mountain Division in the Kuhmo area.
33 VRE performed 266 day missions (flight time 333 h 05 min) and 42 night missions (flight time 70 h), and supported *Osobyi strelkovyi korpus* (Special Infantry Corps) of 9th Army.
13 March 1940 33 VRE was based in Reboly (Repola) with eight R-5 aircraft.

34th Long-Range Reconnaissance Squadron (34 DRAE)

Autumn 1939 34 DRAE was based in Gogolev (Kiev Militray District).

Subordination
VVS KOVO
AG Spirin, VVS 9.A (from 29 February 1940)

Combat Chronicle
29 February 1940 34 DRAE arrived from Gostomil (VVS KOVO) to VVS 9.A, and was attached to AG Spirin. According to a recent Russian article 34 DRAE received no preparation at all for combat operations.
7 March 1940 *fänrik* E. Theler (F19) shot down two SB bombers of 34 DRAE in Utajärvi, four aviators (*kapitan* T.V. Grebennikov, *lt* A.A. Matsnev, *starshina* A.T. Morozov and *lt* A.S. Aleksyev) were taken prisoner, and two crew members were killed.
13 March 1940 34 DRAE was based at Uhtua with seven SBs.

This and next page: E. Theler (F 19) downed two SBs (34 DRAE) at Utajärvi 7.3.1940. SB tactical 2 belly-landed in the soft snow. (SA-kuva)

224

One of the SB-bombers downed by Theler is being transported to VL in Tampere. (Flygvapenmuseum)

38th Heavy Transport Aviation Squadron (38 TTAE)

Moscow Central Airport Commander *polkovnik* S.G. Kurilov was 9 February 1940 ordered to set up 38th Heavy Transport Aviation Squadron (38 TTAE) with 18 TB-3 bombers for delivery of special cargo to the front.

One of the flight commanders of 38 TTAE was *kapitan* N.F. Gastello (who served also as flight commander in 1 TBAP).

TB-3 transport aircraft were used for delivery of fuel to Kuressaare in Estonian Saaremaa. The BZ-35 refueling tank car is based on the ZiS 6 -truck. (G.F.Petrov)

41st Reconnaissance Aviation Squadron (41 RAE)

17 February 1940 41 RAE was attached to VVS 13.A with 12 R-5.

50th Detached Aviation Squadron (50 OAE)

50 OAE was like 10 and 19 OAE a close reconnaissance Squadron attached to 7th Army, and equipped with various R-5 versions.

19 January 1940 50 OAE was based at Kirkkojärvi, which was bombed by Fokker C.X light bombers of LLv 12 after dark. No information on bombing results is available.

56th Detached Army Corps Aviation Squadron (56 OKAE)

Autumn 1939 56 OKAE (or VRAE) was based in Novocherkassk (North Caucasus Military District).

56 OKAE Command
Commander   *kapitan* Nagayev
Chief of Staff   *kapitan* Kirpichnikov

Detached Aviation Units (OAO)

Air support of infantry troops was the topic of M. Smirnov's Vojskovaja aviatsija, *published in 1936 with print run 15,000 copies. (Finnish National Defence University)*

1st Army Corps Aviation Unit (1 KAO)

Autumn 1939 1 KAO was located in Yegoryevsk (Moscow Military District). In January 1940 1 KAO moved to ice bases at Vammeljärvi, Kaukjärvi and Suulajärvi in occupied Karelian Isthmus.

Subordination
  VVS MVO
  VVS 7.A

9 February 1940 two R-5 (c/n 6805 and 8889) were shot down in air combat 4 km west of Boboshino, all crew were killed. *Four pilots of LLv 24 shot down two R-5 aircraft at Summa-Leipäsuo.*

13 February 1940 7 IAP was ordered by *komkor* S.P. Denisov (VVS 7.A Commander) to escort artillery control aircraft of 1 KAO (co-located in Vammeljärvi). 1 KAO participated in an unique test of an A-7bis autogiro for practical artillery fire control at Kaukjärvi.

From 27 February 1940 seven A-7bis missions were flown, of which two were combat missions (total flight time 11 h 14 min). Another autogiro was also earmarked for testing, but this was damaged in Leningrad. Because of the unfinished status of the autogiro, and personnel lacking training, no conclusions concerning possible autogiro operational use could be made during the short test period.

13 March 1940 1 KAO was located in Suulajärvi with two R-5 aircraft and one A-7bis autogiro.

R-5SSS of 1 KAO crash-landed at Perkjärvi 18.1.1940. (RGVA)

Before the Winter War A. Zhavrov wrote a textbook about the use of helicopters and autogiros Avtozhir i gelikopter (published by Osoaviakhim 1939). The manuscript was finished by 15.3.1939, print run 10,000 copies. (Finnish National Defence University)

1 KAO performed field trials of the A-7bis autogiro (designed by Nikolai Kamov). (G.F. Petrov)

2nd Army Corps Aviation Unit (2 KAO)

Autumn 1939 2 KAO was located in Mogilev (Byelorussian Military District).

Subordination
VVS BOVO
VVS 13.A (from 9 January 1940)

9 January 1940 2 KAO was attached to VVS 13.A in Nurmijärvi with seven R-5.
13 March 1940 2 KAO was based in Valkjärvi with five R-5.

227

5th Detached Army Corps Aviation Unit (5 OKAO or 5 KAO)

Autumn 1939 5 OKAO was located in Korostovichi (Leningrad Military District).

Subordination
VVS LVO
VVS 8.A

26 September 1939 5 OKAO moved from Korostovichi to Lisino with 10 SSS aircraft; additional SSS aircraft were received from 9 ShAP (which converted to I-15bis).

6 December 1939 5 OKAO was transferred to VVS 8.A in Lodejnoye pole, and 1 January 1940 to Prääsä. Somewhat later 5 KAO relocated to Suvilahti, Suojärvi in occupied Finnish territory, where 5 OKAO remained until the end of the war. In February 1940 29 AES transferred two SSS-aircraft to 5 OKAO. Main task of 5 OKAO was supply dropping to surrounded troops.

6 January 1940 two SSS-aircraft collided (probably c/n 1132 and 1136) when landing in Prääsä (?) after bombing of Salmi. Three aviators (*lt* S.N. Petukhov, *lt* Ye.I. Zhutskov and *st.lt* V.Ye. Lyadynov) were killed, and one pilot, *lt* Ovcharov escaped by parachute.

26 January 1940 SSS c/n 1367 was shot down by ground fire at Koirinoja on returning from a supply dropping sortie. *lt* I.V. Telegin and *lt* D.M. Pirozhikhin were killed.

31 January 1940 two SSS-aircraft took off from Suojärvi to drop supplies to surrounded troops in East-Lemetti. SSS c/n 1391 was downed by ground fire at Ruokojärvi, Uomaa. *St.lt* I.N. Makletsov was taken prisoner, but died (like three other POW aviators) of CO-suffocation in Otrakkala POW camp 8–9 February 1940. *st.lt* F.A. Rykov was killed by a land-mine. The SSS was captured practically intact.

15 February 1940 *lt* V.Ya. Kirichenko and *st.lt* L.V. Cherezov in SSS c/n 1213 were hit by ground fire at Ylä-Lavajärvi and force-landed at Riihilampi. They were picked up and brought to their home base by another SSS piloted by *st.lt* I.S. Tishchenko, who took the stranded pilot in the cockpit, while *shturman* Cherezov was strapped to the wing. Tishchenko's aircraft was also damaged.

5 OKAO total flight time 544 h 41 min (of which 52 h 51 min at night).

5 OKAO Command

Commander	*major* Filin
	major Chuk
Military Commissar	*bat.komiss* Tuzov
Chief of Staff	*st.lt* Kirpichnikov

9th Army Corps Aviation Unit (9 KAO)

Autumn 1939 9 KAO was based in Smychkovo (Leningrad Military District).

Subordination
VVS LVO
VVS 7.A
VVS 13.A (from 1 January 1940)

Combat Chronicle

19 November 1939 9 KAO moved to Komendantskiy AF base north of Leningrad, and was attached to 19th Army corps (19 AK) of 7th Army, preparing for an attack on the Western Karelian Isthmus. 9 KAO main task was artillery fire control.

1 December 1939 own A-A artillery in Mainila shot down R-5 artillery fire control aircraft (tactical "1"), which force-landed in Alakylä. Pilot *lt* D.S. Tereshchenko was injured. Next day some valuable parts were removed, after which the aircraft was set on fire. Three other R-5s were hit.

18 December 1939 two R-5 aircraft led by *lt* A.A. Knurov were put at the disposal of *komkor* V.D. Grendal at Eastern Karelian Isthmus, and based at Metsäpirtti.

24 December 1939 9 KAO moved to Kanneljärvi.

Late December 1939 seven R-5 were dispatched to VVS 9.A, after which the remaining two R-5 were on 1 January 1940 attached to VVS 13.A.

10 January 1940 *lt* Knurov's flight returned to 9 KAO. From 19 December 1939 to 7 January 1940 the flight controlled the fire of five artillery batteries, resulting in the destruction of five Finnish batteries. On the other hand the activities of the main Squadron was rather moderate, because of bad weather and also lack of fighter cover.

2 February 1940 the aircraft of 9 KAO were split up and distributed to 19 AK Artillery Regiments as follows: 28 KAP – one aircraft, 43 KAP – one a/c, 311 KAP and 320 KAP – two a/c, and as reserve of 19 AK Artillery commander – one a/c. (KAP = *Korpusnoy Artillericheskiy Polk* or Army Corps artillery regiment).

8 February 1940 9 KAO was ordered to move to Suulajärvi.

13 February 1940 own artillery shot down R-5 fire control aircraft c/n 7441 at Perkjärvi. Pilot *st.lt* I.S. Meletashev was killed, navigator *st.lt* F.V. Mishkin escaped by parachute.

On the same day 25 IAP was ordered by *komkor* S.P. Denisov (Commander, VVS 7.A), to escort artillery control aircraft of 9 and 16 KAO, co-located at Suulajärvi and Kanneljärvi respectively.

Up to 23 February 1940 9 KAO had performed 131 combat missions, flight time 222 hours.

25 February 1940 9 KAO an R-5 of 9 KAO observed a Finnish fighter being shot down at Kämärä. This was *alik* T. Bergman (GL-266), who was shot down by an I-16 of 68 IAP.

27 February 1940 an R-5 of 9 KAO observed two SBs crashing after A-A artillery hits. One SB was apparently c/n 10/209 of 5 SBAP, which crashed at Kaukolempiälä. (See 5 SBAP, page 87)

10 March 1940 9 KAO moved to Alusjärvi with four R-5.

15 March 1940 9 KAO moved back to its peacetime base at Luga-Smychkovo.

9 KAO Command
Commander   *kapitan* N.A. Kochanovskiy
Military Commissar   *st.politr* T.A. Korolev

Grave of st.lt I.S. Molotashev in Perkjärvi. His R-5 (c/n 7441) was shot down by own side's ground fire 13.2.1940. (SA-kuva)

11th Army Corps Aviation Unit (11 KAO)

Autumn 1939 11 KAO was based in Mogilev (Byelorussian Military District).

11 KAO performed 97 combat flights in VVS 13.A (flight time 103 h 43 min).

13 March 1940 11 KAO strength was three R-5 and three SSS aircraft. Tasks performed included artillery fire correction (50%) and close-range reconnaissance (50%).

15th Army Corps Aviation Unit (15 KAO)

Autumn 1939 15 KAO was located in Saratov (Volga Military District), equipped with seven R-5 reconnaissance and one U-2 liaison aircraft.

Subordination
VVS PrivVO (until 5 December 1939)
VVS 8.A (from 5 December 1939)
VVS 15.A (from 18 February 1940)

Combat Chronicle
5 December 1939 15 KAO was ordered to move from Kujbyshev to the Finnish front. The relocation started by train to Shuiskaya (Suoju, north of Petrozavodsk), and then by truck to Besovets where the aircraft were assembled.

18 December 1939 Finnish troops found empty U-2 "1" (c/n 11429) at Tolvajärvi, Kotilampi. This aircraft (apparently attached to 15 KAO) is preserved in the Finnish Air Force Museum in Tikkakoski.

Late December 1939 15 KAO relocated via Prjazha (Prääsä, 40 km west of Petrozavodsk) to Uomaa ice base (on occupied Finnish territory), but on 29 December 1939 was forced to withdraw to Kolatselga, strength seven R-5.

Like other KAOs 15 KAO had two "masters" – 15 KAO was attached to VVS 8.A, but in fact subordinated to 56th Army Corps (which incorporated 18th and 168th Divisions, and 34th Light Tank Brigade). 15 KAO ice base at Kolatselga was located only 13 km from 56 AK Command post.

Although the intended task of 15 KAO was reconnaissance, artillery fire control and liaison flights on behalf of 56th Army Corps, more than two-thirds of all 923 missions were supply dropping to surrounded units. Over 116,000 kg supplies were dropped by seven R-5s.

6 January 1940 four R-5 led by *major* Kuznetsov made a reconnaissance and bombing sortie to the operational area of Red Army 18.D at Uomaa-Kitelä. R-5 c/n 6203 was hit by Finnish A-A artillery and force-landed 2 km southwest of Suistamo (between Kitelä ja Leppäsyrjä). Pilot *st.lt* Kukhir was killed, and *kapitan* A.A. Klevtsov was taken prisoner two days later.

26 January 1940 a R-5 (pilot *lt* N.M. Plaksin) was shot down by ground fire at Pitkäranta. The crew was killed.

18 February 1940 15 KAO was transferred to VVS 15.A, strength seven R-5 (of which three were airworthy) in Kolatselga.

15 KAO performed 923 missions. During 659 missions 116,188 kg food stuff and medicines were dropped to the surrounded troops of 56th AK in the Lemetti-Kitelä region, where the intended dropping sites were sometimes only 25 x 5–10 m wide.

15 KAO also performed 32 fire control missions, 17 bombing and 31 photo-reconnaissance missions. All other missions were apparently supply dropping missions. At the end of the war all R-5 aircraft had up to 220 bullet holes.

U-2 c/n 11429 was found empty at Tolvajärvi 18.12.1939. (SA-kuva)

15 KAO Command
Commander   *kapitan* Yevtikov
                                     major Kuznetsov (?)
Military Commissar   *st.politr* Reshetnikov
                                     kapitan Dubinskiy (?)

The U-2 was displayed at the War booty exhibition in Helsinki in late autumn 1941. A swastika has been crudely painted on the fin. (SA-kuva)

R-5 c/n 6203 (tactical 1) of 15 KAO was shot down 6.1.1940 by ground fire at Suistamo. Navigator kapitan A.A. Klevtsov was captured two days later, st.lt A.V. Kukhir perished. (SA-kuva)

231

16th Army Corps Aviation Unit (16 KAO)

Autumn 1939 16 KAO was based in Korostovichi (Leningrad Military District); strength 30 November 1939 seven SSS artillery control aircraft.

Subordination
VVS LVO
VVS 7.A

Combat Chronicle

23 December 1939 SSS c/n 1453 was shot down in air combat at Leipäsuo-Huumola, the crew was killed. Kapt E. Luukkanen (FR-108) and luutn T. Huhanantti (FR-76) shot together down an "R-5" at Leipäsuo.

29 January 1940 SSS c/n 1123 was shot down in air combat at Kaukjärvi-Muolaanjärvi, the crew was killed. *Two R-5 were claimed by LLv 24 at Kaukjärvi-Muolaanjärvi.*

13 February 1940 25 IAP was ordered by *komkor* S.P. Denisov (VVS 7.A Commander), to escort and protect the artillery control aircraft of 9 and 16 KAO, co-located at Suulajärvi and Kanneljärvi respectively.

13 March 1940 16 KAO was based at Kanneljärvi, strength six SSS aircraft.

16 KAO served 50th Army Corps, with individual aircraft distributed to the Corps artillery regiments.

16 KAO performed 249 combat flights, flight time 274 h 20 min. 74 enemy batteries were detected, of which 44 were silenced and 20 destroyed.

16 KAO Command

Commander	*kapitan* T.A. Gorchakov
Military Commissar	*st.politr* Voinov
	st.lt N.P. Antonov

18th Army Corps Aviation Unit (18 KAO)

Autumn 1939 18 KAO was based in Sverdlovsk (Ural Military District).

Subordination
VVS UrVO
152 IAP, VVS 9.A (from 28 December 1939)

This and opposite page: 18 KAO was transferred from Ural Military District to VVS 9.A. Note the underwing cargo containers of the R-5 taking off for a supply mission to surrounded troops. (G.F. Petrov)

Combat Chronicle

18 KAO (seven R-5) was transferred 6 December 1939 from Sverdlovsk by train to Kem, Karelian ASSR, arriving 15–16 December 1939, and further by truck to Pozduzhemye (Usmana). The assembled aircraft were flown to Vojnitsa (Vuonninen) 28 December 1939, where 18 KAO was based until the end of the Winter War. 18 KAO operated in the Puolanka direction, main task supply dropping missions. 18 KAO was attached to 152 IAP in January 1940.

3 January 1940 R-5 *tactical 31* force-landed in Kiantajärvi, Suomussalmi (some 60 km N Juntusranta). *lt* A.A. Svetikov and *st.lt* V.I. Poryvkin were taken prisoner.

18 KAO Command

   Commander   *major* Borzov
   Military Commissar   *bat.komiss* Shokhrin

R-5 tactical 34, 18 KAO, force-landed 3.1.1940 on the Finnish-held frozen Kianta-järvi. Lt A.M. Svetikov and lt V.I. Poryvkin were captured. (SA-kuva)

23rd Army Corps Aviation Unit (23 KAO)

Autumn 1939 23 KAO was located in Podolsk (Moscow Military District).

Subordination
VVS MVO
VVS 7.A (from mid-December 1939)
VVS 13.A (from 1 January 1940)

Combat Chronicle
6 December 1939 23 KAO departed (without aircraft) from Moscow Military District to the Karelian Isthmus. After arrival seven R-5 were received from 3 LBAP (VVS 7.A).

1 January 1940 23 KAO was attached to the new VVS 13.A, strength four R-5 and three SSS.

23 KAO performed 240 war missions supporting two artillery regiments (311 Cannon artillery regiment and 116 Howitzer artillery regiment).

13 March 1940 23 KAO was located in Miestilä, with three R-5 and four SSS aircraft.

23 KAO Command
Commander   *major* S.G. Karpenko
Military Commissar   *st.politr* M.A. Timchenko

33rd Liaison Aviation Unit at 9th Army HQ (33 AO svyazi Shtaba 9.A)

12 December 1939 the unit was dispatched from Krasnogvardejsk with nine disassembled U-2 liaison and ambulance aircraft. Five U-2 aircraft were assembled in early January 1940 in Poduzhemye, and flown to Uhtua.

11 January 1940 two U-2 lost their orientation on a flight from Chiksha to Repola, and force-landed at the Kesseli road, north of Löytövaara. Next day *lt* V.P. Ivanov, *lt* R.A. Bundak and *lt* N.N. Sidyakin were taken prisoner. The aircraft were destroyed by Finnish troops.

17 January 1940 the two U-2 wrecks were detected by Soviet troops at Veselijärvi. The loss of the two courier aircraft had not been reported to 9th Army HQ, which was duly noted by the NKVD *Osobyi Otdel*.

33 AO svyazi Commander   *st.lt* Kruglikov

Liaison Flights (*Aviazveno Svyazi*)

29th Liaison Flight (29 AZv sv)

29 Liaison flight was attached to VVS 13.A with six U-2.

36th Liaison Flight (36 AZv sv)

30 November 1939 in VVS 7.A.

61st Liaison Flight (61 AZv sv)

61st Liaison flight supported 54th Mountain division (56 AK, 9th Army) at Kuhmo with one U-2 and three Sha-2 amphibian aircraft.

69th Liaison Flight (69 AZv sv)

According to a captured document found at Syskyjärvi 18 December 1939 69th Liaison Flight supported 56th Army Corps of 8th Army at Loimola.

85th Liaison Flight (85 AZv sv)

11 February 1940 A crashed aircraft was found on the ice of Lake Ladoga, 2 km east of Järisevä. The aircraft was U-2 (c/n 15631) of 85th Liaison flight of 49th Infantry Division, the wounded pilot *lt* I.I. Mil'ner and navigator *kapitan* M.V. Yenukidze returned to their own lines.

85 AZv sv Commander   *kapitan* Basanov

There may have been still more Liaison Units supporting various infantry divisions.

Aviation Groups

Aviation Group Tkachenko *(Aviagruppa Tkachenko)*

Subordination
VVS 8.A

Combat chronicle
16 December 1939 12 fighter pilots from 5th Squadron of 49 IAP moved to Suojärvi (on occupied Finnish territory), and was named *AG Tkachenko*, directly attached to VVS 8.A.

10 fighter pilots from 2nd fighter Squadron of 72 SAP were also attached to the Aviation Group, which was commanded by *lt* A.G. Tkachenko (HSU 19 May 1940) and equipped with I-15bis fighters. Tasks of AG Tkachenko included reconnaissance flights and artillery fire control. Several hundred war missions were performed.

Kapitan A.G. Tkachenko (13 ORAP, 13. Air Army) with his Pe-2 Za Leningrad in 1944. He performed 175 combat missions, participated in 15 air combats and claimed one personal and four shared victories in GPW. (G.F. Petrov)

18 December 1939 Blenheim BL-118 (LLv 46, piloted by lentom *O. Räikkönen) was attacked by three I-15bis fighters at Hautalampi. MG-gunner V. Laukas reported an uncertain I-15bis kill.*

19 December 1939 on a reconnaissance flight Blenheim BL-121 (LLv 44, pilot kapt *E. Halme) was attacked at Korpiselkä-Tolvajärvi, but was able to escape. MG-gunner E. Pulliainen reported an uncertain I-15bis kill.*

4 January 1940 an I-15bis of 5th Squadron was shot down by Finnish A-A artillery at Aitokoski, *lt* V.P. Galitsin died of his wounds next day.

22 January 1940 *ml.lt* A.F. Rumyantsev (I-15bis, 5th Squadron) did not return from a mission.

13 February 1940 the commissar of 5th Squadron *st.politr* M.A. Kochmala (I-15bis) was killed in air combat at Värtsilä. Ya.F. Mikhin (AG Tkachenko/49 IAP) claimed a taran victory in his I-16 when he collided mid-air with a Finnish Fokker at Värtsilä. *Gladiators of LLv 26, led by Danish volunteer* Løjtnant *C.K. Kalmberg (GL-260) fought against 13 I-153 fighters which were escorting SB bombers. Alik Joensuu shot down an I-15 and Havuvaara, Korpiselkä, but also* Løjtnant *Kalmberg was killed, and another Dane,* Løjtnant *J. Ulrich (GL-257) force-landed.*

18 February 1940 *ml.lt* A.G. Dyatlov (72 SAP, ex 4 IAP) was killed when his I-15bis crashed at Vaksausjärvi after ground fire hits.

Lt *Yakov Mikhin's taran 13.2.1940 was described in Soviet pictorial Ogonëk. In the bottom photo on the left side the wreck of Danish volunteer Carl Kalmberg's Gladiator GL-260 is seen. (Finnish National Library)*

10 March 1940 *lt* N.I. Lozhkov (I-153) was killed in an accident at Suojärvi after engine malfunction.

A reconnaissance mission performed by *kapt* A.G. Tkachenko approximately 11 March 1940 enabled capture of Viipuri "the next day".

AG Tkachenko performed 2,363 combat missions, of which 689 ground attack and bombing missions, 193 bomber escort missions, 17 air combats, 368 supply dropping missions, 702 reconnaissance missions etc.

AG Tkachenko Command

Commander	*lt* A.K. Tkachenko (HSU 19.5.1940). In GPW commanded 13 ORAP.
Military Commissar	*st.politr* Goteyev

Aviation Group Filin *(Aviagruppa Filina)*

Aviagruppa Filina (or Northern Aviation Group of 9. Army) consisted of 145 IAP (with 23 I-15bis), a DB-3 flight (with 3 DB-3s) of 80 SAP and 33 VRE (with 6 R-5s). The Aviation Group supported 122nd Mountain Division of 9th Army in Salla-Kemijärvi direction. AG HQ arrived from 9 LShAP, and Squadrons were based in Kairala and Märkäjärvi.

18 January 1940 a fighter Squadron (14 I-16s) flew to Kairala.

AG Filina was also responsible for air defense of *AG Spirina* (set up in February 1940), based at Fedoseyevka ice base near Kandalaksha.

7 March 1940 *AG Filina* was dissolved, and the Squadrons were attached to *AG Spirina*. (See 80 SAP, 145 IAP and 33 VRE; pages 201, 206 and 223)

AG Filina Command

Commander	*polkovnik* V.M. Filin (1901–1966). In GPW commanded 55 SAD, deputy Commander of VVS 7.A in Karelia, Commander of 10 ShAK etc.
Military Commissar	*st.politr* Rulin
Chief of Staff	*polkovnik* Vorobyev

Polkovnik *V.G. Filin, Commander of AG Filin. (G.F. Petrov)*

237

Aviation Group Spirin *(Aviagruppa Spirina)*

Aviagruppa Spirina (or Special Aviation Group of 9th Army Air Force) was a special blind flying group founded late February 1940, located at Fedoseyevka ice base near Kandalaksha. The Aviation Group was commanded by the Head of the Air Navigation Faculty of the AF Academy in Moscow, *kombrig* I.T. Spirin (who had performed a legendary North Pole flight on 21 May 1937).

Spirin recruited several skilled specialists among academy personnel and student officers for his Aviation Group, which was directly attached to VVS 9.A as "Commander's reserve".

Initially *AG Filina* was responsible for air defense of the ice base, but later an I-16 Squadron was attached to *AG Spirina* (also responsible for Kandalaksha air defense).

AG Spirina Structure
- 12 DB-3 (from 1./80 SAP)
- 8 I-16 (from 145 IAP; C.O. Ledenev)
- 6 TB-3 (arrived 1 March 1940 from 1 TBAP)
- 5 SB (arrived 4 February 1940 from VVS Academy in Moscow, C.O. *polkovnik* Kutasin)
- 34 DRAE (arrived 29 January 1940 from VVS KOVO)

Combat Chronicle
24 February 1940 Kemijärvi was bombed.

7 March 1940 the Squadrons of the dissolved AG Filina were directly attached to AG Spirina.

7 March 1940 Swedish volunteer *fänrik* E. Theler (F19) shot down two SB bombers of 34 DRAE at Utajärvi. (See 34 DRAE, page 223)

10 March 1940 TB-3 c/n 22198 of 1 TBAP went missing. This TB-3 was shot down by Swedish volunteer *fänrik* G. Karlsson (F 19) and force-landed in Kemijärvi. Five aviators were killed and three taken prisoner.

AG Spirina performed some 200 combat missions 1–13 March 1940.

AG Spirina Command
Commander	*kombrig* I.T. Spirin (1898–1960. HSU 27.6.1937. In GPW commanded 9 GvBAK DD etc.
Military Commissar	*polk.komiss* Sukharev
Chief of Staff	*kapitan* Podkorytov

Kombrig I.T. Spirin in his office late autumn 1939. Note map of Finland on the wall. (G.F. Petrov)

Spirin took command of his Aviation Group in the far north in late February 1940. (G.F. Petrov)

Blind flying in Theory and Practise by William C. Ocker and Karl J. Crane was published in the USSR in 1937, edited by I.T. Spirin. The original was printed 1932 in San Antonio, Texas. (Finnish National Defence University)

Civil Air Fleet Special Aviation Group (OAG GVF)

In 1938 one of the first Heroes of Soviet Union, Polar aviator V.S. Molokov was appointed Head of the Soviet Civil Air Fleet (GVF). Molokov remained in this capacity until 1942.

12 December 1939 GU GVF (Main Administration of the Civil Air Fleet) was ordered to perform evacuation of wounded soldiers, transport of medical supplies, military equipment and supplies, fuel, high-ranking officers and medical personnel, newspapers and mail, and various liaison tasks.

Three special *otryady* (units) were formed: 1st in Petrozavodsk, 2nd in Uhtua and 3rd in Murmansk (the names of the various flight groups seem differ). Also 31st *otryad* in Leningrad was attached to this Special Air Group, which incorporated some 125 aircraft of various types (initially SP, S-1, PR-5, R-5, SKh-1, G-1, G-2, PS-7, PS-9, PS-43, PS-89, PS-40 and PS-84; later also U-2 and Ya-6). The Special Air Group was in operation until late March 1940. PS-9 aircraft were modified for ambulance operations, with seven stretchers or 5–6 sitting casualties.

Among the most renowned civil aviators in the Winter War was Aeroflot's Chief Pilot A.Ye. Golovanov (later first Commander of the Long-range Air Forces ADD from 1942), who flew 400 hours in DC-3, crew members M. Vaganov, N. Bajkuzov and K. Tomplon.

Other civil aviators were A.N. Yakovlev (who served in the Civil Liaison Flight of 49 IAP, HSU 20 May 1940), female aviator A.Ye. Adayeva, and polar aviators M.V. Vodopyanov and I.P. Mazuruk (who flew four-engine ANT-6 aircraft in 72 SAP).

Transport tasks performed by the Civil Air Fleet in the Winter War (10 December 1939–20 March 1940) include:
- troops transport:
- over 21,000 injured soldiers (or 15% of all patients evacuated), of which 40% were seriously injured
- 11,600 soldiers and officers
- over 1,000 medical personnel
- cargo transport:
- over 1,420 t, including:
- 164 t war material
- 462 t food stuff
- 227 t medicines (including over 3,000 litres of blood plasma).

More than 1,420 t cargo was dropped to troops surrounded in *mottis*, from which over 6,500 soldiers were evacuated by air.

Almost 10,700 sick and wounded soldiers were transported to Leningrad during the war, mostly with SP (ambulance variant of U-2 with various containers), and also PR-5, K-5 and DC-3.

License production of Douglas DC-3 (named PS-84) was initiated somewhat earlier. Several original DC-3s purchased in USA were also in use.

I.T. Spirin wrote also several of his own books, Polety v oblakah (Flying in clouds) in 1935 and Zapiski vojennogo letchika (Notes for a military pilot). (C-F. Geust, G.F. Petrov)

Aeroflot Chief Pilot Aleksandr Ye. Golovanov flew 400 hours in DC-3 coded UR-SS-D in the war. Golovanov, who commanded ADD from 1942, never received the Golden Star, and his highest decoration was Suvorov Order (1st Class) seen in the photo. (G.F. Petrov)

A Douglas DC-3 carrying a Soviet delegation landed 22.3.1940 in Hanko. According to the peace treaty Hanko with its surroundings was arrended to the USSR for establishment of a naval base. Note Douglas emblems and F-6 code. (SA-kuva)

Polar aviator V.S. Molokov (HSU 20.4.1934) headed the Civil Aviation Fleet (GVF). Molokov's career started in the Imperial Russian naval aviation station Granboda (Åland Islands) later during WWI. (G.F. Petrov)

For fast delivery of mail and "central newspapers" (*Pravda*, *Izvestiya* and *Krasnaya Zvezda*) from Moscow to Leningrad, and also to the remote Army headquarters in Petrozavodsk, Uhtua and Murmansk, a special fast aircraft *otryad* was organized in February 1940 with six PS-40 and one PS-41 courier aircraft (based on the SB bomber). The number of aircraft had grown to 13 (seven PS-40 and six PS-41) when the unit was disbanded 1 April 1940.

Known OAG GVF registrations:

K-5	SSSR-L584, SSSR-L607
PS-43	SSSR-L3000
DC-3	URSS-D (eight leaflet dropping missions to the Finnish rear)
	SSSR-L3400, SSSR-L3401, SSSR-L3407
MT-20	
	SSSR-M138
U-2 (SP)	SSSR-A1152
	SSSR-K267
	SSSR-L2624

240

PS-84 (licence-built DC-3, c/n 2114) SSSR-L3407 (registered 20.1.1940) transported high-ranking officers and wounded. (GA-archive)

Aeroflot PS-84 taking off for a courier flight. Note Aeroflot emblems, engine covers and GAZ-M1 staff car. (GA-archive)

241

One of the first PS-84s assembled in the USSR. The ski-equipped aircraft is apparently only coded SSSR under the right wing. (GA-archive)

Several of the few Kalinin K-5s manufactured were used as ambulance aircraft. K-5 (c/n 79; SSSR-L584, registered 19.8.1934) and a U-2 are seen at an ice base (or possibly Lodejnoje pole). (GA-archive)

Kalinin K-5 connected to an AS-2 starter (constructed on a GAZ-AAA chassis). The bus is apparently a ZiS-8. (GA-archive)

Kalinin K-5 SSSR-L607 (c/n 102; registered 19.8.1934) is taking off. (GA-archive)

A wounded soldier is brought to a Kalinin K-5. Note the civil-registered Tupolev G-2 (transport version of the TB-3 bomber). (GA-archive)

243

This and opposite page: S-3 (SSSR-L321_) and S-1 ambulance aircraft. Red Cross number "2" is subtype S-1 (note long stretcher space). (GA-archive)

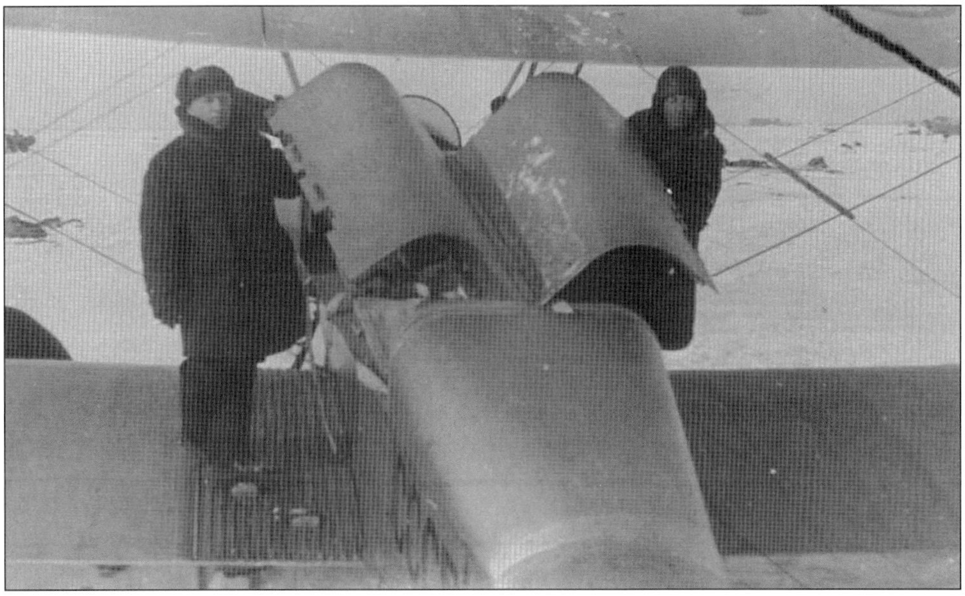

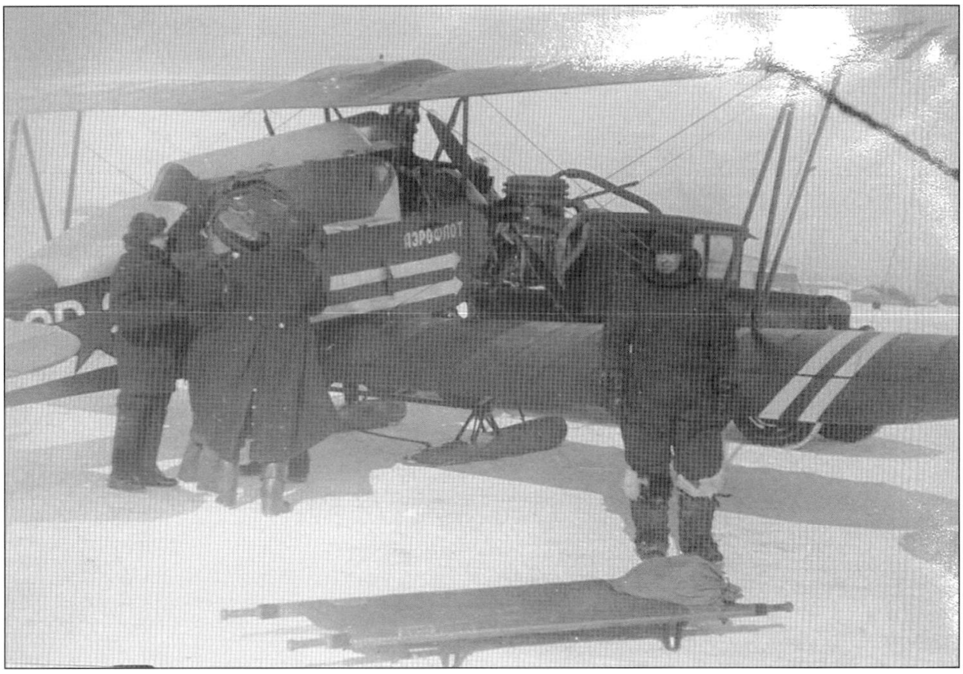
АЭРОФЛОТ

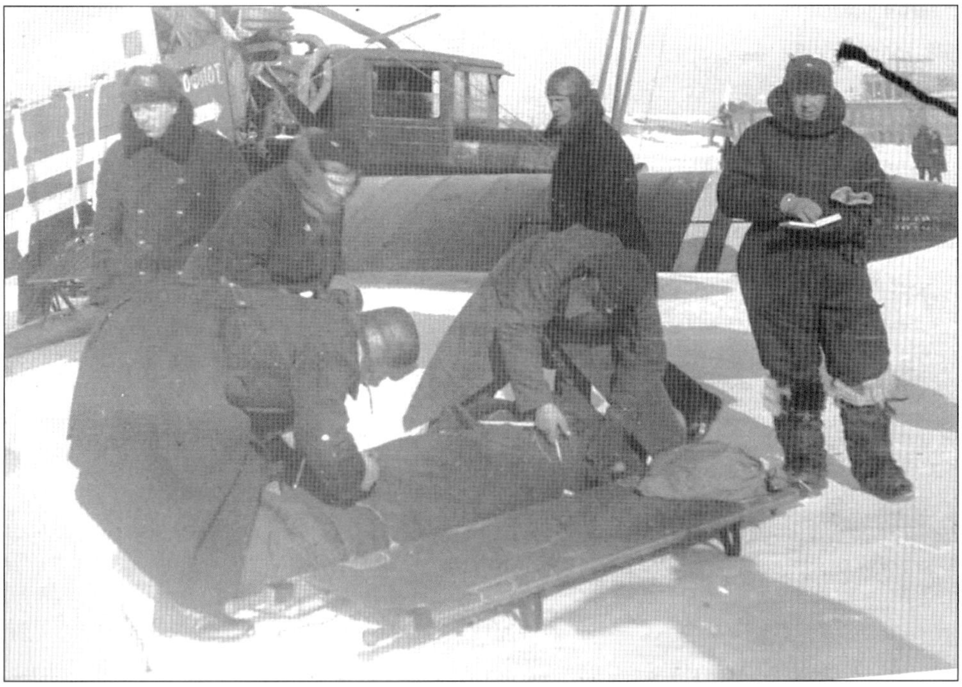

A number of ANT-9 were also used. SSSR-L113 (c/n 113) on skis is depicted (note: the photo was apparently taken during the cold-weather tests in winter 1931). (GA-archive)

PS-40 courier and passenger version of the SB-bomber, coded SSSR-L2469 (c/n 12/V, registered 23.11.1938). (G.F. Petrov)

1st Combined Aviation Unit of the Civil Air Fleet

This temporary unit was formed from aircraft of Civil Aviation Fleet (GVF) in Karelian ASSR. Strength six SSS and nine U-2, base in Petrozavodsk.

Later also a PS-9 was attached.

Subordination
VVS 8.A (from 19 December 1939)

2nd Special Unit of the Civil Air Fleet (2 OO GVF)

This temporary unit was also formed from aircraft of the Civil Aviation Fleet in Karelian ASSR. Strength some ten U-2 and a few PL-5 ambulance aircraft (carrying three wounded passengers), base in Uhtua. Ambulance flights were performed primarily between Uhtua and Alakurtti.

Subordination
VVS 8.A

Combat Chronicle
27 January 1940 2 OO GVF was ordered to drop supplies to 54th Mountain Division surrounded in Kuhmo.

7 February 1940 PL-5 (coded K-19) was shot down by ground fire at Savujärvi. Pilot V.A. Emerik and mechanic F.A. Volokitin were taken prisoner by Finnish units. On questioning the prisoners said that they departed from Saratov in early December 1939, and arrived in Petrozavodsk 20 December 1939. 1 January 1940 the crew flew to Leningrad, for ski undercarriage to be installed, after which they flew back to Uhtua via Petrozavodsk.

2 OO GVF Command

Commander	B.A. Konsulaki
	Zapylionov (late 1.1940)
Military Commissar	Chibisov (13.3.1940)
Chief of Staff	Plyaskin (13.3.1940)

3rd Special Unit of the Civil Air Fleet, also 3rd Combined Special Air Unit of the Civil Air Fleet (3 OO GVF)

This temporary unit was formed from the aircraft of the Kola peninsula Civil Aviation Fleet. Most aircraft were located in Murmansk.

Subordination
VVS 14.A

Strength 6 March 1940
- G-2   2
- PS-9   2
- PS-89   1
- PR-5   5
- SP   5
- S-1   1

PS-43 (Vultee) 1 (SSSR-L3000). Later transferred to 31 OAO in Leningrad.

3 OO GVF command

Commander	Zubarev
Military Commissar	Sychev
Chief of Staff	Pletashin

A civilian G-2 (ANT-6) transport aircraft is exchanging cargo with a horse-drawn sleigh. The last digits of the civilian registration is "41". Possibly L-3041, registered 23.4.1939 49648. (G.F. Petrov)

Baltic Fleet Air Force (VVS KBF)

VVS KBF Organisation

In autumn 1939 Red Banner Baltic Fleet Air Force (VVS KBF) consisted of three Aviation Brigades: **8 Bomber Aviation Brigade** (8 BAB), **61 Fighter Aviation Brigade** (61 IAB), three **Detached Maritime Close Reconnaissance Squadrons** (18, 41 and 58 OBRAE) and three **Detached Aviation Units** (71 OAO and the newly formed 12 and 44 OAO).

VVS KBF strength 30 November 1939 was 469 aircraft (246 I-15bis, I-16 and I-153 fighters in 61 IAB, 111 SB and DB-3 bombers in 8 BAB, 102 MBR-2 reconnaissance aircraft and 10 R-5 artillery fire correction aircraft), which considerably exceeded Finnish Air Force strength.

After the Soviet-Estonian treaty of 10 October 1939 **10 Aviation Brigade** (10 AB) was set up in Paldiski at the mouth of Gulf of Finland. The task of 10 AB was to enforce the blockade of Finnish ports and shipping. After several naval AF units had been relocated to Paldiski 10 AB became operative in mid-December 1939.

During the war Baltic Fleet AF got considerable reinforcements from the Black Sea Fleet (VVS ChF) and Pacific Fleet Air Forces (VVS TOF).

Baltic Fleet Air Force (VVS KBF) High Command
Commander   *Kombrig* (4.6.1940 *General-major*) V.V. Yermachenkov (1906–1963). In GPW
                   commanded VVS ChF etc.
Military Commissar *Brigadnyj komissar* L.N. Purnik (1901–1970).
Chief of Staff   *Major* A.I. Zenkin (to 20.12.1939, then CoS of VVS SF)
                   Polkovnik P.P. Kvade (from 20.12.1939). In GPW CoS of VVS ChF etc.

The border between the operational areas of Baltic Fleet AF and 7th Army AF on the Western Karelian Isthmus was 27° Eastern meridian (or approximately along Kotka–Hogland–Kiviöli, Estonia).

VVS KBF Commander V.V. Yermatshenkov. (G.F. Petrov)

VVS KBF operation area in the Winter War. Cities, harbours and coastal forts along the coast of the Gulf of Finlsnd and Lake Ladoga, and also railway junctions in southern Finland were bombed. Mines were dropped in the waters leading to Turku, Rauma and Pori ports. (RGAVMF)

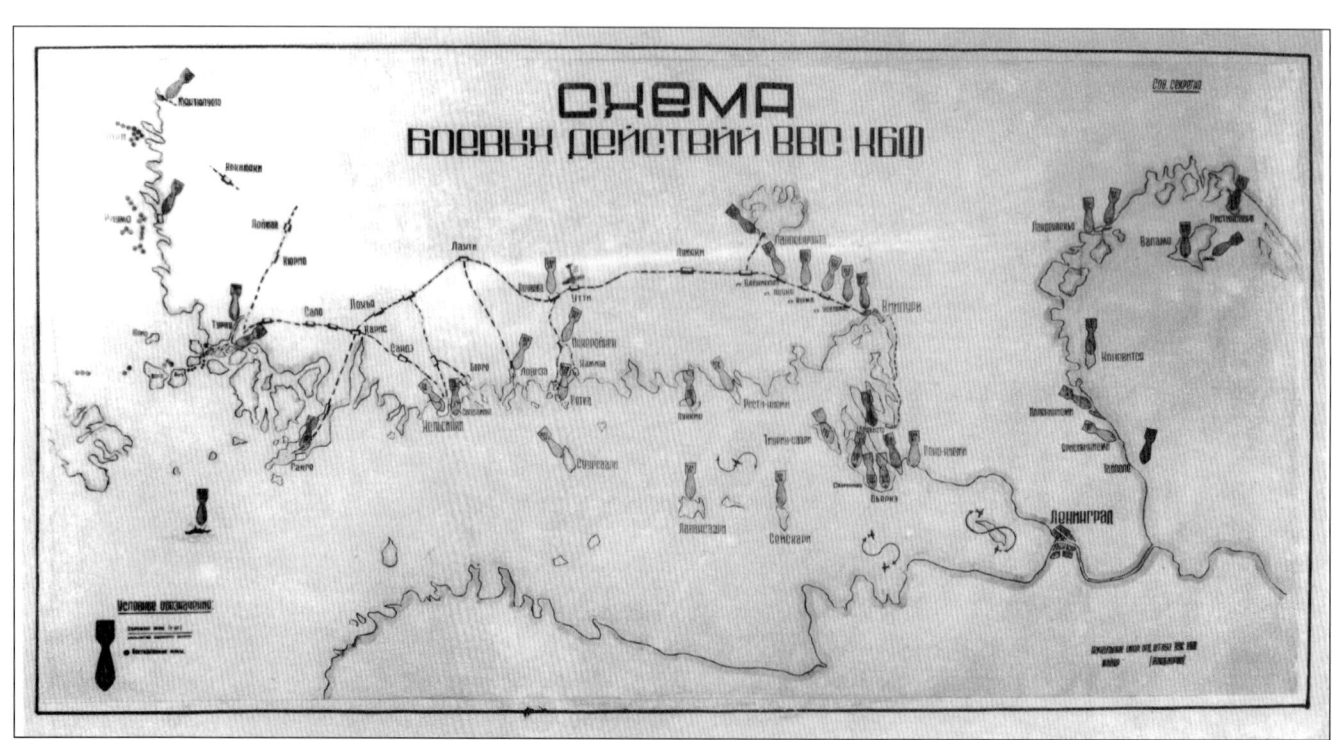

The main task was to maintain the blockade proclaimed by the Kremlin, including bombing and strafing of Finnish vessels, ports, coastal forts and shipping traffic. The explicit order was to prevent use of the vitally important transport route from Sweden by uninterrupted bombing of all ports in Western Finland and mine-dropping in the fairways. This order was fulfilled with rather moderate results only.

The first VVS KBF operation was support of the capture of the islands in the Gulf of Finland: Seiskari and Lavansaari (30 November 1939), Narvi and Someri (1 December 1939), Tytärsaari (2 December 1939) and finally Suursaari 3 December 1939. The islands were virtually empty as almost all the Finnish population and officials had already been evacuated in November 1939. Furthermore they were totally undefended – according to the Tartu peace treaty signed 14 October 1920 the islands were demilitarized.

Nevertheless Soviet Navy organized a unprecented (and unnecessary!) invasion fleet, consisting of 7 destroyers, 12 torpedo boats, 25 patrol boats, 16 transport ships and tugs, 5 transport ships and 28 auxiliary vessels. The massive navy flotilla was protected by AGON – aviation combat group consisting of 43 bombers, 70 fighters and 26 reconnaissance aircraft. The first day AGON performed 22 missions against Suursaari, where the northern lighthouse was set on fire and 20 buildings destroyed.

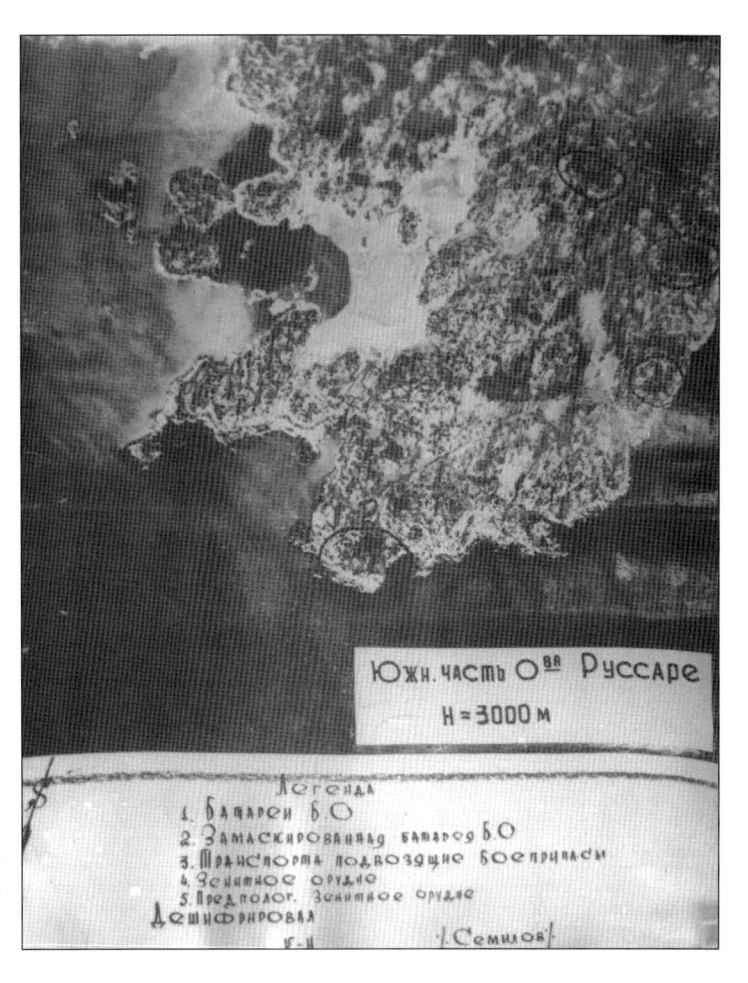

During the operation 30 November-3 December 1939 AGON performed 387 aircraft missions (of which on 30 November 1939 145 fighter and 41 bomber missions) and dropped 2,110 bombs (of which on 30 November 1939 1,052 bombs). "*The enemy did not show any resistance*".
Nevertheless Soviet naval aviation losses were serious: seven aviators killed, two I-15bis fighters, four SB bombers (another two SB bombers seriously damaged) and one R-5 reconnaissance aircraft lost.

Soviet reconnaissance photo of Fort Russarö. The locations of the the heavy coastal artillery guns are marked. (RGAVMF)

Soviet naval forces were badly prepared for combat operations, resulting in numerous cases of loss of orientation and misidentification. Several cases of fatal friendly fire were recorded: at Ruchi six SB bombers were fired upon by Soviet A-A artillery. Naval fighters forced down a SB-bomber of Leningrad Military District (LVO) at Veino after it was misidentified as a Junkers Ju 86(!). In an encounter between seven Soviet naval fighters and SB bombers 30 November 1939 an I-15bis of 12 OIAE was shot down (the pilot escaped by parachute).

17 December 1939 Baltic Fleet Commander V.F. Tributs issued orders to destroy Saarenpää 254 mm coast battery (at Koivisto) in combined attacks by surface ships and naval aviation. Turku and Rauma ports were to be destroyed by bombing attacks.

18–19 December 1939 8 BAB supported shelling of Saarenpää 254 mm coastal batteries by the battleships *Oktyarbrskaya Revolutsiya* and *Marat*, destroyers *Minsk*, *Steregushchiy*, *Karl Marks*, *Artem*, *Engels* and *Lenin*. On 18 December 1939 44 fighters and 22 bombers made 14 attacks and dropped 74 100–250 kg bombs and a large number of small bombs. Next day 35 bombers and 52 fighters made 33 attacks and dropped fifteen 1,000 kg bombs, 199 250–500 kg bombs, 338,100 kg bombs and almost 2,000 smaller bombs.

29 December 1939 People's Commissar N.G. Kuznetsov ordered VVS KBF to lay mine barrages in eleven fairwater points in the Finnish south-western archipelago. Mine laying was to be performed from Paldiski. Six DB-3s of 1 AP were to be appropriately equipped and transferred to 10 AB.

18 January 1940 32 fighters, 10 bombers and 32 reconnaissance aircraft protected icebreaker *Yermak* and the transport *Kazakhstan*, which were stuck in the ice. On the same day 22 SB bombers attacked the Finnish icebreaker *Tarmo* in Kotka harbour, dropping 30 bombs. *Tarmo* was seriously damaged. Next day a Finnish aircraft was forced down by 45 mm gun fire from submarine S-1.

The Baltic Fleet Air Force (VVS KBF) performed 16,663 combat missions (of which 991 were at night), and dropped 2,600 t bombs and 45 mines in the Winter War. VVS KBF claimed 65 Finnish aircraft downed in air combat, claimed 38 Finnish transports and military vessels sunk, delivered 68,500 t cargo and some 300 persons by air. Own losses were 59 aircraft (of which were 12 in combat) and 110 aviators. (According to the calculations of this author VVS KBF lost 97 aircraft, of which 42 were in combat. Flying personnel losses amounted to 110 naval aviators.

8th Bomber Aviation Brigade (8 BAB)

In November 1939 8 BAB had 111 SB-and DB-3 bombers, located at three bases between Leningrad and Koporskaya Guba (Kaprionlahti) on the southern shore of the Gulf of Finland.

8 BAB regiments:
- **1 Aviation Regiment (1 AP)**, later named **1 Mine-Torpedo Aviation Regiment (1 MTAP)** with DB-3b bombers in Bezzabotnoye,
- **57 Fast Bomber Aviation Regiment (57 SBAP)** with SB bombers in Kotly,
- **15 Maritime Bombing Aviation Regiment (15 MBAP)** which was soon separated from the Brigade, and converted into the separate **15 Detached Maritime Reconnaissance Regiment (15 OMRAP)** with two MBR-2 flying boat Squadrons in Grebnoy port, Leningrad; and one DB-3b Squadron in Koporye, which remained in 8 AB when the MBR-2 Squadrons were separated.

8 AB Command

Commander	*polkovnik* A.N. Sukhanov (1907–1978). In GPW commanded 8 BAB, which in July 1943 was converted into 8 MTAD. He served in the Allied Control Commission (ACC) in Romania from September 1944 to March 1945.
Military Commissar	*polk.komiss* N.S. Aleksandrov (1902–1964).
Chief of Staff	*major* B.K. Nevezhin

1st Aviation Regiment (1 AP)

1 AP was formed in autumn 1938 in Bezzabotnoye.

Strength late November 1939: three DB-3 Squadrons in Bezzabotnoye and one DB-3 Squadron in Koporye, total 60 DB-3.

29 November 1939 26 DB-3 bombers moved to Klopitsy, ready for attacks against the Finnish armoured ships *Ilmarinen* and *Väinämöinen*.

30 November 1939 at 0950 six DB-3s (led by *major* Ye.N. Preobrazhenskiy) started from Klopitsy, and searched for the Finnish armoured ships along the coast from Kotka to Turku. At Helsinki the bombers were countered by heavy A-A fire. The target was detected west of Hanko, and bombs were dropped from only 200 m altitude, but no hits were scored. The target location was transmitted by radio. *A considerable part of the Finnish naval fleet was at anchor at Högsåra:* Väinämöinen *and* Ilmarinen, *submarine depot ship* Suomen Joutsen *(former full-rigged school ship of the Finnish Navy), submarines*

Bezzabotnoye AF base 11.5.1940. (RGAVMF)

Ilmarinen *anchored near Turku. The exceptionally heavy armament and fire control system of the armoured ship significantly improved the air defence of Turku, and was a dangerous target for Soviet bombers. (SA-kuva)*

Vetehinen *and* Iku-Turso *and several gun and patrol boats. The bombs were in fact dropped from 3,000 m altitude, but only* Ilmarinen *was hit by bomb splinters. The Finnish ships opened fire on the bombers with their efficient anti-aircraft armament: 105 mm Bofors cannons and 40 mm guns.*

At 1320 eight DB-3s of 3rd Squadron (led by *major* N.A.Tokarev) flew towards the reported location, and reached there at 1510 hours but it was now empty. Tokarev's bombers turned back and bombed the reserve target, the western port of Helsinki and Hietalahti (Sandvikens) Shipyard. Fifteen 500 kg and thirty 100 kg bombs were dropped from 1,500 m altitude. A big fire was observed near the shipyard: several buildings (including Helsinki Technical University), fuel tanks and two mine-layers were burning. *Several bombs fell on downtown Helsinki apartment blocks, killing 91 civilians and 200 persons were wounded. The port and ships got only minor damage. As an ironic twist of fate the Soviet Embassy in Helsinki was also badly hit. The Soviet diplomats had left Finland 3 December 1939 on board the German S/S Donau.*

1 AP suffered also heavy losses: two DB-3b bombers did not return, apparently shot down by Finnish anti-aircraft artillery. At take-off from Klopitsy one DB-3 (carrying three FAB-500 bombs) crashed into an ammunition store. In the resulting explosions six persons were killed and 29 injured, Klopitsy command post was destroyed and two DB-3s, two I-15s, one R-5 and one U-2 seriously damaged. A SB and a DB-3 (originally of 15 OMRAP) crashed at landing in Koporye (DB-3 pilot and navigator were killed, the gunner was injured).

10 December 1939 nine aviators from 35 OBAE (in Yevpatoria at the Black Sea) were sent to Moscow to ferry three new DB-3s to 1 AP. The first two DB-3s arrived in Bezzabotnoye 17 December 1939.

After this the ports of Turku, Hanko, Rauma and Pori, and the Finnish coastal batteries were repeatedly bombed by 1 AP.

26 December 1939 one DB-3 was downed by the Saarenpää 40 mm Bofors A-A battery, all crew were killed (one aviator was seen escaping by parachute).

In January 1940 1 AP was directed to support 7th Army on the Karelian isthmus and to bomb Finnish coastal batteries (Koivisto, Rononiemi, Pukkio etc) and Pentikkälä railway station.

Six DB-3s were equipped for minedropping, and transferred to 10 AB in Klooga/Paldiski. (See 10 AB, page 268) 12 January 1940 the main part of 1 AP was relocated from Bezzabotnoye to Koporye.

18 February 1940 Simola railway station south of Lappeenranta was bombed. Two DB-3 bombers were intercepted and shot down by Finnish fighters over the target, while a third was badly damaged and crashed 12 km NE Narvi lighthouse. One pilot bailed out and was taken prisoner near Simola, while the navigator and gunner were killed, as were the entire crew of the second bomber. The crew of the third bomber was rescued by an MBR-2 which landed on the ice. The pilot was wounded, but the MG-gunner was killed in the air. *LLv 24 scored three victories with Fokker D.XXI fighters at Simola-Vainikkala; pilots were* luutn *J. Sarvanto (FR-100),* lentom *Y. Turkka (FR-83) and* kers *E. Kinnunen (FR-109).*

19 February 1940 Lappeenranta was bombed by 3rd Squadron. On approach to Lappeenranta the DB-3s were attacked six times by 14 Fokker D.XXIs. Squadron leader N.A.Tokarev returned on one engine after air combat damage. Six Finnish fighters were claimed by DB-3 gunners protecting Tokarev's

Major *Vedernikov* (1 AP Head of Intelligence) planning a bombing attack on Ristniemi coastal fort. (G.F. Petrov)

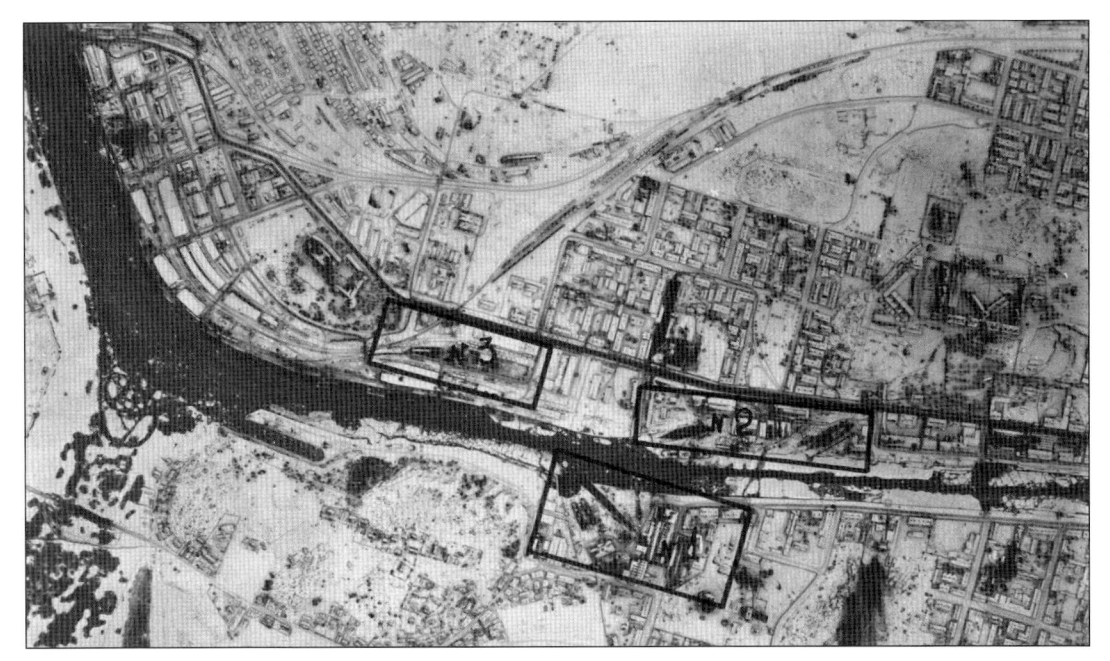

Photo from 3,300 m altitude of Turku 12.1.1940, with the target areas indicated. (RGAVMF)

Photo of Turku 14.2.1940. (RGAVMF)

damaged aircraft. *Only one Fokker D.XXI of LLv 24 was lost: Danish volunteer* Løjtnant *E. Frijs (in FR-80) was killed by MG-fire from a Soviet DB-3, and crashed in Heinjoki.*

2 March 1940 the Finnish armoured ships were attacked by 19 DB-3 and 9 SB bombers (from 8 and 10 AB), escorted by 19 fighters. The SB bombers were first to eliminate the ships' A-A artillery, after which DB-3s should drop their heavy bombs. The SB bombers dropped several small bombs from high altitude on the ships, scoring one 100 kg bomb hit. The bombers were intercepted by twelve Finnish fighters, which shot down one SB which crashed at Hanglax, Lill-Nagu, killing the crew, and one I-153 escort fighter, which force-landed on the ice near Örö (the pilot was killed when resisting capture by Finnish troops). The only lightly damaged I-153 was retrieved by Finnish troops, which were attacked by three Soviet fighters killing one Finnish soldier.

The DB-3s only arrived at the target area 18 minutes later (instead of the intended 3–4 minutes), and dropped fifteen 500 kg and forty-one 250 kg bombs from 4,500 m altitude on the ships without direct hits. One DB-3 was hit by the 105 mm A-A artillery and crashed at Kakskerta killing the crew, while six "Brewsters"(!) were claimed by the Soviet fighters. One seriously wounded aviator of this DB-3 bailed out by parachute but perished later. Both MG-gunners of another DB-3 were killed in the air. *34 bombers were observed over Turku in three waves, 345 bombs were recorded. The SB was shot down by* vänr *P. Massinen (LLv 28) in MS-318, while* kapt *E. Jutila (MS-316) and* vänr *P. Reinikainen (MS-317) shared the I-153 victory. Brewsters had not yet arrived to Finland! No Finnish aircraft were lost at Turku 2 March 1940.*

253

1 AP organisation 20 January 1940

Squadron	Aircraft	Base
1st	10 DB-3b	Klopitsy
2nd and 4th	14 DB-3b	Bezzabotnoye
3rd	8 DB-3b	Kotly
5th	6 DB-3b	Koporye
Not serviceable	18 DB-3	
Transport and liaison aircraft	7 R-6, 1 UT-1 and 7 U-2	

1 AP Command

Commander	*polk* V.P. Vorobyev (to 30.12.1939)
	major S.B. Bidzinashvili (to August 1940)
Military Commissar	*voyenkom st.politr* P.P. Bushikhin (to 17.12.1939)
	polk.komiss R.I. Erenprajs (from 17.12.1939)
Chief of Staff	*major* G.S. Peresada
Squadron C.O. and Commissars	
1st Squadron	*kapitan* V.A. Golub'
	st.politr P.A. Redkov
2nd Squadron	*kapitan* P.P. Popok (to end-January 1940)
	kapitan M.A. Babushkin (from end-January 1940)
	st.politr S.S. Mozgachev
3rd Squadron	*major* N.A. Tokarev (HSU 21.4.40)
	st.politr N.P. Ivanov
4th Squadron	*major* Ye.N. Preobrazhenskiy (to 1.1.40)
	kapitan G.K. Belyayev (from 1.1.40)
	batl.komiss G.I. Soloshchenko
5th Squadron	*kapitan* A.I. Ivanov (from 15 OMBAP 19.12.39)
	st.politr A.B. Kulev (to mid-January 1940)
	st.politr A.I. Polenov (from mid-January 1940)

1 AP Commander major S.B. Bidzinashvili. (G.F. Petrov)

Major N.A. Tokarev, Commander of 3rd Squadron, 1 AP. (G.F. Petrov)

Navigation skill in 1 AP was clearly insufficient. Numerous cases of loss of orientation and bombing of own territory are reported (for instance the coast-artillery batteries at Krasnaya Gorka, own AF base and Kikerino railway station near Krasnogvardejsk – now Gatchina – were bombed). Repeated cases of technical malfunctions and human errors (such as wrongly set trimmers etc.) resulted in tragical catastrophies. 1 MTAP lost 17 bombers (of which 9 in combat) and 40 aviators (or almost 40% of all VVS KBF human losses!).

Contemporary Russian historians are honestly admitting that the unprovoked bombing on 30 November 1939 of the undefended Finnish capital led to international protests against the aggression, after which Soviet Union was expelled from the League of Nations on 14 Decmber 1939. Because of the unsuccessful operations (and in particular the major loss of Soviet international prestige resulting from the bombing of Helsinki) 1 AP Commander *polkovnik* V.P. Vorobyev was on 30 December 1939 replaced with *major* S.B. Bidzinashvili.

DB-3 piloted by kapitan V.A. Golub, shot down 2.3.1940 by Ilmarinen's A-A artillery. The DB-3 crashed at Kakskerta near Turku. (C-F. Geust)

254

The personel of Red Banner-decorated 3rd Squadron of 1 AP, major Tokarev sitting in the middle. (G.F. Petrov)

Nevertheless *major* N.A. Tokarev was on 21 April 1940 decorated with the Golden Star, and his 3rd Squadron, which performed 46 missions, dropped 320 t bombs and claimed 11 enemy aircraft, was the same day awarded Red Banner Order (it is remarkable that 1 AP as such was **NOT** decorated).

In this context the official history of VMF (*Boevaya letopis Voenno-Morskogo Flota 1917–1941*, Moskva 1993) writes incorrectly that *the [30 November 1939] attack forced the Finnish government to hastily escape to Vaasa*. The Finnish government in fact stayed in Helsinki during the entire Winter War, but on early morning 1 December 1939 the Finnish parliament moved to Kauhajoki, staying there until 12 February 1940.

In June 1940 1 AP participated in the *Soviet occupation of Estonia* (these words are exceptionally used in the 768-page history of the Russian Naval Air Forces (*P.V. Levshov, D.Je. Boltenkov: Vek v Stroju VMF – Aviatsija Vojenno-Morskogo Flota Rossii 1910–2010*), published in 2012.

Then 1 AP became guilty of another international incident: 14 June 1940 two DB-3b bombers, led by *polkovnik* Bidzinashvili shot down a Finnish Ju-52/3m airliner *Kaleva* (OH-ALL) on a scheduled flight from Tallinn to Helsinki. All persons onboard *Kaleva*, crew consisting of *Aero OY* Chief pilot Bo von Willebrand, radio operator Tauno Launis and seven passengers including two French diplomats (Paul Longuet and Frederic Marty), two German businessmen (Friedrich Offermann and Rudolf Cöllen) and US diplomat Henry William Antheil were killed (see page 328).

The second international scandal of 1 AP within less than one year (!) led once more to the dismissal of the regiment commander, and in August 1940 *polkovnik* Bidshinashvili was replaced by *major* Tokarev (who apparently was considered a very competent officer, as he was appointed regiment Commander despite the bombing of Helsinki 30 November 1939).

Junkers Ju 52/3m OH-ALL Kaleva was shot down 14.6.1940 by two DB-3 bombers of 1 AP shortly after take-off from Tallinn. All nine persons on board on the scheduled flight to Helsinki were killed. (C-F. Geust)

57th Aviation Regiment (57 AP)

57 Aviation Regiment (57 AP) was formed in autumn 1938 and based in Kotly and Bezabotnoye, equipment with SB bombers and a few R-6 transport and U-2 liaison aircraft. Strength 27 November 1939: 48 SB bombers in Kotly.

In summer 1939 57 AP was attached to 8 AB. In the tense situation in autumn 1939 57 AP got the important task of surveillance of the Gulf of Finland and Baltic Sea, and especially keeping track of the Finnish armoured ships *Väinämöinen* and *Ilmarinen*.

26 October 1939 as already mentioned two SB bombers led by *kapitan* V.I. Rakov located *Väinämöinen* and *Ilmarinen* at anchor near Nagu (in the archipelago between Turku and Åland island).

30 November 1939 at 1136 hours 2nd Squadron (led by *kapitan* Rakov) attacked Santahamina naval AF base (south-east of downtown Helsinki), bombing from 400–500 m altitude. The base was empty, but one aircraft hangar and some other buildings were destroyed. *One barrack was hit, 15 soldiers died.*

The other Squadrons were attached to AGON for the Suursaari operation. Two SB bombers did not return, while another three SB were damaged by their own bombs and force-landed. An 8 kg bomb of

Kapitan V.I. Rakov (Commander of 2./57 AP) in the open cockpit of his SB-bomber. G.F. Petrov)

A "flagman" giving take-off permission to an SB bomber. G.F. Petrov)

Kotly AF base 15.5.1940. (RGAVMF)

an SB exploded under the bomber, causing serious damage (some 50 splinter holes were counted) and killing the MG-gunner. In a similar accident another SB got 98 splinter holes, fortunately both aircraft were able to return.

14 December 1939 a SB of 4th Squadron lost its orientation on a ferry flight from Koporye to Kotly in snowstorm and crashed at Kempolovo (near Klopitsy); all crew were killed.

19 December 1939 1st and 2nd Squadrons of 57 AP (14 SB bombers, commanded by *kapitan* Rakov and *kapitan* A.I. Krokhalev respectively) and three I-153 fighters of 61 IAB flew to Klooga (Paldiski) from Kotly.

5 January 1940 the SB Squadrons were formally attached to 10 AB, and formed 1 and 2 OSBAE.

57 AP was now split into parts, the main part operating in the eastern part of Gulf of Finland, while two Squadrons (1 and 2 OSBAE, subordinated to 10 AB) operated against Finnish ports and shipping at the mouth of Gulf of Finland.

5th Squadron (five SB bombers, commanded by *kapitan* M.N Khrolenko) and five MBR-2 of 58 AE were attached to 41 MBRAE of the Ladoga flotilla.

29 January 1940 two SB bombers crashed: one at Koporye (the pilot *major* Osipov was flight inspector of VVS TOF), and the second 5 km east of Långviran (30 km north of Suursaari). The MG-gunner was taken prisoner, the other aviators were killed. A third SB of 57 AP did not return.

2 February 1940 one SB on a photo reconnaissance mission was forced down by two "Fokker D.XXI fighters" on the ice between Someri and Narvi (within the range of Finnish coastal batteries). One of the Fokkers was claimed shot down by the MG-gunner. The force-landed bomber was detected by *st.lt* A.I. Nefedov (12 OIAE) in an I-15bis, who alerted an MBR-2 piloted by *kapitan* A.A. Gubriy (18 AE). Gubriy landed on the ice and evacuated the stranded crew to Oranienbaum (pilot *lt* G.S. Pinchuk, face burned; navigator *st.lt* V.M. Kharlamov, unhurt; and MG-gunner *st.ser.* A.I. Belogurov, lightly wounded). All three crew members of the SB were appointed HSUs 7 February 1940, and Nefedov and Gubriy both became HSUs 21 April 1940. *Pinchuk's SB was apparently shot down by Danish volunteer Løjtnant. J.Ulrich of LLv 26 in Gladiator GL-259. Ulrich's prey was seen burning at Suursaari.*

29 February 1940 ten SB bombers of 1st Squadron bombed Kouvola railway junction. Several hits on station buildings, trains and the railway yard were observed. The attacking bombers were intercepted by Finnish "Fokker D.XXI fighters" *(in fact FIATs of LLv 26)*. Two escorting I-153s (12 OIAE) were damaged in air combat at Kouvola. One SB-bomber crash-landed on the ice in the Gulf of Finland near

Someri after both engines were hit. The crew were evacuated by Squadron C.O. *st.lt* F.N.Radus who landed with his SB near the force-landed bomber (Radus got the Golden Star on 21 April 1940). *Lt U. Nieminen (FA-13, LLv 26) shot down an SB-bomber south of Kotka.*

57 AP Command

Commander	*major* S.I. Snetkov, to 1.1.1940.
	major Ye.N. Preobrazhenskiy (1909–1963), from 1.1.40. (1909–1963). Bombed Berlin 7–8.8.41, HSU 13.8.1941. Commanded VVS SF 1944–1945, VVS TOF 1946–1950, then commanded Soviet Naval Air Forces until 1962.
Military Commissar	*batl.komiss* A.S. Miroshnichenko
Head of Staff	*kapitan* N.Ye. Cherkashin

Squadron C.O. and Commissars

1st Squadron	(5.1.40 to 10 AB)
	kapitan B.B. Romanov (to 14.1.40)
	st.lt F.N. Radus (from 14.1.40), HSU 21.4.40.
	batl.komiss S.V. Lapshenkov
2nd Squadron (5.1.1940 to 10 AB)	
	kapitan V.I. Rakov (HSU 7.2.40 and 22.7.44)
	st.politr N.F. Polyakov
3rd Squadron	*kapitan* S.I. Smol'kov
	st.politr P.I. Resnyanskiy
4th Squadron	*kapitan* V.F. Gusev
	st.politr
5th Squadron (25 December 1939 to 41 OMRAE)	
	kapitan M.N. Khrolenko
	st.politr M.A. Gurevich

After the Winter War the regiment denomination was changed to 57 SBAP (57 Fast Bomber Aviation Regiment).

In GPW 57 SBAP was converted to a ground attack regiment with Il-2 *Shturmovik* aircraft as 57 PShAP (57 Dive Ground Attack Aviation Regiment) and was also nucleus for the new 73 BAP. Both 57 PShAP and 73 BAP were elevated to Guards status as 7 GvPShAP and 12 GvBAP (on 1 March 1943 and 22 January 1944 respectively). *Podpolkovnik* Rakov commanded 12 GvBAP in summer 1944, and led the sinking of the German A-A cruiser *Niobe* (ex Dutch *Gelderland*, then mistakenly identified as *Väinämöinen*) in the port of Kotka 16 July 1944. Rakov got his second Golden Star decoration 22 July 1944.

St.politr P.I. Resnyanskiy giving preflight instructions to 3rd squadron of 57 AP. (G.F. Petrov)

11th Detached Fighter Aviation Squadron (11 OIAE)

11 OIAE was formed in April 1939 in Kummolovo (subordinated to 61 IAB).
Strength 27 November 1939: 16 I-16 and 7 I-15bis fighters.
In late January 1940 11 OIAE was transferred to 10 AB in Paldiski.

11 OIAE tasks:
Seiskari, Someri, Suursaari and Lavansaari landing operations   237 missions
Strafing of enemy positions, railway stations, road transports, population centres and batteries (eg. Koivisto 2.2.1940, Ristiniemi 20.2.1940)   138 missions
Escort and protection of KBF bombers   209 missions
11 OIAE missions, total   **584 missions**

One pilot was lost: 2 March 1940 *ml.lt* A.M. Ivanov in I-153 c/n 6165 was shot down in air combat with two Moranes of LLv 28 (*kapt* E. Jutila and *vänr* P. Reinikainen, MS-316 and 317) at Örö. After crash-landing on the ice Ivanov was killed at capture.

Four of the best fighter pilots of VVS KBF, from left: 12 OIAE Commander, major A.A. Denisov; 5./5 IAP Commander, major B.I. Mikhailov; 13 IAP Commander major I.G. Romanenko and kapitan Shugayev. Denisov and Romanenko were appointed HSU 21.4.1940. (G.F. Petrov)

I-15bis was one of the most common fighters of VVS KBF in the Winter War. (G.F. Petrov)

11 OIAE Command

Commander	*kapitan* V.V. Antipov
Military Commissar	*st.politr* K.T. Kapshuk
Chief of Staff	*kapitan* M.G. Shapovalov

At the end of the Winter War only 12 I-16 fighters and 23 pilots remained in 11 OIAE, which returned to 61 IAB.

12th Detached Fighter Aviation Squadron (12 OIAE)

Major *A.A. Denisov*, 12 OIAE Commander. (G.F. Petrov)

In February 1939 12 OIAE was formed in Lipovo, equipped with I-15bis fighters. In December 1939 one flight of 12 OIAE was attached to 10 AB.

12 OIAE tasks

Protection of Seiskari, Someri and Suursaari, and Suursaari landing operations	122 missions
Weather reconnaissance, enemy position and truck transport attacks	93 missions
Bombing of enemy coastal batteries and ships	76 missions
Strafing of enemy fire positions, truck transports, ships, AF bases and batteries (eg. Saarenpää coast battery 14.12 and 23.12 1939, Koivisto and Humaljoki 18.1.1940, Koivisto 4.2.1940, Rononiemi 20.2.1940)	188 missions
Interception of enemy fighters at Simola railway junction	15 missions
Bomber escort (8 AB and VVS RKKA; five Fokker D.XXIs and one Bulldog claimed in air combat)	574 missions
Escort of SB bombers and MBR-2 fire control and photo reconnaissance aircraft	120 missions
Photo reconnaissance of enemy positions	16 missions
Protection of own bombers (eg. Lappeenranta 19.2.1940, Utti 20.2.1940)	18 missions
Relocation of AF bases	16 missions
12 OIAE missions, total	**1,249 missions**

30 November 1939 an I-15bis was shot down by MG-gunners in air combat between three SB bombers and seven naval fighters, the pilot escaped by parachute.

14 December 1939 despite the poor weather I-15bis fighters performed separate reconnaissance and strafing of Saarenpää. One I-15bis was lost on the return leg and crashed at Voronino, killing the pilot. A second I-15bis was hit by A-A artillery at Saarenpää and crash-landed in Lipovo. I-15bis flight of 12 OIAE landed at the new base at Klooga base (7 km from Paldiski).

Utti AF base was strafed 7 and 20 January 1940, resulting in considerable damage (hangars and fuel tanks set on fire etc.). Two Finnish aircraft were claimed destroyed on the ground 20 January 1940

19 February 1940 three Finnish Fokker fighters were claimed in air combat in Vainikkala-Vilajoki area when escorting DB-3 bombers of 1 AP to Lappeenranta.

1 March 1940 Utti AF base was strafed by 13 IAP and 12 OIAE fighters, eleven (!) Finnish aircraft (seven Fokker D.XXIs and four Bristol Bulldogs) were claimed destroyed. *On 1 March 1940 Utti AF base was empty – all aircraft were dispersed to well-camouflaged temporary bases.*

12 OIAE Command

Commander	*st.lt* S.A. Gladchenko
	major A.A. Denisov (1907–1976). HSU 21.4.1940
Military Commissar	*batl.komiss* N.M. Kosorukov (1913–1942)
Chief of Staff	*kapitan* N.Ye. Kovshirov

On 21 April 1940 12 OIAE was awarded Red Banner Order. Major Denisov, *st.lt* A.I. Nefedov (WIA 29 February 1940) and *lt* S.M. Shuvalov were decorated with the Golden Star.

In GPW 12 OIAE was 22 October 1943 expanded to 12 IAP.

13th Detached Fighter Aviation Squadron (13 OIAE)

In February 1939 13 OIAE was formed in Kuplya, equipped with I-15bis fighters. In December 1939 13 OIAE was attached to 10 AB with 34 I-16 fighters.

30 November 1939 while strafing Seiskari one I-15bis hit its own propeller because of a defective gun synchronizer, and crashed into the Gulf of Finland (the pilot was rescued).

19 December 1939 the battleship *Marat* shelled Saarenpää battery. Saarenpää was also bombed by 52 fighters and 35 bombers. Six I-16 and I-15bis fighters (13 OIAE) were damaged by the A-A fire. *Despite the massive attacks the battery suffered only minor damage, two soldiers were killed and four were wounded.*

18 January 1940 Several I-15bis (12 and 13 OIAE) fighters strafed Koivisto, Humaljoki and Penttilä railway station.

29 January 1940 one I-15bis crash-landed on the ice in the Narvi-Someri area after A-A hits (apparently at Koivisto). The wreck was set on fire.

4 February 1940 the batteries at Koivisto were strafed by fighters of 12 and 13 OIAE. One I-15bis fighter was destroyed when crash-landing in fog at Kurgolovo.

19 February 1940 Lappeenranta was bombed by 3rd AE/1 AP. Three escorting fighters (12 and 13 OIAE) were damaged in air combat at Vainikkala-Vilajoki.

Kapitan G.P. Gubanov, Commander of 13 OIAE (HSU 21.4.1940). (G.F. Petrov)

On 30.11.1939 the I-16 fighters of 13 OIAE were decorated with patriotic slogans. The I-16 tactical 11 of squadron commander major A.A. Gubanov was inscribed Svobodu udnetennym! (Freedom to the oppressed!) on the starboard side and Za VKP(b)! (For the Bolshevik party!) on the port side. (RGAVMF)

13 OIAE tasks

Protection of Suursaari landing operation, own troops and ships	122 missions
Reconnaissance of enemy troops and aircraft at Viipuri and Virolahti	9 missions
Strafing of enemy ground objects (eg. Koivisto battery, 4 and 13.2.1940)	661 missions
Attacks against enemy ships at Koivisto and water area east of Kuutsalo	40 missions
Bomber escort (8 AB and VVS RKKA; eg. Lappeenranta 19.2.1940)	629 missions
Escort of photo reconnaissance aircraft (four Gladiators claimed) and weather reconnaissance	202 missions
13 OIAE missions, total	**1,661 missions**

Four enemy aircraft claimed downed and several enemy anti-aircraft positions destroyed. 13 OIAE suffered no personnel losses, but several I-15bis and I-16 fighters were damaged by ground fire and destroyed in force-landings.

13 OIAE Command

Commander *kapitan* G.P. Gubanov (1908–1973). HSU 21.4.1940
Military Commissar *batl.komiss* I.I. Volosevich (1909–1941). HSU 21.4.1940.
Chief of Staff *st.lt* D.V. Likhatsiy

21 April 1940 13 OIAE was awarded Red Banner Order.
In GPW 13 OIAE was 21 November 1942 expanded to 13 IAP (note: this was a "new" 13 IAP, as the previous 13 IAP had already 18 January 1942 converted to 4 GvIAP).

St.lt Boruzdin's I-16 tactical 13 was inscribed Za kommunizm! *(For Communism!). (RGAVMF)*

Novikov's I-16 tactical 3 was inscribed Za konstitutsii SSSR! *(For the Soviet Constitution!). (RGAVMF)*

262

The I-15bis of bat.komiss I.I. Volosevich (HSU 21.4.1940) was inscribed Za Stalina! (For Stalin!), (RGAVMF)

61st Fighter Aviation Brigade (61 IAB)

61 IAB was formed in April 1939 in Kotly. 30 November 1939 61 IAP HQ was located in Novyj Petergof.

61 IAP fighter units:
- 5 IAP (Nizino, 39 I-16)
- 13 IAP (Kotly, 42 I-16)
- 11 OIAE (Kummolovo, 22 I-16; and a MBR-2 flying boat flight)
- 12 OIAE (Lipovo, 25 I-15)
- 13 OIAE (Kuplya, 34 I-16).

In December 1939 11, 12 and 13 OIAE were dispatched to 10 AB in Klooga (Paldiski).

Fighter pilots of 5 IAP, from left to right: kapitan P.G. Artemyev (KIA at Rononiemi 14.2.1940), st.lt I.P. Borisov, bat.komiss A.V. Bondarenko and Bashkirov. (G.F. Petrov)

263

61 IAB tasks:
- Protection of KBF main base (Kronstadt), ships and troop transports at Suursaari, Lavansaari, Someri Tytärsaari and Seiskari
- Reconnaissance and strafing of roads, enemy troops, population centres, trains, bridges and fire positions
- Weather reconnaissance in own operation area, air photography of enemy objects
- Escort of 8 AB, 15 ORAP and VVS LVO bombers, strafing of enemy A-A positions
- Escort of 8 AB and 15 ORAP photo reconnaissance aircraft and 71 ORAO fire control aircraft
- Protection of U-2 and MBR-2 aircraft during rescuing of aviators force-landed in enemy held territory
- Escort of R-5 aircraft carrying VVS KBF high commanders
- Independent strafing and bombing missions
- Air combat with enemy fighters

61 IAB 10,141 missions, of which 435 nighttime

61 AB Command

Commander	*polkovnik* A.M. Morozov (1905–1942)
Military Commissar	*polk.komiss* V.M. Pankov
Chief of Staff	*major* V.I. Sokolov

Three fighter pilots of 13 IAP, in the middle kapitan V.M. Savchenko (HSU 21.4.1940) in front of a cannon-equipped I-16 tip 17. (G.F. Petrov)

13 IAP Commander major I.G. Romanenko is planning operations together with his deputy major P.V. Kondratyev. Note the Stalin statue in the background! Both Romanenko and Kondratyev became HSU 21.4.1940. (G.F. Petrov)

Posed photo of 13 IAP fighter pilots. (G.F. Petrov)

I-16 fighters of 13 IAP lined up for inspection, summer 1940. (G.F. Petrov)

5th Fighter Aviation Regiment (5 IAP)

5 IAP was formed in Nizino in April 1939. A special I-16 Squadron manned by experienced fighter pilots participated in August 1939 in the Khalkin-Gol campaign in Mongolia.

5 IAP strength and dislocation

Squadron	Aircraft	Base
1st-4th	54 I-16, 10 I-15, 2 I-153 (from 30.1.1940), 23 I-15bis, 3 I-5, 6 UTI-4, 4 UT-2 and 2 U-2.	Nizino
5th	10 I-15bis	Byche Pole

6 December 1939 eight patrolling I-15bis (5 AP) were caught in a snowstorm, three fighters crashed on landing at Gorskaya and Nizino.

On 18 December 1939 the battleship *Oktyabrskaya Revolyutsiya* shelled Saarenpää coastal battery with 209 explosive projectiles. The attack was preceded by strafing of AA-batteries at Koivisto by six I-15bis fighters. Three I-15s got up to 20 bullet holes from accurate A-A fire. 44 fighters and 22 bombers attacked Saarenpää, dropping fourteen 250 kg, sixty 100 kg bombs and a large number of smaller bombs in 13 waves. One I-15bis (5 AP) was shot down and crashed SW Koivistonsaari. Several fighters (of which four were I-15bis of 5 AP and three of 13 OIAE) and seven SBs suffered damage.

12 January 1940 23 fighters strafed Koivisto in several waves, two locomotives, one warehouse and one field radio-transmitter were destroyed. Several fighters (I-16s of 5 AP and I-15bis of 13 OIAE) were hit by A-A artillery. Because of lack of fuel three I-16s force-landed on the ice in the bay of Narva.

18 January 1940 several tens of I-16s (5 AP) and I-15bis (12 and 13 OIAE) fighters strafed Koivisto, Humaljoki and Penttilä railway station. Several fighters were damaged by AA-fire and crashlanded on the ice.

2, 3, 4 and 14 February 1940 Koivisto and Rononiemi coastal batteries were repeatedly strafed by fighters of 5 and 13 AP, 11 and 13 OIAE. Several fighters were damaged by A-A hits and crashlanded on return. On 14 February 1940 only four of eight fighters attacking Rononiemi returned to their base.

5 IAP tasks and missions:

KBF main base (Kronstadt) protection	3,330 missions
Weather Reconnaissance (Kronstadt and Koivisto)	43 missions
Enemy road transport Reconnaissance	25 missions
Road strafing	15 missions
Enemy aircraft interception	19 missions
Protection of own ground troops at Ino and Tolbukhin light house	95 missions
Strafing of enemy fire positions and railways	294 missions
Day and night bombing	180 missions
Escort of R-5 aircraft carrying high-ranking KBF officers	12 missions
Protection of KBF ships at Koivisto	8 missions
Escort of 8 AB bombers	80 missions
Escort of photo reconnaissance aircraft	8 missions
Searching for MIA aviators	9 missions
5 IAP missions, total	**4,158 missions**

5 IAP Command

Commander	*major* A.Z. Dushin
Military Commissar	*batl.komiss* A.B. Bondarenko (1913–1944)
Chief of Staff	*kapitan* A.A. Martyanov

Squadron C.O. and Commissars

1st Squadron	*kapitan* A.V. Red'kin
	st.politr V.M. Yankovskiy
2nd Squadron	*kapitan* M.V. Okhten'
	st.politr A.I. Asevich
3rd Squadron	*st.lt* N.V. Glinin
	st.politr S.N. Dmitrovskiy
4th Squadron	*kapitan* V.S. Koreshkov
	st.politr P.I. Sidorin
5th Squadron	*major* B.I. Mikhajlov
	st.politr F.F. Petrov

In GPW 5 IAP was on 18 January 1942 elevated to Guards status and became 3 GvIAP.

Night Fighter Group

In January 1940 a special night fighter group was set up with I-15bis fighters and pilots from 32 AP of VVS ChF (Black Sea Fleet Air Force).

18 January 1940 two I-15bis night fighters did not return.

Night Fighter Group Command
Commander	*kapitan* P.G. Artemyev
Military Commissar	*st.lt* V.M. Kostra
Chief of Staff	*lt* Vladimirskiy

I-153-group
Commander	*kapitan* I.R. Novikov
Military Commissar	*kapitan* N.M. Sokolov

13th Fighter Aviation Regiment (13 IAP)

13 IAP was formed in Kotly in August 1938.
13 IAP strength 27 November 1939: 42 fighters (I-16 and I-153)

13 IAP tasks:

Procection of KBF bases, Kotly AF base, ships and troop transports at Someri, Suursaari and Lavansaari	799 missions
Weather Reconnaissance at Koivisto	5 missions
Enemy road and fire position Reconnaissance	62 missions
Strafing of enemy fire positions, Utti and Haukkajärvi AF bases	
Enemy aircraft interception	19 missions
Protection of troop landing at Suursaari	3 missions
Strafing of enemy fire positions and railways	294 missions
Bombing of enemy coastal batteries and ships	82 missions
Escort of R-5 aircraft carrying high KBF officers	12 missions
Escort of photo reconnaissance aircraft	179 missions
Interception of enemy fighters at Simola railway junction	11 missions
Bomber escort (8 AB DB-3 and SB; 15 AP and VVS RKKA); one Bulldog, three Fokker D.XXIs and two Gladiators claimed in air combat)	71 missions
Fire control of MBR-2s at Koivisto	6 missions
13 IAP missions, total	**2,116 missions**

11 January 1940 A Fokker D.XXI was claimed near Kotka by G.D. Tsokolayev (13 IAP). *No aircraft were lost by Finnish AF.*

17 February 1940 Five I-16s of 5 and 13 IAP were damaged by A-A fire at Koivisto. *Lt* V.M. Savchenko (flight leader of 1st Squadron, 13 IAP) was wounded in his left leg and left hand and his I-16 got 14 A-A hits when strafing Koivisto. Gripping the control column in his mouth Savchenko landed at a reserve base before he lost consciousness. 21 April 1940 he was awarded the Golden Star.

1 March 1940 Utti AF base was strafed by fighters (of 13 IAP and 12 OIAE) led by *kapitan* P.V. Kondryatyev (HSU 21 April 1940). Seven Fokker D.XXIs and four Bristol Bulldogs were claimed destroyed. *On 1 March 1940 Utti AF base was empty – all aircraft were dispersed to well-camoflagued temporary bases.*

13 IAP Command
Commander	*major* I.G. Romanenko (1908–1994). Performed 20 combat missions in the Winter War, HSU 21.4.1940. In GPW commanded 61 IAB VVS KBF. From March 1942 to VVS TOF, where he commanded 17 AP, 34 AP and 7 IAD. In 1956 1. Deputy Commander of VVS SF.
Military Commissar	*batl.komiss* Z.F. Lazarev
Chief of Staff	*kapitan* P.L. Rojtberg

Squadron C.O. and Commissars
1st Squadron	*kapitan* T.F. Kamenskiy
	st.politr V.P. Zharnikov
2nd Squadron	*kapitan* A.Ya. Luchikhin
	st.politr G.Ye. Shugayev
3rd Squadron	*kapitan* N.M. Nikitin
	st.politr I.I. Serbin
4th Squadron	*kapitan* A.F. Myasnikov
	st.politr P.I. Biskup

Major Romanenko, P.V. Kondratyev and V.M. Savchenko were decorated 21 April 1940 with the Golden Star.

After the Winter War 13 IAP was transferred to the new AF base in Hanko (which was leased to the USSR for 30 years).

In GPW 13 IAP was on 18 January 1942 elevated to Guards status, and become 4 GvIAP.

10th Aviation Brigade (10 AB)

In late October 1939 10 Mixed Aviation Brigade (10 SAB) was formed in Paldiski, Estonia according to the Soviet-Estonian agreement signed 11 October 1939, initially consisting only of three Maritime Close Reconnaissance Squadrons (15, 43 and 44 MBRAE) equipped with 39 MBR-2 flying boats.

From 12 November 15 MBRAE arrived with 12 MBR-2 flying boats from Khabolovo to Kihelkonna in Saaremaa, and 44 MBRAE arrived with 15 MBR-2 from Veino to Paldiski. The transfer of 43 MBRAE to Liepaja in Latvia was completed only on 15 December 1939. Fifteen (!) of the 19 MBR-2 in Paldiski were seriously damaged by a violent storm 12–13 November 1939.

29 November 1939 10 AB was subordinated to *kapitan 1 r.* V.A. Alafuzov (Deputy Commander of the Baltic Fleet) in charge of the Finnish ports and shipping blockade. Consequently 10 AB attacked mainly Finnish ports and fairwaters at the mouth of Gulf of Finland and the northern Baltic Sea, and together with 8 BAB repeatedly bombed the Finnish armoured ships *Väinämöinen* and *Ilmarinen*. Despite intensive attacks and hundreds of dropped bombs no hits were scored, but well-directed fire of the ships' A-A artillery downed several bombers.

Kapitan A.Ye. Krokhalev (HSU 7.2.1940) commanded 1 OSBAE of 10 AB. (G.F. Petrov)

1 December 1939 Reconnaissance missions to the main operation area was initiated by six MBR-2 flying boats.

3 December 1939 10 SAB was named 10 Aviation Brigade (10 AB).

In mid-December 1939 two Squadrons of 57 AP (with 17 SB bombers), a DB-3 Squadron from 1 AP and a fighter flight (of 12 OIAE, with nine I-15bis) arrived to the terrestrial AF base in Klooga (7 km east of Paldiski). The SB bombers arrived from Kotly, and formed 1st and 2nd Detached SB-Squadrons (1 and 2 OSBAE, commanded by *kapitan* V.I. Rakov and *kapitan* A.I. Krokhalev respectively). Gradually the number of SB bombers at Klooga rose to 27.

Three I-153 fighters (led by *st.lt* I.D. Borisov) arrived 18 December 1939 in Klooga from 61 IAB forming 30 OIAO.

According to an order by Peoples' Commissar N.G. Kuznetsov, six DB-3s of 1 AP were on 19 December 1939 flown to Paldiski forming 3rd Squadron (3 OBAE, Commander *kapitan* M.N. Plotkin) of 10 AB. Their task was to drop mines in Finnish fairwaters to Turku and other Gulf of Botnia ports, in order to prevent supply transports from Sweden to Finland. Altogether six mine droppings were performed: 29 January, 2, 3, 9, 19 and 20 February 1940, and 45 mines were dropped, of which 2 exploded on ice-impact.

14 January 1940 the last air attack against Helsinki in the Winter War was performed by six I-15bis fighters (apparently from 10 AB) strafing the eastern parts of the capital. Six persons were killed and 21 wounded.

10 AB received 27 SB, 15 I-15bis, 6 I-16, 16 I-153 and 3 MBR-2, forming three bomber Squadrons, two fighter Squadrons and one reconnaissance Squadron. The 85-aircraft strong 10 AB was able to bomb Finnish ports practically daily.

Main targets (only major bombing attacks listed, many cities and ports were repeatedly strafed by fighters):
- Turku (20, 23, 25, 30 and 31 December 1939; 1, 3, 4, 7, 12, 13, 14, 16, 17, 19, 29 and 31 January
- 1940; 17, 18, 20, 26 and 29 February 1940; 9 March 1940)
- Uusikaupunki (12 January 1940)
- Rauma (20 and 23 December 1939; 4, 7, 12, 14, 19, 20 and 28 January 1940; 17 and 20 February
- 1940)
- Pori (23 December 1939; 12 and 20 January 1940 and 17 February 1940)

- Vaasa (20 December 1939)
- Hangö (23 and 25 December 1939; 1, 3, 4, 12, 14, 16, 28 and 29 January 1940; 9, 17 and 20
- February 1940)
- Ekenäs (23 and 25 December 1939; 1, 10, 17, 19 and 20 January 1940)
- Karis (1 and 14 January 1940)

10 AB Command

Commander *kombrig* N.T. Petrukhin (1907–1988). In GPW commanded 61 IAB VVS KBF, and 6 IAD VVS SF. In 1954 Deputy Commander of VVS TOF etc.

Military Commissar *polk.komiss* R.I. Erenprajs (to late December 1939)
polk.komiss D.V. Sklokin (from late December 1939)

1st and 2nd Detached Fast Bomber Aviation Squadron (1 and 2 OSBAE)

The first major bombing attack from Paldiski was performed 20 December 1939. Targets: ports of Turku (fuel tanks set on fire, S/S Leo was claimed sunk), Rauma (direct hits on ships observed) and Vaasa (six SBs led by V.I. Rakov, no damage). Two SBs were damaged by AA-fire, Rakov returned from Vaasa to Paldiski on one engine. *S/S Leo (1,243 brt) was sunk in Turku on 1 January 1940.*

23 December 1939 SB bombers attacked Turku, Rauma, Pori, Hanko and Ekenäs-Karis railway. The railway bridge of Ekenäs was damaged. A direct hit on a Finnish ship was recorded.

25 December 1939 25 SB bombers attacked Finnish armoured ships, ports and coastal batteries between Turku and Åland; Turku, Hanko and Ekenäs; and Örö and Jurmo coastal batteries. Ten SBs bombed the ships without hits, but suffered serious damage by well-directed A-A fire. *In the morning the Finnish armoured ships opened A-A fire on three bombers north of Kökar (and east of Bogskär), claiming two bombers. In the afternoon ten bombers arrived from Russarö, and dropped several well-aimed bombs. On board Ilmarinen (NW Jungfruskär) one sailor was killed and some five were wounded. The Finnish ships claimed two bombers – one Soviet aviator was seen bailing out (this claim does not seem to be confirmed by Soviet sources). Five bombers were observed over Turku, where 47 bombs were dropped. Four persons were killed and twelve injured. Several buildings were destroyed and damaged (the medieval castle of Turku was badly damaged).*

31 December 1939 Fifteen SBs flying in waves at 3,500–4,000 m altitude bombed seven transports in the port of Turku. *22 bombers were observed over Turku, dropping 105 bombs. No human losses. The port tug Vetäjä III was sunk by a direct bomb hit, and the dredger Karhu was damaged and sank later. Several buildings badly damaged. Bulldogs of Osasto Heinilä reported some hits on the attacking bombers.*

1 January 1940 18 SB bombers attacked the port of Turku, and dropped some 12 t bombs. 44 direct bomb hits were recorded. Hanko, Lappvik, Karis and Ekenäs were bombed. *30 bombers were observed over Turku in four waves, dropping some 150 bombs. Several buildings were destroyed and damaged, two persons were killed and five injured. In the port of Turku S/S Leo was sunk (later lifted and repaired), S/S Arcturus (1,217 BRT) was damaged. S/S Navigator (3,700 GWT) run aground at Uusikaupunki between Putsaari and Vehainen, remained there for the rest of the war and was repeatedly bombed. The Bulldogs were too slow to intercept the bombers.*

4 January 1940 Turku was bombed by nine SBs. The attack led by *kapitan* A.I. Krokhalev caused considerable damage to the port and railway station. A direct hit on one transport was observed, and a number of buildings were also hit. One Bulldog was claimed shot down. In Rauma two transports were set on fire by three SBs. *Nine bombers were observed over Turku, dropping over 220 bombs (mainly at the port area). No human losses. Two Bulldogs attacked three SB bombers near Turku from 300–400 m distance without results.*

12 January 1940 Six SBs attacked an icebreaker in the archipelago of Turku without success. *36 bombers were observed over Turku in two waves. 250 bombs were dropped, mainly on the port, Crichton-Vulcan shipyard and the urban city centre. The civilians had to stay in bomb shelters for over six hours. Several buildings were destroyed, one civilian killed and four wounded.*

The submarine depot ships Suomen Joutsen and Sisu were bombed near Sottunga, Åland (south of Husö). The submarine Vetehinen was just returning from its last mission and approaching Suomen Joutsen, when a lone aircraft was observed. One hour later a formation of bombers arrived dropping several bombs without damage. After the bombers had departed Vetehinen submerged and was still under water when a new bomber formation arrived. Also this time the Finnish ships were lucky as no damage were caused, but Radio Moscow reported that one Finnish submarine had been destroyed(!).

Pori, Rauma and Uusikaupunki were also bombed. In the port of Rauma one ship was sunk, and another two ships suffered damage.

13 January 1940 The port of Turku was bombed by 17 SB bombers. A direct hit on a transport was recorded. *17 bombers were observed over Turku in two waves, dropping 150 bombs (mainly at the port and Crichton-Vulcan shipyard). No human losses. Several buildings destroyed. S/S* Arcturus *was hit again (already damaged 1 January 1940).*

14 January 1940 Fuel stores in the port of Turku were bombed by ten SBs. *Six Bulldogs of Osasto Heinilä/LLv 26 took off from Littoinen to intercept the SBs bombing Turku. One SB was shot down jointly by lentom L.Lautamäki in BU-72 and A-A artillery. The bomber crashed at Perniö. Several buildings were destroyed in Turku.*

The same day Rauma and Karis were bombed. Hanko was attacked by 57 aircraft, causing 36 fires.

17 January 1940 Despite poor weather Turku were bombed by five SBs of 10 AB, the shipyard was set on fire. *Five bombers were observed over Turku, dropping 40 bombs (mainly on the Crichton-Vulcan shipyard). Two Bulldogs of LLv 26 tried to intercept SB bombers at Littoinen without results.*

20 January 1940 Mäntyluoto at Pori, Rauma and Ekenäs were bombed. One transport was sunk, another was set on fire. *The German S/S Aegir loaded with ore had strangely run aground four days earlier at Granskär (south of Eckerö, Åland) on route from Gävle to Kiel, and was bombed by two aircraft without serious damage. S/S Aegir remained there for the rest of the war, but was able to continue her interrupted trip in spring 1940! Another two bombers attacked Mariehamn, causing minor damage to some buildings. Pilot inspection vessel* Suunta *(170 t) was lightly damaged. The 40 mm A-A battery at Mäntyluoto reported two Soviet bombers shot down (this is not confirmed by Soviet loss reports).*

28 January 1940 1 OSBAE bombed Rauma. Kapitan Krokhalev's electrically heated overall caught fire in the air, but nevertheless he performed his task. Upon return the wounded aviator was hospitalized, and ten days later (7 February 1940) he was decorated with the Golden Star. *The Finnish armoured ships anchored at the entrance to Turku, where they remained for the rest of the war: Ilmarinen at Pikisaari and Väinämöinen at Pikku-Pukari, significantly improving the air defence of Turku. In addition to S/S Notung (1,650 brt; sunk 24 January 1940), Soviet naval aviators claimed two other transports damaged and one armed tug sunk from 23 to 28 January 1940. These vessels have not been identified.*

29 January 1940 Turku was bombed by SBs, and Hanko was strafed by fighters. *This was the worst bombing of Turku during the Winter War. Eight bombers were observed over Turku in two waves, dropping 235 bombs (mainly on the urban centre). 36 persons were killed and 48 injured. The fires lasted 12 hours.*

9 February 1940 SB bombers attacked ports in SW Finland. Two SBs were destroyed in force landings, one of which was in Lithuania (the navigator died of wounds 14 February 1940). The other SB returned with bombs and crashed on landing (the crew was able to leave the aircraft in time). Two SB bombers were hit by A-A artillery, and one Fokker D.XXI was claimed shot down. *No Finnish fighters were lost!*

17 February 1940 A reconnaissance flight to Turku reported that the port was still not operating. Eight SBs bombed oil tanks 3 km north of Turku. Direct hits were scored, and flames seen at a distance of over 100 km. *26 bombers were observed over Turku in two waves. 46 bombs were dropped mainly at the Pansio oil terminal.*

Vaasa, Rauma, Reposaari and Mäntyluoto, Hanko and Lappvik were also bombed. One locomotive and two wagons were claimed destroyed. Two Fokker D.XXIs were claimed by the gunners of the Soviet bombers at Turku and Mäntyluoto. Three SBs suffered severe damage (with up to 130 bullet holes), two of which returned on one engine and belly-landed. Several aviators were wounded by enemy fighters and AA-fire. One SB was destroyed in an unsuccessful take-off for a ferry flight to Paldiski. *A Morane fighter of LLv 28 tried to intercept the bombers at Pori, and scored hits in one SB-bomber.*

18 February 1940 *Five bombers were observed over Turku in three waves, dropping 53 bombs (mainly at the city centre). S/S Rigel (1,739 brt) and S/S Bore IV (1,691 brt) were sunk by bombs at Mäntyluoto. Bore IV was raised five days later and returned to service in early summer 1941. Osasto Ahola intercepted several bombers and escort fighters approaching SW Finland from Estonia.*

20 February 1940 Korpo, Hanko, Rauma and Turku were bombed. Two SB bombers did not return from Rauma, and a third returned on one engine with 75 bullet holes. Three Finnish fighters were claimed. *Eight bombers were observed over Turku in four waves, dropping 48 bombs. No human losses.*

Luutn R. Turkki's Morane patrol of LLv 28 intercepted six SB bombers heading for Rauma. One bomber was shot down by Turkki (MS-307) and crashed at Tankkarit (10 km W Rauma, the pilot bailed out and was taken prisoner). Later luutn V. Karu (MS-321) intercepted another formation of SB bombers north-west of Säkylä, shooting down one SB-bomber near the Estonian coast and setting another bomber on fire. Neither LLv 28 nor Osasto Ahola suffered losses.

A convoy consisting of icebreakers and transports was repeatedly attacked north of Korpo by some 20 bombers and five fighters. At night the attack was repeated at Airisto near Turku. The last bombing attack *against this convoy was made early next morning in the port of Turku, where the powerful A-A artillery of* Ilmarinen *provided protection.*

26 February 1940 Seven DB-3 and twelve SB bombers of 10 AB attacked the armoured ships at Turku. Twenty-one 500 kg bombs were dropped from 3.800 m altitude without success. Four "Spitfires" were claimed shot down. Hanko was also bombed. *As mentioned above the Soviet bombers were intercepted by Morane-Saulnier MS.406 fighters of LLv 28, mistaken for Spitfires. 19 bombers and 10 fighters were observed over Turku. 822 bombs were dropped. Three persons were injured.*

An SB was hit by AA-fire of the ships, and after further attack by Finnish fighters crash-landed on the ice 12 km N Osmussaar. The wounded crew were picked up next day by *major* V.I. Rakov in an MBR-2. Vänr *J. Röhr (LLv 28, MS-308) shot an SB-bomber down in flames at Nagu.*

29 February 1940 The Finnish armoured ships at Turku were attacked by five DB-3 and nine SB bombers of 10 AB, escorted by 16 fighters. The DB-3s dropped fifteen 500 kg bombs on one ship from 4,700 m altitude while the SB bombers dropped eighteen 250 kg and twenty-seven 100 kg bombs on the other ship (at anchor 1 km from the first) from 5,100 m altitude. Despite fierce A-A fire all aircraft returned without losses. Two "Spitfires" were claimed shot down. *30 bombers were observed over Turku in three waves, dropping 207 bombs. No human losses. The opposing fighters were in fact Moranes of LLv 28 which also suffered no losses.*

2 March 1940 8 BAB and 10 AB made a joint major attempt to destroy the Finnish armoured ships, again without success. (See see 1 AP, page 250).

9 March 1940 Two SBs bombed the armoured ships, still without success. *Twelve bombers were observed over Turku, dropping 250 bombs. No human losses. Eight Hurricanes were received by LLv 28 in Säkylä. The Hurricanes had been ferry flown from England via Norway and Sweden by Finnish pilots, and were intended for the new LLv 22.*

1 OSBAE performed 190 missions during the Winter War, and claimed destruction of six transport ships, two trains, four storages, one Finnish aircraft, and the railroad at Ekenäs railway station.

1 OSBAE lost four SB bombers:
- 7 January 1940 c/n 18/233 (piloted by *lt* .I.M. Gutarov) went missing from a bombing mission to Rauma. The crew had arrived from 40 AP /VVS ChF.
- 9 February 1940 c/n 12/207 force-landed in Ukmerge, Lithuania, *lt* V.A. Zorin stepped on a landmine after landing and was killed.
- 26 February 1940 c/n 2/206 (piloted by *st.lt* P.S. Kurochkin) was hit by A-A artillery from Finnish armoured ships at Turku; force-landed 30 km NW Estonian Pakri (Rågö) on the frozen Gulf of Finland. The injured crew was picked up by *kapitan* V.I. Rakov in a MBR-2 flying boat.
- 2 March 1940 c/n 19/240 (piloted by *ml.lt* V.I. Rayazanov) was shot down by Finnish Morane MS 406 fighters of LLv 28 from Säkylä and crashed at Nagu, all crew KIA. The Morane fighters were identified as "Spitfires"!

2 OSBAE lost three SB bombers:
- 16 January 1940 c/n 1/243 (piloted by *lt* R.T. Bastamov) went missing from a bombing mission to Turku/Hanko. The crew had arrived from 40 AP /VVS ChF.
- 20 February 1940 c/n 19/224 (piloted by *lt* P.V. Asadov) and c/n 7/209 (*lt* Ye.I. Ptitsyn). Both bombers were shot down near Rauma by Morane MS-406 fighters of LLv 28 from Säkylä. Lt Ptitsyn escaped by parachute and was taken prisoner near Tankkari island (W Rauma), the other five aviators were killed.

1 OSBAE Command

Commander	*major* A.I. Krokhalev (1910–1994). HSU 7.2.1940.
Military Commissar	*st.lt* Meshcherin

2 OSBAE Command

Commander	*kapitan* V.I. Rakov (1909–1996). HSU 7.2.1940 and 22.7.1944.
Military Commissar	*st.politr* N.F. Polyakov

3rd Detached Bomber Aviation Squadron (3 OBAE, also called 3 Detached Long-Range Bomber Aviation Squadron 3 OBDAB)

From 10 January 1940 six DB-3b bombers of 1 AP were flown to Paldiski, where 3 OBAE was formed. Later six additional DB-3b bombers arrived.

3 OBAE task was mine dropping in fairwaters leading to Turku and to Gulf of Botnia ports in order to prevent transports from Sweden to Finland.

Because of unfavourable weather conditions ferrying of mine-laying capable DB-3s to Paldiski was finished only on 19 January 1940. *Komdiv* Zhavoronkov and *major* M.F.Veis (Head of VVS KBF Mine-Torpedo systems) were personally directing and supervising the operation in Paldiski. *Kapitan* M.N. Plotkin and *major* Veis performed the first reconnaissance flight in order to check the planned targets of 30–50 m wide passages.

29 January 1940 Laying of mine barrages in passages leading to Turku was initiated. Three waves of three bombers each dropped parachute-equipped MAV-1 mines at three locations from 500 m altitude. Only two mines fell successfully. Several mines exploded on impact with the ice, or fell outside of the passages. One bomber opened fire on Finnish soldiers examining mines and parachutes. Despite Finnish A-A artillery fire along the passages and attacks by Bulldog fighters, all Soviet aircraft returned without losses.

The Finns were fortunately able to inspect the mechanisms of some intact mines. Nevertheless the port of Turku had to be closed until 4 February, when a new passage at Airisto was opened by the icebreaker *Jääkarhu*. South of Kökar two water spouts were seen and immediately after two explosions heard, which were assumed to be caused by "parachute mines".

2 February 1940 Twelve MAV-1 parachute mines were dropped. Six mines were dropped at the entrance to the port of Pori, three at Rauma and another three mines at Sottunga, Åland. Eight mines were reported to have fallen in the passages. According to a KBF command report *the port of Turku is closed because of mine barrages*. The port of Turku was reopened on 4 February when a new passage at Airisto had been opened by the icebreaker Jääkarhu (see 29 January 1940). After midnight two bombers were observed over Turku, dropping nine bombs. Of the three mines dropped at Husö (east of Sottunga) one exploded at impact, one was destroyed by explosives, and the third was lifted and disarmed a few days later.

3 February 1940 Nine DB-3s continued mine-laying in Finnish passages. Four MAV-1 parachute mines were dropped at the entrance to Pori, three at Rauma and two at Turku *(in fact at Berghamn west of Korpo)*. Eight mines were dropped in the passages. On the return leg three DB-3s were attacked by Finnish fighters at Kökar. Two bombers were shot down near Korpo, the third DB-3 was seriously damaged but able to limp home (some 60 bullet holes were counted, so this aircraft did not fly again very

No photos have been found of the top-secret Winter War mine-dropping missions. In this photo from summer 1941 the shape, handling and under-belly attachment of the AMG-1 mine is clearly seen. (G.F. Petrov)

272

soon). *Osasto Ahola attacked DB-3 bombers returning from southwest Finland, claiming three victories.* vänr P. Kokko (FR-86) was officially assigned two bombers, while the third victory was shared by Kokko, vänr E. Ilveskorpi (FR-105) and ylik L. Nissinen (FR-98). The pilot of DB-3 No. 1 bailed out by parachute at Jungfruskär, Houtskär, while DB-3 No.2 (which had arrived in Paldiski 19 January 1940) made a force-landing on the ice at Vidskär, Korpo. The navigator and the gunner were taken prisoner, while the other three aviators were killed.

10 February 1940 Three MAV-1 mines were dropped by DB-3s SE Rauma; two mines were observed in the passage. *Parachute mines were observed south of Åland by T/LLv 39 (these mines had been laid by submarine L-1 on 1 December 1939.)* RI-132 of T-LLv 39 was written off after a hard landing in Pori, crew unhurt.

15 February 1940 Six DB-3 bombers were transferred from 1 AP to 10 AB at Paldiski.

20 February 1940 In the sixth and final mine laying mission six DB-3s dropped mines at Svartholm north of Korpo (three AMG-1 mines) and the entrance to Turku (three MAV-1 mines). Only one mine was observed in the passage, all other mines exploded either at impact or sank to the bottom.

Regardless of the significantly increased air defence of Turku, the Soviet Navy considered that *the port of Turku was closed down because of the mine laying operation.* Arriving ships were unloaded directly onto the ice at Korpo, from where trucks transported the cargos further on. *Turku port operation was interrupted only for a few days, and was reopened after a new passage (not observed by the Soviets?) had been opened by icebreakers.*

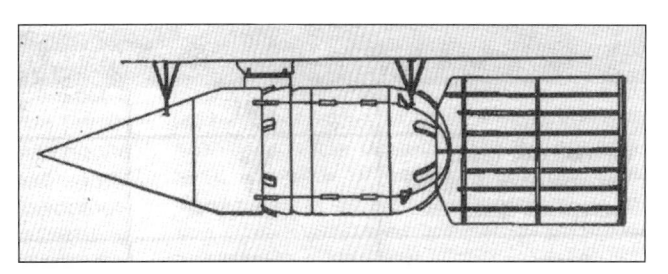

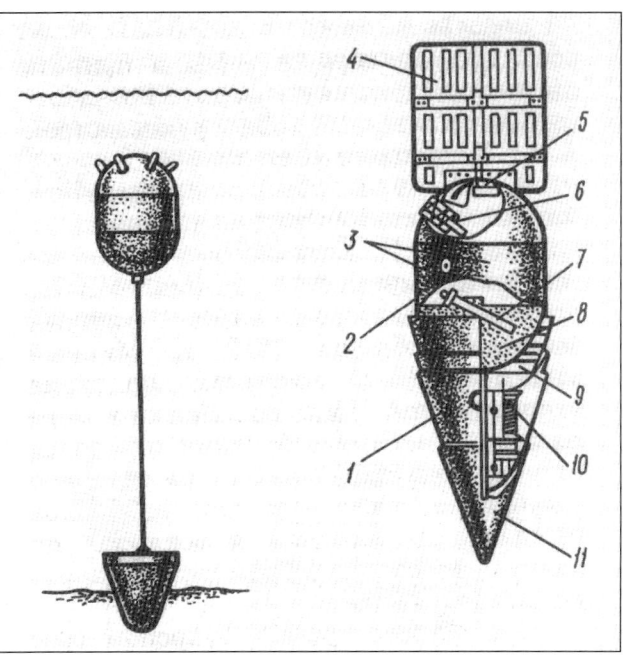

Sketches of the AMG-1 mine. (Finnish National Archive)

Mine Dropping Summary

Date	Area	Aircraft	Mines	Mine location
29.1.40	Turku	9 DB-3	3 groups with 3 mines each	4 in fairwater, 2 exploded at ice impact, 3 on ice
2.2.40	Pori	6 DB-3	2 groups with 3 mines each	6 in fairwater
2.2.40	Rauma	3 DB-3	1 group with 3 mines	2 in fairwater, 1 on ice
2.2.40	20 nm E Åland	3 DB-3	1 group with 3 mines	2 in fairwater, 1 on ice
3.2.40	Pori	4 DB-3	1 group with 4 mines	4 in fairwater
3.2.40	Rauma	3 DB-3	1 group with 3 mines	2 in fairwater, 1 on ice
3.2.40	Turku	2 DB-3	1 group with 2 mines	2 in fairwater
9.2.40	Rauma	3 DB-3	1 group with 3 mines	2 in fairwater, 1 on ice
10.2.40	Uusikaupunki-Rauma	6 DB-3	2 groups with 3 mines each	5 in fairwater, 1 exploded on ice impact
20.2.40	Turku	6 DB-3	2 groups with 3 mines each	4 in fairwater, 1 exploded on ice impact, 1 on ice
Mines dropped	Turku 20 mines Rauma 15 mines Pori 10 mines		45 mines dropped	33 mines in fairwater, 4 exploded on impact, 8 fell on ice

26 and 29 February 1940 DB-3s of 10 AB participated in attacks against the armoured ships at Turku without success. (See 1 and 2 OSBAE sections, page 269)

4 March 1940 DB-3b (c/n 392611) crashed on the ice of Gulf of Finland approx 90 km east of Tallinn on a ferry flight from Paldiski to Bezzabotnoye. Six persons (four-person crew and two passengers) were killed.

After the Winter War the DB-3b bombers were returned from 3 OBAE to 1 MTAP.

3 OBAE Command

Commander   *kapitan* P.P. Plotkin (1912–1942). Bombed Berlin 7–8.8.1941. HSU 13.8.1941.
Military Commissar   *lt* Pavlyuk

273

Both in the Winter and Continuation Wars several mines dropped from aircraft were captured by Finnish forces; photo dated 20 November 1941. (SA-kuva)

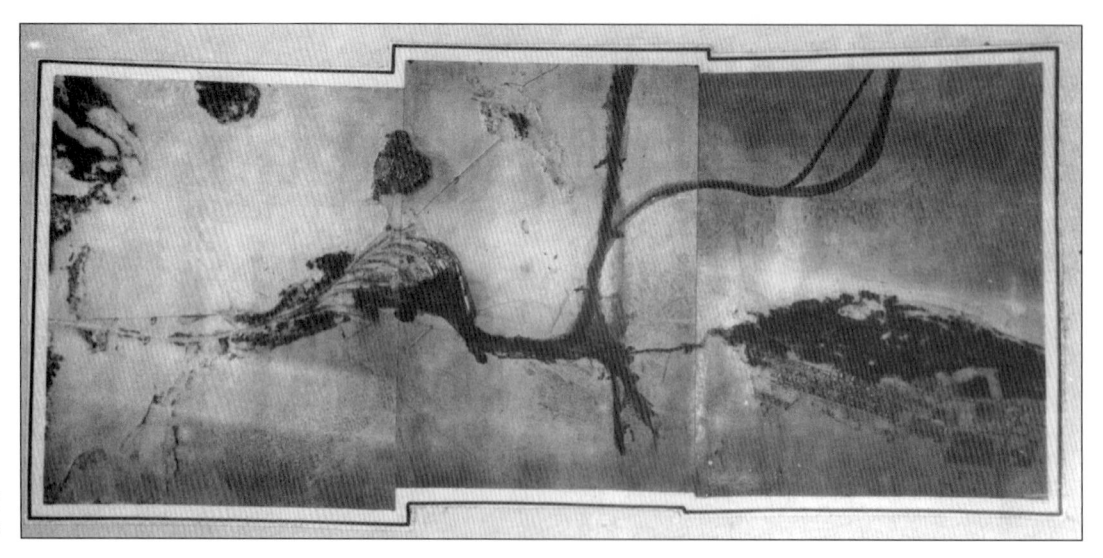

The results of mine dropping operation was checked by reconnaissance photographs. The entrance to Pori (Mäntyluoto-Reposaari) was photographed 2 February 1940, and the entrance to Rauma next day. (RGAVMF)

30th Detached Fighter Aviation Squadron (30 OIAE)

Three I-153 fighters (led by *st.lt* I.D. Borisov) arrived from 61 IAB to Klooga 18 December 1939 and formed 30 OIAE of 10 AB.

23 December 1939 *st.lt* I.D. Borisov in a I-153 shot down a Finnish "Kotka" reconnaissance aircraft in air combat near Paldiski. The Finnish pilot escaped by parachute but was shot dead in the air. *The aircraft was Ripon RI-155 (pilot* kers *K. Söderholm, observer* vänr *E. Huhanantti of LLv 36) on a photo-reconnaissance mission to Paldiski. Both Finnish aviators were killed. The Finnish-produced Kotka – even more obsolete than the Ripons – were only used in the rear for liaison and auxiliary tasks.*

25 December 1939 *st.lt* I.D. Borisov strafed the Finnish battery at Hästö-Busö (west of Hanko), but was hit by ground fire. According to Soviet legends Borisov performed an *ognennyj* (blazing *taran)*, as he directed the damaged I-153 towards a Finnish fire position. Borisov performed 10 combat missions in the Winter War. After his *ognennyi* (blazing *taran)* he was 7 February 1940 posthumously decorated with the Golden Star.

2 March 1940 *ml.lt* A.M. Ivanov was shot down in air combat with two Morane MS.406 fighters of LLv 28 (*kapt* E. Jutila, MS-316 and *vänr* P. Reinikainen, MS-317). Ivanov force-landed near Örö fort, and was killed in combat with Finnish soldiers. His I-153 was virtually intact, and next day a SB bomber tried to destroy the aircraft by dropping bombs.

Soviet artist's impression of st.lt I.D. Borisov's "blazing taran" against the Finnish battery at Hästö-Busö island 25 December 1939. (G.F. Petrov)

Borisov and kapitan *A.K. Antonenko (13 IAP, first HSU aviator in GPW 14.7.1941, KIA 21.7.1941) were buried at the central square in Hanko. (C-F. Geust)*

275

12th Detached Maritime Close Reconnassaince Aviation Squadron (12 OMBRAE)

In late autumn 1939 12 OMBRAE from Khabolovo was attached to 10 AB. In November 1939 twelve MBR-2 were dispatched to Paldiski, and five MBR-2 to Kihelkonna on Saaremaa. In 1940 12 OMBRAE was renamed 15 OMRAE and attached to 15 OMRAP.

19 December 1939 Two MBR-2s bombed Soviet ships *Lunacharskiy* and *Tobol* by mistake at Saaremaa. Although the aviators reported a direct 50 kg bomb hit, the Operations Department of 8 AB was forced to admit that the attack was "unsuccessful"!

2 February 1940 An MBR-2 (piloted by *kapitan* A.G. Groshenkov) sank after forced-landing because of engine malfunction) 6 km NE Ristna. The crew was picked up by the gunboat *Krasnoye Znamya* four days later after extensive searches.

12 OMBRAE Command
    Commander   *kapitan* V.P. Kanarev
    Military Commissar   *st.politr* D.A. Nechayev

43rd Detached Maritime Reconnaissance Aviation Squadron (43 OMRAE)

In December 1939 43 OMRAE, equipped with 12 MBR-2, was attached to 10 AB. The Squadron was subsequently transferred from Gori-Valdaj to Estonia, and in December 1939 further to Liepaja in Latvia. As the Baltic Sea was frozen, seven MBR-2 were equipped with wheeled undercarriages. 43 OMRAE performed only reconnaissance missions in the Liepaja area, and did not actively participate in combat actions.

43 OMRAE Command
    Commander   *kapitan* I.Ya.Vahkterman
    Military Commissar   *st.politr* V.M. Kalashnikov

44th Detached Maritime Reconnaissance Aviation Squadron (44 OMRAE)

Major V.I. Mukhin (C.O. 44 MBRAE) performed a daring rescue operation 27.2.1940, when he together with kapitan V.I. Rakov picked up the crew of an SB-bomber which had force-landed on the ice the day before. (G.F. Petrov)

In November 1939 44 OMRAE was attached to 10 AB. The Squadron was dispatched from Veino to Paldiski with 12 MBR-2.

14 December 1939 Destroyers *Gnevnyi* and *Grozashchiy* attacked Utö coastal battery (four 152 mm cannons) in northern Baltic Sea, supported by six MBR-2 aircraft of 44 OMRAE. The battery opened well-directed fire on the two destroyers, which turned back after 10 minutes exchange of fire. At Lillharu the MBR-2s were attacked by "Bulldogs". KBF Chief of Staff *kapitan 2 r.* S.G. Kucherov reported *previously unknown battery at Lillharu*.

The Soviet destroyers were apparently not aware that the unmanned (and unarmed!) Lillharu beacon (5 km south of Utö) was blown up 2 December 1939. In the snowstorm Utö was apparently misidentified for Lillharu(!), which explains the careless approach of the destroyers (at the moment of turning of the ships Utö was located directly behind Lillharu). The Finns assumed that one of the destroyers was hit by the battery Utö, but the observed explosion was in fact a smoke screen laid to protect the retreat of the Soviet ships. All Bulldogs were still at the Karelian Isthmus, so the "attacking biplanes" at Lillharu must have been Soviet I-15bis fighters (or possibly Ripons searching for Soviet submarines!

44 OMRAE Command
    Commander   *major* V.I. Mukhin
    Military Commissar   *st.politr* Z.I. Pil'vitskiy

Detached Units

15th Detached Maritime Reconnaissance Aviation Regiment (15 OMRAP)

15 OMRAP was formed in summer 1938, equipped with MBR-2 flying boats, TB-1 bombers and MR-6 reconnaissance aircraft.

In summer 1939 the TB-1 bombers of 2nd Squadron were replaced by DB-3 bombers.

15 OMRAP was intially attached to 8 AB, but from September 1939 functioned separately as a detached regiment, incorporating 15, 19 and 58 OMRAE, all equipped with MBR-2 flying boats. From 2 October 1939 15 OMRAP was based at Kerstovo. 30 November 1939 15 OMRAP suffered its only loss during the Winter War: a DB-3 of 2nd Squadron (piloted by *st.lt* G.V. Levchenko) crashed on landing in Koporye. Levchenko and *ml.lt* M.M. Mashtakov were killed.

9 December 1939 12 MBR-2s bombed Utö, Örö and Russarö coast artillery batteries and the Hanko-Helsinki railway. *The small skerry Bänken was bombed by Soviet aircraft 17 km ESE Utö. LLv 36 made a reconnaissance flight in the Gulf of Finland.*

19 December 1939 2nd Squadron (equipped with DB-3 bombers) was transferred to 1 MTAP.

During the second half of February North-West Front Command decided to transfer troops across the frozen Gulf of Finland from the southern to northern shore. In order to facilitate orientation 15 OMRAP was ordered to spread red marking dye on the ice along the route from Cape Kolganpya (Kolkanpää) to Seiskari. The liquid was put into 100 litre containers carried by MBR-2 aircraft, which performed 23 "ice painting" missions.

15 OMRAP performed also supply missions to the "liberated" islands transporting 118 persons (of which 88 were sick and wounded soldiers) and 68.5 t cargo. Two crash-landed aircraft were detected on the frozen Gulf of Finland, five aviators were rescued.

A few examples of the Tupolev-designed MR-6 reconnaissance and transport aircraft were still in use. (G.F. Petrov)

15 OMRAP Command
Commander	*podpolkovnik* D.F. Bartnovskiy
Military Commissar	*batl.komiss* N.G. Safonov
Chief of Staff	*kapitan* V.P. Stroganov

After the Winter War 15 OMRAP was again split up; with eg. 81 MRAE based in Hanko, and 85 MRAE based in Viipuri.

Four of the detached Squadrons and units, namely 18 and 58 MBRAE, 12 and 44 OAO operated some 50 MBR-2 flying boats, based at naval AF bases at the Gulf of Finland, Lake Ladoga and lakes and rivers in NW Russia.Four of the detached Squadrons and units, namely 18 and 58 MBRAE, 12 and 44 OAO operated some 50 MBR-2 flying boats, based at naval AF bases at the Gulf of Finland, Lake Ladoga and lakes and rivers in NW Russia.

MBR-2 flying boats were widely used for bombing, reconnaissance and rescue missions in the Baltic Sea and Lake Ladoga. (G.F. Petrov)

After the sea was frozen MBR-2 was equipped with skies for operations from the ice. (G.F. Petrov)

Map-checking before take-off for a MBR-2 mission. (G.F. Petrov)

18th Maritime Close Reconnaissance Aviation Squadron (18 OMBRAE)

2 February 1940 One SB of 57 AP on a photo reconnaissance mission was set afire by two "Fokker D.XXI fighters" and force-landed on the ice between Someri and Narvi (within the range of Finnish coast batteries). One Fokker was claimed shot down by the MG-gunner. The force-landed bomber was located by *st.lt* A.I. Nefedov (12 OIAE) in an I-15bis, who alerted an MBR-2 (piloted by *kapitan* A.A. Gubriy, 18 AE).

Gubriy landed on the ice and evacuated the stranded crew (*lt* G.S. Pinchuk, face burned; *st.lt* V.M. Kharlamov, unhurt; and *st.ser* A.I. Belogurov, leg wounds) to Oranienbaum. All three SB-aviators were 7 February 1940 decorated with the Golden Star on 7 February 1940, while Nefedov and Gubriy both got their Golden Stars 21 April 1940.

Pinchuk's SB was apparently shot down by Danish volunteer *Løjtnant* J. Ulrich of LLv 26 in Gladiator GL-259. Ulrich's prey was seen burning at Suursaari.

18 OMBRAE Command
    Commander   *kapitan* F.A. Usachev (1908–1970). HSU 20.5.1945.
    Military Commissar   *st.politr* M.A. Syrnikov

19th Maritime Close Reconnaissance Aviation Squadron (19 OMBRAE)

During the Winter War 19 OMRAE, based in Grebnoi Port, Leningrad, was attached to 15 OMRAP as 2nd Squadron.

58th Detached Aviation Squadron (58 OAE)

58 OAE was based in Peipiya, equipped with 16 MBR-2s. On 21 December 1939 one MBR-2 on a submarine search mission was shot down by mistake by MG-fire from Soviet destroyer *Smetlivyj*. Two other MBR-2s were lost in accidents (four aviators were killed).

58 OBRAE Command
    Commander   *major* A.V. Arefyev
    Military Commissar   *st.politr* M.S. Sobolev

12th Detached Maritime Reconnaissance Aviation Unit (12 OMRAO)

12 OMRAO was based in Khabalovo and equipped with 3 MBR-2.

71st Detached Fire-Control Aviation Unit (71 OKAO)

71 OKAO was formed in Novyj Petergof in 1937, equipped with 10 R-5 reconnaissance aircraft. In the Winter War its tasks included enemy ground position and submarine reconnaissance, artillery fire control and bombing of Finnish coastal defense positions.
Strength March 1940: eleven R-5 and two U-2 aircraft.
30 November 1939 One R-5 lost by own bomb exploding at take-off.
9 December 1939 Two R-5s lost (one shot down, the other on an unsuccessful landing).
27 February 1940 A R-5 was destroyed by own bombs on a nighttime mission 6 km NW Seivästö.

71 OAO Command
    Commander   *kapitan* P.I. Vasyagin
    Military Commissar   *st.politr* A.K. Krivosheyev
    Chief of Staff   *st.lt* N.N. Nilov

Line-up of R-5 reconnaissance aircraft of 71 OKAO. (G.F. Petrov)

Ladoga Military Flotilla (VVS LVF)

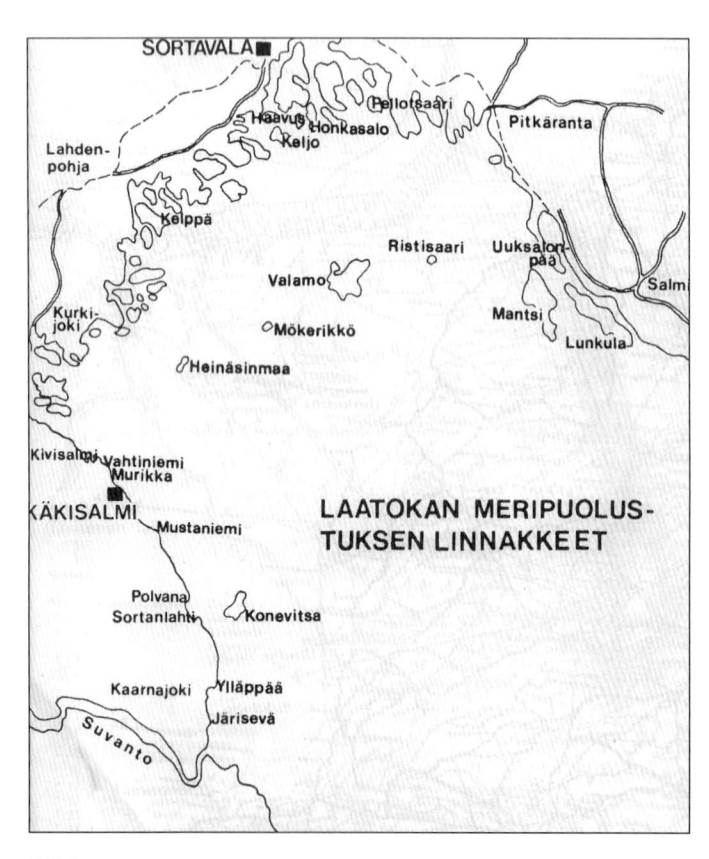

Was set up in October 1939, and was equipped with mobilized civil vessels, KBF and NKVD Border Guard vessels.

Commander: *kapitan* 1 r. S.I. Kobyl'skikh.

Finnish coast artillery forts at lake Ladoga. Note the orthodox monasteries of Valamo and Konevitsa. (C-F. Geust)

41st Detached Maritime Reconnaissance Aviation Squadron (41 OMRAE)

The aviation component of the Ladoga flotilla, 41 OMRAE, based at Novaya Ladoga on the southern shore of Lake Ladoga.

41 OMRAE strength: 8 (later 13) MBR-2 flying boats, one U-2 and one UT-1.

41 OMRAE tasks:
- Reconnaissance and strafing of enemy shipping at Salmi and Sortanlahti ports and Lake Ladoga
- Bombing of enemy objects at Mantsinsaari and Ristisaari
- Destruction of coastal batteries on Valamo and Konevitsa monastery islands.

41 OMRAE Command
Commander	*major* V.M. Bakanov
Military Commissar	*batl.komiss* V.V. Galushkin
Chief of Staff	*kapitan* I.P. Guryev
	kapitan V.S. Kovel (from January 1940)

2 December 1939 At Miikkulainen (Nikulyasy) on the western shore of Ladoga ships of the Soviet Ladoga Flotilla opened fire on an MBR-2 of 41 OMRAE. Fort Järisevä opened A-A fire on the Soviet aircraft. In the evening a crashed Soviet aircraft was found at Sakkola between Vilakkala and Korvenkylä (10 km west of Järisevä). No traces of the pilot were found, only blood-stained maps and documents in the cockpit. (This was probably a VVS fighter?) At night 3./LLv 16 performed a reconnaissance mission over Ladoga to Saunaniemi. No ships were observed.

6 December 1939 MBR-2 c/n 14/629 was shot down 2 km N Tuloksa by four I-16s of 49 IAP (of VVS 8.A) from Nurmolitsa. Three of the four-member MBR-2 crew were killed. (For details see 49 IAP, page 170)

8 December 1939 Two MBR-2 aircraft of 41 AE bombed Valamo monastery without damage. *Some 28 aircraft of VVS 8.A strafed Mantsinsaari in the north-western part of Lake Ladoga. Two I-16 fighters of 49 IAP collided mid-air when avoiding A-A fire from Mantsi coastal battery (see 49 IAP section)*

25 December 1939 5th Squadron/57 AP (with five SB bombers) and five MBR-2s of 58 AE were attached to 41 MBRAE.

6 January 1940 Like one month earlier a MBR-2 was attacked by 5 I-153s (apparently also of 49 IAP, VVS 8.A). This time the MBR-2 force-landed at the mouth of River Olonka.

12 January 1940 Finnish auxiliary gunboat Aallokas (200 brt) was attacked near Valamo by seven fighters.

13 January 1940 Ripons RI-150 and RI-151 of LLv 36 bombed the Soviet icebreakers Yermak and Truvor east of Suursaari without success. The Ripons force-landed east of Nordsjö (Vuosaari) upon return, no damage.

22 January 1940 At Niikkana, Valamo two motor-boats and one icebreaker claimed sunk by SB bombers. *The "icebreaker" at Niikkana was the monastery tourist ship S/S Valamon Luostari ("Valamo Monastery", 133 brt) which received four direct hits and sank in flames. All ship movements on Lake Ladoga had ceased on 17 January 1940 when the lake was frozen over.*

1 February 1940 Despite poor weather Konevitsa was bombed by 41 AE. *Some 130 Soviet aircraft heading west were seen from Ylläppää. Four bombers dropped some 20 bombs on Konevitsa, hitting several buildings. Two soldiers and one orthodox monk were killed.*

2 February 1940 At Lahdenpohja a ship – "probably an icebreaker" – was claimed sunk. *In the early morning seven "desants" or paratroopers (in Finnish uniforms, belonging to 201. Parachute Brigade) were dropped at Lake Pyhäjärvi (some 10 km east of Sortanlahti at Lake Ladoga). All were killed by Finnish troops. Nine bombers performed several unsuccessful attacks against the auxiliary gunboat Aallokas, anchored between Petäjäsaari and Majaniemi south-east of Lahdenpohja. Valamo monastery received considerable damage.*

4 February 1940 Valamo was bombed by some 120 aircraft in several waves causing serious damage to the monastery. Up to 73 bombers were counted simultaneously over the island. The normal activity of the monastery ceased, and most of the monks were evacuated. Only five monks remained in the monastery. S/S Otava was lightly damaged at Valamo.

13 February 1940 A DB-3 of 21 DBAP crashed 15 km from Fort Mustaniemi. All four aviators were killed in the crash. (See 21 DBAP, page 122)

4 March 1940 People's Commissar N.G. Kuznetsov ordered considerable reinforcement of the Ladoga Flotilla, including allocation of a three-Squadron aviation regiment (two SB bomber squadrons and one MBR-2 reconnaissance Squadron) etc. Because of the peace treaty signed on 13 March 1940 the order was not carried out.

After the Winter War 41 OMRAE was dispatched to Latvia.

VVS KBF Aircraft Losses (including written-off and seriously damaged aircraft)

Type	Combat losses	MIA	Catastrophies	Total
I-15bis	8 (Finnish A-A artillery 7, own bomber 1)	3	11	22
I-16	-	1	4	5
I-153	2 (Finnish fighter 1, A-A artillery 1)	-	3	5
Fighters total	10 (Finnish fighter 1, A-A artillery 8)	4	18	32
SB	8 (Finnish fighters)	5	17	30
DB-3	8 (Finnish fighters 5, A-A artillery 3)	2	7	17
Bombers total	16 (Finnish fighters 13, A-A artillery 3)	7	24	47
R-5	-	1	4	5
MBR-2	3 (own aircraft 2, own ship 1)	-	9	12
R-6	1 (A-A artillery)	-	-	1
TOTAL	30 (Finnish fighters 14, A-A artillery 12, own aircraft 3, own ship 1)	12	55	97

Significantly fewer naval aircraft were lost in combat (most aircraft MIA were apparently shot down by Finnish fighters or A-A artillery, bringing total combat losses to some 42 aircraft) than in accidents (55 aircraft). 104 naval aviators were killed in action, and six taken prisoner. Furthermore three mechanics were killed in accidents on the ground.

Northern Fleet Air Force (VVS SF)

The origin of the Northern Fleet AF was the detached maritime close reconnaissance Squadron 29 OMBRAE (equipped with MBR-2 flying boats), organized in July 1937 as the first naval aviation unit in the Barents Sea. In October 1939 *kombrig* Aleksandr Kuznetsov was appointed VVS SF Commander.

VVS SF High Command

Commander *kombrig* (4.6.1940 *General-major*) A.A. Kuznetsov (1904–1966). Commanded VVS SF until 1943. Head of Northern Seaway (Sevmorput) 1948–1953 etc. HSU 6.12.1949.
Military Commissar *brig.komiss* M.I. Skobelev
Chief of Staff *polkovnik* I.V. Kukin

VVS SF Commander Aleksandr A. Kuznetsov (HSU 6.12.1949). (G.F. Petrov)

VVS SF Organisation

In November 1939 VVS SF consisted of only of MBR-2 equipped 118 MRAP in Guba Gryaznaya and 49 OMRAE in Yagodnik, together 45 MBR-2 flying boats.

Mixed aviation regiment 72 AP was formed 23 December 1939 in Vayenga, and incorporated two fighter Squadrons and one SB squadron from Belorussian Military District (BOVO).

Main task of the Northern Fleet was protection of Murmansk against possible Finnish attacks and prevention of possible invasion and capture of Pechenga Bay and the ice-free port of Liinahamari by Anglo-French intervention troops.

118th Maritime Reconnaissance Aviation Regiment (118 MRAP)

118 MRAP was formed in Guba Graznaya in September 1939, and received the first 18 MBR-2 flying boats flown from 15 OMRAP. Gradually the number of flying boats rose to 37.

118 MRAP tasks:
- surveillance of enemy shipping up to Tanafjord and Varangerfjord (in Norway!) and in Barents Sea
- photo reconnaissance of Finnish territory
- protection of troop transports to Petsamo
- "special tasks of the Fleet Command" (which usually means spy and agent dropping on enemy held territory)

Most missions were performed from land airfields, using ski-equipped MBR-2s.

118 MRAP suffered no combat losses, but at Guba Gryaznaya 14 (fourteen!) MBR-2s were destroyed and two more damaged in a hangar fire 14 January 1940. Apparently because of this fire *major* M.D. Nizhegorodtsev was dismissed in February 1940, and replaced by V.N. Vasilyev who was appointed 118 MRAP Commander only in June 1941.

118 MRAP Command
Commander *major* M.D. Nizhegorodtsev (to February 1940)
Military Commissar *batl.komiss* R.V. Obukhov
Chief of Staff *major* L.A. Koleshnichenko

Squadron Commanders
1st Squadron *kapitan* G.S. Sharov
2nd Squadron *kapitan* V.M. Sechkin
3rd Squadron *kapitan* V.I. Bojko

72nd Aviation Regiment (72 AP)

72 AP was set up 23 December 1939 in Vayenga, incorporating two fighter squadrons and one SB squadron from BOVO (Byelorussian Military District).

Komsomol representative in ex-15 IAP Squadron was *st.lt* Boris Safonov, future top ace of VVS SF and posthumously double HSU. (Safonov was killed when his P-40 Kittyhawk fighter crashed into the Polar Sea after engine malfunction 30 May 1942. His HSU and Golden Stars were awarded 16 September 1941 and posthumously 14 June 1942.)

In honor of Safonov's memory in 1954 Guba Grazhnaya was given the name Safonovo (now attached to the city of Vayenga).

Boris Safonov in front of his I-16 inscribed Za Stalina! *(For Stalin!) summer 1941. (G.F. Petrov)*

72 AP strength 23 December 1939

Squadron	Aircraft	Comments
1st	15 I-15bis	Ex 2./15 IAP
2nd	15 I-15bis	Ex 4 OIAE, 70AB
3rd	8 SB	Ex 5 SBAE and 39 SBAP

72 AP Command
Commander *kapitan* V.K. Chernykh
Military Commissar *polk.komiss* A.S. Shabanov
Chief of Staff *major* L.M. Levant

Squadron Commanders
1st Squadron *kapitan* A.V. Ilyin
2nd Squadron *kapitan* A.V. Plotnikov
3rd Squadron *kapitan* D.F. Korenkov

White Sea Flotilla

49th Detached Naval Close-Reconnaissance Aviation Squadron (49 OMBRAE)

In September 1939 49 OMBRAE was formed as the White Sea Flotilla aviation component at Yagodnik near Arkhangelsk.

49 OMBRAE was equipped with 13 MBR-2 flying boats, but did not participate in the Winter War.

Commander   V.N. Andreyev

Claims and Losses

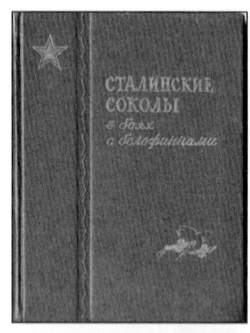

By the end of the Winter War Soviet air forces had received considerable reinforcements. Despite the heavy losses suffered, the Red air forces now counted over 3,700 aircraft against Finland; almost 2,700 aircraft in the Red Army Air Forces (VVS RKKA), over 850 aircraft in the Baltic Fleet Air Forces (VVS KBF), some 50 aircraft in the Northern Fleet Air Forces (VVS SF), and additionally approx. 150 aircraft in the Special Units of the Civil Air Fleet (GVF).

The organisation of the Red Army Air Forces (VVS RKKA) concentrated against Finland 13 March 1940 is presented in table 2.

Red Army Air Forces (VVS RKKA) performed 84,307 combat missions in the Winter War (of which 44,041 were bomber missions and 40,266 fighter missions), while Naval Air Forces (VVS VMF) performed 16,633 combat missions. VVS RKKA dropped a bomb load of 23,146 tonnes and VVS KBF another 2,600 tonnes, totalling some 25,750 tonnes. In comparison to 100,940 Soviet combat missions, *Ilmavoimat* performed 5,993 combat missions, and dropped only 218.4 ton bombs (or only 5.9% of Soviet aviation missions, and some 0.8% of the bomb load dropped by Soviet aircraft).

Decorated Aviators and Air Force Units

91 aviators of VVS RKKA and 17 naval aviators of VVS KBF were awarded the highest Soviet award **Hero of the Soviet Union** after the Winter War, or over 26% of all 412 Winter War Hero awards.

The Red Banner Order was collectively awarded to following aviation units:
- 21 March 1940: 15 SBAB, 44 SBAP, 54 SBAP, 25 IAP and 1 DRAE.
- 11 April 1940: 7 IAP, 10 SBAP, 19 IAP, 58 SBAP and 32 ROAE.
- 21 April 1940: 3rd Squadron/1 AP, 12 OIAE and 13 OIAE (VVS KBF units).
- 7 May 1940: 5 OSBAP
- 20 May 1940: 49 IAP and 18 SBAP
- 21 May 1940: 80 SAP

Six Red Army units were awarded the Lenin Order, one Red Army unit was awarded the Red Star Order, and 53 Red Army units and three submarines of KBF were also awarded the Red Banner Order.

A special Winter War medal was prepared, but never distributed.

The first Soviet publications describing the Winter War in the air was Stalinskiye sokoly v boyakh s belofinnami *(Stalin's hawks in combat with the White Finns) and* Moguchaya sovetskaya aviatsiya *(Mighty Soviet aviation) by N. Volkov. Both books were printed in 1940. (C-F. Geust)*

The Soviet Winter War Order (inscribed Karelian Isthmus 30.11.1939) was never distributed. (C-F. Geust)

Most Bombed Finnish Cities in the Winter War

City	Bomb attacks	Bombers	Explosive bombs	Persons killed
Hanko	72	260	1,100	6
Viipuri	64	1,400	4,700	38
Turku	61	440	2,550	52
Riihimäki	40	620	1,700	20
Kouvola	39	850	1,200	28
Elisenvaara	39	280	1,000	35
Nurmes	37	150	600	22
Lappeenranta	36	550	1,800	37
Jänisjärvi	36	220	900	49
Lahti	23	300	1,500	23
Sortavala	23	200	1,050	31
Rovaniemi	19	170	700	28
Tampere	12	260	1,000	17
Iisalmi	11	80	450	41
Mikkeli	10	110	400	63
Helsinki	8	70	350	97
Hämeenlinna	8	50	200	13
Vaasa	6	85	600	22
Kuopio	5	80	400	38
Seinäjoki	1	27	150	10

Air victories and losses

The first public Soviet account of the Winter War in the air was published by N. Volkov in his book *Moguchaya sovietskaya aviatsiya* (Mighty Soviet air force), printed by the State Publishing House for Political Literature as early as 1940. According to Volkov air victories and losses were distributed as follows:

Date	Destroyed Finnish a/c	Lost Soviet a/c	Notes
1.12.39	10	-	
30.11–5.12.39	11	4	2 shot down and 2 force-landed in Finland
19.12.1939–1.1.40	24	1	
5–6.1.40	10	-	
17–29.1.40	33	?	
11.2–1.3.40	191	11	
1–2.3.40	18		
3.3.40	10		
4.3.1940	-		No Finnish missions observed
5.3.40	21		
7–8.3.40	17		
9–10.3.40	10		
Total	300		

Ilmavoimat claimed 207 Soviet aircraft shot down, and Finnish A-A artillery another 314. According to the first Soviet comprehensive loss figures only published in 1988 VVS RKKA lost 261 aircraft in combat.

Based on archive document analysis published by Oleg Kiselev VVS RKKA lost 269 aircraft in combat (of which 46 were in air combat and 106 to anti-aircraft fire, while 117 aircraft went missing) and 136 aircraft were destroyed in non-combat situations. Thus 405 aircraft were written off, and additionally 200 aircraft were seriously damaged. According to research by Dr. Pavel Petrov in St.Petersburg (mainly based on documents of the Russian State Naval Archive RGVMA), Baltic Fleet Air Force (VVS KBF) lost furthermore 90 aircraft, of which some 40 in combat, and some 50 aircraft in accidents. The Northern Fleet Air Force (VVS SF) did not suffer any losses in the Winter War.

Thus total Soviet aircraft losses amount to some 500 aircraft.

However, recent research by this author indicate that the total losses of the Soviet Air Forces amount to at least 980 aircraft, of which the Red Army Air Forces (VVS RKKA) losses amount to at least 880 aircraft. About half of these tremendous losses are apparently direct combat losses, and the rest are results of accidents, losses of orientation, bad weather etc. At least 770 (perhaps over 810?) Red Army Air Forces aircraft were destroyed or written off. At least 27 aircraft went missing, and at least 30 aircraft were sent for factory repairs, and some 20 aircraft were correspondingly dispatched to field repair depots for lengthy repair of combat damage.

Soviet Air Forces Flying Personnel Losses

	Red Army Air Force (VVS RKKA)	Baltic Fleet Air Force (VVS KBF)	Total
KIA	609	79	688
MIA	58	23	81
POW	100	6	106
DOW	20	2	22
Total	787	110	897

Thus total Soviet AF personnel losses amount to 897 aviators, of which 769 Soviet aviators were killed or missing in action and 106 taken prisoner. All flying personnel losses (KIA, MIA and POW) are listed in appendix 13. In addition some 20 ground personnel were killed in various accidents etc.

The dead Soviet aviators in aircraft crashed in Finland were usually buried by Finnish troops near the crash site. The Soviet diplomatic mission in Finland organised in cooperation with Finnish authorities four trips in December 1940 for investigation of known graves of Soviet aviators in various locations in Finland. After opening the graves some 20 remains of Soviet aviators were brought to Hanko, and reburied with military honors in the new Soviet naval base.

Ilmavoimat lost 62 aircraft (of which 47 were in combat), and 71 aviators were killed (of which three were Swedish, four Danish, one Italian and one Hungarian volunteers). Five aviators were taken prisoner (of which two were Swedish volunteers).

According to the official history *Vozdushnaya moshsch rodiny* (*Air power of the Motherland*, published in 1988 by the Military Publishing House *Voyenizdat*) the Red Army Air Force claimed 362 Finnish aircraft shot down in combat, or almost eight times the real Finnish combat losses (the inventory of the Finnish Air Force had never amounted to 362 aircraft...)!

Fokker C.X (FK-111) was shot down at Saunasaari 29.1.1940, Vänrikki Robert Nenonen and Sverre Roschier were killed. (G.F. Petrov)

Kersantti Mauno Fräntilä force-landed on the ice of Viipuri Bay 5.3.1940, and was able to reach his own lines. The only lightly damaged Fokker FR-76 was captured by the Soviets, and put on display in the war booty exhibition opened in Leningrad 10.5.1940. (G.F. Petrov)

Overall Soviet losses (KIA, MIA and DOW) in the Winter War were approximately 330,000 soldiers. Some 6,000 Red Army soldiers were taken prisoner, of which 5,573 were repatriated in spring 1940. Several hundred POWs died in captivity or refused repatriation to the USSR.

Finnish total losses (KIA, MIA and DOW) amount to 26,662 soldiers and 957 civilians (killed in bombings or in sunken merchant ships). Some 1,000 Finnish soldiers were taken prisoner, of which 847 were repatriated in spring 1940.

Aviator POWs

Almost 6,000 Soviet soldiers were taken prisoner by the Finns, of which some 100 were aviators (while more than 500 Soviet aviators were killed in combat).

Soviet AF losses numbered some 1,000 aircraft, of which more than were half in combat. The rest were lost in frequent accidents because of loss of orientation on long ferry flights, bad weather conditions, breaches against flight discipline, technical failures etc.

Finnish anti-aircraft forces reported 404 Soviet aircraft downed, and *Ilmavoimat* claimed another 281 aircraft (of which 85 victories were considered uncertain). As most wrecks were located, the overwhelming majority of the victory claims are confirmed.

Among the POW aviators were one Major and ten Captains (of which two were Squadron commanders).

Most (but not all) aviator POW interrogation reports (or fragments of them) have been located in the Finnish National Archive. No central filing system for POW aviator questioning reports seems to have been established, and unfortunately cannot easily be found.

By 1 December 1939 nine POW aviators were captured from Soviet bombers downed in SE Finland. Some POWs had escaped by parachute, but some remained in their aircraft and survived a crash-landing on snowy fields or in forests. Some aviators were badly injured, others were almost without bruises. In most cases the aviators were fairly quickly captured by Finnish patrols. The capture was not always a safe process, which became clear on the same day. Between lakes Rieskjärvi and Vammeljärvi at Lempiälä on the Karelian isthmus, two parachutes were seen coming from a Soviet bomber in flames after ground fire hits. A patrol led by Cavalry *kapt* Adolf Ehrnrooth (future General, and recipient of the Mannerheim Cross) was dispatched to capture the Soviet aviators, who were apparently hiding in a nearby empty farm.

As the Finnish patrol approached the house, they were met by fierce gun fire. *Luutn* (res.) Jorma Gallén-Kallela (son of Finland's national artist, Akseli Gallén-Kallela) was killed immediately – he was the first reserve officer killed in the Winter War. The rifle-equipped Ehrnrooth shot one of the two aviators, and *lt* Petr Krivosheya (24 SBAP) was seriously injured, and died later of his wounds. This gunfire exchange between downed Soviet aviators and Finnish soldiers was by no means unique. After other similar cases the Finnish Home Guard was instructed to attempt captures very carefully, which is reflected by ambiguous war diary phrases referring to Soviet aviators "killed at capture".

The Red aviators often committed suicide after crashlanding on Finnish territory, having been told by the politruks that the Finns do not take any prisoners, but execute them after torture.

Captured aviators were in fact initially given first aid or sent to field hospitals as necessary. Thereafter they were taken to the nearest military unit or police station, where interrogation was initiated as soon as an interpreter (often only a Russian teacher or Orthodox priest, without knowledge of aviation terminology!) had arrived.

Thus *lt* Zh.Tanklayev and *lt* Viktor Demchinskiy (41 SBAP) were interrogated on 1 December 1939 in Imatra by *vänr* (res.) Valentin Kiparsky (later an internationally renowned Professor of Slavic Languages – who certainly spoke Russian perfectly, but knew virtually nothing about military aviation).

In November 1939 "frontal questionnaires" for possible POW questioning were distributed to newly-mobilised Finnish army units. After the shocking Soviet attack 30 November 1939 new preparations were quickly made for POW aviator interrogation, and 6 December 1939 an updated questionnaire with 87 (!) questions was distributed.

The interrogation of the POW aviators was initially planned to be performed by intelligence officers of *Ilmavoimat*'s aviation regiments and Squadrons, who naturally were air combat specialists, but seldom Russian-speaking.

As shot down enemy aviators in fact appeared literally all over Finland, it is easily understood that aviation specialists were not available among the infantry or Home Guard ("suojeluskunta/skyddskår") troops which arrested enemy aviators. The interrogating officers were thus not always able to ask "correct" or meaningful questions, and could not even recognize whether the POW was clearly lying. It is self-evident that POWs were evading giving vital information in their answers. When the POW, after recovery from the mental and physical shocks of the crash and parachute jump, recognised that the questioning officer did not understand the relevance of his own question, he could easily give false or evasive answers, and to hide secret matters ("I got lost on my first combat flight, and do not know anything about operational matters" etc).

Preserved reports are thus often of rather low quality with respect to structure and factual contents, sometimes lacking such basic information as POW's name and unit, date and place of capture, aircraft type and tactical number, and description of the last mission. As indicated linguistic and terminological misunderstandings are commonplace.

Questioning of one of the Soviet aviators shot down 1 December 1939 in Enso 4 December 1939. (SA-kuva)

In the brief and intense Winter War the few – and even fewer Russian-speaking – skilled intelligence officers had no time for the special analysis and repeated interrogation required in order to collect the maximum amount of information from the relatively few POW aviators.

Several reports were compiled in Viipuri, where a local office of the General Staff Statistical (ie. Intelligence) Department (with special knowledge of the Red Army and Russian-speaking personnel) was located. Documents found in crashed aircraft and in the pockets of captured or dead aviators were also sent to this office for analysis of Soviet strategic and tactical plans.

After initial interrogation the POW aviators were sent to various POW camps. Because of a regrettable accident in Otrakkala POW camp (located in Ruskeala between Sortavala and Värtsilä) on the night 8–9 February 1940 several POWs died of carbon monoxide suffocation, including four POW aviators: *st.lt* Ivan Makletsov, 5 OKAO (POW 31 January 1940), *st.lt* Nikolai Vorobyev and Vasiliy Palchikov, 42 DBAP (POW 3 February 1940) and *lt* Nikolai Volkov, 24 SBAP (POW 2 February 1940).

All Soviet POWs were repatriated from mid-April 1940, however about 100 refused repatriation and deliberatedly stayed in Finland (no POW aviators are known to have refused repatration).

Finnish POWs in Soviet Union

About 1,000 Finnish soldiers were captured by Soviet forces in the Winter War, of which 847 were repatriated in April-May 1940. *Ilmavoimat* lost 50 aircraft (of which two thirds were in combat) and 70 aviators, of which five were taken prisoner, who all were repatriated in May 1940.

The highest-ranking Finnish POW aviators were two lieutenants, Eino Laasko (navigator in Blackburn Ripon RI-143, shot down by ground fire at Ägläjärvi 6 Deecmber 1939), and Swedish F19 volunteer Per Sterner (Hawker Hart pilot, taken prisoner on his first combat flight 12 January 1940 after a midair collision with another Hart at Märkäjärvi). The other Finnish POWs were *lentomestari* (Flight Master) Viktor Törhönen (pilot of RI-143), *fänrik* (Ensign) Arne Jung (navigator in the other Hart, which collided at Märkäjärvi 12 January 1940), and *kokelas* ("Ensign Candidate") Kauko Nykänen (navigator in Blenheim BL-144, which was shot down by Soviet fighters of 7 IAP at Koivisto 7 March 1940).

Despite their rather moderate military ranks at least the Swedes and Nykänen were interrogated by exceptionally high-ranking Soviet officers.

The Swedes Sterner and Jung were interrogated by the High Command of 9th Army (*komkor* Vasily Chuikov, Military Commissar Lev Mekhlis and 9th Army Air Force Commander *komdiv* Pavel Rychagov), who now got the first proof of the arrival of Swedish combat troops in Finland.

The reports were immediately sent by telegraph to *Stavka* in Moscow, where Stalin was personally informed of the Swedish involvment.

Sterner and Jung (who were interrogated separately) incredibly succeeded in hiding vital information from their interrogators. Thus both confirmed that the take-off for the Märkäjärvi bombing mission was made from Oulu (not saying a word about the temporary ice base at Olkkajärvi north of Rovaniemi, from where they actually took off).

After the shocking information of Swedish air force units in Finland Stalin gave the harsh order to destroy the city of Oulu, which was carried out by 44 SB bombers of 41 SBAP and 80 SAP approaching the city in three waves during the afternoon and evening of 21 January 1940. (See 41 SBAP, page 151)

The Swedes were there after repeatedly questioned, and were exposed to physical and psychological torture (including simulated executions), forcing them to sign "agent" contracts.

After arrival in Finland on 11 May 1940 both Swedish volunteers informed Finnish (and later also Swedish) counterintelligence about their "agent recruitment". After appropriate investigation of the matter both Sterner and Jung were allowed to continue their service in the Swedish Air Force.

Also young Nykänen who was taken prisoner on his second combat flight on 7 March 1940, had the doubtful honor to be interrogated by prominent Soviet AF officers including *komandarm* Yevgeniy Ptukhin (North-West Front AF Commander) and *komdiv* Sergei Denisov (7. Army AF Commander).

It can be concluded from Nykänen's interrogation reports that Soviet Commanders were now extremely interested in the possible arrival of bombers and volunteers from other countries than Finland, which at the moment really was considered at the highest political level in Finland and the Allied Countries (ie. England and France) – about which the poor Nykänen (who had not even got his AF Wings!) was completely unaware.

Five Finnish aviators were taken prisoner during the Winter War. Ripon RI-143 (LLv 16) was shot down by ground fire at Ägläjärvi 6.12.1939. Lentom *Viktor Törhonen (right) and* luutnantti *Eino Laakso (left) were taken prisoner. The photo is taken after their return to Helsinki 20.4.1940. (SA-kuva)*

Finnish War Booty Aircraft

17 February 1940 a War trophy exhibition opened in Helsinki. Exhibited aircraft included SB bombers tactical *yellow 4* and *green 5* and I-16 (already with Finnish code *VH-201*).

Several Soviet aircraft force-landed in Finland were only slightly damaged, and were relatively easily repaired and taken into use by Finnish Air Force. As original Soviet contruction numbers of the recovered aircraft are not always indicated in Finnish documents the origin of all the war booty aircraft in Finland is not known. Following types of Winter War booty aircraft were repaired and used by *Ilmavoimat*:
- I-15bis fighter: five aircraft, of which two were used in the Winter War (Finnish codes VH-10 (ex – Soviet *11*) and VH-11 (ex-19 IAP 173, c/n 4616).
- I-153 fighter: eight aircraft, first used from April 1940 (VH-101).

289

- I-16 fighter: one aircraft, used from April 1940 VH-201 (ex-149 IAP 39, c/n 27P21D54).
- SB bomber: eight aircraft, first used from April 1940 VH-201 (ex-149 IAP 39, c/n 27P21D54).
- DB-3 bomber: five aircraft, VP-101 (ex-53 DBAP red 15, c/n 392320), in March 1940 used in the Winter War.

This and opposite page: The war booty exhibition was opened 17.2.1940 in Helsinki, with two SB-bombers and one I-16 on display. (SA-kuva)

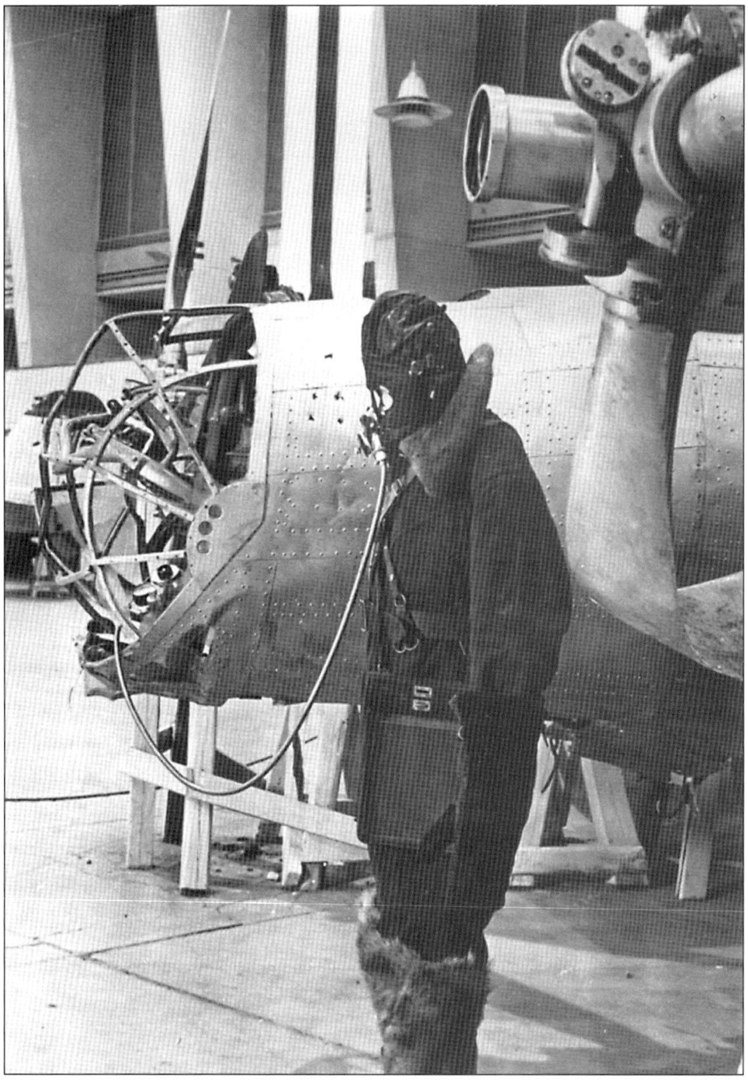

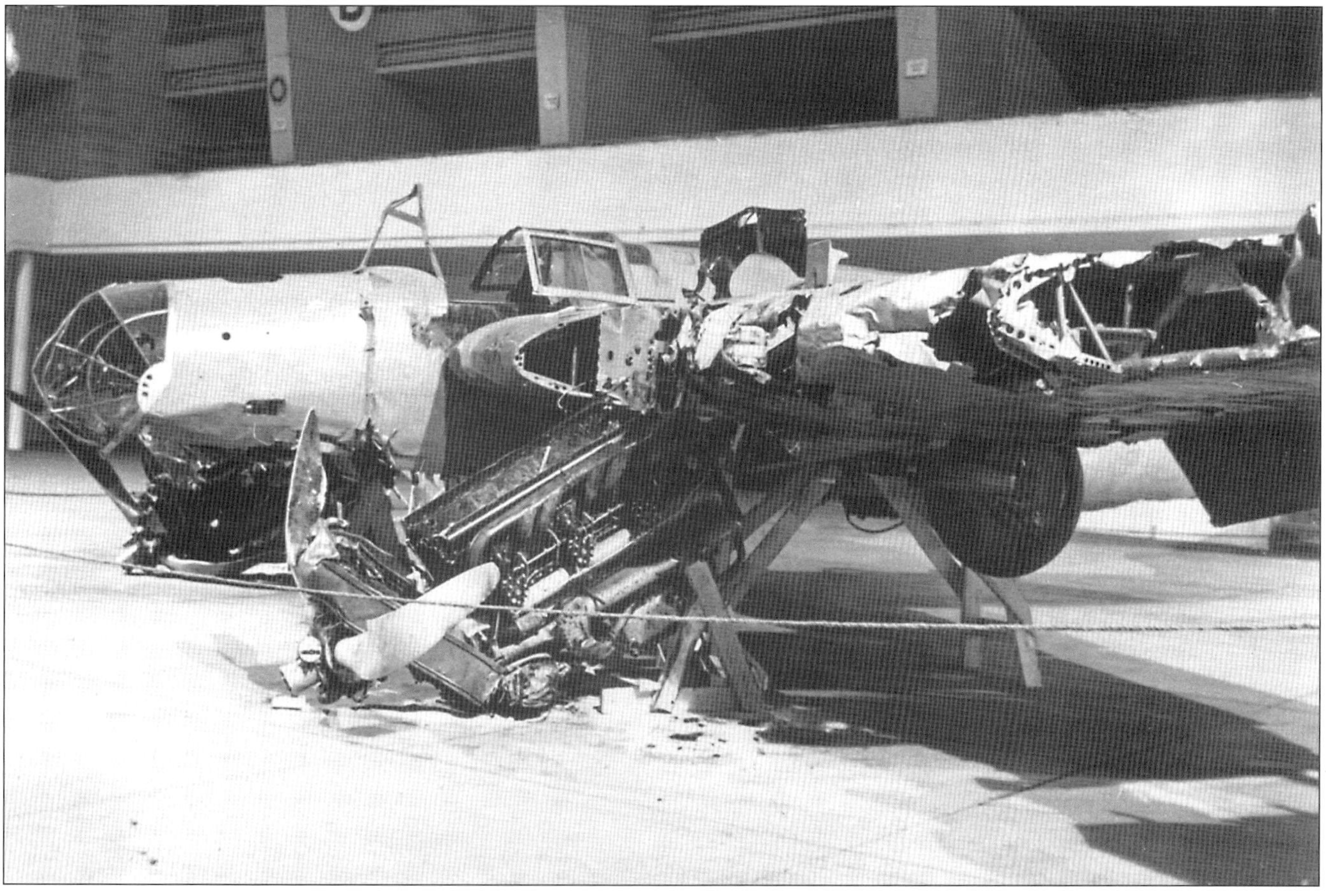

This I-15bis has got fake Soviet colors – VH-5 of Finnish AF was repainted 21.1.1942 for a propaganda film as Soviet white 17. (SA-kuva)

VH-11 was ex-173 of 19 IAP which landed on lake Oulunjärvi 24.12.1939. (SA-kuva)

The first SB repaired by VL (VP-10) in April 1940. (SA-kuva)

Winter War Impact on the Soviet Air Forces

After the peace treaty signed on 13 March 1940 a "post mortem" analysis was secretly initiated in the Soviet Air Forces – like in all armies after a campaign. The large losses and their reasons were analysed behind closed doors. The Soviet people were provided with heroic reports and stories describing the glorious return of the victors from the front. Newspapers were filled with photos of the new Heroes of the Soviet Union, and the lists of decorated officers and soldiers filled many pages day after day. However, the attentive reader could not avoid observing the complete lack of information concerning units and soldiers fighting north of lake Ladoga.

A clear drawback was the low level of preparation and navigation skills of the bomber pilots. Non-combat bomber losses on long ferry flights were practically as great as combat losses. Thus, on 29 March 1940 in Monino, east of Moscow, a new aviation academy called "Air Force Academy for Officers and Navigators of the Red Army Air Force" was inaugurated. This Academy was later to become the most prestigious academy of the Russian Air Forces. Renowned polar aviator Ivan Spirin (Commander of a special aviation group of 9th Army Air Force in the Winter War) was appointed Head of the Academy's navigation faculty. Experienced navigation and all-weather flight specialists and test pilots were invited as instructors to the Academy.

Large bomber formations (like the Special AON-Air Armies and aviation brigades) were far too large to be efficiently controlled, and were simply not able to operate from small, snow-covered and icy airfields. Already in January 1940 the Special Aviation Armies (AON) were dissolved, after which bombers operated in smaller formations only.

A few days after the establishment of the Monino Academy the Special (counterintelligence, or OO) Department of the NKVD sent a detailed, 119 page long report to the State Security Main Administration of the same NKVD. A number of technical deficiencies were listed: low reliability of the M-87 engines of the DB-3 bombers, dead sectors of onboard machine guns, lack of self-sealing fuel tanks, machine gun failures, unreliable dropping mechanism of AO-2.5 and AO-8 bombs in RRAB-3 containers, failing AGN-1 and AGM-3 bomb fuses, low quality radio and navigation equipment, air and ground equipment unfit for winter conditions, lack of long-range fighters for bomber escort etc. Also operational deficiencies were mentioned: erroneously formulated orders and correspondingly chaotic updates and corrections, sloppy intelligence and incomplete enemy information, low quality maps, "friendly fire" at own aircraft, bombs dropped on own troops leading to tragic losses, mid-air and ground collisions on narrow runways, bomber formations without fighter escort. Tactical plans often became unintentionally disclosed to the enemy because of the low security level applied, eg. by use of same flight routes to and from target locations, or by poor radio discipline in the few radio-equipped aircraft.

From 14 to 17 April 1940 a special top-secret post-war conference was arranged by the Bolshevik Party Central Committee in the Kremlin, to which practically all top-level Commanders were invited. The conference was chaired by Kliment Voroshilov, with Iosif Stalin personally present.

The Air Forces were represented by Yevgeniy Ptukhin (*komkor*, VVS SZFr Commander), Georgij Kravchenko (*kombrig*, OAG Commander), Ivan Kopets (*kombrig*, VVS 8.A Commander), Pavel Rychagov (*komkor*, fighter ace from the Spanish Civil war, VVS 9.A Commander) etc. The Head of Intelligence of the General Staff (GRU), former aviator Ivan Proskurov took also part in the conference.

The above mentioned OO NKVD report was apparently available only to the conference chairman. The participants were encouraged to speak openly about deficiencies and observed mistakes. During heated discussions Ptukhin and Rychagov dared to make veiled accusations towards Stalin in their comments, for which both were to pay a high price. Both were executed in the early Great Patriotic War because of the Air Force unpreparedness for the new war, but Stalin had not forgotten their accusations in April 1940.

It is necessary to mention that contemporary documents and the conference report mention above all deficiencies concerning bomber aviation. As there were rather few fighter to fighter combats in the Winter War, fighter problems were not so perceptibly identified.

In 7 IAP (the most efficient fighter regiment of VVS RKKA) it was however noted that the traditional Soviet *trojka* (or three-aircraft) combat formation was less efficient than the Finnish pair formation. Fighter pilots Fedor Shinkarenko and Petr Pokryshev thus started to apply fighter pairs in the Winter War.

Shinkarenko writes in his memoirs how he was unexpectedly invited to speak about his experiences at a reception by North-West Front Commander Semen Timoshenko and Politburo member Andrei Zhdanov in the Leningrad party HQ Smolnyi. Shinkarenko described how 7 IAP successfully applied the pair formation, and how Finnish fighter tactics was studied in the regiment.

During and after the Winter War many Soviet aircraft designers (in particular Nikolaj Polikarpov and Aleksandr Yakovlev) visited Germany, studying the German aircraft industry. As result of these trips some 40 German aircraft of different types were purchased and delivered to the USSR in 1940–1941.

Based on the Winter War experience and on the information from Germany, development of new combat aircraft types was accelerated. In 1941 new aircraft types entered series production, but Shinkarenko's tactical proposal was not supported. Thus the combat *trojka* was still the regular tactical formation of the Soviet AF early in the Great Patriotic war. Because of flight safety reasons use of the "complicated and difficult" new Yak, MiG and LaGG fighters was limited. Consequently Soviet pilots were in 1941 not able to fully utilise the potential of these new fighters in air combat against German (and Finnish!) opponents.

Finally the famous letter of Aeroflot veteran Aleksandr Golovanov should be mentioned. Golovanov served in the Winter War as a "civilian pilot", and wrote his letter to Stalin on New Year's Eve 1940 on a proposal by Yakov Smushkevich. In his letter Golovanov repeated the already well-known bomber navigation mistakes, and proposed to set up a special unit, based on Aeroflot's experience of night and all-weather navigation and technical maintenance in Arctic conditions. Golovanov's letter subsequently led to the foundation of the Long-distance Air Forces (ADD) in early 1942, and his appointment as ADD Commander.

From the book it is clear that a large part of the Soviet Air Force commanders in the Great Patriotic War got their combat baptism in the Winter War. Unfortunately only very few of them wrote their memoirs, telling of their experience of this "infamous" war.

The Soviet aviation delegations in Germany during the Soviet-German honeymoon 1939-1941 consisted of some 60 aviation engineers, including the famous designers Aleksandr Yakovlev, Artem Mikoyan and Nikolai Polikarpov. They toured extensively the German aircraft and equipment factories, and met German colleagues including Ernst Heinkel and Willy Messerschmitt. The test pilot Stepan Suprun flew the experimental He 100 fighter, and also a war booty Spitfire and a Curtiss P-40. The Soviet delagation purchased some 40 aircraft (including Bf 109, Bf 110 and He 100 fighters, Ju 88 and Do 215 bombers). In the upper photo Ernst Heinkel (centre) is demonstration the He 111 bomber to the Soviet delegation, and in the lower photo Stepan Suprun is ready to test the He 100. (G.F. Petrov)

Finnish Air Force during the Winter War 1939–1940

Introduction

The Finnish Air Force was created on 6 March 1918, and is thus one of the oldest air forces in the world. In the 1920s and 1930s a number of partly conflicting air force doctrines were proposed. With the enormous Soviet industrial and military might (quickly developing during the five-year plans of the 1930s) next to Finland, the task to organize Finland's air defense was formidable. Funds available were very limited, and Finns did not seriously anticipate military conflicts.

Up to the mid-1930s naval aircraft were considered optimal for Finnish topography with the long shoreline and multitude of lakes. In wintertime naval aircraft could easily use ski undercarriage. Differing performance of floatplanes and wheel equipped aircraft were not considered critical. However, the fast development of military aviation and its use in military conflicts, showed clearly that land-based aircraft were superior. Bombers were generally seen as instruments of air power.

In 1931 General Mannerheim was appointed chairman of the National Defense Council. Under his direction a development plan aiming at 17 squadrons (3 fighter squadrons, 5 ground support squadrons, 3 maritime support squadrons and 6 long-range squadrons, totaling 221 combat aircraft) was drafted in 1932. At this time the air force numbered 81 aircraft in seven only partially equipped squadrons. Because of economic constraints not even reduced plans could be fulfilled.

Relatively more emphasis was put on fighters than in other countries. Fighter tactics was also very modern, with flexible fighter pairs as the basic tactical unit. Both pair leader and wingman acted according to the *see first –shoot first* principle, stimulating personal initiative. All fighter pilots got extensive air gunnery marksman training.

Aircraft licences acquired in 1935–1938

Aircraft and engine licences acquired in late 1930s turned out to be of the utmost importance for development of Finnish air force and aviation industry.

Bristol Mercury radial engine (840 hp; UK)

A Mercury engine licence was signed in 1935 by Tampella Ltd. in Tampere, and was to be decisive for the subsequent choice of aircraft licences.

Bristol Blenheim (BL, two-engine bomber, Mercury engine; UK)

On 6 October 1936 18 Blenheim bombers were ordered. The Blenheims, coded BL-104-BL-121, arrived 29.7.1937–27.71938. A production licence was signed 12 April 1938, but no licence-produced aircraft were delivered before the Winter War. Used by LLv 44 and LLv 46.

Bristol Blenheim I "short-nose" BL-113 equipped with skis. This aircraft was one of 18 Blenheims delivered from England in 1937–1938 (coded BL-104 – BL-121). (K. Stenman)

Fokker D.XXI (FR, single engine monoplane fighter, Mercury engine; Netherlands)

On 18 November 1936 seven pattern aircraft and a production licence for 14 aircraft were purchased for the State Aircraft Factory (VL) in Tampere (the license was later expanded to unlimited production). The fighters, coded FR-76-FR-82, arrived 4–13.11.1937

The first Finnish produced Fokker D.XXI was ready on 11 November 1938. Two batches of a total of 35 fighters were delivered 11.11.1938–27.7.1939, coded FR-83-FR-117. The Fokker fighters equipped the only modern fighter squadron LLv 24 in autumn 1939, and remined the most important aircraft throughout the Winter War. The Fokker was very robust, and a stable gun platform. Winter War record: 130 victory claims, 13 FR lost (10 in air combat), 8 pilots killed in action.

Pilots of 3/LLv 24 at Ruokolahti in February 1940. From left Luutn E. Luukkanen, kers J. Dahl, vääp I. Juutilainen *and* kers M. Alho. *(K. Stenman)*

Fokker D.XXI was the main Finnish fighter in the Winter War. Seven pattern aircraft and a production license were aquired from Holland in 1936. Before the Winter War 35 aircraft were manufactured by VL in Tampere. The Fokker fighters were coded FR-76–FR-82 (purchased from Holland) and FR-83–FR-117 (manufactured by VL in Finland). (K. Stenman)

FR-79 at the State Aircraft Factory (VL) in Tampere in February 1938. (K. Stenman)

Detachment Luukkanen at Värtsilä, Christmas 1939. (K. Stenman)

Major G.E. Magnusson, Commander of LLv 24, addressing his personnel on 6 December 1939, Finland's Independence Day. The same day Magnusson was promoted to Major. (K. Stenman)

FR-86 in Utti, December 1939. (SA-kuva)

Luutnantti P. Sovelius (Deputy Leader, 4/LLv 24) at FR-92. (SA-kuva)

Luutnantti J. Sarvanto in FR-97, 6 January 1940. (K. Stenman)

Fokker C.X (FK, light dive bomber and reconnaissance biplane, Pegasus engine; Netherlands)
First order for four aircraft (coded FK-78–FK-81) and a production licence was signed on 18 May 1936.

Two batches of a total 30 of Fokker C.X were produced by VL in 1938 (coded FK-82–FK-111). Used by LLv 10, 12, 14 and 16. Winter War record: 587 missions, 8 FK lost, 14 aviators killed in action.

Finland bought four Dutch Fokker C.X dive bombers (FK-78-FK-81) and also a production licence from Holland in 1936. 30 Fokker C.X dive bombers were manufactured before the Winter War (coded FK-82–FK-111), FK-82 was the first aircraft produced by VL in Tampere. (SA-kuva)

In the Winter War Fokker C.X dive bombers were used by LLv 10, LLv 12 and LLv 14, mainly on the Karelian isthmus. FK-90 and FK-78 are pictured at Tikkakoski 7.3.1940. (SA-kuva)

FK-97 on skis, pictured at Suur-Merijoki AF base (west of Viipuri) in January 1939. (SA-kuva)

299

Aircraft procurement in October 1939

In the critical autumn of 1939 Finnish delegations were sent abroad to purchase armaments (in particular aircraft and artillery). However, most countries refused to sell arms after 1 September 1939. Prices were also much higher than expected – arms are very expensive when really needed! Traditional Finnish-German trade relations were seriously impaired by the Molotov-Ribbentrop pact, and Germany blocked all deliveries of goods from its enemy countries.

In autumn 1939 only Italy was ready to sell combat aircraft. Although Sweden reacted positively to Finnish appeals (but had no aircraft to sell), the Swedish government avoided official commitment. Transit via Sweden was the only import route open.

FIAT G.50 (FA, single-engine monoplane fighter)
25 Italian FIAT fighters were purchased on 23 October 1939, with another ten FIATs ordered 13 January 1940 (coded FA-1-FA-35).

The first FIAT G.50 (FA-1) bound for Finland after assembly in Sweden. Finland purchased 25 FIAT G.50 fighters from Italy in October 1939. Only two were delivered via Germany in December 1939, after which a German transit embargo interrupted further deliveries. Ten more FIATs were bought in January 1940. The FIATs were coded FA-1–FA-35, and used by LLv 26 in the last weeks of the Winter War. (K. Stenman)

FA-10 waiting for interception orders at Haukkajärvi ice base in March 1940. (SA-kuva)

The first two FIATs were dispatched 14 November 1939 by train from Italy via Germany to Sweden, and assembled in Malmö. The two fighters were flown to Finland in December 1939, and allocated to the Test Flight of the VL-factory in Tampere. Two attacking SB bombers were subsequently shot down by the test pilots.

In early December 1939 Germany stopped transit of war material to Finland because of Soviet protests. Six FIATs in northern Germany awaiting shipping to Sweden were returned to Switzerland, from where slow transit transport was organized. Remaining FIATs were delivered by ship from Italy to Sweden, and flown to Finland by Finnish pilots, arriving from 11 February 1940. Two FIATs were lost during transit (one Hungarian volunteer ferry pilot disappeared over the Baltic Sea), and the last FIAT arrived only on 19 June 1940. The FIATs were used by LLv 26 from 15 February 1940.

FA-32 is prepared in Swedish Air Force F 6 Wing for ferry flight to Finland in February 1940. (SA-kuva)

Italian volunteer technicians servicing the FIAT A.74 radial engine of a FIAT G.50 fighter at Pyhäniemi 11.3.1940. (SA-kuva)

301

Like the French Moranes, FIATs were mistaken for Spitfires by Soviet bomber crews. 13 air victories were claimed with FIATs, one FIAT was shot down in combat and two pilots were killed in action (of which one was an Italian volunteer).

30 November 1939 – the Winter War breaks out

On 30 November 1939 the Red Army crossed the over 1,000 km long land border with Finland. The Soviet navy blockaded the Finnish ports and the Soviet Air Force bombed Finnish cities (including Helsinki and Viipuri).

The Soviet AF numerical superiority was overwhelming: on 30 November 1939 over 2,000 Soviet aircraft were ranged against only 116 Finnish aircraft (of which only 36 Fokker D.XXI fighters and 14 Blenheim bombers could be considered relatively modern). In order to minimize their own losses, the few fighter pilots were instructed to avoid Soviet fighters, and to concentrate on intercepting enemy bombers, so fighter dogfights were relatively rare.

When weather permitted Fokker C.X dive bombers (LLv 10, 12 and 14) attacked Soviet ground forces on the Karelian isthmus with one or two aircraft only, and LLv 16 operated in Ladoga-Karelia. Blenheims of LeR 4 performed long-distance reconnaissance missions and occasional bombing sorties. All bombing and reconnaissance operations were performed by one or two Blenheims. Nevertheless losses to Soviet fighters and ground fire critically reduced the number of available aircraft and pilots.

Fortunately the Finnish aviators had in general a much better training and were better prepared for Arctic conditions than the Soviet aggressors (although *Ilmavoimat* had also practically no previous experience of flying in extreme sub-zero temperatures). In particular equipment and methods for photo reconnaissance in temperatures less than – 20 C° and at high altitudes (5,000 – 8,000 m) were not available before end-January 1940.

A top-secret advantage of the Finns was their excellent radio intelligence, which after recovery from the initial shock, in many cases was able to give early warning to cities about to be attacked, and direct the few own fighters to optimal interception locations.

One of the few advantages on the Finnish side was mental situation or fighting spirit: while the Red army entered and occupied foreign and unknown territory, the Finns fought for – and on – their own country!

Finnish Air Force operations summary:

- 30 November 1939. Because of poor weather the fighters of LeR 2 were not able to intercept attacking Soviet bombers.
- 1 December 1939. In *Ilmavoimat's* first air combat ever. *Ylik* Toivo Uuttu (LLv 26, in Bulldog BU-64) was shot down and force-landed at Muolaa on the Karelian isthmus. Also his opponent *lt* Petr Pokryshev (7 IAP) force-landed; both fighter pilots were unhurt.
- LLv 24 shot down 9 SB bombers (four SBs of 24 SBAP and five SBs of 41 SBAP) near Imatra; several others were seriously damaged and seen emitting heavy smoke. After this date the weather deteriorated for over two weeks.
- 19 December 1939. LLv 24 shot down 11 SB bombers (four of 13 SBAP and seven of 44 DSBAP) and one DB-3 bomber (6 DBAP) on the Karelian isthmus.
- 21 December 1939. LLv 24 shot down two SBs (24 SBAP) on the Karelian isthmus.
- 23 December 1939. LLv 24 shot down six SBs (five of 44 SBAP and one of 24 SBAP) and two I-16 fighters (7 IAP) in a rare fighter dogfight on the Karelian isthmus.
- 25 December 1939. Eight Fokker fighters were transferred to Värtsilä (Osasto Luukkanen) for air defence of Ladoga-Karelia. LLv 24 shot down three DB-3s (6 DBAP) on the Karelian isthmus, and four SBs (72 SBAP) at Korpijärvi-Äglajärvi.
- 27 December 1939. Four SBs (2 SBAP) were shot down at Imatra by LLv 24, after which bad weather prevented major combat.
- 1 January 1940. Two SBs (18 and 72 SBAP) were shot down in Ladoga-Karelia by Osasto Luukkanen.
- 5 January 1940. Two SBs (54 SBAP) were shot down on the Karelian isthmus by LLv 24.
- 6 January 1940. *Luutn* Jorma Sarvanto shot down six DB-3s (of 6 DBAP) between Utti and Tavastila. The DB-3s were returning from Kuopio, and a seventh DB-3 was shot down near Suursaari.
- 10 January 1940. Swedish volunteer unit F 19 arrived at Veitsiluoto at Kemi with 12 Gladiator fighters and four Hart light bombers.
- 12 January 1940. F 19 performed its first mission attacking Märkäjärvi AF base. Three Harts were lost.

Swedish volunteer squadron F 19 was initially equipped with twelve Gloster Gladiator fighters (coded A-L), four Hawker Hart light bombers (R, X, Y and Z) and three liaison aircraft. A Gladiator on an ice base is seen in the photo. (SFF)

Hawker Hart (M) over northern Finland. In the first F 19 operation 12 January 1940 three Harts were lost: one Hart (Z) was shot down and two Harts (X and Y) collided over the bombing target Märkäjärvi. Löjtnant A. Zachau was killed, and löjtnant P. Sterner and fänrik A. Jung were taken prisoner. In February a replacement Hart (M) was delivered to F 19 in Finland. (SFF)

- 17 January 1940. Three SBs of 31 SBAP and six SBs of 54 SBAP were shot down by LLv 24 on the Karelian isthmus. After the big losses *komandarm* Ye.S. Ptukhin explicitely prohibited bombing attacks without escort fighters.
- F 19 shot down three I-15bis fighters (145 AP) at Märkäjärvi.
- 19 January 1940. Three SBs of 24 SBAP on the Karelian isthmus and one SB of 72 SBAP in Ladoga-Karelia were shot down by LLv 24.
- 20 January 1940. Four SBs of 35 SBAP were shot down at Hämeenlinna by own and visiting pilots of the Test Flight in Tampere. One SB (18 SBAP) and one DB-3 (21 DBAP) were shot down by LLv 24.
- 21 January 1940. Ten long-nose Blenheim IV arrived to Tikkakoski, and were attached to LLv 46, which transferred its Blenheim I to LLv 44. LLv 14 performed the first photo reconnaissance mission with a Fokker C.X to eastern Karelian isthmus (Taipale-Vuoksi sector), which was repeated on 14 and 17 February 1940, and 1 and 12 March 1940.
- 29 January 1940. One SB (50 SBAP) and one R-5 (16 KAO) were shot down by LLv 24 on the Karelian isthmus, and one DB-3 (53 DBAP) was shot down by a Test Flight pilot at Lempäälä. Six other DB-3s of 53 DBAP were lost because of other reasons (ground fire, loss of orientation) in southern Finland.

- 1 to 22 February 1940. One Blenheim of LLv 44 was despatched to Kuluntalahti (near Kajaani) for strategic reconnaissance and bombing of encircled Soviet troops in northern Karelia.
- 1 February 1940. A Fokker C.X of LLv 12 protected by four Fokker D.XXI fighters (of which one was shot down) flying at 7,000 m altitude photographed the central Summa sector of the Mannerheim line where the Red Army was grouping for a breakthrough ten days later. Twenty sets of three photo strips (totalling 30 photos) were produced extremely fast, one photo set was delivered to Marshal Mannerheim. Tragically the Finnish Army had no means to prevent the breakthrough. The western part of the Karelian isthmus was repeatedly photographed by LLv 12 (15, 17, 25 and 26 February 1940).
- 2 February 1940. After a training period combat missions were performed with Gladiators of LLv 26, and two Soviet fighters were shot down: one I-153 (38 IAP) at Bromarf, and one I-16 (149 IAP) near Kotka. LLv 24 downed two SBs (24 SBAP) near Sortavala, two DB-3s (one of 6 DBAP on the Karelian isthmus, the other of 53 DBAP near Hanko) and one SB (57 AP KBF) near Someri. Ten Fokker D.XXI fighters (Osasto Ahola) were transferred to Turku for air defence of SW Finland.
- 3 February 1940. Four DB-3s of 42 DBAP were shot down by LLv 24 in SW Finland, and Osatoa Ahola downed two DB-3s of 10 AB KBF at Korpo in Turku archipelago.
- 9 February 1940. LLv 24 downed two R-5 reconnaissance aircraft (1 KAO) on the Karelian isthmus.
- 11 February 1940. The first FIAT G.50 fighter arrived at LLv 26 in Utti.
- 13 February 1940. Gladiators of LLv 26 shot down three SBs of 39 SBAP at Suistamo, Ladoga-Karelia. In combat with fighters of 49 IAP one I-15bis and one I-16 were shot down, but two Gladiators flown by Danish volunteers were lost (*Løjtnant* Carl Kalmberg was killed and *Løjtnant* Jörn Ulrich was wounded).
- 14 February 1940. LeR 1 resumed daylight reconnaissance flights with Gladiators received from LLv 26. Two SBs of 48 SBAP were shot down by LLv 24 near Lappeenranta.
- 17 February 1940: LLv 24 shot down one DB-3 (21 DBAP) at Enso and one SB (31 SBAP) at Muolaa. Morane-equipped LLv 28 recorded their first victory, downing a DB-3 (53 DBAP) at Utö in the norther Baltic Sea.
- 18 February 1940. Three DB-3s (1 AP KBF) were shot down by LLv 24 at Vainikkala.
- 19 February 1940. Single Blenheims (of LLv 44) performed photo reconnaissance missions on the Karelian isthmus and the islands of Suursaari, Seiskari and Tytärsaari in the Gulf of Finland.
- 20 February 1940. Two SBs (10 AB KBF) were shot down by LLv 28 at Rauma.
- 21 February 1940. F 19 shot down one SB and one DB-3 near Rovaniemi (both of 5 OSAP).
- 25 February 1940. Tytärsaari, Lavansaari, Seiskari and Peninsaari were photographed by BL-117 (LLv 44). Three R-Z reconnaissance aircraft (4 LBAP) were shot down by Gladiators of LLv 26 at Muolaa, but three Gladiators were lost to I-153 fighters of 68 IAP at Muolaa.
- 26 February 1940. Twelve Blenheim I were ferried by British crews to Juva and attached to LLv 42. The FIAT G.50s of LLv 26 initiated combat flights, downing one I-15bis (149 IAP) at Lavansaari and one DB-3 (10 AB) at Someri.
- 27 February 1940. All LeR 4 missions were directed at the Bay of Viipuri.
- 29 February 1940. This was a black day for *Ilmavoimat*, with four fighter pilots, six Gladiators and one Fokker lost. The well-hidden ice base at Ruokolahti (used for two weeks by Fokkers of Osasto Luukkanen and Gladiators of LLv 26) had been detected by the Soviet Air Force, and 68 IAP was given the task to destroy the base. Thus the Gladiators of LLv 26 were surprised at take-off by over 20 I-16 and I-153 fighters, which shot down five Gladiators and one Fokker, while 68 IAP lost one I-16 and one I-153 in the combat.
- 1 March 1940: The remaining Gladiators of LLv 26 were handed over to LLv 12 and 14 to be used for reconnaissance tasks. The sole Douglas DC-2 (modified to carry bombs) performed its only bombing mission in LLv 44.
- 2 March 1940. LLv 28 Morane fighters downed one SB and one I-153 (both of 10 AB KBF) in Turku archipelago.
- 7 March 1940. Two SB bombers (34 DRAE) were downed by F 19 near Vaala. Two Blenheim bombers were shot down by 7 IAP fighters at Bay of Viipuri.
- 10 March 1940. One TB-3 (1 TAP) was shot down at Posio.
- 11 March 1940. Two DB-3 bombers (7 DBAP) were shot down by LLv 28 Moranes at Loviisa.

Top scoring Finnish Fighter Pilots in the Winter War

Rank	Name	Squadron	Claims
Luutnantti	Jorma Sarvanto	24	15.83
Lentomestari	Viktor Pyötsiä	24	10.33
Ylikersantti	Oiva Tuominen	26	10
Luutnantti	Jorma Karhunen	24	9.83

Luutnantti	Pelle Sovelius	24	8.75
Luutnantti	Aapo Nieminen	26	8
Luutnantti	Olli Puhakka	26	8
Luutnantti	Tatu Huhanantti	24	7
Vääpeli	Kelpo Virta	24	7
Vääpeli	Lauri Nissinen	24	6.83
Luutnantti	Paavo Berg	26	6
Vänrikki	Toivo Vuorimaa	24	6
Luutnantti	Yrjö Turkka	24	5.75
Vänrikki	Pekka Kokko	24	5.33
Ylikersantti	Pentti Tilli	26	5
Lentomestari	Jaakko Vuorela	24	5

FINNISH AIRCRAFT LOST DUE TO ENEMY ACTIONS

1939

Date and time	A/C	Sq	Crew	Fate	Location	Comments
1.12.39	FK-93	14	*Kers* Nissilä Urho *Vänr* Ritavuori Ilpo	+ WIA	Kivennapa	Shot down by enemy ground fire, crashed between the lines.
1.12.39	BU-64	26	*Ylik* Uuttu Toivo.		Muolaanjärvi	Forced landing escaping enemy fighter (7 IAP).
6.12.39, 12.55	RI-143	16	*Lentom* Törhönen Viktor *Luutn* Laakso Eino	POW POW	Ägläjärvi	Shot down by enemy ground fire, both POWs returned 20.4.40.
19.12.39	RI-141	16	*Kers* Norvola Kauko *Vänr* Hallakorpi Olli	+ +	Suojärvi	Did not return – wreck and dead pilots found in 1943.
19.12.39, 09.25	FK-95	12	*Vänr* Rintala Kauko *Kers* Mäkelä Sulo	+ +	Johannes	Shot down by *lt* Antonov, 25 IAP
23.12.39, 09.00	FK-96	12	*Luutn* Salo Ilmari *Kers* Saloranta Erkki	+ +	Kaukjärvi-Uusikirkko	Shot down by 25 IAP fighters
23.12.39	FK-80	10	*Luutn* Kalaja Heikki *Vänr* Lintunen Niilo	WIA +	Perkjärvi	Attacked by 25 IAP fighters. Pilot returned with damaged ac, navigator KIA.
23.12.39, 14.00	RI-155	36	*Kers* Söderholm Kaj *Vänr* Huhanantti Esko	+ +	Paldiski	Shot down by *st.lt* Borisov (10 AB VVS KBF).
23.12.39	FR-111	24	*Kers* Kaarma Tauno	WIA	Lyykylä	Shot down by fighter, forced landing in forest.
24.12.39, 12.30	JU-126	16	*Ylik* Hyytiäinen Kauko *Luutn* Alanen Erkki *Kers* Kaurto Paavo	Para + +	Kuolajärvi	Shot down by *kapt* K.P. Sokol in I-15bis (38 IAP).
6.1.40	BL-112	46	*Luutn* Pesola Onni *Lentom* Termonen Matti *Kers* Pakkala Arvi		E Ladoga	Shot down by fighter, forced landing on enemy side. Crew escaped to Finnish side.
12.1.40	HH-Y	19	*Luutn* Sterner Per *Luutn* Zachau Anders	POW +	Märkäjärvi	Swedish volunteers. Collided with another Hart over Märkäjärvi (see below), Sterner POW, returned in May 1940.
12.1.40	HH-X	19	*Vänr* Jung Arne *Kers* Sundsten Matti	POW	Märkäjärvi	Swedish volunteers. Collided with another Hart over Märkäjärvi (see above). Jung returned in May 40
12.1.40	HH-Z	19	*Vänr* Färnström Fritz *Kers* Hansson Thure		Märkäjärvi	Swedish volunteers. Shot down by enemy fighter.
15.1.40	FK-87	10	*Luutn* Mustonen Leo *Vänr* Turtiainen Reino	MIA MIA	Pitkäranta	Did not return from reconnaissance and bombing flight; shot down by *st.lt* Savushkin and *ml.lt* Goryunov (I-16, 49 IAP)
19.1.40	BL-121	44	*Kers* Toivonen Johannes *Vänr* Ranta Tauno *Kers* Toivio Veikko	+ + +	Salmi	Shot down by *st.lt* Savushkin and *ml.lt* Goryunov (I-16, 49 IAP).
20.1.40	FR-107	26	*Kers* Tilli Pentti	+	Uuksujoki	Shot down by *st.politr* Permakov etc, 49 IAP .
23.1.40, 13.10	GL-B	19	*Vänr* Sjökvist John	+	Märkäjärvi	Swedish volunteer. Shot down by enemy fighters.
26.1.40	FK-81	10	*Lentom* Heilä Toivo *Luutn* Vaittinen Reino	MIA MIA	Uuksu	Not returned from reconnaissance flight Uuksu-Uusikylä-Salmi. Shot down by *st.lt* Peskov, 49 IAP?
29.1.40, 16.35	FK-111	10	*Vänr* Nenonen Robert *Vänr* Roschier Sverre	+ +	Saunasaari Metsäpirtti	Shot down by enemy ground fire.
1.2.40, 15.20	FR-115	24	*Vänr* Harmaja Tapani	+	Viipuri	Shot down by enemy fighters.
2.2.40	FR-81	24	*Luutn* Rasmussen Fritz	+	Saimaa	Danish volunteer. Shot down by enemy fighters.

Date	Code	Unit	Name	Status	Location	Notes
10.2.40	FR-102	24	*Ylik* Ikonen Väinö		Lappeenranta	Hits by enemy fighter, a/c destroyed on landing.
13.2.40	GL-260	26	*Luutn* Kalmberg Carl	+	Värtsilä	Danish volunteer. Shot down by 49 IAP fighters.
13.2.40	GL-257	26	*Luutn* Ulrich Jörn	WIA	Värtsilä	Danish volunteer Shot down by 49 IAP fighters.
17.2.40	FR-89	24	*Vänr* Törrönen Iikka	WIA	Koskenkylä	Hits in air combat, forced landing in forest.
18.2.40, 11.15	BL-113	44	*Kers* Westermark Karl *Vänr* Laamanen Erkki *Ylik* Koivuneva Toivo	Para + +	Ladoga	Shot down by enemy fighters, pilot escaped by parachute. *StLt Peshkov*, 49 IAP.
19.2.40	FR-80	26	*Luutn* Frijs Erhard Krag	+	Viipuri	Danish volunteer. Shot down by DB (1 AP/VVS KBF or 21 DBAP),
20.2.40, 11.10	GL-280	26	*Luutn* Berg Paavo	Para	Utti	Shot down by fighter/DB, (Yevseyev, 6 DBAP?).
25.2.40, 15.20	GL-254	26	*Luutn* Tevä Pentti.	+	Muolaanjärvi	Shot down by R-5.
25.2.40	GL-266	26	*Kers* Bergman Tage		Kämärä	Forced landing after air combat.
25.2.40	GL-258	26	*Kers* Sukanen Matti	WIA	Äyräpää	Forced landing after air combat.
26.2.40, 19.15	RI-130	36	*Kers* Tammisto Antti *Luutn* Helin Waldemar	+ +	Hogland	Shot down by ground fire. Parts of wreck lifted from 30 m by Soviet divers 28.2.40.
26.2.40	FR-85	24	*Kers* Kaarma Tauno		Immola	Set afire in air combat at Immola.
26.2.40	BL-119	44	*Kers* Oksala Unto		Salmi	Set afire in air combat at Ladoga (Salmi).
27.2.40	FA-12	26	*Vänr* Malmivuo Eero	+	Utti	Shot down by enemy fighters.
29.2.40	GL-269	26	*Alik* Kosola Pentti	+	Ruokolahti	Shot down by enemy fighters.
29.2.40, 12.00	GL-268	26	*Ylik* Lilja Väinö	Para	Ruokolahti	Shot down by enemy fighters.
29.2.40, 12.00	GL-262	26	*Luutn* Halme Erkki	+	Ruokolahti	Shot down by enemy fighters.
29.2.40, 12.00	GL-259	26	*Luutn* Kristensen Carl	+	Ruokolahti	Danish volunteer. Shot down by enemy fighters.
29.2.40, 12.00	GL-261	26	*Luutn* Christensen Povl	Para	Ruokolahti	Danish volunteer. Shot down by enemy fighters.
29.2.40	GL-263	26	*Ylik* Tolkki Juho	WIA	Ruokolahti	Set afire by enemy fighters.
29.2.40	FR-94	24	*Luutn* Huhanantti Tatu	+	Ruokolahti	Shot down by enemy fighters.
2.3.40, 12.55	FR-84	VL	*Lentom* Heiskala Urho	+	Tampere	Shot down by SB.
5.3.40	FR-76	24	*Kers* Fräntilä Mauno		Karelian Isthmus	Forced landing in "no man's land" after combat. Pilot escaped, a/c evacuated by Soviet troops, later displayed in Leningrad.
7.3.40, 07.30	BL-144	42	*Kers* Hyytiäinen Toivo *Vänr* Nykänen Kauko *Kers* Turunen Eelis	+ POW +	Koivisto	Shot down by enemy fighters (Gejbo, 7 IAP?) Parachuted, returned spring 1940.
7.3.40, 12.10	BL-122	46	*Luutn* Hakala Niilo *Luutn* Salokoski Pekka *Kers* Pakkala Arvi	Para + +	Vilaniemi	Shot down by enemy fighters (7 IAP?).
9.3.40	MS-322	28	*Luutn* Lupari Erkki		Vilalahti	Set afire by ground fire at Bay of Viipuri.
10.3.40	BL-133	46	*Kapt* Piponius Jouko *Luutn* Sopenlehto Arvi *Kers* Tani Erkki	+ + +	Ylämaa	Shot down by enemy fighters.
10.3.40, 11.10	GL-279	14	*Luutn* Ollikainen Tauno	+	Kirvu	Shot down by enemy fighters.
11.4.40, 14.40	FA-22	26	*Ylik* Manzocchi Diego	+	Iitti	Italian volunteer. Forced-landing after air combat.

Finnish AF Order of Battle 30 November 1939 and 15 March 1940 are presented in appendices 5.2 and 5.3.

During the Winter War (which lasted 105 days until 13 March 1940) some 100,000 aircraft bombs were dropped on 690 cities and villages. Approx. 1,000 persons were killed by bombs, 540 seriously wounded and 1,300 lightly wounded. 157 multi-storey buildings and 1,800 wooden houses were destroyed, and another 700 stone buildings and 4,100 wooden houses were seriously damaged.

International assistance during the Winter War

Sweden

Already on 3 December 1939 some Swedish officers proposed a volunteer Corps to be sent to Finland. On 8 December 1940 the Swedish government donated two Bulldog II, two Jaktfalken II and three Fokker C.VD aircraft to Finland, which were immediately flown to Finland. The Bulldog and Jaktfalken were allocated to fighter training unit T-LLv 29, and the Fokker C.VDs to LLv 16.

On 14 December 1940 the Swedish government permitted the formation of a volunteer aviation regiment (named F 19), consisting of twelve Gloster Gladiator fighters and four Hawker Hart light bombers.

F 19 was quickly organised, personnel and equipment mainly coming from the Gladiator-equipped F 8 fighter wing near Stockholm and Hart-equipped F 4 light bomber wing in Östersund.

Personnel strength was some 250 men (of which 12 were fighter pilots and 9 light bomber aviators). Operational area was Northern Finland, with main base at Veitsiluoto, Kemi. Tasks included Finnish

Bulldog Mk. IVa BU-74 on frozen lake Lehijärvi near Parola. This aircraft was one of 17 Bulldogs delivered from England 1934–1935 (codes BU-59–BU-75). (C-F. Geust)

Fighter conversion training unit T-LLv 29 in Parola was equipped with Bristol Bulldog and Swedish Jalkfalken fighters. Two Bulldog Mk. II (BUj-214 and BUj-216) and three ASJA J 6B Jalkfalken (JF-219, JF-224 and JF-228) were delivered from Sweden in December 1939. (C-F. Geust)

307

ground forces support and air defence of the main cities (Oulu, Kemi and Rovaniemi) in northern Finland. Before F 19 arrived no fighters were available for air defence of the northern half of Finland!

F 19 arrived in Kemi 10 January 1940. Already two days later the Soviet AF base at Märkäjärvi (east of Kemijärvi) was attacked by all the Harts, escorted by four Gladiators. Three Harts did not return (two crashed in a mid-air collision, and one was downed by a I-15bis of 145 IAP). Three Hart crewmen were able to reach Finnish lines, two were taken prisoner and one was killed. After its first mission (despite the losses clearly showing that the enemy's air superiority was no longer unchallenged), F 19 fought bravely and skilfully, particularly against attacking bombers.

In February 1940 it was clear that F 19 needed more and better aircraft. Funds for new aircraft were donated by Finnish cities and industries, and also by Swedish organizations and individuals. In late February 1940 twelve FIAT CR.42 biplane fighters were ordered from Italy by the Royal Swedish Air Board

Junkers F.13 liaison aircraft of F 19 with provisional Finnish civil code OH-SUO (ex-SE-ACK Gästrikland of ABA). After the Winter War it was handed over to Finnish Air Force, coded JU-120. (SFF)

F 19 also had a Waco ZQC-6 liaison aircraft (provisional Finnish civil code OH-SLA, ex SE-AHM). After the Winter War the Waco returned to Sweden. (SFF)

308

The third liaison aircraft of F19 was Raab-Katzenstein RK-26 Tigerschwalbe (ex SE-ADK) with Finnish swastika insigna (no individual code). This aircraft was only rarely used because of technical problems and lack of spares. (SFF)

A bomb-loaded Hart ready to take off from a primitive shelter in northern Finland. (SFF)

The Bristol Mercury VIII engine of a F 19 Gladiator is changed in sub-zero arctic environment. (SFF)

The removed Mercury engine is manually transported for further maintenance. (SFF)

Fuel is transported by horses to the aircraft. (SFF)

Really "outsourced" tool box! (SFF)

311

on behalf of F 19. The FIAT CR.42s were optimistically expected to be available within one month, but they arrived in Sweden only after the end of the Winter War.

Meanwhile modern fighters had arrived in Finland, and the Finnish AF was no longer interested in Italian biplanes. Corresponding funds were released for purchase of Brewsters from USA, and the FIATs were taken over by the Swedish AF (coded J 11 in Sweden).

In parallel with the purchase of FIAT fighters the Royal Swedish Air Board wanted to purchase up to 40 Italian bombers for F 19. On 29 February some 12 Savoia bombers were preliminarly promised for immediate delivery. Flygvapnet also planned transfer of heavy B 3 (Ju 86) bombers to F 19 for attacking strategic targets in the Murmansk area. On March 11 a bomber group was ready in Västerås, and corresponding preparations were made in Veitsiluoto. After the peace treaty two days later the Swedish bomber group was dissolved, and the acquisition plans were scrapped. As the Ju 86 bombers were already obsolete, it is highly likely that entering Murmansk airspace would have resulted in considerable losses.

F 19 claimed nine air victories on 464 missions. The regiment lost five aircraft, two Gladiators (one in combat) and three Harts. Three pilots were killed (two in air combat), and two were taken prisoner (both returned to Finland in May 1940). After the Winter War F 19 personnel and aircraft returned to Sweden (except a Junkers F.13 liaison aircraft transferred to Finnish Air Force).

F 19 was unique among the international assistance in the Winter War. The self-contained unit fought on its own, with own supply and maintenance, without support demands from scarce Finnish resources. Both personnel and equipment were adapted to arctic conditions. Full attention of the Finnish AF could thus be directed to the main fronts in southern Finland.

Virtually all Swedish aircraft factories and workshops were also busy assembling Italian, British, French and American aircraft for Finland. Without this effort the Finnish Air Force would apparently not have received any imported aircraft during the short campaign. Almost all deliveries to *Flygvapnet* (also in desperate need for modern aircraft!) were delayed for several months.

Several of the highest officers of Flygvapnet during the 1950s and 1960s were F 19 veterans, including four Generals and AF Wing Commanders, and the AF Chief Medical Officer. F 19 combat experiences were also significant when drafting the Swedish cold-war doctrine.

Assistance offered by allied countries (England, France, Poland)

England

The Finnish Minister in London G.A. Gripenberg was on 3 December 1939 instructed to immediately purchase 30 aircraft:

"Only three days after the outbreak of the war, on Sunday, 3 December I received an order to purchase 30 aircraft immediately – Spitfires, Hurricanes or Gladiators.... After I had received permission to buy 20 Gladiators immediately and 10 later, I was instructed to acquire 25 to 30 Gauntlet planes, but they had already been sold to South Africa. When this order was approved, I was requested to ask for 24 Blenheim bombers. And so it went, day after day." (Although Gripenberg was a skilled and experienced diplomat – to become Finland's first permanent representative to the United Nations in 1955 – he had absolutely no competence to buy combat aircraft...)

The Allied countries expected Finnish defence to collapse rather quickly, and the interest to dispatch weapons, in particular aircraft, to Finland was rather small. As Finland resisted the invaders surprisingly vigorously, with several Soviet divisions bogged down in the Finnish forests, Allied opinions gradually changed.

Especially after the expulsion of the USSR from the League of Nations on 14 December 1939, when member countries were instructed to give Finland all possible assistance, the Allied plans to assist Finland became more concrete. On 19 December 1939 England and France started to plan military invention in Finland.

Gloster Gladiator (GL)

Already on 5 December 1940 the British government promised 20 Gladiators to Finland. One week later (12 December) Gripenberg signed a contract with the Gloster Aircraft Co. (the British avoided signing Finnish contracts directly with Government Agencies "*in order not to provoke the Soviet Union*").

Twenty Gladiators were to be delivered immediately, price £80,000, and somewhat later another ten were donated. All Gladiators were taken from RAF maintenance units. Despite repeated Finnish appeals, only after one month were the Gladiators dispatched by ship to Bergen in Norway, and then by train to Linköping where they were assembled by British and Swedish technicians. Finnish pilots ferried the aircraft to Finland, arriving 18.1–17.2.1940 (coded GL-251-GL280]. The Gladiators were at first allocated to LLv 26, and after heavy losses to 68 IAP fighters at Ruokolahti February 29, 1940 to reconnaissance squadrons LLv 12, 14 and 16. The Gladiator tally in the Winter War counted about 700 missions and 37 victory claims. 14 Gladiators were lost (of which 11 were in combat), and seven pilots were killed.

Kersantti A. Juhola (1/LLv 12) in a Gladiator in March 1940. (A. Juhola)

Fighter pilots of LLv 26 at Ruokolahti in February 1940. Note the white starboard wings and the black port wings. (K. Stenman)

313

In December 1939 30 Gloster Gladiator II fighters were aquired from England (coded GL-251–GL-280). The Gladiators were assembled in Sweden and ferried to Finland in January–February 1940, and equipped LLv 26 and LLv 12. Gladiators of LLv 26 are pictured at the Ruokolahti ice base. (K. Stenman)

Vänrikki O. Marttila (1/LLv 12)is ready for take off from lake Karhusjärvi with GL-277 in March 1940. (K. Stenman)

Hawker Hurricane (HU, later HC)

Minister Gripenberg repeated the official Finnish request for "*at least 30, if possible 60 Spitfires or Hurricanes*" on 9 January 1940 in London. The response concerning delivery of Spitfires was strongly negative, but negotiations concerning Hurricane fighters (with more moderate performance) continued. Although Hurricane deliveries were opposed by the RAF, on 24 January 1940 the British Minister of Air Sir Kingsley Wood informed that Finland can buy "*twelve, not sixty Hurricanes*", which were released on February 2, 1940 (the contract was signed 17 February 1940 by Minister Gripenberg with Gloster Aircraft Co.).

Twelve Hurricanes were taken from RAF stocks, and were expensive (unit price £9,785, compared to ex-works price £6,000–7,000!). From 25 February 1940 the Hurricanes were flown to Finland via Norway and Sweden by rather inexperienced Finnish pilots (using provisional civil codes OH-IPx; in Sweden codes HU451–462 were painted, prefix later changed to HC-). HU461 was damaged in Scotland and left behind, and HC462 crashed in Norway during the long ferry flight. Ten Hurricanes arrived in Finland between 8 and 10 March too late to participate in the Winter War.

HU455 arrived in Säkylä 10.3.1940 and was allocated to LLv 28. (C-F. Geust)

Twelve Hawker Hurricane I fighters were purchased from England in February 1940 (coded HU451–HU462, later prefix HC). They were ferried to Finland by Finnish pilots, and arrived during the last days of the Winter War, too late to take part in combat. HU452 is pictured ready for ferry flight from Scotland at the end of February 1940. (C-F. Geust)

Hawker Hurricanes in transit in Sweden. Note the provisional civil registration codes (OH-IPx) and lack of swastikas. (C-F. Geust)

Bristol Blenheim (BL)

On Christmas Eve 1939 the British Air Ministry agreed to sell twelve Blenheim IV ("long-nose") to Finland, total price £264,000. On 17 January 1940 the Blenheims were handed over to Finnish crews which had arrived in England in early January 1940. As the bomb racks were not modified for Finnish bombs, 1,500 British 120 lb bombs were also purchased. Because of the rack arrangement the Blenheim IV could carry only five bombs, or half of the normal bomb load!

The Blenheims were ferried by Finnish pilots via Norway and Sweden to Finland (coded BL-122-BL-133). Ten Blenheims arrived 21 January 1940. BL-127 (*lentomestari* Rudolf Gottschalk annd kersantti Pekka Kallakari) disappeared 18 January 1940 over the North Sea, and BL-125 arrived only on 31 May 1940 after a transit accident in Sweden.

During the Winter War Finland also received 12 "long-nose" Blenheim IV, which were ferried by Finnish crews. Fuel filling of Blenheim IV BL-129 in Tikkakoski 7.3.1940 is depicted. Because of lack of proper equipment much manual work was required, and horses were used for ground transport tasks. (SA-kuva)

Twelve "short-nose" Bristol Blenheim I bombers were aquired from England, and ferried to Finland by British crews. Provisional civil registrations were used during the ferry flight, This Blenheim batch was coded BL-134–BL-145, and used by LLv 42. Provisional civil codes were used on ferry flights, thus OH-IPA later became BL-134. The photo was taken after landing at Juva 26.2.1940. (SA-kuva)

In February 1940 the Air Ministry released another batch of twelve Blenheims, this time "short-nose" Mk I. Although this batch was taken from RAF No. 2 Group, the deal was signed with Bristol Aeroplane Co. (total price £240,000), and ferried to Finland via Norway and Sweden by English crews, arriving 26 February 1940 to LLv 42 in Juva (coded BL-134-BL-145).

The Blenheim record (all Blenheim batches included) in the Winter War was 423 missions, 12 Blenheims lost (of which seven were in air combat), 21 aviators killed and one taken prisoner. Five Soviet fighters were claimed by Blenheim MG-gunners.

Gloster Gauntlet (GA)

29 (of 30 promised!) Gauntlet fighter trainers were donated by South Africa and released in late December 1939. The Gauntlets were taken from RAF stocks. 24 trainers arrived in crates by ship to Gothenburg. Nine aircraft were assembled in Linköping and flown to Finland between 10 March and 12 April 1940. Another 15 Gauntlets arrived by ship to Finland in May 1940.

24 Gloster Gauntlet fighter trainers were received from South Africa at the end of the Winter War. (coded GT-395–GT-418). (C-F. Geust)

Westland Lysander (LY)

An order for 17 Lysanders was signed on 8 January 1940. Nine Lysanders were dispatched by ship to Gothenburg 24 February 1940. After assembly in Gothenburg they were flown to Finland between 21 March and 3 May 1940.

American-Finnish test pilot E. Davidson with a Lysander in Sweden. (SFF)

Seventeen (of which twelve were delivered) Westland Lysander I reconnaissance aircraft were purchased in January 1940. Three Lysanders were ferried from Scotland, and nine were assembled in Sweden (codes LY-114–LY-125) and ferried to Finland in spring 1940. Two Lysanders (LY-114 in the mddle) are depicted in Sweden. (SFF)

Lysander LY-115 of LLv 12 summer 1940 (SA-kuva)

Eight Lysanders were to be flown by British pilots to Finland via Norway, but only two aircraft arrived in Finland on 5 March 1940 (one crashed in Norway). Only eleven Lysanders arrived in Finland (according to Gripenberg 30 Lysanders were dispatched on 5 March but none arrived).

Blackburn Roc (RO)

Among the many aircraft bound for Finland at the end of the Winter War were also some 30 Blackburn Roc naval fighters (codes reserved RO-141 etc). Four Rocs (RO-141, RO-142, RO-143 and RO-144) are pictured at Aberdeen, Scotland on 12 March 1940. (K. Stenman)

On 28 December 1939 50 single engine and 15 twin-engine dive bombers were requested from England. On 25 January 1940 33 Roc, or 20 Skua and 13 Roc aircraft were promised. In March 1940 several Roc aircraft (with Finnish AF codes already painted!) were to be flown by British pilots from Scotland to Sweden, and on 8 March Finnish pilots were ready to depart to Sweden to ferry the Rocs to Finland. On 13 March 1940 all aircraft delivery plans were cancelled.

Polish government in exile

After Anglo-French plans to assist Finland were formulated on 19 December *Generał* Władysław Sikorski (Polish government in exile Prime Minister and Commander-in-chief) assumed that participation of Polish soldiers on the Finnish side would stimulate the Finns to recognize the Polish government in exile.

The question of Polish aid was also convenient to the French. After a meeting between General Victor Denain (Chief of the French Military Mission at the Polish Government) and *Generał* Józef Zając (Chief of Aviation Command, in March 1940 Commander Polish AF) on 22 January 1940 it was decided to send a volunteer Polish AF squadron (commanded by *major* Józef Kępiński, with *kapitan* Piotr Łaguna as his deputy) to Finland.

In early 1940 no less than 7,000 Polish air force personnel had arrived in France (including some 650 skilled pilots). The appeal for volunteers for the *Finland Squadron* (to include 30 pilots and 30 technicians) met great enthusiasm, with some 150 applications received. On 12 February 1940 the Polish

Caudron-Renault CR.714 light fighter CA-552 seen assembled at LeV (Air Depot) at Tampere on 29 May 1940. It took over three months before the first flight could be made on 3 September 1940. The French construction number was 7. (Finnish Air Force).

The only existing (unfortunately incomplete) Caudron C.714 (CA-556) is currently on loan to the Polish Aviation Museum in Krakow as a reminder of the Polish-French willingness to assist Finland in the Winter War. (C-F. Geust)

military attaché in Stockholm Colonel Tadeusz Rudnicki was instructed to agree the details of the use of the Polish squadron (to be attached to the Finnish Air Force as LLv 20).

A total of 80 **Caudron CR.714** monoplane fighters were promised (some apparently intended for the Polish volunteer squadron; codes reserved CA-551–630). 46 Dutch-made **Koolhoven FK.58** were also earmarked for expansion of the *Finland Squadron* (codes *KN-501–546* reserved 7 March 1940). Fifteen Polish pilots were reserved for *Escadrille Koolhoven* (C.O. Capt. Walerian Jasionowski).

Training and preparation of the *Finland Squadron* was in full swing at Lyon-Bron when news of the peace agreement of 13 March 1940 was received. All plans to assist Finland were immediately cancelled. Six Caudron CR.714 fighters were in transit for Finland, another ten in the port of Le Havre, and three more in transit from Paris to Le Havre. The *Finland Squadron* was subsequently renamed CG 1/145 *Groupe de Chasse Polonaise de Varsovie* in the French Air Force, still using Caudron CR.714 fighters.

After arrival of the first six Caudron CR.714 fighters (CA-551–556) in May 1940, it turned out that they were practically useless for Finnish conditions (weak armament, long take-off and landing run) and were grounded in September 1940. It is questionable whether the Polish Caudron-equipped squadron would have able to provide any positive impact in Winter conditions.

France

Morane Saulnier MS.406 (MS)

50 Moranes were donated by France in late December 1939, but only 30 arrived in Finland. The Morane fighters were dispatched in crates to Malmö, Sweden. After assembly by French and Swedish technicians in Malmö, the fighters were ferried by Finnish pilots 4–29 February 1940.

The new LLv 28 was set up at Säkylä in south-western Finland to receive the Moranes. The ports and cities in this region (especially Turku, but also Pori, Uusikaupunki, Mariehamn etc.) had repeatedly been bombed by Soviet naval AF bombers from bases in Estonia, and were in urgent need of interceptor defence.

The appearance of Moranes was apparently entirely unexpected for the Soviet bombers, which suffered rather heavy losses to the opposing "Spitfires". The French fighter was never correctly identified during the Winter War. The outline, vaguely similar to the Spitfire – possibly combined with misleading intelligence information of Gripenberg's attempts to buy Spitfires – may explain the mistaken identification.

On 7 March 1940 several Moranes were transferred to south-east Finland for ground attack against the Red Army units at Bay of Viipuri.

The Morane fighters claimed 14 air victories on 288 missions in the Winter War. One Morane was shot down by anti-aircraft artillery at the Bay of Viipuri, the pilot was wounded. Frequent ground-loops occurred with the rather unfamiliar new fighters on icy runways, so several Morane became unserviceable soon after delivery.

Danish volunteer Løjtnant M. Fensboe at MS-303 of LLv 28 in Hollola 13.3.1940. (SA-kuva)

MS305 at take-off from Pyhäniemi for one of the last combat missions in the Winter War 13.3.1940. (SA-kuva)

MS306 of LLv 28 in Säkylä in March 1940. (SA-kuva)

France delivered 30 Morane-Saulnier MS.406 fighters, coded MS301–MS330. After assembly in Sweden the fighters were ferried by Finnish pilots, and equipped LLv 28 at Säkylä in SW Finland. MS-310 is pictured in Sweden. (SFF)

MS311 was tested on skis in April 1940. (SA-kuva)

Potez 633 (two-engine dive bomber).

On 12 March 1940 the volunteer *Groupe aérien de volontaires francais en Finlande* (GAVFF) was formed in France. This unit was to consist of twelve Potez 633 bombers, three Bloch fighters and one Dewoitine 338 transport aircraft. Later also separate fighter units (equipped with Morane 406 and Koolhoven FK.58 fighters) were to be formed.

News of the peace agreement was received on 13 March 1940. Already the day before 10 Potez 633 and the Dewoitine 338 transport were to have taken off for Tangmere, England bound for Finland via Stavanger, Norway and Västerås, Sweden. After the peace agreement the aircraft returned from England to France, and all further operations were cancelled.

USA

Brewster B.239 (BW)

In October 1939 Col. Per Zilliacus (Finnish Military Attaché in USA) enquired about American fighter deliveries. When Winter War broke out the rather unknown Brewster factory remained the only feasible alternative. As American legislation prohibited all sales of military material owned by the US government, any possible aircraft deals had to be made with private partners.

Finnish Prime Minister Risto Ryti and Finnish Minister in Washington Hjalmar Procopé proposed to President Franklin D. Roosevelt that 100 fighters under construction for the USAAF could be sold to Finland **before** actual delivery (when the aircraft were still the formal property of the factories!), referring to a precedent in 1927 when aircraft engines were sold to the USSR by the Curtiss Co. (These engines were originally ordered by the US government, and replaced by more modern Curtiss engines.)

Applying this formula, on December 16, 1939 Finland bought 44 Brewster F2A-1 fighters (under production for the US Navy, which later received the newer F2A-2), for a total price $3.4 million. The Brewsters were delivered in crates by ship to Bergen in Norway (the first batch was shipped from New York 13 January 1940), further by train to Trollhättan in Sweden, and assembled by American, Swedish, Norwegian, English and Finnish technicians. The Brewsters were flown from Trollhättan to Finland by Finnish pilots between 1 March (when the first eight Brewsters arrived) and 1 May 1940.

The Brewsters arrived too late to participate in the Winter War, but were to become the best combat aircraft of the Finnish AF during the first two years of the Continuation War 1941–1944.

Germany

After the signing of the Molotov-Ribbentrop pact Germany provided practically no assistance to Finland, causing much bitter feelings in Finland as Germany was considered a traditional ally. In early December 1939 transit of FIAT G.50 fighters purchased from Italy was stopped by Germany, and fighters already awaiting shipping to Finland were returned.

Private donations

Douglas DC-2 (DC)

One DC-2 passenger aircraft was bought by Swedish airline pilot Count Carl Gustav von Rosen from his former employer (Dutch airline company KLM) and donated to Finland. After modifications to carry bombs the aircraft was allocated to LLv 46 on 19 February 1940. One night bombing mission was performed by von Rosen himself.

(Carl-Gustav von Rosen's father, Count Eric von Rosen had donated the first military aircraft, a Morane Parasol fighter produced under licence by the Swedish Thulin company, to the Finnish Army commanded by General C.G. Mannerheim in 1918. The day of arrival of this aircraft, 6 March is since then celebrated as Finnish Air Force day, and von Rosen's family emblem, a blue swastika which was painted on the aircraft, was adopted as the Finnish AF national insignia. On 1 April 1945, the blue swastika was replaced as national insignia by the current blue and white cockade.)

DC-1 was named Hanssin-Jukka in Finland. In the photo the external bomb racks are clearly seen. DC-1 performed only one bombing mission 1.3.1940, when the Soviet AF base on frozen lake Suuri Pyhäjärvi was bombed, crew. Pilot löjtnant von Rosen, navigator vänrikki R. Winqvist and MG-gunner Danish volunteer Sergent R.Rasmussen. (C-F. Geust)

Swedish ex-KLM – Captain Carl Gustaf von Rosen donated a Douglas DC-1 passenger aircraft PH-AKH to the Finnish Air Force. The aircraft was modified to a bomber as DC-1. The photo was taken in Karlborg, Sweden during transfer to Finland, so blue swastikas are not yet painted. (C-F. Geust)

Koolhoven FK.52 (KO)

Two Dutch Koolhoven FK.52 aircraft were also bought by C.G. von Rosen and donated to Finland. The aircraft were used by LLv 36 for maritime reconnaissance from 4 March 1940.

A number of civil aircraft were also donated by non-governmental organizations and private persons in England and Sweden. These aircraft included Fokker F.VIII, DH 86 and Junkers F.13 outdated passenger aircraft (mainly intended for ambulance use), and some light aircraft (Beech 17, Waco, Raab-Katzenstein RK-26) and were of no military value.

Two Koolhoven FK.52 reconnaissance aircraft were bought by Swedish Count C.G. von Rosen and donated to Finnish Air Force (KO-129 and KO-130, ex PH-ASW and PH-ASX). They were used for surveillance of the eastern Gulf of Finland. (K. Stenman)

De Havilland DH-86B Silver Star G-AETM was donated in England to be used as an ambulance aircraft (Finnish code OH-IPA). Because of a ground accident 27.5.1940 the aircraft was practically not used at all. (SA-kuva)

War booty (ex-Soviet) aircraft

24 Soviet aircraft force-landed in Finland were also repaired and taken into use by Finnish Air Force. However only three ex-Soviet aircraft were allocated to AF squadrons before 13 March 1940: one DB-3 bomber which had landed at Hauho on 29 January 1940 was taken into use one month later by LLv 36, and two I-15bis fighters were allocated to a training squadron. Finnish AF had altogether 103 ex-Soviet aircraft in its inventory 1939–1944.

Aircraft production and maintenance

Before World War II Finnish industry lacked practically entirely all high-tech capabilities. The new aircraft and engine licences thus significantly improved the technical level of the industry. Significantly the Bristol Co. had been in big doubts whether the licensed engines and aircraft could be produced in Finland. However, in autumn 1939 production of modern Fokker fighters, Blenheim bombers and Mercury engines was in full swing.

Finnish technical personnel proved capable of extensive maintenance and repair of battle-damaged aircraft, and foreign specialists assisted in handling of new aircraft. Non-compatibility of new aircraft

VH-101 was the first war booty I-153 repaired by VL in Tampere, and was delivered to Ilmavoimat *in April 1940. (SA-kuva)*

however provided tremendous practical problems. Finland received 16 different aircraft types, with 12 different engines and 11 different radios during the short Winter War. Also superficially similar equipment turned out to be non-compatible: although both Brewster and FIAT fighters were equipped with 12.7 mm calibre machine guns, the ammunition was however not interchangeable! Also very few of the new aircraft were adapted to operation in sub-zero arctic conditions, so extensive modifications were requested.

The Chief Designer of the State Aircraft Factory (VL), *Dipl.Ing.* Edward Wegelius apparently got the impulse to devote his future career to industrial standardization as result of the struggles with non-standard equipment during the Winter War. Wegelius ultimately became Chairman of the International Standardisation Organisation (ISO) in the 1960s!

Personnel resources

When new aircraft started to arrive in Finland in January-February 1940 lack of skilled pilots was an acute problem. Ferrying of aircraft from England and/or Sweden was often done by pilots lacking appropriate qualifications. Miraculously only very few aircraft were lost on the long ferry flights, in deteriorating weather conditions, and over long distances over open sea (North Sea, Baltic Sea). New and unknown aircraft were flown in combat immediately upon arrival – after only one or two familiarisation flights, without normal conversion training! A small Test Flight of skilled test pilots was attached to VL, and took part in the air defence of Tampere with any airworthy fighter available.

In order to set up new squadrons the existing squadrons were "thinned out". It is very questionable how long scarce pilot resources would have lasted in the longer spring-time daylight periods. The technicians also faced enormous difficulties with the large number of aircraft types, and with every fighter squadron operating different aircraft. Repeated squadron relocation to temporary bases on frozen lakes did not make life easier, either.

In addition to the well-organised Swedish F 19, a large number of spontaneous volunteers turned up at Finnish missions in various countries and applied for service in the Finnish Air Force. The volunteers were in general unaccustomed to conditions in Finland, and naturally did not know the Finnish language. They also lacked in most cases appropriate flight training, and required excessive attention by Finnish supervisors and instructors. Only very few volunteers could be accepted in combat squadrons.

The rest were sent to various training units, having primarily "public relations" value only. Most volunteers with sufficient basic training were allocated to LLv 22, receiving the new Hurricanes and Brewsters in March 1940. This short-lived squadron (which has been called the "Foreign Legion" of the Finnish AF) was formed near Lahti during the very last days of the Winter War. LLv 22 counted four non-Finnish pilot officers and ten non-commissioned officers, representing ten different nations in its ranks. The technical personnel of LLv 22 were similarly "international".

Many foreign pilots unfortunately got lost during their first (in some cases only!) familiarisation flights over snow-covered Finnish forests and frozen lakes. Take-off and landing accidents on snowy and slippery runways were also very common.

There were however also a few positive exceptions:
- Seven Danes served as fighter pilots with Fokker and Gladiator fighters, and claimed a total of seven Soviet aircraft shot downin in action (see above).

- Italian fighter pilot *ylik* Diego Manzocchi was killed in action with FIAT G.50 FA-22 on 11 March 1940. was killed in action in a FIAT G.50.
- Two Hungarian fighter pilots flew FIAT G.50 fighters. Hungarian *vänrikki* Wilhelm Bekassy disappeared with FA-7 on 8 February 1940 over the Baltic Sea on a ferry flight from Sweden. Disappeared over the Baltic Sea on a ferry flight from Sweden.

In addition to the Swedish F 19 some other Swedish pilots served also in squadrons of the Finnish AF, and made a few operational missions.

In connection with delivery of various new aircraft, factory test pilots and mechanics were also sent to Sweden to supervise assembly, and to test-fly aircraft. Most of these skilled specialists later went to Finland to instruct their Finnish colleagues. They were naturally not "volunteers" in the literal sense of the word, and absolutely not comparable to the above-mentioned group.

Most volunteers departed from Finland in spring-summer 1940. Some British citizens stayed in Finland even up to the outbreak of the Soviet-Finnish Continuation war in summer 1941, when they were interned (and departed later).

A particular case was ex-Russian Duke Emmanuel Golitsyn (alias British citizen Edward M. Graham), whose father Duke Vladimir Golitsyn had served together with Mannerheim in the Imperial Russian Army. Emmanuel Golitsyn arrived in Finland only at the end of the Winter War, and served in the Fokker-equipped fighter squadron LLv 32 from 2 April until end-1940. Emmanuel Golitsyn was twice received by Marshal Mannerheim, who regrettably informed him during their first meeting in October 1940 that his mother, Duchess Yekaterina Golitsina had perished in the German bombing of London. According to an interview with Graham-Golitsyn published in 1993, Mannerheim asked him during the second and last meeting in January 1941 (when Golitsyn was due to return to England after expiration of his contract; and the planning of the coming Finnish-German cooperation was in full swing) to report to his "friends in Whitehall" that he (Mannerheim) does not want to attack Russia, and asked for concrete assistance from the Western powers to resist German pressure! Nothing is known about the

English volunteer Lt P.O.E. Graham (ex Russian Duke Emmanuel Golitsyn) in FR-98 at Siikakangas, spring 1940. (C-F. Geust)

possible results of Golitsin's mission. He served later as a fighter pilot in RAF, and after WW II as an airline pilot and sales representative of British aircraft manufacturer Avro Ltd.

A summary of all foreign volunteers in the Finnish Air Force in the Winter War is presented in appendix 7.

Basic training abroad

During the Winter War training of pilots for the Finnish AF was naturally speeded up. Basic (non-military) flight training was also arranged by the national civil aviation clubs of Sweden and Norway.

Ten Finnish pilot students of the Finnish Air Force College were sent to Sweden in January 1940. Somewhat later another group was sent to Norway. The Swedish course was arranged in Eskilstuna 11.02–09.04.1940. After the shock news of the peace agreement 13 March the enthusiasm of both students and instructors decreased dramatically. The course was discontinued after the German invasion of Denmark and Norway on 9 April, and the Finns returned home.

The other group of Finnish pilot students arrived in Steinsfjorden in Norway only a few days before the peace agreement of 13 March 1940. The Norwegian course was also discontinued after 9 April. Some Finns considered joining the Norwegian armed forces to fight the Germans, but after second thoughts all Finns returned home.

In summer 1940 some Norwegian AF officers (including the legendary Ole Reistad) even wanted to set up a reciprocal Norwegian flight course in Finland. This idea was not approved, and Reistad would ultimately set up the *Little Norway* training center in Canada, where Norwegian aviators were trained to fight the *Luftwaffe* in RAF squadrons.

Offensive plans in March 1940

On 1 February 1940 the Finnish bomber regiment LeR 4 was ordered to perform Blenheim photo-reconnaissance missions to Soviet AF bases in Estonia. This order was repeated on 10 February, when the Finnish Foreign Ministry also proposed bombing of the Soviet naval base at Liepaja in Latvia!

On 24 February 1940 detailed information about Finnish AF bases in south-west and northern Finland, and also detailed information of the Leningrad area was delivered to Anglo-French representatives in anticipation of Allied intervention.

In early March 1940 Allied intervention plans became very detailed. Gripenberg was in continuous contact with British Foreign Secretary Lord Halifax in London, and asked for "*one hundred bombers to be sent immediately to Finland*". On March 6 Gripenberg was finally informed that 36 Blenheims (three squadrons) would be sent to Finland. The number of aircraft was limited by the estimated Finnish capability to receive assistance, Finland was judged able to receive only 12–20 aircraft immediately, the rest would be shipped afterwards.

On 9 March 1940 Lord Halifax told Gripenberg that if Finland were to break off the peace negotiations with the Soviet Union (of which information had leaked), England would deliver 50 bombers to Finland. These bombers were to be flown to Finland by RAF pilots immediately after an official Finnish appeal for military assistance. Eight aircraft would take off in four days, and the rest (42 aircraft) in eight days. The British ferry crews would return to England, but later volunteer bomber crews would be sent to Finland. Halifax stressed that Finland had only three days to make its appeal, thereafter the bomber group would be dissolved as it was urgently needed elsewhere.

The Finnish appeal was never presented, and the peace treaty signed in Moscow 13 March 1940 changed the course of history. The large-scale arrival of British and French bombers in Finland would most likely have resulted in England and France fighting against Stalin´s Soviet Union (in its turn possibly supported by Hitler´s Germany!), or "three days to catatrophe" as phrased by British historian Douglas Clarke.

It is very unlikely that the promised Allied bomber force would have arrived in time to have a decisive impact on the outcome on the Winter War, as the Finnish Army was virtually on the brink of collapse when peace was signed. In parallel with Finnish intervention plans, the Allied forces also planned to bomb Soviet oil wells in Baku. The Soviet willingness to make peace with Finland was apparently influenced by knowledge of the Allied plans, including the intervention in Finland and the bombing of Baku.

War ends 13 March 1940

The peace treaty was signed in Moscow on the night of 12/13 March 1940. All Allied intervention plans were immediately cancelled. Aircraft already arrived in Sweden were ultimately delivered to Finland, but aircraft awaiting delivery in France and England never did arrive. Only less than half of the over 400 aircraft promised by various countries arrived, and most arrived far too late to participate in combat. Except for the Swedish F 19 squadron the numerous volunteers (although far from the "thousand American pilots" mentioned in the Soviet History of the Great Patriotic War published in 1960!) were of no real use to the Air Force, and were in fact only a nuisance!

Finnish Air Force after the Winter War

Finnish Air Force organization, training and tactical methods were reviewed after the Winter War, with due attention paid to combat experience. New squadrons, equipped with aircraft delivered in spring 1940, were combat ready in summer-autumn 1940. Production and maintenance capacity were also expanded, and the Finnish Air Force was at the peak of its relative strength in summer 1941.

Mentally the Finnish Air Force had learned the hard way not to believe in promises of foreign assistance. Own technical competence and independence from foreign sources were fully appreciated. Thus no foreign volunteers were accepted in the Finnish Air Force in the Continuation War 1941–1944 (with the exception of two Swedes; both serving as volunteers already in the Winter war: kersantti Sten Haraldsson disappeared in RI-152 on a patrol flight over the Baltic Sea on 4 September 1942), and vänrikki

Appendices

http://mmpbooks.biz/assets/ WWAppendices.pdf

The young Estonian Heino Kaukula witnessed from his father´s fishingboat how KALEVA was shot down near Keri (Kokskär) lighthouse just north of Tallinn on 14 June 1940. These drawings were made by Kaukula for a TV-documentary produced in 1991 by Bo von Willebrand (whose father was KALEVA´s pilot). (C-F. Geust)

Gustaf-Mauritz Armfelt (distant relative of Marshal Mannerheim), who on 24 April 1944 was awarded the Finnish Wings after appropriate flight training, but never joined any operational unit.

Epilogue

Civil airliner Kaleva shot down 14 June 1940 (see page 255)

Despite attempts to create normal relations with its former enemy, Finnish authorities witnessed continuous political pressure from Moscow in spring 1940 (categorical refusal to accept closer Finnish-Swedish cooperation; problems with the new border line, repatriation of prisoners of war, war reparations, Petsamo nickel mine concession, transit traffic to Hanko naval base etc.). Most problems were hidden from the public and known only to rather few Finnish officials.

One single event of 14 June 1940 would however have a dramatic impact on Finnish official and public opinion towards the USSR. This day a passenger aircraft (Junkers Ju 52 *Kaleva*, registration code OH-ALL) of Finnish flag-carrier Aero Oy was shot down by Soviet aircraft over the Gulf of Finland. The civil airliner, bound for Helsinki on scheduled flight 1631, was attacked by two bombers of the Air Force of the Baltic Fleet (VVS KBF) a few moments after take-off from Tallinn airport. All nine persons on board (two Finnish crew members and seven passengers) were killed. The passengers included three diplomats (two French and one American), two German businessmen, one Swedish businessman and one Estonian woman.

This unprovoked event, comparable only to the shooting down of the Korean jumbo jet in the Far East on 1 September 1983, has never been officially admitted, nor have any regrets been presented by Soviet authorities.

The *Kaleva* tragedy was evidently connected to the Soviet occupation of the Baltic countries in mid-June 1940. Was the USSR ready to prevent diplomatic information to get out of its "sphere of influence" by any means, or was the downing of a civil airliner a mistake by the blockade forces? What was in the first case the unwanted information? Some diplomatic mail bags were picked up by Soviet naval ships and brought to Kronstadt, but their contents have never been disclosed.

The Finnish army had received significant intelligence information (eg. radio intercepts which greatly facilitated the destruction of several Soviet divisions) from both the Estonian and Latvian Armies during the Winter War. Were the diplomats possibly carrying sensitive intelligence information – was this the reason to shoot down the civil airliner?

Apparently not one of the native (mutually opposing!) countries of the dead diplomats did officially protest, nor are they known to have made any contacts whatsoever with the Soviet authorities. Only carefully worded requests for investigations were presented to Finnish authorities. Germany paid out pensions to the relatives of her dead citizens in silence.

The *Kaleva* incident was very soon forgotten outside Finland – the major world event of this day, 14 June 1940 was the German entry into Paris! Although the exact reason of the *Kaleva* tragedy was hidden from the Finnish public, everyone was nervously able to read between the lines of the official communiqués ("*airliner Kaleva crashed due to external explosion not related to any identified technical problems, killing all on board...*").

Finland was once more left alone – for the second time in less than one year.

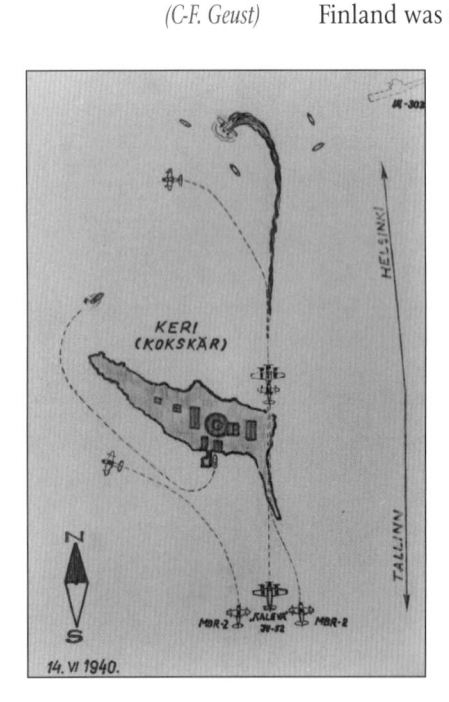

I-15bis blue 10, batl. kommissar I.I. Volosevich (13 OIAE VVS KBF). The inscription reads 'Za Stalina! (For Stalin!)'.

I-15bis red 5, unidentified IAP, winter 1939–1940.

I-15bis white 11. Captured in the Winter war and became VH-10, later VH-1 and IH-1 in Finnish AF.

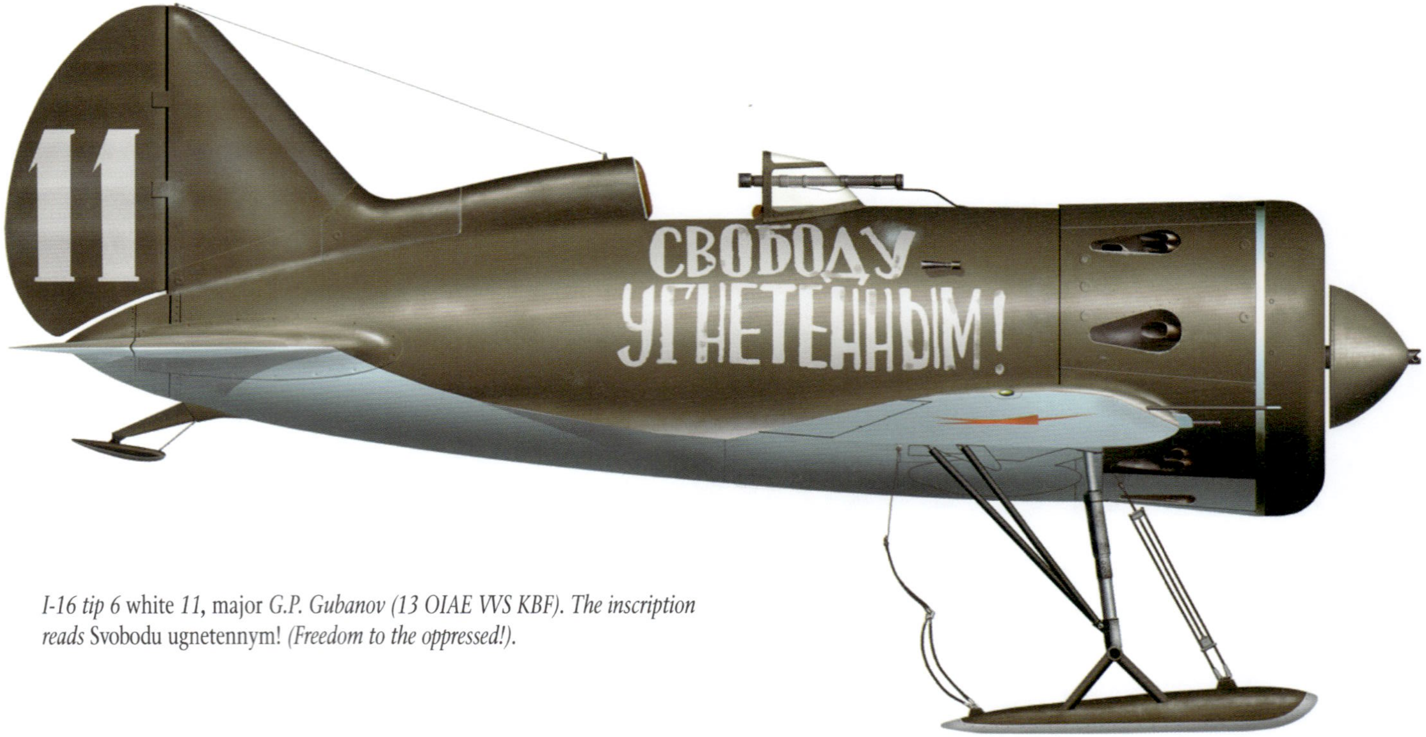

I-16 tip 6 white 11, major G.P. Gubanov (13 OIAE VVS KBF). The inscription reads Svobodu ugnetennym! (Freedom to the oppressed!).

I-16 red 228, lt I.I. Koval'kov (3./68 IAP) crashed at Muolaa 23 December 1939 and was taken prisoner.

I-153 red 16 (c/n 6804) st.lt N.P. Perevezentsev (2./38 IAP) crashed at Kirkkonummi 20 February 1940 and died of wounds.

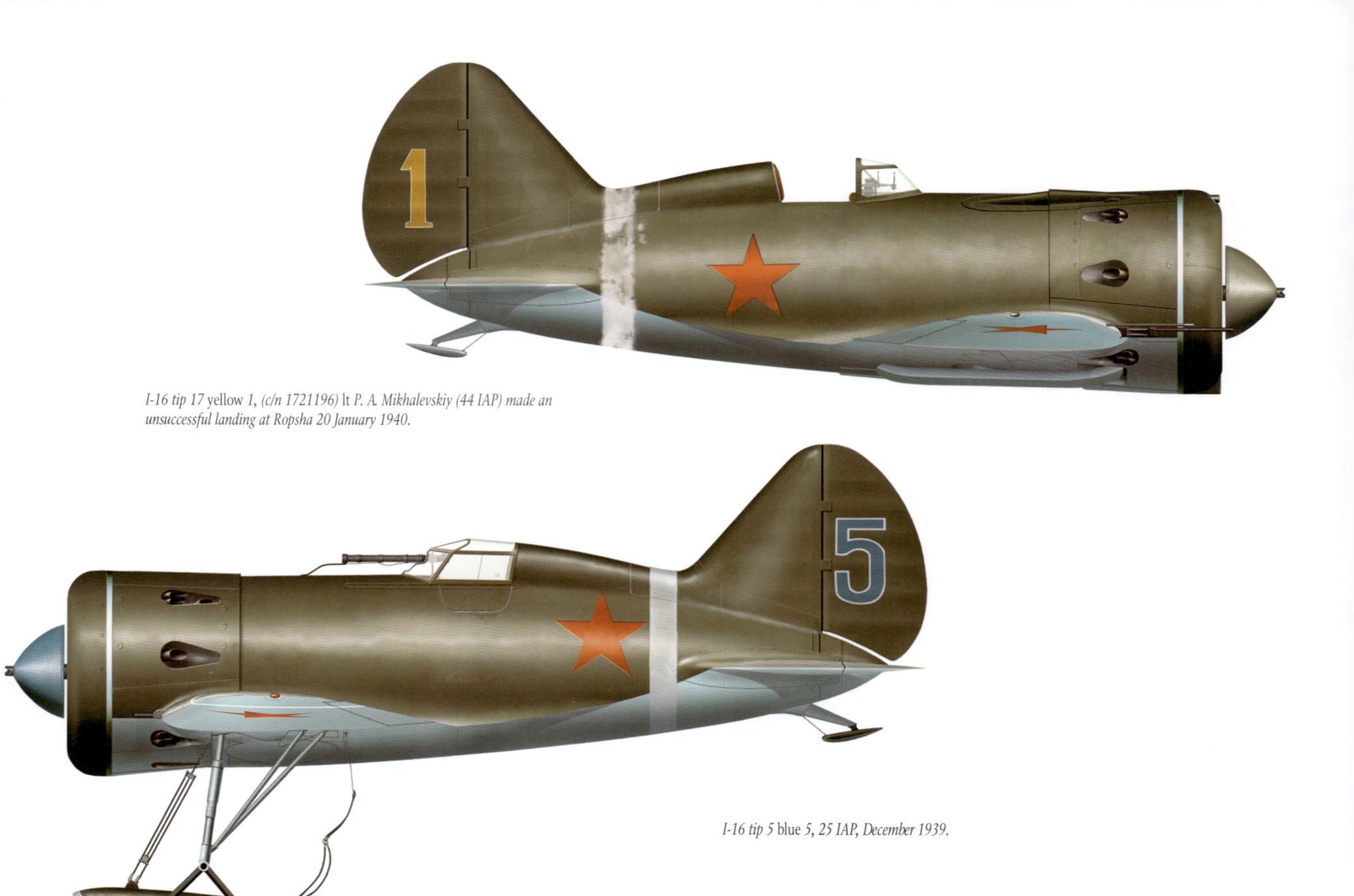

I-16 tip 17 yellow 1, (c/n 1721196) lt P. A. Mikhalevskiy (44 IAP) made an unsuccessful landing at Ropsha 20 January 1940.

I-16 tip 5 blue 5, 25 IAP, December 1939.

I-16 tip 6 white 230, (c/n 5214378), 25 IAP. Destroyed 26 December 1939 in an unsuccessful landing in Manushkino by lt V.S. Tsyganenko (1./26 IAP).

I-16 tip 5 red 3, ml.lt Novikov (13 OIAE VVS KBF). The inscription reads Za konstitutsiju SSSR! (For the Soviet Constitution!)

Fokker D.XXI, FR-97, luutn. Jorma Sarvanto, 4/Lentolaivue 24, Utti airfield, January 1940.

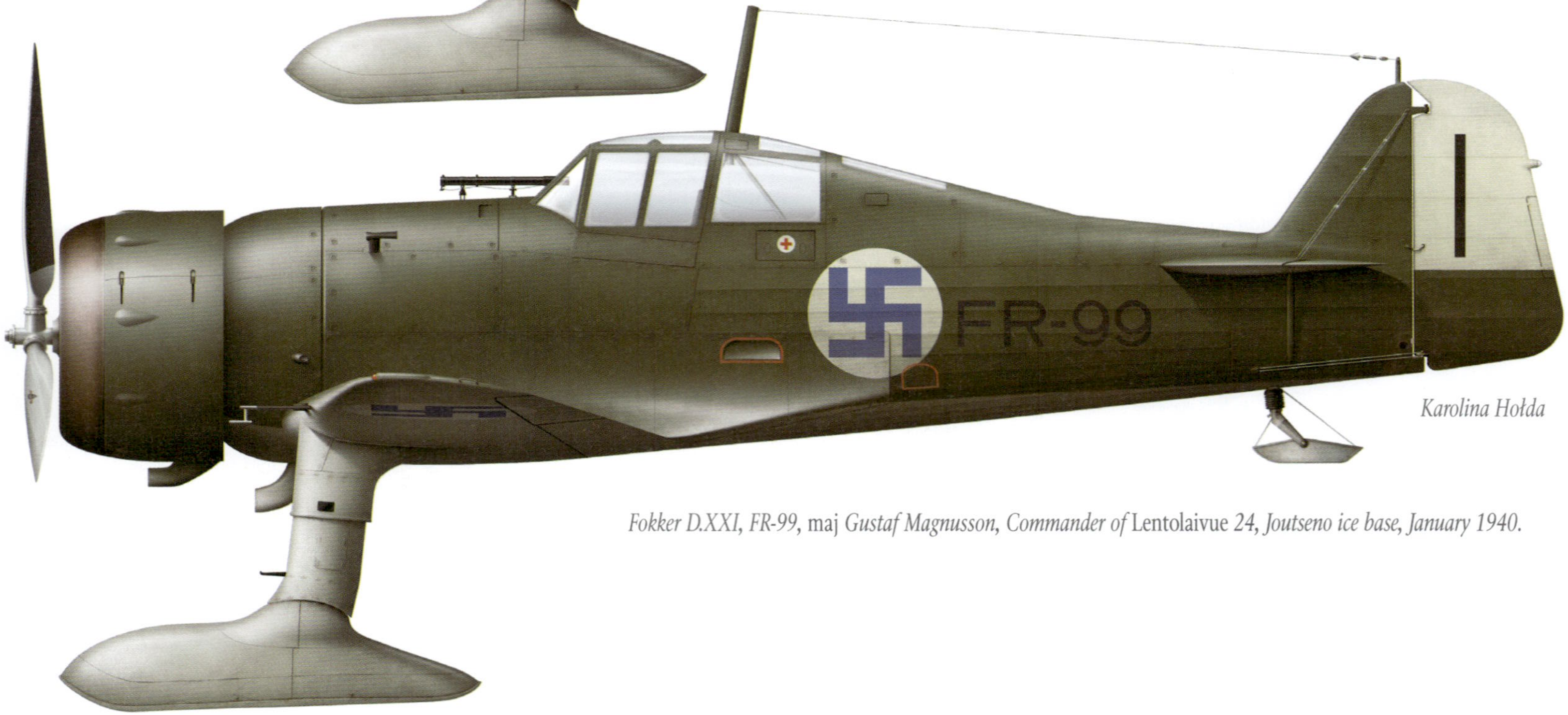

Fokker D.XXI, FR-99, maj Gustaf Magnusson, Commander of Lentolaivue 24, Joutseno ice base, January 1940.

Karolina Hołda

R-Z red 2 of 43 LBAP, winter 1939-1940.

R-Z star (c/n 2251) of 43 LBAP was destroyed in a snowstorm 11 March 1940.

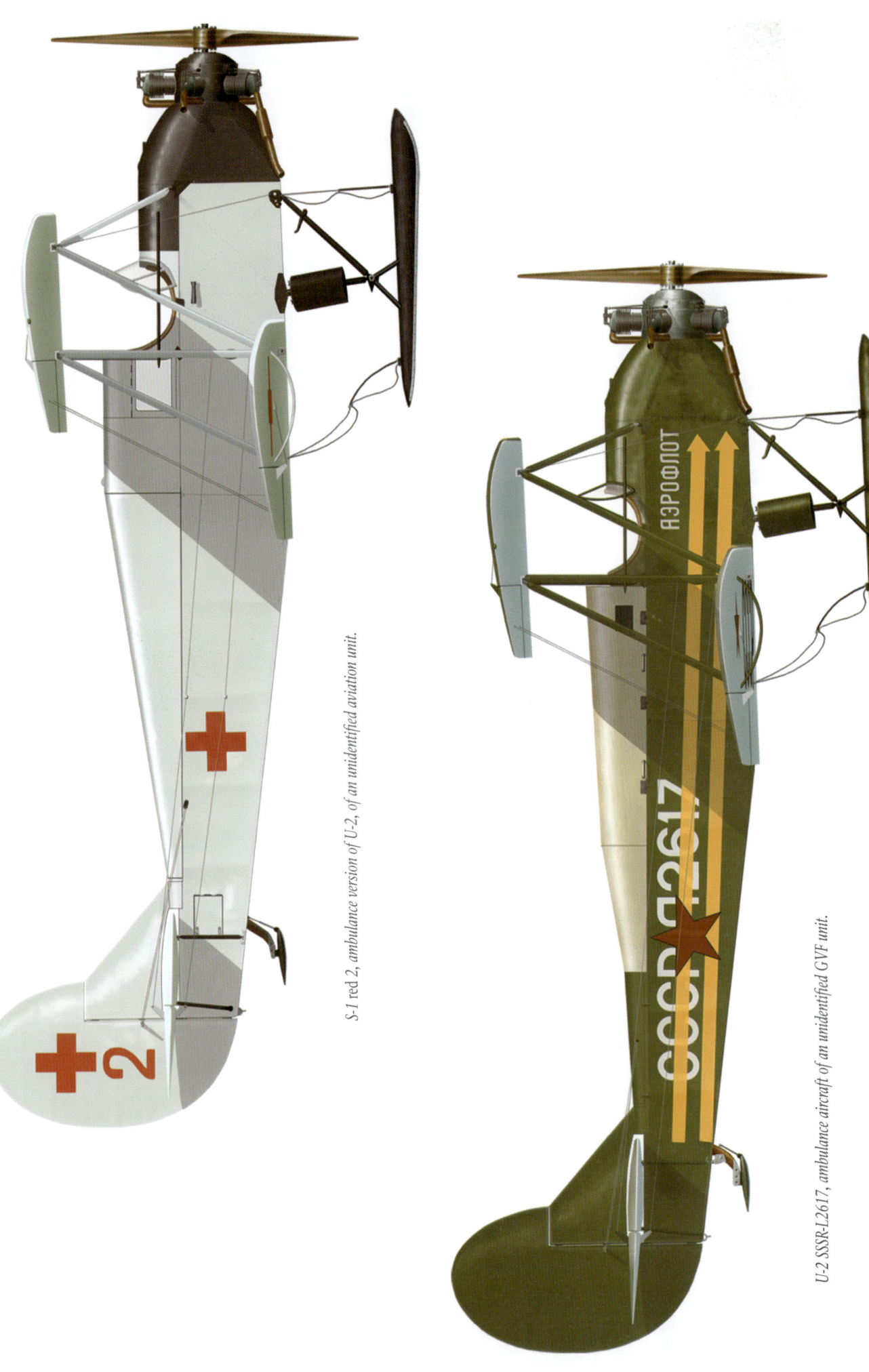

S-1 red 2, ambulance version of U-2, of an unidentified aviation unit.

U-2 SSSR-L2617, ambulance aircraft of an unidentified GVF unit.

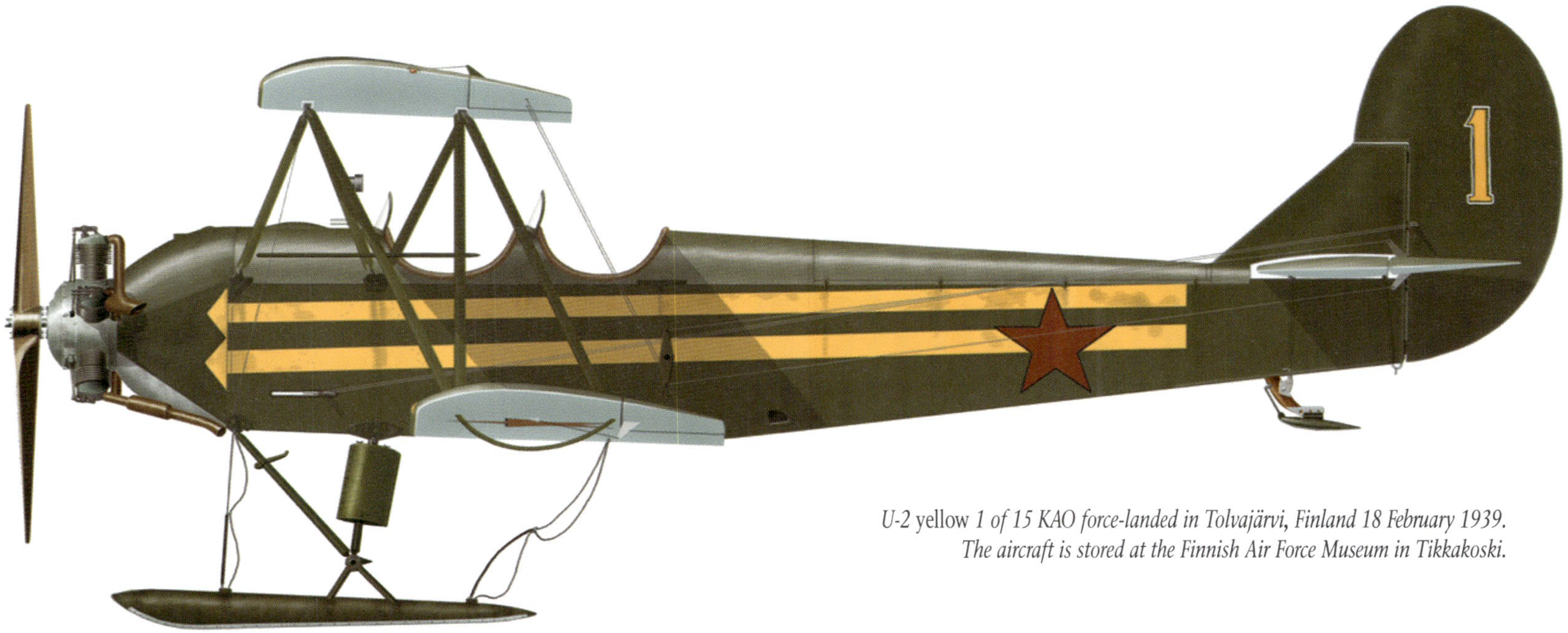

U-2 yellow 1 of 15 KAO force-landed in Tolvajärvi, Finland 18 February 1939. The aircraft is stored at the Finnish Air Force Museum in Tikkakoski.

SSS white 66 of 7 LShAP.

Gladiator Mk II, GL-255, ylik Oiva Tuominen, 2/Lentolaivue 26, Ruokolahti ice base, February 1940.

Karolina Holda

Gladiator Mk I, aircraft A, Flygflottilj 19, Veitsiluoto ice base, March 1940.

Karolina Holda

Fokker C.X, FK-80, luutn Heikki Kalaja, leader of 1/LLv 10, Mensuvaara airfield, January 1940.

Karolina Holda

SB yellow 9 (c/n 20/101) of 2./41 SBAP force-landed 1 December 1939 at Mansikkakoski, Imatra in Finland. Lt G. Tanklayev and ml.lt V.A Demchinskiy were taken prisoner. The SB was repaired and used by Finnish AF.

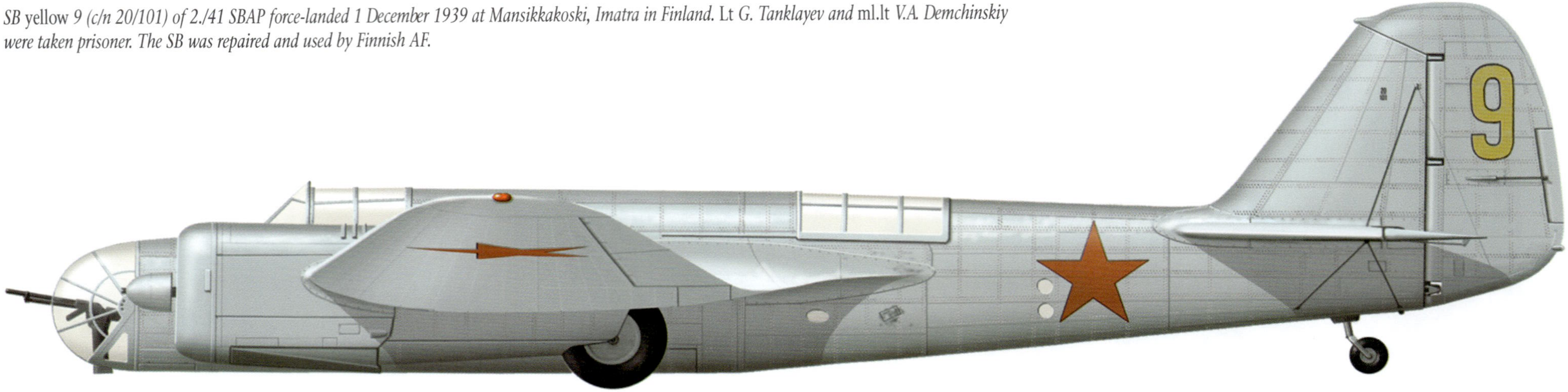

SB yellow 4 of 3./24 SBAP force-landed in December 1939 in Finland. This SB was possibly c/n 15/96 which came down on 21 December 1939 at Lake Yskjärvi, and was exhibited in the War trophy exhibition in Helsinki, February 1940.

SB blue 3 of 2./2 SBAP (c/n 1/224) was destroyed in an unsuccessful take-off from Vitino 2 February 1940 (pilot lt A.A. Kostin).

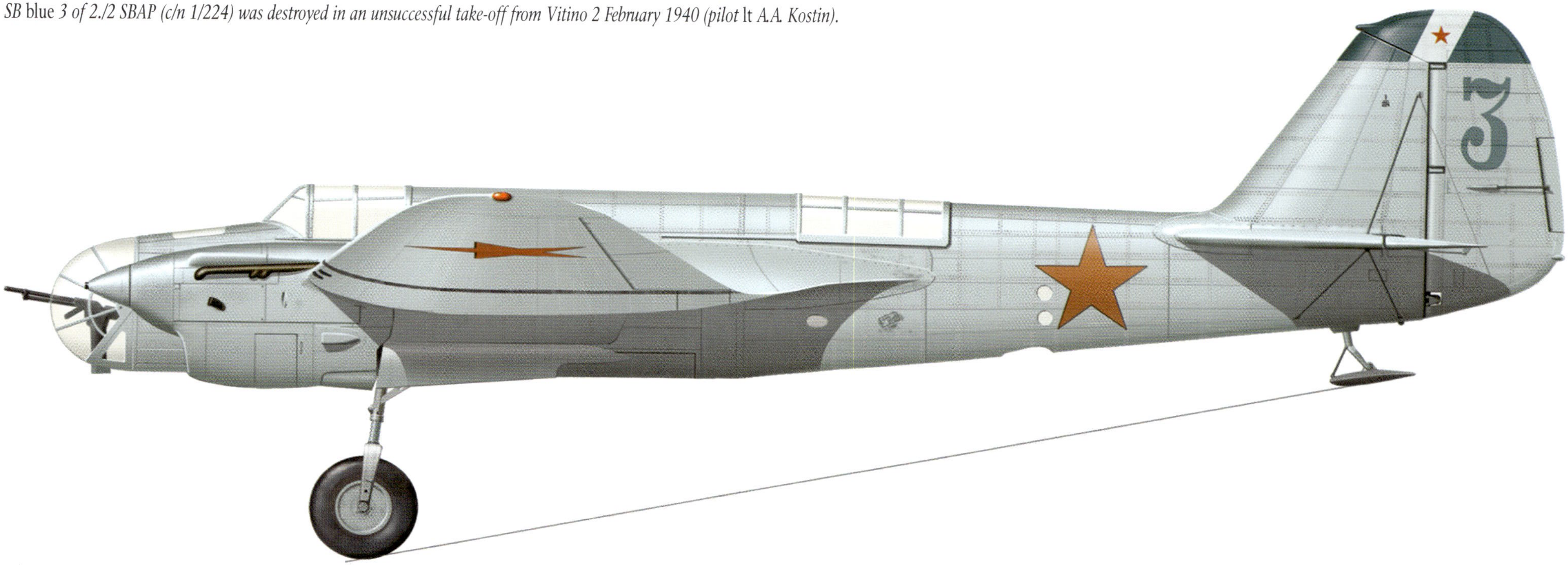

SB green 5 (c/n 16/69) of 2./24 SBAP was shot down 1 December 1939 and crashed near Viipuri. The crew lt A.L. Cherenkov, lt M.V. Pushmenkov and gunner M.M. Novozhenin) were killed. The aircraft was exhibited in the War trophy exhibition in Helsinki, February 1940.

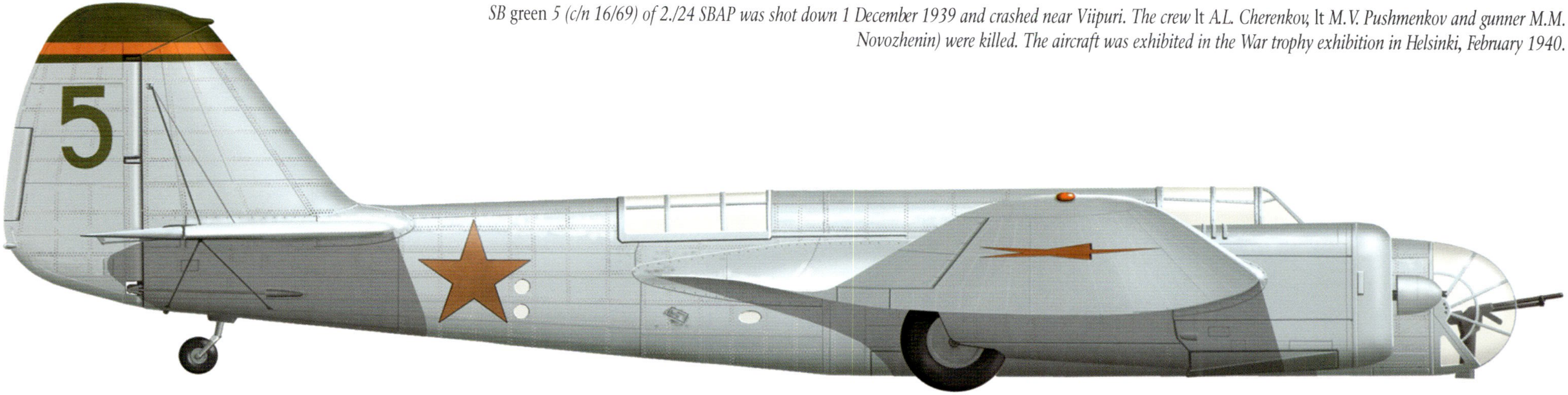

341

SB red 10 of 3./35 SBAP, January 1940.

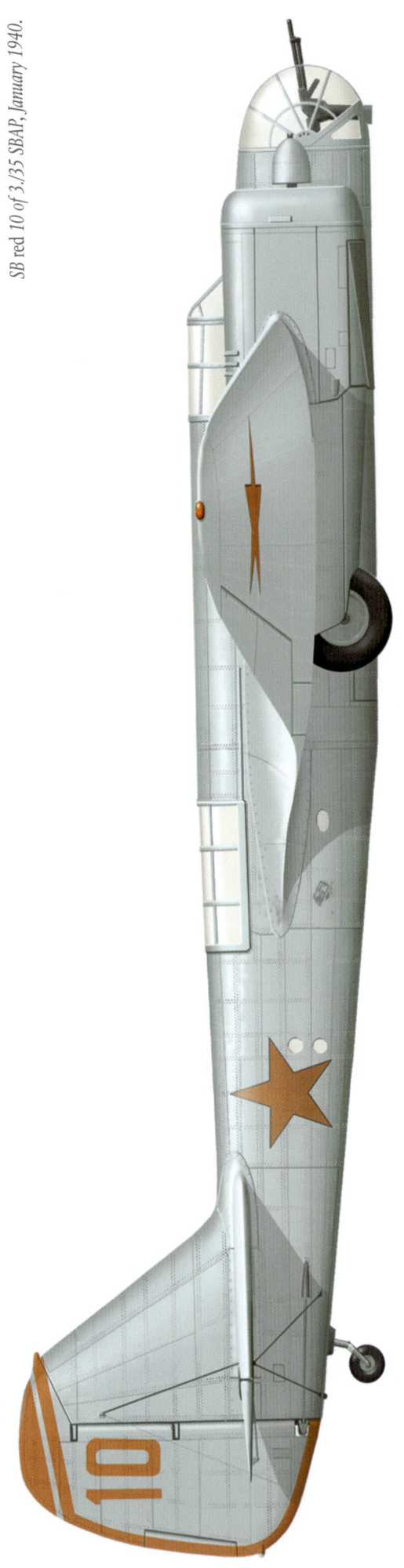

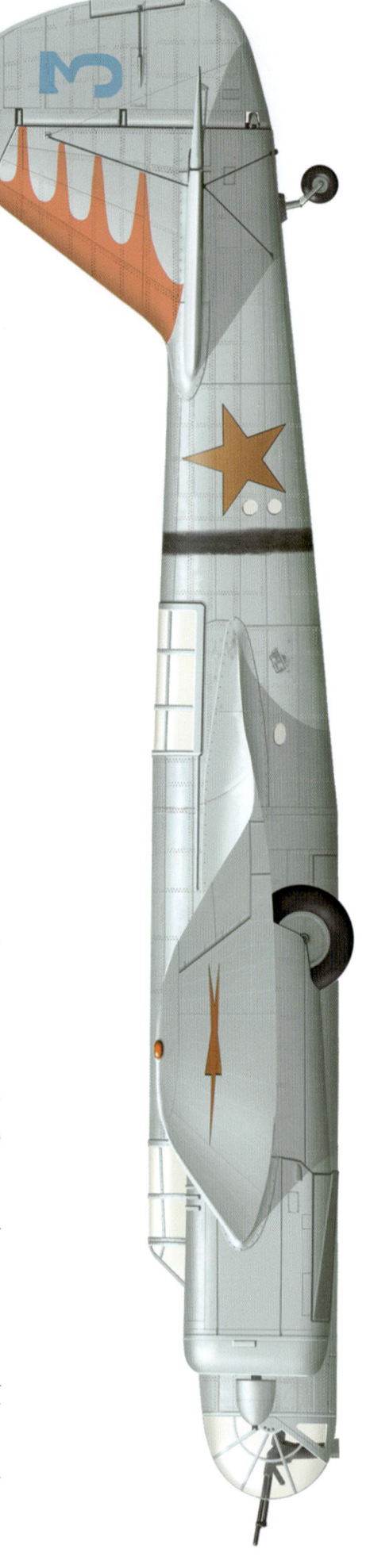

SB blue 3 (c/n 19/136) of 5./44 SBAP was destroyed in Krasnogvardejsk 26 December 1939 (pilot lt N.I. Timoshenko).

SB blue 4 (c/n 11/220) of 3./24 SBAP force-landed 1 December 1939 in Säiniö, Finland. st. lt I.K. Storchilo and Ya.V. Yegorov were taken prisoner, gunner P.I. Petrov was killed. The SB was repaired and later flew in Finnish AF as VP-10, later VP-1 and SB-1.

SB black 2 of 34 DRAE. One of two SBs shot down 7 March 1940 by Swedish volunteer E. Theler (F19) in Utajärvi, Finland. Lt A.S. Aleksyev was taken prisoner, st.lt G.A Sechkin and starshina V.S. Lepekash were killed.

SB star (c/n 11/77) of 1./48 SBAP forced-landed in Sestroretsk 25 February 1940, pilot kapitan M.P. Voronin.

SB red 8 of unidentified SBAP. This SB participated in the Winter War.

DB-3 blue 14 (c/n 391151) of 5./42 DBAP force-landed 3 February 1940 at Läskelä. st.lt N.Kh. Vorobyev and gunner V.Ya. Palchikov were taken prisoner, st.lt K.N. Sokolov was killed.

DB-3 red 15 (c/n 392320, pilot kapitan Podmazovskiy) of 4./53 DBAP landed on 29 January 1940 on Lake Iso-Roine, Finland. Later used by Finnish AF as VP-101, later VP-11 (see page 351).

345

DB-3 yellow 8 (c/n 391505) of 5 OAP force-landed on 14 January 1940 near Sodankylä, Finland. The pilot lt L.F. Zubov was taken prisoner, the fate of st.lt F.I. Kononov and starshina V.Ye. Yerofeyev is unclear. The DB-3 was repaired and later used by Finnish AF.

DB-3 red 12 (c/n 392515) of 4./53 DBAP crashed 29 January 1940 at Urjala, Finland. The crew lt G.A Yandushev, lt G.V. Kurbatov and starshina N.G. Zuyev were taken prisoner. The DB-3 was repaired and later used by Finnish AF.

DB-3 green 11 (c/n 391695) of 5 OAP was shot down 21 February 1940 by Swedish volunteers A. Frykholm and C-O. Steninger (F19) north of Vuotso. The crew st.lt A.N. Isayev and lt F.P. Zapryagailev were taken prisoner, starshina V.F. Volkov was killed. The DB-3 was repaired and later used by Finnish AF as VP-14.

ANT-6 SSSR-N-170 AVIAARKTIKA. In December 1939 this aircraft was attached to 72 SAP, and flown by HSU M.V. Vodopyanov.

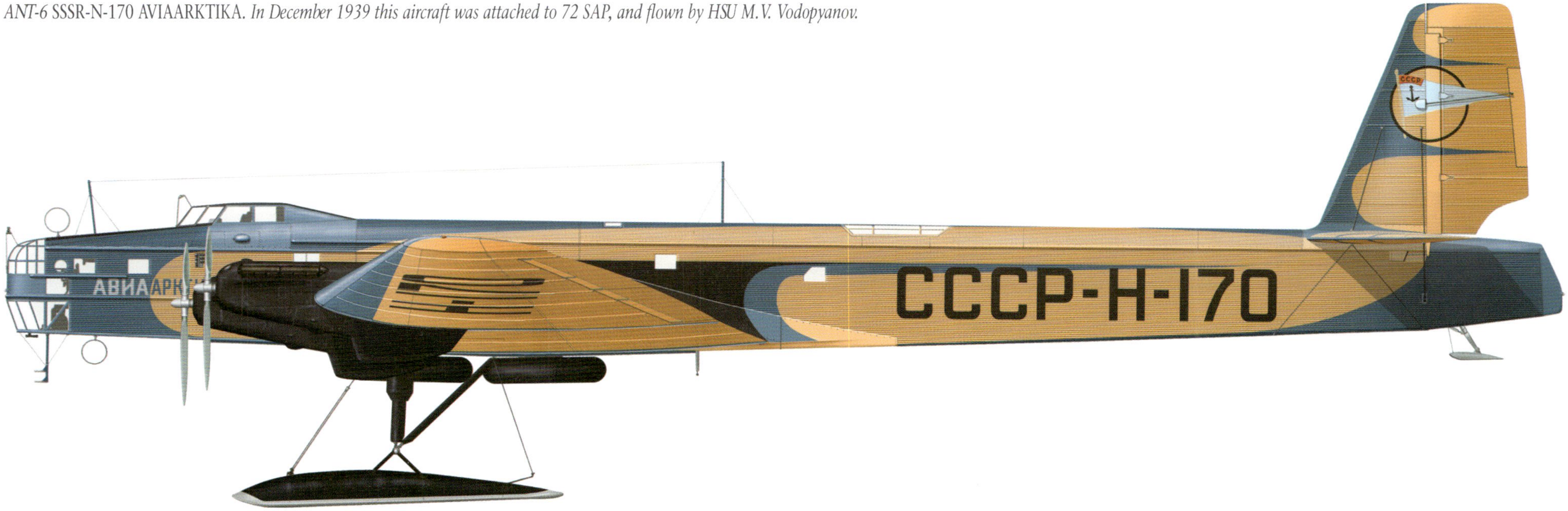

347

TB-3 4M-34 yellow 7 (c/n 22604) of 3 TBAP was destroyed in a ground collision on 18 January 1940 in Lodejnoye Pole.

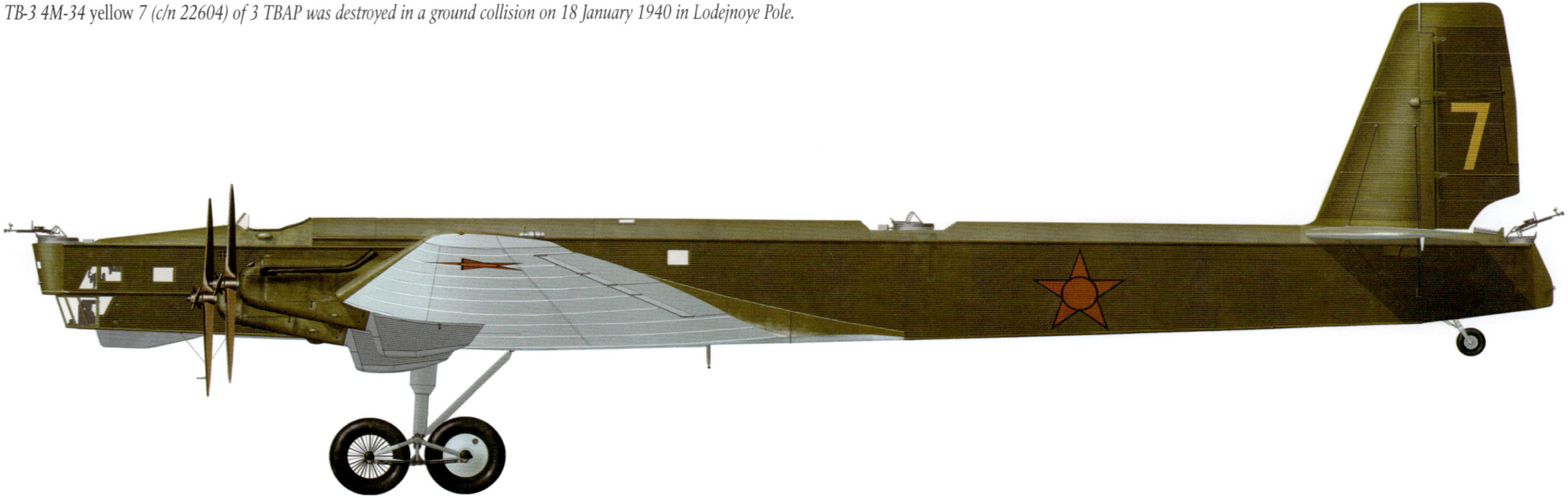

K-5 SSSR-L607 was mobilized from the Civil Aviation Fleet (GVF) and used as an ambulance aircraft.

Douglas DC-3 F-6 transported the Soviet Navy delegation to Hanko on 22 March 1940, to sign the lease of the territory ceded to the the USSR according to the peace treaty of 13 March 1940.

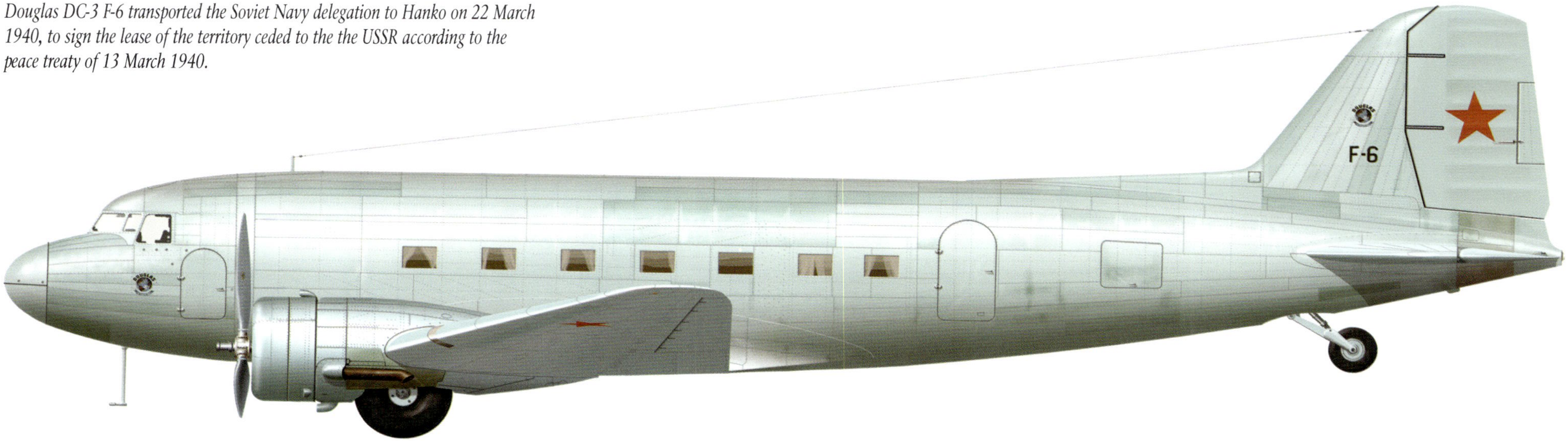

PS-84 SSSR-L3407. PS-84 was the Soviet designation of the license-produced DC-3. This aircraft was mobilized from Aeroflot, and used for special transport of high-ranking officers.

Bristol Blenheim I, BL-117, lentom Viljo Salminen, 1/Lentolaivue 44, Joroinen airfield, February 1940.

Bristol Blenheim I, BL-111, maj Erik Stenbäck, commander of Lentolaivue 44, Joroinen airfield, November 1939.

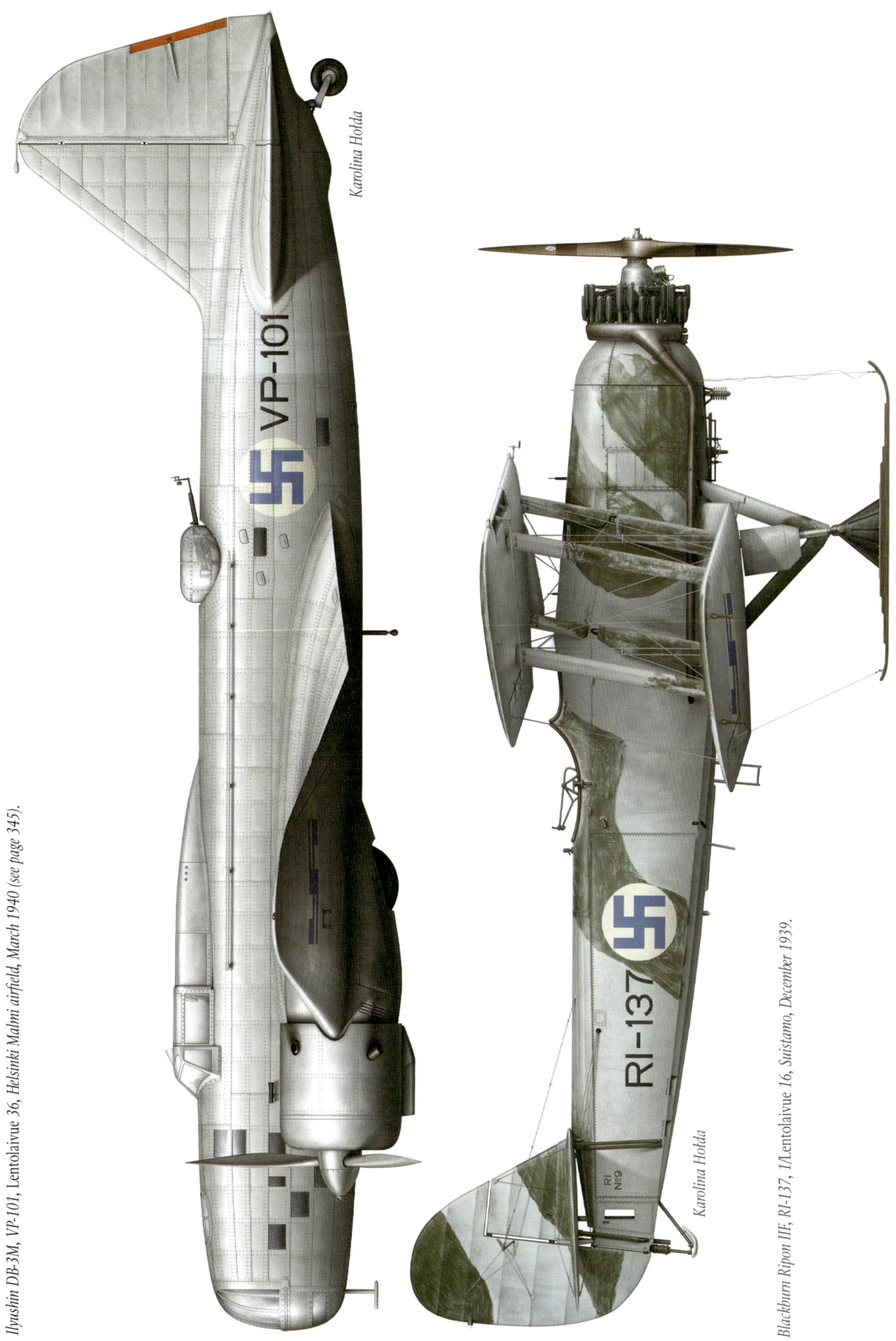

Ilyushin DB-3M, VP-101, Lentolaivue 36, Helsinki Malmi airfield, March 1940 (see page 345).

Karolina Hołda

Blackburn Ripon IIF, RI-137, 1/Lentolaivue 16, Suistamo, December 1939.

Karolina Hołda

351

Blackburn Ripon IIF, RI-138, 2/Lentolaivue 16, Värtsilä, November 1939.

Karolina Holda

Blackburn Ripon IIF, RI-153, 2/Lentolaivue 36, Kallvik, November 1939.

Karolina Holda